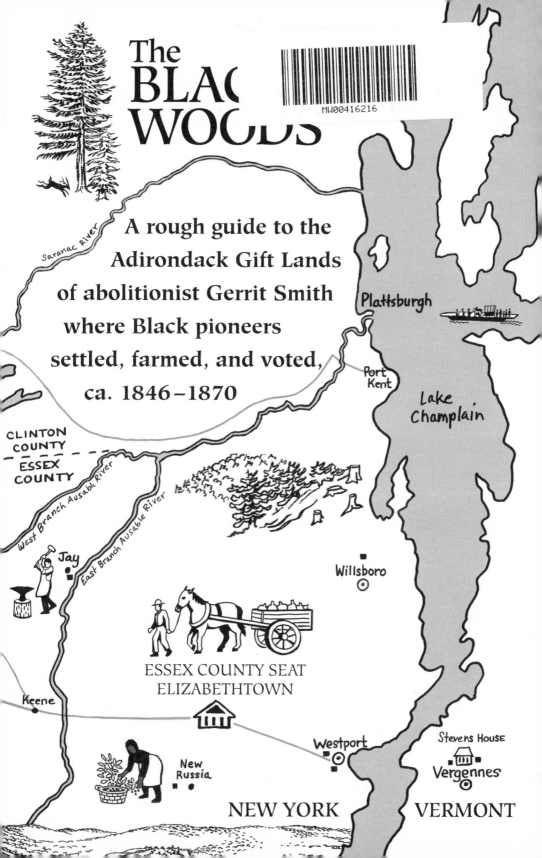

The
BLAC
WOODS

A rough guide to the
Adirondack Gift Lands
of abolitionist Gerrit Smith
where Black pioneers
settled, farmed, and voted,
ca. 1846–1870

Saranac River

Plattsburgh

Port
Kent

Lake
Champlain

CLINTON
COUNTY
ESSEX
COUNTY

West Branch Ausable River

East Branch Ausable River

Jay

Willsboro

ESSEX COUNTY SEAT
ELIZABETHTOWN

Keene

Westport

Stevens House

Vergennes

New
Russia

NEW YORK

VERMONT

THE BLACK WOODS

THE BLACK WOODS

PURSUING RACIAL JUSTICE ON THE ADIRONDACK FRONTIER

AMY GODINE

THREE HILLS
AN IMPRINT OF CORNELL UNIVERSITY PRESS
Ithaca and London

Furthermore:
a program of the J. M. Kaplan Fund

Publication of this book was supported by a grant
from Furthermore: a program of the J. M. Kaplan
Fund.

Endpaper maps created by Peter Seward and Ren
Davidson Seward, Saranac Lake, New York.

First published 2023 by Cornell University Press
Printed in the United States of America

Library of Congress Cataloging-in-Publication Data

Names: Godine, Amy, author.
Title: The black woods : pursuing racial justice on the
    Adirondack frontier / Amy Godine.
Description: Ithaca [New York] : Three Hills, an
    imprint of Cornell University Press, 2023. | Includes
    bibliographical references and index.
Identifiers: LCCN 2023002743 (print) | LCCN
    2023002744 (ebook) | ISBN 9781501771682
    (hardcover) | ISBN 9781501771699 (pdf) | ISBN
    9781501771705 (epub)
Subjects: LCSH: Smith, Gerrit, 1797–1874—Influence. |
    Antislavery movements—New York (State)—History. |
    African Americans—Land tenure—New York (State)—
    History. | African Americans—Suffrage. | North Elba
    (N.Y. : Town)—History—19th century.
Classification: LCC E445.N56 G63 2023 (print) |
    LCC E445.N56 (ebook) |
DDC 974.7/00496073—dc23/eng/20230126
LC record available at https://lccn.loc.gov/2023002743
LC ebook record available at https://lccn.loc.
    gov/2023002744

In memory of my folks, Morton and Bernice Godine, who loved history, and reading about it, and made sure I did too.

And I thought, *It could have worked!* This democracy, this land of freedom and equality and the pursuit of happiness—it could have worked! There was something to it, after all! It didn't have to turn into a greedy free-for-all! We didn't have to make a mess of it and the continent and ourselves! It could have worked! It wasn't just a joke, just a blind for the machinations of money!

—Ian Frazier, Great Plains

Contents

PREFACE

For fifteen years before his death at sixty-eight in 2013, the youth worker and environmentalist Brother Yusuf Abdul-Wasi Burgess took teenagers from Albany camping in the Adirondack Mountains. Brother Yusuf supplied paddles, life jackets, and canoes; his first-time campers brought their wariness and disbelief. City kids from hard-used neighborhoods, they took a cool view of the six-million-acre Adirondack Park. Not only was it famously, unwaveringly white, but it seemed a land of grim dysfunctionality where nothing you relied on worked. You could not text a friend or parent. Nobody moved, dressed, or laughed in any way that made you feel at home. How this big green playpen, this so-called getaway, was anybody's notion of a *good time* was a mystery you did not care to solve.[1]

But Brother Yusuf, Brooklyn raised, never aimed to make his campers nature lovers. Learning bird calls, naming constellations—this was never the idea. The mission, always, was to challenge and relax his teenagers' idea of their turf. With a wider sense of place comes the glint of interest in a world beyond the close-at-hand with its hard-defended codes. Some distant college or line of work may look more thinkable after overnighting in a tent by an icy stream. Test the comfort zone this once, and next time the kids would push it harder. A stretched-out sense of where they fit here may lead to a respect for their historical connection to it, their right to call it theirs.

For this reason, Brother Yusuf always took his campers to John Brown's Adirondack home. He told them about the radical abolitionist's assault on a federal armory in Harpers Ferry, Virginia (West Virginia today), from October 16 to 18, 1859. With a hand-picked band of guerrilla fighters, Brown occupied the armory, aiming to deliver one hundred thousand muskets and rifles to nearby slaves who, he hoped, would join his effort to secure the territory between the Potomac and Shenandoah Rivers, then push south to free more slaves, plantation by plantation.

But stuck in a small engine house, Brown's group was no match for mi-
litiamen and marines. His holdout fell in minutes. Ten men were killed,
two sons of his among them. A Virginia jury convicted him of treason.
On December 2, 1859, "Old Brown" was hanged.

The teenagers Brother Yusuf took to the park knew Brown's name,
but the impact of his raid, how Harpers Ferry blazed the road to the
Civil War, and the war to the legal freedom for four million Black
Americans, how Brown's trial, the first to be reported nationally, has
been judged the most important criminal trial in the history of the
Republic—this was news for Yusuf's charges. Also revelatory: learning
that John Brown came to the Adirondacks to join a settlement of Black
pioneers. Back in the day, said Brother Yusuf, a stretch of Adirondack
wilderness ten times bigger than the city of Albany belonged to thousands of Black New Yorkers. They got this land (and Brown got his)
from a New York abolitionist named Gerrit Smith. From the tiny town
of Peterboro in upstate Madison County, this land-rich white man
hoped his forty-acre Adirondack gift lots would pull poor Black families out of cities and put them on new farms. Back then, Black New
Yorkers had to prove they owned land if they ever hoped to vote. No
property, no ballot—a special rule for colored men alone. That's why
Gerrit Smith came up with his idea in 1846. With their new parcels,
Black New Yorkers could get out of the city, start farming, and gain
the franchise. They could vote for candidates who hated slavery, vote
for equal rights for all. They would be empowered. Working citizens.
That's what land could do.

So, you think twice before you tell me this place is for white folks, Brother
Yusuf urged his campers out of Albany. *You think hard before you say this
place has nothing to do with you. This is your patrimony, your business. You
don't have to buy this story. You own it. You're stakeholders. This land is my
land. This land is yours.*

In 2000, Martha Swan, founder and director of the Adirondack social
action group John Brown Lives!, invited me to curate a traveling exhibit about Gerrit Smith's radical agrarian initiative, the plan that inspired John Brown to move to Essex County in 1849. At the time, what
I knew about Smith's scheme I mostly owed to antiquarian historians
who considered it a lost cause from its conception. Twentieth-century
historians were less dismissive, but their interest in it was still defined
by the slit-like window of Brown's residency. (Brown was away from his
North Elba home much more than he was there, and did the work that

gained him lasting fame far from New York State.) Brown's Adirondack burial in 1859, and his surviving family's removal to points west, cued the end of any deep historical concern with the fate of the Black Woods.

Swan, a civil rights activist in the Adirondack village of Westport, urged me to approach this story differently. The exhibit she asked me to develop, *Dreaming of Timbuctoo*, would focus on the Black pioneers. Would I find much? I didn't think so. There was the inarguable fact that Gerrit Smith's original idea, a Black farm settlement for thousands, was, for the great majority of Smith's deedholders, unrealized. Hence that word *Dreaming* in the exhibition's name. Smith's colony was, for most of its beneficiaries, no more than an eager prospect. Nor, I knew, could I glean a thing from artifacts. The cabins and outbuildings that made up Timbuctoo and other Black enclaves in Essex and Franklin Counties were down to duff and moss. I would be working without ruins, pictures, or, really, anything very tangible except headstones. Epistolary evidence from the settlers' side was scant. No images of the grantees on their farms remained. No pictures of women or children, period. Taken singly, clues that could be gleaned from census data, newspaper posts, legal cases, military pension files, tax reports, school rolls, and local memory seemed inconclusive. Any reconstruction of this history was going to be tough.

Other challenges revealed themselves to me more gradually. I had assumed, for instance, that what I knew about Adirondack ethnic history, something I'd been writing about for decades, could only help. There were a great many nineteenth-century Adirondack enclaves that had slipped through the cracks of antiquarian and twentieth-century regional history. Wasn't Timbuctoo one of these? I figured the exhibit would reunite the Black homesteaders with all the rest of the great unseen and unremarked-on in the Adirondack region—migratory hired hands, Irish tanners, Italian railroad workers, Polish miners, loggers from Quebec. . . .

It didn't. Timbuctoo was not another bright tooth on the cogwheel of diversity. For all the poverty, social precarity, and cultural invisibility it shared with white Adirondack settlements in its time, it also stood apart. What it meant for Adirondack memory—and how Blackness, more generally, resonated in the regional narrative—was not how poor white enclaves were remembered. It was not how they were disremembered. Here was an othering of a different order: more purposeful, intractable, and, for this writer, demanding. I would need to lose ways of thinking about Adirondack landscape and history that had seemed to work for me for decades. My idea of inclusivity, long bound to the documentable (evidence of ethnic enclaves, names in the census, work crew rolls, and other hard proofs of diversity), no longer struck me as sufficient. Did the way I research, the way I *see*, make room for the undocumented, the great ranks of the missing?

Many of Smith's Black deedholders visited the Adirondacks and left without a trace. Thousands more never ventured to the Adirondacks at all. Why was this? Why, until quite recently, did regional accounts of the giveaway make room for one family only, with no notice of scores of others—almost two hundred Black people—who made the Adirondacks home? Also puzzling: the antiquarian emphasis on the Black Woods as a refuge for self-emancipated slaves, even while the influence of slavery in Adirondack life remained wholly unexamined. True, here was no slaveocracy, yet Southern enslavers and their Northern enablers put sugar in Adirondack teacups, cotton on the backs of Adirondack schoolboys, and tobacco in the tins of Adirondack farmers (not to speak of turpentine, indigo, cigars, molasses, palm-leaf hats, and quilt batting on the shelves of Adirondack crossroad stores). Did this not make enslaved people silent but emphatic influencers of Adirondack daily life? In the Black Woods, a veritable army of the unacknowledged and gone missing could pack a census of its own.

I understood the racialized accounts of Gerrit Smith's pioneers in terms of racial bias in its own time. It would be a while before I recognized how the default racism of the mid-nineteenth century was steeped in white ideas about Blackness that took hold in the region maybe centuries before Gerrit Smith's grantees went north. Also far from obvious to me: the shaping influence of white Adirondackers' ideas about *Redness* on how Black people were perceived. Indigenous peoples had sojourned in the Adirondacks for millennia before its "discovery" by Europeans, but their claim on the land would be discounted by Euro-colonizers who measured their entitlement to this new world by very different standards: in-place year-round settlement, land grants, deeds and titles. Early on, then, an exclusionary paradigm pitted the deserving against the rest.

And that paradigm not only preceded the Black farmers of Timbuctoo but persisted long after they were gone. The late nineteenth-century convergence of the conservation discourse with scientific racialism gave the region's members-only residential resorts, hunting lodges, sportsmen's clubs, and other elite strongholds a pseudoscientific rationale for excluding Black people and other "undesirables" for generations. In the name of guarding and defending the new-claimed Adirondack Park, poor white subsistence farmers, immigrants, indigenous people, and migratory laborers were framed as vectors of impurity, and in strokes both offhand and explicit, racialized as lesser, and unworthy of the park's bounty.

Given the fact that a legacy of enslavement was largely absent from the region, and that very few Black people lived in the Adirondacks from the first days of European settlement, this exclusionary culture baffled me. Why was it so entrenched? Why so well defended? I was looking for an answer in demography, which, of course, was not the place to look at all—though it took a book of literary criticism to re-direct my focus. In her canonical *Playing in the Dark*, the novelist Toni Morrison argues for a shadowy Black Other as a shaping presence in our best-known American novels, even when—maybe especially when—these books feature no Black characters and evince no concern with race. This Other makes its imprint, offers Morrison, not directly so much as inferentially, "in implication, in sign, in demarcation," and its work is oppositional; it reinforces authorial ideas of whiteness, offers a foil to the New American—self-made, resourceful, male, white—in many of our beloved novels.[2]

This writer's words shook something loose for me. Her subject was great literature, but was there an insight here as well on how to puzzle out entrenched narratives of regional identity? For all its enduringly white populace, the Adirondacks was steeped in a palimpsestic memory of slavery that stood everywhere for degradation and incapacity. Only scan the racist representations of Black Americans, free and enslaved, in nineteenth-century Adirondack newspapers, where editorials, boys' adventure stories, and dialect columns ensured that ideas about Black indolence and easy criminality stayed evergreen in white minds—and in towns where Black people could be numbered on one hand. As early as the mid-nineteenth century, blackface minstrel shows featuring white performers were a cherished mainstay of Adirondack small-town en-tertainment, and every time Rastus and Jemima cakewalked into Ad-irondack grange halls and opera houses (even into the 1950s), racial stereotypes about "natural-born" propensities and an inherent Black servility were reinforced.[3]

Freedom as the vested entitlement of whiteness was a point made and remade in low culture and high. Whenever an Adirondack county history introduced the courage and resourcefulness of a founding pio-neer in terms of his (always) Puritan forebears, these qualities were conflated with his undiluted Anglo "rootstock"—no small point in a place where the fight for environmental purity defines regional identity. It was a desire to ensure the purity of New York's water that made the winning case for the conservation of the Adirondack wilderness and the creation of the Adirondack Park, and it is the park's achievement *in defense of purity* whose story has dominated the region's history for the last century and a half. Eloquent dispatches extolled the region's vaunted unspoiled beauty and healthful assets along with the cultural and racial purity of Adirondack Yankee "founders." From the 1840s for another century, an emphasis on social purity—who belonged, who didn't, who were stewards, who despoilers—gave this place a name for exclusivity that outshone all competitors (including the Massachusetts Berkshires, the New Hampshire White Mountains, and New York's earlier-settled Catskills). And always against purity stood the Other, Toni Morrison's contrapuntal shadow that lent the normative its clarity and frame.[4]

Even the memory of John Brown was enlisted in this cause. Brown's Adirondack sojourn would be deracialized into a one-size-fits-all fable of courage and self-sacrifice without regard to means and ends. In these tellings, his single-minded focus expressed his purity of pedigree, that oft-noted Puritan ancestry so attractive to historians who were unnerved by what he did. This enshrinement in Adirondack memory and the devaluing of Brown's concern for systemic racial justice should not surprise us. Historians like David Blight have documented how postbellum Blue-Gray commemorative events marginalized the brutal history of slavery in the name of sectional reconciliation. What happened to Brown's memory was happening all over.[5]

And, of course, whatever happened to John Brown's memory affected the memory of Timbuctoo—if only because it was Brown's interest in Timbuctoo that explains history's attention to it, sporadic and impatient as it was. I confess that when I was working on the exhibition, my focus on the Black grantees came as a relief; it spared me the mighty challenge of tangling with John Brown's exacting legacy. But if the exhibit gave me a pass, this book was less indulgent. As I bushwhacked into the afterlives of the Black Woods in memory (lives, not life, because Black memory made one thing of Gerrit Smith's idea, white memory another, and white memory, more confident and empowered, wrote the lasting script), Brown was everywhere, his energy and vision backlit by the presumed *inaction* of Black neighbors who declined to join him. They were the foil—the uninspired, uncompelled.

Research for this book, unlike the exhibition, gave me the freedom to consider the historiography of the Black Woods as a dramatic player in its own right. How did antiquarian historians and John Brown's early biographers use Gerrit Smith's initiative to argue for Adirondack exceptionalism and a racialized regional brand? Recall the suspicion and anxiety among Brother Yusuf's campers. The reputation of the Adirondacks—no place for the dark complected—is deep-set.

In the last quarter century, Timbuctoo has roused the interest of artists, scholars, and racial justice activists alike. The year 1998 saw the publication of the Boston educator Katherine Butler Jones's "They Called It Timbucto," an intimate account in the environmental magazine *Orion* of this college teacher's discovery of her ancestors' gift of Adirondack acreage from Gerrit Smith. In that year, too, Russell Banks's expansive novel *Cloudsplitter* plunged a wide readership into John Brown's North Elba sojourn and his Adirondack world. Timbuctoo looms as well in the Harvard historian John Stauffer's 2001 cultural history, *The Black Hearts of Men*, and four years later in David Reynolds's definitive *John Brown, Abolitionist*, the first biography to give the Brown family's Adirondack years their due.[6]

More recently, Timbuctoo has inspired book chapters and papers from scholars at Rice, Cornell, SUNY Potsdam, and Harvard. The anthropologist Hadley Kruczek-Aaron has explored the sites where the Black pioneer Lyman Eppes lived or farmed. The Rochester composer Glenn McClure gave Eppes, the best remembered of the Smith grantees, a lead voice in an Adirondack folk opera and oratorio produced and performed by the seventy-person Northern Lights Choir in Saranac Lake. Schoolchildren in Adirondack hamlets have turned stories of Black farmers into folk songs and school plays. The saga of John Thomas, the Smith grantee and self-emancipated slave, is a central feature of the permanent exhibition at the North Star Underground Railroad Museum in Ausable Falls. As for the John Brown Lives! exhibit, *Dreaming of Timbuctoo*: in 2015, after fifteen years on the road, setting up in granges, college galleries, museums, city halls, the New York State Library, an Adirondack correctional facility, and the state fair (twice), the state Historic Preservation Office gave it a permanent home in the big barn at the John Brown Farm State Historic Site (which gave me an opportunity to occasionally refresh the script with new findings).[7]

The charismatic luster of this story in this time makes sense. In New York's northern wilderness before the Civil War was a subversive plan to challenge race-based voter suppression, a radical bid for environmental distributive justice, and a case for the bracing value of face-to-face connection as an antidote to bigotry—even if the often neighborly rapport between Black and white Adirondackers was never color-blind. A respect for racial justice did not crown this land (Brown's egalitarian household notwithstanding). The postracial community the giveaway's promoters promised would arise from the homesteaders' recognition of a common good did not prevail.

Yet ground was gained. The exigencies of frontier life ensured it. Good neighbors, honest and dependable, were too few to take for granted. Necessity compelled suspicion to defer to a practical collegiality. The way a fellow tracked a wolf, laid a fire; a helpful pair of hands at childbirth—the human touch was felt. Race prejudice was a given in the Black Woods; it was not unassailable. White Adirondackers took pride in the relative absence of a slaveholding tradition, and if Yankees stamped the region with a racialized Anglo-Saxonism, they also brought their faith in small-*r* republicanism, and the trace memory of Great Awakenings that urged resistance to top-down religious rule and a greater trust in the inner light of conscience. These legacies did not rout "Negrophobia," but between them and the subversive influence the Black grantees exerted through their own examples, some biases relaxed their vigil. The picture, we might say, was vexed.

And in this sense, not because it was utopian but because it was the opposite—imperfect, rangy, and adaptive—the story here suggests a model. There have been Black Woods, after all, all over the land. Vermont, Oregon, Indiana, California, Maine—they all have secret histories pasted thick with hegemonic folklore. But lost as they are, and often misconstrued, these scattered histories still had their triumphs—gains enabled by the common, hardworking love of place. The raw world of the frontier was just loose enough at the joints to let these gains occur. If we can take from them a glimpse, however fleet, of that promised arc that bends toward justice, we see why the Black Woods matters.

So we lean in, and we look hard. A glimpse may be all we get.

Notes on Language, Spelling, and Surnames

When I quote a historical document in this book or invoke a place name that reflects racist word usage at the time the name originated, I have chosen to retain the original spelling and capitalization that speaks for that history.

As offensive as this language is to me and, I suspect, to most readers of this book, I can't see easing my own discomfort by misrepresenting someone else's language whose values are at odds with my own or my readers'. My responsibility is to the unmediated representation of the record, and to the representation of the day-to-day Adirondack world the Black pioneers tried, and managed, to make their own.

This is not a choice every reader will embrace. I write this to explain my reasoning, and to acknowledge and thank my readers for their forbearance.

John Brown hewed to the spelling of *Timbucto* with one *o*; his son John Jr. spelled it with two. Artists and essayists like the two *o*'s better. Historians side with John Brown. Because Brown was an erratic speller, and *Timbuctoo* is more familiar with two *o*'s, and also because switch-hitting in this book between a one-*o* and a two-*o* *Timbuctoo* seems needlessly confusing, I go with *Timbuctoo* throughout. Context should make it clear when *Timbuctoo* signifies a small North Elba enclave where the name, or nickname, likely got its start, or the wider neighborhood of Black grantees in North Elba (John Brown's understanding of it), or the Black settlement in its wide-ranging entirety, a looser reading that includes the St. Armand and Franklin enclaves. In recent years, the name Timbuctoo is sometimes used to stand for all of these. I try to resist this, not always with success.

Dr. James McCune Smith's last name was Smith. I refer to him as McCune Smith in this book to distinguish him from Gerrit Smith.

Several leading families in the Black Woods spelled their surnames in more than one way. Lyman E. Eppes, Gerrit Smith grantee, used two *e*'s in his surname—but not always. His son Lyman dropped the second *e*, except when he didn't. Avery Hazzard used two *z*'s, and his son Charles Henry did also—for a while. Where a preference is very reliably suggested (as with Lyman Epps Jr.), I honor it. Otherwise, and for the sake of consistency, I hew to the more familiar spelling.

Abbreviations

Civil War Pensions

All Civil War pension files noted in this book—veteran, widow, and dependent—are in the National Archives and Records Administration (NARA) in Washington, DC.

CAM   Charlotte Ann [Thomas] Morehouse, widow's pension, 297.189
CHH   Charles Henry Hazzard, military pension, 709.265, 357.887
CM   Christina [Anderson] Mason, widow's pension, 787.162
EC   Eliza [Reed] Carasaw, widow's pension, 381.111
JBr   James Brady, military pension, 608.822
JF   Jane [Oakley] Frazier, widow's pension, 233.302 and 185.533
JH   Josiah Hasbrook, military pension, 302478, 373.818, 372.818
JM   Jeremiah Miles, military pension, 589.087
JSH   Julia [Smith] Hazzard, widow's pension, 427.53
LB   Louisa [Bunyan/Domer] Brady, dependent mother's pension, 342.920
LM   Lewis Mason, military pension, 787.162
LPM   Lucy [Pierce Hasbrook] Miles, widow's pension, 1007183
MCM   Mary C. [Wheeler] Mason, widow's pension, 283.513
SH   Simeon Hasbrook, military pension, 31475, 77173, 30702
TE/TT   Thomas Elliott, alias, Thomas Thompson, military pension, 1376073
THSP   Thomas H. Sands Pennington, military pension, 807815

Newspapers and Journals

AA   *Anglo-African*
ADE   *Adirondack Daily Enterprise*
AP   *Albany Patriot*
A&P   *Argus & Patriot* (Montpelier, VT)

AR-EP	Adirondack Record-Elizabethtown Post
BDE	Brooklyn Daily Eagle
CA	The Colored American
DG	Daily Gazette (Schenectady, NY)
DM	Douglass' Monthly
ECR	Essex County Republican
EP	Elizabethtown (NY) Post
EPG	Elizabethtown (NY) Post & Gazette
FDP	Frederick Douglass' Paper
FG	Franklin Gazette
IC	Impartial Citizen
LPN	Lake Placid News
MF	Malone Farmer
MP	Malone Palladium
NASS	National Anti-slavery Standard
NE	National Era
NS	North Star
NSCF	Northern Star and Colored Farmer
NSFA	Northern Star and Freemen's Advocate
NYDN	New York Daily News
NYDT	New York Daily Tribune
NYHT	New York Herald Tribune
NYT	New York Times
PC	Pittsburgh Courier
PDR	Plattsburgh Daily Republican (1916–42)
PF	Provincial Freeman (Toronto)
PPR	Plattsburgh Press-Republican (1942–66)
PR	Plattsburgh Republican (1813–1916)
P-R	Press-Republican (1966–)
PS	Plattsburgh Sentinel (1861–1931)
RH	Ram's Horn
SL	Signal of Liberty
TC	The Crisis
TS	Ticonderoga Sentinel
VWSJ	Vermont Watchman & State Journal

Agents, Grantees, and Interested Parties

BBS	Boyd B. Stutler
CBR	Charles Bennett Ray

DD   Daniel Dorrance
FD   Frederick Douglass
GS   Gerrit Smith
HHG   Henry Highland Garnet
HWH   Harry Wade Hicks
JB   John Brown
JHH   James H. Henderson
JMB   Jesse Max Barber
JMS   James McCune Smith
LEE   Lyman E. Eppes
LK   Lemuel Knapp
SW   Samuel Warner
TW   Theodore S. Wright
WH   Willis A. Hodges
WPP   William P. Powell

Historic Sites, Libraries, Archives, and Repositories

CTSR   Comptrollers Tax Sales Records, New York State Archives (NYSA)

Du Bois Papers   W. E. B. Du Bois Papers, Special Collections and University Archives, University of Massachusetts Amherst

ECCO   Essex County Clerk's Office (archives, land and court records), Essex County Courthouse, Elizabethtown, NY

FCA   Franklin County Archives, Franklin County Courthouse, Malone, NY

GSLB   Gerrit Smith's *Land Book, v. 88, or, Account of My Distribution of Land among Colored Men,* ca. 1846–53, GSP

GSP   Gerrit Smith Papers, Special Collections Research Center, Syracuse University Libraries, Syracuse, NY

HWHC   Harry Wade Hicks Collection, John Brown Farm State Historic Site, North Elba, NY

JB/BBS Coll./WVMP   John Brown/Boyd B. Stutler Collection, West Virginia Memory Project (https://archive.wvculture.org/history/wvmemory/imls intro.html)

JBF	John Brown Farm State Historic Site, North Elba, NY
JBJr	John Brown Jr. Papers, Ohio Historical Society, Columbus, OH
JBjrKS	John Brown Jr. Papers, Kansas State Historical Society, Topeka
JBjrOH	John Brown Jr. Letters, Charles E. Frohman Collections, Rutherford B. Hayes Presidential Library, Fremont, OH
JBMA	John Brown Memorial Association/Harry Wade Hicks Collection, John Brown Farm State Historic Site, North Elba, NY
LOC	Library of Congress, Washington, DC
LPPL	Lake Placid Public Library, NY
NARA	National Archives and Records Administration, Washington, DC
NE	North Elba, NY
NYHS	New-York Historical Society, New York City
NYPL	New York Public Library, New York City
NYSA	New York State Archives, Albany
NYSC	New York State Census, NYSL, Albany
PIA	Peebles Island Archives, Bureau of Historic Sites, Parks, Recreation, and Historic Preservation, Peebles Island State Park, Waterford, NY
SLFL	Saranac Lake Free Library (Adirondack Research Room), Saranac Lake, NY
SUNY	State University of New York
USFC	United States Federal Census, NARA

Introduction

        In 1921, Alfred L. Donaldson, author of the two-volume *History of the Adirondacks,* summed up a wealthy abolitionist's donation of 120,000 acres in New York's northern wilderness to three thousand Black New Yorkers with a smirk: "The attempt to combine an escaped slave with a so-called Adirondack farm was about as promising of agricultural results as would be the placing of an Italian lizard on a Norwegian iceberg." Donaldson was something. In a breath he managed to sectionalize, racialize, and discount the entire story of the Black Woods. So confident was his dismissal that it skewed the public understanding of this story for another eighty years.[1]

But Donaldson got one thing right: the abolitionist reformer Gerrit Smith's "scheme of justice and benevolence" of 1846 did not produce the crop of Black farmers Smith hoped for. The great majority of Smith's Black grantees judged a removal to the wilderness an untimely, unaffordable idea. His deedholders who sampled life on the Adirondack frontier may, at best, have numbered around seventy, exclusive of family members and fellow travelers who brought the head count closer to two hundred. Most would not remain in the region. The descendants of those who did would not recall a family link to an antebellum strategy to win Black voting rights. By the usual yardsticks of success (longevity, prosperity, and local pride), the radical philanthropist Gerrit

Smith had good reason to judge his plan a bust. So, on he pressed to more urgent, less parochial affairs: the campaign for a "Free Soil" Kansas, the battle for the Union, the abolition of slavery, and, toward the end of his life, the defense of civil rights for four million freed Black Americans in the South. Except for the New York City activist Charles Bennett Ray, all of the great reformers who touted Gerrit Smith's "little colored colony" lost heart. Frederick Douglass, Henry Highland Garnet, Jermain Wesley Loguen, and James McCune Smith all let the coals of their enthusiasm cool to ash.[2]

And these coals had glowed so hotly, and warmed so many souls! The vision of forty-acre lots of land for thousands, land that spoke for economic independence and the right to vote, once held New York's Black reform community in thrall. For twenty-five years since the state's Constitutional Convention of 1821, free men of color in New York had been denied the ballot unless they could show proof of ownership of $250 in landed property. The race-specific property requirement aimed to hobble an emergent Black electorate. With statewide abolition scheduled for July 4, 1827, New York's proslavery interests hoped to nip the threat of Black political empowerment in the bud. This they did, decisively. Notwithstanding the efforts of equal justice lobbyists to get the racist rule rescinded, it would be endorsed at the Constitutional Convention of 1846 and resoundingly reinstated at the polls.[3]

Hence the giveaway (my inelegant name for Smith's land distribution scheme). Gerrit Smith from Peterboro, a small village in upstate New York south of the Mohawk River, had land to spare he did not need. His donation of three thousand Adirondack gift lots would, he reasoned, not only get land into the hands of Black New Yorkers and help them meet an onerous, for-Blacks-only property requirement, but would lure them out of cities and make them citizens of the republic through self-directed labor on their own backcountry farms. How Smith came up with this idea, how it expressed Romantic notions about spiritual regeneration and a conviction that the only hope for Black New Yorkers was to leave urban life behind—all this is taken up in the first part of this book, along with the good work of Smith's adviser-scouts ("agents") who vetted thousands of grantees. These Black reformers kept Smith informed about the rampant "Negro-phobia" in metropolitan New York that crushed any hope of Black economic gain. It was their and Smith's belief that moving to the wilderness would not only ease his grantees' access to the ballot but fire up their souls. On their own land, Smith's deedholders would gain economic freedom alone and dignity, civic pride, community. With their eyes fixed on this prize, Smith and his agents enjoyed an interracial alliance that, while not unprecedented in New York, ranked among the earliest pioneering instances of Blacks and whites collaborating, working toward a shared progressive end.[4]

In this first section, too, are the first hints and rumbles of dissatisfaction with Smith's plan from Black activists outside his inner ring of confidantes. Some had their own ideas about what they needed, plans that worked for them. An enterprising grantee from Albany, the activist Stephen Myers, had the temerity to organize a sort of countercolony for free Black settlers west of the Adirondacks in the Tug Hill region north of Utica. Smith's discomfort with this plan revealed more than he intended about his uneasiness with Black initiative; it was always so much easier to go for Black empowerment when he fixed the terms.

The second section of this book steps down from the high stoop of aspirational rhetoric to the rubbled floor of work and action, and finds the grantees at home in the woods. The land Smith earmarked for his beneficiaries—about forty miles north to south and maybe fifteen miles across, or eight times the size of Manhattan—was not a solid swath. Smith scattered gift lots; he spread the wealth around. Picture the patchy profile of a half-finished Scrabble game, as many squares unoccupied as full. This is how the Smith Lands show up on an Adirondack map. Smith wanted his giftees to range a little, not huddle in defensive clusters. And he may have also wanted to introduce white land reformers to racially distributive environmental justice in action. "Give up your proposition of a separate location for the colored people," he told the land reformer George H. Evans in 1844, and "identify yourself with the whole human family, and have a heart big enough for every afflicted child of Adam to run into; and then you will have a reforming spirit." He was preaching to the resolutely unconverted, who were filled "with horror," as he knew, at "the thought of tessellated, piebald townships." But Smith would have his Adirondack checkerboard, and white land reformers would learn this could be done.[5]

The grantees, of course, saw something else: Smith's scattering of gift lots was a recipe for social isolation and insecurity, and some of them would organize—their deeds be hanged!—Black enclaves that hinted at their old devotion to the memory of towns and cities they left behind. So grantees from Troy stuck tight, as did Brooklynites, and Hudson River Valley families too. Getting to know their new white neighbors would happen when it happened, if it happened, and this would take some time. (Smith's Black land agents would not furnish grantees with the names of sympathetic white people until 1848.) Notwithstanding the Adirondacks' progressive vote on Black voting rights in 1846 (Essex, Clinton, and Franklin Counties all went for equal suffrage), the grantees knew a laissez-faire rural racism was likely. On Election Day, no Black names on the ballot. In schoolhouses, no Black teachers scratching sums on slate. In stores, which doubled as ad hoc banks, no line of credit for the Black farmer looking to enlarge a home or build a business.[6]

Even so, there were locals who were openhearted and square dealing, who offered shrewd appraisals of the gift land and directed deedholders unhappy with their lots to better land nearby. History has recognized John Brown's family for its sympathetic dealings with the grantees, but part two notes many more white people than the Browns who were allies and companions of the Black pioneers. White neighbors stood by an elderly grantee a speculator hoped to evict. White neighbors of a Black farmer, once enslaved, scared away a bounty hunter looking to take him back to the South. Black and white North Elbans founded two North Elba churches together, and a library, and a choir. Black and white homesteaders shared town appointments, brought potatoes to the same starch factory, buried their dead in the same cemeteries. Mountain hikes, ball games, Christmas feasts, and field work were shared pursuits. When the Union Army needed volunteers, Black Adirondackers stepped up, and after the Civil War, white Adirondackers supported the military pension claims of their Black neighbors. Several white households made room for Black boarders, and this worked the other way too. In the great commons of the unregulated wilderness, Black people and white hunted, fished, and foraged together, and bridled at new laws that deemed them poachers and their culture of subsistence something thieving and pathetic. The shared work of place making on this frontier was no perfect antidote for racism, but racism was challenged and subverted in a hundred unsuspected ways.

Strongest Champion and Truest Friend

A few days after Christmas in 1874, Gerrit Smith, seventy-seven, died of a stroke in his nephew's home in Manhattan. Obituaries were long and lavish, praising public work and private deeds alike. Editors who scoffed at Smith's politics and style while he lived put the barbs away to laud a moral icon. In newspapers and magazines, essays honored the equal rights reformer who, offered the *New York Herald*, "was not great, as Clay and Webster and Calhoun were great—[and] was not even so profound a champion of his cause as Charles Sumner, but [who] united the aristocratic bearing of the gentleman with the simplicity of the servant of the bondman, giving to him as a brother, in such equal proportions that he earned for himself a title better than that of gentleman, better than that of philanthropist—that of a man." The *Tribune*, long a thorn in Smith's side, was fulsome: "The possession of great tracts of land makes common men conservative and monopolists. It made of Gerrit Smith one of the most radical and generous of men." Four articles on Smith's career and funeral ran in the *New York Times*. An editorial mourned the end of "the era of moral politics" and reminded readers of the "stubbornness of conviction and moral courage" it took to be an "'out-and-out Abolitionist' (even worse than the cry of 'Infidel' in the Middle Ages) in the antebellum era when so much of New York's trade and commerce was for slavery," and "when a 'nigger's' appearance anywhere near a Tammany meeting meant a broken head, if not an ornamented lamp-post." In Philadelphia, the *Christian Recorder* tolled the losses: "One by one are passing away the noble band of men who were the nation's truest leaders through the wilderness of the dark era of Slavery." Lovejoy, Giddings, Seward, Chase, Greeley and Tappan—all gone, and now, "the prince of them all . . . , Gerrit Smith. Providence could not have given the cause a more efficient ally. He was just the man."[7]

Viewing hours at General Cochrane's home where Smith's body rested under ferns in an ice shell by a window were brief and little publicized. Still, word sifted out and crowds collected, and the reporter from the *New York Times* judged that "fully one-fourth of those who called were colored people, whose grief on viewing the remains of their deceased benefactor was intense." Neither Frederick Douglass nor William Lloyd Garrison attended, but here was Smith's old friend Henry Highland Garnet, and what the churchman offered spoke for thousands: "The colored people without exception looked upon Mr. Smith as their dearest and even their only friend, such was . . . their affection for him. They know that in him they have lost their strongest champion and truest friend, and they keenly feel their loss."[8]

Other Black mourners in the room that day were Peter Porter, the "Railroad Champion for Equal Rights" (his fight for Black access to public transport thrice roused the wrath of mobs), and Charles Reason, a scholar-poet and school head. Elder Ray, Smith's city land agent, was detained, but he sent two daughters in his stead, and all this was duly noted by the *Times*. What the reporter didn't write, however (how could he know?), was that all the Black attendees he named had a tie to Smith's land giveaway of 1846. Reason, Porter, and Garnet were deed-holders. Charles Ray was, like Garnet, both agent and grantee. In fact, when Smith died, Charles Ray was *still* working for the giveaway and would keep working for it until his death in 1886, at which time his daughter Florence took up the baton.[9]

Ray's devotion would have left Smith baffled. *Why still bother? What meaning has this plan for anyone? Who remembers it? Who cares? Out of all the good I've done in my long life, why fix on the deed that so starkly failed to meet my expectations?*

But Smith's expectations are exactly what I've tried to push aside to see how his idea played out in ways he could not anticipate or imagine. He did not expect his grantees to squat on lots that weren't the ones he gave them or guess they would develop mini-neighborhoods of their own. And they did. He did not foresee the interest of Black speculators, who, like Smith, recognized a bargain when they saw one and started trading in Adirondack gift lots as soon as they came up for sale. He may have guessed that the agrarian values he invoked to explain his project would be touted at Black political conventions from the 1840s to the 1860s, but maybe not that activists would obliquely reference the Smith Lands when they promoted farm colonies for fugitives in Canada. After the Civil War, Black reformers also tipped their hats to Smith's great "scheme" of emigration when they urged Southern freedmen to put Ku Klux country at their backs and go west. White land reformers in the postbellum era recalled Smith's gift land, too, when they courted his support and urged him to back a more sweeping land reform agenda. Indirectly, white progressives honored the giveaway when they spun great schemes to head south after the war and establish farm colonies for freed people, impoverished immigrants, or poor white families, "honest and industrious." They knew what Smith tried to do in 1846. Now that slavery was over, maybe it was time to revive an old idea. They, too, were the heirs of Timbuctoo.[10]

Several deedholders, many prominent Black reformers among them, were inspired by their gift land not to move north but head instead for California, Michigan, and Canada West. One deedholder used Smith's idea as a model for an upstate colony of his own (a repurposing from which Smith recoiled). *Non*deedholders, beguiled by the rumor of a corner of New York where Black families were farming, ventured to the

Black Woods and claimed it for their home. And none of this Mr. Smith saw coming. Nor would he extend his giveaway to out-of-staters, but they still came, and mostly from the South. The expectation that only free people of color would respond to his offer was never very realistic, as Smith himself may have understood. The line between the free Black New Yorker and the fugitive was too porous, and without fanfare, freedom seekers would head north. But neither Smith nor his agents likely guessed that enslavers still chafing at the loss of human property would send their hired guns in hot pursuit of one Black farmer who had lived free in New York for a decade. Smith no more anticipated this than he imagined his Black agents might consider setting up an enslaved person with a gift lot of his own. But it happened, and the legal dust-up that attended it would span two centuries, long after the enslaved grantee and Gerrit Smith were dead. Nor would Smith ever learn that a key goal of the giveaway he deemed a failure had been realized, if not as robustly as he'd hoped. It was his bitter conviction that almost all his deedholders failed to retain their land for its value at the polls. But he was wrong. In 1903, the *New York Times* revealed that after the Fifteenth Amendment was enacted in 1870, as many as four hundred downstate Black New Yorkers gave up or sold the gift deeds their parents or grandparents received from Gerrit Smith. They had retained them for twenty-four years, until the hated property requirement was nullified and their rights of citizenship were guaranteed. Then, and not until, they let them go. So the gift deeds helped them vote. This was Smith's idea, and some part of it bore fruit.

If the first meaning of this book's title invokes the settlers who responded to Smith's offer, and the world they made with their white neighbors in the Adirondack woods, there is a second meaning too. There is the blackness of obscurity, of what cannot be seen. Since 1859, a vigilant and little-challenged narrative has kept this story in the shadows. "John Brown Country," the third section of this book, takes up the shaping role of historiography. How and why was a Black agrarian initiative reduced to anecdotal marginalia? From the first days it was publicized, Smith's giveaway was misrepresented in terms, here coded, there explicit, that racialized the Adirondacks as a country made and fit for white people. This prejudice shapes an image of the region even now.

This is not to say this whiting-out was special to this region. Scholars have delved deeply into forgotten or never-documented pockets of

Black social history in Iowa and Indiana, Maine, Oregon and Alabama, and all the old Northwest Territory. A midnight mob, a vanished neighborhood, a once thriving country church put to the torch—no corner of the country lacks a lost-and-found or still-lost story of its own. What distinguishes the Black Woods is the legibility of the process. With its glib and frequent linkages of environmental integrity and racial purity, the Adirondack brand has informed a racialized literary culture for a century and a half. And for this reason, the Black Woods suggests a model for considering this process in many places, Northern, rural, and purportedly all white, where the Black story has been othered. *Lost* and *othered* aren't the same. What happened in the Black Woods reminds us why the difference matters.[11]

How did it begin? Smith's plan was destined to be distorted; the pervasive racism of his time ensured this. But the shelf life of some fantasies-turned-facts has been very long indeed. Early on it was asserted that the giveaway was for "runaways," and, even now, casual summaries of this effort frame New York as a land of refuge and redemption, not as the state whose strident racism was a driving reason for Smith's plan. Another example along these lines: the insistence in antiquarian accounts that in a few years Black families on the ground thinned to one (in fact, the census reveals that as late as 1900, scores of deedholders' descendants resided in the region). Or the offhand, popular assertion that only one Black settlement, Timbuctoo, ever saw the light of an Adirondack day, when, in fact, four communities (Freeman's Home, Timbuctoo, Blacksville, and Negro Brook) were Black-founded, and Black families put down lasting roots in older hamlets founded by Canadians and New Englanders, such as St. Armand, Bloomingdale, and Franklin. Very sticky, too, has been the notion that when Black settlers left, they drifted "home" to cities they all came from and where they presumably belonged. In fact, when families moved from the Black Woods, they often migrated to small towns or other farm districts in upstate New York or New England.[12]

The most egregious historical distortion, the assertion of Black inferiority, did not originate with the sacralized terrain I call John Brown Country. Much older Eurocentric readings claimed this part of the New World for hegemonic narratives of white supremacy. John Brown himself stood for the opposite of this, of course, but the fierce antiracism he preached and practiced all his life would be much transformed—diluted and deracinated—after he was hanged and buried. The enshrinement of the antislavery martyr, which began with the gloomy trip that hauled his body home from Virginia to North Elba, an odyssey that pitched his widow Mary Ann and her companion, Wendell Phillips, from train to sail ferry, oxcart to wagon, and culminated in the sodden winter burial with its sparse mourners, put John Brown Country on the map. And as the allure of John Brown Country brightened with every visitor's rapt account, so would Brown's radical call for a world without caste or race hate grow fainter.

No grand tour of the Adirondacks in the late nineteenth century failed to include a stop at Brown's home; no magic lantern show lacked a slide of his slim headstone in its protective case of glass. Accounts of the pilgrimage to the farm usually put the rigors of the journey on a par with visiting the grave itself, which underscored a hopeful likeness between North Elba and holy sites like Calvary and Jerusalem. In the next century, the faithful included civil rights activists, Cold War zealots, and political progressives. From the 1920s into the 1970s, schools closed and church bells tolled as North Elbans gathered at the grave on Brown's May birthday, joining members of the John Brown Memorial Association from Boston, Worcester, Philadelphia, and New York. Speeches, prayers, and hymns were offered, and wreaths tipped tenderly against his stone. In local history and guidebooks, Brown was embraced as hometown hero and archetypal Adirondacker, resilient, blunt, God fearing, resolute.

But in these visits, the land gifts of Gerrit Smith, the part to do with equal voting rights, went unremarked. And if we have Brown to thank for forcing history to notice Timbuctoo at all, the blessing of his influence is mixed. The emphasis in shelves of "Browniana" on all the white man did for the grantees—the lot lines he set right, the lifesaving stores of food he supplied when famine threatened, the Scripture he intoned at Sabbath—did not extend to a concern with what his Black neighbors did for themselves or *their* impressions of their white neighbor. Except as conduits for John Brown anecdotes, they had no voice in his biographies. How they survived, or didn't, and what the Black Woods meant to them, were subjects not explored. Not so the assumption of the grantees' "natural" inadequacy, lack of mettle, staying power, or grit.

Why, biographers, historians, and memoirists loved to wonder, did so many of them abandon their gift farms? *Why* had none of them followed Brown to Kansas? Did they not see this was all for *them*? It is a fact that Brown moved to North Elba in part to find Black fighters for clandestine work to come, a goal he could not realize. The locals who joined his militant campaign were his sons (not all) and some white neighbors. The grantees in his neighborhood declined. The reason? They were obtuse. Unworthy of Brown's vision. Even Thomas Wentworth Higginson, the Massachusetts abolitionist and Brown's friend who found more things to praise about the Black farmers than most, embraced this judgment. When it came to the right stuff, said Higginson, Brown would find it only in his sons, "reared" to sacrifice and valor.[13]

Not to blame the poor grantees! Not to ask for what they never had to give! Asserted Smith's biographer, Octavius Brooks Frothingham, in 1878, "On the best land they would have done nothing. They had none of the qualities that make the farmer. . . . [Had] the land been the richest in the State they would not have responded, for they could not; it was not in them." Almost a half century later, E. P. Tanner dusted off the verdict for the state historical association, blaming the "failure" of Smith's giveaway on "the character of the colonists who naturally had neither the training nor the stuff in them for pioneering."[14]

Twentieth-century Black memory ought not to be censured for borrowing these essentialist conclusions. That W. E. B. Du Bois's 1909 John Brown biography suggested that Brown alone was responsible for "much if not all of [the giveaway's] success," or that Zita Dyson, a Black scholar writing on the giveaway in 1919, declared the Black grantees "had none of the qualities of farmers" and moreover were "disabled by infirmities and vices," reflected a necessary reliance on white antiquarian perspectives before primary sources became widely available (and before many libraries welcomed Black scholars). In the 1920s, the Black pilgrim-speakers of the John Brown Memorial Association (JBMA) never once spoke proudly of Smith's giveaway or acknowledged the Black settlements that brought their hero to North Elba. In fact, in 1978, the North Elba chapter of the JBMA joined ranks with white neighbors to crush a long-planned state initiative to bring a history center to the farm that would have fixed Brown's Adirondack chapter in the context of Black voting rights and Timbuctoo.[15]

Black Americans who moved to the Adirondacks in the decades of the Great Migration, seeking jobs in the grand resorts, service industry, iron mines, blast furnaces, and foundries, learned nothing of it either. The miner's daughter and social justice activist Alice Paden Green, whose family journeyed to the mining town of Witherbee from South Carolina after World War II, heard about the Black Woods only in her seventh decade. Black history at her Adirondack high school in 1948 was a ten-minute interlude on Booker T. Washington and Jackie

Robinson, "and if you missed that one class, that was it." For Alice and her siblings, the campaign for civil rights and racial justice belonged to blighted cities and a benighted South. Discovering a voting rights campaign that sired a nineteenth-century Black farm colony in her own Essex County thrilled her. But it also got her wondering: *How was she never told? Did her teachers know? Did anyone? Why had this story gone away?*[16]

It didn't go away, of course. What the public record junks is never sheer caprice. The Black Woods was the staging ground of an unprecedented voting rights initiative and the home of a cherished abolitionist shrine, but it also was the stronghold of an Anglocentric narrative of purity and inviolability that saved a wilderness while clinching the region's name as a place where nonwhite Americans did not fit, did not belong, feared they would never feel welcome, and suspect this even now.

We can't resolve this contradiction. The side-by-sideness of this world, the fractured quality of a culture so internally at odds—here gains and there reversals, now boons and later blows—more than characterized Adirondack Country. It enabled it. It defines it still. Far from the ennobled landscape so dear to abolitionists, travel writers, environmentalists, and town historians, this was an all-American roiling mess, a world of stubborn paradox where people said one thing, did another, and then went and did something else. It looked like hypocrisy but that would mean one thing was false and the other true and this wasn't how it was. Both sides were true; both sides were felt.

We chafe at this. The forward thrust of history clamors for coherence and progression but the lives as they were lived, up close, resist. And this confounds us. We want consistency. We ask, How could they manage? How did they bear it?

As if we were beyond this. As if this weren't us.

A Scheme of Justice and Benevolence

CHAPTER 1

He Feeds the Sparrow

> At Peterboro . . . it was all Abolition—Abolition
> in doors and out—Abolition in the churches and
> Abolition in the stores—Abolition in the field and
> Abolition by the wayside.
>
> —Charles Wheeler Dennison, New York
> abolitionist, 1841

In late August 1872, Gerrit Smith, a radical reformer in upstate New York, got a thank-you letter from a flyspeck hamlet in the Adirondack Mountains. All in a day's work. Smith, seventy-five, had a nation-spanning name for philanthropy as rich and deep as his own voice. A life of steady giving had earned him thank-you notes enough to paper every room in his mansion and the columns on his portico besides. He kept some, answered others, and threw away the rest. He spent as many as fifteen hours a day in his high-ceilinged study, whipping off letters in his swift, sometimes impenetrable hand to presidents, land agents, contract farmers, big-city editors, fellow reformers, and cousins twice removed. He wrote about temperance, Cuban independence, Italy's freedom fighters, and the famine-making grasshoppers of Kansas. He had a lot to say.[1]

In 1872, when Smith heard from the Adirondack homesteader John Thomas, he was in his land office near his Peterboro home, penning speeches on behalf of the presidential candidate Ulysses S. Grant. The powerful newspaper publisher Horace Greeley was running on a multiparty ticket against the war hero and incumbent, and though Grant had his liabilities (the chronic tippling, the blatant cronyism), most Republicans felt bound to defend him. Smith, who knew that civil rights for nearly five million Black Americans could happen, if it happened, only with a Republican in the White House, flogged Grant's candidacy with a fervor near fanatic. A friend chided him for his "unaccountable . . . relentless severity" toward the Democrats: "It would seem as if your philanthropy was leaking out." But Smith dug in, arguing that "the Anti-Slavery battle is not yet fought out—and, until it is, we shall need Grant's continued leadership."[2]

Still, caught up as he was in the campaign, Smith saved the letter from John Thomas. His old hopes for his Adirondack land giveaway were dead, and nothing Thomas had to say would brighten Smith's view of it. Yet here was this full-hearted, unexpected thank-you note from one of Smith's three thousand Black beneficiaries, still up there in the North Country, and still farming as Smith had hoped. Smith wouldn't, couldn't, give it to the coals.

Close to a million acres had come to Smith in early manhood upon the death of his father, Peter Smith, a fur trader turned spectacularly wealthy land speculator. Gerrit Smith then bought more land on his own, much of it at auction. But selling Adirondack land proved much less easy than inheriting or buying it. By 1846, he'd had enough. Why labor unavailingly to peddle wild land when he could make a gift of it to those unable to afford it? With 120,000 acres broken into 40-acre lots, Smith could give as many as three thousand Black New Yorkers a reason to leave the city, remake themselves as yeoman farmers, and enjoy the fruits of citizenship when they gained the right to vote. After the 1821 Constitutional Convention, New York law withheld the ballot from free Black men who could not show they owned $250 in taxable property. The point of this racialized voting requirement was to check Black enfranchisement before slavery was legally abolished in New York in 1827, and it worked. A Black electorate was administratively aborted before it could be politically empowered. When Smith announced his plan to give away a portion of his land in 1846, this "mean and wicked exclusion" had already kept a generation of Black New Yorkers from the polls.[3]

1846 was also the year of the first state Constitutional Convention in New York since 1821. Convention delegates from every county poured into Albany to debate a range of changes to New York's constitution, including the question of Black enfranchisement. After a summer of rancorous debate, the issue remained unresolved. The weary delegates handed off the fate of equal suffrage to a plebiscite, and that November, New York voters (white men all) went two to one to keep the for-Blacks-only $250 restriction. When Smith announced his giveaway in

Hon. Gerrit Smith of New York. Matthew Brady, photographer, 1855–60. Brady-Handy Photograph Collection, LOC.

August 1846, this outcome was not certain. But it loomed, and he knew what it would do. For decades free Black Americans had protested the suppression of a Black electorate. More than two hundred national and state Colored Conventions took place from 1830 into the 1890s, with Black rights and suffrage justice, the measure of full citizenship, at the head of the agenda. Smith foresaw how it would resonate for Black New Yorkers in 1846 when white voters, once again, kept them from the ballot. His land distribution effort was a preemptive strike that stood for hope. No one of his gift lots held the worth of the $250 voting requirement, but if land was cleared, fields planted, and holdings doggedly improved, the rising value of these gift lots would be noted by the town assessor, and the voting requirement might be met. "Since the State has... determined [that] Black men . . . must become landholders that they may be entitled to vote they will become landholders," Smith reasoned. "Vote they will, cost what it will."[4]

Land reform was the other great goal of his giveaway, and this Smith deemed quite as urgent as racial justice at the polls. "I am an Agrarian," he told his Black city agents in his explanatory letter about his "scheme of justice and benevolence." "I would that every man who desires a farm might have one." He had pressed for environmental justice before, but in this letter, he clarified the link between poverty and racism, each the stoker and enabler of the other. In New York City, whole fields of working-class employment were closed to Blacks. In public spaces and professions, schools, businesses, and churches, segregation was the rule. Hence Smith's belief that city Blacks would benefit the most from his land gifts in the woods; if poor Black New Yorkers faced hardships unimaginable to poor whites, poor Black *city* people had it worse. The agents Smith chose to cull his grantees in metropolitan New York were as unhappy with Black prospects in the city as he was, and had long urged an outmigration of Black people in the city to small towns and the country. Smith's giveaway gave Black agrarianism a compass. Black urbanites now had a place to go, not just a place to leave.[5]

That destination, the Adirondack wilderness, was imperfect, as Smith knew. Little of the gift land was homestead ready. There would be gift lots under water, or straddling the shaggy spines of mountains. Some would be in country so remote, so impenetrable, it had yet to be surveyed. And Smith's knowledge of it was thin. What he saw from the coach that juddered him around the region to check in with his rent collectors was fleeting, and those journeys, always arduous, were infrequent. Smith traveled only when he had to. Home and office were his keep. Like the baronies of many speculators in his era, his near-million-acre empire surged and ebbed on tides of paper. But about his gift land he could say this: It might not match more richly soiled land out west, and would always suffer from the impatient brevity of the Adirondack summer, but it was free of liens, or close enough, and most taxes were paid up. It had value, and it could gain more.[6]

Other benefits of his new scheme Smith kept to himself. No need to dwell on the fact that these land gifts would relieve his tax burden and the dreary work of long-distance land management. Also left unstated was his hope that Black New Yorkers, once enfranchised, would vote for the Liberty Party, the only dedicatedly antislavery party in New York. Smith, a keen disciple, stumped for the Liberty, attended its conventions, published handbills for the cause, and sometimes saw his name on its ticket. But he never asked for votes from his giftees. He knew better. In March 1846, he had carelessly confessed that he cared less about Black voting rights than about whether the enfranchised Black voter could be relied on to "cast his vote in the right spirit, and for the right ends." Whig newspapers smirked for weeks at this admission that Smith's interest in equal suffrage was motivated by the expectation of Black votes for his party: "So is the *liberty* of the Liberty party of New York!"[7]

The depth of Smith's commitment to his interest in Black voting rights also came under fire in the spring of 1846 when he refused to back a one-time Liberty-Whig alliance that might have beefed up the prosuffrage lobby at the New York Constitutional Convention. Nothing, Smith fumed, not even a better shot at equal rights for Black New Yorkers, could excuse deal making with the Whigs. A party that counted slaveholders among its leaders was in cahoots with Satan. The mere idea of collaborating filled Smith "with surprise, shame and sorrow." Smith's toughness on this point recalled to some Whig editors the Liberty's old name as a spoiler. Hadn't this same radical intransigence as much as put the slave-owning Democrat James Polk in the White House in 1844, poaching precious swing votes from the Whig contender, Henry Clay, and wasting them on the unelectable antislavery "Ultraist" James Birney? For New York Whigs, the bitter grievance had not died.[8]

But the giveaway put party politics to the side. Here was a gift outright, or very close—a gift that asked only that its beneficiaries be Black, poor, nondrinking, and living in Smith's New York. Smith was not dunning for his beloved party or putting principle ahead of practical reform. If his earlier positions gave him a name for obduracy, the giveaway was pointedly conciliatory. It suggested a common cause between white land reformers and Black agrarians; it gave abolitionists Black and white, at odds on points of strategy, something to agree on;

it did not privilege any of the sparring factions in the Black reform community; and, above all, it birthed a new fraternity of Gerrit Smith *giftees*. What bound them? Nothing more or less than the shared fact of ownership, and ownership of something so unknown that it partook (briefly) of the ideal: a land that promised self-sufficiency, a farm economy so productive, so fine-tuned, it had no need of cash or credit, debt or interest. In his cultural history *The Gift*, Lewis Hyde observes that when people share the condition of being gifted all together, they discover a "society . . . where there was none before." The promise of membership in this new-made society was as much Smith's gift as the deeds themselves.[9]

The Perfectionist's Agenda

The giveaway gifted Smith too. Its charitable spirit honored the claims of faith. Notwithstanding his rejection of his father's strict Presbyterianism, Smith was a man of God. Hewing to a usable "religion of Jesus"—a faith-in-action that asked Smith to bring his business into line with Christian goals each day—this was his life's challenge. Through an accretion of conscious acts and gestures, Smith could make the world more perfect, more a facsimile of heaven on this earth. This was how the world was saved, his road map to Perfectionist redemption.[10]

The idea was not his. Smith grew up in the Burned-Over District of rural upstate New York. The land was scorched, it was said, because so many here had been evangelized at camp revivals that no "fuel" was left to burn. Faith through doing, faith inherent in each act and gesture, took vigilance and ingenuity; Smith seized the challenge. Private losses drove him too. In 1837, a nationwide financial panic drained much of his worth, and the same year marked the deaths of his father, Peter, and his and his wife Nancy's son and daughter. Loss on this order devastated, but in radical abolitionism Smith found a working faith that let the world in and helped him find his focus. Abolitionism was not just one available expression of Christian love; it was its culmination. If nothing was dearer to God's heart than the faithful observation of the Golden Rule, nothing could be more offensive than its opposite, and what greater violation of the Golden Rule than the reduction of a God-gifted human soul to chattel? Slavery insulted God's best gift, derailed His plan and subverted any hope of a redeemed, perfected world. A true Christian theology was obliged to challenge this first sin any way it could.[11]

So when Gerrit and Nancy Smith's hometown ministers balked at preaching antislavery Bible politics on the Sabbath, or would not call out slavery as sinful because it might offend the sternly "neutral" policies of distant church authorities, the Smiths formed their own church, the nonaffiliated Free Church of Peterboro. And like the democratic grassroots congregations of early Christianity, Peterboro's church would be accountable to its own members and authority alone. As for "those stupid, nonsensical, absurd doctrines with which the churches have ever been puzzling their poor, pitiable brains"—a lot of mystic claptrap, Smith declared. The sole criterion of discipleship in the "Christ-religion" of the new church was "everyday conduct in the presence of the world." Did the "Comeouter" congregant take Jesus as his model? Reject the "nonsense—that he, whom God has made a man, man can turn into a chattel"? Did she who called herself Christian understand this meant not just enacting the Golden Rule at every opportunity but spurning church denominations that admitted slaveholders, stores that peddled slave-made goods, and parties that counted slave owners among their candidates?[12]

This was a lot to ask. A Peterboro Presbyterian might say she hated slavery and still covet a frock of slave-grown cotton. A Congregationalist could call himself an abolitionist yet dose his tea with slave-milled sugar. Abolition faith said no. Why, asked the proponents of Bible politics, should one portion of one's life be less subject to God's law than another? Why not one unifying standard? Every corner of the secular realm was game for the work of perfectionist redemption. Bring it all under scrutiny, hold firm, and if members of this community squabbled, be a peacemaker. No antislavery reformer in the Burned-Over District did as much as Gerrit Smith to nurse and knit the radicals into a collaborative force.[13]

Another laboratory for a sanctified community was Smith's Peterboro home. With the goal of hastening the great day of redemption, Smith made his daily world a model of love and justice. In the name of "[building] up the Redeemer's Kingdom in this community," he launched his hometown church, organized a Black trade school, and recruited applicants from New York City, some fugitives among them. In the village named for his father, he fenced his village green, improved the creek, and stocked an antislavery library in the spirits-free inn. He spruced up the cemetery and gave neighbors cash to paint their homes and buy them. This was not the easy, incidental charity of the giver who fires off a bank note to the antislavery outfit of his choice. Smith's sleepless philanthropy was as reflexive as his breath.[14]

The farm colonies that Smith hoped to launch on his Adirondack gift land could not replicate his Peterboro, but they were Peterboro's country cousins, suggesting (at least on paper) Smith's dream of a perfected world. Putting antislavery settlers on the ground whose votes might abolitionize their backwoods communities was a beginning. And when Smith made sure the gift land was in a part of his property seeded with antislavery believers, devised rules of eligibility for land that screened God's deserving poor from the impious and intemperate, and encouraged his Adirondack settlers to build an antislavery church "on the Peterboro platform," he honored a Perfectionist agenda.[15]

Smith also offered the Black settlers a proxy version of himself—another rock-hard abolition man who had read about Smith's plan for a Black farm colony on the Adirondack frontier and thought it something fine, even hoped to move his family there to help the pioneers. Would Smith support him? In April 1848, this sheep farmer came to Peterboro to share with Smith his hope to "give [the grantees] work as I have occasion, look after them in all needful ways, and be a kind of father to them." A wonderful idea, Smith agreed, and a year later, John Brown, the name as plain as his garb and speech, moved his family of eleven into a vacant farmhouse in North Elba, hard by a fledgling Black enclave whose nickname, Freemans Home, would endure in local memory another hundred years. This commonsensical, no-nonsense Yankee, Smith believed, would work wonders for the "colored colony." With John Brown in the grantees' corner, Smith may have felt God read his heart.[16]

Yours with Great Respect

What the Adirondack grantee John Thomas offered Gerrit Smith in his thank-you note of 1872 (transcribed with a neighbor's help, since he could not write) was a thumbnail sketch of his own life.

Thomas was not always a New Yorker. For his first three decades, home was Queen Anne's County, Maryland, where Thomas, his wife, and their children were enslaved. The babies died in infancy. Then in 1840, his wife was sold away to enslavers in Georgia. It was the calamity every married slave most feared. Thomas and his wife had made a world, a partnership, and in a day, maybe an hour, that world was loaded up like cordwood and carted out of sight. Thomas was immobilized. He could not think what to do. The next mood, a surging outrage, served him better. "Dissatisfied with my lot of being marketable property and a subject of involuntary servitude for no crime but that of the color which God gave me," the twenty-nine-year-old slave resolved to give his master, Ezekiel Merrick, a very "long farewell." That year, Thomas escaped from Merrick's farm and made his way to Quaker farmers. They directed him to Philadelphia, where he lingered for half a year before he pushed north to New York's upstate Troy, a boomtown on the Hudson River and his world for seven years.[17]

A strange new world he found here, too. No springy fragrance of the peach orchard, but coal-heated tenements and rank canals, and instead of hushed, clandestine meetings, were open speeches about slave catchers as murderers, slavery as sin. No more slave elders cloaking dreams of freedom and escape in homiletics, but bold-spoken activists blasting man-thieves, and young, well-educated Black ministers freely urging "resistance! resistance! resistance! . . . You had far better all die—*die immediately*, than live slaves." And yet this same Troy, for all its Black churches and vibrant oratory, was no easy place to love. Still in the thrall of proslavery interests that kept its mills humming around the clock, it was beset with blackbirders (subsidized kidnappers of fugitives) and white gangs.[18]

Some of Thomas's seven years in Troy were hopeful. Here he met and married his second wife, Mary Ann Vanderheyden. He joined the Liberty Street clapboard church of Rev. Henry Highland Garnet, who, too, was born enslaved in Maryland and had fled north. Garnet, perhaps Smith's most effective land agent, signed on interested grantees from Troy and its environs for two years running. And if he could not go north himself (a boyhood injury put farming out of reach), Garnet still made the gift land glow with all the promise Troy withheld. In 1849, the year Garnet left Troy for Geneva to pastor a small Black church, many congregants in Troy were packing for the Adirondack frontier. John Thomas, Mary Ann, and two children were among them.[19]

Thomas knew that starting over in the North would be daunting. A growing season quick enough to nap through, topsoil frayed as an old map, mosquitoes thick as woodsmoke, blackflies big as bats: the rumors hissed. Would he ever find his forty acres west of Plumadore Pond in Franklin County, Township 9? If he made the hike, his first view may well have been his last. To Gerrit Smith, he wrote that he sold this lot because of "the inconvenience of Church and School privileges at that time," but this was tact talking. "Privileges" in this raw, tangled forest would not come for years. In Township 10, just to the south, Thomas found a better lot handy to both a rough road and a clear-running stream, with enough Black settlers in the neighborhood to explain the (still-used) name of Negro (and sometimes N——) Brook. By 1850, the Thomases were well entrenched, their potato patch full seeded, their fields bright with oats and hay. Twenty-two years later, Thomas could describe to Smith a home "which by labor and necessity has been enlarged into a handsome farm of two hundred acres, with all necessary Stock and farming implements," and well secured, he noted proudly, with earnings of "two or three hundred dollars every year."[20]

Thanks to "your generous donation," Thomas assured Smith, he and his family "enjoy our rural home in peace and quiet." And now that "the toils of life are nearly done," he wanted his rich benefactor to know that he had "breasted the storm of prejudice and opposition, until I begin to be regarded as an 'American Citizen.' Heartily thanking you for the interest you have always taken in the welfare of my people, and hoping to hear from you at your earliest convenience. I remain, Yours with Great Respect, John Thomas."[21]

The Long Silence

Why Gerrit Smith held on to this letter is no mystery. Its two pages vividly revealed one man's life-risking courage, his enduring gratitude and faith in Smith's original idea. Perhaps the more intriguing question is why Smith did not respond (his diligently maintained letter book holds no copy of an answer).

Smith took pains to answer those who wrote him; indeed, this was a reason he got as many letters as he did. Abolition scholars are well acquainted with the ones that came from antislavery activists Black and white; American, British, and Canadian; radical and moderate. Less known (and little studied) is the much greater part of his correspondence with people long forgotten—country ministers, small-town Liberty men, impoverished widows, lonely veterans, crackpot inventors, needy students, temperance zealots, and backwoods farmers from upstate New York. These letters, often appeals for help, were sometimes satisfied, often not. It didn't matter. Regardless of the outcome, Gerrit Smith could be counted on to listen, and for many, this was philanthropy enough. "God cares for worlds, yet feeds the sparrow. He has made you one of his chief Stewards," a McGrawville friend told him in 1861. "Though myself a stranger to you," an upstate farmer's wife observed, "I feel that congeniality which says, such an individual is no stranger to me." An Ohioan knew what she meant: "Although I have never seen you, I seem to be writing an old friend." It was this eager confidence in Smith's empathy that emboldened an Onondaga County woman to believe Smith could help her find her missing son, an African seminary student in New York to ask Smith to buy him winter boots, a Vermont medical student to hope that Smith would underwrite his practice, a bankrupt painter in Philadelphia to invite Smith to pay his rent.[22]

Smith fed the sparrow. He took pains. But the Black Adirondack farmer who asked for no favor, loan, advice or gift, he did not answer. Why this silence?

Smith did not coddle his missteps and mistakes. He stepped past them. He moved on. He outran a youthful romance with African colonization. From 1827 to 1835 he had defended it with zeal, but when abolitionist allies explained its rootedness in white racism, he spurned the "folly of a young man" and never looked back. He quit his love affair with the millenarian William Miller, a Vermont farmer who had devised an elaborate mathematical approximation of the Second Coming from an inventive reading of the Hebrew Bible. With legions of hopeful Millerites in the Northeast (estimates of Miller's followers range from fifty thousand to half a million), Gerrit and Nancy Smith made ready for the Last Days on October 21, 1843. When the Messiah skipped His date with destiny, the Millerites were crushed. Donned in their ascension robes, squinting skyward from the hilltops, many had given up all their worldly goods to embrace the Second Coming. The Smiths were not among them. If they lost their hearts, they kept their heads; their fortune stayed their own.[23]

Smith also walked out on his congressional career, and with good reason, as I'll show later. Well before his term was over, he packed up and returned to Peterboro. He wasn't tired. He was impatient and he was bored. There was work to do, a ton of work, and Congress was no place for a man with plans. In this era in Washington, a brute culture of intimidation stood for statecraft, and the abolitionist could gain no ground. In Peterboro, he knew his strength. From the home place, as Frederick Douglass wrote, he made "his purse strings the common property of the anti-slavery cause."[24]

In Utica in 1835, at the first meeting of the New York State Antislavery Society, Smith had singlehandedly and memorably turned a

catastrophe into a blessing when he invited six hundred radical abolitionists to reconvene at his Peterboro home after their convention was
mobbed by their opponents. History read the meaning of this gesture
in its rebuke to hooliganism, but for the shaken delegates its value went
deeper. Smith's offer shattered old divides between public and private,
rich and poor, rural and urban, and modeled a new kind of antislavery
community, inclusive and empathic. The pies and good hot coffee he
and Nancy fed the pilgrims, the rugs and blankets they passed around,
suggested to their guests (how could they not?) perhaps something of
how enslaved people felt when they were rescued and made safe. And as
the delegates were powerfully moved by the experience, so was Smith
himself. The self-named "convert of the occasion," he there and then declared himself for radical abolitionism and immediate emancipation.[25]

From Smith's home, too, he could underwrite and steward the New
York State Anti-slavery Society, the New York State Vigilance Committee (a Manhattan-based organization that guided hundreds of fugitives
to freedom), a dozen chronically cash-strapped antislavery papers, and
the antislavery campaigns in Kansas, legal and illicit. Other kinds of
gifts, unpublicized, unsystematic, known only to his secretaries, were
no less lavish. The $8 million in gifts that we can track had a worth
that now would exceed $1 billion. But as his biographer observed in
1878, "No one will ever know how much he gave away; no record of it
was made."[26]

From Peterboro, Smith crafted media events that unsettled the slave
power more than any speech he gave in Congress. The two-day convention he pulled together in August 1850 to denounce the coming
Fugitive Slave Act attracted as many as four thousand to the upstate
village of Cazenovia. Press coverage was avid, and news of as many as
fifty fugitives, all "guests of honor" mingling with white activists in
pointed defiance of the Slave Act, whipped Southerners into a fury (and
some Northern editors as well; the *Poughkeepsie Journal* called the meeting "Gerrit Smith's Amalgamation Convention"). Particularly galling
was the keynote. Said to have been written by an escaped slave (actually, Smith authored it himself), "A Letter to the Slaves" called for self-
emancipation and assured Black fugitives that they could count on
help from white supporters in the North. From Georgia to the capital,
slavery's defenders excoriated these lawless "wild fanatics."[27]

"Can any scene be found more disgusting?" raged Tennessee's *Gallatin Tenth Legion*. "If patriots tremble for the safety of our glorious Union,

Fugitive Slave Law Convention, August 21–22, 1850. Cazenovia, New York. Daguerreotype. Ezra Greenleaf Weld, photographer. Seated at table on right is Frederick Douglass, and standing behind Douglass is Gerrit Smith. Courtesy of the Madison County Historical Society, Oneida, NY.

let them not look to the South. . . . [T]hey will find the true cause in such meetings as [this one]."[28] *Let them tremble*, Smith seemed to exult. *Let them panic. Let them know our strength.*

To make things happen: this was his joy, his rich man's privilege. On October 1, 1851, in Syracuse, New York (the city that Secretary of State Daniel Webster had reviled as a "laboratory of abolitionism, libel, and treason"), an escaped slave, the cooper William "Jerry" Henry, was taken into custody. Happily, for Henry, this coincided with a Liberty Party convention, and when the radical abolitionists learned of this arrest, they moved. Two sallies with a battering ram broke Jerry Henry out of custody and put him on the road to Canada—and Gerrit Smith, who participated in the "Jerry Rescue," rejoiced not just for Henry but for himself. Not, for once, to talk, but to risk life and limb to save a captured slave! Working at "the Jerry Level," faith through action, physical and thrilling, was true commitment: "To tell what is right is good preaching. But to do what is right is better. The best of pulpits preaches but in words. The rescue of Jerry preached in deeds."[29]

Smith could not "preach in deeds" in Washington. But in Peterboro, from his study, land office, and antislavery church, his work could resonate across the nation. He was fifty-seven when he left Washington without regret. He knew his strength. He shone when he felt useful, when he did work that made change: bought the freedom of a slave, a score of slaves; bankrolled an antislavery lobbyist, an abolition newspaper, a station on the Underground Railroad; busted a freedom seeker out of jail.

The land giveaway initiative was a big plan too. But like Congress, it let him down. It never struck the Jerry Level he adored, never delivered that Black voting bloc. His zeal for the plan was waning even before John Thomas and his family moved from Troy to Franklin County. In 1848, two years after the giveaway was announced, the land baron was chiding Black New Yorkers at political conventions for "clustering in cities and large villages"—that is, for not moving north. A few years later, Smith's dismay was blunter still. He blasted Black New Yorkers for clinging to their "cities and villages . . . confined to servile employments . . . , your votes at the disposal of your employers. . . . Why do you not scatter yourselves over the country in the capacity of independent and upright farmers and mechanics?"[30]

In 1856, Smith wrote the autobiographical essay that referred to the giveaway so obliquely it was all but unrecognizable, just one of several land gifts he made to "various destitute people." The next year, he was blunter. The Black grantees, he told Horace Greeley, had failed him: "Of the three thousand colored men to whom I gave land, probably less than fifty have taken and continue to hold possession of their grants. What is worse, half of the three thousand . . . have either sold their land, or been so careless as to allow it to be sold for taxes." A few years later, disappointment had chilled to silence. To the editor of the *New American Cyclopedia*, Smith wrote, "I have given to colored people about 125,000 acres & to white people & to institutions of Learning, about 100,000 acres more"—but about his gifting's greater aims for voting rights and agrarian redemption, he wrote nothing. "I do not like to speak of my gifts—& I will speak no more of them."[31]

A Change of Course

Smith also gave, and gave generously, to the sheep farmer who came to him in 1848. Because of how Brown was helping, or aimed to help, the Black grantees, Smith took no payment for either the house he sold him or a land lot; Smith wanted him to stay. Smith could not know that only months after the Brown family moved near Freeman's Home in North Elba, Brown himself would need to go to Massachusetts, then London, Leeds, Brussels, and Hamburg. Unexpected business challenges engaged him, and his Adirondack stays were brief—a month here, a fortnight there, occasionally a season. This is not to say he did not love his Adirondack aerie, or to say historians are wrong to emphasize Brown's deep feeling for it and his interest in the Black grantees. When they needed money, Brown gave them work clearing his fields. If they ran short on food, he opened his larder. When he was home, he helped square away their deeds and boundaries. He asked them to dinner, organized church meetings, delivered sermons and advice. But mostly he was not home. Mostly his dream of mentoring the Black grantees was not realized. Kansas beckoned, then Canada, Ohio, and Harpers Ferry, where Brown's fleeting capture of a federal arsenal won him the page in the nation's story that reads as memorably today as it did in 1859.[32]

Once, in 1855, Gerrit Smith suggested that John Brown stay put for the sake of his Black neighbors. But he did not insist. The growing reach and power of the slaveocracy had shifted both of these activists' agendas. An agrarian experiment in the Adirondacks no longer represented a useful battle strategy in a war against an invigorated slave power. The giveaway's gains were too paltry, its long game just too slow, and maybe worse—distracting and irrelevant. In August 1856, Smith electrified antislavery convention-goers in Buffalo with a brusque, decisive disavowal of political action: "You are looking to ballots when you should be looking to bayonets; counting up votes, when you should be mustering armed men. . . . [And] all the time you are making this mistake, slavery is fortifying itself in Kansas, and weakening and expelling liberty." The meaningful but episodic, quiet victories in the Black Woods (economic self-sufficiency, political empowerment, and peaceful integration) were too far from the war that counted. The cold truth: even if all three thousand grantees moved onto their lots, gained the ballot, and put antislavery candidates in office, slavery would thrive.[33]

So Smith would not protest when his North Elba ally John Brown shifted gears from community building in the Black Woods to a long-nurtured plan to raise a guerrilla band of antislavery fighters and wage a direct, emphatic war on slavery in Kansas, Missouri, and Virginia. Part of a group of Brown's radical abolitionist supporters, which would eventually be described as the Secret Six (among them Rev. Theodore Parker, Thomas Wentworth Higginson, Franklin Sanborn, Samuel Howe, and George Luther Stearns), Smith helped underwrite Brown's quick-as-lighting rescues, command appearances, and raids and skirmishes in Kansas, Ohio, Missouri, and Virginia, for five years. And if, as Smith claimed later, he was ignorant of Brown's designs on a federal arsenal, Smith knew Brown's aim.[34]

John Brown hoped to spark an insurrection, an uprising of slaves who would embrace the chance to join a tiny integrated army secreted in the Allegheny Mountains. From craggy hideouts the holy warriors would swoop down, more slaves flying to their ranks before white men had time to load their guns. The script was never realized, and scholars still debate the extent to which Brown's plan made some sense, less sense, or no sense at all. *Terrorist or patriot? Murderer or martyr?* Since 1859 the question has heated enough debate to float an airship (and nothing in these pages suggests a resolution; for that, there are other books, and very good ones, vividly reported and furiously argued). Smith himself could not resolve his anguish about what Brown did at Harpers Ferry. Much as he loved Brown's courage, shared his outrage at the grudging pace of reform, and marveled at a raid that galvanized a nation and readied it for the war that toppled slavery, he could not reconcile his complicity. What happened at that lightly guarded federal arsenal in the fall of 1859—the people killed, some with pikes and rifles bought with Smith's money, and then Brown's capture, his too-rushed trial and controversial hanging—should not have come as a surprise. Brown himself was ready for it. This was the cost of what he chose to do. But Smith resisted. Horror gripped him to the end.[35]

The worst, of course, was Brown's own fate. Charged with treason, found guilty, Smith's good friend would hang. And Smith faced repercussions too. As details of his long alliance with John Brown surfaced, Smith's notoriety exploded. Arrest threatened, and the prospect of a trial. Soon after Brown's capture, Smith was admitted to the state asylum at Utica (whether by his own consent or the connivance of his family is unclear). Skeptics at the time judged this twenty-two-day medical retreat craven and opportunistic. Others observed that Smith had long suffered from "hyper-melancholia," and that if anything could trip an episode of deep depression, it was the prospect of a trial and a public hanging.[36]

Neither Smith nor any member of the Secret Six would be indicted. And while Smith recalled "much of the year 1859" as "a black dream . . . much of it hazy & uncertain," he rallied. With his Utica physician's guidance (rest, beef broth and cod liver oil, marijuana, no newspapers, and *no writing*), he regained his confidence and vigor. Back in Peterboro in the summer of 1860, the old campaigner was sufficiently revived to accept a nomination for president on the Radical Abolition ticket. Victory was hopeless, but, as with all his bids for office, he hoped a third party would compel main-party candidates to clarify their stance on slavery, and this could be of use.[37]

His renewed political career would not untangle his name from Brown's, however. As soon as Smith's role in the Secret Six was revealed, his biography was remade in John Brown's image. And it must be stressed that until Harpers Ferry, that's not how Smith saw his role, and that's not what he wanted. The John Brown who came calling on Smith in 1848 was one more cash-needy scripture-quoting small-town abolitionist among a hundred looking to do good, another walk-on with a bit part in the great man's script. Smith was more than pleased to see that bit part grow. He helped it grow. The hundred-dollar bank note Brown had on him when he was seized at Harpers Ferry bore Smith's name. But to see his image of himself shaved back from leading man to shadowy accomplice—this was not how Smith expected to be known.

A Waning Reputation

Come the outbreak of the Civil War in 1861, Gerrit Smith at once made the preservation of the Union his first cause. "Stand by the

Government!" he exhorted. Of the nineteen speeches he gave during the war, a dozen might have been thus titled. "Since the Rebellion broke out," he said, "I have been nothing but an anti-rebellion man." The war unleashed a fervor for the Union that so utterly outpaced his Bible politics and eclipsed his abolitionism that Smith's Black friends grew alarmed. Call it triage, he explained: "In time of war, when the question is whether there will be a party left to differ about—nay, whether there will be so much as a party left to us to govern—then, clearly, all should give up party, and join hands to save the country." Smith oversaw enlistment drives and supplied recruits from his upstate district with stationery, stamps, Bibles, and a pig roast. In 1863, he helped finance the new Black regiments in Massachusetts and New York.[38]

He liked to say that the rebellion was a wayward child in need of discipline. This was the homely rhetoric of the Sunday school teacher, reducing history to a Bible lesson. It got Smith into trouble. After Appomattox, when the rebellion (likened, in Smith's figuring, to an impudent, impious brat) was subdued (shamed, disciplined, and back in check), Smith then envisioned the ruined South as a prodigal son, and made ready to forgive. *Our Christian duty insists on this*, he told his fellow Unionists. *Yes, the slaveholders are criminals, but isn't the slaveless North complicit?* Northern merchants who dealt in slave-made products, northern voters who backed slaveholding presidents, northern bounty hunters who pursued fugitives, northern hooligans who preferred to put their cities to the torch rather than submit to a draft in a war for human rights—they all supported slavery, and they were sinners too. Were not mercy and forbearance everybody's portion? Leviticus 19:18: *Do not seek revenge or bear a grudge against one of your people, but love your neighbor as yourself.*[39]

"Slavery is a crime of the north as well as of the South." Other abolitionists made this point, but Smith's grasp of the link between the confidently unconcealed white supremacism of the South and the sedimented racism of the North was unrelenting. "Who are to be held amenable for this crime [at Fort Pillow]?" Smith asked in 1864. "The rebels. Yes, but not the rebels only. . . . All who have held that Blacks are unfit to sit by the side of whites in the church, the school, the car and at the table. All who have been in favor of making his complexion shut out a Black man from the ballot-box. . . . All, in short, who have hated or despised the Black man." To pardon the arrant South required that the North first know and face its own complicity. And after that, and only after, could it forgive itself.[40]

Thus, Smith's controversial gesture of May 11, 1867. With Horace Greeley, Cornelius Vanderbilt, and some dozen wealthy Virginians, Smith stepped up to cover Jefferson Davis's bail. Since the war's end, the deposed president of the Confederacy had languished in Fort Monroe on the Virginia coast. Smith and Greeley felt confining him without a trial or conviction was unjust. Southerners agreed. They hailed Davis's release and the large-minded Yankees who enabled it. Northern Unionists were baffled and dismayed. *This*, of all things, from the great Republican and patriot Horace Greeley and the radical abolitionist Gerrit Smith?[41]

Newspapers across the nation debated the reasoning, or lack of it, behind Davis's release. How to fathom Christian charity for the man that millions called a traitor? For Unionists, Gerrit Smith's bail making for the officer who called for Smith's conviction after Harpers Ferry epitomized the flaw in Smith, the random-seeming changes of heart. But this misunderstood him. Smith's gift of bail was right in line with his devotion to the Golden Rule. How better to express his great faith in the individual's capacity for moral transformation, and an empathic civic brotherhood? And what clearer way to model the human fellowship the white South owed the emancipated slave?[42]

Finally, and not least, what a good way to free his name from John Brown's? Eight years after Harpers Ferry, Smith had high hopes for the impact of this bailout on his public reputation. What he did for Davis earned him the most exposure of his life after John Brown's capture. But while Southerners applauded it, Northerners would never love his charity for the head of the rebellion more than what he did for Brown. Nor would the ex-rebels find in Smith's gospel of lovingkindness a model for a changed relationship with freed Blacks. Smith himself, by the last year of his life, had relinquished any hope of this. Too many reports had crossed his desk that testified to the vigorous resurgence of Southern white supremacism and racialized atrocities. A letter to him from a Northerner in late 1874 was typical. "This is the calm, clear truth," his unnamed correspondent offered. "To-day the old rebel oligarchy is awake, active, vigilant [and] hopeful. It is now more hopeful, hating, bitter and aggressive than at any time since the war." Smith's letter to his old friend George T. Downing defending "Equal Rights for Blacks and Whites" suggested just how great was his late-life retreat from any gospel of reconciliation. The Democrats, he offered, in defending the slaveocracy before and after the war, had committed "a sin not to be forgiven." This was the language of a man betrayed.[43]

Pilgrims started coming to North Elba as soon as John Brown was buried on December 8, 1859. Until recently, however, visitors to Brown's historic farm learned almost nothing about the benefactor who got the Brown family to the region in the first place. Indeed, in memory, both the giveaway and its originator languished in Brown's shadow. By the time Smith got his thank-you note from John Thomas in 1872, the Black Woods that stood for Black civic standing, voting rights, integration, and agrarian reform had been overtaken by John Brown Country, an idealized storyscape of white sacrifice and valor. And Smith, for his part, was sick and tired of them both.

Others in the Secret Six visited Brown's North Elba grave. Never Gerrit Smith. Brown's widow, Mary, hoped the family place would be a monument to abolitionist memory. Smith shrugged. "It does not strike me as important that the farm be owned by the Anti-Slavery Society," he told the caretaker at the farm. "Let it be . . . by some farmer, who will put it [to] use and keep it in good order." The storied pilgrimage from Utica to Peterboro in 1835, the Fugitive Slave Law convention in 1850, the rescue of Jerry Henry in Syracuse in 1851—all this, with his philanthropy, his good work for the Liberty Party, his efforts for the Union, Smith recalled with pride. As would his admirers. "Many thousands bear the name of Mr. Smith in our country. Nevertheless, if a person should address a letter to Mr. Smith, America, it would doubtless reach to the beautiful little village of Peterboro," gushed a fan in Oswego. A Chenango County phrenologist deemed Smith "the man who has encouraged more persons in their struggles from darkness to light than any other man on the planet." From Onondaga County, an activist predicted, "The day is not yet distant when a statue in Central Park, New York, shall be unveiled of the liberator of slavery, the friend of the oppressed . . . Gerrit Smith." Smith was like Moses, like Noah, indeed, in his munificence, like God himself; why, even "the smallest sum" from Gerrit Smith, wrote a petitioner, was "as manna from our heavenly Father, in whom thro' all our privations I have never failed to trust."[44]

There were praiseful letters for the giveaway as well, at least in the beginning. But when Smith's "scheme of justice and benevolence" did not flourish as he hoped, he turned away and moved on. And when he gave up, and John Brown, too, history followed suit. Accounts of the giveaway would snip its threads to voting rights, community building, and environmental distributive justice. In white memory, and only decades after Smith's death, the gift that had once captivated New York's friends of abolition was good only for what it said about the eccentricity of the giver—for who but an "eccentric" would dream of giving land to the poor Black men of New York? This was how the *New York Times* introduced him in an article in 1904. Smith, an instinctive unifier who in a blink could see the common ground that joined the fight for racial justice with the rights of women, immigrants, and children; Smith, the most syncretic of reformers, ever prescient in his grasp of linkages between seemingly uncongenial causes, was down to an "Eccentric Philanthropist."[45]

The self-emancipated slave John Thomas, who stayed in the Black Woods until his death in 1894, did not regard Smith as eccentric. A man he'd never met had changed his life, and in changing his, Smith changed much more. Thomas's white neighbors would be changed by their dealings with Black farmers. Thomas's descendants stayed in the Adirondack region for 150 years. Thomas had urged Smith to answer him, but the absence of a letter in Smith's copybook suggests he never did. Did this pain the pioneer? It may have, but hearing from Gerrit Smith was never Thomas's goal. He wasn't angling for the rich man's blessing. The blessing had been his to give—his own long-pondered gift of thanks.

Then, the right thing done, the letter stamped, sealed, and on its way, he got back to his farm.

CHAPTER 2

Gerrit Smith Country

After a long winter attending to epistolary duties, splitting a twelve-hour workday between his study and his shoebox of a land office on the village green near his Peterboro home, Gerrit Smith craved a change of view. He read too much, subscribed to sixty periodicals, perused newspapers by the score. Headaches immobilized him, and hemorrhoids gave no peace. Funks came on hard, and sometimes allergies so bleared his sight he worried he'd go blind. To leave home for a spring tour in the North Country, before dust dulled the polish of the carriage or the haze of summer palled the fields—what better salve for this gray mood?[1]

The five-week swing around his northern landholdings commenced in May 1845. From Peterboro, Smith, his wife, Nancy, and Smith's secretary, Caleb Calkins, called on their famous Auburn neighbor, former governor William Seward, then headed east along the Mohawk River toward Albany. Smith visited with Thurlow Weed, the powerful publisher of the *Albany Journal*, and his old friend Eliphalet Nott, president of Union College in Schenectady. The resort towns of Ballston Spa and Saratoga Springs held his interest for a spell. But the greater piece of Smith's business in the region was in the Adirondacks, the rough and largely undeveloped country where Smith's father, and now Gerrit, son and heir, owned land. This was the part of his long journey where he got to freshen his alliances with upstate abolition allies, preach Bible politics in small towns, stump for the Liberty Party, and—not least—catch up with land agents in the field. By this time, Smith's fortune had somewhat revived from the devastating Panic of 1837, but he still hoped to lighten his acreage and loosen his liquidity. Thus, two arduous side trips into the Adirondack interior: in Essex County, a sixty-mile round trip from Elizabethtown west to the Keene Plains and back, "22 [miles] on foot," and from Clinton County, a foray out of Plattsburgh to Franklin County's barely settled town of Franklin to the southwest. The land was said to be inhospitable; Smith would judge for himself. The high quality of Essex County ore, the promise of a rail route, and the charcoal-making and lumber potential of Clinton County's hardwoods—all this improved the region's prospects. Smith, smart marketer, was keen to make his own high hopes his readers' interest too.[2]

Of special note were the Keene Plains (the name North Elba came only at the start of 1850). Here, Smith offered, was "a very extensive and very beautiful tract of level land" as wide around as "seventy or eighty square miles," with only fifteen families on the ground. The land was rich, and "the soil . . . so remarkably favorable to the production of potatoes" that homesteaders were already putting up a starch factory. The antislavery scene was hopeful too. Chester boasted "abolitionists of the truest class," Elizabethtown "a few faithful friends of the slave," and Keene "some noble spirits [like] Phineas Norton . . . an ornament to our cause." Keeseville was stepping up: "Scarcely had I arrived . . . when that true friend of the slave, Wendell Lansing, called upon me." And Champlain had its hero, too. "That wise and steadfast friend of the slave, Noadiah Moore, came all the way from Champlain yesterday (twenty-one miles) to hear me." When Smith named names like this in every hamlet, he democratized the abolitionist community. Here was a world where antislavery conviction overrode conventional divides of class and political influence—here, a true nobility of peers.[3]

Abolition's enemies were also noted. The resort town of Saratoga Springs, an early stop on Smith's long trip, was famously dependent on the patronage of enslavers (Smith likened it to Charleston and New Orleans). Farther north in Elizabethtown, Smith could not find a church to host him and had to lead his Sunday prayer meeting out of doors. That was fine. His Adirondack adversaries moved him to prayer, not defensiveness. And he could always preach in the dappled light of a locust grove, the scent of blossoms on the breeze, and no blackflies, not just yet. Sunday preaching about slavery was, for some, a profanation of the Sabbath, but people would turn up. How often did a land baron on his scale rumble into town? Old-timers still recalled his late father, the notoriously stingy speculator Peter Smith. Very different was his son, whose philanthropy was legendary, and who never played the swell but took an agrarian's earnest interest in wheat production and good tilth.[4]

In all, the trip was better than restorative; it was a journey of discovery. Many mapmakers had limned the Adirondack region before Smith's trip—army scouts and surveyors, stage and steamboat agents spreading word of wild cataracts and chasms. The 1842 publication of the state surveyor Ebenezer Emmons' ethereally tinted maps of the geological Adirondacks assured Smith of the mining promise of his land (in Warren County, granite, graphite, and limestone; in Essex County, magnetite iron ore . . .). County maps from *Burr's Atlas* were his to study, along with the updated version of Amos Lay's map of northern New York. Smith's own sheaf of survey maps would steer him to more remote property (all those even-sided lot lines charging blindly over bald and bog). But for an Adirondack map that showed the routes from one antislavery household to the next, Smith was his own cartographer, seizing any flick of interest in the welfare of the slave as proof of northern New York's hunger for the cause. The Albany-based antislavery activist Abel Brown had tramped a northern loop before, hinting at the names and homes of Underground Railroad operatives in the *Tocsin of Liberty*, but in the longer-lasting, better-circulated *Albany Patriot*, Smith's travel diary joined the dots with flair. Radical evangelical perfectionists in northern New York basked in the *Patriot*'s celebration of a far-flung fraternity, with its intimation of a whole so much greater than its parts. And in 1846, when Smith considered where to settle thousands of Black pioneers, he would recall the "noble spirits" of the Adirondack activists he met in 1845, their farms as closely tended as their abolition faith.[5]

The White Man's Proviso

Unfortunately, 1846 would prove to be as devastating as the summer of 1845 was hopeful, with each month bearing a fresh crisis. Manifest destiny, an offhand catchphrase in 1845, would by the end of 1846 be extravagantly realized with the expansion of the great republic by one-third. The bulk of it was gained by "Mr. Polk's War" on Mexico, a brazenly imperialistic land grab. For the boxy piece called Oregon, the United States could thank Great Britain, whose leaders, after years of wrangling, finally figured that the course of empire might run marginally better with one less Pacific colony to manage from afar. Was this land needed? In 1846, the historian of the Mexican conquest, William H. Prescott, wrote the abolitionist Charles Sumner, "One would suppose that millions of uncultivated acres inviting settlement and the hand of civilization that lie within our present limits might satisfy the most craving cupidity"—and so they might have if cupidity were all of it. But hungrier than greed was the habit of entitlement. The population of the United States had grown by one-third every decade from 1800 to 1850, a growth spurt unmatched by any other country. Did not a growth rate so exuberant deserve to be rewarded with more territory to contain it? Would not more land refresh the people's love of nation building and distract them from their sectional disputes?[6]

This was President Polk's serene prediction. But tensions only surged, and for the antislavery cohort, the rush to settle this new land looked disastrous. Slavery would surely prevail at the polls in the newly annexed territory; at the headlong pace that Southerners and their human property were rolling west, how could it not? Concerned about the threat to the fragile balance of political power between free states and the slaveocracy, David Wilmot, a freshman Democratic congressman from Pennsylvania, proposed a law in August 1846 that would bar slavery's extension into the new territories. Approved in the House but twice failing to win passage in the Senate, the Wilmot Proviso tapped a stress fracture between North and South that split into a chasm in a few congressional seasons.[7]

And all the while, abolitionists were powerless. No part of the legislative battle to keep the western territories free of slavery concerned itself with the millions of Black people enslaved in the South. Nor could antislavery activists look to Wilmot's Free Soilers to support the rights of free Black pioneers who wanted to move west. For many in Wilmot's camp, free labor was white labor. Free Blacks would stay east; in the new land they weren't welcome. "Shall the Territories Be Africanized?" rang the panicky alarm. Not if David Wilmot and his Free Soilers had anything to do with it. None of the stern rhetoric about keeping western territories free of the "disgrace which association with negro slavery brings upon free labor" damned white racism itself. Wilmot called his plan a "White Man's Proviso"—to keep out slavery from the new territory was to keep it safe for "the sons of toil, of my own race and own color." At the heart of the debate, Eric Foner has observed, was this "crucial ambiguity. . . . Was it the institution of slavery, or the presence of the Negro, which degraded the white laborer?" For thousands of Free Soilers, one implied the other. Slave or free, competition from Black labor was reviled.[8]

The 3001st Grantee

It is possible that in this hard year Gerrit Smith let his thoughts stray from the raucous frontline of race and politics to more distant scenes, like, say, the discovery of Neptune, or the removal of more than ten thousand Mormons to the West, fresh from the debacle of Nauvoo. The Irish potato blight, two years strong, would have split Smith's heart between pity for the famine victims and horror at the antisuffrage influence that Irish immigrants, new-minted Democrats, now wielded at the polls. Much as Smith talked up his rustic insularity and country ways, he was no stranger to the world. His donations over decades to a constellation of causes—Greek patriots, Hungarian rebels, the starving Irish—showed the ecumenicism of his compassion. But 1846 was not a year to let him reach for the vast, cooling overview. It was a year, as the historian Bernard DeVoto put it, when "something had shifted out of plumb, moved on its base, begun to topple down." With the swelling contours of the nation and the prospect of a much-expanded slave economy, "something was ending in America, forever. A period, an era, a social context, a way of life, was running out."[9]

DeVoto dubbed it, famously, the "Year of Decision." For the resolute white pioneers, bold explorers, and cocky politicians in his enduring history of that name, that's maybe how it seemed. For Black America, free or enslaved, it was the opposite: a year of unremitting impotence just when decisive action was needed. And if free Black Americans, lacking strength of numbers, voting power, money, and public access to debate, were demoralized, so, surely, was a white man as perennially hopeful of his influence as Gerrit Smith.[10]

Smith identified his three thousand beneficiaries in his scrupulously documented *Land Book*. But there was another giftee, never named. This was Smith himself. To give was to claim agency, to make oneself of use, to *do*. In 1846 especially, Gerrit Smith needed this. Without *doing*, he was lost.

In August 1846, two months after the start of the New York Constitutional Convention and two months before it reconvened to tackle equal suffrage, Smith shared his hope of giving away land in a letter to three Black activists in New York City. Rev. Theodore Wright and

Elder Charles B. Ray were Smith's long-standing acquaintances. Dr. James McCune Smith was newer and untested, but said to be whip-smart and politically astute. These activists, whom Smith asked to serve on his New York City Committee, had the job of finding eligible grantees in all of metropolitan New York. Earlier in 1846, these three suffrage advocates and several others had implored Smith to back a one-time Whig-Liberty alliance for the coming Constitutional Convention; the prosuffrage lobby badly needed votes. Smith would not oblige. In fact, their appeal stiffened his opposition. But that was then, and this was now. Smith's August invitation not only aimed for reconciliation, it proved, unequivocally, his commitment to Black suffrage. *Only read my plan. You'll see.* If the Black Laws in the new territories discouraged pioneering in the West, Smith had an alternative. *Here, in our own New York, is a wilderness where Black homesteaders will feel welcome. Here, a fresh frontier for hopeful voter-pioneers.*[11]

After Smith lined up his New York City agents, he organized committees for the Hudson River Valley, the Mohawk Valley and the Southern Tier, and Western New York. In all, thirteen antislavery activists, five white, eight Black, would act as agents for his giveaway and oversee the distribution of 120,000 acres among three thousand Black New Yorkers from 1846 to 1853. Each of the four committees was charged with whipping up interest in the giveaway in its designated regions, and with vetting and collecting the names of eligible grantees. No compensation was offered (though Smith's Black agents would get gift lots, and sometimes more than one). Smith thought hard about the makeup of his committees, and for the New York City group he asked the city abolitionist Lewis Tappan for advice. Tappan was all for Ray and Wright but about the youthful physician he had doubts. Dr. McCune Smith, he feared, had some "peculiar notions about things etc." Ironically, no one of Smith's agents would be a better friend to the philanthropist than the brilliant Black physician. He and Smith shared warm, confiding letters well after the gift land was parceled out.[12]

For the recruitment of grantees in the Hudson Valley, the Capital District, and all points north, Smith fixed on three Albanians and a Trojan. The Troy minister Rev. Henry Highland Garnet was Black, as was Albany's prominent suffrage lobbyist William Topp. The newspaper editor William Chaplin and the lumber merchant Nathanial Safford were white. Between them these four agents covered seventeen counties along New York's northeastern flank. Nine counties in central New York and north into the St. Lawrence River valley were assigned

Dr. James McCune Smith, NYC. Carte de visite, 1855. Johnson, Williams & Co., photographers. Courtesy of the Madison County Historical Society, Oneida, NY.

to three white abolitionists from Utica: Wesley Bailey, George Lawson, and Alfred H. Hunt. All counties to the west of Broome, Chenango, Madison, and Oswego Counties belonged to three Black activists: the churchmen Samuel Ringgold Ward from Cortland and Jermain Wesley Loguen of Syracuse, and James W. Duffin, a Geneva barber.[13]

With thirteen downstate counties on its watch, the New York City Committee bore the brunt of the job. Smith was asking it to find two-thirds of his three thousand deedholders in the great city at the mouth of the Hudson, where most Black New Yorkers lived. Here, he felt, was where the love of caste flourished most robustly, where workshops and the wharves were trip-wired with racial restrictions, neighborhoods mined with slums and rum shops, and white gangs driven by "Negro-hate." Only when the New York agents fell short of Smith's high quota would he direct them to less congested counties beyond Brooklyn and Manhattan, and while this expansion made good sense, it hardly eased their work. Then, nine months after the giveaway was publicized,

Reverend Wright died of pleurisy, and now two agents, Ray and McCune Smith, assumed the work of three. But Smith was eager. Momentum now was everything. Once his critics learned about his plan, they would leap to tear it down. On the first of August, his city agents got their marching orders. If they could round up the first two thousand names as fast as possible, he would date them all September 1, and the grantees could get their deeds as early as October.[14]

He did not write, "in time for a November referendum on Black suffrage." He and the agents all knew that the distribution of the deeds would not impact the outcome of a November plebiscite on equal voting rights for Black New Yorkers. Forty-acre woodland lots, barely surveyed, never settled, could not meet the $250 property requirement or even a fifth of that amount. But clear the land and cultivate it, harvest it for timber, or just hold on to it for resale, and its value would go up. Not in time for this election, but maybe for the next.

Could Smith know what he was asking? His Black city agents were family men with taxing day jobs and no access to the resources that a rich white man took for granted. They had no land office, secretaries, or stables full of carriages and tack. They were expected to cover twelve downstate counties without benefit of legal access to public transport, to lobby for a wild land that, for Black people, lacked any resonance or allure, and to introduce a largely illiterate constituency to deeds and surveys, maps and tax dates. Gerrit Smith guessed that what he expected them to do might entail "no little labor." He had no idea.[15]

CHAPTER 3

Three Agents and Their Reasons

The Physician: "Our Lives Are Much Shortened"

In 1820, a deadly strain of typhoid ran amok in New York City. Seven-year-old James McCune Smith, son of an enslaved Black woman and a white merchant, was too young to measure the gap between Black and white mortality rates. But he experienced it. In the earthen cellars of one tenement, Bancker Street Fever infected thirty-three of forty-eight Black residents, fourteen of whom died; no illness troubled the 120 white people in the rooms above. Smallpox struck in 1823, and six years later, when McCune Smith was a teenager, yellow fever once again filled unmarked graves. By the time cholera ravaged the city in 1832, he could anticipate the outcome. Whether by an outbreak of the above, or tuberculosis, pneumonia, influenza, rickets, dysentery, or bronchitis, Black New Yorkers in the city were disproportionately imperiled. More got sick than their white neighbors, and more died. In the mid-nineteenth century, death rates for Black city dwellers matched mortality rates for enslaved people in the South. And McCune Smith, who had spent five years in a medical school in Glasgow when no American university would have him, knew why. Negrophobia enabled the disparity. Viruses and germs were the bullets, but racism aimed and fired the gun.[1]

When Gerrit Smith tapped McCune Smith to be an agent for the giveaway, he was one of two Black doctors in New York. Between a private practice and his work as staff doctor at the Colored Orphan Asylum, he covered a lot of ground. He had an integrated practice, and was co-owner of a pharmacy at 193 Broadway in the neighborhood now called Tribeca. He and his wife, Malvina Barnet, a graduate of the Rutgers Female Institute, worshipped at St. Philip's Episcopal, where McCune Smith was a vestryman, no small honor in a congregation-owned church with a capacity of two thousand. From his brick home, he and Malvina could stroll to St. John's Park, where two hundred trees cooled their corner of the city. This was an enviable life. But when he signed on to recruit grantees for Smith's initiative, this doctor's mood was bleak.[2]

McCune Smith could publish his incisive columns about racism and the city's racially skewed death rates in the *Colored American*. He could hobnob with the enlightened likes of white radical reformers like Lewis Tappan. But conversation was not action. It worked no lasting change. The laws that kept him out of streetcars meant that bad weather clipped his rounds. When he could not work, his patients suffered, his orphans most of all. The rules that barred him from city medical societies meant he could not keep up with recent scholarship and research, or build a readership for his own. He could not audit anatomy lessons at city hospitals or collaborate with other researchers and physicians. Professional advancement was a sham, while breaking news of treatments, protocols, and medicines was out of reach. It was the iron clamp of prejudice that constrained all Black New Yorkers of ambition. If his friend Thomas Downing tried serving Black diners at his oyster house, the merchants and European tourists who thronged his venue would desert it in an hour. Black barbers who tried taking in the "colored custom" would see their white trade die that day.[3]

There was simply no part of urban life where "caste" did not rule with the confidence of law. Complexion pinned the young Black men of New York City to the worst-paid jobs, with little promise of advancement. Homes were frigid shanties, and some tenements were as shoddy as the single-layer brick facades that fronted them. Rent for city Blacks ran 25 to 30 percent higher than what white New Yorkers ever paid, and this for "rooms" the size of a doghouse, a broom closet, a coffin. For bodily relief there were privies without sewers, or alleys boggy and impassable with excrement. No missing or uneven cobbles to complain of—there were no cobbles, and if there were, how could it matter? In *Five*

Points, the cultural historian Tyler Anbinder describes an aged woman encountering a cobble-cleaning effort in her nook of the city: "Where in the world did all those stones come from? I never knew that the streets were covered with stones before." Garbage, a witches' brew of offal, ashes, litter, animal waste, and trash, was consumed by roving packs of pigs and dogs, and so disruptive were the latter that in 1847 the city hired four Black men to hunt and kill them by the hundreds. Each day every workhorse dosed the streets with a quart of urine and up to thirty-five pounds of excrement, and these horses, gaunt and weary, were ubiquitous, dragging carts and omnibuses until they toppled in the street. Manure stuck and dried to a fine dust that powdered pedestrians and shop windows alike, and toxified the groundwater that spread the typhoid whose long reach McCune Smith knew so well. The proof of poverty's impact on sickness and early death for poor Black people was as tangible as it was irrefutable.[4]

Some illnesses that seemed to target city Blacks were so little understood that they had no name—but McCune Smith saw how they rampaged. Though the Croton waterworks brought running water to Manhattan in 1842, this was no use to poor renters whose landlords would not pay for Croton's installation fee or spring for hookups to the trunk line; tenement and shanty dwellers got their drinking water from wells, cisterns, and hydrants, and risked their health with every sip. Hydrants froze in winter and sputtered dry in summer, coal dust and bird feces befouled cisterns, and, as for wells, when city numbers surged and water usage with it, the water table rose as well, mingling sewage and spring well water to murderous effect. In 1849, cholera, a waterborne disease, claimed five thousand city lives.[5]

McCune Smith, a voracious reader, knew his Emerson, Burns, and Byron (and had his knuckles rapped by a Black columnist for the "idle time" he devoted to "readings of that sort"). He knew all the vaunted uses of Romantic nature, how it imaged God's originality, revived the spirit, salved the soul. But much more than a passion for Romantic poetry made the Black Woods look good to the doctor. City life, he argued in his *Report on the Social Condition of the People of Color around New York City*, was more than hard on Black people. It was killing them. "Our lives in the city are much shortened," he declared. "Look at the preponderance of widows and children among us. They so far exceed the calamities of mere sickness that our benevolent societies have been obliged to cut off the widows and orphans, in order to heal the sick." Middle-class Black professionals like McCune Smith were buffered from these scourges; they had access to more space, cleaner water, better food, and prompt medical attention. But not for them, for any Black city dweller, the mobility of their white neighbors. When white people got wind of a looming epidemic, they packed up for the country to sit out the latest plague. Even poor whites enjoyed this option; cheap hotels and boardinghouses abounded in Long Island and New Jersey. Rich or poor, Black health seekers need not apply.[6]

The Leveler: "Something in It Paradisiacal"

"It almost possesses ubiquity; it is everywhere, doing its deleterious work wherever one of the proscribed class lives and moves," said the churchman Charles B. Ray of the "Monster, Prejudice. One needs to feel it, and to wither under its effects, to know it." Elder Ray, the most devoted of Smith's land agents, was on close terms with the Monster. It assailed his working-class parishioners and hobbled the prospects of his church. With Black clergymen laboring at half the wages of their white counterparts and taking second and third jobs to get by, church pulpits were undermanned, prayer meetings sporadic, and attendance unreliable. Ray himself could not afford to do his job full-time. (Church work was his calling. For a living, he made shoes and copublished a newspaper, the *Colored American*, which he edited and peddled town to town until publication ceased in 1841.) But at least Ray kept his flock. Many Black churches that had been torched in New York's antiabolition riot of 1834 never recovered. And the next year's sweeping fire—"a thirteen-acre ocean of burning waves," the worst blaze in the city's history—took a toll too. Churches were not rebuilt, and Black churchmen could not afford to rent or buy. By 1852, most of Ray's congregants had lost all "relish for God's house." They were numb, and spent. Ray grieved, "The Sabbath is an irksome day to them."[7]

In the country, this could change. There would be a schoolhouse for the children. The invigorating labor and deep slumber of the farmer would rout perennial fatigue. Relish, not resentment, would welcome the day of prayer. And for Ray, this was more than theoretical. His faith in the special power of the small, farm-based community was steeped in early memory. His first home, Falmouth, Massachusetts, was a seaside village south of Boston on the Nantucket Sound, ringed with modest hills, old sheep pastures, and cranberry bogs. His mother arrived there as a girl; she was brought by her enslaver. Ray grew up with the story of townspeople hiding her in the post office cellar the day she was supposed to leave. She stepped out into her new life only when the white man tired of the hunt and sailed away for good. Taking a new name, Annis Harrington joined the Methodist church and married Joseph Ray, the part-Black and part-Native postman who ran the mailboat between Falmouth and Nantucket. Charles Bennett Ray was the first of their seven children.[8]

Before the move to New York City, Charles Ray worked on his grandfather's farm in Westerly, Rhode Island, and apprenticed with a Martha's Vineyard bootmaker. And this, too, bolstered his agrarianism; he knew what northern small-town and rural life might offer that city life withheld. As early as 1829, Ray's old friend Samuel Cornish, the publisher of the newspaper *The Rights of All*, was urging freed slaves to "escape contagion of the vices" and "command a more respectable standing in society" by farming, and later, in the *Colored American*, Ray and Cornish kept beating this same drum. Cornish went so far as to buy a two-thousand-acre riverfront parcel in New Jersey for a farm colony for city Blacks. Cornish aimed to spare his Black friends and family the "corruptions of a city life. . . . If parents would have their children be a comfort to them and a blessing to the world, they must separate them from the snares and abounding wickednesses of our large cities." The project was abandoned when hoped-for colonists did not invest and Cornish's young son drowned in the Delaware River. Back in New York City, the Cornishes put the wretched interlude behind them. Yet the promise of Black farming still compelled. From 1837 to 1842, *Colored American* copublishers Ray, Cornish, and Phillip Bell churned out a wagonload of articles with titles like "Self-Denial, Enterprise, Husbandry," "Brethren, Go to the Country," "Encourage the Colored People to Become Farmers," "The Charms of the Farmer's Life," and "Importance of Agriculture." In 1837, this paper asked its readers, "What is more honorable than husbandry? To till the soil, to be a producer of corn and wheat, and a grower of flocks and herds, has something in it paradisiacal. If there be any calling in the world allied to primitive innocency, it is husbandry. . . . This will honorably connect us with the prosperity, and make us participants in the glories of the American Republic."[9]

Also working to promote the cause of frontier farming was the *white* press, which in the wake of the devastating national depression of 1837, found solace in a vision of a generative American frontier. "We say, then, Mechanics, artisans, laborers . . . Fly—scatter throughout the country—go to the Great West—rather than remain here, consuming the pittance which is left of your earnings," urged the *New Yorker* magazine in 1837. Black New Yorkers read these columns too, and learned about newly opened territories (secured by laws and treaties that swept Native Americans out of the way). Along with whites, they marveled at the long reach of the canal system and new railroad routes, noted the proliferating land offices, and registered the impact of the self-scouring plow. Between 1800 and 1850, half a million square miles were opened to settlement, an expanse larger than any European state west of Russia. Exclusionary "Black laws" were discouraging, but were they enforceable on every acre? Surely in this imperial swath were some safe patches for Black pioneers.[10]

That, anyway, was the determined message of the *Colored American* in the late 1830s, as its westward-faring correspondents filled long columns with proud accounts of new Black enclaves. Working for the American Anti-slavery Society, the Quaker brothers Augustus and John Owen Wattles visited numerous Black midwestern settlements between 1837 and 1839. Here in Cabin Creek, Indiana, was a Virginia shoemaker who bought his wife's freedom and a town lot with what he made cobbling shoes and working a small farm. In Springfield, Ohio, were "30 families, containing 200 individuals. . . . 14 are farmers, 4 are wagoners who drove their own teams, 4 own real estate, and 4 have bought themselves and paid $1,000 for their freedom." Zanesville, Ohio, boasted "a large settlement," and one landowner there had "the name of being one of the best farmers in the county. He settled here when the country was new . . . 17 years ago. Besides . . . bringing up a family of 12 children, he has during the last year purchased and paid for one thousand acres of government land." Smith Township, Columbiana County, Ohio, held a Black settlement numbering "264 individuals, owning 1860 acres of land, valued at $29,200, 70 horses . . . , 213 head of cattle . . . , 328 sheep," plus two schools and four preachers.[11]

Charles B. Ray did not need western testimonials to shore up his agrarianism. He had his grandfather in Rhode Island. He had the Black farmer he met in the Mohawk Valley in 1837, who "lives among an intelligent farming community; he nor his children know very little about prejudice; and suffer nothing on account of it. . . . If we would run away from prejudice, it is not necessary that we should run out of the United States; but scatter thousands of us all over the country; and buy up the soil, and become cultivators of it. In this way, better than in any other, can we get rid of prejudice." Ray offered this almost a decade before Gerrit Smith opened the Black Woods.[12]

Ray also lobbied for farming and the country life at Black politi-cal conventions. "Become possessors of the soil," Ray and Theodore Wright told delegates in 1840 at a meeting in Albany, New York. And in Buffalo a few years later, Ray and convention delegates confidently pictured farming as "the shortest, surest road to respectability and influence." There was simply no better, faster way to *win white hearts*. Farming, Ray insisted, "puts the one farmer . . . upon the same level with his neighbors—their occupation is one, their hopes and interests are one; his neighbors see him now, not as in other situations they may have done as a servant; but an independent man; . . . they are not above him nor he above them; they are all alike upon a level; . . . and as it is only by placing men in the same position in society that all cast[es] are lost sight of; all cast[e] in his case, were he previously of the proscribed class, will fade away and be forgotten." The power of the farmer here was close to alchemical. Subsistence farming on fresh land enabled true distributive justice. Start with level ground, and all the rest—trust, re-spect, even friendship—would follow.[13]

The Perfectionist: "A Perfect System of Agrarianism"

When George Trusty got word of his enslaver's death in 1822, he knew what was coming. Maryland's Colonel William Spencer was heavily in debt. His heirs would want to settle his estate. Assets would be sold, among them some of his twenty-four slaves. George Trusty, his cobbler, would bring good money. Hence the haste with which his family made its getaway from Spencer's 1,100-acre Kent County plantation. Within two months of Spencer's burial, a covered wagon holding ten breath-less fugitives, Trusty's immediate family of four and six other relatives, made a break for freedom. There was no time to lose. As soon as their escape was reported, they would be pursued.[14]

Six of Trusty's relatives were discovered in Delaware and New York. The more fortunate Trustys made it to Quaker-settled New Hope, Pennsylvania, and from there, after a few years, to Manhattan, where the family surname was changed to Garnet, and some first names too. George Garnet resumed making shoes, and his wife, Elizabeth (formerly Henny), enrolled their son in the African Free School on Mott Street. Arithmetic, geography, rhetoric, and navigation were Henry Highland Garnet's portion, and he may have liked the last the best; he went to sea when he was a young teen. On vessels bound for Washington, DC, and Cuba, he was a ship's cook, cabin boy, and steward. Tough work and meager pay, but at least as long as he was boat-bound, "man-thieves" in the pay of Spencer's heirs could not track him down.[15]

His family was less lucky. In 1829, slave hunters broke into the Garnets' Manhattan home. On his return, the young seaman found his family scattered, their rooms in shambles. And though the Garnets weathered the crisis (Henry's sister Eliza persuaded authorities to release her, and Elizabeth was freed with the help of abolitionist family friends), they knew their luck could fail at any time. The bounty hunters were still looking. So again, Henry, now fifteen, left the city, this time contracting with a Quaker farmer in Jericho, Long Island. He liked this labor and might have made it his life's work, but a grievous injury killed that prospect, and back he went to Manhattan, this time to enroll in school at First Colored Presbyterian, the second-largest Black church in the country. Here, the leading pastor, Theodore S. Wright, newly graduated from the Princeton Theological Seminary, preached a fearlessly wholistic activism that waged a hands-on war on Negrophobia. He hid fugitives in his Broadway home, lobbied for Black voting rights, argued for Black uplift, denounced the colonizationists, condemned the sin of slavery, called out abolitionists, both white and Black, who defended segregation—and made sure his students grasped the indivisibility of these concerns.

Garnet had been enslaved, and Reverend Wright, born free in New Jersey, had never known the lash. Yet they felt each other's story. As Wright told a New York antislavery assembly in 1837, "We are still slaves—everywhere we feel the chain galling us," whether freeborn or not. "The spirit of slavery . . . is withering all our hopes. [Its] influence cuts us off from everything; it follows us up from childhood to manhood." It was simply inescapable, like "the atmosphere, everywhere felt." Garnet knew what he meant. He had choked on this same atmosphere in Maryland, Pennsylvania, New York City, and in Canaan, New Hampshire. At the last of these was a new school, integrated, where Garnet, nineteen, hoped to study. But only weeks after Noyes Academy welcomed Garnet and his companion, the younger student Alexander Crummell, white farmers wagoned to the campus, hitched the little schoolhouse to teams of oxen, dragged it to a swamp, and torched it.[16]

The next move augured better. Garnet and Crummell's city mentor, Reverend Wright, urged his protégés to head west to Oneida County, New York, where a radical white abolitionist had launched an integrated school in Whitesboro. Beriah Green's academy promised to steep its scholars in the manual trades, Greek and Hebrew, and the tenets of radical perfectionism. And this place locals left alone. At the Oneida Institute, Garnet cultivated the gift for oratory that early on distinguished a long pastoral career. It would be Gerrit Smith's eventual great fortune that young Garnet's first assignment in the field was in Troy, the city closest to the gift lands in the Adirondack wilds.[17]

Garnet assumed the ministry at Liberty Street Presbyterian in 1839. He was its first pastor, and the congregants his first parishioners. In five years, his vigorous, audacious oratory had more than doubled the church's membership. Four years later, Garnet, only twenty-eight, spoke for ninety minutes at a National Negro Convention in Buffalo. It would be the speech that made his fame and notoriety. In clear, emphatic, scrupulously reasoned terms, Garnet's "Address to the Slaves" called for armed resistance to slavery in the North and South alike. Its eloquence was matched by its unexpectedness, and at its close, the hall full of convention delegates erupted. Garnet's old mentor, Theodore S. Wright, glowed with pride. Elder Ray was on the fence, and Frederick Douglass enraged. Delegates put Garnet's resolution to a vote; this hot call to rebellion lost the day by one vote. But the winds of Garnet's appeal gusted well beyond Buffalo, New York. Antislavery papers quoted him in Ohio, Boston, and New Hampshire. At a Colored Convention in Ohio in 1849, delegates endorsed this six-year-old address and urged its widespread circulation (Garnet had published it himself, along with the late Black militant David Walker's 1830 *Appeal to the Colored Citizens of the World*). John Brown invoked Garnet's address in 1859 before his hanging. At the height of the Black Power movement in the 1960s, the *Black World/Negro Digest* declared Henry Garnet "the first black leader in America to call for a National Liberation Struggle [whose] ideas clearly conform to many of the feelings held by black leaders today."[18]

In 1848, Garnet broke with the Albany Presbytery and declared his Troy congregation beholden only to "God and His Son Jesus Christ"; this way, he could preach his antislavery Bible politics without fear of reproof. (Gerrit Smith may have inspired this; in 1843, Smith left the Peterboro Presbyterians to found his nonsectarian abolition church.) Garnet knew he risked the loss of some parishioners. Not all of his flock were keen on Bible politics. But risk and Garnet were old friends. He took a risk when he left Maryland, went to sea, and attended Noyes Academy, and he took a risk in Troy preaching antislavery in a city jealously protective of its trade with Southern clients. Risk was his daily fare.[19]

THREE AGENTS AND THEIR REASONS   53

The risk he ran in 1846, when he signed on to get Smith "pick'd men" for a new life in the woods, was failure. Some of Smith's agents simply could not meet their quotas. Garnet not only met his, but when he discovered that some of his choices were unworthy, he made Smith scratch them from the list. Some of his devotion to this task reflected his own respect and love for Gerrit Smith himself; for Garnet more than the others, Peterboro was like a second home. But mostly, Garnet was motivated by his own passionate agrarianism. Like Ray, he had been urging Black families to get out of the city for years. The vote was more achievable in small towns where it was easier to save money. To a Black audience in Schenectady in 1844 he pointed out that "in the towns of Syracuse and Geneva, among a colored population of some eight hundred, there are more voters according to the odious $250 qualification, than there are in New York City, which has eighteen or twenty thousand." Prejudice, he added, was "so strong in cities, and custom is so set and determined, that it is impossible for us to emerge from the most laborious and least profitable occupations." Work hard in the country, however, and "there is no prejudice so strong as to be able to roll back the tide of our enfranchisement."[20]

Note the goal here: not Charles Ray's equalitarian pastoral (agrarian hardship as an equalizer), and not McCune Smith's regenerative frontier, but voting rights—civic power enabled by a perfectionist agenda. In a sermon to the Troy grantees before they headed north, Garnet set the standard high. To the deedholders would fall the work of "set[ting] an example of independence" for other Black people and demonstrating "the falsity of the old doctrine, that we are doomed to be the hewers of wood, and drawers of water." "God's design that every man shall have a home" was theirs to claim, "a perfect system of agrarianism" their duty to install. Take your Bibles, Garnet told them. Keep the Sabbath. Save money, and turn away from "rum jugs . . . and whiskey barrels." Rather than join a church whose leaders shrank from damning slavery, start your own church. Remember Bible politics and stay engaged, "interested in the political affairs of the nation." This, to the perfectionist, was key. "Refuse to vote for those who will give honor to oppressors. O, brethren, be faithful to your duty at the ballot box. There, give expression to your prayers." Infusing politics with faith, faith with political resolve, was the Black settler's charge. Garnet's Black Woods would be perfected. Where McCune Smith emphasized the antiurban angle, and Ray dreamed of small, integrated communities driven to egalitarianism by pragmatic need, Garnet saw a sanctified utopia, a city on a hill.[21]

Rev. Henry Highland Garnet. Photograph, 1881. Courtesy of the National Portrait Gallery, Smithsonian Institution.

This message would be heard. While Ray and McCune Smith signed up takers by the thousands, it was Troy's Garnet, the preacher with the voice of "one who wrestled with an angel," who inspired the most grantees to move onto their land. McCune Smith confirmed this twenty years after the giveaway was launched. Not his and Ray's work but his old friend Henry Garnet's "influence and teachings" and his "judgment in selecting beneficiaries" resulted in "the largest number of actual occupants of these lands, the best men in overcoming the difficulties in the new and laborious field, and the only men who yet remain . . . successful cultivators of the soil." This is not to say that these Trojans all stayed put and prospered. But they *went*; they took the chance. True, Garnet's cohort was advantaged by geography, his Rensselaer County so much nearer to the Adirondacks than New York City or points west, and his giftees' exodus more manageable, their destination not so distant as to seem unreal. But before they went, they had to feel this was better than a good idea. They had to feel it as a destiny, a spiritual duty. That's where Garnet delivered. He promised the more perfect world.[22]

The Big Pitch

In the month after Smith divulged his plan, his enthusiasm brimmed. He talked it up to friends, and even to a Maryland enslaver who wanted Smith to buy and free his slaves. *You* free them, Smith countered. "I am now engaged in settling three thousand colored men of this State on lands I own in this State—about 40 to 60 acres each." *Emancipate your slaves and I will set them up with gift lots*, was the gist of Smith's offer. The Marylander balked.[23]

But talking up his plan in private was one thing. Public scrutiny was another. Smith hoped to "keep this whole business out of the newspapers." He couldn't, and, as early as September, his plan, he felt, was being "grossly misrepresented." In Auburn, Ossining, Cortland, Rochester, Elizabethtown, and Manhattan, New Yorkers read that the gift land was in *Hamilton* County, where "the woods are so dense as to be almost impervious to the axe of the settler, and even when by almost superhuman effort they are finally leveled to the earth and their trunks cleared away . . . , there appears naught to reward the woodman's anxious toil but an interminable field of stones." Add to this fake news the dark reports of "flies, punckies, gnats, gallinippers and musquitoes" as bad for "bloodthirstiness" as anything a pioneer might find "on the banks of the Rio Grande"—insects that could "draw blood" through the woodman's "very boots"—and ponder the donor's folly! The Smith grantee, "unused to self-dependence," did not stand a chance. Whig newspapers across the state called the giveaway a rich man's ploy to dump bad land and dodge taxes. Skepticism soured judgments in the *Essex County Republican*, too.[24]

Smith had parceled out about 350 land grants in Township 3, a part of the old Tottenham and Crossfield Patent that straddles Hamilton and Herkimer Counties—hard land to reach, and harder still to farm. This stood for a fraction of the gift land overall. But if misinformation did the giveaway no favors, it did jolt Smith into preparing his deeds in record time; as soon as late October, he had two thousand of them ready and waiting for his agents to fill in names. The next thousand would be distributed when all lingering debt on this acreage was resolved, and when his agents identified the last thousand giftees. Smith also penned a robust explanation of the giveaway for his favorite antislavery paper, the *Albany Patriot*. This "Address to the Three Thousand Colored Citizens of New York who are the owners of one hundred and twenty thousand acres of land, in the state of New York, given to them by Gerrit Smith, Esq., of Peterboro, September 1, 1846," incorporated not only Smith's first long letter to his New York City agents of August 1 but a follow-up letter he sent September 9, and the agents' gracious, hopeful, and highly tactical response. Smith recognized that Black readers especially would value the agents' perspective, and he knew he could count on the *Patriot*'s publisher, William C. Chaplin, one of Smith's Albany agents, to print this appeal for the cause. Then, Smith guessed, Horace Greeley's *Tribune* would scoop it up "as cheerfully . . . and as correctly" as the *Patriot*, and the little papers that spiced their pages with Greeley-vetted dispatches would surely run it too.[25]

The agents' essay, twice as long as Smith's address, made its own argument for agrarianism, and in terms much more ambitious than its value for Black suffrage. Only farmers could hope to achieve lasting self-reliance, Ray, Wright, and McCune Smith declared. Only husbandry could release Black people from "dependent employments at reduced wages . . . thus creating that feeling of dependence and uncertainty which ever . . . deadens the faculties of men." Set us on "our own land," they predicted, "we will be our own masters, free to think, free to act." Once free men of color had land they could work, white neighbors would respect them, and concede their shared humanity. To the agents, it was this simple. "There is no life like that of a farmer, for overcoming the mere prejudice against color," they declared. "The owners of adjacent farms are neighbors. . . . There must be mutual assistance, mutual and equal dependence, mutual sympathy—and labor, the 'common destiny of the American people,' under such circumstances yields equally to all, and make all equal."[26]

The farmer as the ideal citizen of the republic, self-made, unbeholden, happy lord of the vaunted "middle landscape" that straddled wilderness and town—this was nothing fresh. Like Crèvecoeur and Jefferson before them, the erudite Black agents of the New York City Committee knew the classical texts from which the archetype derived. By 1846, the self-providing freehold as an image of American independence (an image, really, of America itself) was an icon of popular and literary culture (never mind the growing irrelevance of the pastoral ideal that, even as Smith pushed it, had begun to breathe its worn-out last). In their homage to the giveaway, Ray, Wright, and McCune Smith, shepherds garbed in native homespun, took their places in a long line of Romantically inspired writers enamored of this cultural cliché.[27]

But that's not all they were after, not all Black agrarianism was up to. The Black farmer would be to his white neighbors a beacon and a catalyst. Farmers were obliged by the nature of their work and isolation to lend a hand to other farmers in times of need. Farmers who'd been helped were bound to repay the favor. And this occupational parity was only the beginning. Living and working near other farmers on the frontier would slowly bless the Black frontiersman with the influence to free white neighbors from the sin of a reflexive prejudice. In aiding himself, he saved the world. In the woods, on his land, he gained the power to change men's hearts.

This was not the first time the Adirondack wilderness was vested with close-to-magical transforming powers, but it was surely its first outing as an agent of racial equity and Black pride. The farmer's life on the Adirondack frontier would more than foster "elements of character" among the grantees and their white neighbors; it would *compel* them. No good farmer could succeed without these qualities, the agents promised. They are as crucial to success as land ownership itself. First came organization, or what the agents called "Mutual system": "Without system you can effect but little, with it, you can accomplish any desirable and practicable undertaking." The role of thrift, or "economy," invited more attention still: "The very uncertainty of a large portion of our present employments . . . have produced amongst us that negative, slipshod economy, which consists in barely making the income eke out the expenditure. If we would be successful farmers, we must abandon this careless mode of living, and substitute therefore a rigid economy of our time and of our means." This, the agents warned, would be the stiffest challenge for the grantees, "the point in which we will have to make the greatest and most thorough revolution in our present habits." Were the grantees up to it? If they meant business, they had better "begin at economy *now*." Start organizing parties of fifteen or twenty, aim for "about one hundred dollars" per grantee. Pool this, and the fund would buy the group "a sufficient number of horses or oxen, farm tools for all, and the means for each to stock his own farm." How to raise the cash? The agents knew exactly: "By avoiding in the winter months the expense of balls, parties and fruit entertainments, you can readily save one hundred dollars each." This way, they promised, you will never have to borrow on your land and thus betray the friend who has given it to you in good faith that you will hold on to it debt free.[28]

After economy came "Self-Reliance" and "Mutual Reliance," two qualities lacking among Black New Yorkers thanks to the "false education" that had gotten them to "regard our own faculties as inferior." More self-trust, beseeched the agents. If white people could follow a "trail of 3 or 4,000 miles over an almost trackless wilderness," downstate Blacks could manage traveling by "steamboat and railroad and stage routes" to New York woodlots that were, they guessed, not more "than 2 miles from well-traveled roads." Black deedholders who worked this land with their "free labor" would live to see their children "cluster round [the] hearth in the robust health of a country life." They could "exert this power, do for yourselves what other men have done for themselves." Hadn't they "the same physical and intellectual power which other men have"? And as you help yourselves, the agents wrote, you will begin to help each other. "Away with mutual distrust!" Live planfully, don't drink, work hard, pool earnings, and in time you'll gain a role in "a great experiment in behalf of long suffering, long crushed, downtrodden and bleeding humanity . . . an experiment for the RACE! not of Africa, nor of Cush, but for the race of mankind! The cause of our common race is, in a manner, entrusted to our hands."[29]

Smith's hope for the giveaway was nothing next to this. He "would that every man who desires a farm, might have one," and if getting a farm could edge a Black New Yorker closer to the ballot, so much the better. As Smith himself was often running for office, some biographers have described this as self-serving. If so, it was an antislavery strategy he was in a very good position to promote. "Since they must become landowners that they may be entitled to vote," he declared, "they will become landowners. Vote they will, cost what it will." The tone was weary (he wrote this a few days after the devastating antisuffrage vote in November), but Smith was no cynic. He was a pragmatist, a "practical dreamer," as his biographer Norman Dann observes. And the city agents, suffrage fighters all, found his logic sound.[30]

But their pitch in the *Patriot* aimed higher still. What they emphasized was how Black settlers on their farms might influence *white* voters, and, specifically, the pioneers' new neighbors. Remember, wrote the agents, how white people welcomed Black families headed to a temperance meeting in 1846? They swarmed the Hudson River banks to cheer steamships bearing Black men to the jubilee. Let Black people take up farming and it would be the same. White New Yorkers would, "in like manner, hail our self-emancipation from the drudgery of the cities, and . . . glory in the prosperity which two or three thousand additional tillers of the soil will bring to the Empire State." And with white respect for Black uplift would come white votes for voting rights. The ballots that Black men gained as a result of owning land were welcome, but just as thrilling, maybe more so, would be the power to change the hearts of white men by the force of personal example. This was more than the promise of self-rule. This was the hope of influence, the tiller all your own.[31]

Smith had not flagged these specific expectations in the *Patriot*, but they came as no surprise. Black agrarianism, much like Black suffrage activism, was a river running long before Smith launched his boat on its bold current. And when Smith's distracted vessel drifted, the river kept on flowing, bearing farmers, miners, Exodusters, to Ontario, Michigan, Kansas, and Ohio. Smith had been an agrarian for a while, but not as long as his Black agents had. That, after all, is why he picked them and why they signed on for this work. His vision for the giveaway drew in good part from Black imaginings and dreams.

And there was another quarter he borrowed from—though its response was somewhat less ecstatic. Two years before Smith gave up land, he found himself the target of a feisty takedown from the land reformer George Henry Evans, editor of the city paper *The People's Rights*. Evans charged the land-rich Smith with enslaving white laborers in northern cities by default. Smith had the power, Evans offered, to liberate legions of the working poor by giving land to them he did not need, use, or plan to farm. Not exercising that power was criminal. Hopeful farmers were denied a crack at self-betterment. Families starved who might be fed. Smith could change this. He had not. Where was the philanthropy in this?[32]

Evans's gamble—that Smith would choose to defend himself—paid off. He and Smith exchanged several letters, all published in Evans's newspaper, and their bright debate on land reform would conclude with Smith conceding that Evans's notions about land distribution to the poor made some sense. Indeed, following this exchange, Smith declared himself a land reformer, inspiring some of that camp to hope he'd prove a benefactor and an ally.[33]

But the kind of voluntaristic land reform Smith practiced when he gave land to poor *Black* New Yorkers was not what George Evans had in mind. And a philanthropy indebted to the arguments of white land reformers was not what Black agrarians expected either. Smith's plan of 1846 borrowed gratefully from both camps to come up with something entirely and boldly new. Did they welcome this? In one case yes, and in the other, likely no. Either way, it hardly mattered. White and Black agrarians alike would see their mission widened, deepened, and enriched—whether they asked for this or not.[34]

CHAPTER 4

Theories into Practice

> In theory, theory and practice are the same. In practice, they are not.
>
> —Albert Einstein

From the beginning there were snags and slowdowns, malcontents and doubters, and cases angling for special consideration. A blacksmith griped that the barber James Duffin, Smith's Black agent in Geneva, played favorites. Not true, Duffin said. This smithy did not deserve a deed. He drank. In Albany, the grantee Jacob Benjamin charged the land agent William Topp with cronyism. Why else had Topp swapped Benjamin's gift land with Topp's uncle's lot, which was underwater and "no earthly good"? Anna Shotwell, the Quaker headmistress of the Colored Orphan Asylum in Manhattan, pressed Gerrit Smith to relax his rules so that some of her young boys could farm too. An Albany woman asked Smith to consider giving farms to Black women who "must contend not only with prejudice against her poverty, prejudice against color, but prejudice against her sex. . . . Which of the three is the most cruel I am not prepared to say. But that all three combined are enough to crush a Lion I can testify." Amos Beman, a New Haven minister, reported "quite a fever in this city among the colored people" to get homesteads and start farming, and hoped Smith could sell him land near the gift lot of his old schoolmate, Dr. James McCune Smith.[1]

The grantee Samuel Cornish, who, years earlier, had turned Smith against the cause of African colonization, was especially aggrieved. Why no deed for him, when his late paper, the *Colored American*, had done so

much to proselytize Black husbandry? Did the agents think him insufficiently impoverished? He was poor enough, and he could prove it. The
Manhattan activist Thomas Van Rensselaer guessed he never got a deed
because he was a Garrisonian, and maybe, too, because he sometimes
tippled. But brandy, in his case, had been prescribed for a medical condition by none other than Dr. McCune Smith![2]

In Johnstown, a white activist, Abel Seaton, feared that a prospective
grantee from his community might not qualify "on account of his color . . . ,
he being a little more *white* than black." The Rochester antislavery attorney Samuel Porter wanted Smith's assurance that all deeds were absolute and unconditional. And poor white abolitionists who had labored
for the cause were moved to wonder—*why not us? Are we not needy?* In
1844, Captain Jonathan Walker tried rowing seven slaves to freedom
from Pensacola, Florida, to the Bahamas. Caught and jailed, Walker
was released with the initials "S.S.," for "Slave Stealer," burned into his
palm. John Greenleaf Whittier wrote a poem about Walker's ordeal,
but literary fame put no bread on Walker's table, and in 1852 he asked
Smith, "Knowing that you was making a liberal dispossession of lands
in your possession," would not the rich man give him "some place for
a home"? Farming for another was only "a little milder form of slavery
than that experience of our Southern friends in bonds."[3]

Decades of long-distance land management had readied the philanthropist for pushback and finagling. The wounded Cornish and com-
bustible Van Rensselaer got deeds (even if, as Smith reminded Cornish,
this was in "manifold violation of my plan"), and Samuel Porter got
his answer: "Yes, the Deeds are *absolute*—and the Grantees have a perfect *legal* right to do what they will with the property—to make a good
use of it, or to drink it up, or waste it in some other way." If Smith
could not satisfy the blunt-spoken Mary Mills of Albany, he still made
exceptions to his rules. Some women would get deeds, as would several self-revealed fugitives. To the Colored Orphan Asylum, Smith gave
five thousand acres to be held in trust. A few years after the giveaway,
he donated yet more acreage to a thousand poor white New Yorkers,
some women among them. As noted earlier, he had even offered to
give gift lots to ten slaves belonging to Judge John Thomson Mason of
Maryland—if Mason freed them first. The judge declined.[4]

Smith also gave deeds to a few non–New Yorkers engaged in equal
justice work—a doff of the cap from one civil rights veteran to fellow
toilers in the field. When grantees lost their deeds, he replaced them. If
a grantee's lot was discovered to be underwater or ravaged by a fire, he

sent a new deed. The Utica agent Wesley Bailey knew a grantee struggling to hoist himself from debt. Might this man's deed be put in his
wife's name so that creditors could not seize it? *Done.* A father and his
son hoped for adjacent lots. Would Smith oblige? *Of course.* When the
Black agents traveled to the Smith Lands, Smith furnished them with
an introductory note that explained their purpose. He encouraged the
formation of mutual aid groups, a tools bank, a co-share plan for livestock. And when a Yankee abolitionist showed up at his home and offered to move his family to North Elba and get the new farmers settled
in, Smith met the offer with delight.[5]

But for Smith, this was no full-time job. During the six or seven years
he oversaw the giveaway, he was also managing his own Peterboro estate,
preaching Bible politics at his church, bucking up the shrinking Liberty
Party faithful, resolutely leveling his mountain of old debt, buying land,
selling land, working up more philanthropic schemes to unload more
land still, buying the freedom of sundry fugitives and their extended
families, hosting visitors, convalescing from his chronic ailments, keeping up his massive correspondence, burnishing his verse and daybooks,
clipping fan mail, underwriting the New York State Vigilance Committee, and, by 1852, stumping for a seat in Congress. Further, the antics
of his "rebel child" Greene, born in 1842, were causing Smith no end
of bafflement and worry. (Another way to fix Smith's land gifts in the
wider context of his work: his archives at Syracuse University's Special
Collections Research Center occupy 155 boxes, 29 oversized bound
volumes, 339 maps, and 77 reels of microfilm. The portion dedicated
to his northern New York land project takes up a few yards of a reel,
or, in hard copy, a folder.) The onerous demands on Smith's working
hours meant that it would fall to the land agents to turn the giveaway
from a beautiful idea into a usable reality. Smith would mail packets
of signed deeds to his agents when they sent him names, but it was the
agents who would need to market the idea, vet the grantees' eligibility,
collect the signatures, and track their progress. All this Smith left to
them.[6]

A Chain That Pulled Itself

Smith's apostles were men of overlapping interests, one cause locked to
the next like links on a chain, church to temperance, temperance to uplift, uplift to political empowerment and reform. Any one of these would
suggest a reason to support Smith's plan. But was this chain attached

to something bigger or did it pull only its shiny self-regarding self? No systematic strategy directed the grantees' recruitment. Congregants at Reverend Garnet's Liberty Street Church in Troy likely heard about it in a sermon. Black seamen staying at the Colored Sailors' Home on Pearl Street may have heard their innkeeper, William P. Powell, preach Black enfranchisement and the uses of the gift lots at Philomathean Hall. Families squatting in Cow Bay, a cul-de-sac in Manhattan's notorious Five Points, likely got the news from Elder Ray, who, like Smith, kept a notebook for all the names he'd culled. Ray's "Receipt Book" also noted street addresses, which tell a story all their own. Families of three grantees shared one home at 17 Sullivan, eleven more grantees and their families shared rooms in a tenement at 55–59 Mercer, and blocks on Chrystie, Leonard, Little Water, and Mulberry Streets were home to congested enclaves of grantees as well.[7]

Doors opened dutifully for Elder Ray. Did hearts? Only two months after Smith's announcement, agents were observing how hard it was for them to recruit prospective farmers who took issue with Smith's temperance clause. James Duffin, Smith's agent in Geneva, was at his wit's end. Black men, he wrote Smith, balked at being ordered to give up their daily dram of beer or cider. Worse (in his view), on learning that their drinking made them ineligible, they blamed not their own "evil propensities" but the agents' "partiality and a desire to crush the poor." Syracuse's Loguen, Cortland County's Ward, and Albany's William Chaplin all struggled to find enough rock-hard temperance men to meet Smith's quotas. Even the downstate agents faced a shortfall. But Smith would not retract or modify his policy. The intemperance his agents lamented seemed only to vindicate the wisdom of his antidrinking provision.[8]

Were Black New Yorkers who flunked Smith's stringent standard of eligibility necessarily drunkards? Was this the only way to read their resistance? Smith and his agents' preoccupation with intemperance may say less about the drinking habits of Black New Yorkers than about the agents' ignorance of the population they wanted to recruit. While drunkenness may have been as rampant as Smith feared, there were reasons besides love of drink why free men of color might resent a temperance clause. Not everyone bought the adamantine logic that a sip of beer was as wicked as a full-tilt dive in a river of rye. The rigidity of temperance evangelism could not dispel considerable anecdotal evidence that showed a fellow could drink without getting drunk or helplessly addicted. If John Calvin's saint-or-sinner absolutism struck a chord with the heirs of Cotton Mather and an elite cadre of Black reformers steeped in this tradition, it did not resonate with Black New Yorkers unimpressed with Yankee pieties. What did they care for temperance when so many white temperance activists cared so little about them? Exceptions notwithstanding (Gerrit Smith and Arthur Tappan among them), many white temperance zealots showed as little love for racial justice as those white artisans and mechanics who banned Black men from their confederated shops and trades. As Frederick Douglass reminded a Scottish audience in 1846, "Such is the prejudice against the coloured man, such the hatred, the contempt in which he is held, that no temperance society in the [United States] would so far jeopardize its popularity as to invite a coloured man to stand before them."[9]

Temperance men said that abstinence on the job could boost business profits by one-fourth. Well and good for employers. Bottom-rung Black laborers did not register the gain. Temperance moralists declared that drink "inflamed the passions," but it was not drunkenness that frightened them. It was the prospect of public sexuality and, specifically, the bogey of miscegenation. That's what brought reformers to Uncle Pete William's joint on Orange Street. In the shadows they stood appalled (yet mesmerized) while patrons whooped and jigged, and what Black New Yorker would not recognize the prurience in this?[10]

The bards of temperance sang the virtues of fresh cold water, that "drink divine." Did they know how hard it was to get fresh water in the slums? In wine, wisdom; in beer, freedom; in water, bacteria—so Benjamin Franklin had observed. New Yorkers with access to a private source were set. Some piped clean water into their homes. Gerrit Smith drew his from a gravity-fed system that directed water from the Oriskany Stream to his own water tower. But no law forced a New York City landlord to plumb the ramshackle dwellings of the poor.[11]

The social reformer Charles Loring Brace was not thinking of Black tavern-goers when he described the lure of a city saloon, but Black or white, the appeal of a defiantly masculine world of "jolly companions, a lighted and warmed room, a newspaper, and, above all, a draught which ... can change poverty into riches, and drive [out] care and labor and the thought of all his burdens and annoyances" was the same. Wrote Brace, "The liquor shop is [the tavern-goers'] picture gallery, club, reading room, and social *salon*, at once. His glass is the magic transmuter, of care to cheerfulness, of penury to plenty, of a low, ignorant, worried life, to an existence for the moment buoyant, contented, and hopeful." Gerrit Smith had his picture gallery, club, reading room, and salon—all the assets of a salon except for firewater—at home in Peterboro. Not needing to leave home to work, he could not know the dramshop's sociable allure. As for the agents he had tapped to round up his grantees, when they craved a collegial space outside their day jobs and home, they had book clubs, suffrage meetings, and conventions. Not so the Black laborer, shuttling between the work site and a verminous dim room he almost surely shared with others. No books for him; if he knew how to read (not likely), there was no light to read by. He might have liked to pray, but churchgoing meant church dues he couldn't pay. And who had leisure time for meetings? Breathing space, a refuge of his own, was a smoky low room with gritty floors, a few mates, a boy behind the bar who recalled your poison without being told.[12]

When James Duffin wrote Gerrit Smith that some Black men felt the temperance clause was nothing but another way "to crush the poor," he did not probe their reasoning. Duffin saw temperance as the road to respectability; they saw a blithe repudiation of the one pleasure that poor men could afford, and the solace of a place, however shabby, where Black working men could unwind. Duffin saw common cause with an antislavery elect; they discerned a bourgeois club they didn't know or trust. Their suspicions struck Duffin as so ungrateful he could only note the "evil propensities" of those who voiced them.

The prospect of the "cold ingratitude of colored men," and poor Black men especially, troubled James McCune Smith too. As early as December 1846, he could guess that Smith's gifts might not raise the robust response Smith expected; Smith, the doctor feared, might not know his "colored friends" quite as well as he supposed. "Have you prepared yourself?" he asked the land baron. Poor Black grantees who rode the "tide of wealth-worship" might hate a man who let wealth go.[13]

The doctor's well-intentioned letter revealed more than he intended. He was worried. Would the grantees be sufficiently appreciative? Would they get that this was heaven sent? Would they assume their part? Gratitude, to this well-schooled uplift abolitionist, reflected civility, respect, and piety, good bourgeois Christian values all the agents shared. The grantees' morality was different. Gratitude, for many, painfully invoked the entitled expectation of the slaveowner and the forced deference of the enslaved. The word right from the gate was loaded, racialized, and implicitly demeaning. What had it to do with the progress or failure of the giveaway? To suggest that grantees might spurn their gift lots not for a range of solid, thoughtful reasons but because they were predisposed to ingratitude—here was a judgment that spoke less of the grantees than of the land agent's fearful worry about *Black men behaving badly*, a bias that hinted at a cultural rift between Smith's helpers and his beneficiaries that would beleaguer the giveaway for years.

Building Up the List

By the end of 1846, Smith's agents had identified two thousand Black men ready to become Adirondack deedholders, and received signed deeds from Smith's Peterboro land office. Most of these proud, unlikely, new-made owners of wild land were from metropolitan New York. Recruiting the remaining thousand would take much longer. Over the next few years, the agents would need to shuffle and adjust their quotas to favor more responsive counties over those where interest in Smith's plan was weak. The agents got a boost from friendly coverage in the Whig papers, and it surely helped that every one of Smith's agents worked or wrote for the abolition press: Garnet, Bailey, Chaplin, Ray, and Ward were newspaper publishers and editors; Wright, Loguen, and McCune Smith, columnists; Loguen, Ray, and Ward, drummers for subscriptions. Topp, McCune Smith, and Chaplin advertised in abolition papers for their businesses or shops. Further, among the loyal readers of these plain-printed broadsheets were publishers of other papers hunting for good copy: a piece about a Troy grantees' meeting in the *Albany Patriot* would be picked up by the *Cortland True American* and Milwaukee's *American Freeman*. What a New York City paper, the *Ram's Horn*, had to say about grantees forming bands to venture north was grist for Rochester's *North Star*. The urban editors Frederick Douglass, Stephen Myers, and Willis Hodges were not land agents by invitation, but they did the work of agents, and sometimes more.[14]

Others who pitched in: William P. Powell of the Colored Seaman's Home in Manhattan vouched for sailors hungering for land (and when McCune Smith visited the Smith Lands in 1849, his friend Powell went with him). In Ray's private "Receipt Book" of city grantees, Powell vouched for eight good men he knew. A Flushing farmer, Jonathan Mingo, "stood" for twenty hopeful deedholders; a city cartman, Anthony Provost, signed for six. The cohort of grantees who could not write their names was hefty: in Ray's notebook, some five hundred men flagged their desire for a gift lot with a hard X dropped into the middle of their names, as in John "X" Dixon of 45 Anthony Street, or Henry "X" Butler of 7 Thomas Street. Almost half of Staten Island's twenty-nine grantees signed with Xs. Their wives signed for them too.

These middlemen weren't necessarily more literate than the grantees they brought on board. (Provost, also represented in this notebook as Pervost, Prevost, and Prevolt, signed with an *X*.) What made their word good was a track record of political engagement at conventions, church rallies, and petition drives. The official agents trusted them to make smart picks.[15]

Black agents also prospected among their comrades in reform; hence the many uplift men whose names spangled the long list. Some of these were from New York City, like Charles Reason, a multilingual professor of belles lettres, his gifted brother Patrick, an engraver, Alexander Crummell, Garnet's old school friend and a published theologian, and Rev. James W. C. Pennington, author, educator, and founder of the first Black missionary society. Buffalo's pages included the barber, poet, and emigrationist James M. Whitfield, and among several Elmirans was the esteemed Baptist sexton John W. Jones, an organizer of his town's Underground Railroad. It was unlikely these men asked for deeds because they planned to farm, but there were other reasons to participate. They could reward the good faith of a white ally, endorse a strategy for equal voting rights, and hope their sudden slice of wilderness would prove a usable investment.

White admirers of Gerrit Smith also volunteered the names of prospects. In Rochester, Smith's friend the attorney Samuel Porter filled a page. The printer E. M. Griffing of Little Falls vouched for three "honest, industrious and sober" candidates, "and the quicker the better," he wrote Smith; his men "would go right upon the lands, if they had it, and undertake the getting in of Corn and Potato crops." A Delaware County farmer, Street Dutton, put in a word for four "worthy Industrious good Citizens," and when Reverend Garnet needed names from Montgomery County, the Canajoharie merchant, John Snell, helped him out. In Washington County near Vermont, Dr. Hiram Corliss distributed Smith's deeds to all of the grantees in his district and advised Smith to take note of Avery Hazzard, the grantee-settler whose surname threads this story from first to last. The giveaway had white friends in the villages of Holley, Cherry Valley, Oneida Castle, and Union Village, and in Middlebury, Vermont. Even the *Berkshire County Whig* gave it a plug.[16]

Perhaps the meager contribution of Smith's white agents (as distinct from other white volunteers) was predictable. Their knowledge of the Black communities in their territories was thin, and for all their wish to please the great philanthropist, they may not have privileged

Black voting rights over other work. Abolition, an end to slavery—was the battle that compelled, and the link between abolition and equal suffrage that glowed so hotly for Smith was a dimmer light for them. Fugitives were one thing; for the freedom seeker these white reformers would preach, petition, endure death threats and prison. In Washington, DC, in 1850, Chaplin spent five months in jail when he got caught helping the escaping slaves of a Georgia congressmen. Utica's Alfred H. Hunt and George Lawson, as well as Albany's Nathaniel Safford, were all Liberty men. Wesley Bailey's *Liberty Press* was the leading abolition paper in central New York. But Black voting rights were not their cause, and their interest only went so far. "We have made all possible inquiry but have been able to find only a very few out of this city [Albany] that seemed trustworthy—I have not yet been able to get a name either from Warren or Franklin County," William Chaplin sighed in November 1846.[17]

"God Bless Mr. Smith and All the Smiths"

When Smith made his last entry in his private inventory of grantees in 1853, he could take credit for something utterly unprecedented: a midcentury directory of virtually every Black reformer in New York State. Single causes like Black enfranchisement, uplift, abolition, and temperance may have generated sheaves of names as well, but nothing this inclusive and diversified. At issue was a time-specific land settlement proposal that offered a kind of paper commons for reformers of all stripes—emigrationists, anticolonizationists, authors of influential slave narratives, charismatic orators, suffrage lobbyists and moral suasion ideologues, abolition church dissenters, affiliated church officers—and all these names mingling with several thousand Black New Yorkers with no activist pedigree at all. For in Smith's *Land Book*, front-row reformers did not preside. The some five hundred city deed-holders who signed their names with an *X* in Ray's Receipt Book were no more or less worthy of a deed than the physician McCune Smith. This is not to overstate class differences among free Black New Yorkers, where the rift between the manual laborer and an aspiring bourgeois could be no wider than a crack. The grantee Philip Bell may have run an employment office for Black domestics and coedited the nation's leading Black newspaper, but he also peddled coal. Both Reverend Pennington and Dr. McCune Smith were blacksmiths before they took up middle-class careers, and if McCune Smith read three languages, he

and his neighborhood chimney sweep still shared a legacy of enslavement and endured the daily slap of bigotry. But putting up with racists
was shared ground for despair; Smith's proposition offered a common
ground for joy. Free land was part of it, of course, but so was the pride
of membership in a picked fraternity of deedholders that put bootblack
and professor, cartman and minister, on one level. With these deeds,
the commonality of deprivation bloomed into its opposite—a hope of
economic opportunity, a route to equal rights.

When the giveaway was publicized in the fall of 1846, delegates to
Black conventions, large and small, saluted Gerrit Smith. At the invitation of Smith's central New York land agents, Black men from nine
central New York counties thronged a "Grand Convention of Gerrit
Smith's Grantees" in mid-December, in Ithaca. That month, too, grantees convened in Troy, Manhattan, Brooklyn, and Westchester. Their
mood, reported McCune Smith, was hugely eager, emboldening him
to chide his Peterboro friend for not venturing "to see a gathering of
the grantees. . . . Tall, stalwart, hard-fisted, they embody a Hope of the
Race."[18]

In October of that year, with the *Albany Patriot* reporting, Troy grantees at Reverend Garnet's Liberty Street Church raised a cheer to the
benefactor they had not met. William Jones, a Troy grantee with a talent for the stump, declared that God "had opened a way for many, by
touching the heart of Mr. Smith. Shame on the human who will not improve the opportunity." Once, Jones said, he used to "drive the carriage
of an old drunken slaveholder." No more! "Soon I hope to drive my own
team, and lead my own horse to water." Once, Jones was "compelled to
clear up ten acres for another, and do other work, and get thumped in
the bargain." No longer! "When I reach my little farm, with my liberty
axe I expect to clear up fifteen acres annually." Thanks to his new deed,
swore Jones, "I will cut down my own tree—build my own cabin—plant
my own grain—eat the fruit of my own stall." And then, in a remark
likely meant for this group only, Jones confessed, "I have received so
much abuse from white people that once I thought all were my enemies." Gerrit Smith proved him wrong. "God bless Mr. Smith and all
the Smiths." To the cheers of fellow Trojans, Jones exhorted, "Come
off from the steamboats—leave your barber shops—leave the kitchen,
where you have to live under ground all day and climb up ten pairs of
stairs at night" (a scenario so recognizable, it brought down the house).
"Tomorrow," this ex-slave promised, "I intend to leave for Essex County
to see for myself."[19]

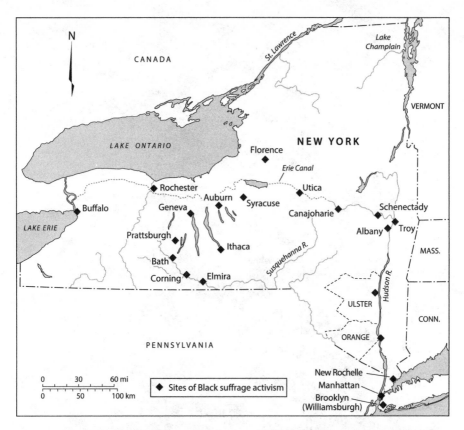

Map of Black civil rights and antislavery meetings and conventions in New York State where Gerrit Smith's "scheme of justice and benevolence" was endorsed by activists. Map by Bill Nelson.

More meetings in 1847 ginned up good press for the giveaway. In March, the grantees of Monroe County gave thanks to their benefactor, and in May, the American Anti-slavery Society hailed Smith's "munificent gifts of land" in the *National Era*. But much of what was done that year was the quiet, unsung work of agents: identifying qualified grantees, getting signatures, and sending names ("these presents," Ray and McCune Smith called them) to Peterboro. And in July, Charles Ray did more. He headed north to Essex County to see his new land for himself—his, and the new lot, too, of his friend and fellow agent James McCune Smith.[20]

Was his mood a little anxious? The Black minister, traveling alone, had no contacts in this wild place. But Smith's land office had armed him with a note of introduction to ease his arrival and make sure his guide would be a good one, and the North Elba innkeeper Iddo Osgood

Rev. Charles Bennett Ray. Engraving, 1887. Courtesy of the Schomburg Center for Research in Black Culture, NYPL.

was better than good. He knew this country cold. He had come to Essex County from New Hampshire forty years before, and when other settlers grew discouraged, he stayed put. Not even the catastrophe of 1816 discouraged him. In that infamous year, a volcano in the Indian Ocean dressed half the planet in a shawl of ash, including everything between the Atlantic and the Great Lakes, and nothing ripened and there was no food. Most of Elba's ruined pioneers (only at midcentury would this hamlet gain its full name) slogged back to New England. But Deacon Osgood looked ahead. He took over old abandoned farms, opened up an inn, and sometimes agented for Gerrit Smith, whose antislavery beliefs he shared. He knew the gift lots well.[21]

Ray's and McCune Smith's lots were wretched—thinly soiled, rocky, hilly, and facing coldly north. But Ray's dismay was Osgood's inspiration. After conferring with his neighbors, Osgood expressed to Ray "a strong desire that we should settle . . . in the center of the settlement . . . out of their regard and wish for our professional services (being in need of a clergyman and Doctor)." Ray did not expect this invitation. It moved him deeply, as it would his friend the doctor when Ray, back in the city, filled him in. The land lot that Osgood was urging them to pursue was near a road, with a wide stream running diagonally across it, the start of a sugar bush, and a swampy part that promised springs. Writing Gerrit Smith about everything Ray had reported, McCune Smith asked that his and Ray's hillside lots be swapped for the better piece near Osgood, and then described another lot they might like to buy as well. Nothing in this letter conveyed any information about the settlers on their land. Maybe what Ray found on that front was too paltry or distressing to report, or perhaps he (or the physician) was distracted by the bounty of Osgood's warm suggestion. Real news about the welfare of the Black grantees would have to wait for the Syracuse land agent, Rev. Jermain Wesley Loguen, who toured the Black Woods in September. His report, published in the *North Star*, would tell a very different story.[22]

"For Want of a Well Digested Plan"

As it worked out, neither minister nor physician ever moved to their North Elba land, or to the other lots Smith gave them in Peterboro and Oneida County's Florence. City challenges—their day jobs, charities, Black uplift work, public service, and now, their labor for the giveaway—claimed every waking hour. Vetting grantees was slow going, and they were late getting Smith their lists. And in 1847 and increasingly in 1848, Smith, too, was distracted, all thoughts and worries now directed at the rapid-changing politics of his beloved Liberty Party, increasingly beset with warring factions. At issue was the platform: some abolitionists wanted a program more diversified and electable. Others, more traditional, felt the party should stick with antislavery work alone.

Conciliation was Smith's strength, but in this case he got nowhere, and his failure in this instance was a blow. He was slow to answer letters from his land agents and slow to send them back completed deeds, and he may have even allowed himself to wonder why he was bothering to build a new Black antislavery voting bloc when the party he hoped his Black grantees would back (*hoped*, never insisted) was bickering itself right off the ballot.[23]

Perhaps the bleakest revelation of Smith's mood in this spell was a letter he wrote Charles Ray when he received the formal resolutions of thanks for his philanthropy from delegates to the National Convention of Colored People in Troy, October 1847. These praiseful sentences, penned by Manhattan's Ray and Willis A. Hodges from Williamsburg, Brooklyn, not only thanked Smith but discerned in the "God-Send" of Smith's land gifts "a Divine Providence directing our people to this mode of life as well as opening the way to it." They urged the deedholders to leave their cities, settle on their land, start farming, "and hereby build a tower of strength for themselves." But another resolution made clear that Smith's gift was one option among many. If deedholders could not head north, they could still "forsake the cities ... and emigrate to those parts of the country where land is cheap, and become cultivators of the soil, as the surest road to respectability and influence."

Were Smith's Black allies already hedging bets, guessing the big plan might fail? If so, Smith's gloomy answer brought no comfort. But for a curt acknowledgment of the "twenty or thirty" grantees who had "comfortably settled" on their land, he did not mention the giveaway at all, except to suggest that its failure to progress was yet another measure of the Black community's inability to act in its own interest. And why was this? Why had so few grantees left the city? Why were Black leaders so slow to join the Liberty Party? Why did they stick with mainstream denominations that would not come out against the slave power? One thing only could explain it: "The free colored people of this country have lost their self-respect." It took self-respect, self-*faith*, to break ranks with a culture that held you in contempt. The lack of it explained a raft of self-destructive choices Black New Yorkers made and just kept making, and Smith confessed the "gravest doubt of their redemption."[24]

That the better-known Black and antislavery papers chose not to run this screed is hardly a surprise. What is surprising is Smith's evident impatience when so much of his land had yet to be distributed. He did not entertain the possibility that Black "self-respect" might be reflected in choices that displeased him, or that *not* moving to their gift lots was, for many impoverished deedholders, an informed choice. His implicit disavowal of Black agency said much less about the grantees than it did about his own ignorance of Black concerns. And the fact was, even as he vented, Black agency was being fervently, and multiply, expressed.

Not only were most grantees *not* streaming to the Promised Land up north, but Black entrepreneurs were hatching settlement proposals of their own, looking for investors and affordable raw land, and lightly patterning their plans on Smith's. There was the Florence Association, the St. Lawrence Anti-slavery and Land Company, and the Temperance and Slavery Land Committee. The first of these sprang up in 1846, and three years later, they were still sprouting, thick as weeds.

Smith's old ally Lewis Tappan, the abolitionist businessman in Manhattan, implored the land baron to look sharp. Things were getting very messy. "Some of the leading men of color put their names to these projects—and even to those of a contradictory character. I am very fearful," Tappan confessed, "that for want of a well digested plan and able executive men, disaster will befall your beneficiaries. Instead of them accomplishing anything beneficial to themselves & families, I fear many will lose their land." Tappan's sources? None other than Smith's own city agents. (Tappan's Broadway office was their mail drop for Peterboro.)[25]

Tappan was especially worried about the absence of a head man. "There seems to be no leading [friend] among [the grantees] who has practical knowledge of agriculture, and the best mode of proceeding to make your generous gifts availing," he wrote Smith on April 15, 1848. And reports of these other unvetted, pop-up, half-cocked emigration parties were the last thing the Black Woods needed. What it *did* need, and at once, was "an experienced farmer . . . to go upon the ground and instruct the owners of the little farms in clearing and practical agriculture." Then "a sufficient sum could be raised to purchase cattle, agricultural implements, feed, etc." Reports of "what seems to be the incompetency of the owners of the land to go forward and convert it into little farms that will give them a living" had Tappan very worried.[26]

Smith may have settled Tappan's jitters with news of a recent meeting with a farmer-abolitionist, John Brown, whose plan to help the homesteaders in Essex County's Township 12 offered a partial answer to Tappan's prayers. But what the new colony proposals revealed was much more than the need for a leader for the grantees. Ray and Hodges had been right to hedge their bets about the gift lands at the 1847 convention: things weren't going according to Smith's plan because not everybody liked the plan. Some Black people wanted to pick or buy their own land. They wanted women in on it, or out-of-staters, and maybe fugitives as well. Some didn't care for handouts. They didn't share Smith's politics. They didn't like his rules. They wanted something more their own.

CHAPTER 5

On Fat Lands under Genial Suns

In 1818, Gerrit Smith, not a half year out of college, bought an eighteen-thousand-acre upland tract in Tug Hill, Oneida County, to the west of the Adirondacks in what, before the American Revolution, had been the hunting territory of the Iroquois. Tug Hill was worse than raw. Every winter, cold winds whipping off Lake Ontario dumped enough snow on this high plateau to give Tug Hill the highest average snowfall in the country east of the Rocky Mountains. The soil here, thin, sandy, and rock cobbled, was no bargain either.[1]

This was Smith's first outing as a land baron. Some were sure he'd rue the day. But the Florence township had its charms. Dense stands of hemlock ranged as far as the horizon, boding well for tanneries, and if wheat failed to flourish, sheep would claim a home on wild land just cleared. The freshman speculator underwrote Florence's first church. He gave new settlers a cemetery lot and subsidized a blacksmith, gristmill, and village store. He recruited skilled mechanics. By the mid-1840s, these investments were paying off. Here were asheries and sawmills, and the prospect of emerging markets thanks to roads that led to Utica and Rome, and the Erie and Oswego Canals, which opened in 1825 and 1828.[2]

In 1846 and 1847, Smith parceled out Florence lots to some two dozen Black grantees. He did this, too, with lots of his in Fulton, Delaware, and Genesee Counties. Five lots here, ten lots there—he was whisking out crumbs. He did not have the same expectations for these gifts that he had for the Black Woods. On the contrary, a Black settlement in Florence, a town already mapped and tamed, was all wrong for what he had in mind—too done, too "found," no kind of tough, transforming proving ground for Frederick Douglass's "sable-armed pioneer" and his long-handled, busy axe.[3]

To one Albany grantee, however, Florence's difference from the Adirondacks was the very thing that recommended it. Not that Stephen Myers, an antislavery reformer and suffrage activist, ever meant to move there. Albany was home. Gainful employment was no bitter hardship for this "indefatigable" multitasker (the adjective was Frederick Douglass's). Steamboat captains wanted him to steward, wealthy clients to cater, fine restaurants to wait tables in high style. His newspapers (too many to name) always seemed to have their backers, and antislavery members of the state assembly respected him as well. Myers and his wife, Harriet, had made this city's Underground Railroad operation the most efficient and effective one north of New York. Even the *Charleston Mercury* joylessly acknowledged Stephen Myers's impact.[4]

Why had Gerrit Smith not made this Albanian a land agent? Myers was well connected; he would have gotten all his names. But he made Smith uneasy. He was a maverick—an antislavery activist who steered clear of the Liberty Party and sometimes worked with Whigs. Smith told Henry Highland Garnet he found Myers's politics "truckling," and he had no love for Myers's irrepressible newssheets either—among them, the *Elevator*, the *Telegraph and Temperance Journal*, and the vexingly successful *Northern Star and Freemen's Advocate*. The last of these was the rag that published the 1846 appeal from Black suffrage activists urging Smith to back a Whig-Liberty alliance for the Constitutional Convention. This was an unhappy memory for Smith, and it was made worse when Horace Greeley reprinted these activists' appeal in the *Tribune*. Smith's memory was long.[5]

Still, in the name of an impartial inclusivity, Smith made Myers a giftee, giving the Albanian a thirty-seven-acre lot in Florence. And Myers, learning of several Albany friends who got Florence land as well, discerned an opportunity. Guessing that this already established village in Tug Hill had some assets that the Adirondack wilderness did not, he broke his gift piece into quarter-acre lots for buyers who liked to keep their neighbors close, their farms and woodlots at their settlement's perimeter. The first meetings with prospective investors were in the late fall of 1846. Myers talked up Florence in Albany and Stockbridge,

Massachusetts (a town known to him from temperance visits). Interested parties were urged to scout for emigrants beyond New York in Pittsfield, Massachusetts, and Bridgeport and New Milford, Connecticut. Unlike Smith, Myers was reaching wide and going public as fast as he could manage, and making sure that every meeting got some coverage. By January 1849, newspapers from Wisconsin to Louisiana were running versions of his eager dispatch, "Gerrit Smith's Colored Settlement in Florence," with its bold plans for grist- and sawmills and an almost finished dormitory for a slew of new arrivals to live in while they put up their cabins, school, and church.[6]

Myers also worked hard and fast to win regional and local buy-in for his project. On December 21, 1848, he spoke about his high hopes for the Florence Farming and Lumber Association to an audience of locals, and made quite a "very favorable impression," one attendee wrote Gerrit Smith. The next week Myers was in Utica; he and the Black minister James Fountain, a Smith grantee, held forth for ninety minutes. Two months later, Myers unveiled his plan in New Bedford, Massachusetts (in the audience, the Boston reformer William Wells Brown listened closely and heartily approved). While a blizzard raged outside the Congregational church in Pittsfield, Massachusetts, Myers spoke for hours.[7]

And always, he took pains to clarify that he and Gerrit Smith were not competing. On the contrary, his aim was to build on Smith's idea. The out-of-staters he was bringing to New York would help the cause of equal suffrage everywhere. "Every colored man of Massachusetts who is a lover of political equality," he said, will recognize his "political duty . . . to emigrate to [the] settlement . . . and join hands with their colored brethren of [New York] to break down . . . prejudices and political inequalities." His praise for the giveaway and Smith's Black Woods was warm. "We bid them God speed in their enterprise," he wrote of grantees he met in the Hudson River Valley who were planning to move onto their land. He hoped "their industry will be rewarded by the speedy possession of a comfortable home." Three Black newspapers published these remarks.[8]

But if Myers was hoping for Smith's blessing in return, he would be disappointed. And when he intimated to reporters that Smith was an interested party, he pushed his luck too hard. Thanks be to Smith, said Myers in Pittsfield, for "appropriating certain amounts of land to the colored people of the State of New York, and the avenue which he has opened to the colored men of other States to come out and purchase, thereby forming among themselves a UNION." And thanks again, he offered in New Bedford, for "the prospect opened to us by the benevolence of that great-hearted man, Gerrit Smith, in the gift lands, and those offered at such low prices, urging upon us to avail ourselves of this opportunity to purchase lands—occupy them—engage in farming . . ." He called his project "Gerrit Smith's Florence Settlement," pronounced "Florence . . . a favorite town of Mr. Gerrit Smith," and called his company's acreage "Smith Lands." He made the Smith name pay. Framed as a Gerrit Smith production and backed (said Myers) by powerful and wealthy white men like New York's Governor Hamilton Fish and Vice President Millard Fillmore, the Florence name ranged wide. In Wisconsin, Indiana, Pennsylvania, Maryland, Louisiana, North Carolina, and Georgia, people read of "Gerrit Smith's Colored Settlement in Florence, New York . . . now in full progress." This was a mistake.[9]

Though antislavery papers still covered the progress of the Black Woods to the north, in the mainstream press it seemed that this brash, unauthorized Florence colony was hogging all the ink! Smith's own agents were beguiled. Five of them, by January 1849, were soliciting donations for the Florence project, and Frederick Douglass had good words for it as well. Cortland's Samuel Ringgold Ward was pushing it in the *Northern Star and Colored Farmer* and its successor, the *Impartial Citizen*; William Topp, Smith's land agent in Albany, was all in, too. Myers had a new paper, the *Florence Telegraph*, talking up his plan. Even Greeley noted it. Why stop at Florence? he offered in the *Tribune*. Black New Yorkers "might club their means and buy a whole County in Iowa or Michigan, each man owning what he paid for . . . under a general agreement to sell only to men of their own race. . . . Such a colony would do more for the Race than any amount of ill-advised philanthropy." He didn't bother identifying the philanthropist. Anyone who shared his smirk would know.[10]

As Did the Israelites in the Desert

Myers's Florence colony registered the first blow in January 1849, when Myers's friend and ally, Rev. Samuel Ward, was preparing to address the New York State Assembly. Myers rather wonderfully had managed to secure a speaker's slot for the eloquent agrarian; Ward had fully ninety minutes to talk up Florence and the value of Black husbandry. Myers, thrilled, flagged the coming speech in the *Northern Star and Colored Farmer*. He also named the assemblymen who hoped and failed to block the speaker, deeming them "political demagogues." Two words! But when this column was read to the assembly, the Democrats pounced hard. The speech was canceled. And just like that, a first-ever opportunity to introduce white lawmakers to Black agrarian reform was crushed. It would not be revived.[11]

This was bad, and February delivered worse news still. The same *North Star* that described the eager turnout for Myers's Florence talk in New Bedford, Massachusetts, included a letter from the antislavery activist Henry Bibb. On a speaking tour in western New York, this Smith grantee had paid Florence a visit. What he found fell far short of anything he'd read. This "humbug," he wrote Frederick Douglass, will "doubtless do great injury to the anti-slavery cause if it is not exposed. . . . Be on your guard." Bibb had never offered his letter for publication. Douglass ran it anyway. In the *Impartial Citizen,* an outraged Samuel Ward charged Douglass with crediting "mere innuendoes"; in the *North Star,* the Florence Farming Association threatened to sue the rattled Bibb for libel.[12]

And through all of this—Myers's first eager trips to Florence, and the great bloom of press about the Florence Settlement in early January— Peterboro said nothing. But after Bibb's revelation of a "humbug," the gavel finally dropped. "There is a strong disposition in some quarters to have the colored people purchase the lands which I have left in Florence," Gerrit Smith wrote the *North Star.* "But these lands are of very moderate fertility, are not favorably situated, and are held by my agent, who resides in that town, at prices probably quite equal to their value." In other words, no bargain here, so "why should the colored people buy them?" It is one thing, argued Smith, for Black people to move to land they get for free, "even if it is of inferior value, as are most of the lands which I have given to them. But, when the colored people buy lands, and especially at their full value, I think they should buy such as are fertile, easy of cultivation, and advantageously situated."[13]

Smith's note was shrewdly parsed. He did not invoke Bibb's concern. He did not mention Stephen Myers; he would not stoop to scold. But Myers was his target. *If you buy this land,* his note implied, *you waste your money. Best keep your savings and stick with land you get for free—from me. Not from a brash pretender who suggests an intimacy with me he doesn't have, affects a knowledge of my land he doesn't possess, and inflates the value of my property beyond its worth.*

And now Frederick Douglass, "undeceived," yanked his backing, offering by way of reasons "the wildness of the country, the infertility of the lands, the distance and the difficulties of the way to market, and the

Stephen Myers. Drawing. Melissa Moshetti, 2020. Commissioned by the National Abolition Hall of Fame and Museum, Peterboro, NY. Courtesy of the NAHFM.

entire absence of water power." In the *Impartial Citizen*, the chastened Samuel Ward beat a retreat as well: "Inasmuch as arrangements are made for a settlement in Florence, we have no disposition to disparage it," *yet!*—"we should not have counseled the settlement of a village in that part of the State. There are cheaper and better lands in the Counties of Tioga and Allegheny." Then, the feisty *Ram's Horn* took a potshot at Myers, "who has put himself at the head and front of this splendid humbug." Douglass reinforced his disavowal when he urged prospective Florentines to recall that the Albany promoter was "a deeply interested party," a front man for a pack of speculators (though who they were, Douglass never said).[14]

Enter Levin Tilmon, a Black minister who had heard Stephen Myers speak in New Bedford. To the *North Star*, he complained, *Enough!* "Though our means are various, let our aims be the same. Let us not fall out by the way, as did the Israelites in the desert." The Florence plan made room for out-of-state settlers who weren't eligible for Smith's free land to the north. Why not accommodate their interest (and gain new Black voters in the process)? Perhaps Douglass, a loyal advocate of Adirondack pioneering, was "not disposed to favor the Florence enterprise"—but why malign a fresh idea? Look at the map, the numbers. Here was booming Oneida County, with twice the population of Essex and Franklin Counties and growing all the time. Look at "its large and flourishing towns," its roads, waterways, and rail lines. "Why . . . throw obstacles in its way?"[15]

Myers, for his part, was equally bewildered. He had never said the land was first-rate farmland. He had represented it as "a heavily timbered country, stony soil, good oats and corn," and also "good for grazing." Local farmers had assured him that "cleared land" could "realize from twenty-five to fifty dollars per acre," and Myers always said it would be two years before a farmer could turn a profit. Hence his emphasis on "forming a village, so as to get up an enterprising spirit." As for rumors about profiteering backstage speculators, Myers had given Douglass accounts of his group's meetings, which Douglass "might have published" and had not. "Your object is not to destroy the influence of good men," Myers remonstrated. But his point did raise the question: why *were* Douglass and Gerrit Smith so dismissive of his plan?[16]

Myers Packs It In

Stephen Myers stuck with the Florence project through the spring and into that summer. In late May 1849, when sixty-two pioneers from Massachusetts detrained in Albany, he and a reporter from the *Albany Argus* welcomed these "mainly hearty, robust looking persons" to New York. But the emigrants' enthusiasm would not survive the shock of Florence's manifold deficiencies. By midsummer, Daniel Dorrance, Smith's land agent, would report that half of them were gone. The management of the colony passed from Myers to Rev. Daniel H. Peterson, a minister from nearby Rome. As Myers had before him, Peterson scrupulously lauded white people in Florence and nearby settlements for their open-handed hospitality, and Dorrance "for his kindness to the settlers, and his exertions to promote the interests of the Association." Thanks were also offered to those New Englanders who sent a pitchfork, shovel, Sunday school supplies, and plow. Peterson's good manners would not keep Florence in the news, however. With Myers out, the *North Star* lost all interest. And Myers, for his part, back in Albany and stumping for Black suffrage, Free Soil, and temperance, looked strictly ahead. On August 18, 1851, the Oneida County sheriff seized Myers's Florence gift lot for back taxes. It was auctioned off October 8 in a Utica hotel.[17]

Maybe Myers had to quit. His blunders had been careless. Overstating Smith's interest was misleading; prophesying a six-hundred-family influx, grandiose; and failing to make timely payments to Elder Fuller, the local builder of the Emigrant House, impolitic and hurtful. But before the rush to judgment, let's recall what Myers got right. He planned an exodus from city to country down to the lot lines, masterminded the mostly very warm publicity, spurred the interest of scores of homesteaders, and responded to his critics. Further, he encouraged the new emigrants to come in groups, not singly, so they would be inclined to work together on their arrival, and he cultivated local buy-in for the colony well before the colonists arrived. None of this had happened in the Black Woods to the north. And if Myers indulged, as Smith had not, a cultural preference among Black emigrants for a cohesive, familial, recognizable community over isolated freeholds in the wild, what was this but just smart marketing?[18]

Had Smith ever thought to build a boardinghouse for newly arrived North Elba settlers, as Myers aimed to do in Florence? He might have done. It might have helped. With more clarity than any of Smith's agents, Myers articulated the link between land ownership and voting rights and, as Smith's agents never did, observed that the voteless plight of Black New Yorkers was the rightful business of Black people in every state. And what difference did it make, really, if land was bought or gifted when land ownership, however managed, advanced Black enfranchisement? What Smith dismissed as an unaffordable distraction from the gift land in the North, Myers deemed an act of political solidarity. (Even McCune Smith would eventually urge Smith to consider an "enlargement" of the target area for the recruitment of Black grantees to a few "adjoining states"—not to populate Myers's colony in particular but for the sake of agrarian enfranchisement overall.) There was more than one way to skin this cat, as Reverend Tilmon had observed.[19]

Smith's longtime Florence land agent, Daniel Dorrance, faulted Myers for selling settlers plots half a mile from a water source. But that's where Myers's gift lot was; he began with what he had. Smith worked with what he had, too, giving grantees Adirondack land that was underwater, on mountaintops, or devastated by flood and fire, and figuring his grantees would trade up as they needed. Myers banked on this as well, and guessed that as the colony evolved, more and better land would be procured. Myers promised an influx of six hundred. He wound up with fifty families. Well, so did the Black Woods, with its head start of three thousand grantees, twelve agents, newspaper endorsements, conferences, and meetings all over the state. And as with the Black Woods, most of those fifty families would peel away. But not all. As late as 1860, several dozen Black people were still residents of Florence. The remains of their settlement have been identified by a dogged zealot for this story, the history teacher Jessica Harney of Rome, New York, working with the Albany archaeologist Mark Kirk. So much for Myers's "humbug." Orphaned and derided, Florence nonetheless apparently endured.[20]

A Gift Defiled

Gerrit Smith liked giving things away, but he did not care to see his gifts used in ways he thought were wasteful, inappropriate, or counter to his goals. And while he anticipated uses for the gift land beyond farming (he knew that some grantees would keep it for its timber value, or bequeath it to their children, sell it, see it seized for taxes, or retain it for the vote), he did not imagine deedholders following his lead and speculating on their own. Speculation was his department, and the business of his several land dealers and secretaries. As close as he was to James McCune Smith and Frederick Douglass, he shared with them few details of this day job. To fellow abolitionists, he cast himself as inadvertent heir to a land fortune he never made or asked for—less a land baron than, as his antislavery friend Samuel May put it, a "steward who would have to give an account of the estate entrusted to his care." Liberty Party allies who read his 1845 diary in the *Albany Patriot* about touring northern New York met a country mapped by pockets of reform and reaction, not by news of auctions, land sales, and rent collection on the road. And when Smith referenced his estate in his third-person midlife autobiography, he did not mention the hundreds of thousands of acres he had bought, managed, and sold over his career, preferring to describe his holdings in terms of his inheritance, his youthful purchases, and his forays into "practical Land Reform."[21]

Yet he was not a hypocrite. What other land baron in his time worked so doggedly, both before and after debts were paid, to give away his land? Far from taking pride in owning land in almost every county in the state, he offered that he would "count it a good bargain" if he could "exchange all the scraps and remnants of my father's wild tracts for five farms, or even three." Nothing, he wrote in 1848, could be "more obvious to him who will reflect upon it than that the right of every person to the soil is perfect—as perfect as to the sea, the light, the air." In 1849, Smith gave away a thousand deeds to poor white New Yorkers, men and women both, then revised the plan so that female beneficiaries could get their gifts in cash and so buy land they actually might want. His land gifts expressed the same adaptive millenarianism that fired his antislavery sermons, emancipatory purchases of slaves, and political abolitionism. Each project promised to accelerate a ready-for-redemption world. And if, in striving for the world's perfection, Smith won some measure of redemption for himself, so much the better.[22]

But with stakes as high as these, he did want things his way. The script was his to write, and at its heart was the idea that the gifted land grants remain gifted. Once a gift entered the marketplace, the sacred trust was broken. In his book *The Gift*, the poet-essayist Lewis Hyde explains this with a metaphor: "When gifts are sold, they change their nature as much as water changes when it freezes, and no rationalist telling of the constant elemental structure can replace the feeling that is lost." The sweetness of Smith's "scheme of benevolence" was that it eschewed the marketplace for the fluid realm of giving. No cash or contract, rent or mounting interest. Smith wanted to decant his wealth, to let it go as freely as his Redeemer sowed His blessings.[23]

So, what to do with Stephen Myers and his pretty map, his sales plan, his rumored (and possibly exaggerated) Whig backers? (For Myers never did say whether they gave him money or merely met his pitch outside a legislative chamber with a vague smile and a keep-us-posted nod.) What to do when Myers took a gift and carved it into stamp-sized parcels and yanked the whole benevolent affair down to a speculator's hustle? Had Smith given away land so that Myers might profit? Even deedholders who never settled on their land but kept it as an investment honored the giveaway's core values; their respect for economy kept the spirit of the gift alive, kept it generous and loving (as would Smith's city agents when they described the grantees' names they sent to Smith as "presents"). Smith could not see how a profit-seeking project and a "scheme of justice and benevolence" might work toward the same end. Myers was mixing up the gift land with the sale land to turn a profit. He was making a big mess.[24]

Admirers or Copycats?

Well, there were a lot of messes. But the others mostly collapsed under the weight of their ineptitude and overblown ambition. There was a land proposal from five Albanians, all Smith grantees, who hoped the land baron would sell them a 75,000-acre parcel in St. Lawrence County in 1846 (part of the 350,000-acre sale Smith was advertising that same summer at fire sale prices). The Albanians' idea was to bust it into sale lots of one hundred to two hundred acres, but first Smith would need to take the parcel off the market while they raised the money to buy it. Since Smith held no land without an advance payment, that was the end of that.[25]

Also in the fall of 1846, George W. B. Wilson, a seaman and a Smith grantee in New York City, went to Peterboro to pique Smith's interest in a land company that had its eye on Smith's St. Lawrence County sale land rolling between Franklin County toward Lake Ontario and the St. Lawrence River. Smith liked Wilson, and he liked the New York Emigration Association's constitution. But here, again, the directors wanted Smith to take sale land out of play while they raised funds to buy it. Smith would not oblige. "The rule of my [Land] Office," Smith said, "is to reserve lands for no one. . . . To refuse to sell when persons offer to comply with these terms is to falsify my word." Worse for Smith, the company's head spokesman, Thomas Van Rensselaer, boasted in the *Ram's Horn* that Gerrit Smith was his land company's "originator." Smith was livid. "That statement will give rise to the remark that I am endeavoring to make money out of my colored brethren." Van Rensselaer stepped back.[26]

More credible was a proposal from a third group, also city based, among whose stockholders were Black reformers Smith quite admired. In addition to his old friend, the antiemigrationist activist and prospering caterer George Downing, were Samuel Cornish, ardent agrarian, and the esteemed African Methodist Episcopal Zion minister Christopher Rush (the first self-freed slave in the nation to become a bishop).

Their Anti-slavery & Land Company had its eye on four thousand acres of Smith's sale land in St. Lawrence County's Township 5. Its board included women, and its directors, Abraham Caldwell and James Blair Webb, were Black city men of means who now and then engaged in racial justice work. But Smith didn't know them, and could get no feel for their long-range plans. He asked his city agents to arrange an interview, which went uneasily, with the agents enduring something of "a little battering." This company, however, did at least give Smith a $400 down payment and the assurance that all purchases were for the on-site use of Black buyers. (Hands-on usage, not long-distance profit, was Smith's interest, not four thousand acres to be flipped for speculation.)[27]

Then Webb and Caldwell switched it up. Would Smith sell them another "20,000 acres more or less? [We] believe . . . that in a short time the same could be possessed and occupied by our people as tillers of the soil. Things are sitting so heavily upon us in this city and there is such an increase from the South here which must have an opening [somewhere] that we believe that an advantage like this would very soon be made use of."[28]

New York City's Black population had been dropping since 1840. Were these speculators expecting a fresh wave of self-freed slaves? Did they plan to make St. Lawrence County a home for fugitives? How would this work? Was this why the group was called the *Anti-slavery* & Land Company, and why it wanted land in this high corner of the state? In 1844, fifteen St. Lawrence County towns or hamlets had an abolition church (Essex County, in contrast, had four, and Franklin County one). Five St. Lawrence County towns boasted more than thirty Liberty Party voters each. Where the slave power had enemies, freedom seekers would find friends.[29]

But this alluring scheme fared no better than the others. Webb and Caldwell never settled on this land, and no records, letters, or local legends suggest that fugitives reached St. Lawrence County with their help. (North Elba, in contrast, fairly groans under anecdotal leads.) Their city company did broker a few Essex County purchases, among them a North Elba 160-acre lot intended for a school for aspiring A.M.E ministers. Named for Bishop Christopher Rush of New York City, the Rush Academy in "Twelfth Township, Essex County," a "Connectional Manual Labor School," was vested with an elaborate constitution, an extensive board of directors (Reverend Loguen among them), and, in 1865, a charter from New York's Board of Regents. On paper, it lasted twenty-five years. It never did get built.[30]

Abraham Caldwell still had his uses for the North Country, however—even when he surfaced in the Black press as an avid back-to-Africa colonizationist in 1852. Just a few years after eyeing Smith's wild acres for his Anti-slavery & Land Company, Caldwell was flogging a farm colony in Liberia as an alternative to Gerrit Smith's alternative to Liberia. Smith's gift land, Caldwell told the *Tribune*, was a fake mecca whose flaws and failures suggested the necessity of the real thing across the sea: "I hesitate not to say that colonization is the only thing to elevate the colored man. It is vain for many of us to talk of settling on Mr. Smith's land, or of emigrating to Canada and settling on land without money, which, comparatively speaking, few have. Africa holds forth inducements whereby the colored man may be elevated without money and without price."[31]

Payback hovered in these lines. Three years earlier, George Downing had invested $250 in Caldwell's St. Lawrence County scheme. His money gone and his good faith abused, Downing was done with Caldwell and made no secret of his dislike. To Black activists in Rochester, he asked why anyone would choose Liberia when "there are large tracts of land in this country, fertile and beautiful, which the colored man can occupy—live an independent life where he can command respect and consideration—thousands of acres of which are already owned by colored men in the State." The allusion to Smith's gift land—an American Liberia, a Timbuctoo *at home*—was pointed. "We claim no affinity with . . . pestilential, inhospitable, benighted Africa," Downing roared to clamorous applause. "This is our home."[32]

When Gerrit Smith was in Congress, he called Liberia "a frightful graveyard" and the Colonization Society "the deadliest enemy of the Negro race." Radical Black abolitionists like Downing spied a foe more deadly still: the race traitors who fronted the Liberia Emigration Association, "a false and deceptive movement because it is an ally of the Colonization Society—the colored man's uncompromising enemy." Anybody working, rooting, or raising funds for it (like Caldwell and his group) "deserves the opprobrium of the people." But in the end, it wasn't the anticolonizationist lobby that put a stop to Caldwell's work. It was a virus he picked up on the mail boat from Monrovia to Sierra Leone in 1854. He got sick the day he went aboard; he went ashore and died. Two years later, a Black reporter took a stroll around his settlement. "There is no greater humbug," William Nesbit wrote. "It consists of a one-story frame house, fourteen by sixteen feet . . . and four very small bamboo huts; and indeed, this description is about applicable to all these settlements, pompous in their representations, insignificant in their reality."[33]

The Lesser Wilderness

Surely, Gerrit Smith's exhaustion with fielding other people's land company proposals while his own project languished explains some part of his impatience with Myers's project. Then there was his long-standing dislike of this Albanian, and his certain fury at the Myers-driven rumor that Smith and the Whigs were now united in their love of Myers's plan. But the main trouble with Florence was its own homely, practical, uncharismatic self. It wasn't what Smith wanted for his Black pioneers. It could not regenerate them, or work a deeper change in them. In a letter to his land agents in 1846, Smith laid out his bold hopes for the gift land to the north. Though white opposition to suffrage justice was despicable, it might, he offered, yield good results. If it made the grantees leave New York City, if it got them to their wild land, they would there "begin a new life, and make for themselves a hard and honorable character." And if the Black Woods were "colder and less fertile" than they liked, this, too, would be a blessing. As they "brave[d] the rigors of the wilderness," they would "work out a far better character than they would were they to choose their homes on fat lands under genial suns."[34]

And in Smith's faith in the Black Woods as a proving ground for "better character" and a more perfected self, he had company. Many promotional comments from the giveaway's best friends embraced a romantic faith in the regenerative promise of the wilderness encounter. From Emersonian transcendentalism to the poems of Burns and Byron (all of which Smith's agents knew and loved), Romantic imagery informed the vision of the gift land as a crucible of manly mettle. And to the diverse currents of Romanticism, I'll add the slipstream of Black pastoralism, for an idea of the yeoman farmer's self-sovereignty informed Black agrarianism too. The shared struggle to survive, Charles Bennett Ray offered, would cauterize all trivial preoccupation with caste and race. There would be no place for Negrophobes under the closely tended vine and fig tree of the democratizing woods. The work of conquering the wilderness deracialized it—and the more rigorous the conversion of wild land into a managed kingdom of cabin, wood-pile, kitchen garden, fence, and clearing, the more likely the grantees' admission into that most American of clubs, the fraternity of pioneers.

Unlike the machine shop or the jury box, the land itself was color-blind. As the activist William C. Nell observed in the *North Star* in 1848 (invoking Gerrit Smith), the land itself "has just as much respect for a Black man as it has for a white.—Let our colored brethren betake themselves to it." Raw land modeled democracy in action. In the wilderness, Black people would get justice because the land itself enacted justice. It was its heaven-sent expression.[35]

Let the "sharp ax of the sable-armed pioneer . . . be at once uplifted over the soil of Franklin and Essex Counties, and the noise of falling trees proclaim the glorious dawn of civilization throughout their borders," Douglass bugled in the *North Star* in February 1848. Late that spring, the *Ram's Horn* echoed the appeal: "The occupation of these lands will form an era in the history of free colored men in this State. We would like to be among the first to occupy the wilderness and strike the first blow toward making it blossom like a rose." In April, the *Northern Star and Freemen's Advocate* asked its readers, "Who, among the . . . settlers of Essex and Franklin counties, will there fell the first tree? The *North Star* will hail the name and hand it down to posterity. . . . Hurrah for the Smith Lands! God speed the plough!"[36]

But no first trees would fall in Florence. Myers's short-of-really-wild colony never fit that bill. "The glorious dawn of civilization" could not arise where the sun was halfway to noon. In the 1840s (and today), the Tug Hill Plateau lacked the brooding mystique of the Adirondack region. The Adirondacks was "The Great Wilderness," Tug Hill the "Lesser" one. And thanks to Gerrit Smith, Tug Hill's Florence was commodified. A market economy was gearing up; one of Myers's stakeholders could buy, sell, or trade his quarter-acre lot like sale land all over. This was nothing like Smith's gift land. This was just another deal.[37]

All along, the rhetoric of the Black Woods had been of clearing land with an eye toward economic self-sufficiency. The objective was not to engage the market but to transcend it, dispense with it (and this was a goal with deep, intangible allure for people who, for centuries, were commodified by the market-driven slave economies of the Americas). The farmer's "primitive innocency," extolled by Charles Bennett Ray in 1837, was defiled, not enhanced, by the encounter with a cash economy. Silver never crossed the palm of the self-providing grantee-farmer. He and his family would make, spin, grow it all themselves. When Myers hawked the benefits of nearby mills, factories, and towns, and offered parcels so small they would force their Black owners to have to do much *more* than farm, he muddied the great dream.

The Romantic prism that lent its glow to the Black Woods did Florence no favors. Its distorting lens made the village look inadequate, a backwater not harsh enough by half to test the grantees' rigor. If the painter Thomas Cole had seen it, he might have judged it lacking in what his "Essay on American Scenery" called those "scenes of solitude from which the hand of nature has never been lifted," scenes that "cast the mind into the contemplation of eternal things." Presettled Florence was used goods. Cole's "deep-toned encounter" might be savored in the pristine Adirondacks, a sylvan Eden where the Black pioneers could be "the first to strike a blow for civilization." An exceptionalist Adirondacks would exceptionalize them too—make them agents of their destinies, *make them men*.[38]

This hopeful vision had its good side. It inspired, gave the Black agents and promoters a shared outlook on the project's spiritual purpose, garbed the giveaway in the rhetoric of salvation, and staked its place in a long parade of divinely favored migrations, from forty years of desert wandering to the westward-swarming pioneers. Further, as the historian John Stauffer has suggested, it forged an unprecedented interracial intellectual alliance among Douglass, Brown, Smith, and

Detail from *Baker's Farm*. Eliphalet Terry, painter, 1859. Courtesy of the Adirondack Experience, Blue Mountain Lake, NY.

McCune Smith. But what it meant for the grantees was something else. They would never find that promised Arcady. Restless Yankees from the worked-over hill farms of New England had been hacking into North Elba's cold soil as early as 1800. Rough settlements peppered the territory—mining hamlets, tanneries, blast furnaces, loggers' camps that rang with French; Irish immigrants in flight from cholera in Montreal; white subsistence farmers struggling to keep up with indentures to land barons from unseen parts, like Boston, Albany, and Peterboro. And none of this the pioneers expected, nor were they braced for another unassailable truth. No Adirondack farmer made a living just by farming. The agricultural economy eulogized by writers of the American scene like the Connecticut lecturer and essayist Rev. Horace Bushnell—that fine-tuned farm that thrived in perfect equilibrium, everybody pitching in, "the house ... a factory on the farm, the farm a grower and producer for the house," production and consumption neatly balanced, did not work here, and never had.[39]

Later in the century, a state report on Adirondack farm initiatives was stark: "All attempts at settlement of the Adirondack plateau by an agricultural population ... have resulted in disastrous failure. ... Abandoned homes and fields are scattered everywhere along the borders of the forest, while the scanty population which ... struggles to compel the inhospitable soil to yield it a miserable existence too plainly shows the hopelessness of the task." Farmers quickly saw that they would need to work as well as loggers, trappers, miners, innkeepers, and, beginning with the rise of Adirondack tourism in the 1840s, furnishers of goods and services to nature lovers, convalescents, and sportsmen shopping for adventure. Further, Adirondack soil did not, in fact, respond equally to every hopeful pioneer. A work ethic and a good back mattered, but so did tools, church alliances, kinship links, bartering partners, credit access, and cartloads of experience. In 1857, Horace Greeley gave voice to what Yankee homesteaders had long understood: "No man born and reared in the city can remove to a farm at thirty and forty years of age and become immediately an efficient, thrifty, successful farmer." The cost of bringing a forty-acre farm into production in the mid-1800s averaged $1,500, a figure well beyond the reach of Smith's grantees, beyond the worth of the land itself, and beyond the means, it should be noted, of white wage earners making $1 to $2 a day. But the long familiarity of early Adirondack settlers from New England with the northern forest gave them a head start. Poor as they were, they knew how to twist a span of birch bark into a sap bucket, and when the pond ice was thick enough to walk on. The grantees were not only short on know-how, they lacked the safety net of cultural familiarity. The Vermont pioneer who bushwhacked into the Adirondacks may not have known the homesteaders he met en route, but when they compared family trees, they stood a chance of sharing second cousins once removed. Maybe they subscribed to the same farm journal or swore by the same almanac. The cherished nut of a New England patrimony was collateral that meant the difference between rebuff and welcome and, in the woods, between hopefulness and misery, and even life and death.[40]

And always, for white pioneers, there was the commonality of race. In his "What Is an American?" Hector St. Jean de Crèvecoeur wrote of "Andrew the Hebridean," a composite settler-immigrant. When this Scotsman from the treeless Isle of Barra stepped onto a wharf in Philadelphia, he had never swung an axe or yoked a team of oxen. His family was penniless; their fate "depended entirely upon chance." Yet at once Andrew and all the "pale and emaciated" arrivals were "pitched upon" by sympathetic locals, "citizens impelled either by spontaneous attachments or motives of humanity." Housed, fed, and well advised, "honest Andrew . . . worked hard, lived well, and grew fat." So ought every hopeful immigrant to be greeted, mused Crèvecoeur in 1782. "Landing on this great continent is like going to sea; they must have a compass, some friendly directing needle, or else they will uselessly err and wander for a long time, even with a fair wind."[41]

The Black families who ventured to the Adirondacks needed friendly directing needles too. But Smith's agents would not publish the names of trustworthy white locals until eighteen months after the giveaway was announced, and then only in response to news of grantees getting fleeced. As early as December 1846, McCune Smith had noted the grantees' illiteracy. To Gerrit Smith he wrote that "of the first seventeen Deeds delivered" to Westchester County grantees, "but *one* grantee could sign his name—and he a *runaway slave!*" Surely, fraud and trickery against illiterate city Blacks was a danger Gerrit Smith foresaw. He knew he had enemies. Some locals would want to punish those who stood for his ideas. When William Jones stood up in Troy and told his fellow deedholders that he planned "to clear up fifteen acres annually," someone knew, or should have known, that the average settler in the northern forest would clear no more than three acres a year, and that Jones and his "Liberty axe" would never *reach* his farm if he fell in with racist guides. And surely the necessity of seed capital was evident before 1849, when Douglass lamented in the *North Star*, "Houses cannot be built and farming utensils obtained without money." Smart farmers well understood the necessity of startup money to float a first year in the woods. But the giveaway's promoters were not farmers. And neither was Gerrit Smith.[42]

As the leaseholder of hundreds of indentures for small farms, however, Smith was familiar with the precarities of rural life. Every week his mail brought him news of failed crops, household crises, the crushing impact of a squall. The Adirondacks was no quilted middle landscape and no Edenic *tabula rasa* either, but an unforgiving, iron-backed terrain scuffed by messy clearings. So why did he not give his agents or grantees advice that might have made the difference between preparedness and ignorance, failure and success? Why deny the lessons of his experience? He had written that some parcels would be unfit for cultivation. This was not the same as telling his agents early on that even the best lots might not support their deedholders through husbandry alone.[43]

He would not let his experience sully his agenda. Florence's commercial possibilities were as good as, maybe better than, what the Smith Lands had to offer, but Florence suffered from what Thomas Cole would call "a meagre utilitarianism." It was too obvious, the land too fat, the sun too warm. It would not build a better character.[44]

The Lesser Wilderness left Smith cold.

CHAPTER 6

Something besides "Speechifying"

> GREAT things are done when Men and
> Mountains meet
>
> This is not done by jostling in the Street
>
> —William Blake, from *Notebook*, ca. 1808–1811

When Willis Hodges was living on the family farm in Virginia's Princess Anne County, his parents, Charles and Julia, hired white teachers to school their children in their home. This was against Virginia law, as were the guns that Charles Hodges kept inside his home to defend his family against white marauders.

His boldness would become his sons'. Willis's older brother William broke the law when he preached against slavery. In 1829, he was arrested on the charge of giving fugitives false papers. Chipping through the Richmond jail's oak walls with a pocketknife, William and his cellmates escaped, and William made it to New York. White vigilantes had been targeting free Black families in Princess Anne County for a while. After William Hodges's midnight breakout, and the outbreak and suppression of Nat Turner's slave uprising in 1831, the stalking and harassment got much worse.[1]

Preaching by all Black Virginians, free or slave, was outlawed. Black travelers had to carry permits. Mobs in masks and face paint roamed the county and stormed Black homes with impunity. A gang burst into Charles Hodges's home, smashed furnishings, slaughtered animals, and assaulted Hodges's wife. Certain this would never end, Charles Hodges pondered moving north. In the early 1830s he got word of a farm for sale on Long Island and dispatched Willis to join his brother William in New York and look this prospect over.[2]

But the sale land was unimpressive, and the "great city of New York" enticed Willis even less. With his older brother he patrolled neighborhoods where Black people lived and worked. So many laborers and servants, so few artisans or self-made entrepreneurs. "I did not like New York any way that it could be placed before me," he later wrote. (A year after Hodges arrived, Frederick Douglass, a recent fugitive from Maryland, reached the same conclusion.) Skilled tradesmen Hodges knew from home were waiting tables, toiling over stoves. Was this the promised land of self-employment and Black pride? Lonely and discouraged, the young Virginian went back south, bent on finding work that offered wages. On a canal in the Great Dismal Swamp, Hodges joined a work gang of five hundred, one of twelve free Blacks in this crew. The other laborers, mostly Black, were most of them enslaved. It may have been his first time working with enslaved laborers, and if so, his enlightenment was harsh. The work was brutal, long, and dull, and worse than the drudgery was Hodges's mandatory muteness. He could not speak up when slaves were beaten by the "drivers" without targeting his own back for the same; in fact, any protest might result in his enslavement. New York was looking better all the time. Maybe no one there would listen to him, but at least up north he could rip off this gag and hear his voice out loud.[3]

By 1836, Willis Hodges was back in Brooklyn, grabbing odd jobs at the wharves unloading saltpeter, or on the docks shoveling snow. Two days a stevedore, Hodges was made foreman (fair advancement, he recalled, for a "greenhorn countryman" from the South). He was night watchman in a merchant house on South Street. With his brother, he opened a grocery in Williamsburg. This made sense; he and William knew good produce and how to move it. But growing food was what he loved. He missed the farm whose acres kept his family in fat supply with greens, beef, pork, and stove wood. The city slights he weathered as a dockworker, cartman, and fruit peddler only clarified his agrarian resolve.[4]

At a Troy political convention in 1841, Willis Hodges implored Black Americans to "move into the country and the small growing villages like Williamsburg, and grow up with the small town." Six years later, same city, new convention: Hodges and his friend and mentor, the minister Charles B. Ray, produced their eloquent "Report on Agriculture," whose third resolution urged Black New Yorkers to abandon cities for the country and small towns. With what he made as a whitewasher, Hodges invested in a new paper, the *Ram's Horn*; his copublisher was the famously blunt-spoken, older city activist Thomas Van Rensselaer. It was a brazen prospect for a farmer's son with no formal education, but Hodges's job as a night watchman gave him time for poring over antislavery papers, and suffrage meetings kept him current with the crises of the hour. The *Ram's Horn*, born on New Year's Day 1847, tackled all of them (abolition, temperance, Black suffrage, and education), and

Willis Augustus Hodges. Etching, Moss Engraving Co., NY. Frontispiece for *Free Man of Color: The Autobiography of Willis Augustus Hodges*, from E. Garland Penn, *The Afro-American Press and Its Editors*, 1891. Digital Collections, NYPL.

won plaudits from Garrison and Douglass, a guarded nod from Gerrit Smith, and a subscription list of 2,500.[5]

It also won a devoted reader in the abolitionist John Brown, then in western Massachusetts, who sent Hodges money, the names of prospective subscribers, and a pseudonymous column, "Sambo's Mistakes" (Brown assumed the persona of a Black adviser seeking to advise Black city dwellers on how to better their lives). Hodges's dealings with this long-distance white contributor would ripen into a friendship that outlived the newspaper by a decade. Beyond their mutual love of farming and devotion to radical abolitionism, both men were lay ministers, reverenced education, and helped fugitives when they could. Brown's hope of starting a school for Black children would not be realized, but Hodges's private day and Sabbath school for Black children in Williamsburg was such a hit that in eight months the public school district embraced his model and opened a Black school too.[6]

Willis Hodges organized a temperance union. He integrated Williamsburg's abolition society. He got a death sentence for a Black felon radically reduced. And a few times in the 1840s, he went back to Virginia to help out on the farm and lead interracial prayer meetings. But heading south was risky. Among white neighbors, rumors simmered that young Hodges ran a "secret society in the county having as its object the 'betterment of the people of color, both bond and free.'" Was he plotting something lawless? Planning some revolt? It was probably inevitable that Hodges's city savvy and abolitionism would earn him three weeks in the Norfolk city jail and a reputation as "a second Nat Turner." Back to New York he sped.[7]

But never gladly, never with relief. Hodges didn't like the city. Nothing in it held a patch on the old farm. If Virginia made him a target, he was nonetheless devoted to it; heading to New York, he "felt like a coward running away from battle." In Manhattan, his and Van Rensselaer's *Ram's Horn* won the respect of New York's Black leaders, but he also registered the harsh rebuke to equal voting rights in 1846. By the time he became a Smith grantee, what Hodges first admitted feeling in 1842 seemed more germane than ever: "Something besides 'speechifying,' making loud and long prayers, writing petitions or passing big-worded resolutions, had to be done if we wanted our rights." A deed was just a piece of paper if it wasn't put to work. Like John Brown, Willis Hodges was bred to action. It was his hope, he told his readers, "to be among the first to occupy the wilderness and strike the first blow toward making it blossom like the rose." He could beat his big agrarian drum in the *Ram's Horn*, and organize fundraisers for the grantees in the social halls of Brooklyn, but he was still a bystander, and he had stood by long enough. In May 1848, twelve years after he landed in New York, Willis Hodges sold his interest in the newspaper, rounded up a band of hopeful pioneers, some with land grants, some without, and headed to the high Adirondack frontier.[8]

From Troy to Timbuctoo

There is no way to know just when James H. Henderson arrived in New York City, how he got there, or where he came from. One New York census indicates that he hailed from Vermont, but another gives his mother's birthplace as Virginia. Since she was born in 1780, she was probably enslaved. Might James and his mother have escaped enslavement? No hint of a backstory is revealed in the bold, straightforward notice for the J. H. Henderson Boot and Shoe Manufactory that ran for three months in the *Colored American* in 1839. The paper trail tells us only that New York was home, and a home that let him thrive. His and his wife Susan's church was the Second Presbyterian Church of Color on Canal Street, which, while nothing on the grand scale of the African Methodist Episcopal Zion Church or First Colored Presbyterian (later known as Shiloh, it held 1,600 people in its great hall), still claimed the Hendersons' devotion. James Henderson, church secretary, penned the notices in the *Colored American* for the church's thrice-weekly coed night school, Sabbath School, and Bible study, all "highly calculated to improve the mind and render each scholar eminently useful to himself and society." Rock solid in his faith that racial justice could be won through a resolute display of piety, respectability, and self-betterment, Henderson was the very model of an "uplift man."[9]

Then in August 1841, the Hendersons lost their baby, William Henry. A notice in the *Colored American* supplied no explanation. Many poor city children who perished in these years were poisoned by "swill milk" from cows feeding on waste products from decrepit urban distilleries. Yellow fever was also storming the metropolis and scything a wide swath. As Dr. McCune Smith documented, the medical challenges that afflicted urban Black New Yorkers were legion. The Hendersons' migration to less congested upstate Troy so soon after their boy's death may have impressed this couple as an environmental necessity. While no less racist than Manhattan, Troy was cleaner, safer, and healthier, and also, offered the *Colored American*, more welcoming. For Troy's Black lodging

SOMETHING BESIDES "SPEECHIFYING"   101

houses' "spirit of hospitality," a reporter wrote, "it might appropriately be called the stranger's HOME."[10]

Troy also boasted a vigorous reform scene, due in good part, the Hendersons discovered, to the work of the minister-activist Henry Highland Garnet of the Liberty Street Presbyterian Church. Only a few years out of the Oneida Institute, Garnet plunged into the campaign for equal suffrage. He made his church a safe house for fugitives, headed up a slew of meetings, published newspapers, and wrote and said things that in the South would have seen him burned alive. Wild, brazen, unthinkable proposals: *The slaves should rise! Should fight outright!* "Now is the day and the hour. Let every slave throughout the land do this, and the days of slavery are numbered. . . . Rather die free men than live to be slaves!"[11]

The Hendersons arrived in Troy a few years after the young pastor, and Susan joined Garnet's church at once. James would too, eventually, but the first conversion, a bracing plunge into Troy's Black justice activism, was political: Old-fashioned "rising up" might get him into heaven, but organizing, petitioning, and lobbying—here was work that mattered *now*. At an 1841 Black political convention in Troy, Henderson was Garnet's secretary and a county delegate for a statewide "Appeal for Rights." In 1846, Black activists from Troy invited Henderson to sign their letter to Gerrit Smith that urged a Whig-Liberty Party antislavery coalition. Then, in 1847, Garnet made Henderson one of his twenty-two "Pick'd Men" for free land in the woods. (The year before, he named forty-three.) Henderson's gift lot was the southwest quarter of Lot 83, Thorn's Survey, Old Military Tract, Township 12, Essex County, a mouthful of a title with an exhilarating specificity. Ten of Garnet's Troy grantees who got Adirondack land moved north, which, out of sixty-five giftees, may seem a meager showing. But if this same proportional response were reflected in the overall migration of Smith's three thousand grantees, the Black Woods would have held five hundred men instead of one-sixth of that. Reverend Garnet picked his pioneers with care, sometimes even retracting recommendations (William Hill, he decided, was "a notorious blockhead," John Adkins was "unworthy," and Moses Philips "a drunkard"). But James Henderson he never doubted. He wanted him on board.[12]

What the charismatic Garnet could not give his grantees were specifics. For these, he and his congregants relied on grantees who visited the Smith Lands in the fall of 1846. Brandishing their spoils (Adirondack potatoes, wheat, corn, a cornstalk cane for their pastor), the returned

Trojans offered their impressions. And no fine rhetoric would there be on the "noise of falling trees . . . proclaim[ing] the glorious dawn of civilization." The news here was of water, soil, and weather. Were the white people up there friendly? Was there a blacksmith, sawmill, store? Henderson made shoes. Would white North Elbans buy them?[13]

The next fall, Henderson, with scores of other Smith grantees, served as a delegate at the National Convention of Colored People in Troy. The nine-state assembly honored Gerrit Smith with speeches and a vote of thanks for Charles Ray and Willis Hodges's earnest "Report on Agriculture." Henry Highland Garnet and the silver-tongued delegate from Massachusetts, Frederick Douglass, praised both giveaway and benefactor. But as ever at these speechfests, hard facts about the land were wanting. On behalf of the delegates, Ray and Hodges urged Black New York to welcome Smith's donation as a gift from God, "not to be slighted," and the route not to voting rights alone but to more social equality as well. "An Agricultural Life tends to equality in life. The community is a community of farmers. Their occupations are the same; their hopes and interests are the same; . . . the one is not above the other, whether of the proscribed or any other class, they are all alike farmers. And as it is by placing men in the same position in society that all castes fade away, all castes in this case will be forgotten, and an equality of rights, interests and privileges only exist."[14]

This was good, and surely inspiring, but more welcome still for pragmatists like Henderson was learning which Troy grantees owned land near his own. The sobersided, long-faced William Carasaw and his wife, Eliza, had gift land in North Elba, along with the devout and stalwart teamsters Samuel and Thomas Jefferson. In 1847, Henry Dickson and his family, and the new-to-Troy Lyman Eppes and his brood, got North Elba gift lots too. So the Hendersons would know some folks. His children would see other children who looked like them. The common history in Troy—ties to Garnet, to certain neighborhoods—would solace the adults.

In May 1848, Henry Highland Garnet blessed the Troy grantees "on the eve of their departure" and, as it happened, his departure too. The Garnets were leaving Troy for Geneva, a lakeside town in western New York and only a day's coach ride from Gerrit Smith's Peterboro, a town the Garnets adored. Geneva would be a challenge. Its Black community was on the rise but its Black church was in the doldrums. Garnet's marching orders from the American Missionary Association were stiff: *Bring it up as you did Troy. Revive the Sunday school. Start a day school.* Garnet was ready. Starting fresh was nothing new. He'd left a forced labor camp, two great cities, and several tough northern towns. But his first flock in Troy—his friends!—he'd miss. "My mind reverts with pleasure to the profitable and sweet communion which we have had together," he told his congregants. He expected them to stay in touch. They would be making a new world up there, pioneering their redemption.[15]

From Washington County to St. Armand

Avery Hazzard wasn't looking for redemption. He and Margaret just wanted their own farm. When he received his gift deed from Gerrit Smith, he was laboring, as ever (it could seem), for white people. The chance to work his own land, free and clear, was an unexpected boon. But Hazzard was fifty. Younger bones than his might make a farm from scratch, but wise farmers knew their limits. He would build on someone else's start, a farm already begun, with clearings, outbuildings, and a house. This, Hazzard felt, could work. It would be challenging, giving up long-settled Washington County for land so raw and unfamiliar. Avery Hazzard and his family weren't long in this rustic region—the eight of them had moved to Washington County from Queens in the mid-1840s—but the Hazzard clan had deep hooks in the long-cultivated borderland between New York and Vermont, and in New England generally. Hazzard's father, Levi Hazzard, from Granville to the east, had fought for three years with a Massachusetts regiment in the Revolutionary War. The Hazzards' antislavery church in Washington County's Greenwich (Orthodox Free Congregational) welcomed congregants of color and preached a Bible politics that would have made Gerrit Smith feel right at home. The Hazzards themselves lived in Jackson, to the east of Greenwich. Quakers had found this country early, and their imprint had given the wider neighborhood a name among reformers for its "many warm hearted abolitionists, true friends to the colored man," as one of these, Diantha Gunn, observed in 1856.[16]

But slavery's defenders were a bold cohort too, especially in Washington County's river-powered mill towns, and strong feeling on both sides could boil over into a bad brawl. One such clash in 1848 in the hamlet called Union Village (today part of Greenwich) involved three of Avery and Margaret Hazzard's teenaged sons. Each was arrested and found guilty of assault. Their accuser, the self-named "Riot Victim" Moses White, turned his account of getting beaten in a street fight into a reason to vote for him for town collector, and in the overwhelmingly

Republican community, this Democrat won handily. Friends of the Hazzards from the antislavery church posted the three boys' bail, but this wouldn't keep them out of jail. Charles Henry, twenty, served three months in the county jail, his eighteen-year-old brother, Alexander, got sixty days, and George, fifteen, was dispatched to a reformatory.[17]

This happened during harvest time, when Avery Hazzard, father of eight, was likely counting on his boys to help him get in the crops. To see them jailed was a misery; to lose them in this season was calamitous. Was this the blow that emboldened them to move? In 1850, the Hazzards got word of a working farm for sale in St. Armand, Essex County, thirty miles north of Timbuctoo. One William Lathrop, a white contract farmer who had hoped to buy this property on installments from the owner, Gerrit Smith, was badly in arrears and despaired of catching up. When Lathrop made to sell, Avery Hazzard made his offer. Recommended by no less than Greenwich's (and later Brooklyn's) esteemed antislavery attorney and former US congressman Erastus D. Culver, and vetted by Gerrit Smith's St. Armand land agent, the "industrious and respectable" Hazzard bought Lathrop's farm contract on manageable terms. In 1851, Avery, Margaret, and several of their children put Jackson to their backs and headed west toward the fifty-seven square miles of water, rock, and woods in northwest Essex County named by a pioneer from Canada for an obscure Belgian saint.[18]

St. Armand had a newly named hamlet, Bloomingdale, hard by the northeast-slashing Saranac River, which since 1846 had been deemed a "public highway" whose passengers were logs. Here, in what the county history, invoking the poet William Cowper, called a "boundless contiguity of shade," the Hazzards made a home, one household among fifty in the township, most of them Vermonters pulling west of New England. For the isolated Hazzards, the temptation to return to New York's Washington County to the east was likely very strong. They'd left behind some family members, their old antislavery church, and Black friends too. Gerrit Smith's Washington County contacts had given Smith the names of twenty-one grantees, twelve of them from Union Village and nearby Easton. The Hazzards were surely gratified when the Murrays, a young Black family, also Marylanders, moved from their old neighborhood to Franklin, just across the county line. But in St. Armand, for some seasons, Smith's great plan was represented by the Hazzard name alone. Did this get lonely? Did this place, even more than their old home, revive the old uneasy double-consciousness, and their awareness of the rift between how they were seen and how they saw themselves? Or was all that nothing next to this great marvel, a new farm all their own, fields waiting for them, no boss in sight, their plans, prospects, failures too, all theirs to name and claim?[19]

From the Hudson River Valley to South Mountain

Hasbrook—also Hasbrock, Hasbrouck, Hasebreucq—has been a reverenced name in the Hudson River Valley for four hundred years. It sailed to the region with the Protestant Huguenots who fled France in the 1600s, when their refusal to convert cost them their freedom, property, and lives. Earlier Dutch Protestant settlements along the Hudson Valley had made this part of New York a safe and hopeful destination, and the fertile soil along the banks of the great river deepened its appeal. With other Huguenot refugees, the Hasbrooks negotiated the purchase of a thirty-thousand-acre patent from the Esopus Indians, launched a multifamily colony, and started farming and then studding this rolling country with their windmills and steamboat landings, flour mills, and churches. Today, the house museums, parks, streets, and college buildings called Hasbrook reflect the luster of the name.[20]

But not everyone who bore it felt the pride. In Europe, Huguenots had no history of slaveholding. Once in New York, however, they followed the example of their proslavery Dutch neighbors, and as early as 1674 began purchasing enslaved Africans at auction. And for Black slaves and their descendants who were assigned the Hasbrook name, there would be no association with a heritage of defiance, exodus, and North American recovery. In their case, the name of Hasbrook stood for an erasure, a rubbing out of language, history and self-sovereignty. The name blazoned their bondage like a brand.

When Josiah Hasbrook was born in 1813, some three thousand enslaved people lived in Dutchess County. In some parts of his district, one-third of the residents were slaves. Politics was driven by proslavery interests, and except for pockets of the county that were Quaker, abolitionist ministers and speakers were reviled. Slavery ended in New York in 1827, and Black New Yorkers in the Hudson Valley who got free land from Gerrit Smith were, like Josiah Hasbrook, at least two decades out of bondage. But behind his decades as a free New Yorker were ten generations steeped in slavery. Stories from those lost generations are not often or easily recovered. Legal documents—estate inventories, bills of sale, wills—offer the commodifying vantage of white enslavers on the outside looking in. How Black people experienced enslavement for themselves, in their own skin, was a very different story. Unschooled and illiterate, slaves were denied the means to keep and steward their own history. Today, a guide at Abraham Hasbrouck's historic home in New Paltz may lead us to the low, lightless cellar and dutifully urge us to consider how things were for the four slaves who lived there, and we imagine what we can, but their view of it, their own truth, we can't presume to know.[21]

We don't know, either, exactly why Josiah Hasbrook, thirty-four, of Fishkill and sometimes next-door Newburgh, moved his large family to his North Elba gift lot near South Mountain in 1847 (today it is called Mt. Van Hoevenberg). He left no record. Around a hundred Black men from these two Hudson River Valley towns were Smith grantees, but those who ventured north were very few, among them, the Hasbrooks and their friends Leonard and Deanna Worts (whose surname, like the Hasbrooks', bore the imprint of Dutch bondage). What made these families migrate when so many balked? It was not the better farming; they knew they'd never coax the crops out of North Elba that flourished along this river. Nor could it have been the promise of Adirondack scenery. With its orchards, river landings, and fine stone walls as long as last week's sermon, the Hudson River Valley was no less picturesque.[22]

But those winding walls between estates were built with fieldstones that had been dug and hauled by slaves, and slaves had felled, hewn, and hauled the great pines for the river landings, and the work that Hasbrook did on the river profited not himself but the sons and grandsons of his ancestors' enslavers. In November 1846, voters in Essex County went for Black voting rights five to one. White voters in Dutchess County rejected equal suffrage by a vote no less emphatic. Where slavery had flourished for so long, Negro hate was in the soil.[23]

The Hasbrooks would go north.

From New Orleans to Freeman's Home

Lewis Pierce was a slave in New Orleans, Louisiana, when his master, Robert Tilghman, took him to Philadelphia in 1848. The wealthy Tilghman was an invalid; he came north for his health. For some months Pierce served as his "body servant." Then, one fall day, he went missing, and not long after, Tilghman was summoned to the Philadelphia County Court of Common Pleas. There Lewis Pierce waited, two attorneys at his side.[24]

Had Lewis Pierce fled to Pennsylvania on his own, had he not been brought to this state by his white master, he would have had no case. He would then have been a fugitive, and federal law would have compelled Pennsylvania to return him to his "home." But Pierce broke no law at all. It was his owner who was in trouble. The year before (and likely unbeknownst to Tilghman), Pennsylvania had revised a fifty-eight-year-old act, and now any enslaved person "brought [by his or her enslaver] within her territory [became] ipso facto a freeman." Tilghman had unmeaningly enabled Pierce's emancipation the moment he and Pierce entered the state. Pierce's lead attorney, Thomas Earle, a Quaker lawyer of repute and an old hand on the antislavery circuit, suggested that Pierce submit a writ of habeas corpus to the court and ask it not to free him but rather to *confirm* his freedom under the new law. In a ruling that ran in newspapers from Alabama to Ohio, Judge Edward King pronounced Lewis Pierce a free man and "at liberty to go where he pleases." Reported one witness about this "important slave case," Pierce "was hurried out of Court in double-quick time, and before the lawyers could gather up their papers was out of sight."[25]

Pierce's hot-stepping triumph was widely noted. Abolitionist papers like the *National Era* and the *North Star* jumped on it, and the *Times-Picayune* in New Orleans gave it a long column. Gerrit Smith undoubtedly took note. Here was reaching for the "Jerry Level"! What spine Pierce had! He knew what punishment awaited him if the ruling went against him, but he trusted a never-tested law to take the side of freedom. Once Pierce had moved north to New York State, Smith gave him land as hopefully as he had given it to the out-of-staters-turned-New Yorkers Frederick Douglass and Henry Bibb. Pierce received two lots in Township 12. The one he built his home on, up on Cascade Pass north of a scattering of Black cabins called Freeman's Home, put him near the first home of John Brown. A hike south brought him to the Hasbrooks near South Mountain, a big family who became his friends (and eventually something more). Pierce's Adirondack cabin was so modest it was valued at ten dollars. But his one-man farm—flush with sheep, horses, pigs, and the most potatoes of any of his Black neighbors—was worth $300. On off hours, resting, considering his gains, he may have matched the two Lewis Pierces in his mind and marveled at the ease of this conversion of the man another called his property into the new-made Adirondack pioneer.[26]

Fellow Travelers

In 1848, Charles Ray received a letter from a Black musician in Philadelphia. William Appo wasn't fishing for a gift deed (on two counts he was unqualified: he had money of his own, and he resided out of state). Appo planned to buy land, and he knew what he wanted: 148 acres in North Elba. Elder Ray, delighted, wrote Gerrit Smith, "I wish more men would do in this like manner, and purchase thereabouts." Appo, forty, had performed for twenty years in the marching bands and traveling ensembles of the popular Black bandleader Frank Johnson. New York City, London, Saratoga, Newport, White Sulphur Springs, Cape May— Johnson's celebrated band from Philadelphia played them all. Appo was Johnson's brother-in-law; their wives owned a city hat shop. Horn player, violinist, and a wizard on the melodeon, Appo won a mention in the 1888 memoir of the esteemed A.M.E. Bishop Daniel A. Payne as "the most learned musician of the race." In November 1837, twelve years before John Brown went to England hoping to woo buyers for his wool, Appo and four band mates sailed to London. The concert series of these "Self-Taught Men of Colour" featured "national music" and light classical favorites. So strong were the reviews that Queen Victoria granted them an audience. And then they sailed home.[27]

Ray exulted when Appo took an interest in an Adirondack farm. The well-connected Appo might have bought a home in Newport or Saratoga, grand resort towns with year-round up-and-coming Black communities. Instead he fixed on swarming, stinging, hard-to-reach North Elba. It was a gesture of solidarity, a vote of good faith in Smith's idea, and an expression of Appo's brand of quiet activism. In Philadelphia, he and his wife Elizabeth backed abolition fundraisers. In New York, he attended Black political conventions and supported the *Colored American*. And when the Appos lived in Troy, William co-ran an abolitionist meeting at Reverend Garnet's church (was it at this 1843 meeting that he met the secretary-shoemaker who would be his Adirondack neighbor some years on?). In Utica, Appo stood for Oneida County on a suffrage petition in the *Tribune*. A hymn he wrote, "Sing unto God," premiered at a city fundraiser for Black captives on the *Amistad*. So he knew what the Black Woods stood for. He was investing in a new community birthed by a belief in voting rights, racial justice, and abolition. He was saying, *This cause is mine*.[28]

Accounts of Timbuctoo have tended to neglect the significance of nondeeded pioneers like William Appo, but these fellow travelers were on the scene from the first. They came from Maryland to Vermontville, and from Ulster County to North Elba. In 1848, the *Ram's Horn* named thirty-eight New Yorkers who hoped to move to the Smith Lands. Only eight were Smith grantees. The rest were women, children, and deedless enthusiasts as keen to share in Smith's great plan as the deedholders themselves. When Hodges named the eight men living with him in the enclave he called Blacksville, four were deedless. It didn't bother Hodges, and it didn't bother them.[29]

Both Hodges and Appo were also intimate with the one fellow traveler who did not escape public notice. Like Appo, the angular, sunbaked white man who appeared at Smith's Peterboro home in April 1848 did not qualify for gift land. But John Brown, the name stark as the man himself, had read all about Smith's initiative. An abolitionist whose horror of slavery ("the sum of all villainies") was as fierce as Smith's, Brown hoped to move his large family to North Elba to "take one of your farms myself, clear it up and plant it, and show my colored neighbors how such work should be done." Would Gerrit Smith sell him a piece?[30]

Smith liked everything about this man. He was planful and direct, and knew his scripture cold. There was no vanity about him either. Cone Flanders's farmhouse, which Brown rented for his brood, was not big enough by half, but the family would make do until Brown and the bigger boys could built a new home of their own. And Smith would help with that project as gamely as he enabled so many of Brown's other plans over their ten years' acquaintance, from buying rifles for antislavery militants in Kansas to a plot to seize a federal arsenal in Virginia and deliver guns to slaves. Brown's attempt to arm enslaved people would polarize a marveling and shaken nation. Now there, as Brown's Adirondack neighbor, Willis Hodges, might have put it, was something besides speechifying, though the speechifying that followed the failed raid, whether for it or against, thunders ever on.

The Black Woods

CHAPTER 7

Trailblazers

In September 1847, Rev. Jermain Wesley Loguen, Smith's land agent in Syracuse, packed up his "conveyance" and set out for the long trip to the Black Woods. After a year of prospecting for deedholders in his part of New York he was eager, and maybe anxious, to see this country for himself. He reached the Essex County settlements (in Townships 12 and 11) two months after Charles Ray did, and sent his much wider-ranging and more specific findings to his fellow agent James McCune Smith, who shared them with Gerrit Smith and the *North Star*. Frederick Douglass published this report in March 1848. This was the first time Black New Yorkers got hard news from the trenches from a designated land agent, along with cautiously high hopes.[1]

I'll begin, like Loguen, with the good news. From everything he heard and saw, he believed the Essex County gift land was, "with very few exceptions, as good land as any man could need." Franklin County was more problematic. Some lots were "first-rate" for farming. And if many "would not be good for tillage," no one of them was worthless. The forest was itself an asset. Sawmills were proliferating. The rising price of lumber promised that "in a few years" deedholders would "derive from [their gift lots] a handsome income." All the more reason to get settled on them fast to protect the land from wood thieves—which pointed to a wider problem that grantee-settlers would need to prepare for.[2]

Some white folks, Loguen learned, were playing "a highhanded game upon our colored brethren." They led grantees to worthless lots (mountainous or swampy) and charged them royally for the deception, urging them to sell their gift deeds for pennies. Or they took them to lots so distant that the discouraged deedholders were moved to sell their acreage for the cost of the excursion. Then the scammers jeered about it (so county clerks told Loguen). Grantees who could not read or write risked getting fleeced if their paperwork was not in order. What they needed, Loguen believed, were local allies who were literate and sympathetic. Happily, Loguen had procured the names of nine right-thinking white Adirondackers who could keep the sharks at bay. Three lived in Franklin and six in Essex County, and all knew the woodlands well. The grantees could also hope for square dealing from Adirondack county clerks who knew Smith's land and had been working with Smith's agents and secretaries for years.[3]

So the letter started on a good note and ended on a bright one too, with news of white intermediaries who were in the grantees' corner. Only hold on to your gift lots, Loguen urged, and you "cannot fail, [in] a few years, to derive from them a handsome income. . . . Don't sell your land for a song." But this part of the letter, the part that assured the uneasy deedholders that *yes, it's worth it, this can work*, paled next to vivid news of grantees getting conned.

The Franklin Pioneers

Whom to trust, whom to avoid? The grantee-settler Willis Hodges would ask this question too. In May 1848, Hodges and his band of New York City pioneers reached the wild land they would spend the summer clearing and then conjuring the enclave he called Blacksville. The landing was not soft. Early charges for teamstering and supplies were much stiffer than Hodges expected. He had a bleak hunch he'd been rooked. Short of funds, he had to mortgage two hundred acres, and his fellow pioneer William H. Smith, also from the city, had to sell a small lot too. But these hits, while daunting, were survivable, and Hodges and his party found relief in their dogged progress in the woods.

From the spring of 1848 until the onset of winter, the Black pioneers grubbed the underbrush, fired up the slash, chopped trees to logs and logs to cordwood until their muscles froze. They chinked cabin logs (unseasoned! would they crack at the first freeze?) with

J. W. Loguen. Photographer unknown, from Carter G. Woodson, *The History of the Negro Church*, Washington, DC, 1921. Schomburg Center for Research in Black Culture, NYPL.

hunks of green moss, and hauled big stones to a chimney site and mortared them with lime and ash. A spring, I'm guessing, was sourced on a light rise (cedar pump logs would have to wait), and a privy likely dug and capped. In Virginia, Hodges used to help his father, an herbalist, hunt for healing plants and roots. In these woods, too, he likely gathered what he could.[4]

Were there things they left behind and missed? Maybe a spare candle mold, some bar lead, linseed oil, a bee box, rope? The air was warm, but how the locals doomed-and-gloomed the coming cold, you might take it for a war. While a coat peg remained to be whittled, a pine torch readied, a span of bark hacked into shingles or squared off for a shelf, the cabin fixing was not done. Coffee, tinderbox, matches, all called for stations. Beds cried out for feather ticks and quilts. Kettle, gridiron, soap pot, long-handled pan, and waste bucket needed cleaning and rinsing, then back to their posts.

Once, just after the Fourth of July, Willis Hodges slipped down to New York City. With him was his friend and fellow activist-turned-homesteader, William H. Smith. In this a summer Manhattan was besieged with wild dogs so numerous the city was paying "dog-killers" fifty cents a head for any "dog unmuzzled," and ragged boys with bats patrolled the streets. Undeterred by either dogs or their pursuers, the self-dubbed "Franklin Pioneers" thronged to Union Hall on Wooster Street to hear Smith and Hodges share news of their progress. Even McCune Smith broke from his long rounds at the Colored Orphan Asylum to hear the settlers and, afterward, to write Gerrit Smith. Also here to speak was the city cartman Anthony Provost, the activist who had made the giveaway his cause, and his friend Edward Marshall, who ran a night school for Black youths in McCune Smith's home.[5]

Provost told the crowd that he was "steadily concocting a plan of operations" to lead "a good-sized well-organized number" of grantees to "Franklin 9th." Further, he and Marshall had set up a mutual aid fund for Franklin-bound grantees that would help pay for surveys, land clearance, and road building. Investor buy-in was $1.25, and monthly dues $0.50.[6]

Provost's carting clients in the city, ranging from rag dealers to tannery tycoons, had brought him a fair living. Hauling everything from commodities to essential goods like firewood or hay, Black cartmen enjoyed good standing in their community; among the carters, the *Colored American* declared, were "our very best citizens, men who for moral worth and industrious enterprise, are the pride of our city, some of them leaders in the holy cause of equal rights." Why, then, was Provost so eager to leave the city?[7]

In 1839, Provost had applied for a cartman's license. He'd carted profitably for years and had wealthy clients in the Swamp (the heart of the city's leather and tanning district) who were glad to give him references. He owned "as good a horse and cart as was to be seen on the dock" (no small feat given the expense of keeping a horse fed, clean shod, and healthy). His "high moral character" was widely recognized. His case, he felt, was rock solid. And the mayor turned him down. It was simply "not customary for colored men to drive carts in the city," Cornelius Lawrence offered, as if evidence of racism were its own justification. The sophistry was bad enough, but Hizzoner's show of sympathy was worse: not letting Provost drive his cart, explained the mayor, was actually for Provost's good; cart licenses would be withheld from Black men to save them from hotheads "who might dump their horses and carts into the river." Better, in other words, to deprive Black New Yorkers of a legal living than to trouble the city with the obligation to enforce the law. Provost soldiered on, but after 1839, he was a marked man, a Black New Yorker with ambition. Seeing him in this light (maybe seeing him for the first time at all), white cartmen struck back. Provost was fined, and had to sell his horse and cart and "betake himself to more menial employment."[8]

There was a joke the Irish liked to tell, a three-part answer to the story that the streets of New York City were paved with gold. First, no gold here. Second, no pavement either. Third, if the streets were to be paved, it would be the Irish who would do it. Provost might have added that at least the Irish got the job.[9]

Then, in 1846, Provost, a fervent advocate for equal suffrage, had to contend with the debacle of the Constitutional Convention, and the white electorate's decisive routing of any hope of enfranchisement. All the old arguments from 1821 against Black voters had been revived, this time bolstered with new fake science about racial inferiority. Convention delegate John A. Kennedy from New York City railed against granting rights to the race with which Caucasians shared "the fewest points of resemblance . . . Nature revolt[s] at the proposal." John Hunt, also from Manhattan, urged the others to please keep in mind that "the negroes are aliens. . . . We might close our eyes in a fit of amiable enthusiasm, and try to dream the wool out of their curl . . . but they knew and felt all the while (that is, the sane negroes) that they were negroes and aliens by the act of God, and there was no remedy." Give Black New Yorkers full rights of citizenship, and New York would be aswarm with ballot-seeking Southern Blacks, an influx sure to drive white workers from the state when a job war heated up and wage cuts followed. Give these men the vote, opined St. Lawrence County delegate Bishop Perkins, "they would never be permitted to come up to the ballot box, or if they did come, it would only to be bought and sold like cattle in the market."[10]

Equal voting rights for Black New Yorkers never had a prayer. Out of fifty-six counties, only ten supported suffrage. Clinton County, close to Canada—farm patched, Yankee settled, and culturally kin to abolitionist New England—would go five to one for equal voting rights. Essex and Franklin were all for suffrage too. But New York County, home to most of Gerrit Smith's three thousand deedholders, recoiled. Constitutional Convention city delegates in 1821 and 1846 were the most strident advocates of *total* disenfranchisement for Black New Yorkers (and the keenest advocates for African colonization), and city voters in November 1846 rejected equal manhood suffrage by six to one, almost three times the state average.[11]

What did this mean for Anthony Provost? In 1839, he had learned how threadbare was the mantle of "free man of color" when a flagrantly discriminatory ruling assailed his right to make a living. Seven years later, he discovered that six out of seven city voters deemed him unworthy of a ballot. If he wasn't valued and he wasn't wanted, why call New York City home? The wonder isn't that he signed up for forty Adirondack acres and offered to take grantees north. The wonder would have been if he had not.[12]

After Provost, it was the newsman Willis Hodges's turn to speak, a familiar name to many in the hall for his late lamented *Ram's Horn*. There was a bold rag! In Baltimore, white people were so scared of it that when a Black subscriber went to claim his issue at the post office, he was arrested and fined $500. Willis Hodges had sold his stake in the *Ram's Horn* before he headed north, and now it seemed his ex-partner, Thomas Van Rensselaer, planned to shutter New York City's one Black paper for lack of funds.[13]

Like his columns in the *Ram's Horn*, Hodges's remarks about his gift lots pulled no punches. He shared his rocky landing at Loon Lake, the high cost of transport, and the unhappy fact that he'd had to mortgage his land—news that came as a profound surprise to Smith's land agent in the audience. McCune Smith and Gerrit Smith had laid such stress on the need to stay debt free, and now, so early in the journey, the threat of debt already loomed. But so enthusiastic were Hodges and William Smith about their prospects, and so hopeful were they for more settlers, that the doctor put aside his worry. "It did my soul good to shake their hard hands," he later wrote his Peterboro friend about the "two foot sore and travel weary Pioneers. . . . [S]uch a good spirit" prevailed among the Franklin Pioneers, it made the doctor himself "very desirous to go on the good land." The audience in Union Hall was smitten, too, soaking up the reports of "log houses and cleared acres, Pine stumps—and want of a team!" The new homesteader, William H. Smith, once a city porter, declared, "It is better to suffer two years in Franklin, than forever in New York." A few weeks earlier, the *New York Tribune* published a rapt description of Smith's cabin (the writer was the Blacksville settler George B. Wilson): "A spacious dwelling on Lime Lake on the main turnpike from Lake Champlain to Ogdensburg. . . . The site is a beautiful one, and several of the granted locations lie near it on various directions."[14]

What raised the loudest cheer, however, were not reports of cabin work and country views but a joke about the city these frontiersmen had left behind. When William Smith told his wife he was making a short trip to Manhattan and urged her to write letters he could deliver to their friends, she "sat down, and in a few minutes exclaimed that she did not know the day of the month. 'How so?' 'Oh, because I am not forced to remember the *landlord's* call.'" The audience roared. The feeling that one's time was not one's own, that every hour in the waking day belonged to someone else—landlord, creditor, or boss—was something everybody recognized. On the new land, time would be theirs to manage—time and space alike. City space was charged with menace and anxiety. The map, unwritten, that Black New Yorkers took with them every time they went into the streets directed every step. *Not this way, that way; danger, go back, eyes down, get away*. The map marked every hospital, church, school, and library reserved for whites only; every worksite, oyster house, dock, and boatyard they were not to venture near; every firehouse, union hall, and public bath that made it clear: *not here, not yours, step back*.

Even as Hodges and Smith bore the glow of the good meeting into the cobbled streets (still rank with the detritus of the glorious Fourth—spent firecrackers, corncobs, charred potato skins, and whatever else had escaped the avid foraging of pigs), and even after two months in Franklin County, the old habits of Black vigilance and worry ruled the view, fixing route, pace, and direction. Blacksville and Lime Lake were waiting for them. It was time to get back to their new home.

Spring Fever, Winter Dreams

In the city, May had always been a hopeful month, the moment for bold resolve and new beginnings, for removals, risk, and planning. We do it every year, McCune Smith marveled in an essay—each spring, Black city folk packing up and moving "with a vigor and earnestness that outdistances all other nomadic tribes on the face of the earth." And not just to new rooms in the city. The warming season was the time to dream of country living too. A few weeks after the city meeting of the Franklin Pioneers in July 1848, Gerrit Smith sent his city agents a batch of deeds for eighty-six grantees, and in his thank-you note, McCune Smith could report with pride that the Gerrit Smith Farming Association was now fifty members strong.[15]

Willis Hodges's party had reached Loon Lake in May 1848, and that same month, Samuel and Thomas Jefferson, two brothers from Troy, moved to a good-sized lot in Essex County's North Elba (having judged their gift lots in Hamilton County too difficult to reach). The lot they picked in Township 12 was Lot 93; a white farmer, Thomas Nash, who was buying it on time from Gerrit Smith, let the Jeffersons rent it on good terms. Already working a five-acre piece of it was their old congregant from Troy's Liberty Street Church, the shoemaker James H. Henderson. His gift lot, also, was too remote and rough to farm, so he moved here in 1848, and may have been the one to alert the Jefferson brothers to this good land.[16]

That fall on his visit to the Black Woods, John Brown met these three "good colored families" and impressions all around were warm and hopeful. The grantees were already familiar with the abolitionist's keen interest in this project from his cheerleading in the *Ram's Horn* ("The colony on the Smith Lands must be got up, and can be, and will be!"). Brown also knew Gerrit Smith, and if he hadn't yet met these grantees' Troy pastor, he was certainly familiar with Garnet's celebrated "Call to Rebellion." James Henderson was pleased enough about his new white neighbor to describe the visit in the *North Star*. "I have seen J.B. of Springfield, Mass.," he reported, "and he says that he will move here in the Spring, and will give us a start if we will try to help ourselves." And Brown, for his part, was champing to get started. "I can think of no place where I would sooner go, all things considered than to live with these poor despised Africans to try, & encourage them, & show them a little so far as I am capable how to manage," he wrote his father. Only outstanding debts and business woes kept him from joining them sooner than May 1849. He knew they needed help. Without a team of oxen or horses of their own, they couldn't yank their stumps and smooth the ground for seed; they were heading into their first Adirondack winter unprovisioned. Brown likely understood more than the grantees just how long an Adirondack winter could be.[17]

Also worrisome were rumors about local merchants overcharging the grantees for food. In October 1848, Brown shipped the homesteaders ten barrels of pork and flour. Three barrels of each went to Hodges for the settlers around Blacksville, and four more barrels (two pork, two flour) Hodges was to get to Timbuctoo. *Make it last*, Brown wrote Hodges, his confidante and proxy among the settlers. *This is all I can afford.* Through Hodges, too, Brown urged the grantees to avoid a post office he didn't trust and always, when he sent packages, to match receipts to contents to make sure nothing had gone missing along the way. He recommended a storekeeper in Port Kent. This was a long pull from the Black Woods, but he knew the man was honest. He implored the homesteaders to pace themselves and, above all, to plan for cold. Don't build, he warned, before you've laid in fuel. Keep on the good side of the locals, and never forget "the vast importance of sustaining the very best character for honesty, truth, industry and faithfulness." Earlier in May, Reverend Garnet had urged the grantees to stay politically engaged, but Brown's counsel was more pragmatic: "I would advise, by all means, that you do not go to any expense about voting next spring, until we can get ready to *take hold of that matter right*." Hodges, it would seem, was so keen to vote in his new neighborhood that he was prepared to go into debt to meet the property requirement. *Don't you do it*, Brown all but ordered. Debt was just another kind of bondage, as he well knew.[18]

Brown's sober counsel was surely welcome. But what Hodges and the homesteaders could have used (what Lewis Tappan had called for half a year before) was a savvy helper on the scene who knew this country and how to read it, how to work it, how to keep pace with its demands. How many logs, for instance, needed to be chopped and split to warm a ten-by-ten-foot cabin for a six-month Adirondack winter? Blackflies, which in early summer were thick enough to choke on, could be held off with a smudge—but to make a smudge pot you had to know the evergreens and mosses. Tracking a bee tree, rendering mutton fat for candle tallow, matching plow tip to soil type, knowing not to build a cabin with just-cut lumber—maybe this came easy to the farmer's son Willis Hodges, but likely not the others. And while Hodges knew his woodpeckers and his screech owls, nothing back in Princess Anne County approached the witchy chortle of a loon. A nine-foot bull moose looming up out of the mist? The heart could stop midbeat. And who would ready the Black settlers for the vagaries of Adirondack summer, how it came on so brightly, promising the world, then lost interest, just skipped away?[19]

In November 1848, the *North Star* ran a letter from John Brown to the grantees that would be read aloud at Troy's Wesleyan Methodist Episcopal Church. By way of reassurance, this longtime surveyor wanted the grantees to know that he knew how to tell good land from bad, and that their land, which he had seen, was possessed of "many very superior natural advantages. . . . Hold on to [it] as [your] most valuable earthly treasure, and sooner suffer nakedness and hunger than part with [it]." Attending this church meeting was the Timbuctoo pioneer Samuel Jefferson, who seconded Brown's good opinion. Not "under any circumstances" should you "part with your land," he told his Troy friends and fellow deedholders. His and Brown's appeal made a hit. Several Troy grantees moved to the Black Woods that spring.[20]

And it had to be in spring, this move, because in winter, nobody was going anywhere. Prospective pioneers put all their moving plans on hold, and settlers, too, deferred to the still spirit of the season. When winter dropped like a hammer in the woods, they might not leave their cabins more than once or twice a day, and then just to thread a path to the barn or woodshed, stream or privy, blinking back the white light, much too focused on the cold to marvel at the snow spilling off the high-branched pines. For some settlers, the Adirondack winter was simply hateful, nothing for it but to wrap yourself in quilts, darn socks, and pray that when the dog growled after dark, she was just having a bad dream and not telling them to get the sheep into the cabin doublequick because the wolves were moving off the ridge.

But Willis Hodges was a writer, and winter was his ally; it curled around the cabin like a cat, let him pull chair to table, put pen to page, and do what he adored. He had no plans for publication. His memoir, if that's what this turned out to be, was written for the family he had yet to start, something to let them know his backstory, how he got from Virginia to Blacksville, near Loon Lake, and, more than this, to let them understand what Blacksville had to do with slavery. Hodges himself had never been enslaved, but, as McCune Smith once wrote, "The one idea of slavery" had so entirely managed to "spread its shoots & roots & its suckers into every institution in this land" that Hodges clearly felt it wholly sensible to claim the slave narrative for his model. Slavery and the battle to dismantle it shaped his past, his purpose, his very presence in this cabin. And although he wrote the book a future editor would title *A Free Man of Color: The Autobiography of Willis Augustus Hodges* when he was only thirty-three, with more than half his life to come, the half at Hodges's back could load a stone boat. Still-fearful memories of his mother being beaten by vigilantes, his family's home in shambles, his brother's jail time and his own, a hellish season digging a canal with several hundred enslaved men and their white drivers, and then his weary dealings with the Negrophobes of Brooklyn and Manhattan—all this mapped the common ground of degradation that free Blacks shared with enslaved millions. This memoir would document the links.[21]

Hodges finished his seventy-page manuscript on his thirty-fourth birthday in February 1849. In the company of his "little band" of Franklin Pioneers, he gave thanks to "the mercy of God and the goodness of the honorable Garret [*sic*] Smith" and praised the good work of his fellow farmers "under our own 'vine and fig trees,' with none to molest or make us afraid." The "aid and good cheer" of John Brown, Hodges's friend since the old days of the *Ram's Horn*, were warmly noted. But interestingly, he made very little of the Black Woods itself. Though Hodges had been ten months on this land, building up his home and the fragile settlement around it, he gave it no more than a page. Years later he would tell his son about the fugitives he sometimes sheltered in his cabin who were moving up to Canada, but in the memoir, nothing is revealed. His cabin mates are undescribed, his dealings with white neighbors unreported. The view from his front door, what Loon Lake looked like in morning fog, a persistent cold of his that had John Brown a little worried—these were of no interest. What mattered, *all* that mattered, was that he'd made it to the finish line, his Adirondack home.[22]

Someday, Hodges wrote in his last lines, his enslaved brethren would occupy "the wilderness of slavery and injustice. . . . [O]ur children or children's children will possess the land, if God is God, and a just God." The analogy was plain. They would possess and vanquish the "wilderness" of bondage as confidently as Hodges laid claim to the wilderness and cultivated his "vine and fig trees" in the North. His occupation of the Black Woods *anticipated* freedom's triumphant occupation of the South. It dramatized it, made it imaginable: if it could happen in Blacksville, Franklin County, it might happen in Pharaoh Land as well. Thus the fuzzy imprecision of his Adirondack pages. At the dawn of 1849, Hodges's Black Woods had to be all metaphor, as big as Canada, as idealized as Charles Ray's conduit to "respectability and influence." And so, instead of bog marsh, blackflies, and white neighbors, we get figs.[23]

There were no fig trees at Wolf Pond. And the Loon Lake home that Hodges described in his memoir wasn't thanks to "the goodness of the honorable Gerrit Smith." Hodges's gift lot was so starkly uninviting that he'd had to buy another one for two dollars an acre. This was a good move. It flanked an old military road in fair repair, with sawmills, iron forges, and rough-cut hotels all within a day's tramp. East of Loon Lake was Goldsmith, a bustling mill town with a schoolhouse, sawmill, and post office. Merrillsville, where he got his mail, was a hike through the woods.[24]

Help Unwanted

In Timbuctoo, this same winter, the grantees were also busy writing, but unlike Hodges, they did aim to publish, and the sooner the better. The North Star had recently reported that a Keene man (Keene is to North Elba's east) would be the giveaway's official surveyor. Reporting on this new helper was Douglass's coeditor, William C. Nell. The surveyor, Wait J. Lewis, had been vetted by Frederick Douglass and Gerrit Smith, Nell explained, and Douglass himself had introduced the white man to the Rochester grantees. Lewis had told them that his knowledge of the gift lands was exhaustive; he'd seen many lots and could say with confidence that "none of the lots were worthless, but the greater portion excellent." His survey fee was $1.50. People who wanted his assistance could send this fee to the North Star, care of Douglass. Many grantees signed up for a survey then and there.[25]

The settlers of Timbuctoo were stunned. They knew Wait J. Lewis. They'd seen what passed for his surveying. He was, they felt, incompetent. They wrote a worried letter to the North Star, but Douglass would not publish it, offering instead only his own summary of their concerns with this rejoinder: since the letter writers had "admit[ted]" that Mr. Lewis was "a Justice of the Peace, and Chairman of the Keene School Committee, and that he has a certificate as Surveyor," these credentials would "sufficient[ly] guarantee [his] character . . . until something definite and tangible is preferred against him."[26]

Douglass's brusqueness is no mystery. An inquiry into a surveyor whom he and Smith had recommended was embarrassing. And what good could it do Smith's project? The giveaway was already beleaguered by the slow pace of migration, and by the emergence of this new challenge from the colony in Oneida County's Florence. What were the jumpy gripes of a few pioneers next to the prospect of an Adirondack surveyor who was game and primed to help? A year after directing "the sharp axe of the sable-armed pioneer [to] at once be uplifted over the soil of Franklin and Essex Counties," Douglass did not conceal his frustration. "These lands must be soon made a blessing to the colored people or they will become a curse," he told the *North Star* that January. "There is no living there [on the Smith Lands] without houses and farming utensils. Houses cannot be built and farming utensils obtained without money—and this the grantees have not got." This was as bleak and blunt a diagnosis of what ailed the Black Woods as anyone had dared to offer. But it would not suggest the cure. And Douglass was not inclined to name the one person in the world in a position to relieve the undercapitalized pioneers. Douglass was building up a newspaper. What would become of it without Gerrit Smith's occasional gifts of money? A fuss about a surveyor was not his cause. *Let this settle, let it cool.*[27]

Instead these embers caught and flared. Outraged by the grantees' complaints, Wait J. Lewis elicited a long deposition from a Keene acquaintance, Elijah Jones, for the *North Star* and the *Northern Star and Colored Farmer*. Lewis, Jones declared, was the best friend the grantees ever had! He had himself given them land, "40 square rods of beautiful land in the village plat" he called Freeman's Home. For this kindness, he was rewarded with the outrage of his white neighbors, who had said they'd sooner "starve . . . out" the grantees than "live in a village surrounded by colored people," and claimed that Lewis was "trying to ruin the town" and should "go armed, or he would get shot." Gerrit Smith and his Negroes (they said) "ought to be banished to Africa," and Wait Lewis with them. But let it be known, Jones offered, that for all this risk to his own person, Lewis stood by his convictions. He hoped to "live to see one member of the Essex County Board of Supervisors a little darker complexion than the rest," dreamed of reading "the speeches of Dr. James McCune Smith in Congress," and aimed to "live long enough to know that Gerrit Smith occupied the White House at Washington." When his neighbors turned Black people from their doors, Lewis made "his house a home for the colored man." When racists menaced the grantees, he would "fulfill all his contracts" with the deedholders and

get them surveys even when the job incurred "a great expense." Lewis
had been postmaster, coroner, justice of the peace, and superintendent
of his town and its schools, and if anyone was fool enough to slander
him, Lewis would see him "in our County or Supreme Courts."[28]

But Timbuctoo held firm. James Henderson shared the concern of
his community in a letter to his old minister. And because this was his
first note to the reverend since he left Troy, he made sure, first thing, to
assure Garnet that the news from the North Country was mostly very
good. North Elba, he wrote from "West Keene Timbucto, Essex Co.,"
turned out to be a pretty fine place to farm. "I have been here eight
months, and I like the land and the country well. There is no better
land for grain. We get 25 to 50 bushels of oats to the acre. New land is
the best for oats, and for potatoes and turnips; of the last two articles
we get from 200 to 400 to the acre. The farmers here get 46 cents per
bushel, cash in hand, for their oats." Further, "I have seen Mr. J. B. of
Springfield, Mass,—and he says he will move here in the Spring, and
will give us a start if we will try and help ourselves." Henderson put
the bright side front and center. Garnet would love to read this, and
several thousand grantees too. And his letter, which was introduced by
Garnet's, was published in the *North Star*, in full.[29]

But regarding Douglass's recommended man from Keene, Henderson showed no mercy. Wait Lewis called himself a surveyor? "Some of
the best men in the town of Keene . . . all tell one story about him—that
is, that he is not a man to be trusted; all that he wants is the money.
We who are here can see and know." Lewis made no new lines when
he surveyed; he just went "hunting" for the old ones. He used a wire
instead of a surveyor's chain, and marked lot boundaries and names
"with a lead pencil, in a hand as fine as this letter." Nor did he bother
to mark internal boundaries of adjacent 40-acre quarter lots. It was true
that backcountry surveyors liked working with the 160-acre square, but
were the grantees supposed to guess the inside lot lines? Further, Wait
Lewis claimed that Reverend Garnet had hired him to help the settlers.
Henderson had a hunch this wasn't so.[30]

Late that spring of 1849, when John Brown appeared with his good
chain, regulation transit, and miles of experience, the grantees' poor
opinion of Wait Lewis was confirmed. Correcting the sloppy work of
a surveyor by whom "many of [the settlers] had been cheated badly"
consumed Brown's first weeks in Township 12, recalled Brown's daughter Ruth Thompson. The unscrupulous Keene surveyor "took advantage of their ignorance, and got them to settle on lands that did not

correspond with the deeds Gerrit Smith had given them. . . . Father felt deeply over the way so many of them had been treated, and tried to encourage and help them in every way he could. He spent much of his time in surveying their land, running out their lines, and helping them to locate on land actually belonging to them." Though Brown's daughter left the local surveyor unnamed, circumstantial evidence points to Wait J. Lewis from Keene.[31]

The Reverend Backs the Cobbler

Two centuries of public history on the giveaway and its travails have canonized this episode, which, like Loguen's grim report and Hodges's bitter dealings with his teamsters, seems to underscore yet again why the giveaway was so beleaguered: *locals had it in for Black people.* This synopsis is misleading. There were Adirondack racists. There were also Adirondackers who were helpful and supportive, and who might well have directed agents or grantees to credible surveyors early on. But no such counsel was elicited, so Wait Lewis filled the vacuum. And while not the "official" surveyor Henderson would have preferred (an arguable distinction since New York surveyors were not licensed until 1920), Lewis was indeed, town records show, just about everything else he said he was: postmaster, superintendent, school committee chair, and justice of the peace. Further, his surveying methods may have been more usual than Henderson realized. In 1885, the Warren County historian H. P. Smith complained about Adirondack surveyors' overuse of compasses ("magnetic needles") instead of chains. And backcountry surveyors who could not afford a regulation hundred-link chain often made do with brass wire on a spool or even long ropes cinched with knots. In the deep woods, rope and wire were easier to manage. Even Lewis's neglect of the grid inside the 160-acre lots was not unheard of. The late Norman Van Valkenburgh, renowned historian of New York surveying, told me that country surveyors often left inner lot lines uncharted, figuring that clients could save expense and sort these out themselves. (He did, however, concede that Lewis's reliance on a pencil was "a bit much.")[32]

One of Lewis's assertions was entirely unfounded. Reverend Garnet had not authorized him "to receive money or otherwise." Garnet didn't know him. He did however know the Troy grantee James H. Henderson, "a Christian, a cautious man, and of the soundest integrity," and someone to be taken seriously, Garnet told the *North Star*. It grieved him to think the grantees had "again been most miserably humbugged, and most shamefully gulled" (a reference, here, to the copycat land settlement schemes of 1847). "The matter must be seen to," he declared. But neither he nor other good friends of the giveaway would do it. When this erupted, Garnet was at or on his way to Gerrit Smith's, and after Peterboro, Geneva. And Peterboro was not a place from which to launch an inquiry into a surveyor Smith presumably endorsed. All that ever "saw to" this crisis was the fortuitous arrival of John Brown in May 1849. Brown reviewed Lewis's surveys and redid them, and Keene's litigious surveyor was not heard from again.[33]

And May brought more energetic hopeful bodies to the Black Woods than Brown. From 1849 into the next decade, homesteader-grantees from Rensselaer, Ulster, Dutchess, Jefferson, Washington, and New York Counties moved not just to Blacksville, Freeman's Home, and Timbuctoo, but to St. Armand, Duane, Negro Brook, Franklin, and Vermontville. Small parties of fellow travelers from Pennsylvania, Maryland, and Delaware joined these settlements, and after the Civil War, freed people from the South came north and made new homes. Numbers remained modest. This scattered, changeable community would never be what Gerrit Smith imagined.

It *would* be what it could.

CHAPTER 8

The Second Wave

Three years after Gerrit Smith published his intentions, his plan designed to draw three thousand Black New Yorkers north had failed to attract more than a fraction. And this was a plan that Dr. McCune Smith, with his friend Elder Ray, had flogged at suffrage meetings, churches, conventions, temperance rallies, and fundraisers all over metropolitan New York. They had envisioned a thoroughgoing outmigration of Black families to the wilderness; they signed up giftees everywhere they went. Yet McCune Smith had never been there. How this wild country looked, how it smelled, what it felt like underfoot, remained a mystery. Hard as it was to wrest the days from his practice and an ailing daughter, he had to make this trip. It was time—well past—to put the Black Arcadia of his imaginings to the test.

Smith's traveling companion would be William P. Powell, who also had a stake in Gerrit Smith's initiative. The proprietor of Manhattan's Colored Sailor's Home, Powell had urged Black seamen to try Adirondack farming. He owned a gift deed himself.[1]

Their visit was well timed. In early fall, the great woods already winked with color. On either side of the rough road, ferns and bracken made a low surf of yellow-green. Swamp maples stretched and flared, and here and there reared up those high-shouldered boulders called erratics, remnants of the glaciers that once rolled over this domed plateau.

Smith, a man of science who had studied medicine in Scotland and France and was a lay scholar of climatology and geography, was entirely enthralled. He may have recalled a verse or two from one of his favorite poets, Robert Burns. But when "Nature's poet" wrote, "Here is the glen, and here the bower / All underneath the birchen shade," he invoked another world. Burns's "woodlark in the grove" would not have lasted long in the cool, brooding Adirondack woods.

And then their coachman lost his way. The doctor made light of it in his letter later on, but getting lost was hardly trivial. A chance encounter with a bear, a rattler, a white person with an aversion to Black skin—these could make for complications. Happily, a white local got them back on track, and in time, the doctor would assure Smith with a sigh, "I . . . would gladly exchange this bustling anxious life for the repose of that majestic country, could I see the way clear to a livelihood for myself and family. I felt myself a lord indeed beneath the lofty spruce and maple and birch, and by the [tr]awling brook, which your deed made mine."[2]

But McCune Smith was not a lord, and Gerrit Smith was not his king. And after the physician did his duty—made his gratitude as plain as he knew how—he got down to the task at hand. *What was happening on the gift land? What could he report?* "We found in North Elba," he wrote, "about sixty colored persons in all, of all ages and sex. . . . As a general thing the parties had not enough money at the outset and had failed in making up the deficiency partly from the backwardness of the season and partly from having waited too long for Mr. John Brown's team. They were however cheerful, many of them hardy and industrious; a fine talk they made too, about their feeling of independence, when I fear they were a little too dependent upon Mr. Brown's meal bin." But several grantees already had cabins up, and the writer was quite confident that before the end of fall they would "make a fair fallow." The wave of settlers who came in May and June of 1849 had fanned new life out of the coals, and this revival the doctor noted with relief. "I think more clearing had been done within a year in [Township] 12 than in any three years together of late," he wrote.[3]

He and Powell would not meet the abolitionist sheep farmer. When they arrived, John Brown was on his way to London and then the Continent, hoping to get a good price for his wool. Brown and his family were also part of this energizing second wave. In Westport, the Browns had met up with the teamster-grantee Samuel Jefferson from Troy, whom Brown had enlisted to haul his family to a farmhouse on Cascade Road he was leasing from its owner. The road was rocky and

Portrait of John Brown. Daguerreotype, 1847–49. Augustus Washington, photographer, Springfield, MA. Courtesy of the Nelson-Atkins Museum of Art, Kansas City, MO. Gift of the Hall Family Foundation in Honor of the 75th Anniversary of the Nelson-Atkins Museum of Art, 2008.

they took it slow (Jefferson's confident, attentive pacing of Brown's newly purchased team won him side work with this family for some years). Brown himself got busy straightaway redoing the grantees' sloppy surveys—good news for them, and a good way, too, for Brown to make himself familiar in the community and get a feeling for which of his Black neighbors might want to help him in his great antislavery work to come.[4]

Already, some were becoming family friends, a visitor to their household would observe. In this same summer of 1849, the Boston lawyer and adventurer Richard Henry Dana Jr. went climbing in the Adirondacks, lost his way, and wound up, famished and exhausted, at Brown's small home, where he was calmly welcomed, fully fed, and introduced to "Mr. Jefferson and Mrs. Wait," Brown's Black friends and neighbors. Dana was an antislavery man but entirely unused to hearing white people address Black people so respectfully. And the next day, stopping by the Browns' to say goodbye before heading home to Boston, his amazement grew. Here were the white farm family and their new Black neighbors "all at the table together"—as if this were something usual, something everyday!—tucking into a feast of "meat, substantial and wholesome, large quantities of the best of milk, good bread & butter, Indian meal cakes & maple molasses." (Twenty-two years later in the *Atlantic*, the esteemed author of *Twelve Years before the Mast* recalled it in his essay "How We Met John Brown.")[5]

McCune Smith and Powell met more Black settlers at a prayer meeting at the North Elba inn and home of the venerable pioneer "good old Deacon Osgood," who (his deep-dyed Congregationalism notwithstanding) conducted the service according to Smith's own "Peterboro platform" of antislavery Bible politics. That was hopeful, and so was a visit to "Mr. Henderson, a shoe-maker from Troy, [who] had his sign hanging out (the first and only in the township) and appeared to drive a good business." The agent also saluted the homesteaders, unnamed, in Townships 11 and 10, "making the woods ring with the music of their axe strokes."[6]

But much more of McCune Smith's report spoke of failure and defeat. Samuel Drummond had dumped his wife and children and made a beeline back to the city. Benjamin Landrine, not finding water on his gift lot or a second one, had also backtracked "in despair." The city was a siren, and the grantees lacked the numbers and the confidence to resist it. "Could we get about 200 settlers in North Elba, and then cut off all communication with the city (burn the galleys) things could be made to prosper," the doctor sighed. A more remote frontier would have forced a commitment; the settlers would not have had a choice.[7]

Did McCune Smith meet more pioneers than these? They were certainly around. In "greater" Timbuctoo, the Hasbrook family from the

Lyman E. Eppes, North Elba. Photographer unknown, n.d. Courtesy Special Collections, Feinberg Library, SUNY Plattsburgh, NY.

Hudson Valley had settled in the shadow of South Mountain. Lyman Eppes from Troy, whose name and family would dominate reports of the Black Woods for another hundred years, had brought his clan to land just south of North Elba, and in his home (until they built their own) were the Dicksons, Henry and Hannah, an older couple also out of Troy. More Trojans, William and Eliza Carasaw and their three boys, were a brisk walk through the woods. Not yet arrived were the childless couple, Isaac and Jane Craig, who would trundle over from a tiny town in Jefferson County. (Of Smith's three thousand grantees, the Craigs were the only ones to find the Black Woods from points west.)[8]

Lewis Pierce, the self-emancipated slave who found his freedom in Philadelphia may have fixed on his chosen lot this early, and begun dropping trees for his new shoebox of a cabin in the Cascade district, and not far from Pierce, the grantee Tommy Brown, who bunked a while in the Cascade home of the early pioneer Robert Scott, might have started limbing trees on the lot that suited him much more the one he had been gifted. (And the so-called Tommy Brown lot was remembered long after the grantee had slipped from view. North Elbans were helping themselves to still-usable timber from his abandoned cabin as late as 1877.)[9]

What became of Tommy Brown? Or John and Margaret Vinson, who lived briefly with the Dicksons, or old Mrs. Wait, who worked as a live-in helper for the Browns? No surviving stories help us guess where they went next. In the summer of 1849, John Brown's son Owen labored with a grantee, Samuel "Pappa" Hall, to raise "a fine log house" near Timbuctoo. When Hall left and the house started to break down, John Brown urged other grantees to either occupy it or salvage saw boards before they rotted. The thrifty Yankee abhorred needless waste.[10]

A Distracted Witness

A modest colony now occupied the woods of Franklin to the north, where McCune Smith may have met John Thomas, parishioner of the doctor's early schoolmate, Henry Highland Garnet. Thomas, the Maryland grantee whose letter to Gerrit Smith revealed his many years in bondage, was on Lot 284, with Mary Ann, their boy Richard, six, and their baby, Charlotte Ann. Their potato patch was seeded, their fields tall with hay, and not far at all were other families, many also Southern-born and newly come from Troy. One was the Maryland-born William Moore, whose farmstead may have straddled the long stream that would take the name of Negro Brook. His grantee-neighbors, Perry Weeks and Wesley Murray, were Marylanders too. To John Thomas's northeast was the Virginia-born newsman-turned-pioneer Willis Hodges, now bunking with the youthful Morehouses, Stephen and Lura (or, census-depending, Laney or Lara), their young teen Warren, already enrolled in school, and his big sister, Jane. On the Essex County–Franklin County line was a homesteader-grantee from New York City, the aging widower Daniel Thompson, who got his deed when he was living in Elizabethtown, the Essex County seat.[11]

Duane, another of Franklin County's undersettled towns and closer to Malone to the north, was now home to the grantees Richard Willson and the Virginia-born Alexander Gordon, whose households expanded the Black Woods by twelve, or 5 percent of Duane's head count in 1850. In his memoir, Willis Hodges had claimed these Brooklyn pioneers for Blacksville (Duane's boundary with Franklin was maybe five miles west of Loon Lake). It seems Hodges understood the reach of his dispersed community in terms as generous as the scattered settlement of Timbuctoo. And these settlers, too, were squatting (Gerrit Smith gave away no land in Duane). Not by title but through labor would they claim their homes.[12]

But these settlers were not noted in McCune Smith's confiding letter. His anecdote about the shoemaker Henderson aside, he gave no details about new homes. He may have thought, *Why bother?* Anecdotes about a light scattering of pioneers hardly evidenced the avid, lush, migration Gerrit Smith wanted. And it was the land agent's unhappy task to let Smith know that if it hadn't happened yet, it likely wouldn't. No wonder McCune Smith waited six months after he was home before he sent Smith his report. He had delayed, he wrote, because of a personal calamity. His young daughter had died of a consuming illness on Christmas Eve. Smith himself had lost young children; the doctor knew he'd understand. But even if there weren't a family tragedy, this would have been a hard letter to write. Sixty pioneers! Set against the wished-for three thousand, the number was a travesty. The doctor sketched a hopeful scene, but the great ranks of the missing—the men who said they'd come, who hoped to come and bring their families, and didn't come—monopolized the view.[13]

If McCune Smith could have put aside his and Gerrit Smith's expectations and judged this modest influx on its own terms, for where it was and what it meant, he might have left the woods with better news. In a few years' time, a handful of all-white Adirondack hamlets had been integrated. White farmers in North Elba, St. Armand, Duane, and Franklin, whose sole acquaintance with Black Americans were the pranksters and buffoons they met in syndicated race columns in their newspapers, now schooled their children with the sons and daughters of Black neighbors. They learned these neighbors' names at the gristmill, and sang hymns with them in church. Years before, McCune Smith had told Gerrit Smith that he felt the only way white racism could be dislodged was by "mind-work," face to face, eye to eye, at so deep a place it would need to seem "molecular." Political or legal victories were not enough.

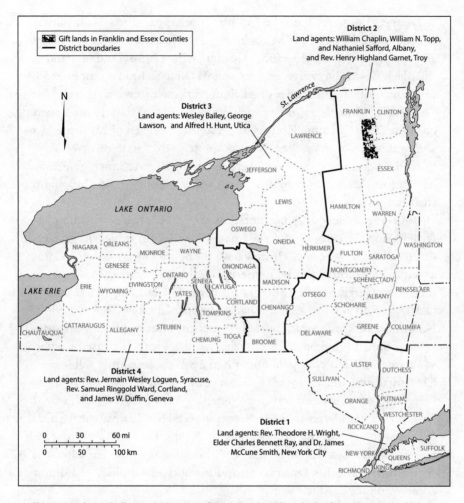

Gift lands in Franklin and Essex Counties
District boundaries

District 2
Land agents: William Chaplin, William N. Topp,
and Nathaniel Safford, Albany,
and Rev. Henry Highland Garnet, Troy

N

District 3
Land agents: Wesley Bailey, George
Lawson, and Alfred H. Hunt, Utica

District 4
Land agents: Rev. Jermain Wesley Loguen, Syracuse,
Rev. Samuel Ringgold Ward, Cortland,
and James W. Duffin, Geneva

District 1
Land agents: Rev. Theodore H. Wright,
Elder Charles Bennett Ray, and Dr. James
McCune Smith, New York City

This New York map indicates the location of Gerrit Smith's Adirondack gift land in Essex and Frank-lin Counties for Black New Yorkers; the four parts (districts) of New York where Smith's land agents scouted for grantees from 1846 to 1853; and the designated agents for each district. Map by Bill Nelson.

The very hearts of white people "needed to be changed, thoroughly, en-tirely, permanently changed." In the Black Woods, a world still evolving, still unfixed, was a stage intimate enough to let this happen. But this, McCune Smith couldn't see.[14]

The Things They Did Instead

The doctor's letter, which held the last thoughts he would care to share about the giveaway of 1846, revealed another blind spot too. While

McCune Smith took pains to explain to Smith just why *he* could not move his family to the Black Woods, he made no such effort for the deedholders. He judged their absence without examining the reasons for it. In his view, the settlers simply lacked confidence and courage to resist the blandishments of city life. In fact, the grantees had good reasons for not moving, reasons myriad enough to pack a volume. This is not that book. But if only for a few pages, we might consider what the grantees were doing instead of going on their gift land, lest we, too, be moved to dismiss them as mere no-shows who missed their chance.

Jonathan Mingo, a hardworking suffrage activist from Flushing in Long Island, was by Charles Ray's lights "one of the most enterprising of the grantees." This "sterling man and . . . excellent farmer" had signed up twenty men for gift deeds, and cared enough about his gift lot to visit it in 1847. When he found it down to fire-blackened stumps, he asked Smith for a new lot, which Smith provided. But Mingo's farm experience, so valued by Ray, was a double-sided flint: if it lit up Mingo's interest in his gift land, it also sparked his interest in better land out west. A web of trans-Appalachian railroad lines, steamship routes, and latitudinal canals now hitched the Atlantic Ocean to the Northwest Territory and beyond. Telegraph lines flanked railroad tracks, and wires sang with news of soil conditions, weather, land prices, and crop sales. In six days, Mingo could get from New York to anywhere in the nation except Texas and the far West. While race laws in western territories and states were daunting, their enforcement varied wildly from state to territory. As the geographer D. W. Meinig observes, the midcentury census revealed Black people living in almost every county in the country, proving that "exclusion laws were never fully effective." There was room for emigration if destinations were picked with care.[15]

In southern Michigan's Lenawee County just north of Ohio, land was low and lush, and the Quaker-founded antislavery community was long entrenched (and some of those old pioneers had come from Mingo's own Flushing). Sometime before 1850, Mingo's family moved to Lenawee's Raisin Township. Jonathan and his oldest boy found day work; the younger Mingos went to integrated schools. Next came Albion in Calhoun County, where Mingo got his farm. On his death in 1869, this "well known and highly esteemed" citizen was remembered by his minister as "a man of good judgment in business matters, unswervingly honest, and a devoted, consistent Christian." Four years later, the lane in Albion that ran along the family farm was named Mingo Street. It is there still.[16]

How many Smith grantees held out, like Mingo, for better opportunities? The minister and newspaper publisher Samuel Cornish chided Smith for not giving him a lot (had this agrarian not been urging Black New Yorkers to take up farming for decades?). But when he received his forty acres in Florence, Cornish did not occupy it but made instead for Johann Sutter's California mill race in the High Sierra, where the riverbanks were flecked with gold and all it took to make it yours was a pan, a pot, and a willow sieve. In 1849, the middle-aged reformer signed on with Black prospectors bound for Tuolumne County's Dragoon Gulch. Also sailing to the Gold Coast were Newport Henry, Jonas Townsend, Philip Bell, James M. Whitfield, and Edward Johnson, all "uplift" men of repute, and every one a Smith grantee. They had read about their fellow activist (and grantee) Reuben Ruby making $600 a month on the Stanislaus River, and the thirty-seven Black New Englanders, not a year in San Francisco, who each were pulling in $300 monthly. These Black Yankees had organized a welcoming committee and an aid group for just-arrived Black miners. Had anybody done this for the Adirondack pioneers? "This is the best place for Black folks on the globe," a Black prospector wrote his wife in 1852. "All a man has to do is work, and he will make money." What Black Adirondack settler could claim as much? Newport Henry and Jonas Townsend joined a mining group from New York City ("Whites are not admitted," the Adirondack *Essex County Reporter* marveled). On the ship, the *Hampden*, they sailed to California the same fall that McCune Smith and William Powell went to the Adirondacks to vet the Smith grantees.[17]

For a century after the giveaway, writers explaining the Black deedholders' rejection of their gift land cited inexperience, fear of hardship, and their horror of the unknown. But first-time mining was at least as new to Black grantees as farming, and as daunting as the Adirondack woods. All things being equal, and all hard work being hard, why not choose the work that promised the best return?

Self-interest, not its opposite, explains why so many did not come. And for New York City's working poor, the better part of self-interest was self-preservation. The biggest reason deedholders did not take up Smith's offer of an Adirondack farm was its unaffordability. McCune Smith knew this, and even hinted at it in his letter, noting that "as a general thing," the settlers "had not enough money at the outset." He could have stopped the sentence there, but then he went on to suggest they *might* have "made up the deficiency" if they had been better prepared for winter and if they hadn't "waited too long" for John Brown's team. His judgments missed the mark. A poor working man in New York City would need to pay one-third of his yearly wages for a team of oxen in this era.[18]

Like Gerrit Smith, the Black agents had never farmed, not for themselves. Some had worked (and slaved) on farms as children, but this was not the same. Their vision of husbandry spoke more of an ideological infatuation than a concern with budget, costs, and how to pace the building of a successful farm. In the Adirondack Experience Library is the memoir of Charles Wardner, whose father, James, had moved to Franklin from the Champlain Valley in the 1850s, westering as confidently as James's schoolteacher-father had hauled his family from Vermont across Lake Champlain fifty years before. Wardner's memoir suggests how much about this kind of removal a Yankee pioneer could take for granted. A move from one region to another could not be managed in one swoop. First had to come the walkabout, noting soil types, water sources, mast trees, and so on. The next visit was for clearing, burning slash, and yanking stumps. Planting, and the getting up of cabins, fences, and woodsheds, all came after. Friendly locals, eager for new neighbors, might point a prospect to a shanty he could borrow while he sized up the terrain. Cash poor he may have been, but James Wardner's eyes were rich in expertise. Southern Franklin County was land he knew how to read as closely as his Bible. High on a ridgeline with his brother on his third visit, he saw and claimed his future:

> Less than a half mile away to the south east of us, we could see one of the finest stands of hardwood timber I had ever seen. "There," I exclaimed to Seth, "is my future farm and where I want to build my home." "What makes you so sure of it?" Seth wanted to know. "That looks like a tamarack swamp between here and that piece of hard wood." "Where you find trees like those you also find good farming soil underneath them," I told him. "I shall build my house on that rise of ground near that bunch of virgin white pine." "But how about this swamp?" Seth asked. "You don't want that in your door yard, do you?" "Don't you see?" I argued. "We can build a dam on this stream and set the water back up here, to cover and make a lake of this entire swamp. See, there is a pond over to the right with an outlet flowing through the swamp and meeting this main stream right over there to your left. It couldn't be a better place."[19]

The downstate grantees could not amortize the steps of their migrations. A multistaged move was entirely beyond their means; it had to be one move or none. And more grantees than the farmer Jonathan Mingo understood this. Several "honest, industrious and sober" grantees from Little Falls could not wait to "go right upon the lands . . . and undertake the getting in of corn and potato crops," a friend of Gerrit Smith had written him. Then they reconsidered. Not inexperience but its opposite was what kept them from moving north.[20]

In May 1849, Gerrit Smith gave away another four thousand acres to one thousand needy white New Yorkers in forty-acre lots. And this time, as if to flag a recognition of the poverty whose depth he had underestimated in 1846, the philanthropist enclosed ten dollars with each deed, explaining, "Where the land is worth removing to, and where there is a disposition to remove to it, this money will help defray the expense of removal. In perhaps every case, it will be sufficient to pay the two or three years' taxes now due, and also the taxes for a number of years to come." But if Smith had learned a lesson from the hobbled progress of his giveaway, it would not help his Black grantees, and it wouldn't put white deedholders on their gift land either. Overwhelmingly, they, like his Black beneficiaries, were too disabled by the lack of capital to manage the migration.[21]

The Black grantees had taxes, too, and could have used a ten-dollar boost. But who among Smith's agents would suggest the extra gift? To imply that he had not done enough—free land for three thousand!— would rouse the specter of Black ingratitude, which, to the proud, scrupulously gracious agents, was anathema. So there would be no tap for help, no beggar's cup from McCune Smith, or from Frederick Douglass, who had written as boldly as he cared to about the settlers' disabling poverty in January 1849. Gerrit Smith had not solicited the input of his Black friends when he shaped his plan. It was formed when he unveiled it, its terms hard set. McCune Smith saw trouble all along and tried, early on, to brace his rich friend for disappointment. He wouldn't ask for more, not now, not after three years. It was time to walk away.[22]

Romance gave way to gritted pragmatism. No more sunny talk among the agents about moving to the woods. *Stay where you're needed, and fight the war at home.* There were nights Charles and Charlotte Ray put up as many as fourteen runaways, weeks when the freedom seekers flowed in and out of their home without a break. James McCune Smith had told Gerrit Smith that his reason for not moving to the country was economic: he would move, he claimed, "could I see the way clear for a livelihood for myself & the family"—and he couldn't. But a livelihood was just part of what city living gave him. At the Colored Orphan Asylum, he cared for children by the hundreds. He was needed. When white "progressives" trotted out their tired schemes to dispatch Black Americans to Africa (that bogey colonization, back from the dead), he drafted furious rebuttals for mass anticolonization meetings. *Needed.* Black children in the city perished at a disproportionately high rate, and his research was proving this. *Needed.* As much as a living wage kept him where he was, duty spoke as well. Charles Ray, Peter Vogelsang, George Downing, Charles Reason, James Pennington, William Wells Brown, James Gloucester, Alexander Crummell, Ulysses Vidal, Louis Bonaparte, John Zuille—these antislavery activists chose a "bustling anxious life" over their free land in the Black Woods for a reason. On isolated farms they could not do the good that city life enabled. The farmer's life might bring the ballots, but city activists would lose their stage of public uplift and resistance. In an era when everything from slave catchers to Jim Crow conspired to yank Northern Blacks out of sight, out of mind, they would surrender visibility. Was this a time to disappear?[23]

McCune Smith would not give up on the country life entirely. At an 1851 convention, he still pled for Black New Yorkers to get out of the city. But no more would he exalt the transformative soul-shaping power of the woods. "Country life is the better life for our people; not consolidated, isolated country life, but a well-mixed country and village life," he now believed. The trick was in the mix. Not just farms, but shops for carpenters and tailors and other businesses and workshops where Black people would not face exclusion "from general mechanical employment" or "white journeymen" who "refuse to work with us." The eager echo here of Florence was hard to miss, but the doctor left that vexed memory unnamed.[24]

CHAPTER 9

A Fluid Cartography

Gerrit Smith never mapped the gift land. Just getting every land grant inventoried in his *Land Book* was all the map he needed. We mapped it for the exhibition *Dreaming of Timbuctoo*, because we wanted to get a feeling for the reach of it, the long, checkered banner of his gift land unfurling south from Township 9 to 12. On taped-together survey maps of Franklin and Essex Counties, we matched each land grant to the forty-acre square (more or less) it claimed, three thousand squares each color-coded by the grantees' counties of origin so we could see where Westchester counties got land, where the Brooklynites were gifted, or where Yates County (cherry red) staked its turf. With fifty-nine counties and a color for each one, our checkerboard was outright gaudy. But this map, a simplified version of which is in the exhibition, breathed in letters, deeds, and notebooks only. A map of the Black Woods where Black settlers actually chose to live would be much harder to construct. This cartography was fluid. It ebbed and flowed, and hewed to its own rules. From the first time a grantee walked a gift lot and said, *Nope, not for me, I can do better*, the Black Woods edited Smith's paper dream.

Of course, Adirondack pioneers had always done this: improvised a better deal, traded legal lots for something better. Their property system, notes the cultural historian Karl Jacoby, was "based on . . . use and

occupation, in which lands that were unused were unneeded and therefore open to settlement by others." And the Black settlers followed suit.
They saw how white pioneers were rewarded with a legal title on easy
terms when they cleared wild land and farmed it, sweat equity trump-
ing the paper claim of an absentee landowner. The fact that a low-born,
hard-toiling squatter could expect the law to take his side against an
owner who left his land unworked was a marvel of the American republic. So, in keeping with the custom, most of the longer-lasting Black
homesteaders did not stick with land they were given. In Timbuctoo,
Freeman's Home, Blacksville, and Vermontville, they squatted. They
wanted acreage already clear, or with a sugar bush or springs, and, of
course, a sun-warmed exposure. They wanted better soil.[1]

And several of them found it. Though the giveaway's critics often
harped on the gift land's insufficiency (too thin, too stingy, never
meant for farming), stretches of it were rich and loamy. It was the
pinched-off growing season that made it moot. The "danger," as John
Brown's son Frederick wrote his brother Watson, "of your crops being cut off by frost or not having time to get them in before winter
is down on you like a brick." The soil might reach five fathoms deep
and the best of farmers could not wrest more out of it than a cellar
full of root vegetables, lady apples, and maybe enough wheat and rye
to just get by. The land, that is, had a way of offering much more than
it could pay, the burst of June promising what September never could
deliver. So it behooved a pioneer to pick with care. Mindful of the
homestead ethic of their white neighbors, the grantees held out for
their best chance.[2]

In North Elba, the Hendersons, Jeffersons, Carasaws, Wortses, Fraziers, Halls, Thompsons, and Browns all chose to farm on undeeded
land. And the upstate New York archaeologist Hadley Kruczek-Aaron,
who has dug extensively on Lyman Eppes's gift lot in the southwest
corner of Lot 84, Township 12, feels Eppes, too, very likely made his
farm not on but near his gift lot. The same held for Black pioneers in
Franklin who spurned their gift land for lots with better roads, fresher
water, congenial neighbors, or nearness to a mill. By 1850, members
of Willis Hodges's Loon Lake party were moving into cabins of their
own. Hodges eventually tucked in with the Morehouse family, whose
cabin (on undeeded land) would be the first of several Franklin homes.
From upstate Rensselaer and Saratoga Counties, the Morehouse
family—Stephen, his wife and their two children, Warren and Jane—might
have set up on their gift lot on the north end of Loon Lake if reaching it

were easier than moving to the moon. The home they made instead, in a cabin south of the lake (their roses marked the place for years), was more sensible. It flanked a road, and along the nearby north branch of the Saranac, enterprising Vermonters were turning an old farmhouse into a rustic inn they would call Hunter's Home. For grantees hoping occasionally to hire out, a sportsmen's hostel augured well. The More-houses all found work at inns and hotels in this district. (But the back-woods life was not for Jane. Early on, she pushed out of South Franklin to the county seat, Malone, married Henry Jones, a prosperous Black harness maker and church deacon, and made a long living in town as a nurse.)[3]

The shifting cartography of the Black Woods also reflected the tug of social networks and alliances, as grantees spurned their gift lots to build closer to old allies, friends, and relatives. Deedholders from the Hudson Valley stuck together, with the Hasbrooks taking in the Wortses on their arrival and then, in time, the Wortses boarding two of the Hasbrooks' teens, and the undeeded Fraziers settling not far off. Troy allegiances made neighbors of the Hendersons and Jeffersons, and cabinmates of the Dicksons and the Vinsons. Southern roots bound the Black households in the town of Franklin. Grantees from Brooklyn and Manhattan followed Willis Hodges to Blacksville. At the front end of migration, the shared memories of the home place, however ambiva-lent and far, offered a kind of comfort.[4]

And some darker dramas, unreported, drew new lines around the social map of Timbuctoo as well. Shortly after 1855, a midlife romance in the Black Woods led to the crack-up of one household and a new one blooming in its wake. After at least fourteen years of marriage, six of these in North Elba, Susan Hasbrook, mother of nine (three of them deceased), left Josiah to marry the grantee Lewis Pierce. And when Susan and the ex-slave from New Orleans headed to Manhattan, they brought with them Susan's three youngest, Sanford, Leonard, and five-year-old Jane. Leonard Worts, Pierce's sometime-hunting partner, took over Pierce's well-tended patch (and maybe bought his livestock, too).[5]

City life dealt roughly with Susan and her new husband. She and Lewis had to bring her three children to the Colored Orphan Asylum, where steady meals, medical attention, and some schooling could be assured. Not so their lasting health. Jane Hasbrook, Susan's five-year-old, did not survive the year. Leonard and Sanford, older, were two years in the orphanage before their mother pulled them out in 1858. The next year, Susan bore her second husband Lewis a child of their own, but Lucy Ann would never know her father well; he died when she was five.[6]

So Lucy Ann eventually explained in her 1913 appeal for a Civil War widow's pension—the sole source of information about the dissolution of her mother's marriage and her early life. Not observed are the circumstances of Lucy Ann's father's death in 1865. By 1860, Lewis and Susan were estranged, and Susan and her three children were living in a Ward 8 sublet with a barber's family and Susan's ex-spouse, Josiah. Susan, back to calling herself Hasbrook, was taking in wash. Her first husband waited tables. Was there to be a renewal of their vows? Why, then, were their names at such a stiff remove in the census?[7]

Vows would come, but not for Susan. By 1865 Josiah had a new bride, Caroline, and was living in Sag Harbor in a frame house with his two younger sons. Susan cropped up that year too, in a letter from North Elba. Reported Jane Thompson to Belle Brown (the young widow of Watson Brown): "Josy" Hasbrook, back from the war, had bought a farmhouse in North Elba, and now his mother was on her way back too. Homeward-bound to keep house for him, she'd written, and bringing, by the way, Josie's half-sister, Lucy Ann, and the baby daughter of his sister, Harriette. (Then Harriette came too.) Every time Private Hasbrook turned around another female was at the door, ready to pitch in.[8]

"So you can see J. is or will be in hot water," Jane Thompson declared. "We are sorry for Josy." It is a confidence so cryptic it fairly pains the reader with the hope of answers, all unknowable, to questions we can't ask. How the neighbors took it when Susan Hasbrook and Lewis Pierce up and left, for instance—were they grieved? Outraged? Sympathetic? Josiah and his two siblings who lingered in North Elba, bunking with the neighbors— How was it for them? Questions throng, but there's no outdistancing our too-few sources, which can seem to move with feet of clay.[9]

Three years later after his return from the South, Josiah married Jane Ann Hazzard, a sister of his army mate, Private Charles Henry Hazzard of St. Armand. The newlyweds (and everybody else) then moved to a farmhouse closer to North Elba village. Next to swell this youthful household were the newborn Stephen (Josiah and Jane Anne's first) and Hasbrook's war chum, the Virginia-born ex-slave and veteran of the Twenty-Sixth United States Colored Troops (USCT), Jeremiah Miles. Three young children in the house kept everybody on their toes, and undoubtedly, the farm and kitchen chores and washing overwhelmed.

But Susan Pierce's daughter Lucy Ann had no complaints. Decades later, trying to explain to the Pension Bureau the mystery of her surnames (why did she sometimes go by Hasbrook, and sometimes Pierce, and sometimes Miles?), Lucy Ann recalled those hectic years in her half brother's farmhouse with warmth. They shaped and stabilized her life.[10]

The Black Woods in Flux

Grantees who were all for living in the country, just not the unreconstructed sticks, also stretched the boundaries of the Black Woods when they migrated from the gift land to small towns nearby, or skipped the wilderness entirely, opting for a small town from the first. Sometimes the loss of a spouse forced a migration, or better access to day work, a family doctor, a dear friend. "High and dry" Elizabethtown, the county seat, "with a surplus of the purest of pure air and water, free from fogs, mosquitos, black flies and malaria" (this from the *Elizabethtown Post*), was blossoming into a popular and lovely town, and all around it mill towns were generating work. Lively Westport on Lake Champlain was a draw. Day work might be found at foundries, bloomeries, mills, and docks. The grantee Edward Weeks and his wife, Hannah, chose Westport over gift land in North Elba. So did a Troy grantee, William Brown, when the Keene surveyor, Wait Lewis, let him know that his hilly lot in Township 12 was "hardly worth paying taxes on" (a judgment that, for all of Lewis's uneasy reputation among the grantees, matched that of an expert Adirondack surveyor in 1804).[11]

Westport was the preference of the Smith grantee Joseph James, as well. In fact, it may have been the two gift lots Smith gave this skilled bloomer that enabled him to stay in Westport and buy his home from his employer in 1850 near the bloomery at Merriam's Forge. Joe's wife, Adeline, the daughter of white abolitionists from the neighboring village of Crown Point, was an herbalist who made house calls; and by the end of her long life, good enough at what she did to be described in her obituary as the "best nurse in the county." Both her and Joe's good jobs suggest why this couple opted not to start again in the unknown infant hamlet of North Elba. Raising a big interracial family in a working-class company village outside Westport had its challenges. But these the Jameses were prepared for. They stuck with what they knew.[12]

And so would the grantee George W. Bell, a Black farmer in Willsboro, a village north of Westport. In this live wire of a town, Bell could amplify his meager living by hiring out to shipyards, bloomeries, limestone quarries, and "coaling" sites (where colliers prepared charcoal for the ironworks). Bell, originally from the South, spurned his gift lot and stayed with his small family in Willsboro for thirty years, working his own farm and other people's fields.[13]

More Than Farms and Farming

The grantees left no aspect of Smith's vision for his gift lands unedited, unchanged. He wanted them to farm, and they did—and then did more. Some used their gift land to secure other land. The Jeffersons hired out as teamsters. Henderson fixed shoes. Lyman Eppes and two grantees' sons—Josiah Hasbrook from North Elba and Alexander Hazzard from St. Armand—were Adirondack guides. Alex Hazzard worked for the celebrated innkeeper Paul Smith. And while William and Eliza Carasaw farmed mainly for themselves, the family also worked a sugarbush that generated four hundred pounds of maple sugar for market. Black settlers picked up day work from their neighbors needing work crews. In the early twentieth century, old-timers in Newcomb, a crossroads hamlet south of North Elba, recalled "some of the colored out of the colony [who] used to go down through what is called Indian Pass through the mountains and work on farms. It is a very short distance by foot across the mountains, [but] 75 miles around by road." The same story rang a bell with the elderly caretaker of Camp Santanoni, an Adirondack Great Camp, who grew up hearing about long-ago Black work crews at Montgomery Clearing, between Moose Mountain and Newcomb Lake.[14]

In Franklin County to the north, Black arrivals adapted too. Their nearness to the fledgling wilderness resort scene got them day jobs as housekeepers, cooks, and guides. Early Adirondack hostelries like Hunter's Home at Loon Lake and its commodious and celebrated successor, Paul Smith's; Merrill's Inn in Merrillsville; and the more modest Rainbow Inn all hired Black settlers. Young Warren "Wash" Morehouse, son of the grantee Stephen Morehouse, was a "waiting man" in hotels on both sides of the Civil War, and camp cooked for hunting parties too (his slow-cooked, maple-syrup-smoky baked beans were in hot demand). The hotelier Paul Smith recalled with delight the woods-wise Wash bringing down a bevy of ruffed grouse with a few sure shots for a hunting party at Hunter's Home. Smith promised his guests that

Adirondack guides at hotel owner Paul Smith's boathouse. A. W. Durkee, photographer, 1884. Alexander Hazzard, brother of Charles Henry Hazzard and son of the grantee Avery and Margaret Hazzard, standing to left of second pillar from right. Courtesy of the Adirondack Research Room, Saranac Lake Free Library, Saranac Lake, NY.

his young employee was "as good as three niggers rolled into one" and would provide "an inexhaustible fund of merriment." He reveled in Morehouse's love of fancy words ("Now, doctors, what kind of tea do you diagnosticate upon today?"), even if the comedy of Morehouse's diction tells us less about the camp cook than it does about the reflexive condescension of his boss.[15]

But not every memory was smirking. Wash Morehouse was also "handy . . . useful . . . [possessed of] rollicking good humour . . . great muscular strength and agility," and was, overall, "a valuable addition to our party." Morehouse also made an impression on an English traveler, who made the Black cook one of the handful of locals he profiled in a piece about his trip to the region in 1860. Morehouse likely never knew it, but Londoners were reading all about him in a popular weekly journal, *All the Year Round*, which was published by Charles Dickens.[16]

There was other part-time work that Adirondack pioneers, white or Black, took on when farmwork slowed or failed. At midcentury, and within a day's wagon ride of Franklin and North Elba, were all the clangorous, unruly hamlets spawned and nurtured by the iron industry—sixty of them in the saddles of the wide Ausable Valley spanning Essex, Franklin, and Clinton Counties. Thanks to these rough boomtowns,

day work could be had. Farmers with a horse or two matched their labor to the season, splitting wood for the voracious forges in the winter,
chopping trees to open skid runs for the loggers. Maybe when they first
arrived, in the glow of all the hype, Black settlers dreamed of living off
the vaunted farm that subsidized and ran itself. But after a few seasons,
nobody was banking on Reverend Garnet's "perfect system of agrarianism" to keep the family clothed and fed.[17]

And no grantee better exemplified this frontier versatility than Lyman Eppes, even if this Troy farmer, the longest-lasting of the North
Elba grantee-settlers, was never really honored for it. In Adirondack written memory, he was singled out for one thing only: his friendship with
John Brown. In fact, his connection to the abolitionist—as confidante,
sometime employee, acolyte, and lifelong mourner—so dominates accounts of him that it can seem he had no life outside it. He did, and it
was rich. In North Elba, Eppes helped found a library, religious school,
and choir. He was a voter and a family man (six of his and Annie's eight
children survived infancy; seven of them were Adirondack born), a temperance zealot, and belonged, with his daughter Eva, to the town chapter
of the International Order of Good Templars. Relative to other newly
arrived subsistence farmers in his neighborhood, his farming was more
than creditable. No other neighbor in 1854, white or Black, raised such a
lot of corn, along with fifteen bushels of rye, twelve bushels of peas, and
three hundred bushels of turnips. The Eppeses' four cows made milk
enough for three hundred pounds of butter; their twelve sheep gave
the family thirty pounds of wool. During the Civil War, he expanded
his production on the eighty acres on Bear Cub Road he purchased
from John Brown's daughter and son-in-law, and this he worked for
thirty years, only moving to the village when he could not manage a
team.[18]

The Lake Placid historian Mary MacKenzie confidently credited
Eppes's farm skill to his free-born father, a Pequod Indian in Colchester, Connecticut, but his mother, long enslaved, likely had farming
skills as well. Kate, or Candace Eppes had Lyman in 1815 when she
was forty-one. By the letter of state law, her baby was born free. If Lyman's mother was enslaved when he was born, however (a fair assumption since Connecticut only got around to abolishing slavery in 1848),
state law would still compel Lyman to work wageless for his mother's
enslaver until he was twenty-one. New London County in Connecticut
was the greatest slaveholding pocket in colonial New England, with the
most enslaved people and the highest number of Black residents. Yet

Colchester itself offered Black youths an unlikely and much-valued asset. In 1800, a woodworker turned philanthropist, Pierpont Bacon, endowed a town academy and a village "Negro School." Bacon, an enslaver, wanted to ease the transition of ex-slaves' children in the slaveless age to come. By the time Lyman Eppes was old enough to attend, Bacon's Negro School was drawing applicants from all over Connecticut. Was this where young Lyman learned his cursive and gained his regard for literacy? In North Elba, all of his and Annie's children went to school.[19]

What distinguished Eppes's Adirondack chapter, however, was neither his zest for education nor his prowess with a hoe, but his range. He made the Adirondacks work for him not because he farmed, but because of all he did when he didn't farm. When city sports and adventure seekers craved the best fishing hole, highest outlook, whitest falls, Eppes guided them; he cut the first trail through Indian Pass. He had an eye for property, making purchases over the years and managing an absentee grantee's lot in Franklin County. His letter in *Frederick Douglass' Paper* on the surging price of Adirondack lumber in 1854 suggests a shrewd feel for emerging markets: "A few years since, lumber contractors could get standard logs delivered on the banks of the Saranac for thirty-four cents apiece; now the same command nine shillings." Eppes urged grantees to keep their gift land for its future value (as had his friend John Brown, who, too, had stressed "the importance of saving as much as consistent the spruce timber in North Elba"). Eppes also hired out as a house builder—hence the signature he scratched into an attic beam in John Brown's home.[20]

And Eppes hunted. Wolves were a favored target; a neighbor would recall how much Eppes did "to rid the Adirondacks of that pest" (headlines honored him and a white neighbor when they tracked and shot a wolf in 1865). And when there was money to be earned as a teamster or a music teacher, Eppes took it on—and was "a very excellent teacher," according to John Brown's daughter Ruth.[21]

Eppes and other grantees who compounded farming with other kinds of work stretched the giveaway's ambition. Not all expansion in this other map, a living map, was topographical. It could be aspirational as well.

Gift Land without Gifts

The dynamism of our human map gained, too, from the arrival of *non*deedholders seeking an integrated rural community. John and Mary Brown's family was the best known of these, and William Appo of Philadelphia we have met. But there were more. The Frazier, Vinson, and Brady families, all deedless, were welcomed by grantees. The Delaware-born Mary Bailey, who came to Franklin with the Bradys (and may have been a Brady too) would eventually marry the grantee's son Alex Hazzard. Between the deeded families and those without was no hierarchy, no divide. If being gifted with a deed suggested a virtual community when the giveaway was announced, once Black families were in the woods, what bound them wasn't paper. It was skin. For their white neighbors made no distinction between the deed-bearing "Gerrit N—— s" and the others. To the bigot, all dark faces were equally offending. To the unbigoted, what newcomers chiefly signified was the promise of more hands and help on the frontier.[22]

And just as lines faded fast between grantees and pioneers without portfolio, so would distinctions between free and fugitive be little labored over, notwithstanding Smith's emphasis on gift land for Black New Yorkers (free people) only. But then, what else could he have said? To publicly encourage Black freedom seekers to the gift land would rouse a storm of fury from the proslavery press, and, worse, prick up the interest of bounty hunters, which could imperil his grantees. If, on the other hand, fugitives were to quietly arrive in the Black Woods on their own steam, well, that could not be held against him.

So the lines were fuzzed from the beginning—blurred and shifting here as they were across the nation. Grantees who were free New Yorkers brought aging parents with them who were once enslaved, and in these Adirondack households in proudly "free" northern New York, slavery remained a tangible fact of life. Survivors of enslavement carried lasting proof of trauma into the heart of the Black Woods. When young Lyman Epps Jr. saw scars on the back of his grandmother in North Elba, the vivid sight stuck fast. Sally Henderson, born in Virginia in 1770, also joined her son James's family in Timbuctoo, and she, too, was likely once enslaved. The grantee-settler Thomas Jefferson and his wife, Jane, were enslaved decades before they got their land, as were the late parents of the giftee Josiah Hasbrook in the Hudson River Valley. In Franklin, the southern origins of James Brady, Mary Elizabeth Bailey, and the grantee Wesley Murray hint at earlier enslavement, and Louisa Brady's first years as a slave are noted in her 1894 obituary. Her friend and neighbor, the farmer John Thomas, was a fugitive. John Brown's family housed the young fugitive Cyrus Thomas for a spell. Little wonder local memory early on embraced the notion that the giveaway was

made for fugitives. It was not. But it was, anyway. In every nook and corner of the Black Woods, slavery was as near as an elderly Black neighbor
peeling apples on her stoop, as lasting as the sight of Candace Eppes's
welted spine.[23]

A Sleepless Law, a Colder World

After the passage of the 1850 Fugitive Slave Act, this sense of slavery's
at-handness quickened. What did freedom mean when half the nation
regarded fugitives as self-stolen property? How strong was the divide?
In his own eyes, the grantee John Thomas was free, but to his old Maryland enslaver he was a marketable commodity gone AWOL, never mind
a ten-year residency in New York. And if he was property, then his free-
born children, too, as the property of property, could be Merrick's to
reclaim as well.

Thus, politics, in 1850, would also influence the map of the Black
Woods, and not for the more vibrant. Smith grantees viewed the unknown Adirondacks with unease even before the Slave Act was enacted.
Reverend Loguen had furnished names of friendly contacts in several
Adirondack towns, but how loyal might white strangers be when the
new law outlawed any effort to defend a Black person said to be a fugitive? Help a runaway, defy a slave catcher, and a white Adirondacker
faced a $1,000 fine and six months in jail. Fail to help a federally ap-
pointed slave catcher pursue a suspect, he broke the new law too. Track
a fugitive, on the other hand, and a poor local could make some badly
needed money. The grantees had already been told to keep an eye on
profiteering surveyors and mercenary guides. This new Slave Act only
multiplied the risks. Local whites resentful of the gift land were now
armed with legislation that rationalized the harassment or pursuit of
anybody with dark skin.[24]

No wonder some prospective Adirondack pioneers, like Dennis and
Phillis Washington, lost heart. Self-freed slaves from Kentucky living
in Michigan, these out-of-staters did not qualify for a Smith gift deed,
but what they read in their Ann Arbor abolition paper about Smith's
"scheme of justice and benevolence" in 1846 electrified them, and, poor
as they were, they put down money on Adirondack land. Then Congress
passed the Slave Act, and that was the end of that. No Black American
dared build a life in this Negrophobic republic, declared Dennis Washington in the *Voice of the Fugitive* in 1852: "Emigration from the United
States is absolutely necessary as long as the Fugitive Slave law exists."

Far from the Adirondacks, in Chatham, Canada West, he and Phillis made their next start.[25]

Was this their first choice? It was, they felt, their only choice, and one to which they were likely urged by another fugitive, Henry Bibb. A few years before he moved to Canada, Bibb published an unflinchingly graphic account of his years in and out of bondage. His oratory and autobiography, detailing five escapes and numerous recaptures, took the antislavery world by storm, and in the same spirit with which Gerrit Smith welcomed Douglass to New York with a gift deed, Smith gave Henry Bibb free land. The grateful activist wrote Smith that he had often dreamed of a farm where he "could get a living for my famley," and in 1849, he told the *North Star* that moving on the "land which has been so generously given" was a prospect "far better than gold or silver." With the passage of the Slave Act, however, this happy prospect dimmed. Like the Washingtons, the Bibbs moved to Canada. And so did the fugitive Walter Hawkins, a Florence Colony pioneer who moved his family to Ontario, and never would regret it, but well recalled his sorrow when he fled his just-built Florence home.[26]

William Jones, a slave-born congregant of Henry Highland Garnet, expressed no fear of slave catchers when he spoke to Troy grantees in 1848 about removing to his gift lot. But when the 1850 law put Black New Yorkers, slave born and otherwise, at risk of enslavement, when it denied suspect fugitives recourse to a jury trial or the right to testify on their own behalf, Jones's prospects changed. The shared destiny of the enslaved southern millions and the now free-in-name-only Black citizens of the North was not news that broke with the passage of the Fugitive Slave Act (kidnappers and slave dealers had been stalking free Black Northerners since the first years of the republic). It was the 1850 law, however, that ripped up the illusion of government protection for Northern Blacks and compelled the recognition of a common cause with three million slaves.[27]

The world was colder, and the stakes were huge. If the new law clarified the bond between free and enslaved African Americans and hastened the maturation of the Underground Railroad, it also tightened the connection between slave owners and their Northern defenders, especially those bankers, lawyers, merchants, and manufacturers determined to keep the machinery of a slavery-driven economy well oiled and efficient. In New York City, the proslavery Union Safety Committee drummed up $25,000 to cover the expense of enforcing the act and funding the reconnaissance of slave hunters. Businessmen in Albany and Troy also defended slave owners against any threat to their shared interests. Almost 90 percent of the 330 fugitives arrested in Northern states from 1850 to 1860 were reenslaved. Along New York river valleys and water routes on either side of the Adirondack region, Black people made for the border to the north, as many as 3,000 lighting down on "Freedom's Soil" within three months of the Slave Act's passage. The flood was epic, unprecedented, and unstoppable. Church congregations picked up and migrated en masse. In Douglass's Rochester, the departure of a Kentucky-born pastor was followed by the exodus of all but two of his 114 congregants. At the urging of their minister, 130 members of a Baptist church in Buffalo went to Canada. Even before the law was signed, several hundred Black Pittsburghers made for Canada, armed and ready to do battle with any party that might presume to interfere. In a few weeks' time, Cincinnati lost almost all of its 300 Black hotel waiters. In Columbia, Pennsylvania, 450 Black people—more than half that city's Black population—headed north.[28]

Might not the Adirondack region have seemed safer for its remoteness? If this ever was the case, it wasn't after 1850. The New York–based American Anti-slavery Society documented every kidnapping attempt it learned of. Bounty hunters were tracking fugitives to rural hamlets and drowsy county seats all over: Dayville, Connecticut; Cedarville, Cumminsville, and New Athens, Ohio; and Byberry, Coatsville, and Christiana, Pennsylvania, among them. Harrison Williams, a teenage runaway from Virginia, was milking a cow in Busti Corners, Chautauqua County, New York, when slave catchers found him. Bound and thrust into a wagon, he was hauled to Buffalo. His employer, William Storum (a Smith grantee), tried to intervene, but Williams was reenslaved.[29]

Moses Viney, a self-freed slave and Smith grantee, glimpsed his old enslaver at a Schenectady hotel just after the new law was passed. Did he make for his gift land? Viney was twenty-two when he escaped from the Maryland tobacco farm where he was Richard Murphy's butler, the "pet slave" of the house. In slaveless Schenectady he'd found a fine job as valet to Eliphalet Nott, president of Union College. The antislavery Nott hoped to persuade Viney's enslaver to let him be, but Murphy would not be deterred. And when Viney heard this, he may have wondered, *If President Nott can't stop this man, how would I fare in the Adirondacks, where I have no friends at all?* Viney went to Canada, as would John Van Pelt and his family when slave catchers showed up in Glens Falls looking for his wife, a self-freed slave. Like Moses Viney,

Van Pelt had a gift lot in the Adirondacks, but if the "blackbirders" came this far, they might well push farther north. He and his family made for the border, fast.[30]

The new law was a game changer for the giveaway's promoters, too. Those who felt themselves to be at risk went to Canada. Jermain Loguen was half a year away from his Syracuse home. Samuel Ringgold Ward went from Canada to Britain, and from there to Jamaica, and he never did come back to the United States. In New York City, Ray and McCune Smith, who had always put up fugitives, harbored more. It is, of course, impossible to know how many grantees who hoped to move to Essex or Franklin Counties changed their minds because of the new legislation or, for that matter, whether any of the Black settlers read it as a reason to get out, go to Canada, play it safe. Some may have felt, *We're so close to Canada anyway—why bother?* But those of Smith's grantees who were still, as far as they knew, regarded by long-ago enslavers as self-stolen goods well knew that the difference between the Smith Lands and Canada was no longer measurable in miles alone.[31]

The Phantom Map

As much as the Black Woods was a work in progress, always shifting, revising its cartography, it was never so chimerical that it didn't leave a mark. Place names inspired by Smith's giveaway endured for generations after grantees left. The name of Blacksville, conceived by Willis Hodges, would not outlast his use of it, but his name clings to Hodges Hill in Franklin County northeast of Loon Lake and to Hodges Bay below. To the south in Essex County, Craig Brook recalls the vanished cabin of Isaac and Jane Craig; as late as 1907, North Elbans were picking apples from the Craigs' gnarled trees. The pond named for the Craigs' neighbor, the "fighting" Silas Frazier, kept its name thirty years after his death. North Elba children living in the Cascade Pass along today's Route 73 played in the abandoned "Tommy Brown lot" well into the Depression, generations after the man himself was gone.[32]

In these ways, local memory pays a debt to this lost history where biography, historical signage, and regional history turn away. Freeman's Home in the Cascade district outlived the Black grantees who furnished its name by a century, and even the state botanist's 1889 monograph on North Elba plants recalled "Freemans Home" for its prolific cranberries and Sweet William ("introduced and cultivated for ornament but sometimes escaping from gardens and front yards"), which kept blooming long after grantees had left. A year later in the *Troy Times*, a Glens Falls publisher, C. H. Possons, called it Freedomville. But local memory kept it straight. In his Lake Placid history of 1946, Arthur Hayes reported stagecoaches stopping at Freeman's Home just after "Keene Cascade," and as late as 1965, a Keene physician recalled poking around Freeman's Home when he was young: "Negro settlements comprised the whole area of Cascade and the surrounding territory. . . . In rambling around I have run across several of their little plots of land, and old log cabins—decayed logs with stones in the corner. One of those cabins was back of Bushy's filling station. There was one on the bob run road [Bobsled Run Lane] near the bridge, one on the grounds of North Country School, and one in the woods back of Goff's house."[33]

The toponymic origins of the tiny hamlet of Ray Brook also invite a speculative suggestion. Town chronicler Mary MacKenzie believed the name of this North Elba hamlet honored an early white homesteader, Daniel Ray, who ventured here in 1810, drifting away seven years later. But Ray Brook doesn't crop up on maps until the 1870s, more than half a century after Daniel Ray moved on. The agent Charles Bennett Ray visited Essex County in 1849, and with Dr. McCune Smith parceled out some thirty deeds for lots near Ray Brook to people in Brooklyn and Manhattan. At least two grantees from Manhattan, Samuel Drummond and Samuel F. Hall, settled—or took a stab at settling—close to Ray Brook. Is it not imaginable that they or other Black pioneers named this place for Charles Bennett Ray, the giveaway's great friend? In the spring of 1903, both the *Plattsburgh Republican* and the *Elizabethtown Post* offered the suggestion that "a man named Ray acted as Smith's agent in New York City, and that Ray Brook, the site of the state Tuberculosis Hospital between Saranac Lake and Lake Placid, is probably named after him."[34]

Racist place names recalled the giveaway as well. In 1871, a Vermont-published tourist map of the Adirondack region showed a Negro Brook (or "N—— Brook," to many locals) just west of Vermontville and southeast of Rainbow Lake. According to James Wardner, father of the Franklin memoirist Charles Wardner, this wide brook took its name from Black pioneers who were encouraged to develop farms along its banks by the St. Armand guide and farmer Ahaz Hayes. The problem with this explanation is that at midcentury, Ahaz was a baby. But someone gave the grantees a start here, even if the town historians never took their names and stories. The name white neighbors gave the settlement itself hung on for more than a century, and it is said the onions the Black settlers planted by the brook waved their bright green wands for years.[35]

To the south of Negro Brook, near Averyville, was the "N—— Clearing" some old-timers were still talking about as late as the mid-twentieth century. Hunters, especially, recalled stories of a "forest hideout" where, it was offered, John Brown secreted fugitives. Rumor had it that a party of these unfortunates ran out of supplies during a bitterly cold winter, and, as "less and less food was brought to them [and] the game became harder to trap, cut off from their friends and deserted by Brown, they died one by one. And there they lie in a neat row of graves"—this from a Lake Placid sportswriter in March 1944. (Apparently these accommodating martyrs, though blizzard bound and starving, still managed to dig their graves in the dead of winter, carve their headstones, get themselves into their graves, and install their headstones too.) Later, in the spring, this columnist resolved to find these graves, "dig 'em up . . . as soon as the snow and ice goes," and unearth the "buried booty from some unlawful raid. . . . Want to come along?"[36]

Would that early mapmakers' interest in the homes of Black Adirondackers was as robust as the local memory for racist place names. Black settlers' names crop up on midcentury town maps of Franklin and St. Armand, but in North Elba, a mid-nineteenth-century map of this community omitted them entirely. Even the town historian Mary MacKenzie was unsettled. To another history buff she mused in 1994, "Did it ever occur to you as very odd that French's map of 1858 showed not one name or house of a black colonist? This despite the fact that several of the families remained here into the 1860s and even the 1870s. Was French a racist?" (John Homer French was a New York mapmaker who organized the first comprehensive statewide map and created the still-used 752-page state gazetteer.) Not the refusal of credit or insurance, but this blithe erasure of cartographic visibility—what was this if not redlining before redlining had a name?[37]

We can thank no mapmaker for our knowledge of Timbuctoo but we know it existed because John Brown, his son, and the grantee James H. Henderson reference it in letters—John Brown writing to Willis Hodges, his son John (who spelled Timbuctoo with two *o*'s) in a letter to his mother, and Henderson in a letter to his former pastor, Henry Highland Garnet. No airy symbol or mere idea, Timbuctoo marked a *place*. Some used it to signify just the enclave where three families put up homes. John Brown's "Timbucto" ranged wider; for him, it seemed to reference about a dozen Black North Elban households, not just the early three.[38]

Who gave it this name in the first place? The even-weighted, slow-stepping syllables of this elegiac word still evoke the mystery of the ancient kingdom-city on the Niger. But even the scholar Caleb McDaniel, who has parsed this riddle with Talmudic rigor, concedes we may never know who gets naming rights for this community. When Gerrit Smith alluded to the best known of his Black settlements, he described it merely as his "little colored colony." The Black agents recognized the Black enclaves only by the numbered townships that contained them; they never named the settlements themselves. Richard Henry Dana, recalling John Brown's old neighborhood, did not name Timbuctoo. Nor did Seneca Ray Stoddard, the artist-writer whose impression of the North Elba colony made such a mark on public memory.[39]

Casual toponymy recalls what history forgets—except for the unmapped Timbuctoo. Here it's the opposite: history recalls what toponymy has forgotten. Partly this was the doing of the Adirondack historian Alfred Donaldson, whose mirthful sketch of a jerry-built shantytown littered with small square huts from which "little stovepipes protruded at varying angles," distinguished by a "last touch of pure negroism . . . a large but dilapidated red flag . . . bearing the half-humorous, half-pathetic legend, 'Timbuctoo,'" captivated generations of journalists and scholars. Mary MacKenzie, the town historian who first documented North Elba's Black community in the early 1970s, despaired of Donaldson's influence. Timbuctoo, she felt, was a label John Brown slapped on the settlement to distinguish it from Willis Hodges's Blacksville, and one that locals mocked. Timbuctoo—that's how out-of-place and far from home were the "Gerrit N—— s" here. Timbuctoo—where Black Americans belonged, in Africa, across the sea. She loathed the name, felt it demeaned. But would an insult strain for delicacy? Until Governor Mario Cuomo outlawed racist place names in New York in 1988, all the Adirondacks was amply salted with N—— Hills, Brooks, and Points. MacKenzie gave naming rights to John Brown because he loved history and Timbuctoo reflected this great passion, and she could not think who else *but* Brown would know this name, or register its value.[40]

Let me offer some suggestions. "Perhaps no foreign name, thanks to the rhyme of 'hymn-book-too,'—is better known in America . . . than Timbucktoo," declared the *Hartford Courant* in 1879. But Black activists in New York were reading about Timbuctoo much earlier than this. *Freedom's Journal*, the nation's first Black newspaper, ran dispatches on European forays into sub-Saharan Africa as early as 1827, and speculation about the far-famed Timbuctoo (also Timbuktu, Tombucktoo, and Tambouctou) was rife. And never mind if this once commercial capital of the Mandingo and Songhai empires, renowned for its architecture, university, royal court, and libraries (eighty of them), blessed by the sweetness of its water, envied for the gold ingots in its treasury (as heavy, one traveler reported, as one thousand English pounds), was, by the early nineteenth century, three centuries past its prime. Fantasists were not discouraged. Observes Sanche de Gramont in *The Strong Brown God*, "Timbuctu the powerful became Timbuctu the mysterious. Its reputation, embellished beyond all measure, fired the imagination of explorers and poets"—and Black reformer-editors in the United States. The legendary crossroads for a thousand caravans bearing fine cloths, salt, and gold was a catalyst for Black orientalist fantasy no less than white.[41]

In 1827 alone, *Freedom's Journal* published nine articles on African exploration, culture, and geography. It noted the Scots adventurer Alexander Gordon Laing's doomed bid to penetrate Timbuctoo in 1826 (he was discovered and beheaded). It tracked the better-favored efforts of the Frenchman René Caillié in 1828, who survived his visit only because he learned Arabic and garbed himself as a trader. That year was also when the self-freed slave Prince Abdoul Rahahman introduced a great many Americans to slavery through his lectures. The grandson of the king of Timbuctoo, Rahahman was leading a war party when he was captured and delivered to British slave traders in 1788. Sold to a farmer in Natchez, Louisiana, he worked forty years on a plantation, raised a family, and never did stop yearning for his ancestral home. With the help of allies like Secretary of State Henry Clay, Rahahman won his freedom. A speaking tour to raise funds to free his African family took him to eight Northern cities. He wore royal robes, recited from the Koran, and reminisced about the world he left behind. His Timbuctoo, *Freedom's Journal* reported, was "probably as large as New York," "a place of great business," "extremely fertile," rich in coffee, seamed with gold, and studded with walled towns. If white subscribers to the *New York Journal of Commerce* thrilled to Rahahman's reports for reasons more mercenary than culturally enthralled (here was an enormous territory traversed by a marvelously navigable river fairly leaping to be harnessed to American extractive interests), the Timbuctoo that roused the interest of Black reformers was a symbol of Black economic self-sufficiency, political independence, military prowess, and unassailability. Little wonder that in 1828, *Freedom's Journal* ran thirteen features on the "Prince of Timbuctoo."[42]

This African American portrait of Timbuctoo did not lack for irony; among Christian abolitionists, the real Timbuctoo may have roused unease. It was Muslim. Its natives were polygamous. Its slave trade was robust. The most willful reading of the map would never get Timbuctoo near the Land of Cush, "Blameless Aethiopia," or (another darling of Black Africanophiles) Pharaonic Egypt. But if Henry Garnet never named Timbuctoo when he rhapsodized about Black America's debt to Africa, Ethiopia, or "Egypt, Africa's dark browed queen," it hardly mattered. Notes Wilson Jeremiah Moses in *Afrotopia*, "It was an exotic and heady brew of contradictory ideas that invigorated the Afrocentrism of those decades. . . . Christian, Jewish, classical and Germanic mythologies were combined in the making of an image of Africa suitable to the needs of Westernized Africans"—and nineteenth-century Afrocentrism had a gift for inclusivity. What Rahahman's Timbuctoo signified was not a slave economy but a legacy of independence, not a violent xenophobia but a tradition of self-reliance and a quality of urbanism. Timbuctoo was civilized. Its attractive layout, robust markets, famed literacy, and schools were a match for any city in the West.[43]

From 1837 until it folded in late 1841, the *Colored American* published thirty articles on Africa; references to Timbuctoo abounded. Black upstate reformers learned about Timbuctoo (Tomboktu) in William Desborough Cooley's *The Negroland of the Arabs Examined and Explained* (1841), and in the antislavery reformer Wilson Armistead's tome, *Tribute for the Negro* (1848), packed with the Moorish explorer Leo Africanus's bold impressions of Timbuctoo from the 1500s. Black activists could ponder "The Interior of Africa" in the *Albany Patriot*, or "The Progress of Discovery in Central Africa" in the antislavery *National Era*. In 1848, Reverend Henry Highland Garnet introduced the Black women of Troy, New York, to his idealized ancient Africa, home of the queen of Sheba.[44]

But Timbuctoo had another meaning in this era. To Black and white Americans, it also meant an outpost grievously forsaken, out of reach, irredeemably obscure. So maybe, as Caleb McDaniel muses, white North Elbans who didn't care for Smith's ideas or his beneficiaries *were* the ones to gift the enclave with a name they deemed a slur, and then "defiant Black settlers . . . repurposed [it and] made the name their own." If so, it wouldn't last. When the Hendersons and Jeffersons left their big lot, the name left with them, and it would not be revived until 1921 when the Adirondack historian Alfred Donaldson used it to denote the settlement at large. Or maybe it *was* Brown who named the enclave. Or those of Smith's Black agents or subagents who read and wrote for antislavery papers, which might mean, really, any one of them. Ray. McCune Smith. Ward. Pennington. Garnet. Especially Garnet, with his fierce passion for African history and culture.[45]

A gold mining enclave called Timbuctoo in Yuba County, California, emerged around the same time as North Elba's. In Burlington County, New Jersey, a Timbuctoo was on the ground almost thirty years before Smith launched his giveaway. Might these have inspired the North Elban model? Called "Tombucktoo" in early deeds and legal documents, the name of the New Jersey settlement employed the spelling of early French explorers and cartographers but was dropped for "Timbuctoo," maybe because the latter was a better fit for Anglophones. And this Timbuctoo took off! Bearing the ancient name was not just the settlement itself but its A.M.E. Zion Church, its school, and its burial ground. By 1860, this Timbuctoo was 125 people strong. In 1883, forty-four children were enrolled in Timbuctoo School District, No. 33.[46]

All of which is to suggest how lushly Timbuctoo flourished in the Black American imagination before Gerrit Smith dreamed up his plan. Settlements were named for it. Editors reported on it. And mostly it meant something good, owned a resonance, a luster. It claimed an ancestral patrimony to a city, never seen, and a devotion to a name that still inspired. It invoked an idea of Africa much as white Americans honored Old World hubs of industry and culture when they named frontier outposts after (sticking just to upstate New York) Rome, Syracuse, Amsterdam, Lisbon, Potsdam, and Florence. And it tweaked and tugged the cultural geography of the Black Woods beyond anything Smith had imagined. It said, Not *that* Timbuctoo, but *this* one. In a green galaxy of towns and hamlets named for white men and their worlds, it said, *This* one's ours.

Chapter 10

We Who Are Here Can See and Know

In 1854, Lyman Eppes was six years in North Elba, time enough to find the best high ledge for sighting whitetails and learn how to tell the difference between a buck's bed and a doe's. But six years was not enough to give Eppes the eyes to see what had gone missing. By midcentury, the once prolific Adirondack beaver (estimated at one million in 1600) faced extinction. Wolves were more memory than threat, and moose largely dispersed. Lynx, wolverines, and fishers were sighted only rarely. Salmon were getting scarce. Dams and mills had slowed stretches of the Saranac and Ausable Rivers from their wild gallop to a crawl.

Deer, on the other hand, now facing fewer predators, were bearing up pretty well in Eppes's part of Essex County, and as long as the *illusion* of abundant Adirondack wildlife saturated dispatches from the region and brought sportsmen by the coach full, Eppes could not complain. Excursionists found Squire Osgood's venerable inn south of the Old Military Road. Robert Scott's home on the Cascade Pass took in hunters too. For part-time guides like Lyman Eppes, the influx of eager outdoorsmen was nothing but good news.[1]

On Christmas Day in 1854, the Eppeses and their neighbors, white and Black, gathered for a wild game dinner. The hunter who furnished some of it was Lyme Eppes Jr., nine years old and already a crack shot.

Lyme Jr. had a younger sister, Albertine, whose twin died in infancy when Lyme was a toddler, and undoubtedly, this loss blighted the young family's first seasons in the woods. But more babies had since joined the clan, and in 1853, the household gained again. Now savoring her second Adirondack Christmas was Candace Eppes, Lyman's octogenarian mother, the former slave from southern Connecticut. So many grandchildren to keep track of, all of them taking to this life like loons to lake water, and her Lyman and his Annie—did they ever take a breath? In addition to readying the land for seed, managing the animals, and guiding for the "sports," Lyman was dropping trees in his woodlot and hauling logs to market. He had civic duties too. He served as North Elba's inspector of elections (an unimaginable prospect in the Connecticut village of his youth).[2]

Other welcome gains: North Elba had a post office, a wood-frame common school, and churches. There were new rules too, and you didn't want to break them. If anybody's dog bit or hounded your sheep, they got fined, and you, too, risked a fine for spearing trout, or hunting deer out of season. (But if you killed a wolf or panther, the county gave you twenty dollars!) There was a new road out of North Elba clear to Wilmington, a plank road that ran from Franklin Falls to Lake Champlain, and a path, finally, from Bear Cub Road to the Eppeses' farm. Railroad spurs were needling toward the hem of the frontier, and ever since Adirondack rivers had been legally defined as New York "highways," lumberjacks were skidding logs and hacking out clearings. This was never very pretty work, but when slash slumped to brush and clearings greened to glades, everybody gained—deer hunters, the innkeepers who put them up, the farmers who provisioned them, the camp cooks who brewed their coffee, the guides who led them to their quarry, and the day hires in the camps, laundries, and hotels.[3]

The Eppeses' social world was richer too. By 1855, Avery Hazzard's family was installed in their St. Armand farm, only a few miles to the north. William Appo, the Philadelphia musician, was spending more time in his North Elba home, and while the eminent performer was socially a world apart from Lyman Eppes, they had in common a fierce devotion to the Browns, their love of music, their political literacy, and perhaps some overlapping memories from past lives in New York City and Troy. Also new to North Elba: a childless couple from Ulster County, Silas and Jane Frazier, who, after a year or two on their plot on Averyville Road, could report some seventy bushels of oats, two tons of hay, and six bushels of wheat. To the north of Freeman's Home, the solitary pioneer Lewis Pierce was working his new lot with all the zeal one might expect from the man who, in 1848, strode into a Philadelphia courthouse and clinched his own emancipation. And new Black faces were in Franklin too; three generations of the Brady family now claimed Vermontville as their home.

Hard Losses, Deep-Felt

But big losses still kept pace with these gains, and the Eppeses registered them all. John Brown had planned to give more time to his farm and Black neighbors after his return from Europe in the fall of 1849. But the business trip that was supposed to fix his economic woes did not. He failed to interest English brokers in buying wool from a consortium of New England sheep farmers, and as a consequence he and his Ohio business partner, Simon Perkins, found themselves $40,000 in the red. So full-time living in North Elba was out; he could not both live in Timbuctoo and hope to salvage his and Perkins's troubled enterprise. He would need to shuttle between Perkins's farm in Akron, Ohio, the warehouse in Springfield, and offices in Virginia, Pennsylvania, and Ohio, to settle his accounts. Adirondack farming would fall to his wife and children and the Brown's young hired hand, Cyrus Thomas, a family friend and formerly a slave.[4]

Some sweet interludes would brighten this long, rather stressful spell. In September 1850, Brown witnessed the marriage of his daughter Ruth to her young neighbor, Henry Thompson, and at the Essex County Fair, Brown's calves and oxen took nine awards in six categories, an achievement notable enough to earn a nod in the *Essex County Republican*. The new farmer on the scene would be praised for bringing "improved stock" to the region, and for "his public spirit and enterprise." But by September 18, 1850, when the Fugitive Slave Act was passed, Brown was back in Springfield, meeting with the city's many Black abolitionists and calling for an antislavery militia he named the League of Gileadites, a secret fraternity bound by oath to drive slave catchers from the city. Half a year later, Brown and the better part of his big family had returned to their rented home in Akron. Only the newly married Ruth remained in the Black Woods. Except for Ruth, and a few fleeting visits from her father, North Elba would not see the rest of this big family for three years. Brown's Black neighbors had grown accustomed to Brown's here-and-gone appearances, but the wholesale removal of his family was a loss.[5]

Then, in the winter of 1852, the Black Woods absorbed a new blow when Timbuctoo's energetic shoemaker James H. Henderson perished in a blizzard. It happened just a few days before Christmas. Henderson was visiting a neighbor, the abolitionist schoolteacher Gilman Fay, when the snow outside began to thicken. Fay implored the shoemaker to spend the night. But back home was Henderson's wife Susan, their children, and his octogenarian mother. They would be watching for him and getting worried. He stepped out.[6]

In a squall as thick as this, stars hid themselves, and familiar landmarks too. A white wind tossed the flakes in all directions. Henderson, unmoored, may have taken comfort in the thought of John Brown, who, a few winters earlier, had also been caught short on a long hike home in heavy weather, and became badly chilled and very tired, but persevered and made out fine, still had his toes and fingers. The idea, Henderson well understood, was not to panic, let the shivering shake out the cold, keep the head clear, eyes on the compass—no easy thing at night. He took a seat on a tree stump to ponder his next move. Then he dozed, and hypothermia slowed his heart, and stopped it. He was half a mile from home. John Fay, son of the schoolteacher who saw him last, reported, "He had torn his compass to pieces, become tired, sleepy and foggy, and he was sitting in what the searchers called a peaceful sleep."[7]

As Adirondack ways of dying went, this was far from the worst, but it yanked a strong bright thread out of the fabric of Henderson's community, and it showed. The Black Woods needed James H. Henderson. If John Brown was an advocate and friend, Henderson was something more, a watchman and defender. When Smith and Douglass promoted their big-talking surveyor, Wait Lewis, it was Henderson, the cobbler, who declared the white man to be as crooked as a dog's hind leg. When Smith would not back a Liberty-Whig coalition to help Black suffrage at the polls, Henderson signed the letter that implored him to reconsider. While Smith's advocates indulged fine fantasies about a "glorious dawn of civilization," Henderson learned and shared the price of oats. He paid his taxes, stepped up to serve as a town inspector of elections, hung a shingle blazoning his trade in the heart of the frontier, and dressed his home in good milled lumber. A man of grit, and sudden as a March squall, stilled.[8]

As for his wife and children and his mother, Sally—what were their prospects now? Their oldest boy was hardly big enough to swing a hatchet. Their closest neighbors, the Jeffersons, were no great help. No sooner were their cabins up than one of them returned to Troy and the other moved to Westport. Henderson, who was renting land from them, was increasingly uneasy and, as early as the late 1840s, looked to Gerrit Smith for reassurance:

> I have heard that one of them [Samuel or Thomas Jefferson] intends to sell the Lot if he can. I know that he has tried to do so and he has not said anything to me. I would like to have the lot and if you would let me . . . , I will be thankful for it, and will make my payments regular. . . . I have worked the farm this season, and . . . I would not like to lose my house and improvements. They [the Jeffersons] have not said anything to me that they intend to sell the lot, but I have seen them that want to buy the lot, and think that if the lot is to be sold, I ought to have it as I live on it.[9]

Clearly, Henderson was caught short. To maybe lose his neighbors, and on top of this to suspect they might sell his land from under him and leave his family unhoused, was horrifying. But no response from Gerrit Smith is recorded in Smith's letter book; his priorities were elsewhere. As Henderson's white neighbors had hinted, he had bigger worries in this season than a grantee's five-acre farm that wasn't even on his gift land. No time to quell a tempest this minute while he was running a congressional campaign, and maybe, too, Smith doubted Henderson's ability to make payments on a contract. Whatever the case, on Henderson's death, his young family was left with a patch to which they held no title, and no grown man to work it.

Susan Henderson might have brought her family to the county home, an airless building mobbed with paupers, many of whom were alcoholic or spoke no English, and who were permitted to mingle indiscriminately—old, young, foreign, native born, men, women, sane, demented, peaceable, and violent. In a place like this, would her small boys, *Black* boys, be safe? And how could she ask another household to take in all her children, or invite another family into her house when she could not know her home was hers?[10]

So back to New York the widow went with all her brood in tow. She found work as a nurse in the city's Colored Orphan Asylum, where she was able to install all six children and deduct their three-dollar monthly boarding fee from her own pay. This institution had long accepted "half-orphans" whose single working parents could not raise their little ones at home. Some of these inmates were the children of Smith grantees. The grantee's wife Susan Hasbrook had lodged a daughter and two sons in the orphanage when she went back to New York City. So would the grantees Samuel Drummond, Abraham Caldwell, and William Smith. It could not have escaped the notice of the asylum's founder, Anna Shotwell, that James Henderson's surviving family came to her establishment only a few years after Shotwell had asked Gerrit Smith to consider gift lots for her teenaged boys who hoped to farm. Smith had declined.[11]

Susan Henderson was lucky on two counts. Most single parents were limited to visits of four hours a month. Because she worked where her children lived, she could see them with some frequency, and doubtless counted this a blessing. And it may have helped that the staff was mindful of her losses. "Father found dead in forest December 19th 1851," the intake report offered. "A man of an excellent character, he was a shoemaker by trade, and resided on his little farm given to him by Mr. G. Smith the Colored Man's friend." But sympathy would bend no rules. From ages ten or twelve until twenty-one, her children might be indentured, likely to people outside the city. Finding ways to visit them was going to be hard.[12]

At least while they were on site, the children could count on schooling, clean clothes, Bible study, and, from Dr. McCune Smith, vaccines. But this was still a toxic city for poor Black children, as she well knew. In 1841, she and James had lost their firstborn son in infancy. In Troy and then in Timbuctoo, they had raised their little ones in health. Back again in Manhattan, Susan's streak of good luck failed. Three of her six youngsters died: the baby Susan and five-year-old Benjamin very soon after they came to the orphanage, and thirteen-year-old James, her eldest, ten days after he was released in 1855. Charles would stay in the asylum five years, and Joseph and Sylvester four, before their mother could take them back.[13]

Blacksville and the Franklin Pioneers also lost a charismatic leader at midcentury. In 1851, Willis Hodges left Stephen Morehouse's household and returned to New York City, and while he never spelled out why, some reasons do suggest themselves. His little colony at Loon Lake had failed to flourish. His good friend and adviser, John Brown, had moved away, and most of Brown's family, too. And Hodges's family's situation in Virginia had been violently disrupted. In 1851, a lawyer had convinced Willis's widowed mother and his brother Charles to sell the Hodgeses' family farm and move away rather than contend with hostile neighbors. Far from Virginia, in William Hodges's Brooklyn home, the lawyer argued, the family would be relieved of its tax burden and finally reunited. In time, the Hodges family would determine that this attorney was a swindler, and after the Civil War, they took him to court. In 1851, however, they were sufficiently intimidated to migrate to New York. Willis, always loyal to his family, likely left Loon Lake to help William get the family settled in.[14]

And while he may have visited the Black Woods, he never went to stay. In Brooklyn, the longtime bachelor met another emigrant from Virginia's Princess Anne County, and in 1853, he and Sarah Ann Corprew Gray married. The next year, Hodges was ordained as a minister in Brooklyn's Apostolic Church. He kept in touch with John Brown (and the fact that his wife was moved to burn most of their correspondence after Brown was seized at Harpers Ferry suggests it held more evidence of Hodges's knowledge of Brown's plans than was safe). Hodges also, in this antebellum decade, resumed his suffrage work and fervent advocacy for more public schools for Black children. But there would be no more urging Smith grantees to the Black Woods, and no talk of Gerrit Smith, at least not until Smith's run for governor in 1858. Then, and with feeling, the Hodges brothers would offer up their thoughts.

The Grantee Points a Finger

In 1854, the year that the newly married Willis Hodges was setting up in Brooklyn and John Brown had moved back to Essex County only to decide, once again, to leave it, the farmer Lyman Eppes discovered that some of Gerrit Smith's downstate friends were planning an event in North Elba, "a contemplated celebration . . . in honor of Gerrit Smith's benevolence in the matter of lands donated to our colored brethren."

Eppes was vexed. Stretching from Eppes's farm in all directions was a wilderness, much of it the property of thousands of Black New Yorkers, hardly any of whom were here. Smith had pitched the giveaway seven years before. Where were the "sable-armed pioneer[s]" bound to make the North Woods ring with "the noise of falling trees"? What was there to celebrate? Would it not "be far more wise in us, as well as more pleasant to our honorable friend," Eppes asked the *North Star*, "if, instead of making a vain show, spending our time and means, we should so husband those means as to be able to settle on those lands, or otherwise make them available in securing a homestead for ourselves and for our children after us?"[15]

If Eppes didn't name the organizers of the proposed event, he could guess who they were. Reverend Garnet was living in Jamaica, doing mission work with his wife, Julia. The city agents McCune Smith and Ray were the only two positioned to make something like this happen. And the gulf between their agents' notion of what was good for the Black settlement and Eppes's own now seemed as wide as the divide between Timbuctoo and Brooklyn. "I wish to say there are some lands in this country (in the vicinity of the Saranac) densely covered with beautiful pine lumber," Eppes wrote the *North Star* in 1854. "As the demand for this lumber increases, and as the supply is becoming scarce, these lands are rapidly increasing in value." Had Smith's city agents informed the grantees about the rising price of lumber since Reverend Loguen visited in 1848? Had anyone reminded the grantees about the tax sales of 1852? Did they understand that unless they paid their taxes "within two years from the day of sale," fast approaching this December, they would lose their land forever, and that, as gallingly, "those who bid them in [would] realize from what they term 'Nigger Lands' handsome fortunes"? Surely, Eppes suggested, Gerrit Smith would deem an all-out effort to alert the grantees to the need to hold on to their land more useful than some costly commemoration![16]

"Deeds and services, rather than . . . vain show and empty declamation"—that's what Black New Yorkers needed, Eppes declared. As James Henderson had told Reverend Garnet years before, "We who are here can see and know." Smith's Black agents, who were not there and did not know, had failed to do their job. "It seems to me, Mr. Editor," Eppes wrote, "that were the grantees apprised of the fact that these lands are very valuable, and still increasing in value, they certainly would redeem them.—I take this method to inform them of these facts." (A letter to a Black newspaper was the one method available to a farmer in North Elba; the agents may have known others.) But then, Smith's agents, conjectured Eppes, had "most probably" let their land go for taxes along with everybody else. They were done with it. They'd given up. That is how it seemed to him.[17]

Farm your land, log it, save it for speculative uses down the road—it little mattered to the pioneer. *Just don't lose it.* And this was not about some sentimental agrarian ideal or a notion that the alchemy of rural living would transform Black and white neighbors into equal citizens and friends (in Eppes's mention of what his white neighbors called "Nigger Lands" was cold intelligence indeed). This concerned the market. The state law of 1846 that made the Saranac River a public highway for saw logs had driven up the price of the standing timber on the riverbanks. Lumber merchants had taken note. Back in Troy, Eppes may have been drawn to North Elba by the dream of a self-sustaining freehold, but that old dream had found the market. Adirondack forests had gained value. Woodlot owners stood to profit. To this pioneer, the glory of an Adirondack freehold was no romantic abstraction but as real as the big logs bucking down the river to the mills.[18]

In October 1854, McCune Smith and Ray answered Eppes's letter in the *North Star* with a circular, "To Gerrit Smith Grantees: Redeem Your Lands!!" Dispatched to Black churchmen all over New York who were urged to read it to their congregants for three consecutive October Sundays, the circular reminded the grantees that those lots sold for taxes due in 1849 might still be reclaimed in the last months of 1854. All a deedholder had to do to redeem his lot was to figure out his debt and pay it. "This done, your Land is saved," the agents promised, "and the men who haven't bought it, and are eager for it, and who are hoping that you will not redeem it, are defeated." Grantees could write the state comptroller or get help from the land agents. And at the urging, maybe, of Eppes's letter, this flyer stressed good reasons to hold on to gift land beyond the hope of a farm, such as new roads that would increase land values and the emerging market for good saw wood.[19]

This was not the first tax sale of the grantees' land. The redemption period after land was sold for unpaid taxes was a roomy two and a half years. A grantee who had registered his deed in 1846 did not have to pay his taxes until late 1848, and if he missed that deadline and his land was claimed in the tax sale of 1849, he still had two years to redeem his property and get the purchase canceled. Hence the urgency of these land agents' eleventh-hour appeal. For grantees who had failed to pay taxes for five years or so, 1854 was the end of the line.

Douglass Turns His Back

Frederick Douglass printed Eppes's letter. He did not offer his support. Years before, he shared his misgivings about the giveaway, and by 1853 his concerns had only grown. That year, Harriet Beecher Stowe, the world-renowned author of *Uncle Tom's Cabin*, tapped him for ideas about projects she might fund that could lift the lot of free Black Americans. *Anything but a Black farm project*, he told her. Homesteading would never work for Black families, notwithstanding the brave hope of that "prince of good men, Gerrit Smith." Husbandry, such a "noble and ennobling occupation," might be a "remedy for the evils of poverty and ignorance among us," but what good was a remedy when it could "not be applied"? Smith's failed effort proved that Black people were city stuck: "From some cause or other . . . [they] will endure any amount of hardship and privation rather than separate and go into the country."[20]

Douglass still acknowledged the fateful impact of undercapitalization on the giveaway, but something else, worse even than a lack of

Frederick Douglass. Photographer unknown, 1856. National Portrait Gallery, Smithsonian Institution.

funding, now cooled his view of Smith's idea. The big issue, he believed, was lack of faith, confidence, and will. "Slavery, more than all things else," he wrote,

> robs its victims of self-reliance. To go into the western wilderness [and here Douglass meant not just the Smith Lands but all of the great frontier] and there to lay the foundation of future Society, requires more of that important quality than a life of slavery has left on us. . . . The Black man (unlike the Indian) likes civilization. He does not make very great progress in civilization himself, but he likes to be in the midst of it, and prefers to share its most galling evils, to encountering barbarism. The dread of isolation—the lack of adventurous spirit—and the thought of seeming to desert their "brethren in bonds," are a powerful and perpetual check upon all schemes of colonization, which look to the removal of the colored people.

Generations of enslavement had robbed them of the habit of initiative, and the wilderness would not restore it. Whatever power Douglass once invested in the wilderness to work an awakening of Black manhood, he now disavowed. All a Black man could expect from the wild woods was loneliness and terror. White men might manage it; Black men, no. (Yet, oddly, in June 1854, Douglass's paper ran an excerpt from S. H. Hammond's *Hills, Lakes, and Forest Streams*, a rhapsodic Adirondack travelogue that extolled the very wildness and isolation that purportedly paralyzed Douglass's Black readers with fear.)[21]

There were other points the influential editor might have made. He might have noted that for the grantees, an "adventurous spirit" was a luxury; that their preference for the city stemmed from a stern assessment of their means and the relative safety they felt in urban communities (especially after the passage of the Fugitive Slave Act); and that four centuries of forced labor on white-ruled fields tinged the thought of farming with an enduring dread. He also might have called to mind a piece from his own paper by his activist-poet friend Joseph C. Holly. In 1851, Holly had offered tough ideas on how to harness white philanthropy to Black advantage. First would need to come the public recognition of centuries-deep white privilege at the expense of Black advancement. If "our friends" would only understand this simple economic truth, Holly felt, they would find much to do for colored people "besides expressing their abhorrence of slavery and disapprobation of prejudice." With the capital and resources that white Americans had accrued along routes of economic gain "from which we have been al-most entirely excluded," white people were positioned to reward Black initiative with the preemptive means to become mechanics, merchants, professionals, *and farmers.* The American Colonization Society had done as much for Black Americans looking to move to Africa. Why not a so-ciety that underwrote Black enterprise at home, and not with charity but with investment strategies that allowed Black farmers to, say, repay startup loans for stock and tools "when their success enable[d] them"? Holly was a Smith grantee. He revered Gerrit Smith enough to write a poem about him; the *North Star* had published it. But admiration would not soften the analysis. Was preemptive capitalization exactly what was missing from the Adirondack plan?[22]

Douglass himself had said much the same in his own newspaper in 1849. Insufficient startup funding had brought Smith's project to its knees, he wrote. Stowe's offer to invest in a Black initiative was an occasion to correct this. Though much of the Smith land had been taken and resold by the state for back taxes, a great many deedholders still retained their deeds. Fresh funding might encourage prospective farmers to make the move, and cover tools and taxes for those already farming. But Douglass would not invoke the cost of structural white racism. Instead, in his note to Stowe, he censured Black people, who, "from some cause or another," were stuck, and needed, more than any-thing, job training in the "mechanic arts." Not free farms they would not use (though the "zeal, industry, perseverance and self-reliance" of some Eppesian exceptions were acknowledged), and not schools for the profes-sions (why read law if nobody hired Black lawyers? why read for divinity if it could not make a living?), but an industrial college "where colored youth can be instructed to use their hands as well as their heads. . . . At this moment, I can more easily get my son into a lawyer's office to study law than I can into a blacksmith's shop. . . . We must build, as well as live in houses—we must make, as well as use furniture—we must construct bridges, as well as pass over them. . . . We need workers in iron, wood, clay, and in leather." No more "barbarism" in the woods! Prac-tical, well organized, closely administered, a trade school could meet a range of needs. Its curricula would balance agricultural training on a community campus with trade craft in small cottage industries. Its alumni would disprove "the injurious opinion of our natural inferior-ity" with living proof. The Black worker's "usefulness to Society" would be made plain as he "fasten[ed] himself to our countrymen through their everyday and cardinal wants."[23]

Well into 1855, Douglass flogged this notion, and the more he colored in the dream, the more confident his tone. Call the place the American Industrial School—a good solid name! Place it within one hundred miles of Erie, Pennsylvania. Make the budget a hefty $30,000, two-thirds in common stock, $10 a share. Douglass would be the agent stateside. Stowe could pass the hat abroad. McCune Smith might be trustee. Take the plan to the Black reform community, convention-goers, pundits; put a notice in his newspaper, and investors would sign on in force.[24]

That, anyway, was the idea. But while Douglass's plan won plaudits from Scotland to California, and a why-not shrug from Horace Greeley's *Tribune*, many urban Black reformers (Willis Hodges, Philip Bell, James Duffin, and Charles Lenox Remond, among them) were unmoved. How far would agents need to travel for support? How could this school be self-sustaining? If Black men would not take their families to free land in the Adirondacks, why would any of them *leave* their families to go to school so far from their homes? And why invest so much in one initiative that would graduate so few, rather than underwrite apprenticeships in up-and-running Black-owned workshops or, for that matter, at Black farms?[25]

Smith's giveaway was not explicitly a part of the debate, but its function as a cautionary tale was plain. No more big plans like Gerrit Smith's unless they were sure to thrive. No high-aiming failures, wrote Peter Clark in Cincinnati's *Herald of Freedom* (echoing, ironically, Douglass himself, who, in the first issue of the *North Star* in 1847, had quietly warned, "Our race must be vindicated from the embarrassing implications resulting from former non-success"). Clark, a Black educator in Ohio, believed Douglass's trade school plan was bound to fail, not because Black Americans were innately unambitious but because they had been made "apathetic . . . from the repeated failures of the high-wrought plans which their leaders have presented for their adoption. Forgetting the materials with which they must work, and the resources upon which they must rely, they [the leaders] have looked upon the enterprises of the whites, and laying their plans of the same scale . . . have called on an ignorant, poverty-stricken, and divided people to accomplish this work." Was there ever a "high-wrought plan" that dramatized this "failure" as succinctly as a bid to seed the Adirondacks with Black pioneers?[26]

Clark was a rising star on the Black convention circuit, and James McCune Smith, who took up Douglass's plan for a school with the zeal he had brought to enlisting Smith grantees, resented Clark's suggestion that Black leaders were to blame for the failure of bold initiatives. Under his pen name, "Communipaw," McCune Smith shot back: *Leaders? What leaders?* "As essential to the idea of 'leaders' in relation to any people," he wrote, "is the assumption that said people can be led. We have no 'leaders among the common people.'" Black men of "public spirit" enjoy about as much influence with "the masses . . . as children sitting in the markets and calling unto their fellows and saying, We have piped unto you, and ye have not danced." Why, it was practically "molecular," this "repulsion" between Black "leaders" and "the masses," the doctor fumed. Look what happens when a Black tradesman sets up shop "in a colored neighborhood; he will find that his brethren so far from supporting him . . . will, on the contrary, pass his door to trade with the whites." Look how Black people treat their ministers, he continued—not one in the land is paid what he deserves. No wonder Black reformers move to England or Canada, sick of the "blame and ridicule" of their own people. Black "men of public spirit . . . zealous for the advancement of the down-trodden . . . alas! . . . have never had the masses to support them, nor even to give an approving cheer or God's speed to their well-meant efforts."[27]

It was not the first time the frustrated physician had lit into a recalcitrant Black underclass. In 1846, he wondered whether Gerrit Smith was ready for the "cold ingratitude of colored men" whose "wealth-worship" made them mock those who defied it. More disappointment showed in his letter to Smith of February 6, 1850, when he reflected on the grantee-pioneers' too-quick retreat to New York City. But those complaints were made in confidence. In *Frederick Douglass' Paper*, what McCune Smith had to say about the rift between a Black political elite and the unschooled, working-class majority he called "the masses" was for anyone to read. And anyone would not. Hence his evident frustration: he was preaching to a converted Black elite. The "masses" either couldn't read Black newspapers or simply wouldn't care. Peter Clark blamed Black leaders for "'forgetting the [human] materials' with which they must work," when, claimed the doctor, it was the wary and distracted masses who rejected *them*.[28]

Nothing came of Douglass's trade school. By 1855, two years after the project was cautiously endorsed at a meagerly attended Black political convention in Rochester, Douglass had yet to raise a penny, and Harriet Beecher Stowe was on to other things. But for the purposes of our story, the debate among leading Black reformers over Douglass's

hard-argued project offered some important news. It glimpsed significant mistrust in Black leadership, a retreat from Black agrarianism, and
a tacit disavowal of the "scheme of justice and benevolence" from 1846.
Far from forgotten in this conversation, Smith's initiative was in active
disrepute.

Mr. Smith Goes to Washington

Eppes was surely troubled by Frederick Douglass's disavowal of Black
agrarianism in his newspaper. These words from a once-faithful ally
could do the Black Woods no good. But the aforementioned rumor of
a "contemplated celebration" was the news that provoked his letter to
the editor in July, 1854. What the farmer may not have considered was
that the celebration that seemed so off the mark (and that never came
to pass) was probably conceived less to honor Smith's philanthropy
than to console and divert "Nature's Nobleman" in the dog days of his
congressional career.[29]

A perennial candidate for office on a range of third-party tickets (if
always with reluctance, and at other people's urging), Smith ran four
times for president, three times for governor, once for the US Senate,
and again for the state assembly, losing every time. With wry wonder an
Albany friend observed, "There is no doubt of one fact, that no man in
the State, will draw to an audience so many approving listeners, and then
get so few of their votes, as you." But central New York's loathing for the
two-year-old federal Fugitive Slave Act swept the candidate into Congress
on the Free Soil ticket in 1852, and come winter, the country radical went
to Washington. The hosannas were downright giddy. Smith's victory was
deemed "but a beginning!" (Horace Greeley), "the greatest victory for the
cause of humanity (if not in the world) that has been gained since the
American Revolution" (John Brown), "among the most extraordinary
political events of this most extraordinary age" (William Lloyd Garrison),
and the herald of "a new era" in civil rights reform (Frederick Douglass).[30]

Smith's hopes were high as well. That first rancorous session, he
waded stoutly into every controversy of the hour. Tolling out the oratory in his lovely bell-toned voice, he spoke on temperance, Hungary's
freedom fighters, a federal war school, and always, and for hours, slavery. But while the 219 legislators (78 Southerners among them) who
Smith invited to his spirits-free Washington home freely ceded his like-
ability and warmth, these qualities won his hard-line antislavery position no new friends. Smith's gift for making a connection, his talent

for calling up a bond that cut through differences of faith, class, race, and politics, worked no magic here. The *New York Times* nailed it early on: "Mr. Smith will probably enjoy the personal respect of all . . . , but after the first curiosity which may wait upon his appearance . . . shall be satisfied, he will have less influence upon many of the great interests of the country, than the veriest cipher." While Smith's speeches (which, anthologized, ran to over four hundred pages) were noted for their eloquence, they hardly mattered when nobody was listening. Persuasion was impossible when the lines were so hard-fixed. Congressional debate, with its asphyxiating clouds of cigar smoke and eruptive curses, drunken taunts, and fistfights, was, by 1852, largely performative.[31]

Smith did make an impression, though, but not for what he hoped. A rumor that he had skipped a vote on the Kansas-Nebraska Act whipped up outrage among Whigs and radical abolitionists alike. This sly piece of proslavery legislation from the Illinois Democrat Stephen A. Douglas dispensed with the balance-keeping Missouri Compromise of 1820 and authorized settlers in Kansas and Nebraska to use majority rule to determine slavery's territorial admissibility. Smith and the Northern abolitionists saw the act as part of an "atrocious plot" that would bend the nation to "the yoke of a slave-holding despotism." But when Smith and five other "Ultra-ists" (a derisive term for radical abolitionists) published their concerns in advance of a congressional debate, they were charged with trying to preempt it and called spoilers and naïfs. And what better evidence of their incapacity for politics than Greeley's insistence in the *Tribune* that Smith missed the Kansas-Nebraska vote because it came at a late hour and Smith, good man of steady habits, preferred to be in bed? Even after the *Congressional Record* showed that Greeley had it wrong, Whig papers painted Smith as an amateur unfit for realpolitik.[32]

Particularly hurtful was the outrage of some Black abolitionists, Smith's longtime allies, who, Smith felt, had been "befooled and bewitched by the Whig press." Had one baseless rumor driven all his work from memory? For a quarter of a century Smith had labored for racial justice. In Washington, he had secured the emancipation of twenty-five enslaved people, and these but a fraction of the freedom seekers he had aided over the years from his Peterboro home. "'A lie well stuck to' can overcome almost any truth," he despaired. "These plaguy Whigs are the ruin of me!—they have taken all the wind out of my abolition sails!" Even the Garrisonians were against him. When he treated Southern lawmakers with his usual (and helpless) cordiality, they were appalled.[33]

With still half a year left in his two-year term, Smith returned to Peterboro. Abolitionist friends were disappointed, and critics would call his foray into politics a failure—he wasn't tough enough; he couldn't take the heat. It is true Smith wielded no great influence, but he was himself profoundly influenced by his congressional adventure, and it might be argued that the change in Smith would change the course of history. He left Congress, he wrote Frederick Douglass's readers, bereft of any "hope of the bloodless termination of American slavery" through political means. Congress would do nothing for the enslaved millions. Smith returned to Peterboro not chastened but more resolute, and prepared for harder measures. This was not flight but reengagement. At home, at his desk, he could bring his words and deeds to the Jerry Level of utility. Home was where he did the work that mattered, and where the terms were his to set.[34]

His Black agents understood this. Hence the idea of a reception, an event to welcome his return. Though Smith's brush with politics was "unlucky," they wanted him to know their loyalty. But Lyman Eppes was having none of it. Let them show Gerrit Smith their love by finishing what they had started. *Get the grantees up here! Get them to their land!*

Deeds for Votes: A Belated Vindication

In fact, numberless grantees were supporting Smith's idea, but not with the hoes and hatchets Eppes was looking for. Their chosen tools were far from view. From 1849 to 1854, past-due bank notes from grantees packed the canvas-bound ledgers of the New York state comptroller, and many of these weren't covering these deedholders' back taxes. They covered neighbors, friends, and relatives. These notes trickled in from Brooklyn, Troy, and Manhattan, and also from Painted Post, Schoharie, Peekskill, Westport, and Ghent. A paper drama to be sure, but in these records is evidence of abiding interest in the gift land, of deals struck and tacit collaborations, fathers spelling sons, brothers stepping in for brothers, and wives and widows sending money in their husbands' stead.[35]

These proxy payments were made for many reasons, not all of them self-evident. Did John Tappan of Steuben County pay Samuel Mann's back taxes to help Mann or himself? Was McCune Smith doing the antislavery lecturer Henry Bibb a good turn when he redeemed his lot while Bibb was in Canada, or hoping to add it to his own holdings?

Several of Gerrit Smith's Black agents paid back taxes on lots not their own. Charles Ray paid taxes on or redeemed Adirondack properties at least sixty times from the late 1840s through the 1850s. Nonagents who had long endorsed the giveaway, such as the wealthy restaurateur George T. Downing, the printer-teacher John J. Zuille, and the seaman's advocate and innkeeper William P. Powell, tracked the tax sales and picked up gift lots at cheap rates.[36]

In many cases, surely, these redemptions were driven by a concern with suffrage justice, and a desire to help poor Black New Yorkers retain the proof of ownership they required to claim the right to vote. But there is another explanation for these quiet interventions. As the cultural geographer D. W. Meinig has observed, all over the mid-nineteenth-century United States, the settlement process was "suffused in speculation," and if you had the money and the price was right, you bit. Gerrit Smith's secretary and land agent, Caleb Calkins, never missed a tax sale. In fact, so frequently were grantees' lots conveyed to Calkins, and from purchasers who were Smith's friends or subagents, that it seems clear that Gerrit Smith was nowhere near as done with Adirondack speculation as he liked to suggest. Well into the 1860s, he or his proxies bought Adirondack land at auction, some of which he'd deeded to grantees. So did many white abolitionists in the Adirondack region, and so did Adirondackers who called the gift lots "N—— Lands." Lyman Eppes's unhappy mention of this epithet conveys his certainty that speculation in his neighborhood was all the work of racists. Doubtless racists read the auction listings, too, but Eppes's explanation missed a wider trend. Nonresident antislavery activists speculated in this land because it was a good way to make money, and money from these investments helped them do the work they loved—good work, lifesaving, but also costly. Charles Ray's speculative investments helped him cover mission work in city slums, set up fugitives in safe homes, and get to civil rights conferences far from home. Ray's partner McCune Smith, whose loathing for "wealth-worship" struck such a chord with Gerrit Smith, also knew the uses of a deal. By 1860, the physician set the value of his real property, much of it in rentals, at $25,000—income that bought him time to write, help fugitives, do suffrage work, and do battle with the emigrationists. Jermain Loguen and his wife, Caroline, may have helped more freedom seekers get to Canada than any other abolitionist couple in their time; some fifteen hundred fugitives streamed through their Syracuse home, each one needing food, clothes, housing, and transportation. Between those grantees who wanted to make money and those who wanted to do good works was no divide at all.[37]

Were any of these speculators picking up gift lots at tax sales with an eye to settling fugitives? Many Black speculators with an interest in the gift land were active in their cities' Underground Railroads. In addition to McCune Smith, Ray, and Loguen, John Z. Zuille speculated in the gift land. A city educator and printer, Zuille was rumored to have helped as many as 120 fugitives get north, sometimes by way of Adirondack hamlets. The "neat and gentle" Hawley Green, a hairdresser in Peekskill who captained his small town's Underground Railroad activities and ran a day school for Black children, bought a slew of Adirondack lots. But no evidence has surfaced that joins the dots between these speculative forays and a master plan to get fugitives into the Black Woods. Right now, it is a teasing notion, and no more.

Not so vaporous, however, is evidence of another outcome of Black speculation in the Adirondack gift lands, and one that suggests that Smith's scheme worked better and for longer than he ever understood.

An old friend of Gerrit Smith, the New York City restaurateur George Downing, never got a gift lot. He didn't qualify. He had money of his own. But he revered the giveaway, and at a Black political convention in Rochester in 1851, he framed an Adirondack homestead as the alternative to African emigration, asking why Black New Yorkers would choose to move to "benighted Africa" when "there are large tracts of land in this country, fertile and beautiful, which the colored man can occupy . . . , thousands of acres . . . already owned by colored men in the State." Downing was so enamored of this vision that he started buying gift lots as soon as grantees let them go for back taxes, and he kept at it for some twenty-five years. He evidently hoped his grown children would enjoy this sylvan bounty after he was gone.[38]

His papers would reveal that 1870 was his biggest year for buying land, and this was no mere happenstance. That year, Congress ratified the Fifteenth Amendment. When federal legislation compelled New York to nullify its for-Black-voters-only $250 property requirement, and Black New Yorkers who'd held on to their land deeds for decades no longer needed them to vote, they released them. Downing likely bought some of these deeds from sellers in the city and purchased more at auction when they reverted to the state. Especially well represented was gift acreage in the Raquette Lake region in Hamilton County (a region where no Black deedholders are known to have settled). And then, it seemed, this busy reformer put his paper duchy out of mind, because his six children learned of this inheritance only after his death in Newport in 1903. A glorious discovery! But what to do about the fact their distracted father had failed to register his deeds with Adirondack county clerks?[39]

Because his land was never registered, New York was free to claim it for nonpayment of taxes and not give Downing notice of the sale. After the 1880s, his paper kingdom was the rustic playground of the Gilded Age tycoons. On Downing's canceled holdings, Alfred G. Vanderbilt, J. P. Morgan, and former New York attorney general Timothy Woodruff bought Great Camps both renowned and, in some circles, notorious for their ostentation and social exclusivity. ("Camps" was a pet name, really; these compounds were about as rough and rugged as Versailles.)[40]

George Downing's heirs had not been raised to dodge a challenge. Born to one of the most prominent Black activist dynasties in New York, they hired the boldest lawyer they could find. The erudite son of a Baptist minister and Africanist scholar, Brooklyn's Rufus L. Perry Jr. told reporters he planned to argue that New York ought never to have transferred ownership of the land without first informing Downing about this impending tax sale. That the speculator had failed to claim title to his land was, Perry allowed, regrettable, but not a reason to strip Downing's heirs of their due. Perry guessed this was the best case he'd taken on in his twenty-year career.[41]

By Thanksgiving, headlines from Boston to Seattle were blazoning the lawsuit that aimed to evict some of the richest families in the country from their wilderness estates. "Negro's Heirs Claim Vast Game Preserves," offered a front-page story in the *New York Times*, followed the next day by "Tale of Gerrit Smith behind Adirondack Suit." The *Times* alone took pains to fix the "eccentric" Gerrit Smith's land giveaway of 1846 in the context of voting rights and racial justice—and it is thanks to the *Times* that we know Downing was able to buy this land in the first place only because grantees held on to it until their voting rights were federally guaranteed. After 1870, and *only* after, as many as four hundred gift lots reverted to New York. "Mr. Smith, after having given away the land, naturally did not want to pay taxes on it," Rufus Perry told the *Times*, whose reporter then observed, "It seems the colored men to whom he gave it did not go to the expense of doing so either *after the property qualification had been removed*." The italics are my own.[42]

So offhandedly, so breezily, did this news come to light that one could miss it in a blink. But here we have it: evidence that Smith's grantees had used and kept their gift deeds to exercise the franchise, and kept them for a quarter of a century, until the right to vote was theirs. Smith likely never knew this, and if coverage of this high-profile dust-up hadn't noted this detail, we wouldn't know it either. At the time, it excited no attention. Democratic papers, indifferent to this backstory, preferred to focus on the prospect of a legal challenge to an insular, undemocratic, mercenary elite. That's what sizzled in an age of glaring wealth disparity and populist unrest: a courtroom blow against a master class that withheld rights of access and usage, a takedown (sneered an upstate editor) of those "millionaires who have invaded the Adirondacks, buying from the State great tracts of wilderness. They have taken possession of the lakes and made camps which are in reality abodes of luxury."[43]

If Rufus Perry had pressed his case half a century before, and if his plaintiffs had themselves been Adirondack farmers, their bid for retroactive compensation might have had a fighting chance. Before and maybe a little after the Civil War, while an idealized Adirondack farmscape still held an allure, local and regional authorities were apt to favor tax-delinquent farmers over long-distance buyers, letting settlers redeem land that had been long sold for unpaid taxes. Farmers did God's work with every axe stroke; it was in the public interest to keep them on the land their sweat and zeal had improved. But by the time Perry took this case in 1904, that narrative was decades out of step. What voters wanted weren't freeholds in the woods but a healthy watershed that kept the Hudson River in good supply, and a wild park that promised not just recreation but regeneration and escape. Further, Downing's heirs were bourgeois urbanites who didn't know this purloined patrimony. The rapidity with which this lawsuit dropped from public notice suggests how decisively it was discredited. No resolution or compensation from the co-defendants was reported, and all public notice of the pending suit ceased within a month. In the summer of 1912, a couple of Adirondack papers ran a notice urging those "whom it may concern . . . in litigious possession of property in . . . Essex and Franklin Counties, belonging to the heirs of the late George T. Downing" to "procure clear titles by applying to the heirs who hold the original deeds." But this legal notice was a formality. Somebody was clearing off his desk.[44]

And so, we wheel back to 1854, the last year that Smith's New York City agents urged the Smith grantees to pay their taxes and redeem their land, and the last time they spoke out publicly for Smith's Adirondack initiative. Now and then, McCune Smith tipped his hat to the settlers in a column, proudly noting the several Black Adirondackers who "hold office in the gift of the people in Essex County," or a "former boot-black . . . now . . . a self-relying farmer in Essex County." But he would not take the prompt of the downstate reformer J. N. Still, who hoped he'd organize a gathering of Smith grantees at a World's Fair in Brooklyn to revive public interest in the undersettled lands. "Shall such a good opportunity for sowing and reaping be allowed to pass?" Still asked. Yes, it would, and with no regrets. After 1854, McCune Smith and Ray launched no giveaway initiatives, called no meetings, and drafted no resolutions of support.[45]

Lyman Eppes called this retreat neglect, and the Black land agents might not have disagreed, so great was their dismay at having parceled out so many deeds that were never put to use. But who in this new decade could say with confidence that more circulars and meetings would bring pioneers north to the woods? Between 1846 and 1854, the lot of Black New Yorkers had changed dramatically. Small towns and wild places in the backcountry that once seemed safe were now fraught with menace. And in the cities—Brooklyn, Albany, Syracuse—agents who once had time for Smith's giveaway were now consumed with a looming crisis: namely, an influx of frantic fugitives needing shelter, sustenance, and guidance. A new political party that promised to do much more for Black rights than Smith's pet party ever had was gaining prominence and power. (And in due time, Eppes himself would join the Republican Party, and never miss a vote.) The agents' disengagement only mirrored, if much later, the example of the benefactor.

The grantee-settlers were on their own. Their few settlements would not grow, and their efforts would no longer be observed in the Black press. In a few years they had gone from exemplary to anomalous and perhaps even embarrassing, performers declaiming to an empty hall.

John Brown, their neighbor, adored the isolation of frontier life (the nearest neighbor two meadows and a sugar bush away, the blizzard swallowing the woodpile without a sound, a toppled headstone in the woods). The human puniness he felt in the woods was food for the soul. Living on the edge, waking to a brutally demanding world "where every thing you see reminds one of Omnipotence, and where if you do get your crops cut off once in a while, you will feel your dependence," kept him humble, and any challenge that checked his vanity was a blessing. But his Black neighbors? Dependence—one way or another, on jobs they could not count on, landlords who overcharged, white voters who withheld the ballot—was what they came north to escape. And they hadn't. Dependence—on a thieving storekeeper, sloppy surveyor, prying postmaster—dogged them still. Their dependence on the team of the late-arriving John Brown almost doomed them to starvation in 1849.[46]

Their dependence on the false promise of Reverend Garnet's "perfect system of agrarianism" would starve them, too, if they didn't give it up. In these Adirondacks, the pioneers discovered, smart farmers improvised and scrambled, shoring up their fields with logging, guiding, teaming, and hiring out. Brown himself was no exemplar of a "perfect" self-sufficiency. Though one of the better farmers in the neighborhood, he still had to lean on wealthy city friends to keep his wife and family provisioned when he left for Kansas (and luckily, they all came through). Nor, it seems, did he pay Gerrit Smith the asking price for his farm near Timbuctoo. Smith forgave some or all of this outstanding bill.[47]

But dependence, the grantees learned, was not always a liability. The pioneers may have felt marooned on what an Adirondack writer called the "Island of Northern New York," but they could not fail to observe that isolation and discouragement were everybody's portion. White neighbors had their own hard times. Whether friendly dealings between Blacks and whites were spawned by principles of racial justice or the cool prod of necessity was not, finally, as important as the outcome. The peculiar genius of frontier life was how it rustled people into common cause who might otherwise have kept their distance, and framed practical alliances firm enough to bear the weight of friendship and respect.[48]

CHAPTER 11

I Begin to Be Regarded as an "American Citizen"

> we are each other's harvest:
> we are each other's business:
> we are each other's magnitude and bond.
>
> —from "Paul Robeson," by Gwendolyn Brooks

In 1844, a restless pride of Lyons—Isaac, Isaac Jr., George, and Freeman—moved their families from Vermont to the northern New York wilderness and made their homes in Franklin, the Adirondack township whose southern half in this decade had a name for intractable terrain and dramatically bad roads. More Vermonters followed in their wake and, too weary for invention, called their settlement Vermontville. The new name worked no magic. While the Yankees briskly introduced the made-in-England town posts that organized their hamlets (poormaster, fence sitter, constable . . .), theirs was one imprint among many. Scatterings of Irish immigrants, woods-wise French-Canadians, New Yorkers washing up from the Hudson Valley, lumber magnates and their work gangs, mill hands, English adventurers, and, by midcentury, clusters of Black families from New York and beyond forged a frontier culture of marked social and cultural diversity. Things were harder, more unruly here than in Vermont. (On voting day, for instance, the good people of Vermontville customarily honored the results of an election with a lively round of bumping, or grabbing winners by the arms and legs and throwing them at walls.) If none could call this frontier lawless (no lynch law here, and banditry was rare), the pioneers of Franklin—peppered with stump-raw settlements, and a long pull from the county seat, Malone—were in the habit of sorting out their troubles for themselves.[1]

Isaac Lyon Jr. got his house up, bought a sawmill, and sold his chairs and tables all around. For running water, he stitched a pipe of augured cedar logs into a feedline one-third of a mile long from a hill spring to his house. The overflow filled an outside trough for anybody's use. Lyon was a justice of the peace, town surveyor, and friend of education; the town's first attempt to organize a school was in his home. By 1850, six years after his arrival, he had fifty of his seventy acres in production, crops to render for his larder and his horses, cows, and sheep. His sugar bush was fruitful; as a Vermonter, he knew to come with kettle, buckets, and spiles.[2]

The Marylander John Thomas, whose farm was near the Lyons', had never tapped a maple tree or boiled sap to syrup. If he had sugar maples on his piece, he would need to find or make his gear. He had no barn back in Vermont, no close-by family with lendable supplies. Lyon's Franklin kin were as thick on the ground as beechnuts. If he wrenched an ankle, his brother Freeman, an "eclectic physician," made a poultice. If a loan was needed, a relative could help. Thomas's new friends among the Black grantees could spare prayers and goodwill, but for sap buckets, spiles, credit, or tips on managing a one-act growing season, he was on his own.[3]

So it ought not to surprise us that by midcentury the white Vermonter had the jump on this new neighbor. Lyon's tools and farm gear held more value than Thomas's, and Lyon had two horses and two cows to Thomas's one and one, and six sheep to Thomas's none. What *is* notable is that for oats, potatoes, hay, rye, and buckwheat, Thomas's production was twice as great as Lyon's, and on less land overall. Resourcefulness on this order would not have gone unnoticed by the farmers from Vermont. *This colored fellow held his own.*[4]

In 1846, an Adirondack lumberman, Thomas Goldsmith, paid Gerrit Smith a dollar an acre for a wide tract of densely wooded land on the Saranac River in southeastern Franklin County. Goldsmith built a sawmill and boardinghouses for his workers. In time, a narrow-gauge railroad hauled lumber from his sawmill to a station at Loon Lake. The village that bore his name bloomed with barns, granaries, and workshops for a blacksmith, wheelwright, and cobbler. There was an inn, a store, a school, even a rough-cut ballroom. Yet ambition and achievement would not save Goldsmith from old debts. When he fell behind on taxes, New York sold his fourteen-thousand-acre property to a long-distance buyer at auction, and it was years before Goldsmith learned of this in 1864. By order of state law, he was a squatter. He could be evicted at any time.[5]

His much poorer Franklin neighbors were more vulnerable still. Isaac Lyon Jr. and many of his neighbors faced eviction for not paying taxes. Their appeals to redeem their land from the 1850s through the 1870s are housed in twenty cubic feet of tax sale and redemption records at the New York State Archives in Albany. These affidavits (brittle lashed-together packets that cover land dealings from the second half of the nineteenth century through the first quarter of the twentieth) are a trove of news about frontier farming in New York, since the more detail Adirondack farmers crammed into their appeals, the more credible their claims. Farmers needed to provide these fine-grained proofs, backed by their neighbors' testimony, to document their residency and redeem their titles. And mostly, as we've seen, these bids worked.[6]

As to why appellants failed to pay taxes in the first place, sometimes for decades, Isaac Lyon Jr. spoke for hundreds. Never had he witnessed any "'Notice' of any Tax Sale on [his] Lot, and . . . never [was] any formal tax sale notice served on himself or his family on any day . . . in any shape, style, form or manner." Nobody had clued him in, and if the local paper ran a notice, he missed it, or maybe didn't read that paper, or didn't read at all.[7]

And if Isaac Lyon Jr., a year-round resident who had owned and worked his land for decades, could miss this notice, what were the odds for a nonresident Smith grantee? Taking a cue from Gerrit Smith himself, critics of his giveaway were quick to fault the grantees for losing gift land for unpaid taxes: here, they felt, was proof of Black ingratitude, carelessness, and indifference to Smith's plan. Yet if a farmer as entrenched and public-spirited as Lyon did not know what he owed, if he would need, like Thomas Goldsmith, to find witnesses to back his claim to his own farm in the hamlet he helped *found*, what about grantees in Brooklyn, Rochester, or Queens? How much fainter was the chance of any "formal tax sale notice" reaching them? How would they know the sale dates when these were published only in those papers serving counties where land was being sold? How many downstate grantees subscribed to the *Franklin Palladium* or *Elizabethtown Post*? How many could read?[8]

Resident grantees, who faced some of these same obstacles, would also say, like Lyon, that they never knew about the tax sales, never knew their land was at risk. John Thomas was twice threatened with eviction for failing to pay taxes. And twice, in 1863 and 1873, his Vermontville neighbors bore witness to his occupancy. The first set of affidavits was compelled by a tax sale in 1859, and the second by a sale in 1853. At the first hearing, two witnesses were on hand to back his claim. At the second, there were ten, including Isaac Lyon Jr. All were white, and almost all were middle-aged Vermonters, among them an innkeeper, a carpenter farmer, and Lyon Jr.'s homeopath brother. And when the Lyons and other locals needed witnesses to stand for them, John and Mary Ann Thomas stepped up.[9]

About neighbors standing for each other, finding common cause against unknown speculator-buyers and a distant (if forbearing) state bureaucracy, was nothing so remarkable. In North Elba and St. Armand, the Hazzards, Eppeses, and Carasaws sought and won the backing of white neighbors when they redeemed their land. What is notable is that their neighbors never—not once—mentioned race.[10]

This quiet but emphatic rural solidarity also revealed itself on Election Day. As early as 1849, in North Elba and the town of Franklin, Black grantee-settlers were casting votes. In the Saranac Lake Free Library are Town of Franklin poll lists which name seven Black grantee-settlers who voted, intermittently, from 1849 to 1889. Richard Williams voted in 1849 and 1850; Willis A. Hodges, Perry Weeks, and William A. Smith in 1850; John Thomas in 1860, 1863, 1864, 1867, and 1889; Wesley Murray in 1863, 1864, and the last year of his life, 1867; and the grantee's son, Warren Morehouse, in 1869. And in 1855, the state census named ten of the eleven Black farmers of North Elba as voting-worthy, despite their documented poverty and the inability of most of them to meet the $250 property requirement. The 1855 New York census suggests that Avery Hazzard of St. Armand enjoyed the right to vote as well.

This was not the case in upstate villages like Union Village and Elizabethtown, very few of whose Black residents were named as voters in the census. And in Troy, a city with a good-sized Black population, Black voters, too, were rare. Why did Franklin and North Elba buck convention? Perhaps because there *was* no inherited or fixed convention; these towns were just that fresh. In late 1849, when the Essex County Board of Supervisors approved the carving of a new town out of West Keene, it named three locals to run North Elba's first town meeting and keep a "poll list." All three were farmers, each knew Gerrit Smith, and each in his own way had helped out one or some grantees. In this raw, emerging neighborhood, suffrage justice bolstered solidarity, and everybody gained. So poor Black men would be deemed voteworthy who, strictly speaking, did not qualify. The new North Elba played by its own rules. And if St. Armand's town records had survived a devastating fire, the odds are good we'd find a poll list for this hamlet that named Charles Henry and Alex Hazzard voters along with Avery, their father.[11]

After the Civil War, some Adirondack rhapsodists would go so far as to suggest that the Black Woods was color-blind. With its harshly volatile weather, whited peaks, and far spans of pure frontier, Adirondack country could seem to embody the drama and spirit of the freedom struggle and the obduracy of the radical abolitionists themselves. And after John Brown was hanged at Harpers Ferry and enshrined at North Elba, his posthumous residency only burnished the belief that this place was a stronghold of antislavery feeling. "With the mighty northern hills looking down upon him, the rush of strong rivers, and the songs of resounding tempests, and the mystery of the illimitable wilderness all around him," was it not inevitable, intoned one nineteenth-century historian, that John Brown "should easily come to think himself inspired to descend like a mountain torrent, and sweep the black curse [of slavery] from out the land"? As went Brown, so, presumably, went the rustic hoi polloi: the self-appointed honor guard who kept stern vigil through the night over Brown's casket in the Essex County Courthouse on Dec. 6, 1859 . . . homesteaders standing in the driving rain to hail the widow in her carriage bearing the plain box across the sleet-puddled Plains . . . stouthearted farm boys and millhands who thronged enlistment offices in Plattsburgh and Malone to whip all the "misguided people of the Southern States" into line. So, anyway, opined the New Yorker journalist Burton Bernstein, in his regional profile The Sticks: A Profile of Essex County, New York, from 1972. Bernstein packed his take on the Civil War–era Adirondacks into a sentence: "They were all good Republicans and they all supported Lincoln."[12]

Well, they weren't. And in fact, they didn't. Pro- and antislavery positions were robustly represented in Adirondack politics before the Civil War. Local feelings about abolition, antislavery reform, the Fugitive Slave Act, and the Underground Railroad ran as hot and icy in the mountains as they did in Manhattan. And for every early founded antislavery society in Keeseville, Plattsburgh, or Malone, there was a fast-forming gang to bust it up. Antislavery publishers sparred with Democratic editors whose contempt for radical abolitionism was exceeded only by their disdain for Black people. Village worthies stood guard over Brown's coffin in Elizabethtown to honor and defend his memory, but also to keep other locals from hacking it to bits. The fact that Essex as a county went three to one for equal voting rights for Black New Yorkers in 1846 gives no hint of the drastic range of opinion from one town to the next. In Wilmington and Jay, the pro-suffrage vote was twenty-five to one, but in Schroon, just south of Keene, the suffrage vote was three to one against. In the winter of 1860, Democratic editors from Albany to Alexandra were delighted to report that North Elba, alone among the towns of Essex County, and the home of the late abolitionist John Brown, voted Democratic. "Brown's neighbors," an Indiana paper crowed, "do not approve of that raid."[13]

The economizing authors of high school history books may be forgiven for asserting that all the antebellum South was of one mind on abolition and all the enlightened North of another; textbook writers have to cover a lot of ground. But sentimental histories that simplify a rough-textured, fast-changing local scene by cloaking the Adirondack story with a flowing mantle of political solidarity obscure the granularity of life as it was lived. A North Elban I spoke with after the annual John Brown Day near Brown's home and grave told me how much Brown had meant to his father, whose family had resided in the town since the mid-nineteenth century. Yet the old man, he confided, also went to local Klan meetings. *Funny, right? He just didn't see a problem there. He liked both.* No less than Walt Whitman's Brooklyn, the Adirondacks had its clashing multitudes—from one hamlet to another, and sometimes in the same unsettled heart.

Skin distinguished John Thomas in his white adoptive community, but what moved his Franklin neighbors to defend his right to keep his land was not color-blindness but something else. He was, like them, a keeper. Where hundreds of prospective Adirondack settlers were bailing out in these tough decades, Thomas had taken hold and hung on.

A Democracy of Need

"I should like to describe an Adirondack village, made up of some half-dozen log houses of the rudest description, with sometimes an unpainted frame-house, with the sign 'Post-Office' on it," a travel writer offered in the English journal *All the Year Round* in 1860. The "sublime mountain scenery" was one thing, but this visitor deemed the human scenery rather less intoxicating:

> The only appearance of thrift is seen at the smithy; no hotel, no "meeting house"; a school-house, falling to decay; "Cash Store,"

in drunken letters over some doorway; a lazy deer-hound or two; some ragged, timid, tow-headed children playing in the road; a frowzy, gipsy-looking face peering through a window; a dense forest hemming in the whole. Sometimes we passed a pretty group of plastered cottages, with white window curtains, and women in snowy caps, belonging to French Canadians. Anon, one of Gerrit Smith's Black settlements, the houses more dilapidated than the rest, with perhaps a laughing black boy, with a rim of old hat upon his wooly head, dancing in the doorway. We saw one village utterly deserted; a freshet swept away its mill several years ago, and the inhabitants abandoned it. It was called New Sweden. Then, we met a long train of waggons, drawn by mules, coming from the iron villages, the chief of which is Ausable Forks.[14]

The sloppy mishmash of the Adirondack scene left this London writer cold, notwithstanding the affection he had for his Black camp cook and marksman, the grantee's son Warren Morehouse. But whether he liked what he was looking at is not the point. What matters is how he framed Gerrit Smith's Black settlement as one poor, stubborn Adirondack enclave in a strand. And it is noteworthy that he did not remark on John Brown's nearby home, though Brown's trial and execution happened not long before his transatlantic visit. What compelled him were the people he encountered, this piebald Adirondack tribe.[15]

The writer was mistaken, though, when he suggested that these enclaves were distinct. Company towns aside, there was no segregation. John Thomas's neighbors were French Canadian laborers and farmers, a smattering of newly settled Irish, and Yankee pioneers. After the Civil War, the last of these—the Lyons, Lamsons, Skiffs and Bryants—would assume the role of patriarchs, but at midcentury, they were all young impoverished farm families on the make, a little longer on their farms than their Black neighbors, and somehow still indifferent to the siren lure of the West that seemed to steal one able-bodied homesteader for every new arrival. For although the town of Franklin was growing (bolstered by a lumber boom, its population from 1850 to 1860 almost doubled), demographic stability was elusive. Consider the Black community alone: In 1850, twenty-nine Black people lived in Franklin. Ten years later, that number was down by half. Yet the giveaway still exerted an appeal. Fifteen of the sixteen Black household heads who migrated to this remote town between 1855 and 1860 came nine years or more after the giveaway was announced.[16]

Most left, of course, but not all. Louisa Brady made Franklin her last home, and descendants of the Morehouses, Thomases, and prolific Hazzards made the Adirondacks their home for generations. That's why they won the loyalty of their white neighbors, and why, in one celebrated instance, those neighbors rallied to the side of one Black family when its existence was suddenly, appallingly, imperiled.

When this happened, we don't know. Local memory gave no year. But sometime after his family's midcentury move to Franklin, John Thomas was threatened with reenslavement. Whether the men who came for him were dispatched from Maryland, Malone, or Troy, or working for "Blackbirders" in New York City, we can't say. But these bounty hunters meant business: they got as far as Franklin Falls, a village six or seven miles east of Vermontville and Negro Brook (as the crow flew; by wagon, the way was longer). This was J. & J. Rogers country, the western stake of an iron-making empire that stretched the length of the Ausable River watershed and once sustained as many as sixty rough-cut settlements. Stagecoaches stopped at the Franklin Falls hotel on route to the pristine interior; they did not linger. This hamlet was a world apart from nearby farm towns in spirit and appearance, the land around it raw and stumpy, kilns, sawmills, and sleepless forges souring the air. Strung along a deep ravine, it made a greedy funnel for the fire that surged its length and leveled all but two of thirty buildings in 1852. But home was home, and that same year the orphaned villagers rebuilt the settlement entirely, all shoulders to the wheel, wood choppers from Quebec, Irish millworkers and sawyers, unsentimental working people happy to vote Democratic if that's what the bosses said they wanted and doled out enough beer. No zeal for abolition here.[17]

It was the right place, in other words, to start asking around. *We're looking for a Black farmer. One of Gerrit Smith's holy fools. Property is property, and this man is an outlaw. We need to get him home.*

A reminder here: in 1840, Thomas, then a slave on the Maryland plantation of Ezekiel Merrick, endured the wholly unexpected sale of his wife to a slaveowner in Georgia. The trauma of this loss, which thrust Thomas into a spell of "terrible dispair . . . and desolation," also fixed his nerve to break for freedom, and that same year, he escaped from his Queen Anne's County enslaver and got to Philadelphia. After this came seven years in Troy, New York, a sojourn brightened by a second marriage and the acquaintance of a charismatic minister, who had also fled enslavement in Maryland many years before. The gift deed that Reverend Garnet secured for Thomas in 1847 eventually enabled him to move his new family north to Franklin. Some ex-slaves felt a positive aversion to all things countrified and rustic, but farming was what John Thomas knew and liked. Did he worry about slave hunters? To Merrick he would always be a self-stolen asset, an investment gone awry. But surely, after all these years, his enslaver had moved on.[18]

The Malone journalist Frederick Seaver anticipated his readers' incredulity. That's why he made a point of all his fact-checking. In his 1918 county history, he claimed to have interviewed people in three Franklin villages, and all confirmed the story. Merrick's unnamed kidnappers got as far as Franklin Falls—and on learning that John Thomas was aware of their approach, that he "was armed and would never be taken alive," and, what's more, that "the local whites would stand by him, with certainty that some one would be killed," they gave up and went away.[19]

Could this be true? When I first read this, I was struck by all the markers of Underground Railroad fakelore: the high drama, the heroism of the white defenders, the eleventh-hour resolution. Like so many tales of its type, it seemed mainly to reveal a postbellum storyteller's hopeful bid to stake out a local angle for the struggle between North and South and to claim a bold, preemptive role for a rural neighborhood at such a great remove from the sublime conflict to come. Yet evidence of antislavery activity in this part of Franklin County was weak, as Seaver himself noted. Among Thomas's Vermontville neighbors were no names on the rolls of the Liberty Party lists or the Franklin County Anti-slavery Society, no antislavery convention-goers, no candidates for the abolition cause. In 1846, equal voting privileges for Black New Yorkers won the support of 58.8 percent of Franklin's voters—hardly the grand showing of Essex's 70.8 percent and Clinton's 72.8 percent. Smith's agent Jermain Loguen alerted the grantees to six white abolitionists in Essex County who could be relied on for support. For Franklin County, he could name but two. In 1850, no northern county delivered so few votes to the Liberty Party as Franklin: a mere ten abolition votes, compared with Essex's seventy-seven and Clinton's thirty-five. And in 1850 when Gerrit Smith dispatched an agent to northern New York to raise bail money for the Underground Railroad operative William Chaplin, then languishing in a Maryland jail, Franklin County yawned. In "especially *Franklin*," Smith's agent sighed, "there appears to be but little interest felt in the anti-slavery enterprise—and but little sympathy for the noble Chaplin."[20]

But if we can't know whether John Thomas's Franklin neighbors were good antislavery men, we do know of their regard for Thomas as their neighbor. Had he once been enslaved? Well, that was somewhere else. Right now his farm flanked theirs, their youngsters and his warmed their palms at the same box stove in their Franklin school, and everybody's backsides made the same sad peace with the hard benches at church. As for this new slave law about handing over fugitives—recall a temperance advocate's unhappy summary of this hard-drinking corner of Franklin County at midcentury: "This region, so far back in the woods, was regarded as outside and beyond the reach of any law whatever, whether human or divine." Laws in these parts got kept when they made sense. When they made hard lives harder (kept homesteaders from squatting on land nobody was using, fined them from taking cordwood from the huge estates of far-off speculators, penalized a father of five for bringing home an out-of-season buck), laws might be ignored.

Cockamamie legislation from long-distance lawmakers that wreaked havoc with Adirondack life was nothing new. In county newspapers,

Arguing the Point. Lithograph, hand-colored, 1855. Arthur Fitzwilliam Tait, with Louis Maurer. Courtesy of the Adirondack Experience, Blue Mountain Lake, NY.

Thomas's neighbors read about big-city magnates hogging profits from iron ore hauled out of mining hamlets in the region ("It pains us to see our county robbed of its very life blood to make non-residents rich," an Essex County editor anguished in 1854. "Will our citizens never see their true interests?") John Thomas's neighbors knew all about the hated scrip system that kept Adirondack miners in thrall to the company store, bank, and barber. They saw the handiwork of logging gangs in their woodlots timber poachers in the pay of outside speculators who hogged the high-selling softwoods. Subsistence pilfering, a longtime Adirondack custom, was one thing, but these weren't locals gathering stovewood and forsaken roof beams, but hired guns who roved around. And always, back of these turkey vultures, were the land barons of Troy, Plattsburgh, and Malone, all of them outsiders, interlopers, little loved. If Thomas's neighbors could handle them, they could surely manage a few pesky *man-thieves* after one of their own.[21]

This, anyway, is how I make sense of Frederick Seaver's story and justify the proposition that Thomas's neighbors came to his defense. I don't see a sudden bloom of antislavery conviction making rifle-grabbing minutemen out of Thomas's neighbors. Maybe that was part of it, but I'm more persuaded by need. Why might a Black farmer have expected his white neighbors to defend him? Because on the agrarian frontier Thomas had made his presence felt. Recall Ray's mantra: "Mutual assistance, mutual and equal dependence, mutual sympathy—and labor, the 'common destiny of the American people,' under such circumstance, yields equally to all, and makes all equal." Much more than an abstract integrationist agenda, practical need prompted Iddo Osgood to urge McCune Smith and Ray to exchange their deeds for property closer to the struggling settlement of North Elba, where their medical and ministerial talents were wanted. Plain and pressing need made an overseer of roads out of Lyman Eppes, an inspector of elections out of James H. Henderson in North Elba, and a tax collector out of Willis Hodges in Loon Lake. Black settlers were asked to sign a petition for a new road because the more names on the list, the more effective the appeal. Volunteerism and collaboration steadied everybody's boat.[22]

Need also helps explain the many racially mixed households in the midcentury Adirondacks: in Essex County, twelve of the twenty-eight homes with Black residents in 1850 were integrated households. Nor was it merely happenstance these were the homes of farmers. In chronically shorthanded frontier households, boarders, hired hands, and housekeepers were a boon. Black single laborers lived with farm families. White workers lived with Black families. Boarders looked after the elderly, took care of children, worked on "shares" for bed and fare, helping farm families get by. When Adirondack homesteading began to stale for the grantee Josiah Hasbrook Sr., he moved away, but his teen-age children lingered, two boarding with Black North Elbans, one lodging with white neighbors. Silas Hicks, a grantee from New York City, spurned his remote gift from Gerrit Smith for a pallet in the crowded farmhouse of the Elizabethtown farmers Milo and Abigail Durand and their ten children. (A few years later, Hicks and his bride, Harriet, were in a log shanty of their own.)[23]

White homes took in Black women too. Hannah Dickson, a grantee's wife, lived with John Brown's daughter Ruth when Ruth's husband, Henry Thompson, was away, and Harriet Hicks boarded with Irish immigrants when she was widowed, and then she joined the household of a white woman (two widows growing old together in a cabin in the woods, giving up only when a fire drove them out and forced Harriet to the poorhouse). Sometime after the death of the Smith grantee Isaac Craig, his widow, Jane, opened her cabin to an English farmer, Charles Willard, who had once worked for hire for John Brown's daughter Ruth. Whether Jane and Charles, a widower, were romantically involved, the census does not say. But their joint occupancy of the farm surely relieved their isolation.[24]

It seems obvious that several of these integrated households reflected the equalitarian culture of their abolitionist owners, like the Liberty Party stalwarts Jesse and Elizabeth Tobey of Jay, who took in Avery Hazzard's niece Eliza, or the antislavery Durands, who housed the grantee Silas Hicks and worked with John Brown to help fugitives get north, and of course, Brown's own family, who for many months sheltered and employed Cyrus Thomas, a young fugitive from Florida. But while a racially progressive home culture prepared the way for integrated households, it's not the reason they existed. Cyrus Thomas lived with the Browns because they were grievously shorthanded and needed live-in help. And not all farmers with integrated homes were white. In Elizabethtown, the grantee Lafayette Mason put up two white charcoal burners from Canada (one lived with the Masons for years). In 1855, George W. Bell, a Delaware-born grantee-farmer in Willsboro, shared his family's home with a French Canadian wood-cutter's family of eight.[25]

These pieced-together Adirondack households defied conventions of segregation less from principle than from rank necessity. This was why the Franklin pioneers, white and Black, circled their wagons when the tax collector came to town, and why John Thomas's neighbors sent the bounty hunters packing. Much more than hot talk from the pulpit or the antislavery press, it was the exigencies of pragmatic, place-based need that helped to integrate and, in John Thomas's case, abolitionize the Adirondack frontier.

Labor, Which Makes All Equal

Pragmatism also drove the tacit argument for Black migration to the gift land in the antislavery paper the *Impartial Citizen* in 1849. At the request of Smith's hard-traveling land agent Jermain Loguen, the Franklin pioneer Jerry Merrill sent the *Citizen* an appraisal of a typical Smith gift lot near his home. Loguen solicited the opinion of this white local because he guessed the grantees were tired of hearing about the land from city activists who did not farm and knew next to nothing about these woods so far from where they lived, and because the Merrills, like their neighbors the Wardners of Rainbow Lake, had the right eyes for the task. Merrill knew his trees and herbs (lady slipper root for nerves, thoroughwort for colds, horseheal for consumption . . .); he hunted (a shot pouch on one shoulder, a powder horn on the other, bullets tucked between his fingers); he was a surveyor, and his society was wide. The family inn in Merrillsville on the Hopkinton-Port Kent highway was as famous for the welcome it extended to perfect strangers (including some grantees) as for the heat that blasted from its huge stove. Ask Jerry Merrill for an opinion of a typical Smith Lot, and Loguen knew he'd get an answer.[26]

Merrill wrote:

I have this day been and examined the North East quarter of Lot No. 151, Township No. 10, Old Military Tract. . . . The said quarter is about one-half swamp, not so wet as swamps in general in this country, timbered with cedar, balsam, tamarack and spruce.—The other part, upland, [is] rather uneven, very heavily timbered with beech, birch, maple, spruce and hemlock, which denotes good soil, and not very stony. Said lot is the fifth lot directly South of my father's. There is an improvement on the lot adjoining it

on the North, which improvement borders on said quarter, and a
passable road to it.

This early in April, the forest floor was still patched with snow, the
maple leaves still stiff enough to crackle, but, to the point: "I should
think the lot was about an average with lots in general in this town, and
a thorough-going, smart man, acquainted with clearing land, might get
a living on it."[27]

The *Impartial Citizen*, the Black agent Samuel Ward's abolition sheet
in Syracuse, framed Merrill's note to Loguen as a rebuke to Smith's detractors: "Read it, you who defame this great man." And maybe Merrill
had this in mind too. For Gerrit Smith, his family had for years collected payments from contract farmers and negotiated sales. They put
up the grantee Jonathan Mingo at the inn and alerted him to a sale lot
much better than his gift land. They held mail at their post office for
Willis Hodges and his pioneers.

But Merrill had another reason beyond family loyalty to Smith to
push for the Black Woods. The "South Towns" of Franklin County—
Brighton, Franklin, Harrietstown, and portions of Duane—were much
slower to develop than the early settled, more populous villages to the
north. This somewhat benighted district needed settlers badly. More
farmers on the ground meant more state and county funds for road-
work and public services. More families meant more hands for shingle
making, sugar boiling, and barn raising. Cleared land would make
browse, more deer would bring city "sports" to the family inn, and locals would find work as guides. A practical urgency at least as much as a
respect for Smith's initiative explains Merrill's obliging but blunt tone.
The simple truth, he suggests, was not everyone was made to homestead. Would a settler work his land hard and steadily? Respect its limits
and potential? In Franklin was no John Brown offering to school the
first-time farmers in their work. All the Franklin grantees' neighbors
were disadvantaged by good-enough-but-not-great land that provided a
living, little more. Not ideology but need, pragmatic, blunt, and steady,
would suggest the common ground, and membership in this fraternity
would come (Ray's promise, once again), through "labor, which yields
equally to all, and makes all equal."[28]

Compare Merrill's letter with Douglass's purple exhortation about
"the sable-armed pioneer" and "the glorious dawn of civilization." Pro-
saic and precise, Merrill did not fancify. He reported what he saw. For
those who'd had their fill of pomp, this measured view was better than

inspiring. It was credible. It said, *This is how it is up here. You can hack it, or you can't.*

Those who did persist, however meager their accomplishment, commanded neighborly respect. Some miles south of Merrillsville, in a cabin on the Essex County–Franklin County line, dwelt a pioneer named Daniel Thompson. It isn't clear when this grantee first moved to this patch. From New York City but residing in Elizabethtown when he was deeded, Thompson lived alone on his gift lot, a mile from a road. By the mid-1850s he was a widower in his seventies, his children grown and gone. But his neighbors knew him. They looked out for him. They described him as "a devoted Christian" well known to "all the Christian community." And they worried for him. "Many a cold morning" the farmer Augustus Porter "look'd to see if he could see the smoke rise from [Thompson's] log cabbin during the winter past fearing he might have suffered from the cold so as not to be able to help himself."[29]

Why did anybody care? Thompson was no community builder. He did little with his land (clearing only about eight acres), never built it up into a "fine cultivated farm" like John Thomas, or earned Thomas's good name as an "honest, upright, and fair-dealing man, much respected in the community." Nor would he cofound a library like Lyman Eppes or a village cemetery like Avery Hazzard's sons. All he offered was tenacity. And for his neighbors, this was enough. For the simple feat of holding on when so many lost heart and packed it in, his small square in the fragile quilt would be defended, and woe betide the man who tried to rip it out.[30]

John Brigham considered trying. A lumberman from the Adirondack mill town of Clintonville, Brigham bought a batch of land in Franklin in 1854, only to discover that one of his new lots was occupied. More problematic still, the resident, Thompson, declared that the land was his own; he had a deed from Gerrit Smith, and this was surely true. But he had built his cabin on Lot 201, St. Armand, Essex County, southeast of his legal property. His gift piece, Lot 200, was just across the county line in Franklin (or ten rods north and west from where Thompson built his home). It was an honest error, and not at all unusual. Years before, the Franklin farmer Isaac Lyon, meaning only to be helpful, had led Thompson to Lot 201 and assured him this was his. (Lyman Eppes built his first home on land not his own but very near it, and a surveying error may have been the cause here too.)[31]

John Brigham had no wish to make this old man suffer. But in 1856 someone offered him $400 for Lot 201, and Brigham, who dreamed of a second home, hoped to "improve the opportunity." He did not "feel justified in putting Mr. Thompson off," he wrote Smith, because to "remove him" might well "far . . . shorten his days." *And yet!* Brigham did not spell it out, but his expectation was plain. He wanted Smith to compensate him for what he stood to lose if he declined this offer, or to underwrite Thompson's resettlement. For was it not a fact that without a gift deed from Gerrit Smith, Thompson would not be on this piece? Was Smith therefore not implicated in Thompson's plight? After noting many reasons why Thompson might be better off elsewhere (so old, so poor, and his soil worn to nothing, his means exhausted, his farming no great shakes), "all" Brigham asked was "that the man may be cared for & provided for without an expense to me."[32]

A colder man than Brigham might have served the squatter with a warrant and let the law take its course (though who knows if a court would find for Brigham after Thompson's nine-year occupation). But Brigham was uneasy. A radical abolitionist and member of Keeseville's antislavery First Congregational Church, he knew all about Smith's effort to fight voter suppression by settling Black grantees on Adirondack land. He sometimes worked for Smith, serving warrants on his delinquent contract holders. He had helped Smith's own longtime land agents buy back land in Township 10 from uninterested grantees. His politics were principled and bold; he once made a hopeless bid for Ausable town clerk on the Liberty Party line. But here was this old squatter, standing in the way of this speculator's dream house. Could Smith please help?[33]

The issue was perceptual. Brigham saw Thompson in light of Gerrit Smith's philanthropy of 1846, a perpetual beneficiary, a farmer of Smith's making. But by 1856, Thompson had improved "his" property, made a home, joined a church, and earned the affection of his neighbors. In the Black Woods he had made good on Smith's design to the point where he'd outdistanced it, and now it was up to the beleaguered Brigham to adjust his view of Thompson not as the object of Smith's charity but as an aging woodsman who would not give up his piece, legitimate or not, without a fight.

This was a lot to ask of Brigham, or of anybody making a living dealing land. But if Gerrit Smith commiserated, he did not think enough of Brigham's plight to note it in his letter book. What he wanted was to build communities, not weaken them. Nor was it his custom to bail out grantee-settlers or speculators in distress. Further, the idea of paying an abolitionist to do the right thing would have left him cold. Bad enough to have to compensate slaveowners for their human "property." Those were necessary dealings with the helplessly benighted. John Brigham, good abolitionist, knew very well what he should do, and in the end, it seems, he did it. He did not sell this lot until 1864, by which time Thompson was lost to the public record. Maybe a young relative or friend took the old man away, or he died in his cabin, a plume of woodsmoke thinning to a whisker, a line of saplings already lifting at the edges of his field.

Not There Yet

The first time I read it, John Thomas's 1872 letter to Gerrit Smith struck me like a vindication. For all that I could find to show that the Smith Land giveaway had a longer lifespan than supposed; that many Black grantee-farmers flourished in the Adirondacks; that John Brown's enclave, Timbuctoo, was just one spoke of this far-flung rural community; and that the integration of this Yankee-settled frontier was in some ways quite profound, I had yet to read a Black grantee's opinion of the gift land in his or her own words. A few white pioneers left their impressions, but this was not like hearing from the grantees. Black reformers who visited (Ray, McCune Smith, Loguen, and maybe Myers) spoke from the outside looking in and, in any case, had their agendas. Nor could I set much store by white-authored accounts like Seneca Ray Stoddard's buffoonish take on Henderson's sad death, or his caricature of the Eppeses, or Lyman Epps Jr.'s interviews with reporters, who much preferred to mine for anecdotes about his father's friendship with the martyred Brown than to learn about the giveaway and anything it meant. John Thomas's letter to Smith was a great boon, but in my wish to have it mean what I hoped it meant, I missed the fuller picture.

Overwhelmingly, that news was good. John Thomas had made out well, and a more stirring endorsement of Smith's idea from a grantee (maybe the one such letter Smith received) is hard to imagine. Thanks to "your generous donation" of a deed, Thomas wrote, he had moved to Franklin County and built himself a home "which by labor and economy has been enlarged into a handsome farm of two hundred acres, with all necessary Stock and farming implements," a farm that produced enough of a surplus to earn him "two or three hundred dollars every year." Thomas and his wife and two daughters, he told

Smith, "enjoy our rural home in peace and quiet: but advancing years notify me that the toils of life are nearly done. . . . I have breasted the storm of prejudice and opposition, until I begin to be regarded as an 'American Citizen.' Heartily thanking you for the interest you have always taken in the welfare of my people, and hoping to hear from you at your earliest convenience. I remain, Yours with Great Respect, John Thomas."

But had farming "made all equal," as Charles Ray and the Black agrarians hoped? When Thomas wrote his letter, he had been on his land for twenty-two years, with eighteen more to go (despite his certainty that his remaining days were few). From 1846 to 1860, electoral support for equal voting rights among the voters of Franklin, Essex, and Clinton Counties plunged. In 1863, the year of the Emancipation Proclamation, New York voters had yet to approve equal voting rights for Black residents of the state; the despised $250 property requirement was still in force. Nor would Lee's surrender bind and heal this political divide. A decade after Appomattox, the *Plattsburgh Republican* was still railing at Black suffrage, calling it nothing but a crude ruse to beef up the Republican electorate, undermine white labor, and position enfranchised Black men to "hold office—as Jurors, Sheriffs, Aldermen, Representatives, and Governors!" And how long before they claimed the liberty to bed and marry whom they pleased? In the rural North no less than in the South, a horror of miscegenation drove objections to social and political equality.[34]

By 1872, John Thomas was saving money. He had already voted four times and he would vote again. Two of his grown children and a pack of grandchildren lived nearby. A tranquil neighborhood and relative security were his to savor. But this was not equality. Advancement, yes, and no disputing it. But he would never join an Adirondack jury. He might have tried to run for office. He could not have won. Nor could his daughters dream of teaching in a Franklin schoolhouse. Full equality in the armed forces would be denied his people for another seventy years. And to some of his white neighbors he would be a "Gerrit N——" until he died.[35]

Only in death, it seemed, could the Black Woods be called colorblind. Cemeteries in the hamlets of Vermontville, Bloomingdale, Wadhams, Westport, Whallonsburg, and North Elba hold the graves of Gerrit Smith grantees, their spouses, and their extended families, which mingle freely with the stones of their white neighbors. They face the same green, breezy views, survive the same heaping blizzards. The headstone here of one John Thomas, eighty-four, "Born in Queen Anna Co., Md., Oct. 30, 1810," may cause a visitor to wonder how this old Southerner ever managed to end up in a remote rural cemetery in the Adirondack hills. But whose bones belonged to Black bodies is nowhere revealed.[36]

CHAPTER 12

If You Only Knew How Poor I Am

I have seen a number of very libral donation to
help the Oppress and of late another to help the
poor Irish and I was glad for I do not Belive in
Oppression in none of its forms. I am poor and
hope that you will not make me unnecessary
expenses for I am trying to pay you as fast as I can.

—Contract farmer Chester Converse to Gerrit
Smith, 1847

In October 1855, fourteen months after the
enactment of the Kansas-Nebraska Act and the eruption of that violent, episodic, unnamed war before the Civil War to win Kansas for free
soil or slavery, John Brown went west. "Something more than speechifying," his old friend Willis Hodges had exhorted. *Something more* was
Brown's hope too. The South would learn that abolitionists were good
for more than speeches and conventions. No less than their enemies,
they could load a rifle, stage an ambush, shoot to kill. Before the year
was out, John Brown and his hand-built company of antislavery guer-
rillas had gained a national reputation for their fleet, aggressive tactics.
Mississippians no less than Vermonters followed the raids and gambits
of "the old terrifier"; Brown's name was twinned with abolitionist defiance and, in the slave states, brutality and cunning.[1]

Less dramatic in their methods, and not known, but also willing to
risk life and family in the effort to resist the slave power in the half
decade before the Civil War, were some of Brown's Adirondack neighbors. In the fall of 1854, when Kansas was not yet "Bleeding" (just
bruised, and braced for worse), the farmer Lemuel Knapp, his wife,
Nancy, and their five children left St. Armand for the Kansas Territory. Its "Virgin Soil," promised the New England Emigrant Aid Company, would be seeded with ballot-hungry pioneers primed to vote the

antislavery ticket—twenty thousand of them, it was hoped, traveling by rail, boat, and wagon to several reservations. Small subscriptions totaling $5 million would defray the cost of these removals; the orderly emplacement of sawmills, gristmills, cabins, boardinghouses, schools, and churches would follow. "That's the way to do it, instead of blustering and spouting impracticable abolition nonsense, and indulging in wild and insane ravings against slave-holders and dough-faces," declared the Democratic *Franklin Gazette*. "No sensible, practical plan like the above could ever originate in the boiling, seething cauldron of an abolitionist's brain, but it is eminently the emanation of a thinking, reasoning, rational mind."[2]

Proslavery homesteaders on the east side of the Missouri ("pukes," some Yankees called them) saw things differently. To them, these antislavery arrivals were land-lusting, big-talking interlopers backed by citified political insiders and the eastern press. Their land companies, it was rumored, packed the emigrant trains with paupers, armed them, and goaded them to drive squatters from their farms. No slave-owning household was safe from thievery. This was an invasion.[3]

In fact, the delivery of Kansas into the ranks of the free states would be the haphazard, undirected doing of farmers drifting in from the Northwest Territory, and not the work of emigration parties out of the Northeast. Many Free Soilers were not abolitionists at all. The Emigrant Aid Company never raised a fraction of the cash it needed and sent fewer than two thousand settlers to the West—and a third of them came right back east. But not Lemuel Knapp. In Albany, the Knapps of St. Armand joined the Fourth Party of the Emigrant Aid Company, headed west, and stayed.[4]

The largest of all the emigrant groups, the Fourth Party had problems from the beginning. The Aid Company had promised low-cost hotel rooms in Kansas City and Chicago. Where were they? Where were the low-priced provisions? The cheaper fees for transport? Running out of cash before they reached the wide Missouri, many settlers lost their zeal. "Of our company which numbered 230 when we landed, I do not think 100 can be found in the territory," one pilgrim complained in 1854. A group letter warning emigrants against "too much reliance" on the Aid Company went east. The first name on it belonged to St. Armand's Lemuel Knapp.[5]

Even so! This wide sky, the coal-black soil, the sheer cracked-open freshness of the place! Go back to St. Armand? A Kansas acre ran a dollar and a quarter. Flocks of parakeets lifted out of grass so high it hid your horse's hocks. The growing season was as long as the horizon. Knapp, like many in his party, made for Fort Riley, a long day's canter west of Lawrence and Topeka. When cholera bared its teeth, the Knapps pushed on to Pawnee City, where Knapp pitched a mighty tent. A blizzard buried it; he dug out and built a hostel. And then, when the US government, claiming this site for itself, started ripping down his boardinghouse while his guests were still at table, Knapp moved his family to Ogden, southwest of Pottawatomie. He built a cabin, chopped wood enough to last the winter, and ran a probate court for the community. Proslavery neighbors put his woodpile to the torch.[6]

Knapp launched another farm in Wildcat Creek. Proslavery men stole one pony and shot another. Seed was sown but not in time; a scheme to keep Free Soilers from farming by forcing them to "danc[e] attendance on bogus courts, as witnesses or jurymen" fatally delayed his planting. Then illness bloomed, a "bilious fever and inflammation on the lungs." Thirty months after the Knapps had put St. Armand to their backs, all they had to show for their great gamble was a Job-sized heap of loss.[7]

Yet hear Knapp's words to the Kansas Relief Committee in 1857: "From my experience, as a practical farmer, both in the States and here, I believe Kansas to be one of the best Agricultural countries. It is unsurpassed for stock growing, sheep raising and dairy farming. It will be one of the finest States in the Union and it will be a Free State." Three years later, Kansas joined the Union. By 1870, two of Lemuel Knapp's sons were working Riley County farms all their own. Their combined worth approached $10,000.[8]

That's part two of the Knapp family saga—blows beating down like the plagues of Egypt, but at the end, the proud payoff: a new expansive home. Part one, a story of farm failure and dispossession, raises other questions. Why did the Knapps give up on St. Armand? Their participation in the Emigrant Aid Company's colonization plan suggests their politics: they joined an antislavery initiative because they liked what it stood for, read the news from Kansas, and chose to make what the *Essex County Republican* declared "the great leading practical duty of the North" their own. But a ballot for a slavery-free state was just one reason they left home. The Knapps bolted because they had to. If they jumped, they were also pushed.[9]

At midcentury, Lemuel Knapp had $900 in assets and the esteem of his backcountry neighborhood. He had served as St. Armand's school superintendent, village justice, election clerk, and overseer of roads.

But these jobs paid no bills. In 1844, Knapp needed surgery and had to deed his farm to get it. When he tried to buy it back, the price had leapt beyond his means. He bought another farm on contract, but his bad back slowed him down, and as debt soared, so would worry. "My boys if they live will soon help," he wrote in 1850, but his eldest, then, was eleven. Though Knapp enjoyed the confidence of his long-distance leaseholder (Gerrit Smith asked him to keep an eye on timber thieves, and to collect rent from other contract farmers), this side work paid indifferently. Knapp needed help. He hadn't met Smith himself, but he knew Smith's Peterboro land agent. Everyone buying land on time knew Smith's proxy, Caleb Calkins, whose rent-collecting turn around the region was an Adirondack ritual. And Knapp knew Smith's radical ideas. Because of these, Knapp's world was integrated. Black deedholders were his neighbors. Knapp welcomed them. It was Knapp who urged Gerrit Smith to set up Avery Hazzard with his St. Armand farm.[10]

If Knapp had no quarrel with Smith's philanthropy, however, he would contest the application. The appeal he made to Calkins in 1850 was striking as much for its bluntness as for its absence of apology: "I am yet lame, afflicted & poor. . . . My only hope is to make a living on & out of the lot I live on, . . .—As Mr. Smith is giving land to the poor that have none, and that are needy—why may I not share of his bounty—can it be so[?]"[11]

What He Said, and What He Did

This was a good question, and more white homesteaders than the exhausted Lemuel Knapp would ask it. *Why not us? Are we not worthy?* Poor Adirondackers read about the land or money the philanthropist gave to downstate Blacks, indigent widows, impoverished Irish immigrants, and needy residents in Smith's own Madison County. They also recalled his dealings with his Hudson Valley leaseholders in 1844. In these years, while the Anti-Rent War was at its peak, poor farmers camouflaged in calico and war paint protested the long-term leases of the patroons, and sheriff's posses roamed the hill country, brandishing eviction papers, wrecking crops, and breaking into homes. Gerrit Smith, alone among the prominent Hudson Valley landholders, gave his restive Delaware, Columbia, and Otsego County leaseholders six months rent-free to collect and furnish legal proof that showed that his title to their land was invalid, telling them that if they got him evidence, he would release them from all claims.[12]

In the North Country, too, Smith counseled leniency, often urging land agents to scale back interest fees and defer rent collection for a season. But the same generosity of spirit that inclined Smith to treat tenants with forbearance also meant he sometimes couldn't: his passions were so many, his priorities so jealous and demanding, that his land work (what he bought, sold, and managed, not what he gave away) would always seem encumbering, the thief that pilfered from the holy work he loved. So prolific was his abolition work that it moved his biographer Ralph Harlow to "wonder how the man ever found time for anything else." Smith found it with the help of his secretary, managers, and land agents, as well as his own driving work ethic. (Railroad, canal, and highway investment schemes intrigued him quite as much as they did other mid-nineteenth-century land barons. His youthful purchases in Oneida and Oswego Counties were prescient.) His own debt, especially what he incurred in the Panic of 1837, he had worked for many years to shed, not only because he wanted to reclaim the fortune he had inherited and almost lost, but because debt embarrassed him, putting him at odds with his own eager perfectionism.[13]

In 1846, Smith still owed creditors close to $500,000. Selling land he didn't need at fire sale prices, and giving some of it away outright, would at least reduce his tax burden. Three years later, his debt was down to $100,000. But cutting back the debt meant calling in his chits. Each of his thousand farm contracts with his buyers was a legal version of a vow between consenting parties. Benjamin Franklin had taught generations of Americans, "The Borrower is a Slave to the Lender." To give while he still owed made Smith worse than thriftless. It made him a kind of thief. By 1849, bankruptcy no longer loomed, but he would toughen up on debt collection. He could be a big-hearted philanthropist or a big-hearted landlord. When either undermined the other, he could not be both at once.[14]

With the exception of the historian Ralph Harlow, still unmatched for his zealous focus on Smith's complex pecuniary culture, Smith's biographers have preferred to follow Smith's own lead and dwell on his philanthropic deeds and efforts. And with reason! Smith the land baron and rent collector was one in a crowd; Smith the philanthropist was in a league all his own. Smith himself discounted the income-generating "day-job" that enabled his largesse. In his third-person autobiographical essay, he crushed the land work into a sentence: "He soon took upon himself the care of his father's immense property, the charge and improvement of which, though naturally a very industrious man, have made his life a very busy one." Money was an accident of birth. Smith took no credit for making it (beyond the loaded word "improvement"); he wanted only to give it up; he had a great estate but never meant to; he would be happy with much less. Fair enough—Smith's public face was his to groom. What makes less sense is why history let Smith's emphasis on what he wished were otherwise to count for more than what he did.[15]

But if the gap between what Smith preached and what he practiced has been largely lost on Smith's biographers, it was not lost on poor contract farmers who, like Knapp, pled earnestly, and sometimes hotly, for better terms, more patience, one more break. Perhaps because these appeals are so drably classified in the microfilms of Smith's papers, they have not enjoyed the scrutiny that favors, say, reel 75 ("GS and John Brown: Correspondence") or Smith's letters from other celebrated allies. But the hard-labored notes in "Land Sales" are newsworthy. They reveal a Smith we rarely meet, the sort of market-minded manager from whom Smith himself professed to recoil. Not the land giver but the debt and rent collector, the enforcer with the resolve to send the sheriff to the cabin and put a delinquent homesteader out of doors. Never mind that this was a muscle Smith rarely flexed, that he was comparatively openhearted. Smith's good name would not obscure the recognition of an imbalance of power, or stifle the resentment of a seeming double standard in which one impoverished cohort was advantaged with gifts of land and money while his own contract farmers were ignored.

From a lessee in Schroon, Essex County, 1847: "I have seen a number of very liberal donations to help the oppressed and of late another to help the poor Irish and I was glad to see it for I do not believe in oppression in none of its forms. I am poor and hope that you will not make me unnecessary expenses for I am trying to pay you as fast as I can." From another in Athol, Warren County, 1847: "Sir—I have paid your father $175.34 and I have paid yourself $85 and have done business for you to the amount of about $25 and that is more than the lot ever was worth and I do feel as you are a rich man and I am a poor one . . . that you would not be desiring more than what would be right if you should discharge your payment you hold against me and take your land and fill me out a deed."[16]

To Smith's Peterboro land office came letters from the Catskills, the Mohawk and Hudson River Valleys, Lake Champlain, Cherry Valley, the Tug Hill Plateau, and, of course, the Adirondacks, where Smith owned so much land. From Franklin, St. Armand, Keene, North Elba,

Elizabethtown, and Westport, all hamlets where Black giftees settled, came appeals for Smith's forbearance from poor whites. Farmers wrote of epidemics, fire, flood, arson, theft, and their own botched investments. A homesteader had bought land only to find that when the snow went, it was a swamp. Health crises abounded: "A reason for my not paying you sooner is that my wife has laid under the doctor's hands for 11 months & finally died the 23rd last—& left me a widower with 6 children." "I was taken with the fever & ague at a very severe rate & my oldest son was taken eight days after with the same complaint. I was obliged to use up the money I intended for you." Bad things happened on the frontier. It was Smith's Christian duty to make allowances. In these letters, regret was signaled, but no remorse, and never shame.[17]

"If you only knew how poor I am and how much trouble I have had you would not think hard of my sending you so small a sum," wrote the farmer Alden Speer from Moriah in 1850. If Smith could see Speer's iron-threaded hamlet, walk his fields, step into his low-roofed home, understanding would surely bloom and charity prevail. But as striking as this farmer's assumption of Smith's empathy was his resignation: Smith could *not* know how poor he was because Smith, in Peterboro, was paring down his sinful debt by trawling for back payments from his contract farmers so that the springs of his largesse might flow as lavishly as ever. Stealing time from his great work to tour a scratch farm in Essex County was a theft he could not justify. It was hard enough managing an estate this large at such a distance from his home. In Potterville, Warren County, vandals wrecked his mill. Lumber thieves were rustling logs from Johnsburg lots and hauling them to tanneries in Thurman. Several hundred cords of firewood went missing from a Keene lot, and though poachers said they'd stop, who was there to make them? A contract farmer died, and Smith, distracted, sued his corpse. Another farmer hoped to learn why he was being penalized when so many lumber thieves had not paid Smith "the first shilling." Inefficiency, inconsistency, out-of-touchness—such were the liabilities of the nonresident rent collector.[18]

So when Mason Whiting of Binghamton begged Smith to repurchase a piece of land Whiting had bought on contract, Smith would not bail him out. "I am greatly embarrassed by my foolish and sinful liabilities for friends and in great need of a large payment from you," he wrote. Assuming debt and then enabling it in others from a sentimental leniency was not merely a legal problem; it was impious. Smith owed it to the grantees, to *all* his needy beneficiaries, to make the gifts he gave his own.[19]

When he started cracking down, however, what made perfect sense to him came as a hard shock to longtime contract holders. "I have paid you nothing for nearly 6 years," a Franklin farmer fretted. Why all at once this note "saying that your patience is exhausted"? Wrote a baffled lumberjack in Keene, "We have heard from you and it come very unexpected to us although I acknowledge we were in the rear." A frantic Glens Falls lumberman told Smith in 1848, "I cannot raise $1,000 to save my soul now. . . . You promised me that you would hold off until June. Will you hold this note until June and not sue me?" Some pressed for understanding ("I am sorry you sued me for I was doing as fast as [I] possibly could"; "I have done the best that I could since I have been on the place. . . . I want to pay the remainder as much as you want it."). Others, quite as sick of Smith as he was of his debt, came back swinging. "Finding myself unable to pay," wrote S. Huntington of Franklin, "I have sold my right to John & Hugh Collins, brothers . . . from the Emerald Isle, that land of oppression, who have paid me $26 and promised $10 more all told. . . . You see [what] I realize for my $82.50 which I paid you, and 7 years of toil, hardship and privation." A few years earlier, Smith gave $2,000 to the victims of the Irish famine, and now two Sons of Erin were the proud new owners of a Franklin County farm that "7 years of toil" failed to deliver to a contract farmer in chronic debt to Gerrit Smith.[20]

Smith sympathized with his debtors. The letters to them that he copied in his letter book are respectful, even warm. But even when Smith gave his Hudson Valley contract farmers half a year rent-free to search for defects in their titles, he never offered to turn leasehold assets into freeholds, or to forgive outstanding debts before or after the six-month respite. If his leaseholders' titles were legally unassailable (and overwhelmingly, they were), the old despised arrangements stood. As to those radicals who urged leaseholders to challenge the patroons, Smith was so repelled by their "lawless, violent and bloody Agrarianism" that he invoked it in his initial letter on the giveaway, taking pains to distinguish his agrarian initiative (orderly, legally admissible, and voluntary) from land reform forced by mobbism and fear. His insistence on this point suggests that his Adirondack giveaway was conceived in part as a response and a rebuke to the Anti-Renters' challenge.[21]

Smith also spurned a chance to forgive long-standing debt among his contract farmers in 1849, when he gave one thousand land lots, mostly in the Adirondacks, to poor *white* men from all over New York. *But why not, this time, make poor Adirondackers your giftees?* wondered his ever-sensible uncle and adviser, Daniel Cady. A veteran lawyer in Fulton County (he was practicing law when George Washington was in the White House), Judge Cady pointed out that "poor men who are already in the northern counties—and who wish to remain there—might be benefitted by your bounty—but the expense of removing from the southern country to the northern part of the state will equal the value of 50 acres of land"—and what poor prospective pioneer could afford that? Cady urged him to gift the people already living there. They liked the place and would use it. Cady's exasperation with his nephew's unconcern with the disabling poverty of his giftees invoked similar complaints from Frederick Douglass and McCune Smith, though they were never so direct.[22]

But Smith stuck to his new plan, scattering this new batch of Adirondack gift deeds to takers all over the state for the sake of fairness and, perhaps, his own visibility. He asked county judges and supervisors to make his choices, and to the poor white men of Essex County, he allotted ten gift deeds, and to Franklin County, eight. No poor Franklin contract farmer in his debt benefited from the giveaway of 1849; no town of Franklin, St. Armand, or North Elba farmer got a gift deed, period. The letter Lemuel Knapp wrote Gerrit Smith about lightening his debt—"as Mr. Smith is giving land to the poor that have none, and that are needy"—went unanswered. And the next time this St. Armand farmer wrote Peterboro, it was to tell Smith he had leased his home to a minister and contracted for another piece nearby. "So, I shall not leave the woods yet," he reported, "but will make one more trial to pay you for a lot of land, don't know as I can"—and he couldn't, as we know. The move to Kansas followed.[23]

A Grantee's Forced Diaspora

One of Smith's Black grantees would also find himself caught short by Smith's adamantine respect for contracts. Lafayette Mason received his gift deed when he was living with his wife and young family in New Russia near Elizabethtown. One of the very few native-born Adirondackers on Gerrit Smith's long list, Mason was from Clinton County, south of Canada, and was likely born enslaved. A collier and scratch farmer when Smith sent him a gift deed, Mason was surely pleased; he'd just gotten married, and this new deed would make it easier for him to vote. But

Untitled: Nine Views of the Adirondacks. Drawing, pencil with gouache, 1861. Arthur Fitzwilliam
Tait. Ninth image in a series. Courtesy of the Adirondack Experience, Blue Mountain Lake, NY.

starting fresh on a Franklin gift lot held no appeal for this laborer. New
Russia, in the long-settled stretch of eastern Essex County along Lake
Champlain, was ablaze with kilns, furnaces, sawmills, and forges. Work
crews and their bosses needed all the milk, charcoal, venison, and eggs
that Mason could provide. This subsistence farmer had a sugar bush; a
rum distillery would buy his syrup. He knew where to drop a line; the
fresh-caught fish he brought to Hiram Putnam's store got him tobacco,
flour, and seed. On every side, the prospects rose like cream, and with
them his ambition. In 1860, Mason put a hundred dollars down on a
351-acre wooded lot in Roaring Brook Tract, where he and his young
family were raising wheat, oats, corn, turnips, and potatoes, and tending milk cows, chickens, and a pig. Gerrit Smith, the seller here, gave
Mason ten years to pay a $600 balance in annual installments.[24]

Then the long shells found Fort Sumter, and Mr. Lincoln asked for men. A few weeks shy of Christmas in 1863, Mason's fourteen-year-old son, Lewis, left New Russia for Brooklyn to join the Twentieth Volunteers, USCT. Lafayette Mason, who was light enough to pass for white, earned a $350 bounty when he joined a local company of the 118th Infantry Regiment, or the "Adirondack Regiment," as it was proudly known. Private Mason (the elder) fought at Petersburg, Richmond, and Fair Oaks. At the last of these, in late October 1864, he was taken prisoner with six hundred Union troops. It is likely Mason counted himself lucky: Union casualties at Fair Oaks were 1,603, and Confederates fewer than a hundred. But Mason, once "a man of iron constitution," emerged from the long hell of a prisoner-of-war camp a ruin, or, as his doctor wrote, "a skeleton of his former self."[25]

Reunited with his family in New Russia in 1865 (Lewis, back home as well, was still recovering from dysentery and a racking cough), Mason tried to pick up where he'd left off, but with his soldier's bounty spent and his contract payments in arrears, he could not keep pace. A year after his and Lewis's return, Mason's land contract was annulled. Gerrit Smith sold Mason's contract lot to a secretary's niece in New York City. The abolitionist who had given a Black pioneer free land in the name of political empowerment and economic freedom bowed to the speculator/landlord who yanked a farm contract from a war-disabled, late-paying veteran and father of fourteen, and sold it to a white, long-distance city buyer with no intent to settle. And from Gerrit Smith's perspective, this made sense. He gave Mason land, and he took land back, and in each case his reasoning honored a perfectionist resolve to honor charity and justice and live in and up to God's exacting image. No contradiction here.[26]

At wit's end, the Black contract farmer took Gerrit Smith to court—a desperate move; he had no case. He had paid nothing to his leaseholder beyond his first deposit. Not only was his plea dismissed, but he now faced court costs and eviction. In 1866, the un-cabined Masons moved to Iowa. Singly and together, they farmed in Vernon Springs and Steamboat Rock. Then, in 1877, Lafayette and Mary pushed west to Minnehaha County in the new Dakota Territory and claimed a 160-acre plot under the Civil War Homestead Act. Their new frame house measured twelve by fourteen feet. When Lafayette died in 1879, he and Mary had broken eighteen acres and planted four hundred fruit trees. And here the widow stayed, tending her young orchard, keeping faith with the old self-providing agrarian idea, until solitude and need compelled her to move to Minneapolis, where her son Lewis, disabled by the asthma he had picked up in the war, worked as a janitor and a deacon for his church. No farming for him.[27]

"You and I Want No Controversy"

Class shaped local responses to Smith's idea much more than histori-cal accounts of it admit. Class allegiance, inflected by culture, church allegiance, and local politics, influenced how poor white Adirondack-ers understood Smith's giveaway and his defense of it. In fact, if Smith concerned himself too little with how a projected wave of poor Black metropoles might impact Essex County, white Adirondackers did the opposite. Since 1839, the cost of poor relief in Essex County had risen every year, and by 1849 the *Essex County Republican* judged it "the great pecuniary burden of the county." Would Smith's grantees end up as public charges? And would public oversight of such an influx result in higher taxes? The prospect of this outcome raised considerable alarm.[28]

Rev. Jermain Loguen, reporting on the gift lands to McCune Smith and the readers of the *North Star*, was keenly attuned to rac-ism on the frontier, but neither he nor the other agents plumbed the boiling working-class anxiety that stoked Negrophobia, too, es-pecially when powerful opinion makers fanned the flames. In 1853, the Adirondack Democratic legislator Winslow C. Watson asserted in his Essex County history that Smith's munificence had "exercised a depressing and sinister influence upon the prosperity and repu-tation of the country. The Negro [has become] in many instances an impoverished and destitute object of public or private charity." No evidence suggests that the fledgling enclaves of the Black Woods flooded county poorhouses as Watson claimed. Decades later, a very few aging grantees or their spouses repaired to these facilities (as was the long-standing country custom among poor Adirondack whites), but at midcentury, lists of recipients of poor relief who lived in North Elba, Franklin, and St. Armand included no Black pioneers. Watson also predicted a power grab by Black radicals whose "ulte-rior" ambition was to seize political control of North Elba, an effort, he predicted, that might result in "the anomalous spectacle . . . of an African supervisor occupying a seat in the county legislature." This did not come to pass. But Watson's rumor only ramped up the anxieties of poor Adirondackers long predisposed to fret about the influence of "outside interests" on their lives.[29]

They weren't wholly paranoid. Outside interests muscling in—from colonial-era military strategists in Albany or Montreal to fur brokers, land barons, lumber magnates, tannery tycoons, iron ore speculators, and stockholders in upstate mills—were an Adirondack tradition, helming the regional economy since the first days of the European discovery. And despite the fondness of antiquarian historians (Winslow C. Watson among them) for the Adirondacks' "rootstock" in next-door Vermont, this was no replicate New England. From the first days of non-Native settlement, other influences staked a claim. Wars and skirmishes between the French and English and their respective Indian allies along the Champlain Valley had famously delayed the region's settlement, so infrastructure here was raw and markets slow to mature. Add to the poor soil (some choice bottomlands aside) a harshly corrugated topography, a blackfly habitat of singular efficiency, and winters longer-seeming than New England's by a month, and the shadow of Vermont grows fainter. Extractive industries—tanning, mining, charcoal-making, and logging—dependent on migratory or immigrant labor gave great swaths of this region a demographic profile at sharp odds with Vermont's (or, at least, with Vermont's hard-defended brand). In 1850, for example, one in three residents of Clinton County was foreign-born.[30]

After the Civil War, invisible strings hitched hundreds of tiny Adirondack settlements to a far-flung network of nonresident investors, bosses, speculators, and developers, and very early on, their interest in the region's industrial potential lent it the character of a dependency. In the Gilded Age, proprietors of the famed Adirondack Great Camps and elite clubs constituted a potent outside interest too. The conservationists and legislators who devised the Adirondack Park and the tough laws that protected it would also be long-distance overseers of the region's destiny, inviting the resentment that off-site bosses always will.

This is not to suggest that in the mid-nineteenth century, thousands of Yankee farmers no longer toiled in the Adirondack woods, or that they had given up on farming as a good use of their land. But many who had once hoped to buy now rented or bought on contract, and between those who owed and those who collected was the hard divide that turned nonresident landlords like Gerrit Smith into yet another kind of outside interest suggesting a despised dependency—and never mind if leaseholder and lessee shared all the same convictions. Let one of Smith's antislavery land agents miss sufficient contract payments, and all the shared values in the world would not buy him a pass. Smith was an equal opportunity enforcer; neglect a debt, and legal action loomed.

Smith sued the abolitionist surveyor Wait J. Lewis of Keene (despite Lewis's blustery insistence that Smith would someday occupy the White House). He sued Monroe Hall, an antislavery storekeeper and speculator in Jay. He sued the aging abolitionist Samuel Warner of Moriah, who had convened the first meeting of Essex County's Liberty Party in 1845, subscribed to *Frederick Douglass' Paper*, and called for an armed "revolution" after the passage of the Fugitive Slave Act—strong medicine from an Adirondack farmer in 1852. "Is there any remedy for the slaver or colored Americans?" Warner asked. He saw "but one, and that is revolution. Sad and awful as it is, the thing will come. . . . Arouse, then, from your lethargy, my colored friends. If you would be free, you must strike the blow." And when it came to picking a side, Warner recognized his duty: "I will help the oppressed."[31]

This was fire-breathing after Smith's own heart. But Warner's zeal could not paper over debt. He had bought several lots on time from Smith, and seven years after he signed for them, not one was fully paid for. From Peterboro, Smith assured him, "You and I want no controversy with each other." Still, Smith sent a summons, and Warner counterstruck at once. Was Smith aware, he wondered, that when he bought these lots, one of them was occupied by a squatter? The man was on the land for decades—even before the purchase of this lot by Peter Smith, Gerrit's father. Knowing "your liberality in relation to giving away land," Warner assured Smith he had never tried to move him. But if he did pursue eviction, he supposed the squatter would "contest it strongly, and I fear with success." The message was as bright as noon: *If I'm in trouble here, so, Mr. Smith, are you.* Warner, no innocent, knew that Smith's name for "liberality" would suffer if the rich man's claim drove Warner to evict a homesteader three decades on his farm. Had Smith not said that in a just world, no person would own more than "his needed portion of the soil"? That money would be made irrelevant, and every household would sustain itself? Had he not declared the soil no more purchasable than air and light, but a thing more "like salvation . . . 'without money and without price'"? Warner's counteroffer: if Smith dropped his suit, Warner would send him sixty-two dollars for two lots and drop *his* complaint that Smith had sold him land that was already occupied.[32]

Warner liked to end his notes to Smith with a nod to common ground ("The fire of freedom cannot be smothered. Take courage, brother. Let the course be onward and upward"), and Smith was no less comradely ("We had rather fight slaveholders than fight each other—I send you a pamphlet . . ."). But in the end, Smith *would* prefer a bank note to War-ner's courage, and a pamphlet would not fix Warner's debt. So when Smith served Warner with papers, the debtor got himself a lawyer, a tough one: the former Essex County district attorney, and a Democrat to boot. For this world was not perfected. Not just yet.[33]

Smith's Bespoke Fraternity

That long-distance land barons like Gerrit Smith preferred to work with local agents who shared their way of seeing things, their values and morality, was only natural. Like called to like. Long-distance land magnates needed people on the scene they could trust, and it made sense that Smith was drawn to Adirondack brokers who shared his an-tislavery vision. Who better in North Elba than Squire Iddo Osgood, or the radical newspaper publisher Wendell Lansing in Wilmington, or, in Keene, Phineas Norton, that "ornament to our cause"? Smith had a man, it seemed, in every town, and this far-flung fraternity of like-minded community builders, many of them descended from the early Yankee pioneers, provided his trusted portal to local goings-on. But was their window on the scene wide enough to represent it?[34]

At midcentury and after, Smith's Adirondack abolitionist allies held no great influence. They were mocked and marginalized by main-stream public servants and editors, and their old name as political spoilers stuck fast. After the 1844 defeat of the Whig candidate for president, Henry Clay, Whig pundits insisted that Clay, not the pro-slavery James Polk, would be in the White House if the Whigs had car-ried New York State—but the hated Liberty Party of New York, which siphoned votes from Clay, and in so doing handed state and then the nation to the slave power, effectively installed the enemy. "Go it slave-dom! How proud northern abolitionists and doughfaces must feel at the result of their labors!" Jonathan Tarbell, Whig editor of the *Essex County Republican*, fumed in 1844, and would keep calling out the abo-litionists for their "treason" for a decade. In 1854, the brazen Tarbell went so far as to liken abolitionists to slaveholders, and Adirondack Whigs to their oppressed lackeys who "have not dared to speak of them above a whisper, and have stooped and crouched before them like a slave to his master." He added, "It is the time now to put an end to this disgraceful submissiveness. Whigs have crawled around the feet of Abolition leaders long enough."[35]

Imagery that framed the Adirondack abolitionist as a slaveholder was ludicrous, yet Tarbell's ugly imagery may have resonated with Adirondackers on the losing end of a summons from Gerrit Smith. When the fellow brandishing a warrant that threatened homelessness and destitution was also, as it happened, the local face of Bible politics, you might not love the cause he stood for. To the immigrant Tierneys, Ryans, and Volins facing eviction, the Bible-quoting, New England–rooted land agents stood for another world.[36]

And what would the Black grantees have known of this? Smith's introduction to the giveaway, the agents' too-few published reports, and Jerry Merrill's land appraisal described the land, but the grantees would learn nothing of the local population and its rent worries, ethnic rifts, town-to-town rivalries, and doctrinal dustups. Reverend Loguen warned of racist knavery in the *North Star*, which was helpful, but racism was just part of what accounted for local fears. Class aggrievement mattered too, and not because the grantees were less impoverished than their neighbors. They had, however, been privileged (as white Adirondackers were not) by a rich man so hugely favored by an accident of birth that he could hand out land he'd never seen to perfect strangers who never hoped or asked for it and had no notion of where it was, land that had been pictured to those strangers as a *tabula rasa*, as if their own cabins, stone walls, sawmills, foundries, kilns, churches, orchards, roads, barns, and workers' shanties were not as real as the wilderness itself.

The grantees had a lot to learn. The Black Woods the agents promised them was gauzed in gorgeous, wishful generalities. The passage of the Fugitive Slave Act in 1850 compelled more interest in the social culture of this destination, but things were still vague and hazy, more rumored than understood. And what the settlers found when they got there and bore down was just the opposite. Here was a land of hard, jostling specificity, where hamlets only miles apart were as unalike as people, and where from one cabin to the next was all the irreducible originality and human mess their white friends would discern in them.

CHAPTER 13

Nothing Would Be More Encouraging to Me

The slumlord's knock, the smutty air, toxic water, slave hunters, street thugs, whites-only work sites, parks, schools, and churches—the injuries of city life were behind them now. The pioneers were out of range. But there was no dodging the bad news gusting north from Washington, DC. Only a few years after the 1850 Fugitive Slave Act was passed, the Missouri Compromise was repealed, turning Kansas into a battle zone and reviving the threat of slavery's tarlike spread. Then, in 1857, the highest court in the land ruled that no Black American had a legal claim to citizenship or freedom. And if the grantees had no access to (or could not read) Greeley's *New-York Tribune*, the *Essex County Republican*, or the antislavery *Northern Standard*, there were other ways to stay informed. Peddlers, preachers, transients, and well-traveled neighbors brought the news. John Brown and Lyman Eppes subscribed to *Frederick Douglass' Paper*, which closely covered Gerrit Smith's headlong gallop into Congress and his just-as-swift retreat. The broadsheets also paid attention to the story of Solomon Northup of Saratoga Springs, tricked and kidnapped, transported south, and rescued from enslavement only after twelve horrific years. In 1853, Adirondackers could buy his memoir, *Twelve Years a Slave*, at Hasbrouck's Store in Keeseville, alongside Morse's Compound of Yellow Dock Root, birdseed, and paint. Northup, from Minerva, only thirty miles south

of Lake Placid, was a free-born Adirondacker. His capture and enslavement brought the "peculiar institution" very close to home.[1]

Some good news broke in 1854 with the formation of a new political party formed by disaffected Whigs and former Free Soil Democrats. The Republicans, as they described themselves, were making the
antislavery campaign the core of their platform, and activists fed up
with Bible politics and its right-thinking but unelectable candidates
rejoiced, many Black New Yorkers among them. Especially heartening
was the thrilling presidential run of the antislavery Republican hopeful, John Fremont, in 1856. He lost but carried all of the Northeast, a
stunning coup for a party barely born. Black activists took note. More
and more it seemed to them the radical antislavery party took their
support for granted, and saw their votes as needful tribute to white
largesse. That's what a "professed abolitionist" told the Black activist,
William J. Watkins, in 1855. With a "sort of masterly nonchalance," the
white man said, "Your people will never, sir, be done paying us for our
efforts in your behalf."[2]

Watkins, then working at *Frederick Douglass' Paper*, was stunned. "In
our behalf? Why sir, you are laboring for yourself and posterity." The
white man, he wrote, "sighed over the mental and oral obliquity which
prevented us from discovering the obligations we, as a people, are under." And here, Watkins reflected, was what came of playing for so long,
too long, the lackey in the abolition cause. In the political arena no less
than on the plantation, Black Americans were "hewers of woods and
drawers of water." Keep on this path, warned Watkins, and "we will
ever be regarded as hangers-on, as miserable dependents." The time had
come to "give orders as well as execute, command as well as obey," and
put aside all thoughts of "the obligations we are under to our white
brethren."[3]

Watkins, the son of a school principal in Baltimore, said that the
cost of white patronage was just too high: "The first man who dares
whisper the word 'ingratitude' to me in this connection will be treated
as he deserves." In 1855, Watkins did not name Gerrit Smith, who had
hosted him in Peterboro. But in 1858, the rise of the new Republican
Party nerved him to speak bluntly. Black voters in New York, few as they
were, could keep trying (and failing) to gain the summit of uncompromising right, or find their footing on the rough floor of realpolitik. No
one could confuse the new Republican leaders for die-hard abolitionists, but in this party were antislavery men who might really get elected.
That's what mattered and maybe all that mattered. Even a friend of

Bible politics as staunch as Douglass was now loath to waste his vote on someone unelectable. After the passage of the Fugitive Slave Act, the stakes were just too high.[4]

In 1856, Gerrit Smith ran for president on the National Liberty ticket. He got 165 votes. There was a message here if Smith could hear it, but in 1858, he ran again, this time for governor on the People's State ticket. It was an eleventh-hour sally, cooked up by the American Abolition Society and temperance advocates the summer before the fall vote. Smith claimed that Republicans had betrayed the antislavery cause when they backed, or didn't fight, a plebiscite to fix the fate of slavery in the territories. Even though a popular vote would likely favor the side of Free Soil, this concession to majority rule struck Smith as unprincipled. Clearly, he argued, a new party was needed. But it wasn't really new at all. It was the Liberty Party all over again, rising like a phoenix from the embers of defeat.[5]

Once he finally agreed to run, Smith ran in earnest. He hit the trail hard, spent $5,000, bankrolled three campaign newspapers, and logged four thousand miles stumping all over New York. Many antislavery activists despaired. Would a third-party rival for the antislavery vote reprise the disaster of 1844?—Would Smith be filching ballots from the antislavery Republican incumbent? Could he possibly deliver New York to the proslavery Dems? Swing ballots could claim as many as twenty-five thousand votes; Smith himself was shooting for an abolition turnout of fifty thousand, and felt he just might get it if disaffected Republicans could be wooed to his camp. Smith made fifty campaign speeches and introduced a question-and-answer format, enthralling his white audiences from Brooklyn to Glens Falls.[6]

But Black activists recoiled. In Ohio and in Troy, New York, Black political convention-goers urged the Black electorate to vote Republican—and at the fall convention in Gerrit Smith's home state, by a decisive majority. To no avail would Smith's loyalists—Garnet, McCune Smith, and Duffin among them—argue for Smith's tiny party as the standard-bearer of the antislavery cause. By 1858, Black Republicans (and by 1858, New York's 11,500 Black voters were overwhelmingly Republican) would not be diverted from an achievable agenda by perfectionist politics. To this generation of Black Republicans, Smith's latest campaign seemed worse than irresponsible. It was heedless and subversive. "We can accomplish almost nothing . . . save over the defeat and ruin of the so-called Democratic party, our most inveterate enemy," Troy delegates asserted. "In order to secure this defeat, it is absolutely necessary to consolidate the strength of the opposition to said party. And we regard the Republican Party . . . as more likely than any other to effect this desirable end." The obscurity of Smith's latest fringe party and its unelectable candidates could only "give aid and comfort to the enemy." The time had come to break with Bible politics, its advocates, and all good works that imposed an expectation of lasting gratefulness—like Gerrit Smith, and his lovely but impossible land giveaway of 1846.[7]

Black Activists, Pushing Back

One especially keen anti-Smith Republican was Stephen Myers, the Albany reformer whose short-lived bid to organize a Black colony in Florence had so aggravated Smith in 1849. That failure had not slowed him down; like Smith, Myers looked ahead, resuming his temperance work, his work with fugitives, his lobbying for Black suffrage, and now, his promotion of this new party. In 1858, Myers put out six issues of a Black Republican campaign sheet, the *Voice of the People*. The pages of the one surviving issue are a revelation. Again and again, Smith's giveaway figures as the image of a hated Black indebtedness to white patronage, with Smith the face of white paternalism. In this Black paper, Smith's star was worse than flickering. It was dead.[8]

"What have I, what have colored people to do with Gerrit Smith's lands, when great eternal principles are at stake?" demanded William J. Watkins in Myers's paper. "Let the lands go to the winds, let everything else slide—but stick fast to principle. The man who tells me that I shall vote for Gerrit Smith because he has given me lands . . . insults me to my face, and I will tell him so before he gets through." And not only had Watkins gone "over to the enemy" (as a gloomy Henry Garnet reported to Gerrit Smith), but he was working Smith's own campaign trail, chasing Smith's oratory with his own as if in cold pursuit, and winning happier reviews. "Rich, Juicy and Able!" gushed the *Troy Daily Times* about one of Watkins's speeches. "His statement of the position occupied by Gerrit Smith . . . was a perfect crusher of that gentleman."[9]

Smith himself was mystified. Why had this abolitionist turned on his own cause? Watkins shrugged. "I have no more changed my Rad. Abolition Principles than did the majority of Rad. Abolitionists who voted for Fremont, and who will vote for the Republican nominee in 1860," he wrote to Smith. "It is with me a question of Policy, as well as of Principle; and I maintain that we may when a great end is sought . . . consult the genius of Expediency, without sacrificing one iota of Moral Principle." Watkins's point: he would vote for Smith if Smith were Republican, but Black voters could not afford another gestural campaign.[10]

Watkins was not alone. Almost every piece in Stephen Myers's campaign sheet framed Smith and his benevolence in dark and wary terms. Warned the poet "E.B.W., "

> Election's fast approaching,
> And friends you know it well;
> Then go up to the Ballot Box,
> And make your Ballot tell.
>
> That precious little ballot
> Should not be thrown away,
> Because some white men choose
> To lead us all astray.
>
> And friends do not be led astray,
> They'll delude you if they can
> And beware of all such "Trickery,"
> As "The Hour and the Man."

The Hour and the Man was Gerrit Smith's election sheet. The allusion to the Peterboro "trickster" was as subtle as the verse.[11]

Willis Hodges's older brother William J. Hodges took a shot at Smith in Myers's paper too. The pastor of an Evangelical Apostolic Baptist church, Hodges had no use for Bible politics or Smith's charity. He implored Black men not to "embrace the pernicious doctrines of Gerrit Smith, through the agents of the Democratic party, or his Colored Land Committee, that he has made his agents to try and deceive us, and make us sell our manhood as well as our birth-right for a small quantity of land, money, or favor." By 1858, Smith's Land Committees had long disbanded and Smith's agents were on to other things, but Hodges made their agenting for Smith the salient peak of their careers, and reduced Smith's thirty-year campaign for racial justice to a twelve-year-old initiative Smith had long since disavowed.[12]

Williamsburg's Samuel Scottron was just as tough. Why, demanded the young activist, were "some of our Gerrit Smith men" obliged to "consult the feeling of one man at the expense of 40,000 colored persons who inhabit this State"? Why would they "throw away their vote to the advantage of their most deadly enemy, or a party who has in every instance proved a most deadly foe"? The habit of Black deference was so deep, feared Scottron, that maybe Black men did not deserve the vote.

"The sympathy we have for our political friends, and the dependence we put in them, is really too great, and must some day be subdued . . . or we will never reach . . . the common platform of Man's Equality and Rights. . . . What credit to us if we are set free only by the exertions of the white man?" Editor Stephen Myers went further still, indicting not only Smith's giveaways and candidacies but the reformers who supported him: "We know that [Smith] has been the champion of the oppressed ever since he has held any influence," but "we also know he cannot be elected. . . . Such men as the Rev. H. H. Garnet, Dr. James McEwen [sic] Smith, and J. W. Duffin, leaders of the GERRIT SMITH faction, are recognized by us as men of intellect, deservedly beloved by all the colored men of this State." Nonetheless, "by their example we can plainly see how easily some great intellects are deceived."[13]

Myers's targeting of Smith may have been inspired by more than his devotion to the Republicans. He and Smith had been at odds for decades. Was there a whiff of payback in these columns? It is easy to imagine. A decade earlier, Myers had flogged the giveaway with zeal, and modeled his own Florence colony on it too. William Hodges's brother Willis once liked the giveaway so much that he led a band of settlers into Franklin and organized the enclave of Blacksville. Samuel Scottron's father had a gift deed, a fact his son left unremarked. For all these writers, a close tie to the gift land was no source of pride or even something to acknowledge. By 1858, the Hodges brothers (Willis by then long back in Brooklyn) were making speeches that, according to the *Brooklyn Daily Eagle*, "denounced Gerrit Smith and the Abolitionists generally." The intervening years, the promise of the Republicans, the fruitlessness of Smith's campaigns, and the growing boldness of the Black political community had done the memory of Smith's philanthropy no favors. A plan devised to help Black New Yorkers get the vote devolved into its opposite. For seeming to impose a debt of gratitude that stuck Black voters with a party that could not win, Smith's "scheme of justice and benevolence" was derided as an obstacle to suffrage, a heavy, hated yoke.[14]

Gratitude is slippery—easy to acknowledge when you feel it, not so easy to sustain. When Smith gave land away in 1846, he never asked for gratitude. Skeptics linked the land gifts with a bid to buy votes for his beloved Liberty Party. Smith hoped for votes, but he never spelled this out. Nowhere is there evidence that he blamed a Black grantee for betraying his land gift with a vote for parties he despised. No quid pro quo or public expectation of a show of gratitude was stated. Smith held back, hoping only that these grants would help Black people farm and ease their access to the ballot—not votes for his party, but the simple right to vote.

The rapidly revealed failures of the giveaway—to make farmers out of thousands, to build a voting bloc that could swing an election to the antislavery side—tested Smith's restraint. In 1856, his autobiographical essay glimpsed his disappointment when it pointedly omitted any mention of his land gifts to Black New Yorkers. But not until 1857, when the *Tribune*'s Horace Greeley prodded Smith to report the true fate of his "noble gift . . . whatever the facts may be," did Smith confess his hurt.[15]

"Of the three thousand colored men to whom I gave land, probably less than fifty have taken and continue to hold possession of their grants. What is worse, half of the three thousand . . . have either sold their land, or been so careless as to allow it to be sold for taxes," he told Greeley. True, he conceded, he had been wrong to give away land that was so difficult to farm. But the greater problem was something else: "White men who live there can support their families only by very hard work and very frugal habits. Why then, considering the character of the colored people, should we expect them to do much in such a country?"[16]

Smith was not the first critic of the giveaway to racialize its failure. In 1853, Winslow Watson and Frederick Douglass invoked the giveaway as proof of the unfitness of Black Northerners for husbandry. But Smith's widely circulated verdict from the *Tribune* was worse. His dismissal of the land as second-rate and his judgment of his grantees as incapable of the same "very hard work and very frugal habits" as white Adirondackers would fix the script for generations. He would take credit for his initial gift of acreage, but not for his own part in his plan's failure. He would not acknowledge the impact of his ignorance of Black impoverishment, or his blindness to the need, unmet, for startup capital, structure, oversight, or guidance. And misled by Smith's confident indictment, subsequent accounts of the giveaway let the giver off the hook.

The trouble was, even after—and long after—Smith put the giveaway behind him (and with the same grim resolve with which he shed his romance with colonization, the Millerites, and his congressional career), the giveaway kept mattering, especially in election years when Smith was waging a campaign. In Myers's 1858 election-year campaign paper, the very mention of Smith's land gifts of 1846 triggered an idea of white expectations of Black gratitude. And this happened in white newspapers too. "Gerrit Smith has the fortune to experience from

Abolitionists, white as well as black, a very small measure of gratitude," opined the *New York Times* in October. In these pages, long opposed to equal suffrage, Black reformers were ingrates for not voting for the man who gave them land, even while the editor cheerfully observed that Smith's party could never win. And while affecting to praise Black delegates at a recent Troy Convention for the "practical sense" they showed in endorsing the Republicans, what the *Times* implied was that Black activists were opportunists: "When there is money to be made, land to be given away, or Jerrys to be rescued, Mr. Smith is a man much lauded and sought after. But let him take the field for Governor, and even the black men turn their backs upon him."[17]

So this was what Black voters were supposed to do—assume a posture of quixotic gratitude at the ballot box whether it helped their cause or not. Vote for Smith and prove themselves, once again, dependents. Be grateful; *know their place*. Be grateful; *it would keep their votes from counting*. Be grateful, loyal, impotent. Here was the idea.

Eppes Weighs His Options

Nothing tells us what the people of the Black Woods made of this election-year fallout between Black Republicans and Smith. But any take on the giveaway that framed it as a symbol of Black indebtedness to white beneficence could bring no comfort. To see the giveaway dismissed by Black activists, some grantees among them, as nothing but a bribe for votes, to see the settlers cast as dupes, and then, in white papers, to see Black voters mocked as ingrates for not backing Gerrit Smith's latest party—the insults never slept. At least New York's fall election put an end to hand-wringing about the divisive influence of the third radical abolition party (Republicans won every seat; Gerrit Smith, aiming for 50,000 ballots, got 5,470 abolition votes). But this would have no impact on the "impending crisis" between the proslavery South and the outraged North, or on the brutal skirmishes in Kansas detailed in Adirondack papers. Three of John Brown's sons—Owen, Frederick, and Salmon—went to Kansas from Ohio in early 1855. Brown's sons John and Jason and their families joined the others in Osawatomie that May, and Brown followed in the fall. And as news reports soon revealed, John Brown's party, unlike Lemuel Knapp's, did not go west to settle, farm, and vote.[18]

Brown had shared his master plan for a revolutionary "Subterranean Pass Way" with Eppes, Avery Hazzard, and some other Adirondackers.

This alternative Underground Railroad, which he'd mulled over for years, aimed to free slaves, then arm them, train them, and build a mountain-based guerrilla army whose raids on slave-owning households would so rattle and unnerve enslavers that they would conclude the work of keeping slaves wasn't worth the risk. "Twenty men in the Alleghanies could break slavery to pieces in two years," he declared.[19]

The raid on the arsenal at Harpers Ferry, which Brown was pondering as early as midcentury, was but one piece of this elaborate project, which Brown described to Lyman Eppes at the same time he revealed it to his family. He wanted Eppes to join his war party in Kansas and points west; in fact, in April 1858, he wrote his family in North Elba, "nothing would be more encouraging to me" than if his son Watson, his neighbor Alexis Hinckley (a white North Elba farmer), and "Mr Epps," could be persuaded "to take hold." In May, he asked "Wife & Children every one," to convene a family meeting specifically to encourage his son-in-law Henry Thompson, his sons John Brown Jr. and Watson Brown, and Lyman Eppes to join him.[20]

Brown believed in Lyman Eppes. He wanted him on board. But no Black Adirondack settler would join him on his antislavery raids. And if, as his daughter Ruth Thompson recalled after his death, Brown moved to North Elba in the first place to find Black recruits for his long-range revolutionary plan, we can imagine his dismay. Some have suggested that this is why he spent little time in North Elba and gained a local reputation as "a wolfish kind of man, always coming and going on his expeditions." North Elba's fields, for his purposes, were barren; his recruitment drive had failed.[21]

As to Eppes's own decision: if his precise response is lost to us, his actions spoke his mind. He knew what it would mean to join John Brown. He read the dispatches in Douglass's paper. He knew what "Captain Brown" had taken on, the risks he ran, the deadly raids and take-no-prisoner showdowns with an enraged, prolific foe. All of the antislavery papers were full of him; Brown was becoming a celebrity. After 1856, Eppes was reminded of the stakes of this engagement each time he visited Brown's home. When Frederick Brown was slain at the Free Soil outpost of Osawatomie, Kansas, Brown had the boy's name etched on the back side of his grandfather's colonial-era headstone, which he leaned against the side of his new house, a positioning that turned the house itself into a memorial to the young picket "murdered for his adherence to the cause of freedom."[22]

Nor was death the only risk. As his wife, Annie, reminded him, if Lyman cast his lot with Brown, he gambled with his family's fate. She could not run the farm alone. She would take the family back to New York City, which would require $200. Could Lyman raise $200 to support his family in his absence? (All this his son, Lyman Jr., told a reporter in 1939.) Some years earlier, the death of the grantee James H. Henderson left his widow with five children. Overwhelmed and desperate, Jane Henderson moved the family to Manhattan—and see what became of them! Mary Brown famously went it alone when John was away (her selfless stoicism—a "Ruth," a "Roman mother," a "modern Penelope," Brown's friend and biographer, Franklin Sanborn, called her—is as much the stuff of legend as her husband's yearning for North Elba). But Mary Brown had help. One or more of her grown children or their spouses were usually around, and she could also hire hands. Further, since April 1857, the Boston abolitionists who supported Brown's Kansas efforts had been raising funds for John Brown's family "in case," Brown confided to his son John, "I never return to them." Could Lyman Eppes hope for "the permanent assistance of . . . wife and family" if he took off for Kansas or Virginia and failed to return? Could any of Brown's neighbors, white or Black?[23]

Let us remember, too, the closeness of the Eppes family, three generations in one cabin, and how firmly this clan was invested in this community. Lyman Eppes was North Elba's choirmaster, Bible teacher, and wolf slayer. He made the Baptist church ring with hymns. He, Annie, and others in the hamlet would organize a library, the first for miles around. Six of their eight children were born, reared, and schooled in the Adirondacks (but for the son who died in infancy soon after they arrived). Eppes's daughter Albertine was so enmeshed in the community that she would marry her Black neighbor, the widower and sometime farmer William Appo of Philadelphia. Eppes's son Lyman Jr. worked the farm with his father and would later work for a rich neighbor, and for the town (he also ran a trotter at the ice races at Lake Placid).[24]

In 1846, the year Smith gave away his land, Charles B. Ray had claimed, "There is no life like that of the farmer, for overcoming the mere prejudice against color." The Eppes family was making Ray's hopeful vision an imperfect, working truth. Let Eppes take up Brown's invitation, and all bets were off—and not just for the Eppeses. The loss of Lyman and the departure of Annie and the family would strain the walls of their community and leave a great gaping hole.[25]

So we can see what the Black Woods stood to lose if Lyman joined his neighbor and left home. The trickier question may be what he felt he might gain. In hindsight, it looks obvious: a hero's luster if all went well, lasting martyrdom if it didn't, and, either way, an opportunity to beat back "Satan and his legions" on the ground. But here, hindsight might be hindrance. What needs to be considered is how Brown's plan—how Brown himself—struck his friends and neighbors *before*, not *after*, Harpers Ferry. We know that Black families in North Elba liked and respected Brown. We have some idea, too (we'll never know the whole), of what Brown did for his Black neighbors. A brief recap: in that first winter of 1849, the food Brown shipped the grantees may have meant the difference between survival and starvation, and he organized a search party when the grantee Josiah Hasbrook got lost in the snow. In the summer, he helped set up the Jefferson brothers and James Henderson with a shared lot for their farming. He righted grantees' lot lines, got them settled on their acres, and furnished fabric when their clothes were thin and frayed. In their cabins and a schoolhouse, he preached Bible politics; he had them to his house for dinner, and hired them in his fields. With the grantee Willis Hodges as his proxy, he mentored them on dealing with white neighbors. Several women from the Black settlement (a Mrs. Reed, a Mrs. Dickson, and an "excellent colored woman," never named) found work on his farm. Samuel Jefferson was the family teamster. Eliza Carasaw sewed dresses for the girls. Lyman Eppes taught the children music.[26]

These dealings were prolific, and in Brown's biographies they are cinched as tightly as I've bundled them above. But the Brown family's correspondence reveals that in real time his encounters with the Black community were scattered over months and years and only rarely noted in his letters. And while he surely meant to make the grantees' progress on the land his priority when he first wrote Smith in 1848, this was not what happened. He could not be an on-site mentor with a steady, guiding hand. For the ten years Brown called North Elba home, from the year he moved his family to their first Adirondack farm to the winter of his hanging in 1859, Brown was at North Elba for no more than eighteen months, a sojourn chopped into hurried visits, most no longer than a fortnight. And this took a toll. It meant that, "on his flying visits to his farm" (Thomas Wentworth Higginson's description), "every moment was used," and that Brown's focus was, of necessity, on his farm and family. It also meant that his letters home allude to specific Black settlers only rarely and to the Black settlements almost never.[27]

This was not from any lack of sympathy. The letters Brown wrote Hodges, almost all of them destroyed, would have surely demonstrated his interest in the grantees. He admired his Black neighbors and valued their advice. He worried about the comfort of the family housekeeper, Mrs. Dickson, and "grieved," his daughter Ruth reported, "over the sad fate of . . . Mr. Henderson," who froze to death in 1852: "Mr. Henderson was an intelligent and good man, and was very industrious, and father thought much of him." Writing from North Elba, Brown gave his wife, then traveling, a thumbnail report on "the colored families'" progress: they "appear to be doing well, and to feel encouraged. They all send much love to you. They have constant preaching on the sabbath; and in intelligence, morality, and religion appear to be all on the advance." But references like these were fewer every year. *Were the boys feeding the cows too many potatoes? Cleaning out the mess vats? Making sure the cattle had fresh bedding and didn't wallow in the muck? How were Ellen's table manners?* These were the concerns that consumed the homesick Brown in his letters home until his death.[28]

Nor would Brown's family evince much interest in the grantees' progress overall. The letters that flew thick and fast among Brown family members make clear that they had their hands full on the farm. Subsistence agriculture was every shoulder to the wheel, all seasons, dark and sunny. Victories were local, hard gathered, and infinitely precious—four acres of rye sown and sprouting, a croupy baby healing up, a bumper crop of spring peas. Crises and losses exploded out of nowhere. A wildfire scarfed up Brown's son-in-law's grain, grass, and fences. A rooster froze to death, a calf choked on a potato, Watson battled typhoid, the girls needed shoes. Ruth Brown spent her first winter in North Elba bent over a needle: overcoats, frocks, pillowcases, pantaloons. Her mother and her brothers tapped the sugar bush and made maple cakes and syrup. The warm seasons turned every child who could toddle into a berry picker, each harvest in its turn, spring for wild strawberries, then raspberries, and pails full of blackberries and blueberries, and August sticky-sweet with wild grapes, with high bush cranberries still to come, and only sweeter after the first frost. Rueful musings on the suitability of North Elba as a place to live are frequent. Some of Brown's children warned against it; others liked it "middling well." Ruminations about Gerrit Smith's intentional community of Black pioneers are absent. Ruth and her husband, Henry Thompson, boarded Simeon Hasbrook for a while. The grantees were the Browns' neighbors, well known to them from church, school, and work parties. Occasional allusions crop up here and there: *Simeon Hasbrook climbed Mt. Whiteface with the Brown children and the Thompsons. . . . Mr. and Mrs. Eppes lost one of the twins.* But nobody was dwelling on Timbuctoo's symbolic value in the larger fight for voting rights for Blacks.[29]

The girls need shoes.

"To Benefit the Colored People on the Whole"

When John Brown first approached Gerrit Smith in 1848, he hoped to join a highly localized, slow-working agrarian experiment that might stand as an example to the region, even the nation. He dared to dream— as Abraham Lincoln had put it just before the Civil War—of an "easier triumph." But the antislavery movement in the 1850s endured a beating as relentless as an enslaver's caning of the abolitionist Charles Sumner on the Senate floor. To merely list the blows—the stunning laws, the overlapping crises—cannot convey the cumulative devastation. There was, as Brown stressed in his constitution for his Subterranean Pass Way, a war on, undeclared. An easier triumph would not deliver slavery's abolition. And from Brown's wide-angle vantage, the way to justice was as clear and rushing as a river, and North Elba was an eddy. He would not be diverted. Not even by the Black neighbors' vote he solicited himself.[30]

Brown put the question to those neighbors in the fall of 1854. At this point all his family but Henry and Ruth Brown Thompson, his son-in-law and daughter, had been away from North Elba for three years. Brown himself intended to return; on a farm lot in North Elba, Henry Thompson was getting up a house for him (the clapboard home that stands today). Brown's sons Owen, Frederick, Salmon, Jason, and John Jr. were on their way to Kansas, along with thousands of other Free Soilers on the move, aiming to take down the proslavery cohort with new farms, numbers, votes, and guns (their brother Oliver, in Illinois, would join them later in the summer). Mary Brown and others in the family were staying put in the rented Akron farmhouse of Brown's old partner, the wool dealer Simon Perkins. Brown himself was caught up in a weary shuttle between courtrooms and lawyers' offices in Springfield, Boston, New York City, Troy, and Vernon, New York, trying gamely, unavailingly, to salvage the good name of his and Perkins's battered wool business and reverse their epic losses in an unforgiving market. It wouldn't happen; the partnership dissolved, and by the end, Brown was nearly destitute. But there was liberation in worldly failure. In his sights now, nothing to block the view, was his lifelong enemy, more confident than ever, and Brown was going to war.[31]

The question was, which battlefield would bring the greater victory? On September 30, 1854, Brown wrote his North Elba family,

> After being hard pressed to go with my family to Kansas as more likely to benefit the colored people *on the whole* than to return with them to North Elba; I have consulted to ask for your *advice & feeling* in the matter; & also to ask you to learn from Mr. Epps and all the colored people (so far as you can) how they would wish, & advise me to act in the case, all things considered. As I volunteered in their service (or the service of the colored people); they have a right to vote, as to the course I take.

Brown also solicited advice from Gerrit Smith, Frederick Douglass, and James McCune Smith. How the latter two responded is not known. Gerrit Smith hoped Brown would resume his perennially interrupted work in the Black Woods, and Brown's family expected this as well, because that November, when Brown was home on a visit, Ruth Brown Thompson wrote about her father, "We are rejoiced to hear that he has given up the idea of going to Kansas, but will move here this winter, if he can get feed for his cattle." As it happened, the poverty that followed the failure of Brown and Simon Perkins's wool business, made worse by the drought that ravaged his Ohio crops, stalled Brown's move home for months. But in late May he was back, settling into the new frame house with its wide view of the High Peaks. Then, in July, Brown left for Kansas, and he would return to North Elba only a few times before the last ride home in a coffin on a drenched December day.[32]

In 1910, Brown's eminent biographer Oswald Garrison Villard chalked up Brown's change of heart about sticking with North Elba to that chronic, helpless "restlessness [that] left him no peace." Louis Ruchames (*A John Brown Reader*, 1959) offered only that Brown was "touched by the contagion that had already seized his sons." Richard O. Boyer (*The Legend of John Brown*, 1973) stressed the galvanizing impact of the letter Brown got from his son John Jr. in May, which sang the praises of the Kansas Territory as eloquently as it foretold the bloody fate of the Free Staters if they weren't prepared, and soon, to meet the enemy with guns. It was this letter that steadied Brown's resolve and put him "for the first time in years . . . at one with himself." Inviting a vote from his Black North Elban neighbors, according to Boyer, revealed weakness; broke and weary, Brown had lost faith in his own

John Brown's Home, North Elba, NY. Photographer unknown, ca. 1860. The *Pageant of America* Collection, Digital Collection, NYPL.

judgment. His son's appeal revived his sense of usefulness and called him back to his great mission.[33]

But Brown knew his mission before he asked the grantees for their thoughts. However they might vote, he was going to do what would "benefit the colored people *on the whole*." That meant Kansas, and the fact that he was inviting his Black neighbors to advise his course of action in terms of "the whole" was their pointed cue to take the long view, too, and privilege the dire crisis of their brethren in bonds over their own needs. They had "a right to vote," and he would listen, but the silent votes of that greater "whole"—a majority of enslaved millions— would need to win the day. This is not to say that his interest in hearing out his neighbors was disingenuous. On the contrary, as David Reynolds notes, it was proof of an egalitarianism close to freakish in its time, and of an interest in a distributive justice that favored all opinions with respect. If, however, Brown's request for a vote is noteworthy, so is the uneasy fact that we do not know what followed the request. Did the grantees suggest he stay or encourage him to go? Nobody took minutes. All we know for sure is, vote or no vote, Brown would not betray his conscience, or his reading of God's will.[34]

Beautiful Dreams

Years before, Brown had promised to be "a sort of father" to the grant-ees. In truth, he could not help being fatherly—it came as easily to him as prayer. But as the antislavery struggle grew more militant, the object of his paternalism changed. In addition to his far-flung family and the grantees, Brown would also be a father—confidante, morale booster, mentor—to forty-four Black men he met in Springfield, Massachusetts, after the passage of the Fugitive Slave Act. Many of these men were doing racial justice work before he met them; Brown was not their or-ganizer. But his passion surely thrilled them, especially when he gave their group a name, the League of Gileadites, and articulated their goal—to fight slave catchers—in terms as confident as they were plain. Black Northerners, free or fugitive, ought not only to resist the law's enforcers, but to strike preemptively, and should "not do [their] work by halves, but make clean work with your enemies." A white man urging Blacks to armed, organized resistance—some activists in this new club would have surely caught the backbeat of Henry Highland Garnet's fu-rious "Call to Rebellion" of 1843 and the Black militant David Walker's earlier appeal of 1829.[35]

Preaching to an ad hoc vigilante group of activists in Springfield was not like "fathering" a widely scattered, underpopulated flock of Ad-irondack farmers, but it satisfied the same need to inspire and to lead, and it reminded Brown, as the slower-working Black Woods could not, that he was good at this. He had a gift. And Brown would exercise this gift through the remainder of the decade. In Kansas, August Bondi re-marked on Brown's expressions of "the most affectionate care for each of us. We were united as a band of brothers by the love and affection toward the man who with tender words and wise counsel . . . prepared a handful of young men." The prisoners he seized in 1858 were invited to join daily prayers, and any taunting of them by his men was forbidden. And when he asked "all [his] family to imagine themselves in the same dreadful condition" as the Springfield Blacks at risk of arrest under the Fugitive Slave Act, he meant not to alarm them but to refresh their memory of his ability to calm. *While I am gone, imagine me still at home in my actions, still fathering and succoring those in need, and if you can imagine how they feel, if you can be them in your minds, so may I succor you.*[36]

The imagination! Brown's faith in its transformative power was boundless. How often had he written Mary of how he imagined her, their children, their home. In 1847 or 1848, Brown's imagination nerved this white wool merchant to write an essay for the *Ram's Horn*, Willis Hodges's city paper, from the vantage of a Black reformer. It let him claim a plain-faced farmhouse he visited only rarely as his heart's home; helped him elaborate his scheme to rescue enslaved Blacks; and gave him license to envision his death as an event that might spur the antislavery world to action (and of his martyrdom, Brown was certain; it was virtually encoded in his plan, right down to the "poor, little, dirty, ragged, bare-headed and barefooted Slave Boys; and Girls, led by some old grey-headed Slave Mother" he imagined bearing witness to his hanging).[37]

Fifty years after Harpers Ferry, Katherine Mayo, a Boston friend, put it thoughtfully: "He could form beautiful dreams of things, as they should occur, and forthwith go into action on the basis of those dreams, making no sufficient allowance for some things occurring as they should not." What overrode Brown's "beautiful dream" of his role in the Black Woods was another dream, a vision close to holy, and as far as we know, no Black Adirondack settler ever wished he'd made another choice. But they would not make it theirs.[38]

Brown's biographer Richard Boyer attributed their noninvolvement to their advanced years; these old men, he indicated, were "demoralized by the hardships of Essex County." In fact, the 1855 North Elba census reported thirteen Black settlers from their late teens into their early fifties, nine of them between the ages of twenty and forty-six. The Hazzard household in St. Armand held three able-bodied twenty-year-old Black farmers. And in five of six Black Franklin households in 1860, the census revealed men of age to take up arms with Captain Brown.[39]

Assuming that able-bodied, slavery-despising Adirondack farmers like Lyman Eppes, the Hazzard men, and John Thomas were welcome in John Brown's ranks, why would they spurn a chance to serve with Brown's guerrilla band? Worcester's Thomas Wentworth Higginson believed he knew the answer (other chroniclers never thought to ask the question, assuming as they did that the Black settlement was dead). In his eulogy for Brown, Higginson, Brown's boldest backer in the "Secret Six," claimed that Brown planned all along to find his fighters among grantees ("Where should he find his men? He came to the Adirondacks to look for them.") but gave up that expectation when he realized that "such men as he needed are not to be found ordinarily; they must be *reared*. John Brown did not merely look for men, therefore; he reared them in his sons." Higginson meant to underscore the extraordinary courage of Brown's family, not to denigrate the grantees. (Alone among Brown's memorialists, he blamed the failure of Smith's giveaway not on the grantees' ineptitude but on the corrosive impact of local racism.) All the same, Higginson's comparison—ordinary mortals versus heroes—suggested that the Black settlers let Brown down. Brown's from-the-cradle rearing of his children in the principles of justice had "given them a wider perspective than the Adirondacks." The Black grantees, by contrast, were stuck. They couldn't give Brown what he needed—they didn't have the vision, the martyr's holy zeal, to back their own best friend. In the end, Higginson declared, it would be other Blacks, "freed slaves and fugitives," who "repaid" Brown "for his early friendship to these New York colored men."[40]

Repaid! So, the Black farmers of the Adirondacks had shirked their duty and revealed themselves to be (compared with Brown's own vigilantes) provincial and ungrateful. Whether the Black settlers were condemned for being unsoldierly, too old for the job, or "demoralized" by the rigors of the frontier, their noninvolvement in Brown's guerrilla war and his assault on Harpers Ferry always seemed to evidence some lack. That they did not join Brown because of their own ideas about his prospects, track record, or goals was not addressed. The choice to stick with what they had started, honor a commitment to their farms and families, was racialized, emasculated: they were weak, fearful, and unfit. Such was the hagiography that exalted the redeemer by discounting Black agency and self-determination.

In this context, the biographer David Reynolds's stern summary of John Brown's career bears repeating: "Few successful people in history have failed so miserably in so many different pursuits as John Brown. He failed as a tanner, a shepherd, a cattle trader, a horse breeder, a lumber dealer, a real estate speculator, and a wool distributor." There were credit conflicts that defied enumeration, and overall, a track record of reversal revealing something worse than just bad luck. It showed a pattern of poor judgment and mismanagement that would have registered with Lyman Eppes and the grantees as surely as the insolvency so chronic that Brown once had to borrow money from his hired hand, the fugitive Cyrus Thomas. Then there were Brown's absences, and his family's long disappearance. From 1851 to 1854, all the Browns except Ruth Brown Thompson were nowhere near the Black Woods.[41]

Nor would it be lost on Eppes and the grantees that only the abolitionist Thompsons, one family among Brown's *white* neighbors, took his side, though many others were aware of his plans and might have joined him. "Brown was at North Elba during a large part of last summer, engaged everywhere in disseminating his opinions," a North Country cattleman told the *Utica Observer* after Brown's arrest. In Vergennes, Vermont, where Brown often sojourned, he remained "a man of mystery," yet "rumors . . . concerning Brown's activities" blew around the town like pollen, the *Springfield Republican* reported. In North Elba, Brown's plans were more than rumored. "Reliable hearsay is that Brown gave others in the community a chance to share the fate of his three sons and two of the Thompson boys at Harpers Ferry—and thus share in the praise of Emerson, Thoreau, Wendell Phillips, and Victor Hugo. But no more there than elsewhere was the call to martyrdom an appealing one," recalled Judge O. Byron Brewster in 1952. In 1902 Judge Brewster's aunt, Adaline Brown, would be described in an obituary as "an intimate and confidential friend of John Brown" who "knew of Brown's plans and purposes before he started on his desperate mission." Yet no male Brewsters joined the Browns, and neither would young Alexis Hinckley, though Brown hoped he might, and Hinckley had told him he was "ready to move at a moment's warning."[42]

Abe Sherman heard Brown talk about his plans at the old Holstead House in Westport. Brown's neighbor William Peacock was privy to them too. An English immigrant who settled in North Elba a year before the Browns arrived, Peacock and his boy Thomas learned all about the abolitionist's plans at a meeting at Brown's home. Later, Peacock was one of the first North Elbans to answer Lincoln's call for volunteers; he served for three years and all his life cherished his friendship with John Brown. But though able-bodied and for the slave, he would not go to Harpers Ferry. At this he drew a line.[43]

The Franklin County pioneer James Wardner went one better: he and his white neighbors tried to "persuade John Brown to give up his foolish notion of trying to liberate the slaves through an uprising." The Wardners were first-vintage Adirondackers, a tight clan of Vermont-bred farmers, innkeepers, and guides. Wardner himself met John Brown on a squall-tossed steamer bound for Plattsburgh in 1857 (Brown helped him calm his horse). Wardner's unpublished memoir, conveyed in old age to his son Charles and transcribed by his grandson Walter, has its starry flourishes (he calls Brown "a tall, broad shouldered and heavy bearded giant"), but there is news here nonetheless. Wardner liked the abolitionist; he and Brown always hoped they might go fishing. But about Gerrit Smith's bid to get up a farm colony for Black people he had misgivings. Nor would he go for Brown's suggestion that he secrete escaping slaves in haystacks built especially for the purpose. A "disgusted" Brown told Wardner he "was not much of an abolitionist. However, we remained friends."[44]

On his visit to Brown's North Elba farm, Wardner and his friends each "took a turn at trying to make him see the futility of [a raid at Harpers Ferry]," Wardner recalled. "'Jawn,' Nokes [John Nokes, from Franklin] said, 'you're going to get yer damn neck stretched down there. You try to seize a government arsenal and they'll hang ye for a traitor. Won't ye give it up?' 'No! I will not!' he thundered. 'I know I am going to be a martyr. I want my body to be brought back and buried right by that rock.'" And then, said Wardner, Brown not only showed his visitors the massive boulder he hoped would flank his grave, but carved his initials into it, then and there.

A bit thick, this. Hideaways tucked into haystacks from a man who openly housed a fugitive in his North Elba home? Initials chiseled, just like that? The boulder that Brown adored is hard as schist. But these fine points matter less, finally, than Wardner's need to partake of an Adirondack rite of passage—laying a postbellum claim on a corner of the John Brown story even while justifying his remove from it. If radical abolitionism, in his self-exonerating reading, meant cockamamie schemes to turn haystacks into hideaways, then no, Wardner was not much of an abolitionist. And he would offer no apology or second-guessing about not joining Brown on a suicidal mission. Wardner acknowledged "the earnest efforts of those who desire . . . reforms," but he would not join their pioneering ranks.[45]

Others held back too. Mary Brown chose not to join her spouse, figuring she could do more good at home with her young children and a new granddaughter than with her husband and his band. Her beloved son-in-law Henry Thompson, a veteran of Pottawatomie, would not go to Harpers Ferry. To join Brown now, he felt, was suicide, and he could not justify the risk of leaving his wife a widow, his children fatherless. Salmon and Jason declined too. Brown's son John Jr. had offered to participate, but when the raid occurred, he was in Canada—and this may not have been accidental. The trauma he experienced when he was captured, tortured, and beaten by proslavery vigilantes in 1857 never wholly eased its grip.[46]

Lyman Eppes and the Black grantees knew some who went. But they knew so many more who didn't—and from no lack of abolitionist conviction (Henry Thompson was not just a radical abolitionist but a husband, son, and brother of abolitionists as well). The grantees would have sensed the skepticism with which Brown's subversive plans were viewed by his white neighbors. His erratic track record as a businessman was no secret, and farmers as observant as Eppes had good reason to suppose that Brown's plan for the seizure of a federal arsenal might end as badly as other high-reaching schemes he had driven into the ground.

Then there was Eppes's faith. Did he want to kill? Brown's plans for Harpers Ferry may have been semisecret, but his bloody exploits in the antislavery struggle out West were widely covered in the Republican and abolition newspapers. Frontline columns in Greeley's syndicated *Tribune* pulsed with news of the undeclared war between "Free Staters" and Missouri emigrants, and here the name "Old Brown" loomed. For Adirondackers, *their* John Brown of North Elba, ribbon winner at the county fair, always talking slavery, always with a plan, was the local link, the connector. He made the far-off intimate. He brought the struggle home.[47]

He was also, by 1859, a wanted man with a price on his head. The Pottawatomie slayings were widely (if imperfectly) reported in many eastern newspapers, and in some reports had been described as outright murderous. How did violations of the sixth commandment resonate with Brown's Black neighbors? Brown, while a believer, was a tepid churchman unless the preaching was his own. Not so his Black friends. The Eppeses, Carasaws, Jeffersons, Hazzards, and Hendersons were devout. Eppes cofounded two congregations in North Elba. So let us suppose that divine law held at least as much meaning for him as it did, say, for Brown's pacifist son Jason. Let us not assume that Eppes and the other grantees, simply because they were Black, automatically condoned Brown's bloody actions or shared his justifying vision of a higher morality. If Brown was disappointed when Eppes declined to join his war party, the disappointment may have worked both ways. Eppes may have been distressed by Brown's disregard for his own first promises, unhappy with a brand of antislavery violence that violated Eppes's spiritual convictions, and uneasy about Brown's long legacy of worldly failure.[48]

A Yes as Resonant as His No

The fact that Brown was unable to get one Black settler in Essex or Franklin Counties to join him has never been linked to his subsequent, better-chronicled failure to win the spontaneous, militant support of Black people living around Harpers Ferry. It should be. North Elba was the proverbial miner's canary, a portent of the debacle of 1859. Brown hoped Eppes would join his ranks for the same reason he expected Black Virginians, free or enslaved, to flock en masse to his defense. Eppes would do it because Eppes was a Black American of conscience, and as such would embrace the opportunity to battle slave owners and the proslavery government that enabled them. How could he not? "In [Brown's] view," David Reynolds explains, "slaves needed no special circumstances to motivate them to rebellion. By definition, they longed to rebel as a result of their oppressed condition." Brown had studied slave revolts; he knew how these things worked. While Eppes was no slave, surely his skin color ensured that his identification with the slave's plight would be, "by definition," at least as great as Brown's.[49]

It is a pity that the Christian vision that let Brown embrace Black Americans as equals did not translate into a keen appreciation of human nature in its particularity. Black people, as it happened, did not act or answer "by definition." If there were "two thousand distinct forms of oppression scattered among the hundred and seventy-six thousand free colored people in the free States," as James McCune Smith wearily observed, there were as many ways that those "forms of oppression" might be fought. Lyman Eppes and the Black Woods enacted one modest, localized approach. Harpers Ferry offered another. Eppes didn't want a martyr's glory in Captain Brown's war; he was captaining his own integrationist campaign at home. And if Eppes's decision was bad news for Brown, it was very good news for Eppes's family and community and for the idea of this community, an idea of Black and white people living peaceably on the frontier, drawn into a shared vision less by a scheme of justice than by good sense. It was, that is, as meaningful a yes as it was a no, as significant a validation as it was a disavowal.[50]

But this was not what was remembered. Eppes's obituaries in 1897 would mostly *not* extol the church-loving citizen who helped bind a smattering of homesteads into a lightly knit community. They would not recall the wolves he shot, the library he cofounded, the conservationists and sportsmen he guided, the trails he cut, or the four ministers who spoke at his funeral. Posterity buried his biography as a pioneer, saving only John Brown's friend and neighbor, the silver-voiced colored man who sang "Blow Ye the Trumpets, Blow" at Brown's funeral. The Connecticut-born Eppes, the *New York Times* obituary reported, was "one of the negroes brought from the South by John Brown." For a century, that's how it stood.[51]

John Brown Country

CHAPTER 14

To Arms! The Black Woods at War

White Adirondackers fought with valor for the Union in the Civil War, and Black Adirondackers did too. But white people fought for one thing; the men and boys of the Black Woods fought for another. There was overlap, but their Civil Wars were not the same.

Black men fought slavery. Its centrality in their lives ensured this. Some settlers on the Smith Land had been slaves in their youth, or were the children of ex-slaves, or had ex-slaves for ministers, grandparents, or spouses. Even when their families were decades out of slavery, reenslavement was ever thinkable. Upstate Black New Yorkers recalled how useless was Solomon Northup's free status was when, in 1841, he was lured from upstate Saratoga Springs to Washington, DC, with the promise of a job, then drugged, jailed, and sold to a Louisiana planter—and Northup the son of an Adirondack farmer-voter. Especially after the enactment of the Fugitive Slave Act, enslavement menaced every free Black person in the North. And because Black Northerners felt slavery as an existential threat, they knew, as white people could not, why only war could smash it. A system as entrenched, confident, and profitable as the one that stole John Thomas's first wife and snatched twelve years from the life of Solomon Northup—a system whose defenders would sooner leave the nation than cede the right to hold human beings as chattel—would yield only to force.

So Black Northerners felt no ambivalence about John Brown's wild raid that pitched half the nation into a lashing paranoia and roused the other half to the grim defense of nationhood and law. The raid that hastened the long war that, alone, offered the hope of justice and relief for millions was a reckoning. *Let it come.* The man Herman Melville called "the Meteor of the War" changed the world.

And this meteor had been their friend! It was another thing that set the Black settlers' Civil War apart. Long before his name was claimed by Union soldiers on the march, John Brown belonged to the Black Woods. His Black neighbors knew his wife and children, his facility with a surveyor's transit, his fierce faith, his taste in hymns. Private Hasbrook's father got lost in a snowstorm and was led to safety by John Brown. Private Carasaw's wife, Eliza, mended clothes for Brown's wife. Private Appo's father sold Brown's daughter a melodeon when she got married. If the men of the Black Woods fought for the slave, they also fought to honor the memory of their white ally and true friend.[1]

For most of them, however, there would be no fighting until the war was halfway over. Until January 1864, Black men who lived within a wagon ride of John Brown's grave were denied the right to bear arms for the Union—as were Black men all over the free North whose efforts to enlist were categorically rebuffed. In New York City, mobs broke up ad hoc Black militias; in Providence, Black-initiated drills were outlawed as "disorderly gatherings." As Benjamin Quarles observes in *The Negro in the Civil War*, "There seemed to be a common sentiment that the only military command that Negroes should hear was, 'As you were.'" But in the Black Woods, the rejection registered as more than legal. It took aim at the hope of justice and equality that drew Black families to this wilderness in the first place, and that had seemed to set this land apart.[2]

Avery Hazzard and his white neighbors in St. Armand were of one pioneering generation. They knew each other's barns and crops, took the other's side against the tax collector. Avery's father, Levi, fought for three years with his Massachusetts regiment in the War of Independence. At the outbreak of the Civil War, three grandsons of this patriot—Charles Henry, Alexander, and George—hoped to fight as much as their white neighbors, who were so keen to enlist that they were making city headlines. ("In St. Armand, N.Y., [near] where John Brown lived and was buried, of the eighty voters in the town, seventy have enlisted," the *New York Times* reported in 1862.) But when the war began, the pliable constraints of caste hardened into federal policy. So white Adirondackers marched to fife and drum, and Black men stood apart with women, children, and old men, cheering on white patriots even as they struggled to ignore this bitter insult here about the white man's greater worthiness for battle.[3]

And this, of course, was the third thing that set their Civil War apart: they, not their white friends, had to deal with an army that held them stiffly at arm's length—or, as historian Benjamin Quarles put it, to suffer a wartime government that "measured out . . . rights for Negroes . . . in homeopathic doses and administered with a long spoon." The formation of Black regiments in New York would be delayed fully a year after federal policy gave Black men fighting rights (and delayed by the same governor, Horatio Seymour, who in 1868 made his campaign slogan for the presidency "This Is a White Man's Country. Let White Men Rule"). Even after February 1864, when Black volunteers were finally, grudgingly, allowed to serve, given rifles, and dispatched to fight, the army stalled their progress. Black fighting men were paid less. They got worse gear. They got less medical attention than white soldiers, and suffered greater rates of injury and a death rate 35 percent higher than what white troops endured. In the South, these soldiers would be exposed to racialized atrocities and war crimes that white soldiers seldom faced. In effect, they fought three adversaries to the white man's two. White enlistees went to beat a sectional rebellion, and those who were abolitionists (never a majority) battled slavery as well. Black soldiers fought the rebels, the slaveocracy, and (maybe worst of all) an enemy their white friends never knew: the rote presumption of Black inferiority.[4]

And this foe, unlike the enemy of white fighters, was unconcerned with legal treaties or military defeat. When General Lee raised the flag of truce at Appomattox, white Union men knew victory was theirs, and they were done. Black soldiers reveled in the defeat of the Confederacy too, but white racism did not surrender. It lost a uniform; it kept its guns.

That only eight men from the Black Woods joined the Union army suggests how much the Black community had dwindled since the giveaway's debut. And while this meager list would double if I beefed it up with grantees or their sons who joined the army from elsewhere in the Adirondacks (Westport, Willsboro, Elizabethtown), or who enlisted after they were well out of the region (like Willis Hodges, who scouted for the Union in Virginia, or the fighting sons of Samuel and Thomas Jefferson), or if I stretched it with the names of emancipated African Americans who discovered Franklin and St. Armand when the war was over, this would only obscure the view. If the point is to track what the Adirondacks signified for African Americans who were living in the Smith Lands when they enlisted, and to consider how the war years shaped their prospects and their expectations on their return, the focus has to stay with those for whom the Black Woods was the starting point. And so we have these eight, and offer here, in the rough order of their enlistments, a bit of what we know about the war years of North Elba's William Appo Jr., Silas Frazier, William Carasaw, and Josiah Hasbrook; St. Armand's Charles Henry Hazzard; and Franklin's Warren Morehouse, James Brady, and Samuel Brady.[5]

William Appo Jr., first in this list to answer President Lincoln's call for volunteers, signed up in North Elba in early 1861. He was nineteen and had been living in North Elba for perhaps a year with his father, William Sr. Why did he not enlist from his parents' year-round home in Burlington, New Jersey? Maybe he tried and was rebuffed, and that's why he was here. He was mixed-race. Nonwhites were not welcome in the army. But Appo Sr.'s 1848 purchase of a good-sized lot in North Elba was a significant investment that pioneers, both Black and white, probably appreciated. And when the light-skinned Appo Jr. (both of his parents were listed as "mulatto" in the census) volunteered to serve his country, some North Elbans, eager for volunteers, may have recalled his father's first show of faith and thought to return the favor. Whatever the reason for this exception, young Appo made the cut. From North Elba, he registered in the all-white US Army and was directed to the Thirtieth Regiment, New York Infantry, Company I, in Troy in 1861. He was the first man from the Black Woods to join a white regiment in defiance of the color law. Surely his father, an army man himself when he was a youth in Haiti, saluted his resolve.[6]

Appo's officers would flag their confidence in this volunteer early on. Only five months after he mustered in, Appo was made corporal. His regiment engaged in twenty-six skirmishes and thirty battles. With the Army of the Potomac, it fought in the First Battle of Bull Run (also called Manassas) and other battles, and it returned to this old killing field with the Army of Virginia in late August 1862. The Second Battle of Bull Run was distinguished by a day of legendarily horrific carnage in an abandoned railroad cut corralled with weedy culverts, digs, and embankments, which gave Confederate general Thomas W. "Stonewall" Jackson all the breastworks and protection his men would need to seize the day. Sixty-two thousand Union troops fought in the Second Battle of Bull Run. A fifth of them, some fourteen thousand men, died in one day. In the Deep Cut, Corporal Appo joined his comrades in a mass grave. His remains were not recovered.[7]

Some years after the war, his father had a stone with his son's name on it placed near his own marker in the Lake Placid cemetery, and much later, in the late twentieth century, a World War II veteran and retired schoolteacher in Lake Placid, Charles Thomas, honored this slain soldier's marker with a Grand Army of the Republic star and a flag. But the flag and star would be removed in 2001 at the insistence of the town historian. Only graves or markers with bodies in the ground were entitled to these honors, she declared, and Appo's body wasn't buried. Never mind that there was no body. None that might have been identified had ever been recovered. Mary MacKenzie was unswayed.[8]

Not so Greg Furness, an Adirondack friend I shared this story with when I learned about it in the summer of 2022. Greg, his old job in state historic preservation well behind him, has spent a lot of time in his retirement in old Adirondack cemeteries, cleaning and repairing old graves, making sure Civil War veterans get their due. On Veterans Day 2022, a message with a picture showed up in my inbox. A small flag rising from its holder in a new-ordered GAR Civil War marker in back of William Appo's stone looked right at home.[9]

Franklin's Warren Morehouse was also keen to take up arms. And when New York's Negrophobic governor, Horatio Seymour, failed to reward the interest of New York's prospective Black volunteers, Morehouse, with 223 other Black New Yorkers, thought of Massachusetts, whose antislavery governor, John Andrew, put out a call for Black enlistees after President Lincoln's Emancipation Proclamation of January 1, 1863. A few months later, Lincoln signed the federal Enrollment Act, directing every congressional district in the Union to meet a soldiers' quota, either by a draft or by voluntary enlistment. Compulsory conscription was never popular, North or South, and Union states hastened to expedite enlistment with bonuses and bounties. These were meaningful and timely boosts for poor men who could not leave dependents for three years unsupported. That six of the eight volunteers from the Black Woods enlisted after the passage of the Enrollment Act indicates they took their domestic obligations seriously. Now that their families were assured of some relief, they could leave them in good conscience. Morehouse headed east.[10]

At the railway depot in Boston that September in 1863, this Adirondacker, not a knuckle over five feet tall, told the recruiter for the

Massachusetts Fifty-Fourth Colored Infantry that he was twenty-one. He was actually more like seventeen, but fudging birthdates was a venerable military tradition. Did the gray Atlantic, with its tang of brine and wheeling gulls, bedazzle him? Not half so much, I imagine, as the sight of Black enlistees rolling into Boston from as many as twenty-four states. Black men and boys from all over the East! In his Blackness, Morehouse now had company. Blackness, in his regiment, was for once not outside of things (not the young Black axman in William Sidney Mount's painting, lingering outside a barn to eavesdrop on the white fiddlers sawing out a tune inside). Blackness was his world now. It had his back; it gave him standing, friends, and mentors. It made a home.[11]

Morehouse's years with the Fifty-Fourth also stretched his understanding of the hundred ways the enemies of Blackness schemed to break his body, soul, and heart. He expected a rough time from the rebels—but from his own side too? Not only did Black volunteers receive less pay than white soldiers (and had to buy their uniforms, as whites did not), but they could expect less expert medical attention, their hospitals were undermanned and insufficiently supplied, and they endured significantly higher rates of injury and death. They hoped for glory in the battlefield; instead they dug encampments and trenches for amputated limbs, tended horses, emptied latrines, heaved coal, cooked for their white officers, and brewed their tea. (The Ninety-Sixth New York Infantry, a northern New York regiment that organized in Plattsburgh, signed up seven "colored cooks"; Malone's Ninety-Eighth Regiment Infantry had thirteen.)[12]

Also new for this backwoods youth: his first encounter with Black men from New York City, many of them still reeling from the draft riots that shocked Manhattan in mid-July. This four-day rampage, ostensibly a protest against President Lincoln's call for compulsory conscription, left as many as 1,200 Black people dead. "Satan has been let loose in this city upon the poor negro," a reporter wrote Gerrit Smith about this American pogrom. Rev. Henry Highland Garnet recalled rioters hacking Black bodies to bits and peddling "Nigger meat." McCune Smith's Colored Orphan Asylum was put to the torch, and he took his family and medical practice from Manhattan. Elder Ray shut his church down, and when the riot was subdued, he returned to the old neighborhoods to solace traumatized survivors with food and medicine. "None know excepting those who have witnessed it the extent of the suffering among them," the minister despaired. Some of the New York recruits Morehouse met at the Camp Meigs training ground south of Boston were here as much to get out of Manhattan as to join the army. And what an irony that the first refugees Morehouse encountered in the service would not be contrabands down South but free Black men in flight from white rage in the North.[13]

Morehouse also learned from his new comrades about the Fifty-Fourth Massachusetts Colored's harsh defeat that summer at Fort Wagner. Frederick Douglass's eldest son, Sergeant Major Lewis H. Douglass, survived that battle (but later injuries would kill his military prospects). Outside Charleston, the Fifty-Fourth had led a charge of many regiments to retake Fort Wagner's earthworks, but without cover or sufficient numbers, and immobilized by crossfire, the Black troops, Douglass reported, were simply "cut to pieces." One witness saw the bodies of Black soldiers heaped so high a man could walk fifty yards across them and never touch the ground. Yet—here was the thing—no other regiment did so much damage to the rebels' fortifications, or made such a lasting name for guts. Garlanded by Union editors and churchmen, the martyrs of the Fifty-Fourth Colored inspired thousands of Black hopefuls to enlist in the Black regiments. So, while devastating to the Fifty-Fourth, this regiment's good work that day also signified a victory, a vindication of Frederick Douglass's promise: "Once let the black man get upon his person the brass letters U.S., let him get an eagle on his button, and a musket on his shoulder, and bullets in his pocket, and there is no power on earth or under the earth which can deny that he has earned the right of citizenship."[14]

Colonel Robert Shaw, the abolitionist Bostonian who headed up the Fifty-Fourth Colored, was killed and buried in a mass grave with his men. To Confederates who judged this a deserved insult, Shaw's family would say their slain son would count an integrated grave the highest honor. And Morehouse may have deemed it an honor to join a regiment so renowned for its abolition leadership. He had been hearing about slavery and abolitionists—such as Gerrit Smith, his family's benefactor, and Troy's Garnet, who made his father one of his "Pick'd Men." At dusk at the Readville parade ground, Boston's abolitionists gathered on the sidelines, there to "take the greatest pleasure in watching the development of the negroes as soldiers," join them at their evening prayer, and salute the new band's "steady and daily improvement" in its one martial tune. So recalled the writer Henry Bowditch, whose family lived close by.[15]

But the more lasting memories would be what Morehouse witnessed in the South, and as he marched with his company into the South

Carolina backcountry, the dry dust swimming up around his boots, the young private saw all he needed to know why he was here. Old men and children in feed sacks and string belts, shoeless, straggling out to greet him; cotton fields hazed with smoke; slave quarters the size of corn cribs next to fine pillared homes; and sometimes (recalled the regimental memoirist) the only sound "the tinkle, tinkle of pans and cups, striking the bayonets for music." Most Black people here were welcoming, of course, but some, of course, still registered their incredulity. *Black men in blue, eyes front, bearing arms. What cold new trickery was this?*[16]

Private Morehouse's war was long, and in the course of it some of Black America's best allies would lose patience with the abolition course. In stumping for the Union, Gerrit Smith, the Black Woods' benefactor and the bondsman's long and faithful friend, now repeatedly declared the Union cause a greater passion, or at least priority, than his devotion to Black freedom. Well, the old man could speechify away. Morehouse fought for the slave—and, according to the regimental history, fought nervily and well. In Olustee, Florida, the Adirondacker, "chaf[ing]" for "aggressive action," "crept out" to take aim at the enemy. At Boykin's Mill (the last skirmish in South Carolina), Morehouse, walking point, spied "Johnnies" in a barn, intelligence that led his captain to change the plan of attack (and to note this private's contribution in his memoir). Morehouse would be tapped to serve in his regimental hospital, a repeat assignment that spanned months. At notoriously short-staffed, under-supplied Colored Regimental Hospitals, the work was ceaseless, urgent, and demoralizing. Morehouse was unfazed. Before the war and after, Adirondack inns had hired him as a camp cook, waiter, and hunter; versatility was his gift. Toward the end of his service, the army made him a regimental marker. Quickness, confidence, precision—troops in formation relied on the "RM" as an orchestra looks to the conductor. Morehouse kept the lines straight, then turned them on a dime. When he mustered out in August 1865, he looked forward to a hundred-dollar bounty and, like his mates, had plans for every cent.[17]

From St. Armand, the farmer Charles Henry Hazzard enlisted with the Adirondack Regiment, the NY 118th, likely delighting the enlistment officer since Hazzard's signature could help this village meet its quota. But higher-ups would catch the breach of army policy, and within a week this volunteer was redirected to the NY Twenty-Sixth US Colored. Just after Christmas in 1863, Hazzard mustered in at Rikers Island. His younger brother, Alexander, also hoped to serve, but left no military record and may have joined a home militia.[18]

Also headed for the Colored Twenty-Sixth: North Elba's grantee-farmer William Carasaw and his younger neighbor Josiah Hasbrook, who, like Hazzard, was a grantee's son. These two went to Clinton County to enlist, accompanied that day by the farmer Leonard Worts, long a Hasbrook family friend. Josiah's older brother, Simeon, already living in Manhattan, had enlisted too. In the US Navy was no lower rank than landsman, but the pay was regular and the job was sure. Simeon served on a half-dozen navy vessels and a whaling bark before he quit the sea in 1870.[19]

From Plattsburgh, Black enlistees in the Twenty-Sixth Colored took the train to New York City to collect their guns and uniforms and start training at Rikers Island. Still in his civvies, a stony-faced Carasaw got his picture taken at the Cady Photo Gallery on Canal Street, close to the Union League Club. This powerful fraternity, staunchly pro-Lincoln and the Union cause, oversaw the recruitment, training, and provisioning of three Black New York regiments representing 4,125 men in 1863 and 1864. Gerrit Smith gave $3,000 to these regiments (to the Massachusetts Fifty-Fourth he gave $500), and he and the philanthropist George H. Stearns bankrolled the whistle-stop recruiting tours of Douglass and the Albany reformer Stephen Myers for Black regiments in Boston and New York. Also working for the new regiments were some of Smith's old land agents for the Black Woods. At Rikers Island, Reverend Garnet ministered to Black recruits (Gerrit Smith gave money for their medicine and nursing). Rev. Jermain Loguen lined up Black enlistees in central New York (a Binghamton militia, "Loguen's Guards," joined Black regiments as they were formed).[20]

The Twenty-Sixth USCT never suffered the frontline casualties of the Massachusetts Fifty-Fourth. In South Carolina, where Hasbrook's Company B was engaged, the long humid days were occupied with the isolating work of manning forts and batteries (in Hasbrook's case, near Hilton Head Island in the Port Royal Sound). The regiment was also charged with busting up Confederate-held rail lines, sallies that never came to much but let these soldiers test their guns at Honey Hill, Tullifinny Station (Devaux's Neck), and McKay's Point. Here, in the Carolina low country, disease would be the soldiers' most malicious foe. Private Carasaw caught the "Southern fever," which saddled him with asthma, bouts of fever, and a weak heart all his life. Prolonged exposure and malaria left Private Hazzard with recurring fevers, a bad kidney, and bouts of bloody urine. Chronic chills and disabling fevers, along with deafness from the measles, were the

Private William Carasaw, 26th Reg. USCT. Photograph, carte de visite. Cady Gallery, NYC. New York State Military Museum and Veterans Research Center, Saratoga Springs, NY.

war-made, enduring lot of Private Hasbrook. Rheumatism plagued them all.[21]

Still, some interludes were joyful. In Beaufort, South Carolina, Hazzard wooed Julia Smith, an emancipated slave and the laundress of a Union officer. They were married by the regimental chaplain, Benjamin F. Randolph, in May 1865. Witnessing their vows were Julia's daughter Clara, and Private Hasbrook from North Elba. Hazzard, Carasaw, and Hasbrook belonged to different companies, but in Beaufort they sought and found each other, and the home ties were a life saver. When Hasbrook was laid up with the measles, his old friends got him medicine, and when Carasaw, the oldest of the three, seemed too weak to muster out, his comrades saw to it that he got home alive.[22]

Private Hazzard and his bride may have thought of staying south. Ex-slaves were starting up small farms on appropriated rebel land. The ex-slave Private Jeremiah Miles, a new friend of the Adirondackers, worked for hire on these reclaimed lots. In 1866, this army teamster raised cotton for a government "collector" at the Gabriel Capers plantation on St. Helena Island. At the outset, it looked promising. Yankee speculators and the Federals talked a good game about the collaborative role of wage labor in the postbellum plantation economy. But Black hands were often paid late and sometimes not paid at all, and those who farmed for themselves were learning how easily Yankee contractors could seize their land. Private Hazzard, used to running his own show, would have grasped what Black freed people were fighting in this postwar economy. Not only was the pay inequitable and the labor contracts ironclad, but the race hate of the old guard was as strong as ever. Some bosses working for the Yankees were the same overseers who had terrorized Black families under slavery. Many vanquished whites bridled at any bid for Black economic autonomy, and Black veterans from the North were particularly despised. Hazzard, Julia, his new stepdaughters Clara and Genevia, and the ex-slave Jeremiah Miles were wise to push on north. Forced evictions would eventually displace tens of thousands of Black homesteaders all over the South, forever shattering the emancipated slaves' long dream of forty acres and a mule.[23]

As for the chaplain who heard Charles and Julia's vows, Benjamin Randolph remained in the South, working for the Freedmen's Bureau, writing for a Black reform newspaper, and pushing for integrated public transportation. He was a delegate to a South Carolina Constitutional Convention. In Orangeburg County he ran for state senator and won; an "electioneering tour" followed. It was while on tour in Abbeville County, changing trains, that this Northern reformer was accosted by three white men brandishing pistols. Witnesses to the group assassination were many. Local rumor credited an ex-Confederate colonel with the idea. No arrests were made.[24]

The same Christmas of 1863 that Charles Hazzard got to Rikers for his training, his North Elba neighbor, Silas Frazier, forty-three, enlisted in a white regiment, the Second New York Volunteer Cavalry then seeking Essex County volunteers. Not one of Smith's "pick'd men" but a fellow traveler who bought thirty acres in the Black Woods from a grantee, then settled on another lot he liked better, this discriminating homesteader and his wife, Jane, came to North Elba from Newburgh on the Hudson. Childless and undistracted, they built their farm up fast. They kept pigs, sheep, cows, and oxen, raised hay, wheat, and rye, made butter for the market, and tapped enough maple sap to sell. Known in Westport as a "strong, healthy, able-bodied" fellow, Frazier also hired out.

In Keene, onlookers at a turkey shoot recalled the day this "fighting man" of "mixed blood" took on "Riley Blood, a staunch Democrat and a hotelkeeper. Blood had no use for colored persons," recalled John Brown's son Salmon. Frazier knocked him flat. Army mates in the Second New York Cavalry described Frazier as "one of the strongest and most robust men in his Company," the "perfect picture of health."[25]

That picture cracked for good a year after Frazier donned his blues. On a Louisiana wintry day in 1864, his company was canvassing the territory around Union-occupied Morganza, checking for rebel vigilantes at surrounding farms. When the horse ahead of Frazier's stumbled and went down, Frazier swung off his horse and rushed to his army mate now pinned under his mount. Kicking wildly, the injured horse caught Frazier in the gut. The damage never healed. He quit the cavalry—he had to—and he never rode again. But he owed the Union two more years, and he was counting on that government pay. Frazier found work as a galley cook on a navy steamer, the *Augusta Dinsmore*, and then he picked up dysentery. This new blow disabled him completely, and he finally mustered out. Back in the Adirondacks, Private Frazier and his wife settled on a twenty-acre farm lot in Westport, which put him within reach of a physician and the kind of "choring around" he could manage. But the life of a frontiersman was a memory. Until his death in 1874, this veteran contended with unremitting pain.[26]

The last of the eight from the Black Woods to take up arms for the Union were James and Samuel Brady. Neither were grantees. They found the Black Woods from New Jersey in the mid-1850s. All the gift lots were parceled out by the time they got to Franklin, and in any case, as out-of-staters, they did not qualify for Smith's largesse. They didn't care. What tugged them north was the bright thread of a rumor. Here was country, wild, still unmade, where Black people could homestead and white people would leave them be—an important asset here, since, as circumstantial evidence suggests, the Marylanders James Brady; his wife, Louisa; her son, Samuel, by a previous marriage; Louisa's father, Josiah Bunion; and a young friend or relative of this family, Mary Elizabeth Bailey from Delaware, were fugitives.[27]

Were the Black Woods what they hoped for? So many Black families had given up. But from those who'd stayed and their white neighbors they found work and a welcome. By 1860, James and Louisa Brady and Mary Bailey occupied a cabin near the home of the grantee Wesley Murray and his young family. Samuel Brady, Louisa's teenage son, was a hired hand living in the home of a white family nearby. Old Josiah Bunion bunked with George Holland, a young grantee from Westchester. John Thomas, originally from Maryland, and his wife and two daughters were farming in this neighborhood (a hard year for this family, marking the death of Richard, just sixteen). Fifteen Black people lived in this small rurality in 1860. And of the nine who hailed from the South (and likely formerly enslaved), four were farming land they called their own.[28]

James Brady joined the 118th Regiment, NY Infantry, Company C, in June 1862, fourteen months after the war began. Not so his young stepson Samuel, whose mother, Louisa, needed help on the farm. As the army beefed up incentives to enlist, however, Samuel reconsidered. From 1863 to 1864, the Franklin County budget shot up 500 percent (a reflection of this county's determination to offer bounties that might stave off the need to launch a dreaded draft). If Samuel joined the 118th and collected every available bounty from town, county, and state, he might make as much as $800, a sum that in 1863 held a present-day value of $27,000. The Brady patch was not the meanest farm around (in 1860, the farm was worth $450, which to the newly arrived Quebecois and out-of-steerage Irish may have seemed a fortune), but like all poor farmers, the Bradys needed cash. This war dividend could keep Samuel's mother on the farm while he and James were in the service, and if Samuel went for the 118th, he and his stepfather might even reunite.[29]

Samuel gave his bounty to a trusted neighbor to make sure his mother's needs were met, and headed to the 118th's training camp in Elmira. A few weeks after, he made his report (spelling and punctuation corrected): "Dear Mother, I now [seat] myself to inform you—that I am well and hope that my few lines will find you the same. Well, Mother, I begin to know what a soldier life is. It is no play. But there is one thing I can say and tell the truth. That is this. That I aint drink anything stronger than [soda] since I left Platt[sburgh], nor none of the boys." She kept this letter all her life.[30]

Two months after he enlisted, "per order" of the War Department, Private Brady was "unassigned" from the white regiment and redirected to the Twentieth Regiment, US Colored Troops, Company A. And he might have counted it a blessing if he'd never set foot in Elmira, so bitter was the difference between the white camp and what Rikers Island held in store. At the training camp in New York Harbor, Black soldiers dealt with shortages of tents, camp stoves, bedding, and winter clothes. Dysentery, frostbite, and pneumonia were epidemic. One recruit's legs froze solid; a surgeon sawed them off. That at least there *was* a surgeon and a place for him to operate was probably the doing of Reverend

Garnet's volunteer parishioners, who built a camp kitchen and a make-shift hospital at Rikers when the army failed to bother.[31]

Bounty fraud, another pestilence, also stalked the Black trainees. Il-literacy made hundreds of enlistees vulnerable to the fast talk and prac-ticed hustle of city swindlers. And here, as everywhere, a rising grievance for the Black enlistees was the absence of commissioned officers of color. With few exceptions (Hazzard's chaplain, Benjamin Randolph, was one), officers in the Colored Troops were white, and not all of them were concerned with equal rights and the antislavery cause. Many, in fact, resented the assignment and trained their men indifferently, sub-jected them to heavy discipline, and court-martialed Black recruits when they pushed for equal pay. But in early March 1864, when Brady and the newly formed Twentieth USCT marched from Rikers Island to Manhattan and down Fifth Avenue, these injuries were not yet felt. If two years earlier, the city's mayor said he hoped New York would leave the Union, and nine months earlier, the worst race riot in the nation's history lashed Manhattan like a whip, this day belonged to President Lincoln. Onlookers packed the balconies and treetops. A cloud of wav-ing handkerchiefs made the spring air jump. On the long avenue below the lushly garlanded Union League Club, Private Brady stood stock-still in his white dress gloves and woolly blues while the president of Colum-bia College assured him that "when you put on the uniform and swear allegiance to the standard of the Union, you stand emancipated, regen-erated, and disenthralled; the peer of the proudest soldier in the land." All the way to the Hudson River piers, the 1,300 men of the Twentieth were buoyed by the "cheers and tears of those who felt the significance of the spectacle." "Everywhere," exulted *Harper's Weekly*, "the soldiers were greeted as a great city ought to greet its defenders, and as it has sa-luted every departing regiment since the Seventh marched on the 19th of April, three years ago."[32]

That proud send-off for the Twentieth would be a cherished memory for the recruits. New Orleans, where they were headed, was an ordeal. They did not fight (they were never favored with a chance), but the fronts of this long war assumed unexpected guises. "More lethal than Confederate bullets or shells," observes the war historian William Se-raile, was the sodden air that sang with malarial mosquitoes: of the 1,325 men in the Twentieth's regimental descriptive book, one died of war wounds and 263 (one in six) succumbed to illness. And darkening this buggy fug was the toxic Negrophobia. A train ride in New Orleans put Regimental Chaplain George LeVere in mind "of going through an

Irish ward in New York; you can see the serpents looking through the window blinds, hissing like the adder, and their young ones along the street hallooing, 'nigger, nigger.'" Nor were the soldiers' spirits helped by late wages and thin rations, the latter sometimes as little as a scoop of corn mush and molasses. Diarrhea felled them, and for this, there was no help. Dysentery was the most rapacious killer of them all.[33]

Fortune did not favor the young soldier from Vermontville. Black soldiers dispatched to segregated army hospitals faced a one-in-three chance of dying. Not a year into his term, Samuel Brady, "farmer," died of dysentery near New Orleans in the for-Blacks-only Corps d'Afrique military hospital 1,500 miles from his Adirondack home. Over half of the twelve thousand Civil War troops in Chalmette National Cemetery outside New Orleans are unidentified, their headstones marked by numbers. At least Private Brady's bears his name.[34]

Very different was the Civil War of Sam Brady's stepfather. Inspired, maybe, by the ease of his assimilation in his all-white Adirondack 118th, James Brady rejiggered his biography from stem to stern. During the war, he did not keep up with Samuel's mother or send her money, as an appeal from a worried neighbor suggests. "Please accept these few lines from a friend," Franklin's Sara Muzzie urged in February 1865. Herself the mother of a prisoner of war in Richmond, Mrs. Muzzie gave news of Brady's wife: "Her health is very poor & everything is in a very bad condition. She is not able to sit up more than one-half of the time." Could James not get a furlough? The snow was very deep that winter, and "your wife has no-one to do her chores for her. . . . She said she would soon be out of wood." There was no more to say. "Come home if you can."[35]

Private Brady kept this letter; it was in his last effects. But it wouldn't bring him home. He had been admitted to a very privileged fraternity. Could he hope for preferential treatment afterward? Claim the perquisites of whiteness back in Franklin with his Black wife? To leverage his provisional enrollment in a white world into full-bore acceptance, Brady chose to leave the Black Woods entirely. The chance to reinvent himself would not come again; the rupture had to be complete. So he did not seek a furlough, and when he was discharged in Plattsburgh in June 1865, he headed to Malone, the Franklin County seat. There he met a war widow, Adeline Spinner, white, Catholic, and very young. Brady, too, became a Catholic and joined Adeline's Notre Dame Church. They married, raised a family, and worked a modest farm outside Malone. It seems James's first marriage to Louisa, the older wife, posed no impediment (if they were enslaved when they met, their marriage may not have been legalized). James and Adeline's descendants, all white in the census, were raised unaware of Brady's Black identity, his Black family, or his link to the Smith Lands.[36]

In the 1990s, a Brady family genealogist happened on James Brady's service record in the Civil War. "I never could get [my parents] to talk much about my great-grandfather, James Brady," Susann Hoskins wrote me from Binghamton, New York. "The more I asked, the more I knew something was out of sorts." James Brady of family legend was Irish, but when she got hold of his pension papers, she learned her ancestor was biracial. ("Bingo!") Census records led Hoskins to Brady's first wife, Louisa (unmentioned in his 1890 appeal for a pension), and to his antebellum farming years in Vermontville. Hoskins was intrigued to learn that her Maryland forebear may have been a fugitive, but the revelation of his first marriage, the Black partner he jilted for the new bride in Malone, and the sad death of his unremembered stepson, Samuel, was unsettling. This ancestor, she mused, was one "wily kind of guy."[37]

Making Shadeism Pay

From the Black Woods, William Appo Jr., Silas Frazier, and James Brady all joined and served in white regiments. This was not supposed to happen, but it did, and it happened elsewhere in the Adirondacks too. In Elizabethtown, near Lake Champlain, a white company mustered in Lafayette Mason of New Russia (the grantee served with the 118th Adirondack Regiment, with many of his neighbors). Two sons of the Westport grantee Joseph James joined white companies as well. Given all we know about hard-and-fast rules of segregation in the US Army (rules that would not be struck until President Harry Truman's executive order in 1948), these exceptions bear notice. What might they reveal about the small-town upstate worlds where they occurred?[38]

Maybe white neighbors gave James Brady a pass because they liked the man, or because they just couldn't see the point of cutting out a reliable, hardworking neighbor. In North Elba and in the town of Franklin, no stories of enslavement bedevil local history. In fact, as far as I know, no one in these hamlets bought or sold another human being. This distinction was a badge white Adirondackers wore with pride, much as they took a guarded, proprietary pride in "their" John Brown. Especially in the 118th and 96th Regiments, Brown's posthumous celebrity may have moved some Adirondack soldiers toward a quiet liberality regarding Black recruits. In Brady's Company C were Brown's good friend William Peacock, an English immigrant and antislavery man long privy to Brown's plans, and the abolitionist sharpshooter Willard Thompson, whose twin brother was murdered at Harpers Ferry.[39]

But for every northern New York Yankee who fought to bring down slavery, there were ten who fought to have a whack at the "Secesh," and another five who simply earned for any kind of break from the dawn-to-dusk routines of home. And it should be noted that no abolitionists distinguished James Brady's Franklin company. Republicans abounded, Brady's Captain, James H. Pierce, among them, but love of party was no measure of abolitionism, and antislavery conviction was no assurance of racial equalitarianism. Recall the Adirondack minister Nathan Wardner, regimental chaplain of the NY Ninety-Sixth, whose Methodist church in Wilmington was said to be all for radical abolition. In the South during the war, Wardner ran a Sabbath school for contrabands. When he came home, the "little slave girl" he had in tow was proud proof of his commitment. But he *would* see to it that the child did not look the part: she was, marveled a reporter, "as white as most of the children we see in our streets."[40]

Cue Private Brady's skin tone. White soldiers admitted James Brady to their ranks for the same reason they suffered Appo Jr., Frazier, and Lafayette Mason. Brady was "mulatto" and light enough to pass. Not so his stepson Samuel, whose complexion favored his much darker birth mother's. At the sight of Samuel's bold Blackness, white men drew a line (and would have drawn a line at Mason's son, the dark-complected Lewis, if he'd given them a chance, but from the family patch in New Russia, the fourteen-year-old farm boy went to Brooklyn to join the Twentieth USCT). Neighborly familiarity was a boon for all these hopefuls, but the base determinant when these Black men joined white companies was light skin. Not that their Black ancestry was unknown, but lightness made the situation bearable. A white soldier might tell himself his comrade wasn't Black at all. Squint hard enough and maybe Appo, Brady, Frazier, and Mason were *Canucks*.[41]

Black soldiers in white companies knew their enlistment in these companies was enabled by white racism. But if the bigotry at the heart of shadeism meant they would be spared other gross injustices, they could live with this sad irony. In white regiments they could bank on higher wages, better medical care, fuller rations, and, after the war, more substantial and easily obtained pension dividends. So they worked shadeism to their advantage, and in this strategy, they weren't alone. Before the war, the Flushing farmer Jonathan Mingo (the grantee who Charles Ray so hoped would use his gift land) shunned his twice-visited Adirondack gift lot for a new home in Michigan. In Albion, he reconstructed his family history in favor of the side that was indigenous, pointedly ignoring his New York life as a Black activist (which included agenting for the *Colored American*, attending Black political conventions, signing Black suffrage petitions, and accepting a gift lot from Gerrit Smith). Today, Mingo's Black ancestry shows up nowhere in his online biography; family memory and local history honor the Native American lineage alone.[42]

Another one to go this route: Maud Eppes Appo, granddaughter of the grantee Lyman Eppes. Maud's parents were Lyman Eppes's daughter Albertine Appo and the Philadelphia musician William Appo (forty years his wife's senior when they wed). When Appo died at seventy-two, Maud, his daughter by his second wife, was seven. Six years later in 1885, on the late John Brown's eighty-fifth birthday, a crowd in North Elba's White Church heard thirteen-year-old Maud Appo recite a poem about "Old Brown." But if John Brown country thrilled to Maud's family's closeness to the martyr, she, it seems, was less enthralled. In Fresno, California, she married an Iowa-born mechanic (white), taught music for a living, and told a census taker that her parents were French. She herself was born in France; she was a naturalized citizen. The year her family immigrated? Couldn't say. Further, "Maud" was out. In Fresno, she was Enid.[43]

John Brown scholars know Enid Maud Eppes Appo LaFollette as the Eppes descendant who peddled family heirlooms to a San Francisco bookseller. Boyd Stutler, an eminent Brown scholar and avid hunter-gatherer of "Browniana," happened on this cache in 1932, fourteen years before the widowed Enid, seventy-three, a piano tuner and, like her father and her grandfather, a music teacher, died of heart disease in the San Francisco City Hospital. Indigent at the end, she is buried in a potter's field. In the cache that Stutler picked up in a used bookstore were a tintype of her grandfather Lyman Eppes, a lock of John Brown's hair, a book about famous Adirondackers, and an obituary for Phineas Norton, the grief-struck abolitionist who invited the sodden funeral party to take a meal with him on their way to Brown's home. Boyd Stutler, writing another Brownophile about his purchase of Maud Appo's effects, seemed doubtful that Lyman Eppes's granddaughter could ever willingly have given up such tender, intimate mementos: "How [had] they got out of her hands?" The suggestion that they'd lost their meaning for her—that they didn't "get out"; she *put* them out—was beyond him.[44]

And of course, it is beyond us too—what this meant to her, and what it didn't. In the last month of her life, when she was dying in a charity ward, Enid LaFollette did reclaim her birth name, Albertine Appo. But she still described herself as white. She wasn't changing that. Were she and James Brady cultural adventurers who, in shaking off the tokens and allegiances of their Blackness, freed themselves to revel in the great American game of reinvention? In their assault on the unsteady posts of Blackness's construction, were they warriors, saboteurs? Or were they just that sick of it, tired of difference, tired of Blackness, even to the point of scrubbing out their memories, family ties, history itself?

Privates Hazzard, Morehouse, Carasaw, and Hasbrook, who made it back to their Adirondack homes in the same Black skins they started with, were also weary and yearned for fresh starts too, using what they learned in the service to advance their interests after the war. But re-invention was not their option or, in any case, their choice. Blackness shaped them, and they shaped it back. They claimed it, and respected it. Thanks in no small part to the army, they understood its strength. Their Black past was usable, and they put it to work.

CHAPTER 15

An Empowering Diaspora

> It is you yourselves who have made yourselves men.
>
> —Colonel T. H. Barrett's mustering-out speech to the 62nd US Colored Infantry of Missouri, 1866

Solidarity with the freed people of the South did not abate when the Adirondack Black enlistees mustered out. After he was discharged, Private Hasbrook lingered in the South, visiting ex-slaves, explaining just what the war's end might mean. Perhaps he urged them to pick new surnames, build a schoolhouse, negotiate a wage. Maybe he shared some stories about his boyhood friend, the legendary abolitionist. Captain Brown who once saved Private Hasbrook's father from freezing in the woods! Old Brown the terrifier—the grizzled farmer from next door. . . . That would have kept them rapt. Private Charles Henry Hazzard took three Black Southerners back home to St. Armand, and when Hasbrook headed north, he brought home young Jerry Miles, the ex-slave from Virginia the North Elbans befriended in the Twenty-Sixth.[1]

Freed people touched down in a score of northern villages and towns, and not only at the urging of Black soldiers. A white officer from Franklin, Alfred Skiff, invited home the once enslaved teenager Walter Scott, from North Carolina. Isaac Johnson, an ex-slave from Virginia, and a young woman, Bettie Burns, accompanied Luther Bryant, an officer with the NY 118th, back to his Franklin farm. The drift of freed people after the war swept refugees into small towns all over the Northeast. What happened in John Brown country belonged to a wider trend.[2]

Thomas Elliott, a self-freed slave from North Carolina who discovered New York's Ninety-Sixth in Suffolk, Virginia, and joined up as a cook, registered this tug. In Company K of the Ninety-Sixth were several North Elbans who knew Old Brown the abolitionist as a neighbor. John Brown himself—*who had captured Harpers Ferry with his nineteen men so true, and frightened old Virginy till she trembled through and through!*—was buried in their village. Here, Elliott would learn, Black and white worked side by side, labored over sums together, swapped seed, thread, and soap. No church or school was segregated. Privates Hinckley, Demmon, and Thompson were joined to Brown by marriage. Second Lieutenant Judson C. Ware had enlisted at the urging of Brown's son Salmon. Two of Brown's little band who were killed at Harpers Ferry were Private Leander Thompson's *brothers*. All over Elliott's Old South, just uttering Brown's name could get a Black man's tongue cut out. These Yankees were tossing it around like a baseball.[3]

Elliott went north and made the Black Woods his home for about twenty years. For the first half of these or so, he worked for the North Elba farmer and town notable Alpheus Demmon (whose son Ben, in Elliott's company, likely urged Elliott to come up north and tap his father for the job). In North Elba were not only a few members of John Brown's family but Black farmers like Josiah Hasbrook and Leonard Worts, and farm laborers like Jerry Miles, who, like Elliott, was once enslaved. Other ex-slaves were settling to the north in Franklin, here living with Black Adirondackers, and there with white.[4]

Bringing It All Back Home

This demographic pop—more Black people, most of them young—resulted in a surge of marriages after the war, and this, too, notes the Civil War scholar Donald R. Shaffer, was a rising trend all over. Black men, having finally claimed "the ultimate manly role—warrior," brought to their postwar lives a war-tempered pride and confidence that extended to the pursuit of all domestic entitlements. How long had enslaved people been denied the right to choose a spouse, marry freely, and raise families in their own homes? Legal marriage, for so long the privilege of whiteness, was now every ex-slave's portion, and free Black New Yorkers would make this a time to marry too. In Essex and Franklin Counties, Josiah Hasbrook, Alexander Hazzard, Charles Henry Hazzard, and Warren Morehouse all got married (and Private James Brady, already married, got married again). William Appo, a widower since 1863, found a second bride after the war. His young wife, Albertine Eppes, was one of seven women from the Black Woods who found a partner in this time. Charlotte Ann, an older daughter of John Thomas, was thirteen when Warren Morehouse went to Boston and joined the Massachusetts Fifty-Fourth, but the regimental marker kept her memory in mind. On his return in the fall of 1866, "Wash" and the now seventeen-year-old farm girl swapped vows in the home of a Franklin justice of the peace. "Josy" Hasbrook also married local, and his St. Armand bride, Jane Ann Hazzard, was one of several of grantee Avery Hazzard's children to take a postwar spouse. Avery's daughter Adaline Hazzard married a Black veteran from Vermont; his son Alexander married his neighbor, Mary Elizabeth Bailey, the ex-slave who came to Franklin with the Bradys some years before the war; Charles Henry Hazzard married Julia Smith in Beaufort; and after Julia and her several relatives were settled in the Black Woods, those relatives found spouses too.[5]

Decades after county historians like Winslow Watson declared Smith's giveaway dead and done, these fresh alliances were turning neighbors into families, in-laws, and new kin, deepening the legacy of Smith's giveaway and double-knotting the long threads of its web.

Their history of military service and a devotion to the Union also amplified the social world of Black veterans on their return. In Vergennes, Vermont, the Ethan Allen Post of the Grand Army of the Republic (GAR) welcomed a new resident, Private William Carasaw (and what a coup for this post, to see a neighbor of the sainted John Brown in its ranks!). His farming days behind him, Carasaw found work as a whitewasher and hostler at the Stevens House (where Brown's body rested in its casket before it crossed the lake), and he tried canal work, too. His employer, Lewis Mott, aware of his employee's war-made disabilities, kept Carasaw's work as light as possible. He liked this older veteran, found him trustworthy and reliable. Carasaw's fellow congregants at his new church in Vergennes (Methodist), the veterans he met at the Vergennes post of the GAR, and fellow members of a new political reform group, invigorated his postwar society as well. On the stormy day of his crowded funeral in 1886, Vergennes's high school principal was so moved by the pastor's "tribute of respect" that he directed his students to make a model out of Private Carasaw, a "man without wealth or station, a plain laboring man" widely esteemed for his "Christian uprightness and integrity."[6]

In Middlesex, Vermont, Jerry Miles joined the GAR, as would his neighbor Josiah Hasbrook. James Brady never missed a GAR meeting in Malone (eventually declaring himself the oldest GAR member in New York). Warren Morehouse may have belonged to a Bloomingdale post as well; after he died, the GAR helped out his widow and their children.[7]

The war opened up the lives and livelihoods of Black women, too, who headed up their households when their men were away, and when husbands came home disabled, or did not come home at all, hired out as cooks, washerwomen, hotel helpers, and housekeepers. Jane Craig farmed when Isaac died or disappeared, and when Jane Frazier's husband was in the navy, the census taker called her "farmer." On Silas's return ("all broken down"), she cooked for a hotel, a job the widowed Susan Hasbrook Pierce took, too. In Franklin, the unhusbanded ex-slave Louisa Brady was a laundress, housekeeper, and farmer of her patch. No longer able to work his farm as hard as he once did, Charles Henry Hazzard now looked to his wife, Julia; she made money selling home-woven cloth and keeping house for neighbors. From the first, the Black Woods had been framed by its white founder and Black agents as a proving ground for Black manhood. Would a Black man get along up here as well as any white? He would, and so might a Black woman. But it would take the war to call to light all that she could do.[8]

Was this what Black women wanted? They didn't have much choice. Not one of their returning men or boys could work the way he had. The war came home with the Black veterans in knotted joints and wheezy lungs, fevered sleep, bloody urine, swollen hearts, blinding headaches (sunstroke's legacy), malaria, and chest colds that laid them out for seasons at a time. "I was a stout and healthy man [and] always ready to do a day's work," wrote Josiah Hasbrook on his return. "I have not been able to perform one half the labor I could before I went in the army." Charles Henry Hazzard, a man "without a blemish" on enlistment, came north too weak to pitch hay. So bloody was his urine that a white friend said, "I think his kidney affliction would long ago have killed you or me, or anybody, but a colored man."[9]

Hence the resolute pursuit of federal pension aid, a campaign that Black Civil War veterans and their descendants in the Black Woods waged into the twentieth century. White veterans also pressed their pension claims with zeal, but federal examiners demanded more evidence and paperwork from Black claimants and rewarded them with less, so the Black pursuit of pension justice was different; the odds against success were worse. It took Black veterans time they couldn't spare and funds they didn't have to track down long-distance witnesses who could vouch for prewar health and war-caused injuries, hire court officers or attorneys, and travel to review boards days away from home. Some Black veterans (Carasaw, Morehouse, and Frazier) deemed it not worth the effort. Their widows disagreed. On their husbands' deaths, female heads of households needed pension money more than ever, and alongside Josiah Hasbrook, Charles Henry Hazzard, Lewis and Lafayette Mason, and Jeremiah Miles, the widows, too, put in their claims.[10]

Veterans, widows, and their grown children fought for that monthly stipend even after appeals were challenged or denied, enlisting help from doctors, bosses, army mates, and neighbors, Black and white—and maybe white especially. Not until the 1960s would scholars document the bias that skewed the Pension Bureau's review process, but Black veterans felt it keenly. Why did federal examiners press the seaman Simeon Hasbrook for hard proof of his birthdate when, as his brother Josiah wearily explained, "There is no public record of his birth, nor no family Bible. Our parents were slaves in the State of New York and neither of them could read or write"? How could Josiah be expected to recall the "Reble Dr." who tended him in Port Royal when, at the time, he was deranged with fever? Why would Charlotte Morehouse be pressed to name her husband's army friends twenty years after his death? On these petty points, Black veterans' bids for pensions were delayed. Charles Hazzard's pension file is hymnal-thick because it had to be. The call for one more affidavit, medical report, or wartime witness was unrelenting. Hasbrook's exasperated doctor told the Pension Bureau that this aging veteran was so disabled that his hand may as well be "amputated . . . at the wrist," and that the only work he could do was "drive around a little with an old horse, gathering swill," and still the government resisted. Hasbrook got his upgrades only after multiple appeals.[11]

This is not to say that a hostile administrative culture targeted Black Adirondackers in particular. Military racism afflicted Black veterans all over the North. In the war they suffered higher rates of fatality and sickness than white soldiers, and after it, they died younger (at age forty years on average for Black veterans, and age fifty for white). Their portion of awarded pensions was much lower than what white men received: Black claimants won pensions 75 percent of the time, and whites 92 percent. What Black Adirondackers endured was part of a wider pattern of abuse.[12]

What was not usual, however, was the help that Black Adirondack veterans got from their white neighbors. More than thirty Adirondackers attested to the prewar health of Charles Henry Hazzard, vouching for this "remarkably powerful" grantee's son who returned from the war "utterly broken down in health and constitution." So convincing were the testimonials on behalf of this farmer (and later on, his widow), and so "excellent [his] character among his neighbors," that pension investigator Clement Sullivane expressed an incredulity close to outrage when a New York Board of Surgeons rejected Hazzard's appeals because he could not furnish doctors' notes confirming his good health before the war. *Of course he can't! One doctor's dead. The other has moved to who knows where.* Further, Hazzard's health history was readily available. "No man is better known in his community where he has lived straight along from his earliest manhood to the present time," wrote Sullivane of Hazzard. Added a white neighbor, Hazzard's "bad health has been a notorious fact in this neighborhood where he has lived, and he ought to have had a pension long ago."[13]

Private Josiah Hasbrook also found he could count on neighbors, white and Black. Before the war, said Samuel Dickinson (white), Hasbrook was "a perfectly healthy man—never knew him to be sick—was a neighbor and worked with him in the Lumber woods the winter before he enlisted." Betsy Torrance (white) echoed this: "I never knew him to be sick before he enlisted." But after: "He came to my house and was taken with the chills and feaver and I nursed him up the best I could untill the [Hasbrook family's] removal to Vermont." After, swore the Hasbrook family doctor, the unhappy veteran was so stiff with rheumatism that he could not manage "more than one fourth of the day good manual labor."[14]

Veterans' widows and children who looked to white neighbors to back their appeals were also buoyed by the response. When the heart disease that Warren Morehouse contracted in the service killed him in 1882, his young widow, Charlotte Ann, appealed for a government pension. Alone with four young children, one of them bedbound with pediatric hydrocephalus, she got by with help from the Franklin poor fund and the GAR, but this would not be enough. As they had backed the pension claim of Louisa Brady, Charlotte's neighbors rallied, ten of them vouching for her need.[15]

It must be noted, though, that this solidarity was not driven by any special pride in the Black veterans' war service—or no more, surely, than what they felt for their disabled own, many of whom had served longer and suffered more in combat than their Black neighbors. Nor did these affidavits hint at a concern about racism in the Pension Bureau; white locals may have shared these biases themselves. What white affiants were defending was not racial justice but the right to own and name their memory, their ownership of place-based knowledge. Did a pension examiner in Plattsburgh say Charles Henry Hazzard was just fine? Well, that surgeon had no clue. He didn't know the history. He never knew the man.[16]

"We are farmers, so is Charles H. Hazard—he has employed us—so have we him, on our farms," said the St. Armand farmer Sylvester Reid in 1891. And Reid, not the Pension Bureau, knew for a fact that when Hazzard was on the farm, he could be so convulsed with pain he had to be carried from the field. "I knew her when she was a small girl," said Eunice Swinyer of Charlotte Morehouse. "I knew her at the time of her marriage to Stephen Morehouse and know she was never been married before and has not been married since he died. She has always lived within a few rods of me and if she married I should have known it." Eunice also knew all of Charlotte's children's birthdays, their middle names, and when Henry first had "fits" and was seized by paralysis. Who told her this? *She was in the room.* What greater authority was there than what she knew "by Personal Knowledge"? It was the sense of a fellow you got from growing up with him, watching him gut a fish, prune an apple tree, soothe a fretful child. Not just anybody could claim the patrimony of community. New people with big estates and clubs and second homes and camps were cutting up the country like a currant cake, but they couldn't touch the birthright of lived experience. Not everything was up for grabs.[17]

Diasporic Prospects

When the names of the Black farmers dropped from Franklin and North Elba censuses in the quarter century after 1850, antiquarian historians assumed they had ditched the Adirondacks and farming altogether—quit because they had to, weren't suited to it from an innate incapacity, and simply vanished or beelined back to the cities they probably never should have left. But these assumptions missed the mark.[18]

Many grantees, such as Samuel Drummond, Samuel "Poppa" Hall, and the Jefferson brothers, did head back to cities. Widowed women, like Susan Henderson, Phebe Murray, Eliza Carasaw, and (briefly) Susan Hasbrook Pierce, found city living more consoling and survivable, and maybe some single men felt this as well—like Blacksville's Willis Hodges who, by 1853, was back in Brooklyn, betrothed and taking up the ministry. Also city bound were some of his Blacksville friends. But after the Civil War, several Black settlers used their bounties to stretch their wings and swap out for better farms, or sometimes homes in villages. Country life still suited them. They weren't giving up.[19]

The Hazzards bought a farm lot in St. Armand, and Walter and Rachel Scott contracted for a fifty-acre Vermontville farm from Alfred Skiff, the officer who encouraged Scott to give Franklin a try. Before he went to war, Josiah Hasbrook Jr. bought a farm in North Elba, and on his return he and Jane Ann bought another. His mother Susan, done with cities, came to join him. She missed the country. She missed a home. In 1871, Josiah Hasbrook's extended family moved to Westport on Lake Champlain (that most New Englandy of upstate shoreside towns, where ferries out of Albany docked every day and the air rang with the racket from the factories and forges), and touched down fleetingly in tiny Wadhams Mills. Next would come the big move to Vermont.[20]

There was an echo here, albeit faint, of the wider, more dramatic migratory trend that followed the 1862 Homestead Act. This legislation, which offered free 160-acre land grants to hopeful pioneers, eventually pulled over half a million settlers to the trans-Mississippi West, among them many upstaters, European immigrants, Black freed people determined to get shut of the South, and, from the Adirondacks, the grantee-veteran Lafayette Mason, who rode this tide to Iowa and then to his and Mary's last homestead in the Dakota Territory. But many more Black Adirondackers preferred small, affordable migrations that spoke less of John Soule and Horace Greeley's romance with the West than of their hope the next frontier might be as close as the next hamlet, county, or state.[21]

In 1870, Josiah Hasbrook Sr., patriarch of his big clan, was a farm worker in Glastonbury, Connecticut, along with several of his veteran-sons, including "Josy," who came down from North Elba to lend his father a hand. The war-disabled Silas Frazier and his wife, Jane, were in their small farm in Westport. Jane Craig, left or widowed by her husband, stayed on her North Elba farm as long as she could manage, then joined a sister's farm in Saratoga County. The grantee George Holland put his Franklin farm behind him, but not for a city; he launched a truck farm in Canandaigua near the Finger Lakes. Alexander Gordon, long gone from Blacksville and his squatter's patch in Duane, was farming in Monmouth County, New Jersey.[22]

Enos Brewer, a sailor and grantee who homesteaded with Vermonters on Tupper Lake, left his cabin too, eventually surfacing at a new farm near Malone, where James Brady was farming. As for Avery and Margaret Hazzard's brood: five of their eight children kept farming after the war, and three of them (Alexander, Charles Henry, and Adaline) farmed in the Black Woods of their folks.[23]

Alone among Smith's Black land agents, Samuel Ringgold Ward still spoke of farming. But when the aid he gave to fugitives raised the threat of legal action, Ward fled to Canada, then moved to England, where a Quaker activist gave him a fifty-acre farm in Jamaica. In 1855, Ward made Jamaica his last home. He didn't farm, however. Pastoring a small church was the work that filled these years.[24]

The grantee's son, Josiah Hasbrook Jr., farmed as long as he could swing it. Bucking every westward trend, the Union veteran took his family out of Essex County to make their future in the Green Mountains of Vermont. In the late 1870s, when white farmers were ditching their Vermont ancestral homes for points west, the Hasbrooks staked out a new home in Bear Swamp north of Middlesex, not far from Montpelier, the state capital. Their new home was aptly named; sheep and dairy farmers kept rifles loaded and at hand.[25]

Why here? Land—so much of it cleared and abandoned—was surely a good buy, and in Montpelier (twelve miles southeast) and Burlington (thirty-two miles northwest) were relatives of wife and husband both. It could be, too, that Jane Ann and Josiah, both the children of pioneers, had cooled on the postbellum Adirondacks so dear to tourists, outdoorsmen, and health seekers, and where, increasingly, the best prospect for poor Black people seemed to be working for well-off whites. This son of a suffrage-seeking pioneer may have recalled that fifty years before New York, Vermont abolished slavery, and a hundred years before New York, Black Vermonters got the vote. No sooner was the Fugitive Slave Act passed than Vermont legislators raced to outlaw it (a move that so enraged some Southern legislators that they tried to get Vermont kicked out of the Union). Vermont's long legacy of agrarian egalitarianism was hopeful too, as was the Hasbrook tie to John Brown and his family. In Vermont, Brown's good name gleamed.[26]

The Hasbrooks made a sturdy home in Bear Swamp. They leased an old farmhouse and enrolled the boys in school. Jane Ann tended Adeline, her first daughter, and Josiah bought more land and started logging. Soon enough, locals were calling a stream near his home Hasbrook Brook. He joined the local GAR and was eventually made post commander, no

Josiah Hasbrook Jr. Photographer unknown, ca. 1880–95. Courtesy Special Collections, Jones Public Library, Amherst, MA.

small feat for a Black man in white Vermont. Sometimes he worked for white neighbors; sometimes they worked for him. And here, as he had done in the South when he made the rounds of freed people to alert them to the Union victory, he got the word out. *This place works. Come see for yourself.*[27]

Hasbrook's half sister Lucy and her husband, the ex-slave Jerry Miles, came to Middlesex and never left. Leonard Worts, a grantee-farmer from North Elba, moved to Middlesex when his wife died. Jane Ann's aging mother, Margaret, from St. Armand, and Eliza Carasaw, William's widow, who each had grown children living in Montpelier, stayed in Middlesex for long spells. And it wasn't only Adirondackers whom the Black Vermonters welcomed. In 1883, eight years after they arrived, the Hasbrooks gave themselves a fifteenth-anniversary party. So many Black guests came from Montpelier it took a four-team coach to haul them.[28]

Ten years later, a reporter from the *Vermont Watchman & State Journal* covered the Hasbrooks' silver anniversary. The family built a dance hall for their revelers near their farmhouse in Bear Swamp. In attendance: "republicans, democrats, populists, prohibitionists, Americans, negroes, Irish, Canadians and Low Dutch, mulattoes, maroons, quadroons, octoroons, creoles and orioles, without regard to politics, race, religion or previous condition of servitude." Toasts poured like cider from local politicians, farmers rich and influential, a minister, and the hosts. There were card games, spirituals, gift presentations (mostly silver), a feast, a fistfight, a three-piece band, and dancing until dawn. And the Montpelier writer made no apologies for his exuberantly long account: "The excuse is that *this was no ordinary wedding.*" Not ordinary for him, anyway—a city guest stunned by the social and racial diversity of the occasion. He didn't know what Hasbrook knew, or Charles B. Ray before him. The frontier was a leveler. It might not last, but it happened. People met you eye to eye.[29]

Unfortunately, and no surprise in this tough era, Hasbrook's zeal to expand his farm outran his ability to pay for it. His creditors were losing patience, and he was losing heart. His neighbor and old army friend, Jerry Miles, had played it safer, working mostly on small farms near his own. (Jerry's son Frank did this too, managing eventually to buy a farm and win a warm obituary in the local paper in 1934 as a "well known and highly respected farmer.") But Hasbrook could not stay the course. The rheumatism that stole into his joints during the war had turned his legs to stilts, his hands to clawhammers. He couldn't milk, and so he sold his cows, and without manure, what good were his fields? Then in 1894, the beleaguered father was blindsided by the loss of his and Jane Ann's middle son, George, age twenty, who succumbed to "ulcers in the head."[30]

Was it time to leave the farm? The new statehouse in Montpelier wore a gilded dome that seemed to glow all the brighter against the tree-stippled hillside lifting high behind it, and the legislature, Hasbrook learned, needed an assistant doorkeeper. Were his frozen hands

Stephen, Lloyd, George, and Carroll Hasbrook (sons of Josiah and Jane Ann Hasbrook), Middlesex, VT. Photographer unknown, ca. 1890. Courtesy Middlesex Historical Society, Middlesex, VT.

up to the job? He and Jane Ann had family here. Their children would have cousins. With endorsements from fellow veterans, Vermont senators, and an ex-governor, Josiah applied for the post in 1896. Between his war service, the state's hard-core Republicanism, its proud history of slavelessness, and his own ties to Captain Brown, he was confident he'd get it.[31]

A generation earlier, he might have. But by the 1890s, Vermont, like Adirondack Country and so much of the North, was refining the old narrative. Burgeoning anxiety about the heavy tide of immigrants and racial degeneration now spoke more loudly to Vermonters than the old rote devotion to racial justice. With despair, a Vermont poet described a boneyard of deserted farms littering the land:

> You now behold the shattered homes,
> All crumbling to decay,
> Like long-neglected catacombs
> Of races passed away.

Had Yankee emigrants pushing west taken with them all the enterprising, can-do spirit of their forebears, leaving only torpid layabouts, now joined by lesser "races" from French Canada, Ireland, and southern Europe? And what would the black face of Josiah Hasbrook in the statehouse say about white Vermont's concern with its imperiled racial purity?[32]

To a reporter pressing for a response from Hasbrook when he didn't get the job, the Black man tersely offered that perhaps "the Republican Party does not look after those who have always stood by it." Likely so, but the legislative disavowal glimpsed a more systemic truth: Vermont's vaunted antislavery legacy had not produced an antiracist culture. After Montpelier dashed his hopes, the veteran and his family prepared to leave Bear Swamp for good. And no farewell party marked their abrupt departure for "parts unknown." They were there, and then, a reporter noted with some puzzlement, they vanished. Where to? Why the hurry?[33]

Hasbrook's creditors understood. Farm desertion in New England, so common in these decades, was a proven way both to dodge debt and to beat it; Hasbrook's long-worked contract hill farm went into foreclosure, and he wouldn't see a dime. But he also wouldn't go to jail. Vermont law forbade the interstate prosecution of a debt, and in his new home, the leafy college town of Amherst, Massachusetts, Hasbrook was free and clear to start again.[34]

Hatter's pressman, handyman, post office worker, quarryman, caretaker, chambermaid: Hasbrooks held all these jobs, except his Addie. Tuberculosis killed her when she was twenty-three. In Amherst, Hasbrook's son Lloyd Garrison farmed (though not on land he owned). Until his death in 1915, Josiah Hasbrook himself got by painting houses, delivering mail, and hauling firewood and junk. And in this town, as in Middlesex, he joined the local post of the Grand Army of the Republic.

Private Josiah Hasbrook, Decoration Day, Amherst, MA. Detail from panoramic photograph, 1895. Photographer unknown. Courtesy Special Collections, Jones Public Library, Amherst, MA.

On Decoration Day he bore a wreath to the cemetery with other veterans who could still manage the stroll. A picture of them hangs in the Amherst town library. The bespectacled Private Hasbrook, still tall and lanky in his old age, if slightly stooped, stands in dress gloves and a formal jacket, the wreath hanging from his hand. Amherst on Decoration Day would have been awash in blooms, but Hasbrook's drawn face reveals nothing of the moment. He looks tired and preoccupied. Maybe his thoughts were back in Middlesex with the land and farm he lost to debt. There was a stream there that bore his name. Did anyone remember Hasbrook Brook? One of his three dead children was buried there. How long since anyone dressed George's grave with blooms?[35]

Or perhaps he was preoccupied with his ongoing battle with the Pension Bureau, still refusing (and would keep refusing) his appeals for an increase. Even after Hasbrook's death, justice would be denied this pioneer. Newspaper accounts routinely and mistakenly described Josiah as Mary Brown's "servant." The ever-driven, hopeful arc of his long odyssey from Fishkill to North Elba, then south into the slavelands, back again into the Black Woods, then east into the Green Mountains of Vermont, moving finally to this Massachusetts college town when age and infirmity caught up with him at last, was whittled down to service for the Brown family, and his family's North Elba stay of fifteen years shaved back to one point alone: *They came, and then they left. Another colored family, vanished.* But the Hasbrook family's great migration was no parable of Black incapacity. It was as deliberate and resolute as any bold removal to the West.[36]

On the Trail of Tommy Elliott

The migration of Private Thomas Elliott, the self-freed slave who cooked for Company K in New York's Ninety-Sixth and accompanied his white army mates to North Elba after the war, was also trimmed in public memory, his bold life contracted to one chapter, and this the one that wasn't true: Tommy Elliott (town historian Mary MacKenzie was assured by North Elbans) was a fugitive who found his way to John Brown's farm in the early 1850s and worked for the old man and got to be his friend. Brown (or a descendant) gave Elliott his Bible. Why, Elliott and Brown were thick as thieves![37]

MacKenzie sensed these dates were out of whack, and my own review of Elliott's military pension records confirms her intuition. Private Thomas Elliott saved himself from bondage, and didn't move to

North Elba until years after Brown was hanged. It was an army mate that urged him to North Elba, where "Tommy" Elliott worked on Alpheus Demmon's farm for years (likely overlapping at some point with the veteran and sometime Demmon farmhand "Josy" Hasbrook). Then, and well before the Demmon farm was sold, Elliott pushed east into the Adirondack iron-making district and got work as a hammersmith in Jay, headquarters of the J. & J. Rogers Iron Company, a family-managed empire whose mines, bloomeries, and forges webbed the wide Ausable River valley with scores of rough, teeming settlements. In 1880, only Michigan's Marquette County produced more iron ore than New York's Essex County. No Essex County company employed more full-time workers or made more iron than Elliott's employer. And in Jay, as in North Elba, Elliott boarded with a white family, their brick home hemmed with apple trees. He went to church (First Methodist Episcopal), taught Bible, gained a name for "industry and frugal habits," and voted. It may have been in Jay, too, that he changed his name to Thompson, the surname his Virginia father took when he was freed. In 1882, when this ironworker put down $1,200 for a town lot on the Ausable River, staked at the corners by old "hot pipes" from long-gone blast furnaces, Thomas Thompson was how he signed his name.[38]

Unfortunately, Thompson took up iron work right when market trends began to favor consolidated operations to the west. The resultant layoffs and site closures hit Adirondack iron miners hard. Ethnic strife and wildcat strikes were on the rise, and Thompson, a Black Methodist in an increasingly Catholic, culturally embattled workplace, may have been moved to wonder whether this place was his best home. He had tried working at a small forge in the hamlet of North Hudson, and also at the New Russia Iron Works, where all night long the racket from the giant trip-hammer echoed off the hills. By 1880, he had moved to Elizabethtown and was (again) boarding with a white family while he scouted for a homesite of his own. But only two years after he put down money on a piece of riverfront in Jay, he gave up on the whole idea, and left for good.[39]

In New Jersey's Newark, migrants from the South were arriving every hour. Here were Black neighborhoods and schools, Black baseball teams and Black-owned stores, and, in striking contrast with the Ausable valley mining district, a supply of viable romantic prospects. This is not to say that late nineteenth-century Adirondack censuses record no interracial marriages. But they were few, and public notice scowled. When Frederick Douglass married a white woman in 1884, the editor of the *Elizabethtown Post*, anticipating an eruption of interracial unions, suggested that evidence of race mixing be met with old-time vigilantism. Riding miscreants out of town on a rail—was not interracial marriage a reason to bring this hoary custom back?[40]

In Newark in 1888, Thomas Thompson met, courted, and married a Black woman from Virginia. She took his self-chosen, nonslave name for hers, and that surname would be her daughters'. The house they rented and then bought, freestanding on a Black block, was in his name as well. Fine and cherished gains for sure, but losses were felt, too. Never would he build that dreamed-of home on the banks of a wild river. Nor would his daughters know an integrated classroom, or his family an integrated church. The proud work of the artisan, the thrill and risk of working with hot iron and a forge, was behind him now. Thompson was a night watchman at a lime works and a factory. No meteoric spray of sparks or manly yelling here. He had three people who looked to him for school clothes, church dues, good shoes, and fresh milk, and while he had never sought a pension, perhaps figuring that his two names would complicate the process, he could no longer put it off. In 1906, the former army cook, age sixty, readied his appeal. For backup, he got two white officers from his old company and neighbors from North Elba, Sylvanus Paye and Judson C. Ware, to assure the government that the names Elliott and Thompson belonged to this same veteran. The pension was approved.[41]

And what better time for this former Adirondacker, his memories now stirring, to make a trip to Lake Placid, the old road gleaming with macadam, the hotel windows glimmering with filamented light, and at the village edge, a smartly painted train station with pillars, portico, and a shiny hardwood floor? Intervale was spruced up too—not that Company K's assistant cook would have been invited in to look around. By 1908, Private Elliott's first Adirondack home, once a stronghold of radical abolitionists, belonged to the Lake Placid Club, among whose exclusionary rules was the one that kept Blacks out.[42]

Out of Sight, Out of Mind

What happened to Thomas Elliott/Thompson in local memory— the vanishing of his biography, his reinvention as an acolyte of John Brown—was nothing new. Both Lyman Eppes Sr. and his son would be misremembered in these terms, and Josiah Hasbrook Jr. too. Stories that dramatized Black agency were appropriated and absorbed into narratives that exalted white courage and initiative. Early histories of the Underground Railroad indulged this tendency, as did the careless revisionism that turned the free-born Lyman Eppes into a fugitive. Timbuctoo itself was reinvented in the service of John Brown's martyrology. As Elliott/Thompson was said to have mysteriously vanished from North Elba, so was Timbuctoo assumed to have simply self-destructed, its settlers drifting back to the cities from which they presumably came.[43]

But it wasn't Elliott/Thompson who disappeared. What vanished was an interest in his story when it slipped beyond Brown's orbit. Too often local history reads an absence from the home place as desertion, disappearance, a failure to commit—and between disappearance and diaspora is a difference. Flight and purposeful migration are not the same. Nothing about the Smith grantees and their descendants who kept farming when they left the gift land—who went on to work in North Hudson and New Russia, or to farm in Vermont, Connecticut, or the Dakota Territory—was uncommitted. The faithlessness was history's: out of sight, out of mind.

This is not to sentimentalize these unremarked migrations. If moves to new farms and better prospects expressed agency and nerve, they also suggested the unrelenting pressure of distant market forces that kept Adirondackers—Black *and* white—scrambling to stay afloat. Across the nation in the postwar years, economic trends drove poor farmers, wage laborers, and hired hands off the land, and in the Adirondacks, as in neighboring Vermont, farm abandonment was long the norm. From 1870 to 1925, Essex County lost a third of its farms. Subsistence farming had no future in a new market economy. Rising taxes, surging land values, and higher prices all around (for farm machinery, seed, livestock, hired help, and simple upkeep) clamored for more income. And poor farmers, lacking cash or collateral and unable to make costs, could not keep up. In his compendious *A History of Agriculture in the State of New York*, Ulysses Hedrick kept the explanation simple. With the modernization of the farm, "the economic hazards of farming are increased. A man must have money to begin and keep going. His cost of doing business is sometimes greater than the income. . . . At every turn of country roads, insolvent farmers can be found—some have been insolvent all their lives." You might meet the challenge if you had collateral to start with or knew a local banker or merchant who would favor you with credit. But if your holdings boiled down to two cows, a chicken coop, and a scratch farm in the woods, who would risk a loan?

Only those blessed with assets could catch the updraft of opportunity. For the rest, writes the historian Jack Beatty, "freeholders slipped down the ladder to tenants; tenants to farm laborers; farm laborers to migrant workers," and, within a generation, "the representative American of 1860, the farmer, in a Gilded Age coinage, had become the 'hayseed' of 1890."[44]

Add to the economic uncertainties of rural life for a poor farmer in this era the further liability of race, and the picture darkens more. Civil War bounties and pensions for the families of Black veterans were useful, but the more meaningful capitalization that might have helped Black Adirondack farmers compete in a commercial market stayed out of reach. As for Black women, if the postwar era meant they sometimes worked out of the home, this likely did not translate into the confidence observed in the Black veterans. Out-of-home employment would not have lightened household chores, which now included tending debilitated, sometimes bedbound men. And to bone-weariness, add anxiety, for low-wage jobs offered no reprieve from poverty. If the shift from farm wife to wage earner brought a glimmer of empowerment, illness or old age could snuff it out in a season. After six years living with her son Josiah, Susan Hasbrook Pierce (the ex-wife of one grantee, the widow of another, and the mother of a third) took her eleven-year-old daughter, Lucy Ann, to Westport. There she cooked for a living, and cooked again at the Stevens House in Vergennes, in Vermont. When her son Josiah moved his tribe to Wadhams Mills, she and Lucy went there too, and likely moved in with him. This working widow was the image of postbellum Black mobility. But was this movement upward? Did life improve for her and Lucy when she worked out of the home?[45]

On John Brown's death, his abolitionist allies made sure that two of his daughters got out of North Elba and into Franklin Sanborn's boarding school in Concord, Massachusetts. No Boston abolitionist stepped up to swoop away the fourteen-year-old Lucy Ann and set her up with schooling when her mother Susan, fifty-five, died in Wadhams Mills in 1873. There would be no school at all. Lacking resources of her own or any nearby family, Lucy reviewed her options. Bunking with the Hasbrooks in Wadhams at this time was her brother's old army mate Jerry Miles, the Virginia-born ex-slave who made the Black Woods his new home after the war. Jerry, in his twenties, and Lucy Ann, fourteen, were married four months after her mother's death. The next year they were living in Middlesex, Vermont.[46]

In the dispatches from Middlesex in Montpelier newspapers, the Mi-
leses' domestic triumphs were warmly noted. Jerry once returned from
Bear Swamp with seventy-one trout. Their prize hen laid an egg as big
as a potato. Sixty guests attended their wedding anniversary in 1894.
The farmhand Jerry Miles, "known to everybody and always favorably
known," made a sturdy world in Middlesex. His funeral was thronged,
"showing the great esteem in which [he] was held." His employer, the
town judge, was a pallbearer. But a good name promised no marked advancement. Miles never owned his home, not outright, and like North
Elba's Lyman Epps Jr., he could not make a living farming for himself.[47]

The progress that the ex-slave and deedholder John Thomas proudly
reported to Gerrit Smith in 1872 would not be realized by any of Thomas's descendants. Things did not pick up for them. Things did not no-
tably pick up for any of the descendants of the early grantee-settlers.
After the war, the children and grandchildren of the "first families" of
the Black Woods, the Thomases and Eppeses, Carasaws and Hasbrooks,
Hazzards and Morehouses, got by, and that was it. Hired hand, house
servant, laundress, teamster, waiter—these were the jobs that whisked
them into the next century. For the dark skinned, hard times just stayed
hard, whether in Franklin and Essex Counties or in Brooklyn, Baltimore, and Amherst, and no rags-to-riches hagiographies of African
Americans brighten nineteenth-century Adirondack county histories.
Not that we would read a Black success story in these volumes. The
approving sentences on Thomas Thompson in the Essex County history of 1885 were a fluke. Behind the confident biographies in county
histories simmered the anxiety of Main Street authors and subscribers
who were all too mindful of a new pluralistic culture that threatened
their hegemony. Up-from-under stories of Catholics and non-Anglos
were suffered rarely, and town-proud accounts of Black Americans not
at all.[48]

This was the age, let us recall, when centuries-old race prejudice was
girded by the emerging discipline of physical anthropology and the
pseudoscience of renowned exponents like Louis Agassiz of Harvard,
Samuel George Morton of Philadelphia, and the Alabama physician
Josiah Nott. From these and other well-born pundits, stern "proofs" of
the innate inferiority of "lesser" races and the calamity of "race mixing"
would make their way into public policy and legislation. The case for
a natural racial hierarchy and Black biological inferiority based not on
habit, faith, politics, or profit but on the "neutral" study of skull size

and body type stiffened white anxiety with scientific respectability. And university lecture halls would not contain the reach of these cold influences. The rural North registered them too.[49]

When she was young, John Thomas's granddaughter Rosa Scott was a laundress in Vermontville. Two decades later, living in Englewood, New Jersey, she still washed clothes. In the Adirondacks, her brother Richard was a hired hand and blacksmith; in New Jersey, forty years later, he worked at a city dump. William and Eliza's sons were laborers, truckers, boiler stokers, and grooms. Hellen "Libby" Hazzard, another of Thomas's granddaughters, cleaned homes in Saranac Lake and ironed laundry, a skill as tightly identified with Black women as peddling was with immigrant Eastern European Jews—with a difference. White peddlers leveraged wagons into storefronts, and these into fine mercantile emporia. In the Adirondacks were a score of them, from Ginsberg's, the beloved department store of Tupper Lake, to D. Cohen & Sons Hardware in Saranac Lake, where John Thomas's great-grandson Marshall Morehouse worked for thirty-five years. Would a lifetime on the job earn this shop hand a promotion to store manager, supervisor, or part owner? Morehouse got a paycheck. He would not move up. Nor would his Aunt Libby own a laundry of her own or see her children buy an Adirondack business; they made for cities as soon as they were grown, and drove laundry trucks for others, hauled mail, and swabbed floors. This was honorable and valued work, with paychecks that were steady, but no hope in this of trading in the mop for the life of the mop's manufacturer, no rising up, no office with a view.[50]

In Saranac Lake, James Morehouse, the youngest son of Charlotte Ann, was a stonemason and a construction worker. In New York City, he worked on construction projects for the WPA. He lived alone in Corona, Queens; his neighbors were Italians and Argentinians. During the Depression, his mother came down from the Adirondacks and lived with him for her last years—and what a shock for this octogenarian daughter of a self-freed slave, the girl whose late husband broke camp for one of Charles Dickens's stringers. Charlotte Ann took in her father John Thomas when he was failing. Now it was her son's time to do the same for her.[51]

Was it hard? Did she miss Vermontville? She was a lifelong child of the woods, and she surely recalled some of her youth with joy. Eggs so fresh they warmed the palm. Woodsmoke, fireflies, the gilded haze of late summer. Private Morehouse courting her, and she still such a girl!

Then, Warren's death, the children young, and winter rolling toward them like a great ragged army. In 1934, the last year of her life, thermometers in parts of the Adirondacks registered fifty-two below. And her Sicilian neighbors were so proud of how they stood it, these big-city winters. They had no idea.[52]

When North Elba was a wilderness and Vermontville a crossing in the woods, the Black grantees and their pioneering wives were *needed*. It was all hands on deck when a wolf needed tracking or a farmer late with taxes needed help getting his place back in his name. The new frontier community was as vulnerable as a newly made nest, finding its resilience in each woven twig. That the Black veterans and their widows could look to white friends for help when they applied for pensions, and that many of these neighbors gave that help so freely, was a testament to the community and its small strength. But this was never about building a utopia or honoring an equalitarian agenda. This was the daily application of the old dictum *ex unitate vires*, and when community building was less a matter of *strength through unity*, the adhesive of expedience relaxed. It was a sure fact that in 1847, the estimable Iddo Osgood invited Charles Ray and James McCune Smith to ply their trades in his home hamlet. But the squire died. North Elba grew. When sufficient white folk were on the ground to preach a sermon and set a bone, the invitation was not repeated. Casual racism and Christian fellowship were easy bedfellows in the Black Woods. The agrarian Charles Bennett Ray had promised that on-the-ground daily dealings between farm families would point to trust, respect, and maybe even something like affection, and a great many stories from the Black Woods—revelations in the redemption records and pension files especially—suggest the pastor got this right. But as crossroads settlements burgeoned into hamlets, and hamlets into towns, the social landscape shifted. *Need*, that eager conjurer of frontier fellowship, no longer cast much of a spell.[53]

Something for the Son of Ham

In 1885, the grantee's son Charles Henry Hazzard learned just how much his good standing in his St. Armand home could help him. That year, a county constable came to his farm with a summons from the court: Hazzard had been found guilty of nonpayment of a debt. The constable was here to escort the aging farmer to the county jail for three months.[54]

Hazzard knew he owed the money. The debt was for a horse he had bought in Ausable Forks in 1884. Though the horse was wheezy and "poor in flesh," the seller (white) promised it would rally with a little time and care. Hazzard got the horse back to his farm, but when it wouldn't drink or eat and then collapsed, both hind legs snapping, he had to put it down.[55]

What was his obligation? The white veterans he tapped for advice were good neighbors and community-builders, like himself. Six years earlier, he and his brother Alexander joined ranks with fifteen neighbors to found St. Armand's Brookside Cemetery, and when forest fires lunged, the Hazzard men helped beat them back. Captain James H. Pierce had founded the St. Armand lumber hamlet Bloomingdale and served as its first president, town supervisor (repeatedly), and postmaster. Black farmers brought potatoes to his starch factory. He backed their claims during the tax sales and, after his return from the war, their appeals for military pensions too. Hazzard's other confidante, 2nd Lieutenant Judson C. Ware of North Elba, was credible as well. A former county sheriff and town supervisor, he grew up in the Black Woods. In July 1857, while John Brown was in Kansas, Ware, three Browns, two Thompsons, and the grantee's son, Simeon Hasbrook, camped out on Whiteface and had themselves, wrote Annie Brown, "a first rate time" despite their ill-made, over-smoky campfire. Back from the war, Ware took the side of his Black neighbors against farm seizures for back taxes, bought property from them, and saw them take their vows. And when he and Pierce reviewed Hazzard's situation, they gave their best advice. This horse seller was a swindler. Hazzard owed him not one cent.[56]

But the confident reassurance of these white men, advice that might have worked for Hazzard in St. Armand, could not help him where he wasn't known. Elizabethtown was only thirty miles from St. Armand, but where a Black man wasn't known, the presumption of his criminality was apparently a given. And when a county constable turned up at his farm, the good word of his neighbors couldn't help him. The county jail would be his home for three months—or would have been but for an unexpected intervention.

A decade before Hazzard's case was brought to Byron Pond's attention, when this prominent Elizabethtown attorney was the Essex County judge, Pond heard white farmers in St. Armand neighbors side with the Hazzards against the threat of land confiscation for back taxes. He heard about the Hazzards's roomy fenced-in garden, and about the twelve acres of wild grass they mowed for their animals. Pond, an estate attorney, had helped sort out Avery Hazzard's will. And if Pond's occasional dealings with Gerrit Smith were strictly business, and his devotion to the antislavery cause no match for his older brother's (Alembert Pond was active in the Underground Railroad), Pond still made sure he got to Deer's Head Inn for orator Wendell Phillips's remarks about John Brown's last days in 1859 (the room was packed, and Phillips lived up to his name). By 1886, Pond had served his town and county in every available capacity: county judge most famously, but also school board head, postmaster, town clerk, Republican convention delegate, and district attorney. He was sixty-three when he gave Charles Henry Hazzard's case a look. And as far as he could see, what happened here was casebook plain.[57]

Franklin Rowe, the horse dealer's lawyer, had grossly, even criminally, overreached. Hazzard had never had an opportunity to find a lawyer, plead his case, or organize an appeal. Further, the fellow who sold him his horse never asked for or expected him to go to jail. Sheriff, constable, and attorney, each had overstepped the law. Pond saw to Hazzard's early release, and at Pond's insistence, the court acknowledged that Hazzard's jail time was a mistake (only after extracting Hazzard's promise, however, that he wouldn't countersue). It would be at Hazzard's own insistence, however, that Pond pressed for more. Why, Hazzard demanded, had he still to pay a fine? Was no compensation owed to *him*? Was no one here accountable? Pond apparently agreed, and said as much to Rowe, the horse dealer's attorney: "Hazzard is anxious that something be collected for his being improperly kept in jail for two months. The plaintiff would naturally be the party to call upon in such a case . . . but the judge saw fit . . . to protect him, but to leave you exposed. Now, I don't like to do anything that shall look like punishing a fellow lawyer, still it seems under the Fourteenth Constitutional Amendment, something must be done for the Son of Ham. What do you say about it?"[58]

This was delicately put. For all the condescension of that "Son of Ham" remark and a consoling nod to the shared fraternity of class and whiteness, Judge Pond knew that his word and reputation were not enough to force a change; the "slow democracy" of personal acquaintance and grassroots loyalty was, by itself, no guarantor of justice. Pond invoked the Constitution because pressure had to come from local vigilance and federal law alike—that is, from top and bottom both. The appeal to the highest law of the land let Rowe know Judge Pond's grasp of the stakes here, and while Pond did not spell it out, his expectation was transparent: *Do more for this Black man or we may meet in court.*[59]

Court costs and fine were cancelled. Hazzard's name was cleared. He went home early, his purse intact. These were gains, and this was something. But had a breach of justice been redressed? For Hazzard's two months behind bars, for the blow to his and Julia's subsistence farm (half the planting season stolen), for the trauma to his once enslaved wife, who surely figured she had put these blows behind her (white men seizing, *stealing* people, presuming Black culpability a given)—for this, there was no compensation. The Hazzards of St. Armand never saw a dime.

Hagiographers and Hayseeds

Toward the end of the century, the heyday of the Adirondack homesteader was over. Railroad tracks that once girdled the Adirondack region now bore "summer tramps" and late Gilded Age tycoons to the watery interior. By 1893, sixty private Adirondack parks held more than 940,000 acres; grand hotels added laundry rooms and servant quarters and wide sloping lawns. Rumors of mill-made pollution, scarifying clear-cuts, soil erosion, and the risk of waterborne epidemics had finally claimed the interest of downstate voters: in 1894, they overwhelmingly approved an article for the state constitution to maintain the Adirondack Forest Preserve in a condition "forever wild." Now tourism and the conservation lobby would shape the image of the region, sweeping the old-time subsistence farmer, that quaint and now somewhat comic "hayseed," to the unlit, dusty wings.[60]

That same year, Louisa Brady and John Thomas were buried in the Vermontville Union Cemetery under slim headstones in the second row. I like to imagine the widower and the widow (that's how the 1880 census enumerator described her status; in fact, her errant soldier-spouse outlived her) making the best of things in their last years, two old friends occasionally meeting up over a slice of pie to count the season's blessings: a good run of sap, hollyhocks higher than the gate latch, a better price for potatoes at the starch factory at the Eight-Mile Schoolhouse, or maybe a new dope for the pestilential blackflies (not that these foul potions ever did a thing).

Other topics—the lonely death of Samuel Brady, Louisa's only son, the vanishing of her second husband, the ruination of John Thomas's first family in Maryland, or the death in 1860 of his and Mary Ann's one boy—these survivors may have kept to themselves. And they may have held back, too, about more recent disappointments. The hope that legal freedom for four million Black Americans would conjure a new age of justice and equality. The assumption that their little colony of Black farmers would keep and eventually thrive. The wish that at least a few of the younger folks could scratch out a better deal on the land than their folks. By 1885, Eugene Thew's shingle mill sprawled across the bones of Freeman's Home. Four years later, John Thomas sold his hundred-acre farm to a white man for $800, enough money to see Thomas through his dotage—but how hard to part with that good land! Thomas's son-in-law, Walter Scott, once a farmer, was down to day work, as were Warren and Charlotte Ann's boys. All the grandchildren answered to bosses. Not one could say, as Thomas wrote Gerrit Smith in 1872, that he worked for himself. Even old Mr. Eppes in North Elba was giving up his family farm. His grown girls had made for distant cities, and Lyme Jr. could or would not shoulder it alone.[61]

To a reporter, Lyme Jr. allowed that he might have married if more Black women lived nearby or if he'd ventured to a city. His parents met in a city. His sister Kate met her husband (Black) in Manhattan, moved

Lyman Epps Jr., North Elba. Photographer unknown, ca. 1935. Courtesy Lyman E. Eppes Collection, Lake Placid Public Library, NY.

there, and never left. But Lyme was a homebody. North Elba was his world. Here were old friends, work, his parents' graves. So he stayed single, and having no young family to help him, never did farm solely for himself. Nor would he enjoy his parents' upward mobility. In effect, the casual constraints of Jim Crow apartheid paralyzed his prospects as they almost did those of Thomas Elliott, who only found a partner when he left the North Country for Newark. Lyme Epps's parents, with their children's help, beefed up assets and social standing alike, but the bachelor son was stuck. All his life he worked for others—hauled trash, tended oxen, groomed the links at a whites-only resort. The job he wanted, caretaker and guide at the John Brown Farm, he never got. That was a state hire, and would stay a white one as long as any poor white farmer wanted it, however tepid his connection with John Brown.[62]

At least Epps was always on the scene at the events that brought the crowds. In 1896, when the State of New York took charge of the farm from Kate Field's John Brown Association, the Eppes family sang Brown's favorite hymn. And on August 30, 1899, the anniversary of the Battle of Osawatomie, there was another fine to-do when the remains of eight of Brown's twenty-one "Raiders," redeemed from damaged or unmarked graves in Harpers Ferry and elsewhere and now gathered in one casket, gained an honor long denied them: a proper burial with speeches, prayer, military salute, and place of rest by the gray stone of their commander. Elsewhere in Lake Placid that last week in August was a golf tourney, a ladies' euchre competition, and a minstrel show and cakewalk. But what summoned a throng of thousands (the *New York Times* guessed 3,500) were the goings-on at John Brown's farm. On foot and by carriage, tourists, pilgrims, and native Adirondackers hiked the road to Brown's clapboard home.[63]

Part of the thrill of the occasion was the by now well-published story of what had made it possible—a heist, a traveling trunk, an illicit plan that, in its unlikeliness and bravado, seemed to suggest the spirit of Brown's raid itself. Earlier in July, three passionate admirers of John Brown had resolved to locate and retrieve the boxed-up remains of Brown's eight followers who, not long after the raid, had been buried (more like dumped) with some secrecy in a muddy riverbank near Harpers Ferry. Their plan was to get these bones back to North Elba and see to their reburial, with honors, near John Brown's grave. In July, the organizer of this effort, Thomas Featherstonhaugh of Washington, DC, tracked down a photographer in Saranac Lake who, in 1896, had self-published her elegiac photo essay, *A Hero's Grave in the Adirondacks*.

The booklet, which he chanced on at the John Brown Farm, moved him deeply. Perhaps Katherine McClellan, the photographer, would wish to help him? His scheme was wild and illegal, but if justice long denied could be delivered, McClellan was all in. In early August a large trunk came to her Saranac Lake home bearing the remains of eight raiders, painstakingly recovered from three crude pine boxes half a century in muck. Then it was McClellan's turn to bring the thing to closure. She prevailed on North Elba to provide a silver-handled casket. The burial would happen at the August anniversary of Osawatomie at John Brown's grave.[64]

Here, as in 1896, Katherine McClellan was a principal photographer. Her fine pictures showed men in bowlers and stiff coats, and ladies in wasp-waisted gowns, hair pinned high, parasols lifted to the haze. Also documented: the speakers in their good suits, firm of visage, thin of hair. Bishop Henry Potter of New York spoke (this churchman, veteran pulpiteer, and avid club member loved the Adirondacks; he had a big camp on a little island in Lake Placid). Potter's friend Whitelaw Reid

Reburial of followers of John Brown at Brown's grave. Katherine McClellan, photographer, August 1899. Courtesy Smith College Archives, Katherine McClellan Papers, Northampton, MA.

of the *Herald Tribune* prepared remarks as well. (His camp, Wild Air, was at Upper St. Regis Lake.) The master of events was the Lake Placid hotelier George Stevens, who introduced, from Groton, Massachusetts, the cotton-bearded Rev. Joshua Young, ever honored for his prayer at Brown's funeral, a kindness that half a century before had cost him his first ministry in Burlington, Vermont. Speaking for the veterans were Colonel Richard Hinton and Captain James Holmes, the latter of whom had fought with Brown at Osawatomie.[65]

Hinton, resting heavily on his cane, talked about the raiders. Bishop Potter gave thanks to William Lloyd Garrison and Gerrit Smith. The Eppes family, John Brown's old friends, sang Brown's favorite hymn, "Blow Ye the Trumpets Blow," Charles Wesley's mystic, stately anthem of apocalyptic liberation, and a newer tune, "In the Sweet By-and-By," an everything-is-coming-up-roses crowdpleaser that would have made Brown wince. But this wasn't John Brown's show, not Brown the plotter of seditious raids. That Brown ("crazed," "unbalanced," "misguided," "blinded by fanaticism," as accounts of this commemorative event described him) was no hero here.[66]

This day's great man was Brown the catalyst, whose actions sparked the fuse that led to war, an awful war, but necessary, purifying, and at least as much an object of reverence as Brown himself. For it was the war, not Brown, that put a stop to slavery, as this day's program drove firmly home. The event that set the war in motion might belong to Brown and his men, but thanks for the death of slavery went to Lincoln and his army. So there would be no agitators at the podium today, no latter-day Wendell Phillips among the speakers, no W. E. B. Du Bois to speak for Black Americans and represent Black sentiment on issues that would certainly compel John Brown if he were alive—like Jim Crow, or voter suppression, or lynch law, or the dead letter of Reconstruction. To invoke these crises would suggest that Brown's business was unfinished, the deeper purpose of the war unresolved. And this was not the thing. The point was to say, *Done here*, to walk away that summer afternoon calmly certain that John Brown and his raiders were now at rest. Three regimental salutes from the NY Twenty-Sixth Infantry, the singing of "My Country 'Tis of Thee" and "John Brown's Body," and finally the sweet strains of "Taps" fixed the raiders and their story in a narrative of war and victory, reconciliation and recovery, and claimed the day for patriots. No dissent, no protest, no dwelling on the grievances of Black Americans. Slavery was dead.[67]

It is a pity that Katherine McClellan did not train her lens on the crowd itself. Always, at events at the farm that honored "Old John Brown," were Black people. Black Adirondackers had been coming to the shrine for fifty years. They came for Brown's burial, for GAR events, for the transfer of the farm to the State of New York in 1896. This particular event would have held a singular appeal for Black Adirondackers, since it honored Black raiders along with white. As late as 1899 and not counting the Eppeses, at least thirty direct or extended-family descendants of the Black Woods pioneers were in the region, calling it their home. There were Appos, Hazzards, Morehouses, Scotts, Langleys, Princes, Johnsons, Williamses, Ricketsons, Davises, and Gardineers—and some still farmed. That year, north of John Brown's farmhouse, were two farms run by Black families. Charles Henry Hazzard and his wife, Julia, worked the farm they bought after the war. Next to them, Alexander Hazzard's widow, Elizabeth, ran the old family farm with some of her children.

In 1902 her enterprising daughter Adaline and son-in-law, William Langley from Vermont, converted part of their Bloomingdale farm into a cure cottage for Black invalids afflicted with tuberculosis. In the Resorts section of the *Brooklyn Daily Eagle* in May 1902, the Langleys advertised the "first resort house for colored people" in Saranac Lake. It would never be a moneymaker, and the family's fiscal woes were not improved by Adaline's brother Avery's failure to distribute earnings from the sale of a Hazzard home among his siblings (they wound up suing him to get their share). In 1911, the county sheriff put the old Hazzard farmhouse up for auction for unmet debts (mostly owed to the Bloomingdale storekeeper Sydney Barnard). Yet somehow, Adaline and William kept their eight-bed "Langley Cottage for Colored Patients" going. It was still listed—at seven or eight dollars per diem—in the 1916 directory of the National Tuberculosis Association (the only designated resort for Black people among the approximately seventy Saranac Lake directory listings that year). No less than her settler-grandfather, Avery Hazzard, and her father Alexander, an Adirondack guide, Adaline Hazzard Langley was a pioneer, a Black woman blazing a trail into the frontier of recovery and health.[68]

Were there Hazzards at John Brown's farm in 1899? For all of history's abiding interest in the Eppeses, it was this family from St. Armand who stuck with farming long after the Eppeses gave up. And the Hazzards, noted McClellan in her 1896 essay, were as cozy with the Browns as the Eppeses. Perhaps Adaline's uncle, Charles Henry Hazzard, knew about Brown's plans, and had an opportunity to join him. He would have made a good fighter. Recall the teenage street brawl in Union Village, 1848, that landed him in jail, and then, in 1886, his fierce demand that Judge Byron Pond push for a better settlement from the lawyer who got him locked up for no reason.[69]

This may be why, when I imagine Hazzard there at John Brown's grave in August 1899, I see no breathless celebrant. I see someone pondering the impact of his celebrated neighbor and wondering, not for the first time, if he should have made Brown's destiny his own. I see him imagining *his* bones mingling with the martyrs in their casket, *his* name offered to the throng by the white man leaning on his cane. This could have been his long home too, his green grave next to "the Meteor of the War." Instead he had held out for another war, another call, a choice that consigned him to obscurity even while enabling his blessings, which for all the hard times did add up. There was this fine sunlit day, for instance, and Julia and his stepchildren, their hard-worked farm, his "best of reputations" among his St. Armand neighbors, and these long years of his, three-quarters of the century, and here he stood, still on the warm side of eternity. In 1877 and then again, in 1898, St. Armand made him village constable—this in the same New York whose laws had twice put him behind bars! But this was how things blew in the Black Woods, on winds so careless, you couldn't take a thing for granted. Anything could change.[70]

To speculate so nervily, however, I would need to know that Hazzard was there. I would need him to have been seen and, moreover, recognized as a presence whose history was essential to the day's meaning. And who would do this? Who would turn that day from the old men with their snowy beards and self-regarding speeches rolling out like waves of foam, and notice Private Charles Henry Hazzard? Or contest the rifles booming and the strains of "Taps" declaring this thing over, done with, put to rest? Who could, would want to, break this spell?

Rest was the allure, the great prize, after all. Rest for the raiders, for the veterans, and for the pilgrims too. Rest from the past but, more, especially, rest from what Dr. Martin Luther King Jr. would call the "fierce urgency of Now."[71] So the Black pilgrims in their soft caps and dark plain coats remained unnamed and unremarked, and as "Taps" gave up its notes, they, too, dispersed into the loose drift of the crowd.

CHAPTER 16

White Memory, Black Memory

"Every generation gets the stories it wants to hear."

—Austrian historian Heidemarie Uhl at the Bergen-Belsen International Conference, Germany, 2009.

In 2009, the novelist Russell Banks, author of several works of fiction set in the Adirondacks, was invited by the New York State Writers Institute to pick an entry for a master list of New York's most influential books. Banks's choice, *The Adirondacks Illustrated*, by the writer-photographer Seneca Ray Stoddard, honored this travel memoir's lasting imprint. Stoddard and his books and postcards, tinted maps, humorous sketches, and travel guides did more than any other writer to introduce the nation to the Adirondack region and define its brand and image.[1]

And what had the Glens Falls master-influencer to say about the late John Brown and Gerrit Smith's "scheme of justice and benevolence"? Fifteen years after Brown's hanging, a visit to his storied farm and grave was indispensable to any grand tour of the region. Stoddard made his approach through Wilmington Pass, at one point catching a lift on a wagon whose driver Stoddard never named. When the "darkey" told him he belonged to "the only family of colo'd folks in town," Stoddard asked about the long-gone Black colony he heard John Brown "established." Offered his informant, the "not much account-Niggers" vanished when "they couldn't make a livin'; too cold for 'em; wan't much used to work, I guess; and couldn't stan' the kind they got heah. Most of 'em were barbers an' sich, who thought they wouldn't have nothing

295

to do when they come heah, an' after the old man died they couldn't
get along noway, so they dug out, some of 'em, and some of 'em died.
An' . . . one ole niggah froze to death."[2]

Stoddard urged him on.

"Well, he went out huntin' one day in de winteh an' got lost in the
woods. He had his compass with him, but when they found him they
found where he had sot down on a log and *picked his compass to pieces*,
and then sot there till he froze to death!"

Chasing down Stoddard's errors is no great sport. He never claimed
to be a scholar. He was a brilliant photographer and a fluid, easy ra-
conteur, especially about the woodsy characters in the deep North
he adored. John Brown was too pungent for his repertoire; Stoddard
called him a "fanatic" and a "murderer." The match Brown put to the
battle that burst into a war made a North Elba visit compulsory, but
when Stoddard entered the martyr's aerie through an offhand yarn
about "one ole niggah" who froze to death, his distaste for John Brown
showed. The story of a Black man's solitary death underscored Brown's
absence; the "old man" left his "pet lambs" high and dry, defenseless
against their incompetence. No very loving shepherd, he.

As to what actually happened—Stoddard got some of it right. The
Troy grantee and pioneer James Henderson did freeze to death, as others
had before him. One was the North Elban Arunah Taylor. This settler
perished in a snowstorm in the very early 1800s, and like Henderson, he
belonged to a colony of homesteaders that did not last. But what befell
the white man was, local history implies, any pioneer's hard luck. The
death of Stoddard's subject suggests ignorance and torpor. Slumped on
his tree stump, unable to read his compass, waiting witlessly for death,
Stoddard's frozen settler embodied all that seemed early doomed about
Timbuctoo itself (and that paralleled, and thus reinforced, Stoddard's
cold judgment of Brown's plan). The Black man was done in by the
deluded notion that he could make it in North Elba in the first place,
that he belonged, that this corner of the world could ever be his own.[3]

And why was Stoddard's "sable friend," the driver, without a name?
At the time of Stoddard's visit, his informant was almost surely Lyman Eppes or his son Lyme Jr., but to name either man would have
tasked the writer with respecting someone real. Stoddard was more interested in his driver as a *type*, a spectacle "decidedly attractive in his
way, even if his skin was a few shades darker than regulation and his
hair unexplorable in its kinkiness." Stoddard saw what he hoped to see,
heard the South in the teamster's speech because his readers expected

the shuffling slur of minstrelsy. But the real Eppeses were from Troy, and before that, New York City and Colchester, Connecticut. And when Lyman Sr., a devout man, wrote "Nigger Lands" in a letter to the *North Star*, the pointed quotes around it were meant to underscore the racism of the white speculators who used it. His son, Lyme Jr., would be remembered in Lake Placid as "a quiet, well-spoken and highly respected member of the community." And the shoemaker-grantee James Henderson, was, as we have seen, nobody's "pet lamb." Nor did he die old but at the height of a vigorous middle age.[4]

North Elba, Disavowed

Taking a cue from Mary MacKenzie, modern chroniclers of Timbuctoo hold Alfred Donaldson to blame for the casually racist portrait of the Black pioneers. But it didn't start with Donaldson. It didn't start with Stoddard. Pocket histories of Timbuctoo that reinforce a racializing agenda are as old as the giveaway. As early as 1852, the upstate Democratic legislator Winslow C. Watson judged Smith's scheme doomed because its giftees were inherently undeserving, "ill adapted in [their] physical constitution . . . , with neither experience or competency to the independent management of business affairs, and adverse to them from habits and propensities." Never mind concerns about the climate or the soil—the problem was "the Negro." Because of his "propensities," Smith's plan "bore in its inception inherent elements of failure." After John Brown's raid, this assertion of a flaw, a lack, would be extended to indictments of the grantees' benefactor. Smith's two months in the Utica Asylum gave his critics a perfect opening to discount his philanthropic work for Black New Yorkers as evidence of mental illness—for who but a lunatic would give free land to Blacks? Northern editors invoked Smith's "mania for negroes," expressed in gifts of "small farms to as many of them as choose to take them," as proof that "he was not exactly a person of sound mind." The *Albany Journal* called Smith's philanthropy a symptom of the "state of political hallucination" that kept him on "the borders of insanity for a quarter of a century." This was beyond marginalization. Smith's land gifts were pathologized— madness that had gone too long by kinder names.[5]

After the Civil War, this dire spin relaxed. The assertion of Smith's lunacy reverted to a default charge of eccentricity. At least until the demise of Reconstruction while Northerners still had a use for John Brown as an icon of Christian rectitude and Yankee courage, Smith's reputation gained. He noted it himself in his 1867 *Manifesto* ("The more the public identifies me with John Brown, the more it honors me"). Cherishing this link to Brown fulfilled a debt to public memory; Smith tried to live up to the billing. As Harpers Ferry transformed the Black Woods into John Brown Country, so was Smith recast, foremost, as John Brown's Friend.[6]

But it could be a very dull assignment. Smith heard from people wanting to track down Brown's family, from artists wanting funding for their Brown-themed exhibitions, and from autograph hounds thirsting for Brown's signature. An Ohio medium knew Smith would like to hear Brown's messages for him from the spirit world beyond: "Glory to God, Liberty to the Slaves. I greet you on the prospective freedom of the colored race in a short time. God aid you in this course. Farewell, John Brown." For the rest of Smith's life he would hear from the Liberty Party faithful about his providential role in Brown's career. A reformer asked Smith to represent the "Murdered Patriarch" in Vermont, noting Peterboro's proximity to "John Brown's Tract" (in fact, the John Brown of this tract was a Rhode Island land baron and no kin to the abolitionist, and the tract itself was far from the Black Woods). An Illinois publisher named Eastman hoped Smith would ornament a reunion of career abolitionists, because, he said, "I believe you did more than any other ten men to place John Brown where he is—John Brown's action at Harpers Ferry was the *doing* of your doctrine as taught in your address to the Slaves."[7]

In 1872, Smith, guest of honor at the Republican National Convention in Philadelphia, was introduced as "the oldest pioneer in the cause of emancipation in this room." Governor Richard Oglesby of Illinois called Smith "that venerable, sublime man of New York," a living icon, "the impersonation of American dignity and benevolence. . . . [To] see and hear that great agitator, who long before the Republican party had, at its birth, recognized our duties toward a down-trodden race, and waged earnest battle for their rights, at a time when most of us here today were young and useless"—all this, said Oglesby, "rejoiced my heart." But it was not Smith's name that whipped up "the grandest scene in the history of any political assemblage" and brought the delegates to their feet with "scarcely a dry eye in all that great assemblage." Only the "familiar, electrifying strains" of one anthem could do that, and it wasn't named for Smith.[8]

Years before, Smith predicted his friend Brown would emerge as "the most admired person in American history." It didn't happen, and it won't. But in Gerrit Smith's lifetime and for a generation after, Brown's fame was unassailable. His trial riveted all of Europe; his story was the world's. In Vladivostok in 1900, Russian troops sang his praises (a Black American diplomat was amazed). Surely that summer day in Philadelphia, Smith, with the Republicans, raised his age-faded voice and sang the old familiar song. Duty beckoned. He was the vestigial conduit, the lone link to the martyred icon. Smith knew Brown well, had funded him, got him rifles, given him a farm.[9]

But what Smith did out of the public eye—not his acts so much as his own inaction—reveals a relationship with Brown more ambivalent than history admits. Smith could have visited Brown's family in North Elba after he was released from the asylum. George Stearns, Thomas Wentworth Higginson, and Frank Sanborn made the trip, but not Smith, whose upstate home was nearer to Brown's grave than any one of theirs. Nor would he send a sculptor to the Charles Town jail to make a bust of Brown or hire a mason to etch Brown's name into his grave. Stearns did that. A fund to help Brown's family in the years after his death? That fell to Higginson and Sanborn. Also Sanborn's contribution: the full account of the Secret Six's contributions to John Brown's plan. No public record reveals any trip Smith made to John Brown's grave before Smith died in 1874.[10]

In 1869, Smith heard from Isaac Gates, an aging abolitionist in Iowa. "You must allow me to congratulate you," Gates wrote, "on the fact that you have out lived 'Slavery,' survived its *persecution* & have lived to see the day when to be called the '*friend*' of '*John Brown*' are 'words of *good repute*.'" Smith would not have argued, but his words and actions stayed at odds. Smith was grateful for the restoration of Brown's reputation, but how do we explain his answer to abolitionists who hoped to buy John Brown's North Elba farm and preserve it in Brown's honor?[11]

Never mind that the farm's leaseholder, Alexis Hinckley, told Smith that Brown's widow, Mary, in California since 1864, "would greatly prefer to have the place sold in that way." Smith said no. If he could not stop the conflation of his name and Brown's, he was not obliged to prolong it. He did not want the farm memorialized. Let a farmer take it, he told Hinckley. Let the cult subside. In 1872, the year he rose to sing "John Brown's Body" at the Philadelphia convention, Smith told Sanborn that the very mention of "this John Brown affair" made him so jittery that he feared "a recurrence of my insanity." Better to push it out of mind, and to let the woods and fields that Smith's philanthropy once made synonymous with "justice and benevolence" go back to being just another farmscape, with no deeper resonance, no higher purpose.[12]

Better, anyway, for him. Others would be slower to forget.

The Making of a Shrine

Alexis Hinckley was pitching hay in Brown's old field when the approaching stranger caught his eye. Fresh from a first-time Adirondack camping trip (a thrilling jaunt she wrote up for the *Tribune*), the St. Louis journalist Kate Field had come to tour the grave and home of Old John Brown. But in 1873, the house was empty, picked clean except for Brown's picture on a wall. Did no one live there? Not these days, Hinckley told her. Even he, the "sad, thin man" who owned the place, came around only occasionally and, anyway, had plans to sell.[13]

"*For sale*! For sale with the bones of John Brown lying there!" The reporter was aghast. Surely the old abolition cohort in Boston, stronghold of the Secret Six, would give $2,000 to buy and rescue John Brown's farm. But Massachusetts balked. Even Brown's own family seemed not especially invested in it, Ralph Waldo Emerson reminded Field. And he had seen the place. It "did not look attractive." Why make it more than what it was?[14]

Then Field tried New York. The Union League Club, the fraternity of civic-minded merchants, pressmen, and politicos who stood for Lincoln, had lobbied sternly (if unavailingly) for martial law and federal intervention during the draft riots, and collaborated with Black activists to get relief to city Blacks made homeless by marauders. The league had also—and this less than a year after the city's "rabbledom and rebeldom" claimed hundreds of Black lives—organized three Black regiments, raised money for the US Sanitary Commission, and, after the war, promoted Reconstruction with suffrage drives and speeches. And the Union League came through.

How recently, after all, had many of these Leaguers marched to the tune that bore Brown's name? When so many civil rights initiatives were imperiled, when equal voting rights for Black New Yorkers had again expired at the polls, and when even the Liberal Republican Horace Greeley was hawking a reconciliationist line that would repeal federal protection against the Klan for freedpeople in the South, Union Leaguers agreed that salvaging the modest home of "God's Meteor" was not so much to do.[15]

Kate Field had her cash in two days. Members of the newly formed John Brown Association each chipped in one hundred dollars. The historic farm would not be sold to an indifferent farmer who might eventually raze it or turn it into an inn, camp, or club. It would be a place of pilgrimage, and its eleventh-hour rescue would become part of what pilgrims came to honor too—a drama without bloodshed, heroic action without trauma. There would be no invocation in this story of Brown's guerrilla days in Kansas, the massacre of proslavery settlers at Pottawatomie. Visitors to *this* shrine would not be made uneasy. And when, in 1896, the aging representatives of the John Brown Association passed on the title to the farm to the State of New York, the pilgrims' way of loving and explaining John Brown's home was passed along as well.[16]

One consequence of this was a tilt away from the suggestion of some parity, or balance, between the Brown family's intimate domestic life (farm-bound family, sugarbush and fields, house and barn), and, a little walk away, the grave and boulder that stood for the more storied rest—the Kansas raids, bid for Harpers Ferry, Brown's capture and his hanging. These two realms, the secular and the sacralized, made a fitted, balanced whole. But in the late nineteenth century, the balance skewed toward the latter, and enshrinement overwhelmed. A granite "Donors Monument" commemorated Field and the white knights of the Union League Club (1896); a bronze marker honored John Brown's raiders who fell at Harpers Ferry (1899); another marker flagged the remains of Oliver Brown (1899); a spear-tipped wrought-iron fence went up around the graveyard (1900); a marker was erected for the fallen raiders whose names were left out in 1899 (1916); Brown's headstone got a cover made of bronze and plate glass (1941); and local white women, Browns and Thompsons, who sacrificed their "men-folk" to the raid, were honored with a plaque as well (1945). (Not quite a part of this, for reasons I'll explain, is the statue erected by the John Brown Memorial Association, set a stroll away from home and shrine in its own traffic turnaround in 1935.)[17]

The plaques and markers bore their own proud explanations. But the little home stayed stark. Why the Browns came here to live, how they lived, and how the family fared when Brown was gone were questions left unanswered. No tour or signage addressed them. Artifacts that might have animated the Browns' off-and-on residency were held to a small room of the farmhouse; until 1926, the caretaker and his family took up the rest. With fields to mow and cows to milk, the farmer-caretaker who was supposed to show visitors around often lacked the time.

And when visitors were acknowledged, some were met with grievance (*See that leak? The Conservation folks told me they'd get to it months ago. . . .*) and with historical accounts that were fanciful at best. Among the nuggets of misinformation that visitors reported were the confident assertions that Brown named North Elba "as a result of [his] partiality" for Napoleon, carved his name and death year in the boulder just before he left, rescued Lyman Eppes and family from enslavement and brought them north in covered wagons, "laid out" the Black enclave at Freeman's Home, came to North Elba to build a lumber empire, complete with paper mill, tanneries, and towns, and was dispatched to points west by a rousing send-off from a village band.[18]

And riding like an empty raft on all the speculation was everything left out: Smith and the agents' devotion to Black voting rights and agrarian reform, and the scope of Smith's idea, which encompassed territory well beyond Brown's farm. Unremembered: families besides the Eppeses who stayed in the Black Woods for years. Unesteemed: Brown's good friendship with the Brooklyn grantee Willis Hodges, the Franklin homesteader who parceled out the lifesaving supplies that Brown sent to Timbuctoo and Blacksville. Unobserved: Lyman Eppes the citizen and farmer, community builder, guide, and standard bearer for Smith's idea.

This is not to hold the caretakers responsible for these lacunae. The rift between what happened and how selectively it was remembered started widening at Harpers Ferry. Until Brown was imprisoned, North Elba was just a name—no special resonance, no aura. A hard place, too, from what Brown wrote. *Don't worry about me. Worry about my family in North Elba who will be "left very poor" on my death.* Only when Brown published his wish to be buried by this home, and for his name to be inscribed on the headstone of his Connecticut-born ancestor from the Continental Army, along with the names of two slain sons, would the homeplace gain a glow. Brown's conflation of two movements, one aspiring to free a nation, the other to liberate a race, sacralized the neighborhood—though, admittedly, it was a while before Brown's abolitionist allies discerned how North Elba could be used. After all, where *was* this place? How to get there? Was it even on a map? At the patriots' Olympus, Mt. Auburn cemetery in Cambridge, Massachusetts, Brown would gain a properly imposing monument and a shrine that would be marvelously, continuously thronged—or so claimed the abolitionists Henry C. Wright, Thaddeus Hyatt, Lydia Maria Child, and Wendell Phillips. As early as Brown's hanging, Phillips remonstrated with Mary

Brown for a burial in prestigious, pilgrim-worthy Cambridge. Sixty thousand people visited Mt. Auburn annually! How many would ever get to the Adirondack woods?[19]

Maybe it was a stiff rejoinder from Brown's widow on the way to Essex County (on sopping roads "found to be even worse than was anticipated") that restored Phillips's wayward tact, or his discovery of the devotion of Brown's family and neighbors (white and Black, for here, at the funeral, were Eppeses, Hasbrooks, and likely Hazzards too, all bearing witness to Gerrit Smith's original idea). Whatever the cause of his change of heart, Phillips quickly saw that if pilgrims could not visit North Elba as easily as they might Old North Church or Bunker Hill, they would find other ways to know the place. In the *New York Times*, Greeley's *Tribune*, Garrison's *Liberator*, *Douglass' Monthly*, the *Atlantic*, and the proliferating biographies of Captain Brown, North Elba took on the literary allure that limns it still. Within months of the interment, what the Boston abolitionists deemed a hopeless liability, the grave's great distance from hubs of antislavery activity, would register as an advantage. Any Sunday tourist could stumble on an abolitionist's headstone at Mt. Auburn. That North Elba called for effort, inconvenience, even risk, only brightened its allure.

"'All of Us!' Was the Hearty Response"

This pilgrimage took time, planning, a willingness to be transformed by not just the object but the perils of the journey. Rough roads? Hair-raising precipices? Plunging cliffsides looking "as if ready to fall each moment upon our heads," and breathless views that loomed abruptly, then vanished behind mist in an "enchanted land" of "wild grandeur"? All were stations on a via dolorosa that cast the pilgrim, however faintly, in Brown's hardy mold, and earned the pilgrim's right to honor Brown at his grave. The jolting passage through a rough, unyielding wilderness before arriving at Brown's home helped make sense of Brown himself. "Stern and strong," harsh and fearful, the aloof, self-regulating wilderness was made in John Brown's image, and John Brown returned the favor.[20]

Then might come (and not before the fraught preamble) the literary pilgrim's description of the grave and the massive boulder behind it. If the Revolutionary War headstone invoked the patriotic legacy that drove Brown's sense of national mission, the big rock declared a greater calling still. Seeming (from the *Liberator*) "to have been upheaved from the farthest depths of earth in the convulsions of some mythical age," this "primeval relic" bruited how lasting were the laws that made it—unlike human rules, which rationalized the enslavement of God's children. In its agelessness and immobility, the big rock honored God and Brown's conscience, both beyond the reach of perishable legalisms. No human hand made the boulder he adored; no human law constrained the inner law that drove him.[21]

And more than Adirondack nature was destined to be idealized. In 1866, the Civil War veteran officer Col. Francis Lee, and Lee's friend the Boston attorney George S. Hale, paid a stoneworker to chip Brown's name into the side of the great rock. Hale immortalized the undertaking with an "Ode":

> And at thy feet the massive monument
> Whose Native grandeur best thine own befits,
> No "storied urn" is needed for thy deeds,
> On every side their wide-sown ripening seeds.[22]

In a half century of writerly accounts of visits to Brown's home, those "seeds" "on every side"—among them, Brown's white neighbors—won a role in John Brown country as the faithful chorus that fanned the flame of freedom. In the much-syndicated account of John Brown's funeral in the *Tribune*, Northerners read about the "dear good men and women of Old Essex" (Frederick Douglass's words) and the frontier patriots who stood vigil over Brown's coffin in the county courthouse, the aged abolitionist Phineas Norton who solaced the funeral cortege with a midday lunch for all, and Brown's unnamed neighbors who braved the frigid weather to meet the funeral party and lantern-light its way to the widow's home. John Brown, said Wendell Phillips at the funeral, was "not alone" in his good work here, but rather "the majestic centre of a group." At a July 4 memorial service at the farm eight months after the funeral, Francis J. Merriam of Boston, one of five raiders at Harpers Ferry who was not captured, praised North Elbans for their fighting spirit. How many in this crowd would defend abolitionists and fugitives from the "bloodhounds of Virginia?" he called. "'All of us!' was the hearty response." And if we stayed right here, he pressed, and the New York governor issued warrants for our arrest, would you still defend us? "'I would,' and 'I,' 'I,' came from a large number of persons." That day, too, Thaddeus Hyatt, a Boston abolitionist, saluted Brown's Adirondack allies. Gaze into the eyes of Brown's family and neighbors,

Hyatt declared, and you see at once that "Charlestown has not put out the hero; his fires still live and burn in his descendants, burn in the seething blood of the third generation . . . Charlestown throttles in vain! God and the Adirondacks still stand." Once no more consequential than a jot on a map, North Elba now stood for Brown himself, even to the extent that if the frontlines of militant abolitionism fell, and the last of the antislavery men were driven from Philadelphia, Boston, even Plymouth Rock!, they would take "the Ark of Freedom" and "retire to North Elba, that Calvary of our cause."[23]

Out of History, into the Divine

North Elbans as Brown's apostles? Well, maybe. Brown had some white neighbors who shared his antislavery convictions. Others were more interested in his ideas about sheep breeding. Some loved the man but deemed his politics deranged. Brown's social culture in North Elba was as checkered as the antislavery movement itself. People who heard him out on slavery when he took a wayside meal in Westport, Elizabethtown, or Vergennes knew what he stood for and respected him, and nobody objected when North Elba (later on Lake Placid) gained a reputation as John Brown country. But this hardly made his neighbors his disciples. The John Brown brand was good for business. It brought pilgrims and tourists both, and never mind politics. Frame his story as a generic paean to conscience and anyone could find a reason to like John Brown's home. As travel writers proved, it was no hardship to reverence Brown's elegiac grave and disavow his life (*Love the bones of the old martyr, not so keen on what he did. . .*).[24]

Seneca Ray Stoddard kept his distance from the "monomaniac" but made a visit to Brown's grave a core vignette in *The Adirondacks Illustrated*. The Adirondackophiles Alfred Billings Street, Charles Benno Hoffman, and Martin Ives favored the site too—and none were fans or friends of Brown's ideas. Tucking a visit to Brown's home into the grand tour of the northern wilderness claimed the home for nature—another scenic wonder in a strand. Guidebooks, stereoscopic images, and articles positioned visitors to respond to the farm, and especially the grave, with the reverence they brought to a waterfall or gorge. In 1903, Mary Ellis Nichols recalled her "Adirondack Pilgrimage" in the *National Magazine*. First came the dramatic approach, the silent peaks and stippled woods and streaks of silver where water beaded down a rockface, followed by a landscape of enchantment, vistas "in ever widening circles of amethyst, topaz and sapphire" opening, at long last, to the object of her quest: "At our feet, set like a ground bird's nest in the midst of green pastures, stood the little woodcolored house just as the owner left it forty-four years ago." Nichols's rendering of Brown's farm nested it and tamed it. Field, woodland, bird's nest, farm—all partook of a peaceable divine.[25]

The whole neighborhood was haloed with a nimbus of divinity, declared the Connecticut essayist Charles Dudley Warner in 1866. This "region" was "consecrated with his spirit. Everybody here had something to tell us about the old man." Warner was glad the bid to bury Brown in Massachusetts came to naught. "It is better as it is," he wrote. "In these wilds there is something consonant with his own untamable spirit." In the *New York Times*, one "G.S." confessed he had no use for Brown's militancy, but entering "this circle through dark and deep mountain passes" worked a change in him: it freed him from the awkward job of having to judge and defend Brown historically. North Elba's Brown was more than an insurrectionist—he was part of nature, centerpiece of a design. "It does appear as though God prepared this spot for some specific object. Was this rock placed here purposely as a monument for the one who alone and silently lies at its base? Was this mountain chain designedly reared to wall this spot around?" For "G.S.," the culmination of his trip to Brown's shrine was the "whisper" of his conscience saying, "This is sacred ground." And "G.S." spoke for legions of visitors who liked the idea of Brown much more than the deeds that fixed his fame. What Brown did at Pottawatomie and his plans for Harpers Ferry—all this, for the law-abiding, was problematic, and for some, outright repugnant. So what was reverenced was not the physical reality of Brown's career—the bloodied swords, the severed arms, a moonlit creek pinked with blood—but the certitude that drove it. Not the raids, but the conviction. Not the dull work of the body moldering away, but the goes-on-marching soul. And as Brown's legacy was dehistoricized, the story of that other historical reality, his work and hopes for Timbuctoo, grew ever more peripheral, uncompelling, and easy to dismiss.[26]

Black Memory and the Gift Land

In December 1847, only two months after he left Boston to write and work for Douglass's new *North Star* in Rochester, the Black writer William Cooper Nell got a welcome-to-New-York gift deed from Gerrit

Smith. Nell, a civil rights activist up to his stiff collar in committee work and book projects, was never going to farm. Boston-bred, he was all city. But he did like owning that gift lot in the Adirondack woods. In 1860 (he let Smith know), he was still paying his taxes on it. He might have tried to sell it, but its value was more than fungible. It looked ahead, urged faith, patience, and the sweetness of an unused option. And maybe these, for Nell, were gifts enough.[27]

Hundreds of grantees (as George Downing's mass buy of gift deeds in 1870 revealed) held on to their deeds for decades for their value on Election Day. But Nell was not a New York voter, and still he kept his land. And other grantees kept gift deeds after the passage of the Fifteenth Amendment. Why was this? Thirty years after the 1846 distribution, Susann Owens of New Haven asked Smith to replace her late husband's missing deed. She'd paid taxes on it and did not want to lose the lot. In 1874, an Ausable Forks attorney asked Smith to send him deeds for his clients, the Payne family, deedholders who hoped to replace the titles they had mislaid. Rachel Webb of New York City, a steamboat steward-ess "of great industry and intelligence and moral worth" (so offered John Jenkins of Manhattan, who scripted her appeal), inherited five gift lots from her late husband, the speculator James Blair Webb, and when she mislaid the deeds in 1869, she tapped Smith for duplicates. Twice from London, the reformer William Wells Brown directed his Boston friend Wendell Phillips to cover his taxes for "my Gerrit Smith farm." There was no farm. The acreage in North Elba was wild and unworked. But the possibility, the mere promise of a homestead, now stood for hope itself.[28]

The activist and author Willis A. Hodges clung to his Franklin land on Loon Lake for three decades. It stayed his after he returned to Brooklyn, and while he scouted for the Union Army in Virginia, and when he made a mark after the war as one of the most engaged and forthright delegates to Virginia's first integrated Constitutional Congress in 1867 and 1868. The land was not his destiny; he did not dream of moving back. But it stood for something beautiful; it gave him heart and hope. One visionary resolution in particular bore the imprint of his Adirondack adventure. For the benefit of poor Virginians in need of wild land to "hunt, gun and fish in," Hodges called for unimpeded public access to "all woodland, swamps, marshes, creeks, rivers, lakes and bays in this State." The resolution did not pass, but the memory of Blacksville and the open-hearted wilderness endured.[29]

And long after Hodges died, his Adirondack land retained a sentimental value; in the early 1930s, his descendant Alexander Augustus
Moore ventured north from New York City to see Loon Lake himself. Mary Chase, the aging innkeeper who, with her husband, a Civil
War veteran, bought Hodges's lot in 1878, offered this Black pilgrim
"quite a little history of what her father knew of the settlers." The
old woman, whose inn would welcome Oscar Wilde, Irving Berlin, Sir
Arthur Conan Doyle, and three US presidents, steered her visitor to a
place in the woods where he could see the hand-hewn sills of Hodges's
log home and icehouse still "rot[ting], 86 years after erection." She also
told him she would be "glad to see any of the descendants of Hodges
and would deed back one acre centering from Hodge Hill if they would
live there."[30]

How many others? How many like Mary Ann Brown, an impoverished
Brooklyn widow who asked her family doctor to urge Gerrit Smith to
make over her late husband's deed in her name? Or John J. Johnson of
Manhattan, who beseeched Smith to sort out a wayward deed for him
in 1874? Nathan Johnson of New Bedford would not accept a gift deed
in 1846 because, he wrote, "At the time I was doing well, and would not
take what I thought [belonged] to the more needy," but by 1873, Johnson was in a bad way and wondered if Smith might spare "a pittance,
peradventure a loose, unappropriated greenback," to stand for the farm
he had so gallantly dismissed a quarter century before.[31]

Lyman Eppes, who kept a sharp eye on real estate, was twice tapped
by faraway grantees or their descendants to help broker the sale of a
gift lot. In 1890, Eppes found a buyer for a bank worker in Manhattan
whose father was a Smith grantee. Two years earlier, Eppes did the same
for a Manhattan deedholder, Silas Harris, who kept up taxes on his gift
lot for forty-two years before he let it go.[32]

Revelations from the Courts

One story in particular underscores the resonance of the gift land in
Black memory—in this case, the hundred-acre south half of Lot 277 in
Essex County's Township 11. In 1847, this big lot was assigned to Stephen Pembroke, an Ulster County grantee. Charles Ray had Pembroke
listed in his book, too, and living in Manhattan. In fact, both residences
were invented. Stephen Pembroke lived in Maryland. He received his
gift land while he was enslaved. And he would not learn he was an Adirondack landowner for years.[33]

Did Smith know? He didn't pick the grantees; that fell to his agents. To give land to a slave ran afoul of his rules of eligibility and of state and federal laws too. And while this may not have troubled the reformer who urged antislavery Southerners to give pocket compasses to prospective fugitives so they could guide themselves to freedom, and urged escaping slaves to steal "whatever is essential to your escape," it would not go well for Smith if his detractors learned he gave land to slaves. He would be judged a liar and a criminal. He might be tried, sued, and jailed. And he would put his own grantee-settlers in danger, since rumors of self-freed slaves in the Black Woods would rouse the appetite of bounty hunters. Risks these reckless were not Smith's style.[34]

It was all the more important, then, that Smith have confidence in his Black land agents to uphold his rules. But sometimes the agents didn't, and maybe they let Smith know and maybe they chose not to. The esteemed Rev. James W. C. Pennington, a Smith grantee and a great advocate for Smith's idea, had escaped his own enslavement in 1827. Back then, when he was very young, he was simply "Blacksmith Jim," one of the large and close-knit Pembroke clan on Frisby Tilghman's Maryland plantation. James (Jim) Pembroke changed his name to Pennington when he got to Pennsylvania soon after his escape. After sojourning with antislavery Quakers, he pushed on to New York, where he wrote the harrowing account of his enslavement and escape that put him at the forefront of the abolition cause. Mark Twain borrowed details from *The Fugitive Blacksmith* for *Adventures of Huckleberry Finn*. Gerrit Smith was so moved that he gave Pennington a gift lot with a warm note marveling at his "wisdom and integrity" (praise that so delighted Reverend Pennington he published Smith's note in an edition of his book). The self-taught Pennington, a gifted orator, would lecture about slavery to audiences in Jamaica, Heidelberg, and England. He was pastor of the First Colored Presbyterian Church of New York, one of the largest Black churches of that denomination in the nation.[35]

But Pennington could not fully know his freedom while his family was enslaved, and his failure to do for them what he'd managed for himself made him despair. He had tried to buy the freedom of his older brother. Stephen's enslaver never answered. Gerrit Smith's land gifts suggested another way to help. If and when Stephen escaped, his brother James could make sure land was waiting for him, an Adirondack getaway, a place for a new start. Pennington numbered several of Smith's agents among his closest friends. One of them would help him, surely. And, indeed, on page 3 of Charles B.

Ray's receipt book is Stephen Pembroke's signature, with a great *X* in the middle of it that Ray likely penned himself, just as it was likely Ray who made sure these brothers' gift lots were near each other, and ensured that Pembroke's name was in his book of grantees, and Gerrit Smith's.[36]

Preemptive planning on this order for enslaved people who were not yet free was not unheard of. Black Northerners sometimes lined up situations, jobs, or homes for fugitives in advance of a prayed-for escape. But the flagrant disregard for Smith's intent in this case, and by two of his good friends, raises some beguiling questions. Was Pembroke an anomaly? Or were there more among Smith's three thousand who got New York deeds and fake addresses while they were enslaved? If one story flags no trend, it surely prods the imagination. Most of Smith's Black agents were active in their cities' Underground Railroads. If one did this, why not more than one, and more than once? Why not furnish scores, even hundreds of enslaved Black men with fake New York addresses so they could qualify for deeds?[37]

"Novels arise out of the shortcomings of history," mused the German writer Novalis in 1799. Someday a novelist may meet the challenge posed by this scenario, and bless Timbuctoo with what Philip Roth called the "ruthless intimacy of fiction." And someday a tireless historian may give us something more to coast on than eager speculation. I stick with Pembroke's story because it furnishes an usually well-blazed trail, and where one trail shows the way, more might be discovered.[38]

Stephen Pembroke did join his brother, finally, in May 1854. After his wife died and seven years after he was made an Adirondack deedholder, Pembroke and his two teenage sons escaped from their Maryland enslaver, making first for Philadelphia. At once William Still, the lead conductor of Philadelphia's legendarily well-managed Underground Railroad, got word to Pennington of this party's plan to join him in Manhattan. The astonished and elated (and also frantic) Pennington moved fast to find a safe house for his family that was within walking distance to his own, and to prepare for this reunion with the older brother he hadn't seen in thirty years, and whose boys—his nephews!—he'd never met.[39]

And what a sight they were! For two enchanted hours, the four of them soaked each other up, talked and wept, recovered and caught up. Then fatigue blindsided all of them, and the exultant churchman returned to his own bed.[40]

Rev. James W. C. Pennington. Etching. William Irwin, 1848, England. Courtesy National Portrait Gallery, Smithsonian Institution.

That one enchanted night—first glimpse, full gaze, embrace, first words and last—would haunt Pennington for the rest of his life. While he slumbered in his home, before the city sky began to pale, Philadelphia slave hunters armed with warrants broke into the rooms of his brother and two nephews and took them into custody. Father and sons were led to jail. Special Commissioner G. W. Morton scheduled their hearing bright and early, before the press could rally. Happily for Morton, and so much more efficient, the Fugitive Slave Act spared him the necessity of offering the defendants legal counsel, and his court aides, very shrewdly, assured the panicked Pennington and his attorney that a hearing would come later on that day. It didn't. And as fast as Pennington raced to get a writ of habeas corpus, the commissioner was quicker: that afternoon, and under guard, James, Robert, and Jacob Pembroke were on a southbound train to Maryland. The Fugitive Slave Act authorized a five-dollar fee to special commissioners when an alleged fugitive was released, and ten dollars if the fugitive went "home" with the claimant. Thirty dollars richer, Commissioner Morton surely counted this a very nice day's work.[41]

Fifty-year-old Stephen Pembroke had aimed to deliver his two boys to freedom. Instead he saw them bound, chained, and "twice sold before my face.... My master's son lay in the room where I lay with a brace of pistols under his head; and when I turned over, he would start up and lay his hand on me." Frederick Douglass, outraged, ran updates on the Pembrokes in his newspaper for six weeks; this case especially, he felt, was an emphatic call to arms: "Stephen, Robert and Jacob Pembroke should never have been taken from the house in which they were lodged without bloodshed.... Every colored man in the country should sleep with his revolver under his head, loaded and ready for use." Pembroke's captors weren't complaining. The more fuss the Northern papers made of the captives' plight, the more compensation might be wrung out of their antislavery friends. From Sharpsburg, Pembroke made his stark appeal to Pennington: "Do my dear brother, make arrangements, and that at once, for my relief.... I will work daily when I get there to pay you back. If you only knew my situation and my feelings you would not wait." His sons had already been "sold to the drivers"; for them, it was too late. A North Carolina lumber merchant owned them now. They were assets—back to stuff. Soon Stephen Pembroke, the past property of three masters, was sure to share their fate.[42]

James Pennington pounded every door. Abolitionists, an ex-governor, even the New York Colored Orphan Asylum pitched in to help him meet this ransom. The "man-thieves" had their thousand dollars in a month. Pembroke moved to Brooklyn and worked as a whitewasher. Sometimes he joined his younger brother at the lectern or pulpit to speak of his ordeal. And it seems he remarried (the 1865 state census has him living with a woman from Virginia). But his public footprint was not deep. She moved out, and then he died, and where his home was at the end was anybody's guess. Somebody was keeping up the taxes on his land, though. Someone aimed to keep it in his name.[43]

The land Pembroke never saw was not as lovable in 1846 as it may seem today. Lot 277, South Half, Township 11, Old Military Tract, one hundred acres, "much water," Gerrit Smith had written in his *Land Book*. Just how much was *much*? Was it mostly water, and the rest a marsh? Were there hardwoods? Was there access? It would take several decades and the gilded lens of recreational tourism to make this lakeside piece enticing. But the Elizabethtown attorney Oliver Abel had always loved this wild stretch. As a boy, he camped here, and his memories of the brilliant fishing and the long paddles were rich. In the last quarter of the nineteenth century, waterfront lots on lovely lakes with misty mountain views were gaining value fast. The Westside, a hotel he and Mary owned and ran on Lake Placid, now had a following. On Oliver's hundred-acre childhood getaway, their good fortune might be trebled.[44]

In 1870, Oliver Abel's close review of county land records met with encouraging results. Though a few boathouses and small buildings had sprouted on Lot 277, no one had pursued a title, which, since 1847, had remained in Stephen Pembroke's name. Could this be one of Gerrit Smith's long-gone or never-got-here colored people? Abel was familiar with the giveaway. After the Civil War, he gave Black veterans a hand with their pension claims, and it may have been these clients who suggested he and Mary consider speaking with the one Black agent who still seemed to take an interest in the deedholders. Elder Charles B. Ray was living in Manhattan. The Abels tracked him down.[45]

Their delight in this new ally can scarcely be imagined. Yes, Elder Ray had known the late Stephen Pembroke. He knew his late brother, James Pennington. He knew they both were Smith grantees. And he knew that Pembroke had some sons. A wretched story there. Last Ray heard, they lived in Alabama. And he *would* help the Abels find them, though he was far from idle, with obligations at Bethesda Congregational, his mission outreach, and now stumping for Mr. Lincoln's GOP, a dearer cause than ever. He would find the "twice-sold" nephews of his old friend.[46]

Streetlights were the business of the day when the Greensboro attorney James E. Webb heard from Charles Bennett Ray in 1882. Greensboro, the Hale County seat, didn't have a one. Come sundown, this town worthy couldn't see the tips of his own shoes. The good news was that the mayor had approved a town petition to get Greensboro illuminated, and Webb would be in charge. This was a tall order, installing thirty kerosene streetlamps, but Webb, a Democratic Party operative, liked a challenge. And this letter out of nowhere from New York City—here was a challenge for the archives. A Black minister in New York City was asking him, Colonel Webb, a four-year veteran of the Army of Virginia, to take time out of his day to track down two Negro laborers with a proposition so outlandish, a piece of news so unimaginable—*how could he say no?*[47]

These Negroes, Robert and Jacob McCray, had inherited a piece of New York's Adirondack wilderness. Would they know the Adirondacks from Bessemer or Eutaw? If he pulled a map out, they'd look at it and nod. But they couldn't read a map. They couldn't read, period. They were ex-slaves. As for Charles Bennett Ray, what was he to them? Less than nothing, likely, but this Ray certainly knew plenty about them. He knew their father and their uncle. And he knew all about this land. The father, Stephen Pembroke, came into it (somehow!) in the late 1840s, and now there was a New York lady who would pay these brothers three hundred dollars for it, free and clear.[48]

In January when Webb was asked to find these men, nobody was picking cotton. Everything was baled up. The wide, hard-lit fields were listless. But somewhere in Hale County these gentlemen were working, "day clear to first dark," maybe chopping wood, or at the sawmill. Two poor Black men name of McCray—Webb, a man with many friends, would find them soon enough. In Alabama's Black Belt, Hale County took its name from the Confederate officer who, on President Lincoln's election, predicted "all the horrors of a San Domingo servile insurrection, [the consignment of] her citizens to assassinations, and her wives and daughters to pollution and violation, to gratify the lust of half-civilized Africans." Greensboro was also where Walker Evans took his photographs for James Agee's documentary opus of 1941, *Let Us Now Praise Famous Men*, and where Dr. Martin Luther King Jr. found refuge in a family's modest home from hooded men in pickups trawling the back roads. That night in 1968, Dr. King was fortunate. Before dawn, his Black friends got him out of Greensboro to safety. In Memphis two weeks later, the good luck he never trusted abandoned him for good.[49]

Hale County was impoverished when Dr. King visited, and it was poor in the time of the McCrays. The odds are good that when the aging brothers heard what the white lawyer had to say, they had been farming shares for a quarter of a century, work that held them rigidly in debt and bound them to a peonage that was, in all but name, a variant of slavery. The sum that Oliver and Mary Abel had told Ray to offer the McCrays was a splinter of the land's true value—as Ray (a shrewd speculator in his own right who had amassed a minor fortune in wild land

and city real estate) surely understood. Did he feel the Abels should offer more? Or fear that any greater compensation might invite predatory schemers and put the sharecroppers at risk? If the offer's stunning insufficiency troubled Ray, the McCray brothers, he may have reasoned, would not object. Three hundred dollars in 1882, which today would hold a $7,000 value, could go a distance for two croppers with families. It could turn them from farmworkers to subsistence farmers, buy them livestock, clap a Bible on the table, pay a debt, and lay in seed for fall. It could sweeten the idea of the future. In 1882, the year the Supreme Court declared the Ku Klux Klan Act unconstitutional, stripping federal patrols of the power to protect freedpeople from lynch mobs, anything even a little hopeful was big news.[50]

So, yes, said the McCray brothers to the white lawyer about this never-dreamed-of windfall out of the clear Yankee blue. They would mark the title Charles Ray had sent to Mr. Webb with their Xs, claim it, then at once sell back land and title to the New Yorkers and get paid. And here we may be tempted to wrap things up and count the story (like the news of gift deeds held for voting rights by hundred of grantees) as one of several that gave the giveaway a warm pulse long after history declared it dead. But more would be revealed than the McCrays' unexpected fortune. White memory had other plans for Pembroke and his heirs.

Verdicts and Reversals

The Abels were hell-bent on nailing down Pembroke's title for a reason. In the lot they'd set their hearts on lived, intermittently, a squatter. Gaining title to the land would mean they could evict him—and eviction it would need to be since Benjamin T. Brewster would not go without a fight. No backcountry trapper clad in buckskin, Brewster had his eye on this lot too, and he badly hoped to buy it. A speculator and a businessman with one successful inn already going strong, he (just like the Abels) also had in mind a second hostelry, maybe with a piazza lined with rockers and Chinese lanterns twinkling overhead. In Essex County in this era, lakefront hotels were pushing up like mushrooms after a May rain. Capillary trails widened into coach roads and railroad spurs, and prize lots were selling and reselling as fast as developers could flip them. Some local folks were saying that the hundred-acre Lot 277 was worth as much as $50,000.[51]

Thus the Abels' race for legal standing. Brewster had paid taxes on the property in a desultory way and put up some modest structures, which would boost his case in court. But if the Abels owned the title? That might give their team the edge. But further work awaited. Pembroke's death and the disappearance of the original title compelled the use of circumstantial evidence. And while Smith's *Land Book* and Ray's Receipt Book held Pembroke's name and the number of his lot, neither document was legally binding. Witnesses would need to be called up who could verify these notebooks' value, speak for Pembroke's credibility, confirm his marriage to the boys' late mother, and vouch for Pembroke as the father of his Alabama sons. By the last quarter of the century, who was left who knew about the giveaway? Pennington had died in 1870, Smith in 1874, and Ray, most unhelpfully, in 1887. Also gone to their long home: the Black land agents Wright, McCune Smith, Loguen, Garnet, and Ward.[52]

Charles B. Ray's daughter Florence grew up with the giveaway; the tribute to her father she wrote with her sister, Henrietta Cordelia, vividly described Ray's devotion to Smith's scheme. Garnet may have been the best recruiter, and McCune Smith the sharpest thinker about the giveaway's larger value, but Ray was on the ground, the fixer, the one who lobbied for the grantees after other agents gave up. So when Ray's schoolteacher daughter Florence journeyed from Manhattan to Elizabethtown in 1889, she did more than stand up for the Pembrokes. She defended her father's mission. Brandishing his receipt book with the grantees' names, she told the all-white jury, "I have known of the existence of this book all the years I can remember anything. It remained in my father's possession as long as he lived." She knew how he worked to get deeds dispersed to thousands, knew all about the Pembrokes and how her father tracked down the old slave's orphaned sons. Her defense of her father's notebook defended the giveaway itself.[53]

Unlike Florence Ray, Gerrit Smith Miller did not grow up with the giveaway. He was an infant when it was launched. But this grandson of the late philanthropist, and manager of the family's vast estate, shared Florence Ray's devotion to Smith's initiative and, like her, came to court with evidence in hand: Smith's *Land Book* with Pembroke's name inscribed within. From Peterboro to craggy Essex County on bad roads in early winter was a trek, but Smith's namesake would find the courthouse. For the sake of justice, history, and the collaborative effort that made a bold idea flicker fleetingly to life, he showed up.[54]

The finding for the plaintiff in this "important real estate case" (so judged the *Essex County Republican*) may seem easily explained: Stirred by stories of John Brown's body in this courthouse; roused by the oratory of Mary and Oliver Abel's lawyer, Richard Hand (who as a young man stood vigil over Brown's coffin in this room); moved by the testimony of Gerrit Smith's grandson (the striking and well-spoken Miller, who introduced pure-bred Holsteins to American dairy, was, for many farmers, something of a hero); possibly beguiled by the eloquent schoolteacher from the city; and maybe even disposed to tender feelings about the grand old "scheme of justice and benevolence" that lured Brown's family to Essex County years before, this jury ruled for Mary Abel and, in so doing, for the legitimacy of Stephen Pembroke's deed.[55]

But a harder look at court records suggests that the real reason for this ruling was anything but sentimental. This jury had been given a directed verdict from the judge, a state supreme court justice from Montgomery County then presiding over circuit court in Elizabethtown, the Essex County seat. In this decade in New York, a judge might introduce a directed verdict when he feared a jury would ignore the rules of evidence and law. Judge Frothingham Fish of Fultonville knew the law favored the Abels' claim, but he was enough of an upstater to guess that Adirondackers would never challenge a local as venerable as Brewster, whose taproot in the region reached as deep as Mirror Lake. And the judge may have expected, too, no small resistance to a Black deedholder's posthumous claim to Adirondack land, and a concern among these jurists about other long-dead claimants lacking any visible connection to North Elba who might gain the legal power to oust a local from his land.[56]

Hence the directed verdict. This way, Judge Fish knew that justice would be served. But his ambivalence showed starkly in a summary so fraught with his misgivings that it might have served as a blueprint for the defense—and maybe did. When the case moved to Albany, Ben Brewster got his way: New York Supreme Court justice W. J. Learned and two junior judges dismissed the Abels' claim outright. Why, Judge Learned groused, was Pembroke's name in Smith's *Land Book* not written by himself? Learned was also troubled by the mismatch between Pembroke's name and the surnames of his sons. Could anyone know these men *were* his sons? Was there proof that their parents were even married? In his deposition, Robert McCray hardly seemed to know his father. Why, he could not even name his father's trade![57]

The judgment for Mary Abel was reversed. And the relief that met an outcome favoring Ben Brewster, founder-pioneer, is easy to imagine. What resonates about this case, however, is not so much Brewster's victory as the blithe, untroubled ignorance of slavery that the appellate panel revealed in its response to the McCrays—and this despite the fact that the presiding judge was an erudite legal scholar, well traveled and politically informed. Judge Learned knew the late Stephen Pembroke was a slave. He knew Robert and Jacob McCray's mother, Surena Pembroke, died enslaved in Maryland. Why, then, his dullness on their mismatched surnames? Learned was forty-two when President Lincoln freed the slaves. That enslaved people were property, that slave marriages were not recognized by law—was any of this news? Surely he could infer that when slaves and their enslaved children held different surnames, they had been named (and owned) by different people. Even if this judge knew nothing of Stephen Pembroke's flight, or his recapture and the sale of his boys to a North Carolina lumber merchant, he understood that slavery stood on the wide shoulders of a terroristic culture that brutalized Black families. Yet all the esteemed jurist could suppose was the McCrays were born out of wedlock: "No explanation is given why they do not bear their father's name. . . . No proof of the marriage of the parents, except the witness says his mother's name was Surena Pembroke. . . . It does not appear that they ever lived together. . . . Certainly, if a man and woman cohabit, the ordinary inference is that the children are illegitimate."[58]

Ordinary inferences did not apply to life under slavery. On their return to Maryland in 1854, Robert and Jacob Pembroke were reenslaved at once. McCray was the name they got from their new enslavers. But either Judge Learned knew nothing of the ghastly pressures and lasting ruptures that slave families endured, or he did not care. Why would he? The temper of his era favored his response. This was, after all, the 1890s, dawn of a new age of forgetting, when, writes David Blight, Civil War memory "fell into a drugged state, as though sent to an idyllic foreign land from which it has never fully found the way home." If Northern memory was slower to forget than Southern, it was glad enough to endorse the notion that emancipation freed not only slaves but all of white America from an obligation to concern itself with slavery's causes or lasting toxins. Thus Judge Learned's selective memory. He had testimony from the Pembrokes' neighbors that made it clear this couple was considered married; that their children were not considered bastards; that this family was churchgoing, stable, and intact. But the judge required a certificate of marriage—as if a slave could pick one up as freely as a stick. He needed proof that Stephen and Surena shared one address—as if married slaves with different masters chose their beds. He would read the details of a slave's life as he might his own, and when those details were lacking or confused, when a witness, for example, recalled the McCrays as the McCrarys, or when fifty-four-year-old Robert McCray could not say what his father, whom he had not seen in three decades, did in New York City, the judge assailed his credibility.[59]

The indifference to the injuries to which slave families were exposed, the imposition of Northern mores on slave culture, revealed more than a failure of imagination. Girding Judge Learned's response was the iron of denial; his blind spot was the nation's. Nothing in his upstate world (law school dinners, social clubs, Democratic Party meetings) urged a deeper knowledge of the facts of slavery; nothing said, *Remember how it was*. In fact, to fight the reflex of a purposeful forgetting in the name of sectional reconciliation might have been judged subversive, even unpatriotic. Judge Learned's readiness to find reasons to discredit the McCrays was vicious but not personal. It was the habit of the land.

The dogged Mary Abel won a retrial in 1890, and two years later a new judge heard the case. Once again, Florence Ray and Gerrit Smith Miller testified in Elizabethtown, and with them was Oliver Abel, now brandishing fresh evidence of the Pembrokes' marriage from a Sharpsburg druggist whose father owned Pembroke's first wife Surena, and from a laborer who knew the Pembrokes too. The late Rev. James Pennington's adopted son, Thomas H. S. Pennington, a retired pharmacist in Saratoga Springs, also testified for Abel. This Civil War veteran, once a regimental hospital steward for the Twentieth Regiment, USCT, was a scholar of his late father's activist career and well informed about his uncle's ruptured family.[60]

Another witness for the plaintiff in November 1892 was Robert Grove of Sharpsburg, Maryland: merchant, magistrate, and kin to Stephen Pembroke's last owner. Grove came a long way in late November to wade into a dustup between these Yankee speculators. Did the Abels make it worth his while? Since Ray tracked down the McCrays, the value of this lakeside acreage had surged to $80,000. But the Marylander may have had his own less mercenary reasons for this trip. He knew the McCrays when they were Pembrokes; Jacob and Robert were boyhood friends. He knew what stood for a marriage between slaves, and maybe his white Southern memory registered a cut when a Yankee judge called the Pembrokes' union fake.[61]

In the end, Judge Leslie Russell invoked the antebellum US slave code to "non-suit" the plaintiff once and for all. *Being property himself, he can own no property, nor make any contract.* When Stephen Pembroke got his lot, this was the law. Property can't own itself. Therefore, reasoned Russell (Fourth Judicial District, ex-attorney general, loyal Republican), Pembroke's deed was illegal from day one. Yet if this point was quite so obvious, why was it not made by Brewster's first attorney or Judge Learned of Albany? Did they balk at calling on an article of law so virulently tough it took a civil war to kill it?[62]

Even if Judge Russell had no such qualms, he might have urged a more nuanced reading of the slave law. Slaves did own property before emancipation. They owned horses, clothes, crops, and wages. Land rights had more to do with privileges of access, not ownership of title. But Judge Russell might nonetheless have argued that since slavery was illegal in New York when Pembroke was assigned a deed, *state* law made him eligible to own land in New York that would be held in trust for him (and, indeed, effectively was) until his emancipation was secured. But an argument like this would have marked Russell as a trailblazing radical. This was not his wish. So Ben Brewster got his way, along with $1,000 in court costs. Over the years he would expand his holdings to 517 acres. He built fine lakefront hotels. He filled a boathouse with guide boats and canoes. His beard grew long and pillowy. In 1914, a film company in Lake Placid gave him a bit part as Father Time.[63]

As for the McCrays, did anyone alert them to this case's final disposition? They got their $300. Would they care how it panned out? I think they might have. They had reason.

Robert McCray, "Negro," had registered to vote in Greensboro as early as July 1867, only five months after the passage of the federal Reconstruction Act that legalized this right. But legalized or not, this remained Alabama. The war was over, and, of course, it wasn't. By 1874, Alabama Democrats had overtaken the state legislature and routed every nonfederal reform measure on the books. Black voting rights, a federal entitlement, remained, but the brief shining spell of *equal* voting rights, interracial jury duty, fair elections, government employment, an integrated legislature, and government-mandated protection against white terrorist attacks was already a fading dream.

But Robert McCray had registered to vote, and I'm guessing that if he took this step so early in the process, he meant business. He voted because he was a citizen; it was his obligation and his right. And I want to think he kept voting even when it meant he had to pay a poll tax, pass a literacy test, prove he owned property, or abide by any of the other white-enforced restrictions that would, by 1957, reduce Black voters in Hale County to 1.8 percent of the population.[64]

I'm also guessing that because he knew the risks he ran each time he cast a ballot (risks that ranged from intimidation to joblessness, eviction, whippings, and the lynch mob), he might very much have *liked* to know the disposition of a court case involving his own blasted family. In New York City in 1854, a New York judge had enabled his and Jacob's reenslavement with a ruling that resulted in a lifelong separation from their one living parent and their loss of freedom for eleven years. In Albany in 1892, another New York justice refused to recognize his and his brother Jacob's ruptured lives in slavery. Which legal outcome was the worse is hard to know—the feel of freedom for less than half a day before the resumption of his chatteldom, or the injury embedded in the cool, abstracted language of a court hearing twenty-seven years after the Fifteenth Amendment, a ruling that stripped two aging men of the right to their own remembered lives. One insulted their humanity; the other made it plain that their history, their lives in slavery, as Pembrokes, as their parents' sons, had no meaning, had never happened.[65]

For the message here from Albany was plain: You have no story. You have no past. We don't see you. You aren't there.

CHAPTER 17

Pilgrims

"Civilization is going to pieces," broke out Tom violently. . . . "Have you read 'The Rise of the Colored Empires' by the man Goddard? . . . It's a fine book and everybody ought to read it. The idea is if we don't look out the white race will be—will be totally submerged. It's all scientific stuff. It's been proved."

—F. Scott Fitzgerald, *The Great Gatsby*

May tends to be a good month in Lake Placid—"the most luxuriously beautiful month of the Adirondack year," judged the *New York Times* in 1922 (every hillside "filled with a delicate green mist the effect of the infinite number of tiny leaf buds opening on shrubs and trees"). At Landon's Drug Store, anglers scrutinized new tackle. Boy Scouts whittled lancewood into rods and grubbed for bait. No out-of-towners yet; sidewalks and lunch counters still belonged to locals. Strangers would be noticed. And Black strangers in their long city coats and gleaming shoes would be maybe more than noticed, which is why Jesse Max Barber and his friend Spotuas Burwell came prepared.[1]

Months before they made this trip, these activists took steps to smooth their reception. Barber, a dentist and the president of the Philadelphia chapter of the National Association for the Advancement of Colored People (NAACP), wrote the New York conservation commissioner and other Lake Placid notables, alerting them to his long-dreamed-of plan for a Black pilgrimage to John Brown's home and grave. If this was courteous, it was also a shot across the bow. *Black men coming! Don't be alarmed.* Elder Ray did something like this in 1847, when he asked Gerrit Smith's secretary to write a few North Elbans in advance of his arrival. But Barber and Burwell didn't know this. Nobody was thinking about Smith's "scheme" in 1922.[2]

Half a century before, on May 11, 1873, the *Essex County Republican* boldly envisioned a day, "not remote," when "a splendid monument will rise over the remains of the martyr. . . . [T]he day will come when the colored people who have accumulated wealth will visit North Elba to look upon the grave of their greatest Friend." But while there had been pilgrimages in 1889, 1896, 1899, and 1903, and visitors could number in the thousands, these events, white organized, were mostly white attended. In August 1916, Byron Remembrance Brewster, a local judge with deep roots in the region (and, yes, related to the canny squatter-speculator who bested the unlucky Abels), organized one too. He knew the Browns. His older sister, Martha, married Oliver, who died at Harpers Ferry, and when Byron was a boy, he lived at the Browns' old farmstead, likely napping, between chores, under the attic beam that bore Lyman E. Eppes's signature. The "substantial enduring monument" he envisioned for Brown's farm would honor not the abolitionist alone but all the raiders in the shrine, Black and white, who had yet to be identified. And Brewster's pilgrimage, unlike all predecessors, would reach for racial inclusivity and social relevance. He wanted speakers who could argue for John Brown's value *now*.[3]

This they did, with all the urgency he hoped for. The 1916 John Brown Day featured speeches by Howard University's Kelly Miller, a Black sociologist who had argued before Congress against antimiscegenation laws and segregated streetcars. Franklin B. Sanborn, at eighty-five the sole survivor of John Brown's storied Secret Six, made the trip from Concord, Massachusetts. Manhattan's eight-year-old NAACP dispatched the Adirondack-born progressive John J. Milholland. "Until the United States stands for equality of race and color, and for freedom all along the line, John Brown's mission will not be fulfilled," this activist intoned. Rabbi Stephen Wise, a cofounder of the NAACP and head of the Free Synagogue in New York City, agreed: "Many John Brown tasks now remain today. . . . Justice now we demand for the negro race, as in 1859, justice to wipe out the scenes of Waco Texas." Four months earlier in church-proud Waco, outside Dallas, a Black farmhand convicted of rape and murder was abducted from a courthouse, lynched, and mutilated, charred bits of his body sold as souvenirs. The horrified response to this, on top of rising worry about President Woodrow Wilson's Southern Democrat–dominated Congress, may have encouraged Brewster to hope Lake Placid was ready for a John Brown pilgrimage that historicized as well as honored.[4]

But the rain fell hard that day, and the turnout was indifferent. A reporter for the *Lake Placid News* was mortified. The indifference of "5,000 summer residents, wealthy, cultured, men and women of leisure, those who hypothetically should represent the patriotic, thinking class, with consideration of the virtues, right values, and things of good report," was inexplicable. Where were the pilgrims? "God knows—and perhaps the moving picture show."[5]

By 1922, the mood had shifted. Adirondack newspapers, more sophisticated, less parochial, did not shy away from tougher stories. In 1919, twenty-six race riots ripped across the country. The next year saw fifty-three Black people lynched, and in June 1921, a year before Barber and Burwell's Lake Placid visit, a prosperous Black neighborhood in Tulsa, Oklahoma, was torched while white policemen stood idly by— thirty-five city blocks incinerated, eight thousand Black Tulsans homeless, as many as three hundred people killed. Each week brought fresh atrocities ("The Great American Pastime," the *Survey Journal* called this spate of lynchings). By the time two Black activists from the Philadelphia chapter of the NAACP pilgrimed to North Elba in 1922, John Brown country was ready to extend a welcome. And when, after this launch, the NAACP quietly disengaged (its deeper interest was in its own present-focused legal work, investigations, and protest rallies), the Philadelphians organized the John Brown Memorial Association (JBMA), which took charge of the North Elba event and kept it up for sixty years.[6]

A Wonderfully Enjoyable Affair

Not every JBMA pilgrimage raised a throng. During the Depression, and in the war years, too, attendance waned and local interest flagged. The big-ticket orators of the first decades of the twentieth century— the trial lawyer Clarence Darrow, who packed Town Hall to standing room only; Oswald Garrison Villard, author of Brown's first literary biography; A. Philip Randolph, founder of the nation's first Black labor union—gave way to speakers much less luminous. Barber's successors (he died in 1949) did not share his gift for programming or promotion. But in those first decades before the Second World War, when the JBMA raised chapters in Brooklyn, Manhattan, Springfield, Worcester, and Baltimore, John Brown Day was something fine. Early May brought a mayoral welcome, organ concerts, church services, and speeches by townspeople of influence, and, usually, some passionate and edgy oratory by a racial justice advocate of renown. Adirondackers were especially taken with the folksy, suspender-popping style of the wide-shouldered Darrow, the celebrated provocateur. "The white man gives the negro inferior wages and mean jobs," he declared, "then says the negro is lazy and won't work; but when the white man does work good and hard one day, he says he has 'workt like a nigger.' . . . If any of you white people, leaving this meeting tonight, had to choose between losing a leg or being Black, which would you prefer?"[7]

By the late 1920s, Lake Placid was claiming John Brown Day as a tradition, and so confident was Barber of its acceptance that he pitched it as a vacation in its own right, a "wonderfully enjoyable affair. . . . The automobiles carry copiously filled lunch baskets and the cars are decorated with John Brown Memorial Pennants. They all stop to lunch together far up in New York State. . . . Pictures are snapped, jokes are swapped and the whole atmosphere is permeated with jolly camaraderie." All of this may seem to bear no relation to a day of solemn homage. But to Black travelers in this era, the link between this spring pilgrimage to a hero's grave and the freedom to go "excursioning" was as bright as May itself. For three American centuries, the open road was ruled by whites. Where Black travelers could go, what they did, where they slept, and how they got around was determined by white bosses. They might know the road as construction workers, cooks, porters, drivers, or maids, but not as citizens charting their own course. Train travel to the North in the first half of the twentieth century meant a siege in a Jim Crow car with hard benches, sooty air, and flooding toilets. Traveling by foot could put a Black man afoul of a vagrancy law and hitch him to a chain gang. The JBMA pilgrimage more than spurned this legacy; it stood it on its head. The promise of a safe, welcoming vacation for Black Americans in an all-white rural region (all white, that is, as far as the pilgrims knew) subverted all the old conventions. Barber reveled in the upset.[8]

From a JBMA brochure in 1928: "The people of Lake Placid delight to welcome us and give us the freedom of the Village." Self-determination and freedom of assembly, movement, speech—this was the promise of John Brown Day. A few years later in the *Pittsburgh Courier*, Barber's claim was bolder still. "The pilgrimage is an event in the Northwoods," he said. "We have established contacts up there which, to say the least, few Negroes have anywhere else. There is a respect for us which I have not seen given to any colored group in any of their conventions."[9]

Much more, then, was in the offing than a "good time coming" and a balsam-tingled breeze. For Black pilgrims, the long trip to Brown's grave was as salving as the laying of the wreath. Where white pilgrims made a cult of the hardships of the journey, the twentieth-century Black pilgrims loved this getaway for its *lack* of risk, its normality and ease—and, too, for the pleasure of a historic site where they were plainly welcome. At George Washington's Mount Vernon, Black tourists could not use the picnic grounds or reach the place except by a segregated streetcar or a steamer that docked far from the entrance. In Washington's lovely home, they were subjected to a "lost cause" version of enslavement with throwback "darkeys" and "Uncle Neds" happily engaged in household service. What a relief to find in remote North Elba a state historic site where slavery was actually called out as a crime.[10]

Barber had a second goal for his organization too, though he waited until 1924 to announce it. He wanted to see Brown's Adirondack grave honored with a monument from Black America, a monument whose design, funding, siting, and installation would be overseen entirely by his new John Brown Memorial Association. The pilgrimage was fine for the few days it lasted, but a monument might bring Black pilgrims to North Elba every day, and claim a stake here for Black visitors the long year round.[11]

Fancy Our Surprise

Who was Jesse Max Barber, the Philadelphia activist who launched this plan? What made him want to do this? After college (where he edited the campus newspaper and another publication), this aspiring journalist, a son of former slaves in Blackstock, North Carolina, moved to Atlanta and got work editing and writing for a periodical, the *Voice of the Negro*. By 1904, the *Voice* claimed a readership of fifteen thousand. Observing this meteoric rise was another Black Atlantan, the writer, sociologist, and reformer, W. E. B. Du Bois, who asked the youthful journalist to join his coalition of some thirty Black professionals engaged in civil rights reform. The Niagara Movement, as this group was called, was gaining fame and notoriety for contesting Booker T. Washington's ideology of racial accommodation. It wasn't true and it wasn't right, Du Bois insisted, that only Blacks who toed a line of "non-resistance, giving up agitation, and acquiescence in semi-serfdom" could gain a public voice. "Bookerism" had a stranglehold on Black civic progress. Du Bois aimed to snap its grip.[12]

Young Max Barber made his Atlanta journal a mouthpiece for these subversive notions and a venue, too, for his and his mentor's shared devotion to John Brown. For four days in August 1906, Barber and the Niagara Movement activists honored Brown at Harpers Ferry. One attendee from Chicago, the socialist churchman Reverdy Ransom, urged his fellow radicals to model their resolve on John Brown's "sublime courage." So moved was Barber by Bishop Ransom's appeal that he published it in his *Voice*: "Like the ghost of Hamlet's father, the spirit of John Brown beckons us to arise and seek the recovery of our rights. . . . No weak and ordinary voice can call the nation back to a sense of justice."[13]

Hard on the heels of that summer's triumph, however, was the three-day September race riot that swung across Atlanta like a scythe. Was Barber thinking of Bishop Ransom's challenge when he furnished the *New York World* with a report? In this anonymous indictment, Barber charged Atlanta's white newspapers and political elite with inciting a race riot with unsubstantiated reports of sexual violence and lurid stories about Black "fiends" infected by a "rape germ"—fake news that Barber countered with evidence of white racist conjecture. This was bold, and more than risky. When white Atlantans learned who wrote

John Brown Memorial Association founders at John Brown's grave, May 9, 1922. Photographer unknown. Standing on left, Dr. Spotuas Burwell, and on right, Jesse Max Barber, DDS, from Philadelphia. Kneeling, front, Rev. J. A. Jones, Oneida, Madison County, NY. From the John Brown Collection, gift of Harry Wade Hicks, at the John Brown Farm State Historic Site, Division of Parks, Recreation, and Historic Preservation, NY.

the piece, they gave the editor his options. He could leave the city, and at once, or expect to find himself on a chain gang. The alacrity with which Barber moved his family to Chicago suggests the gravity of the threat. Just as traumatizing, Barber's adversary, Booker Washington, made this forced migration an occasion to paint Barber as a coward, a mocking stigma that effectively derailed the editor's career. Only when the family moved to Philadelphia and Barber took up dentistry and joined the NAACP would he find his second act.[14]

In 1922, when Barber and Spotuas Burwell first visited North Elba, Barber was forty-four and his sponsor, the NAACP, was the nation's boldest voice for civil rights reform. So the wreath-laying at John Brown's grave seven years after Booker Washington's death did more than break a long spell of Black disengagement with John Brown. It defied the cautious strategies of Bookerism ("counsels of submission," Du Bois called them) that stood for all that the arch-antiaccommodationist John Brown despised. Indeed, the Lake Placid ceremony was as much a paean to post-Bookerite public activism as it was to Brown himself.[15]

And a highly scripted celebration it was, too. On John Brown Day, May 9, 1922, the Philadelphia pilgrims would claim to be *shocked! shocked!* when they were thronged by white locals at John Brown's farm. "Fancy our surprise," Barber told the NAACP magazine, *The Crisis*, "to find that . . . the public schools had taken a holiday for the occasion, the Chamber of Commerce sent a delegation to welcome us, and the distinguished people of the town came out to be at the memorial services. . . . There were perhaps one hundred and fifty automobiles parked around the grave and a thousand people there to do honor to her. The school children walked the three and one-half miles to be with us." Among his audience "was a judge from the town . . . lawyers, doctors, school board members, and members of the aristocratic clubs. Old soldiers embraced us. Men who knew John Brown wept for joy that this long-deferred occasion had come. Our photographs were taken by a dozen cameras. School girls took pictures for their civic class. Our pictures are now on sale as souvenir postcards in Placid, and at the caretaker's place at the farm." Anchoring the ecstatic dispatch in *The Crisis* was a photograph of Blacks and whites clustered around and standing atop Brown's boulder under a postracial Yankee sky. In truth, Barber had labored hard behind the scenes to win town backing. But describing white people *just showing up* would help convince Black readers of *The Crisis* that Lake Placid was safe to visit—as would Barber's suggestion that white locals asked the pilgrims to return. A yearly pilgrimage was always part of Barber's long-range plan, but crediting the locals made John Brown country look especially hospitable. And with these hopeful exaggerations, Barber joined an old fraternity. Willis Hodges, Frederick Douglass, Henry Highland Garnet, and Charles Bennett Ray had each burnished an idealized Adirondacks in hopes of stepping up Black interest.[16]

But Barber would not have known this. With the exception of Lyman Epps Jr. (always honored on John Brown Day for his friendship with the Browns), the grantees and the Black Woods of Gerrit Smith were of no interest to the Black pilgrims. On no John Brown Day would Barber mention Timbuctoo, Freeman's Home, Blacksville, or any of the Smith grantees' descendants still in Vermontville, Saranac Lake, and St. Armand. The family likeness between an 1846 bid for equal voting rights for Black New Yorkers and Barber's generation's push for Black enfranchisement was not noted. JBMA speakers made no mention of the Black antislavery reformers who plugged the giveaway (John Brown's good friends among them). Nobody knew that near Brown's home were gift lots, never claimed, of Frederick Douglass and William Wells Brown. When Lyman Epps's clan was hailed, it was never for its early stake in a Black voting rights initiative. The kinships between the nineteenth-century Black grantees and the JBMA activists (their shared delight, for instance, in their freedom of speech, movement, and expression in the Adirondack region, with schools, churches, roads, and back trails and fishing holes accessible to all), were unobserved.[17]

Uneasy with Agrarianism

Partly this may have reflected Barber's own impatience with Black agrarianism, which for so long had been the pet cause of his nemesis. *Buy land, build your farm, own your home, and gain your self-sufficiency*, Booker Washington had promised, *and white respect will follow*. But it hadn't. In the *Voice of the Negro*, Barber once published a piece about one "Simon Elijah Constant," an imagined devotee of Washington's school of quiet industry and uplift, whose "every effort tend[ed] toward the ownership of land, the accumulation of wealth, and the right-shaping of his personal career for the weighty responsibilities of honorable citizenship," yet who, for all his effort, never could get further than "Alas, Simon the Serf." As late as 1920, sixty years after emancipation, only a quarter of the nation's 218,612 Black farmers owned their farms. The rest were stuck in peonage. There was no rising up for them.[18]

"No race can prosper till it learns there is as much dignity in tilling a field as in writing a poem," Booker Washington had said. Gerrit Smith would have agreed. But Smith envisioned husbandry as a path to political empowerment. Each deed he dispatched to a hopeful pioneer struck a blow at a racist law that kept Black men voteless; all along, his goal was to empower a landowning antislavery electorate. Did Barber's generation of Black pilgrims know this? Or did one back-to-the-farm promotion sound just like another? And what, anyway, *could* they know of Smith's "scheme" in 1922?[19]

The JBMA was entirely dependent on white memory for its view of the Black Woods, for what it knew (and didn't) about Gerrit Smith, and even for what it loved about Lyman Epps Jr. And where did this leave Barber? All he knew and maybe could know about the giveaway was that Brown got land from a rich reformer and hoped to lend the Black farmers a hand. After that, he relied on historical accounts much skewed by ignorance and racial bias. Archival sources that might have set the record straight were not yet publicly available, and Black scholars who may have hoped to challenge the clichés lacked access to relevant collections. Frothingham's Smith biography would have assured Barber that the grantee-settlers had "none of the qualities that make the farmer," and Du Bois's biography of Brown went no deeper since he, too, relied on all-white, biased sources. Villard's Brown book made much better use of primary material but offered little insight into the pioneers, whose experience, as ever, was winnowed through the Browns'. As for what Barber gleaned from local memory, this, too, reflected the pinhole focus on John Brown, his neighborhood, and his family. Nor would Barber have picked up much from county histories. By the late nineteenth century, the writers, artists, and environmental lawmakers who shaped the image of the region privileged the imagery of wilderness—mountains, woods, and water—over homelier, less charismatic farmscapes.[20]

So I don't blame Barber, Burwell, or any of the pilgrimage's promoters for saying nothing about the giveaway, a subject that was undervalued, little studied, and poorly understood. Even if they had read Brown's biographies or heard North Elbans' stories about a vanished Adirondack farm colony for Blacks, they still may have not have seen what that fragile, failed, long-ago experiment had to do with them. *That . . . embarrassment. That best-forgotten bust.*

Nor would the one living source of information ever challenge this assessment. It was, after all, Lyman Epps Jr.'s link to John Brown, not his tie to Timbuctoo, that garbed him with his cloak of visibility. The Epps that Barber reverenced was a portal, a living witness to the martyred saint. *And I only am escaped alone to tell thee.* And fine with the grantee's son! The more esteemed was Epps's link to Brown, the more removed he was from a narrative of failure. He was not one of those "lazy good-for-nothins" who "just took one look at the place and turned around and went right back." He was of this place now, a lifelong North Elban and proud to be "the only Negro who [had] 'stuck out the snow and the cold up here.'" I've gone native, he told a white interviewer. Woolly mackinaws and hard-as-iron winters were his joy. Every day he marched a mile to the post office with a cane made out of a hickory golf club he salvaged from the links of the Lake Placid Club. At his birthday party in 1941 (he claimed he was one hundred), he pulled a cross-cut saw. He was feted by the Grand Army of the Republic at a campfire at the John Brown Farm. "People don't treat me as though I was colored," he mused. "They act as though I was just like them, and that's how I want to be."[21]

He wasn't just like them, and not so much like his father either. Between the antebellum grantee-settler's upward trajectory and the son's failure to prosper was a world of difference. Eppes Sr. was a resolute pioneer who farmed into his eighties, an Adirondack guide, a charter member of North Elba's Union Church, and contributor to Douglass's broadsheet. His judgment won John Brown's respect and the confidence of city deedholders who trusted him to sell their land. The five of his and Annie's eight children who survived to grow up in North Elba sang at school, church, and civic events. When he retired, or he and Annie celebrated their golden anniversary, or lodged the Hampton minstrels at their Newman home, the newspapers took note. Four ministers spoke at his funeral. Eppes Sr. was a man of parts.[22]

His son Lyme Jr., the only one of Eppes's children to stay in North Elba, never owned a home outright. He was a farmhand with bosses. He worked for his father, and in 1872 tended oxen for Anna Newman, a rich Philadelphian with a sprawling farm near Brown's home. He groomed the links at the Lake Placid Club, a place that hired no Black caddies, waitstaff, cooks, or housekeepers. He worked at the town dump. He hoped he might be hired by the state to be the caretaker at the historic John Brown Farm. He knew he could do the story justice, and others knew it too. "There is now a movement under foot to provide a place at the farm for Lyman Epps," a reporter wrote in 1921. "Lyman Epps is now 71. He is perhaps the only man living who was intimately in touch with John Brown. . . . He relates many interesting incidents in

connection with JB and would be of great value at the memorial in receiving visitors at the grave and recounting intimate stories of JB's life."
But that tap never came.[23]

Local news items about Epps Jr. were doting. At the 1935 ceremony at
Brown's grave, Lake Placid mayor George P. Owens called him a "faithful Negro saint." Readers learned about the birthday cake baked by his
neighbors, and how he never missed a vote. (His long hike to the polls
in 1940 was said to cause the stroke that compelled his removal to the
Essex County Home.) But public fondness would not ensure security.
Epps started poor and got poorer. He never could afford to visit his
brother, a resident for fifty years in an insane asylum downstate. When
Albert died in Wingdale, Epps could not pay to bring him home. This
the town did, and interred him with his family. Lyme Epps had twenty
dollars to his name when he moved to the Essex County Home.[24]

Epps's death in November 1942 was noted from New York to Fresno.
Lake Placid's mayor lamented the loss of a "venerable figure . . . esteemed and respected by all while he lived among us." But the hometown hero could not pay for his own headstone; that bill was picked
up by the Lake Placid chapter of the JBMA. Max Barber organized a
service for him in Manhattan, but the town's observance of his death
was slight. Epps's burial brought a dozen mourners, among them the
funeral director, the village clerk, a few Black women from the village,
and two pallbearers from the Lake Placid Club: Godfrey Dewey, the son
of the club founder, and the club's secretary and vice president, Harry
Wade Hicks.[25]

This was the double-sided quality of Adirondack race relations: on
one hand, a public show of easy tolerance and inclusion, and on the
other, a casual indifference. The fifty thousand readers of *The Crisis* who
marveled at a photograph of a peaceably integrated gathering in the
Adirondack Mountains honoring a militant advocate for Black rights
saw one side, and that is how Max Barber wanted it. Almost every year
until his death, even in the thick of the Depression when Black pilgrims
from hard-hit Philadelphia could not afford to travel, he went to North
Elba. His commitment never dimmed. But he would learn that the John
Brown so dear to him was not the man revered by his Adirondack allies.
John Brown country was a much more complicated place—here welcoming, there aloof, here accommodating, there the image of Langston
Hughes's "cold-faced North"—than he believed in 1922. He had called
for a pilgrimage as committed to "the new abolition of evils of this new
day" as it was devoted to "the memory of one who nobly gave his life

against the evils of his day." But one commitment did not ensure the other. And if, as Barber first exulted, "the people up there regard John Brown as a saint," this did not mean they saw Brown as a redeemer for *their* century, embraced a civil rights revival, or wanted any part of a year-round interracial "new abolition" spirit in their backyard.[26]

Barber did not argue. He was a guest here. Good guests did not reproach their hosts. In no speech in North Elba would he assail or even acknowledge Adirondack racism. But he heard about it. He knew the middle-class Black families in Lake Placid and Saranac Lake who put up pilgrims in their homes. He saw how Jim Crow mapped their lives.

The porch-fronted cottages of Saranac Lake, so renowned for the healing rest they offered guests and patients racked with tuberculosis, were as segregated here as they were elsewhere in the nation; most Adirondack sanitoriums spurned Black patrons out of hand. The Klan was active in this region too. In the first third of the twentieth century, flaming crosses lit up hills and fields only a hayride away from John Brown's farm. Three hundred people signed up for the Klan in Ticonderoga. In Wilmington, Klansmen were so sure of their acceptability that they built a clubhouse on Route 86. In 1924, Lake Placid saw three crosses illuminated in a week. In this era, Adirondack Kluxers were mostly targeting French Americans, Irish Catholics, and backers of the downstate Democratic politician Al Smith (four-time New York governor and the first Catholic candidate for president in 1928), but Black Adirondackers would not have been consoled. They knew the crosshairs of Klan terror could find them anytime.[27]

Social culture in the region was deeply racialized. Locally produced minstrel shows, for instance, were a staple of small-town Adirondack entertainment long before Barber was born. In 1914 and 1915, the *Lake Placid News* republished John Brown's family letters, heartfelt notes that left no doubt as to his outrage with racism—right next to ads for blackface revues of "Sambo" and "Jungletown." Adirondack opera houses and parades regularly featured blackface routines that reinforced impressions of Black incompetence and guile. From 1916 into the 1920s, Adirondack movie houses in Malone, Lake Placid, Ticonderoga, Saranac Lake, and Plattsburgh steeped Adirondack viewers in *The Birth of a Nation*, D. W. Griffith's Dixie-doting, exuberantly racist take on the Great Conflict and the heartache of a Union-ravaged "stricken South."[28]

And none of this moved Barber to comment. His outrage at the *Southern* lien system ("a camouflaged form of slavery") and his descriptions of "the misery and fear which rises like smoke from every Negro

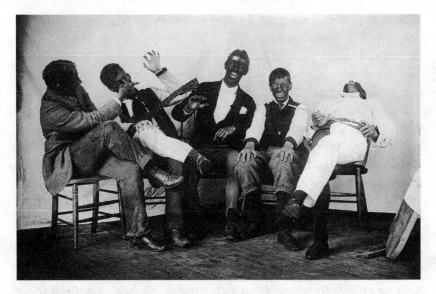

Minstrels at Putnam Camp in Keene, NY. Photographer George F. Weld, ca. 1885. Courtesy of the Adirondack Experience, Blue Mountain Lake, NY.

hovel" *down there* were full-on. Not so his public recognition of John Brown's "cold-faced north." But he felt it. Putting up with it was the price of getting what he wanted. Eyes on the prize, not on the heart.[29]

The Lake Placid Club

In 1895, New York's celebrated state librarian and regent, Melvil Dewey, founded a small residential colony in Lake Placid with a mission close to evangelical. No Gilded Age frivolity and ostentation for his new club. Here would be revived and invigorated the sturdy Yankee values of plain living and high thinking. Food would be healthy, fresh, and locally produced. Activities would honor physical fitness, literacy, and a reverent engagement with the Adirondack wilderness. The club's hotels and cabins welcomed guests the whole year round.[30]

And it took! By the time Max Barber first visited North Elba, the Lake Placid Club was 9,200 acres strong and the employer of 1,100. Its wooded acres were garlanded with bridle paths and ski trails. It had golf courses, a post office, and a toboggan run pitched so high it shot the long sleds clear across the lake. Most enticing to its advocates, and the key to its bright brand, was the "nation's model rest and recreation" community's scrupulously vetted membership. A thousand clubs and colonies were restricted in this era, but Melvil Dewey's "Anglo-Saxonist" criteria for club membership were more than social. They were rooted in racialized eugenics, the pseudoscience of the late nineteenth-century Progressive Era that aimed to improve human "gene stock" through selective breeding. Other clubs left their exclusionary policies implicit, but the Lake Placid Club spelled out its tenets in a handbook, unmodified for decades.[31]

Welcome: white, financially secure, Protestant Republicans who had been vetted by club members. Excluded: Black people, "new-rich groups," Cubans, and especially, emphatically, Jews, "even when of unusual personal qualifications." A member of the national Eugenics Committee, Dewey seeded his club with members who shared his vision of a master race, such as Cornell professor Jeremiah Jenks, coauthor of *The Immigration Problem*, the Yale economist Irving Fisher of the American Eugenics Society ("Breed Out the Unfit and Breed in the Fit"), and the Brooklyn minister Newell Dwight Hillis, eager drummer for the Race Betterment Foundation.[32]

Apologists for Dewey's racism (many Adirondackophiles among them) are quick to invoke the rampant bigotry of the age. The wider backdrop of the era (President Woodrow Wilson's stringent immigration policies, the resurgence of the Klan, the reflexive social antisemitism of resort hotels and clubs) suggested his defense: he was a man of his time. But as Wayne Wiegand, Dewey's biographer, observes, Dewey's racialized worldview did more than glimpse a trend. It advocated and promoted it. It meant that the wife of a club member would be refused membership because she was one-quarter Jewish, notwithstanding her sixteen years as a practicing Christian Scientist. It meant that Dewey derided public inquiries into his discriminatory policies as "Jew attaks [sic]." It meant he urged club members to buy up land along the Cascade Pass as a preemptive prophylactic against Jewish buyers and other "undesirables."[33]

What, exactly, had any of this to do with Barber's pilgrimage? There were no Jews among his pilgrims, and his dealings with Melvil Dewey were insignificant. Not so, however, his exchanges with Harry Wade Hicks, the club's secretary and vice president, and Dewey's close friend and supporter. Barber met Hicks at one of the first pilgrimages (Hicks may have been the member of one of the Adirondack "aristocratic clubs" Barber proudly noted in *The Crisis*). Hicks not only shared Barber's devotion to John Brown; he had made "Browniana" part of his club's culture. He filled shelves and drawers in the club's wood-paneled library with Brown ephemera and hung Brown's portrait above its mantle. He corresponded with a score of lay enthusiasts whose devotion to "the Martyr" ensured the survival of Brown's papers in the first half of the twentieth century when academic historians yawned. A passionate outdoorsman, he also inspired numberless club guests to visit Brown's historic home—sometimes by starlight on long wooden skis. And when the Black Philadelphians launched a pilgrimage in 1922, Hicks, a year-round resident of the club with strong ties in North Elba, made himself the JBMA's on-site Adirondack intermediary, and not just for a pilgrimage or three, but for close to forty years.[34]

Hicks helped Barber get the permits from the state Department of Conservation for the JBMA's yearly visits. He tapped local clergy and town notables to speak at John Brown Day. He pressed his club to pay for a protective cover for John Brown's headstone. For the JBMA organizers, he sometimes led a special tour of the club itself, an offer for which Barber was particularly grateful. An exclusive club tour from a white man of refinement was a delectable reversal of the old script of Black servants ministering to whites. In stretching the show of interracial solidarity from public space (a town hall, a state historic site) to private, the tour amplified the JBMA's influence and territory. Its marketing value was superb.[35]

This worked for the club too. By the early 1920s, its discriminatory policies were widely known. And while a once-a-year guided tour for "worthy" Blacks posed no threat to the club's exclusionary culture, a gestural enactment of interracial fellowship made the club look good. But a gesture, Barber learned early, it would stay.[36]

No, Harry Hicks would not act on Barber's suggestion that the club host an interracial conference. Nor would the club welcome a concert by a Black women's gospel choir. When the club bought and shut down an old railroad hotel in Lake Placid in 1926 (a convenient rest stop favored by the pilgrims), Barber implored Hicks to reopen it for the John Brown Day weekend, only a few months away. He knew of nowhere else to put the pilgrims, not on such short notice. And he had been making such a point of this town's vaunted hospitality: "What a bustle the town is in! The pilgrims have arrived. Homes and hotels are thrown open to us." But here it was late March, and his pilgrims were unhoused. He sent worried letters to town officials, postage stamps provided. No answer. With mounting frustration, Barber wrote Hicks, "Since your Club cannot accommodate us maybe you can perhaps help by waking these men up and asking them to answer my letters." And

Hicks did. Several Saranac Lake boardinghouses made sure the pilgrims all had beds. But this late-breaking club-made housing crisis made the precarity of Barber's status painfully apparent. He needed Hicks and valued him, and maybe the influential clubman, for reasons more obscure, needed him. But *was* Hicks on his side? Were they allies, or was Hicks, in fact, his keeper?[37]

This uneasy possibility may explain why, after many years, Barber stopped asking, in each case, for Hicks's help. There were times he did not need it, and in one case, he avoided it. The JBMA John Brown monument was a project whose progress and detailing Barber planned to manage himself. By 1934, he had been raising money for this memorial for over a decade. He had a vision, he'd pursued it, the state had given him permission to put the monument where he wanted it, and everything looked good. Then someone got ahold of Franklin B. Kirkbride. A fervent champion of eugenics and other "race betterment" initiatives, Kirkbride was the secretary of the venerable and steadfastly exclusive Ausable Club in Keene. What he'd heard about something "unsightly or inappropriate" in store for John Brown's shrine was concerning. Kirkbride knew of Hicks's special tie with the JBMA. He would let Hicks tackle this one. One reliably right-thinking clubman to another.[38]

Any visitor to the John Brown Farm Historic Site has walked by Joseph Pollia's statue of Brown in the traffic turnaround at the entrance. Zeus-sized at eight feet tall, with bulging forearms and tangled beard, midstride and on the move, Pollia's Brown is accompanied by a Black youth, unnamed, who gazes gravely up at "the Liberator" as if to memorize his every word. The boy is shoeless and his clothes are ragged, his need as plain as Brown's authority. Is he a self-emancipated slave, and Brown his guide and liberator? Brown told Gerrit Smith he hoped to be a "kind of father" to the Black grantees. He wasn't, as fate had it, but here in weathered bronze, his palm on this boy's back, he is guide and patriarch essentialized. And this memorial was no solely white-made vision. It took Barber thirteen years to raise the money for it, and he was much too invested in this project not to engage with the design. Together, Barber and Pollia, a classically trained sculptor with an imposing track record of historical commissions, conceived of a monument that would sit on top of John Brown's boulder inside the gated shrine and near the grave. On "nature's pedestal," as Barber put it, the statue would loom triumphant, a symbol of Black gratitude through the ages. At a press conference in August 1934, Barber explained that "the natural stone would serve as a picturesque and practical base for the figures which would be silhouetted against the sky at a much greater height than if placed nearer the ground." In the company of Brown, his raiders, and the women, the monument not only was in the shrine but was itself enshrined, and with it the idea that Brown's devotion to Black America was not just the chief thing but (literally) the highest thing, the jewel in this reliquary's crown.[39]

This siting plan had been approved by William G. Howard, superintendent of lands and forests for the New York State Conservation Department. Everything was good to go. But five weeks before John Brown Day, Barber got a letter from Harry Wade Hicks, who wanted to know whether the statue, shrine, and pilgrims might not all be better served if "points of historic interest" were "decentralize[d]." Would not

John Brown Memorial Statue. Sculptor Joseph Pollia, 1935. John Brown Farm State Historic Site, North Elba, NY. Photographer, Nancie Battaglia, Lake Placid.

this statue on the rock crowd the shrine? The landscaping might suffer too. Barber resisted. He had his permit. This was his to oversee. Hicks did not relent. He wrote to Howard's superior, the state conservation commissioner, Lithgow Osborne. And when Hicks got Osborne on his side, Barber saw how things stood. "I yield," he wrote Hicks. "The pressure is such that of course we shall have to yield." The statue would be erected in the turnaround—decentralized, as Hicks preferred.[40]

Just a problem of aesthetics, Hicks had said.

It was a little more than this. For three-quarters of a century, the graveyard at the farm had been curated by white people whose every plaque and presentation valorized Brown's martyrdom. In contrast, John Brown with a Black boy next to him on the great boulder, a peace-loving Brown, alive, engaged, would divert visitors from the sacred rock itself—that oft-described embodiment of Brown's granitic spirit, his courage out of history—and redirect their gaze to a man whose work with other people, Black people, meant as much as his momentous death. Barber's plan, its shift in emphasis, challenged the ownership of John Brown's memory. And if he had not looped Hicks into his planning because he guessed Hicks might object to this, he guessed exactly right. When Hicks told Barber to find the statue a home outside the sacrarium, he rejected a more inclusive vision of Brown's meaning. The fighter for racial justice and integration had no standing (literally) in the white-made fraternity of graves and markers inside the wrought-iron fence.[41]

In the parking circle, the Black-sponsored monument got its place. It's what we see when we head to the grave. It sets the stage but isn't on it. It's an usher; it sees us in. And what could Barber do? For thirteen years he had looked to Hicks for backstage help. Hicks was calling in his chit. The question was not what Hicks might do if Barber failed him but what he might not do. Would he still urge the mayor to get school-children to the farm on John Brown Day? Still burnish the respectability of the pilgrimage with the approval of his powerful patrician club? Hicks said he was making a suggestion and that Barber did not have to take it. But if Barber's choice diminished Hicks's engagement, the JBMA might be orphaned. Barber could not run the risk.[42]

The standoff was a long time coming. Each reformer had taken pains to protect the other from a version of himself that would have powerfully offended. In North Elba, Barber tamped down the civil rights agitator who excoriated Northern Jim Crow in the *Pittsburgh Courier* and *Abbott's Monthly*. And Hicks, when near Barber, kept the bigot under wraps. For a few days a year, their love of Brown carved out a piece of common ground where they "performed" a drama of race-blind tolerance and mutual respect. And it worked! They knew their lines! But nothing in this script addressed an interracial statue on Brown's rock. And when the clubman found an ally in the accommodating Osborne, the Black activist's true standing in John Brown country was laid bare. Guest and host were far from equals. Barber was, had always been, a supplicant—dependent yet again.

Mindful of Barber's disappointment and the JBMA's Depression-ravaged coffers, Hicks took charge of the unanticipated costs that this unexpected change incurred. He got the new plot graded and land-scaped, ordered a sub-base and a plaque. But what Barber wanted was Hicks's assurance that the displaced monument would still meet his expectation of some stature. A pedestal of six feet couldn't match the eight-foot boulder, but if the pedestal was any shorter than six feet, or five at the lowest, the monument would lose its impact.[43]

The thirty-six-inch pedestal Hicks secured is no higher than a card table.

Barber had fourteen years to get used to this stump before he died in 1949. It may not have been enough.

Better Than No Dream at All

When the JBMA's statue was dedicated in May 1935, the crowd was full, the speeches of a piece. Everyone loved freedom in the abstract. But the call for equal rights for Blacks was less robust. With other speakers, Harry Hicks cast John Brown as a generic model of elemental courage, a martyr for every cause and season. His catalytic role in the Civil War was noted—Harpers Ferry the portal to the calamity that let the nation die and resurrect. The state historian, Alexander Flick, proclaimed that Brown's death "tore away the last resistance to a pent-up volcano which deluged the land for years and filled it with woe" (but a *noble* woe! *restorative*!). Only Byron Remembrance Brewster's son, Judge Byron O. Brewster, the latest Brownophile from his clan, observed Brown's value for the present: "Slavery is a relative term. It may be said that there are many kinds of it still imposed on the human race." And as long as this was so, there yet remained "a crying need for that same fearless and sublime devotion to justice that still emanates from the spirit of Old John Brown—a spirit dedicated singly to the brotherhood of man with justice for all." Yet this same bold speech also indulged the notion that the Civil War was, perhaps, unnecessary. Had "natural economic causes been allowed to work out the problem, slavery would have disappeared from the South long since," the good judge mused. Perhaps more than any remark that day, Brewster's confident aside made clear how little John Brown Day had unsettled racist historiography. At this event and especially before this audience—before Max Barber!—to invoke "lost cause" ideology, and its counterfactual notions of the natural death that was slavery's presumed and rightful destiny? Was this what the Black pilgrims, some, like Barber, just a generation out of slavery, came from Hartford, Brooklyn, and Philadelphia to hear?[44]

But this was no Niagara Movement, and no NAACP either. And Brewster only reprised what white memorialists had said for decades about a Brown who waged war on one front, and whose cause was spent when the conflagration he ignited led to slavery's abolition. Their Brown cared little about equal rights after slavery was outlawed because he cared little for equal rights before—only the divine right to legal freedom. On postbellum disenfranchisement, the injuries of Jim Crow, class grievance, or social racism (embodied, say, in the eugenicist agenda of an Adirondack residential colony), this Brown's legacy was mute. The slaves were free, his work was done, his antislavery career deracinated—painted white. What the *New York Times* had to say about the shrine in 1890 still held: "No enemy of [Brown] who believed he was justly and properly hanged could criticize the manner in which his name is commemorated."[45]

The real surprise in 1935 was not anything white speakers had to say (or not say) but Barber's own remarks. Like the others, he saluted a catalytic Brown whose actions let a president fulfill his destiny: "He it was who kindled the beacon fires of freedom on a thousand hills. He was the grim grey herald of that awful conflict which robed the nation in fire and blood . . . a conflict which had to come." But about Brown's value for the present, Max Barber could only offer heavily, "His work is done."[46]

Barber's work was done, in any case, or that part of it that ever hoped to weaponize John Brown Day in the wider war on racism. And it might be argued that Barber's reticence was the thing that ensured the pilgrimages' survival. In another, painful lifetime, he saw his cherished Atlanta periodical snuffed out in its prime. His pilgrimage and monument were its successors, and these he would not lose. Barber had lived in three Southern states and two Northern cities. Like the grantee-farmer John Thomas, his experience of white racism was wide.

His grasp of the meaning of this monument was well beyond Hicks's own. In May 1925, the same spring that the JBMA held its interracial John Brown Day in Lake Placid, the white people of Greensboro, Alabama, hosted a great event of their own: five hundred Klansmen in full regalia, bearing torches and marching single file down Main Street, six riders at the lead, horses draped in white trappings. This would have been unimaginable in John Brown country, but not to the slaves' son Max Barber, who had every reason to suppose that if a larger-than-life monument of an abolitionist who made war on his own government went up anywhere but North Elba, it would not last a night. Barber settled for a hobbled dream because it beat no dream at all.[47]

The JBMA's annual John Brown Day limped along for decades after Barber's death, its attendance sometimes waxing, mostly waning, its speeches reliably devotional and bland. Calls for a nationwide antiracist agenda were perfunctory and unspecific. In 1946 the Lake Placid JBMA chapter introduced a handsome plaque to Brown's shrine that honored women in Brown's abolition circle who had never been identified. Not included and likely not considered were the Black North Elba women who had joined a radical agrarian initiative to help Black men get the vote. Also missing from the speakers' list in the World War II years and beyond were leading lights in civil rights reform. Barber's mentor, W. E. B. Du Bois, never spoke at John Brown's grave. Nor did the diplomat Ralph Bunche, the NAACP legal wizards Roy Wilkins and Thurgood Marshall, or the Urban League's courageous lawyer, Sadie Alexander, from President Truman's Committee on Civil Rights.[48]

In the summer of 1947, two years before Barber's death, the celebrated artist-author Rockwell Kent and several of his friends made a bid to repurpose the pilgrimage at John Brown's farm. To reporters gathered at Brown's grave, Kent called for a pilgrimage explicitly devoted to racial justice in midcentury America. Nineteen years earlier, Kent had left Manhattan for a new life on a four-hundred-acre dairy farm in Ausable Forks. Here he made his art, wrote, and preached the glories of Adirondack life, and when city friends visited, he often brought them to Brown's shrine. Waist-deep in Black rights initiatives, the left-leaning Kent held John Brown as a hero. With wreath in hand at Brown's grave, Kent, the war correspondent William L. Shirer, then cottaging at the Lake Placid Club, and the Chicago Communist educator William Patterson, whose parents had been enslaved, described a plan to make Brown's home "the objective of a yearly pilgrimage of rededication to John Brown's ideals," and to "stress the importance [of those] ideals in our national life today." The idea was to attract "thousands of Americans annually to North Elba"—as the JBMA had not done for years.⁴⁹

The demise of this high-aiming plan was as abrupt as its inception; Kent, the project's originator, simply had no time for it. Federal investigators were poking into his political affiliations, his art sales were off, and his Ausable neighbors were boycotting his dairy because his milk bottles advertised a socialist presidential candidate, Henry Wallace. Kent's own run for Congress on Wallace's American Labor Party ticket was risible. Out of 14,000 ballots, he culled 350 votes. As for his pilgrimage, to Adirondack families three or four generations in the region, Kent's nineteen years at Asgaard Farm conferred no claim on John Brown's meaning. Didn't John Brown country already have a pilgrimage, with the colored people and their wreath, the statue, everybody so respectful, no hotheads, nobody looking for a fuss?⁵⁰

Just give the thing a rest. One pilgrimage was enough.

Right Here in Franklin

There was another Adirondack pilgrimage that did, finally, credit the racial justice initiative that integrated this frontier and brought John Brown to the region. But it didn't call itself a pilgrimage, and it didn't head for John Brown's grave. It was a local affair, a combination family reunion and town Pioneer Day in Vermontville, town of Franklin, in July 2007. To guests I spoke with during and after the festivities, however, it had the long-time-coming feel of a pilgrimage. It was the first reunion of the long-separated Morehouse family since 1957, and the first time this fifth-generation Adirondack family was honored in this community for its connection to three pioneering Gerrit Smith grantees: Stephen Morehouse, John Thomas, and Avery Hazzard. These Adirondack settlers—in Loon Lake, Vermontville, and St. Armand—received gift land in the Black Woods, and some descendants were right here, two of them living in Vermontville.

Not that they knew they were descendants, at least not until that year. Until the history buffs came knocking, Oscar and Victor Morehouse didn't have a clue. No one told the brothers about a reformer's prescient effort to bring voting rights to Black New Yorkers before the Civil War. About the family in a country graveyard down the road they were wholly unaware. It seems the old people weren't so big on backstories. Looking back was what you did when the view could lift the heart and you had time to take it in.⁵¹

John Morehouse, Oscar and Victor's grandfather, was the son of the
Civil War veteran Warren Morehouse and the fugitive-farmer's daughter Charlotte Ann Thomas. It was John's widowed mother who mostly
raised him; his father died when he was young. John left high school
early, worked as a teamster, and later poured shots at the Dew Drop
Inn. His wife, Mary Hazzard, took in laundry and worked from home.
Their oldest, Kathleen, quit school in the sixth grade and a little later
met Wilbur Prince, a Black Vermonter working in a village bowling alley. She was fifteen when they were married by a justice of the peace;
they moved in with her folks. At sixteen, her younger brother Marshall
was identified in a county newspaper as the "first Saranac Lake boy to
be arrested for nonattendance of part time school." Marshall made the
news again in 1927 when he and a friend broke into a store, cracked
the cash register, and stole a car. They got as far as Albany. A stint in
the Elmira Reformatory followed.[52]

Life steadied for Marshall Morehouse on his return to Saranac Lake.
He got a job at David Cohen's famously stuffed-to-bursting hardware
store—shelving, loading, stocking up—and he did this for years. In 1931,
he married Betty Garrow, a Mohawk girl from the St. Regis reservation
on the US-Canada border. Their family would be big. Also in this town
were several cousins from the Hazzard side. Long out of farming now,
they, like Marshall, had solid jobs that paid the bills but promised no
advancement: line cook, day laborer, porter, laundress, stockboy, maid.
This is not to say that Black Saranackers gained no economic traction
in this era. But among the Black entrepreneurs who opened village
boardinghouses for cure seekers in the first third of the twentieth century were no descendants of Smith grantees.[53]

In the decade after World War II, the Morehouse children did what
all youngsters did in this small town. They joined the Scouts, got bit
parts in school pageants, played ball. This was the Adirondack story:
fireflies in summer and, in winter, slogging off to school in snow so
deep it hemmed your coat. But some Morehouse memories were not
like everybody else's. Most everybody else was white. The Morehouse
children ran the gamut. Some were Black, some pale, some, as white
Saranackers put it, "salt and pepper" or "sort of in-betweenish."[54]

In 1955, Marshall's wife, Betty, age fifty-one and the mother of ten,
was diagnosed with stomach cancer. She died the next year on a raw,
sleety day. Morehouse, a man of tense reserve and tight means at the
best of times, might have tried to keep his brood together if household help had been forthcoming. But in 1957 it was determined that

the younger Morehouses would have a better time of it with Marshall's older sister in Baltimore. The older boys remained in Saranac Lake. The split halves of this family would not be reunited for forty-seven years, and if it weren't for Rob Lagroome, a young Baltimorean, there might have been no reunion at all.[55]

Every Christmas of his life, Rob Lagroome's aunts and mother pulled out their memories of Saranac Lake like playing cards and started dealing out the stories. Rob heard about his grandmother, the Mohawk with the lustrous braids who sang lullabies everybody loved and no one understood. He heard about the old house on the Saranac River and his grandfather's daily tramp along the tracks to Mr. Cohen's store. Marshall, the patriarch, was gone, but two uncles were still up there. Would Rob ever meet them? He made a brisk start—found a people-finding database, hit the keys, and up it popped, Uncle Oscar's number, easy-peasy. So do it, he told himself. Just call the man. But when the lady on the other end wouldn't put his uncle on (*Yes, he's here, this is our home, but he'll need to call you back*), Rob hung up. He knew how this would go. He had tossed his hopes into the air, and for what? For this?

Then the phone rang, and he lunged.

The Morehouse family get-together was scheduled for late July under a pavilion in the town park. Advance press was exuberant, and the big crowd eager and robust. Besides the family, old schoolmates, and longtime friends of the Morehouses, like the event's organizer, town supervisor Mary Ellen Keith, there were independent scholars like Don and Vivian Papson, who had papered a long bulletin board with maps and letters documenting Morehouse family history as wide and far as they could track it. The *Plattsburgh Republican* reporter Robin Caudell shared her research on the Morehouses' clan. The historical reenactor Cliff Mealy Oliver did a musing turn in a slouch hat and overalls as the self-emancipated slave and pioneer John Thomas. Don Papson explained what Gerrit Smith was up to when he gave away his land in 1846, and all he'd learned about Private Warren Morehouse, the sharpshooter of Boykin's Mill. He also spoke with moving candor to the crowd about his considerable anxiety when he introduced himself to Oscar and Victor Morehouse. While he was thrilled to find descendants of Gerrit Smith grantees "right here in Franklin," Don wasn't sure how much to say. Oscar and Victor were light complected and perhaps had never been identified as Black. How would they take it? "There are white people in the Adirondacks who don't want to know," Papson said.[56]

But what had never been called out was always understood. All his life, Oscar and Victor's father, Marshall, was *N* or *B* in the census (except in 1910, when the census taker registered all the Morehouse family as Montauk Indians). So Papson's revelation did not rattle Marshall's sons. Nor would the Morehouse brothers shrink from learning that their ancestor, John Thomas, had been enslaved. "This, for me, was the best moment," Papson recalled. "That moment of acceptance."[57]

The best moment for the Baltimoreans at the reunion was different. John Thomas was from Maryland, their home. Surely something here had come full circle. In the 1830s, a Black marriage was destroyed, and Thomas made a life-risking escape from Maryland to Troy and, after several years, the Adirondack frontier. And back again, five generations later, were Thomas's descendants, who, too, had seen their family blasted by calamity, the death of a beloved mother that dispatched half their number from the Adirondacks south to—Maryland! *Here* was a pilgrimage! Speaking for the Baltimoreans, an exultant Rob Lagroome thanked the white people of Vermontville and his newfound aunt and uncles for their welcome. Mary Ellen Keith spoke stoutly of her town's frontier culture, saying of the antebellum Black pioneers, "They were of the community. They worked with the people. They were respected. Everybody loved everybody. *This* was a neighborhood. We did not see race." The Baltimorean Joan Morehouse Queen turned tearfully to her Adirondack brother, Oscar, and they embraced. Then everybody cheered, and Oscar found a chair.[58]

I'm no fan of staged reunions, and genealogy, the stark fact of some nominal connection, leaves me cold. John Brown country's reverence for Brown's vaunted Anglo-Puritan blood, Melvil Dewey's obsession with racial hygiene, Madison Grant's catastrophically influential call for ethnic and racial cleansing (a shaping influence on Adolf Hitler), indeed, our long American romance with the myth of racial purity—nothing here beguiles me. But that summer afternoon in 2007, Papson's and Lagroome's faith in the uses of genealogy bore fruit. I never thought I'd see an interracial family reunion feted at an Adirondack Pioneer Day. Gathered here was more than a ruptured clan. The reunion brought the present face-to-face with a never-dreamed-of past. History, as the Alabama activist Bryan Stevenson might say, "got proximate," and proud.[59]

But I did not share Rob Lagroome's hopeful feeling that a newfound Baltimore connection meant that diaspora and return balanced out. Between the exuberance of the pilgrims who had driven up from Baltimore and the cautious faces of the Morehouses of Vermontville was a remove. Did the Adirondack side of this family welcome a public celebration of its ancestry, or were they putting up with it because, after all the hoopla in the papers, what choice did they have? Just stay home? I couldn't tell. Their reserve was hard to read.

A few summers after the reunion, I talked about that day with Bob McKillip, a fifth-generation Adirondacker whose people came from Ireland's County Antrim, during the Great Famine. McKillip reveled in the history of the occasion: the family link to Gerrit Smith, John Thomas's self-emancipation, his new life, his farm. But McKillip, too, had found some aspects of the day disquieting. He recalled the Morehouses from school. He was a little bit in awe of them, he admitted. "Tough kids. You definitely wanted them on your side in a fight." And the part of Pioneer Day that made so much of race, this bit he didn't get. "People didn't used to think about that," he told me carefully, parsing his unease. "Racism. This was not a word in Saranac Lake. When all that stuff came up on the news about civil rights for colored people— well, we were already doing that. Here we were living it all the time. And we didn't even know it." In his view, Pioneer Day took an openhearted decency and made it knowing and self-conscious. And seeing his old schoolmates being called out as Black, "singled out as something different," made him wince. It rattled the Morehouse brothers too, he sensed. "That was new for them. That was just not part of their—dialogue." It seemed overcooked.

I suspect more reunion-goers than McKillip shared his sense of a misunderstanding. The idea of a John Brown country beyond racism, beyond hate, has a proud grip on the region's image of itself—and has since long before the Town of Franklin supervisor made her hopeful claim on a postracial past. Douglass's rhapsodic sketch of the Smith Lands was inspired by the idea of a regenerative wilderness, God fashioned, God favored, that, too, "did not see race." In the republican frontier, Charles Ray predicted, hard work and good behavior would win the grantee-settlers the color-blind esteem of their white neighbors. The assumption of a morally exceptionalist Adirondacks was a keystone of John Brown country—from Charles Ray's high hopes to Max Barber's giddy dispatches from North Elba ("Everybody here regards John Brown as a saint!") to a 1961 editorial in an *Adirondack Record-Elizabethtown Post* that asked readers, "Aren't you glad you live in good old Essex County? Here we don't have racial violence and hatred. There is no need of 'freedom riders' in our region." No need of anything, apparently. Up here in the good place, we've got the whole thing licked.[60]

The Blinders of Exceptionalism

Exceptionalism is a problematic legacy in the Adirondack story. On one hand, it's been a lifesaver, or anyway a park saver, making an emphatic and compelling case for the lasting preservation of this green Adirondack world. But if exceptionalism got us the park, it also planted a stubborn culture of social exclusivity. If it moved Smith's agents to wax lyrical about the alchemical potential of the wilderness encounter, it also obscured their recognition of the settlers' real needs. And in one account after another, an exceptionalist perspective would explain the settlers' "disappearance" from the Black Woods in terms of a racialized, inherent incapacity.

In the late 1970s, the rhetoric of exceptionalism would once again be deployed at the John Brown Farm State Historic Site to devastating (and now largely forgotten) effect. The messaging at this sleepy site had not been refreshed for decades. Young curators and site historians at Parks and Recreation's Bureau of Historic Sites were keen to shake it up. No other site of the thirty-four under Parks' wide wing (there are six more today) was, in their view, better fixed to offer visitors a perspective on the outbreak of the Civil War through the antislavery campaign and the struggle for Black rights. Inspired by Black studies and the "bottom-up" history movements of the seventies, they aimed to crack the notoriously tough shell of enshrinement around the place and contemporize the script. New scholarship had tracked a tangle of alliances between John Brown and the radical Black abolitionists of New York. Was this not central to the story? What about Brown as an Adirondacker, and Gerrit Smith, whose "scheme of justice and benevolence" got Black pioneers, and then the Brown family, into this wild country in the first place? And who were the grantees? Weren't their stories part of this as well?[61]

With Parks and Recreation Commissioner Orin Lehman was all for a site makeover, and when Parks won a hefty grant to bring this thing to pass, the Parks' interpreters got busy. They focused on the Browns as Adirondack pioneers. They profiled the Browns' Black neighbors, and the settlement called Timbuctoo. They considered Timbuctoo and Brown's arrival in light of the larger campaign for Black justice and equal voting rights, and then, how that connected to the antislavery discourse, and how, for Brown, the two movements were joined at the hip. And hoping for support, they got in touch with the John Brown Farm site manager, Ed Cotter, and the town historian, Mary MacKenzie.[62]

They would be disappointed. Mackenzie was appalled. To her garden club, she observed that North Elba's John Brown was not an easy hero. His Kansas chapter in particular she deemed "unpalatable and indigestible," and all that bloody business would be hauled out in an interpretative center because that's what these places *did*. They covered everything. And was this necessary? "Much better that John Brown and the John Brown Farm remain symbolic," she offered. "Better for people to just stand in that sublime spot, look at the sublime mountains, and think sublime thoughts about an incredible man who had an incredible dream." Her friend the John Brown Farm Historic Site's supervisor, Ed Cotter, heartily concurred. This new upgrade left him cold—the part of it that made anything of Timbuctoo and Gerrit Smith especially. Visitors to this site, said Cotter, knew nothing of this "obscure nineteenth century reformer.... Of the thousands of people who visit the site every year . . . only a mere handful have ever heard of Gerrit Smith and *his* Negro colony," and they did not need to be enlightened. "Talk with our foreign visitors, members of the John Brown Memorial Association and visitors we get from all over our country reveals that they are interested in what John Brown tried to do for human rights and not in Gerrit Smith's failures."[63]

By 1978, the JBMA to which Cotter alluded was a specter of its old self. The North Elba chapter now oversaw John Brown Day—a formulaic, sparkless business with prayers, spirituals, a wreath. This threat to local memory, however, yanked the sleepy outfit to its feet. An interpretive center at the site, a JBMA member wrote the *New York Times*, would attract visitors to Brown's home who would not *get* it, mere unenlightened idlers who would think nothing of "trampling over the grave, dispensing beer cans, soda cans, and litter." (Again that Adirondack bogey: an invasion of the unsuitable, the undeserving.) The JBMA's anxiety freed the *Times* to admit its own distaste for "historic-site circuses," and then the Department of Environmental Conservation confessed concern about the impact of the "trampling" hordes on alpine vegetation.[64]

"We got clobbered," one of Parks' team recalled. "Blindsided like you wouldn't believe." Schoolchildren were writing postcards. *Leave John Brown alone!* Parking lots, tour buses, *facilities*! Who needed it? And Parks backed out. Two years of planning, research, and architectural proposals were abandoned. A new center would have to wait. It's waiting even now. Retired staffers who worked on that junked project told me it was the toughest setback of their professional careers.[65]

Yet was it so surprising? For 120 years, in county histories, newspapers, and memoirs, the Adirondacks stood for John Brown, and Brown's story had returned the favor. It helped locals know who belonged to this tough country. It helped them say they knew who didn't. It was the tough nut of regional identity, this confident exceptionalism, and nothing, not one part of it, recalled the story of Smith's plan, Black voting rights, or the Black pioneers. Long before Parks killed its project, John Brown's passion for racial justice and his equalitarian convictions had faded from his hometown resume, his sublime courage neutralized to the point where even racists could embrace him. By the time Parks got on the job, local ways of thinking about John Brown and the Black Woods were as hard-sunk as an Adirondack frost. Parks' new spin in 1977 was more than fresh. No one *got* it. How did it *belong*?

This Place Is My Land, It Isn't Your Land

It seems all roads in this story eventually swing back to this question: *Who belongs? Who gets to say this place is mine?* The Black agents put deeds into the hands of Marshall Morehouse's ancestors with the promise of a healthful, color-blind, wide-open frontier. This new country, which, as William C. Nell put it in the *North Star*, had "just as much respect for a Black man as it has for a white," would equalize Black opportunity as a Negrophobic Northern city never could. But it wasn't new or so wide open. Long before Smith gave up his acres, native people had inhabited this region, and had claimed it for millennia. European colonizers who observed the absence of year-round settlements were quick to proclaim a clear, uncluttered *tabula rasa* inviting white dominion. The racializing discourse that defended this perspective emphasized the unfitness of the native people for the Adirondack wilderness—from their intransigent indifference to the rules of settlement and ownership right down to the region's self-incriminating name. Adirondack means "bark eater." That's how helpless were the natives, how wholly unevolved. They ate tree bark "like the brutes, and bore, from thenceforth, degradation's low mark" (so offered an Elizabethtown village history of 1905). The rift between the worthy and the undeserving was articulated long before the Adirondack historian Alfred Donaldson treated his readers to his eager fantasy of an ill-built shantytown with "little stovepipes" sticking out of "flat roofs . . . at varying angles," crowned with ("the last touch of pure negroism") "a large but dilapidated red flag" that read, "Timbuctoo."[66]

In 1853, and long before a penciled Blue Line corralled the region, county historian Winslow C. Watson boasted, "Thanks to . . . the settlers of Essex County . . . of New England origin . . . no county of the state embraced a population of higher intelligence, of purer morality, of more industrious and frugal habits." The vaunted purity of Adirondack Yankeedom defined the regional brand even before the Civil War. White antislavery settlers like John Brown idealized an Adirondacks of Puritan incorruptibility, a soul-testing stronghold fashioned in God's image. Social reformers (Gerrit Smith among them) predicted brilliant changes in the "rough and untamed natures" of the "monsters" in Clinton Prison after they worked in the Adirondack wilderness. The harsher the inmates' wilderness encounter, the more profound their redemption.[67]

Nativists who discerned a threat to the vaunted Yankee Adirondack rootstock posed by the rolling swells of immigrants (twenty-five million of them between 1880 and 1924) found a rationale for their alarm in the burgeoning new field of eugenics. A pseudoscience would be weaponized to justify the defense of Adirondack purity in all its incarnations: the balsam-scented air, healthful water, mountain views, and, with them, of a piece with them, the racial or genetic purity of Adirondackers themselves ("next to the bottom in number of defects found" in drafted men, declared the American eugenicist Charles Davenport to the War Department in 1920). Racial ideologues like Melvil Dewey observed with gratitude the Adirondacks' saving distance from mongrel city hordes, a remove that felt like destiny. To leave a world behind, it had to stay behind, and because of how hard it was to get there, New York's northern "Central Park for the World" would remain largely free and clear of poor Black people, immigrants, and impoverished whites. All to the good, claimed race-betterment ideologues (and, as recent scholarship suggests, some geographers as well, who would deploy these arguments to spatialize hierarchical ideas that also, indirectly, advanced a racialized agenda). Only the conservation of good Anglo rootstock ensured the survival of the race. Cross a pure-bred Nordic specimen with an African, Native American, Hispanic, Jew, or any "lower type," and the nation would be worse than changed; it would be irreversibly degraded, and "Old Stock" Americans ("*Homo Europaeus*, the white man par excellence," as the prominent conservationist and eugenicist Madison Grant proudly offered) would grow scarcer than the Adirondack moose.[68]

Environmental history has noted the lead role of public health in early arguments for the Adirondack Forest Preserve (concerns fueled by the threat of befouled watersheds and rivers), but more than drinking water was at risk. Predatory forces from without imperiled woodlands, wildlife, oxygenated air, and Edenic views. Suspect spoilers (loggers, market hunters, railroad hands, migratory work crews, and immigrants) were judged as harshly as their suspected carelessness. Class, race, and ethnicity divided the pure of heart from the unprincipled, the pure of mind from the uneducable, the pure of pedigree from the polyglot and "unevolved." Between the immigrant or impoverished Adirondacker (Black or white) who shot deer out of season and the clubman who fished and hunted for sport and proudly stewarded the wildlife he tracked was a divide as deep as it was necessary. "We, the mothers of this generation, ancestresses of future generations, have a right to insist upon the conserving of not only our soil, our forest, birds, minerals, fishes, waterways, in the interest of future home-makers, but also upon the conservation of the Caucasian race in our land," the president of the Daughters of the American Revolution declared in 1910.[69]

The stewards of Adirondack hunting clubs, private preserves, family compounds, and residential colonies guarded this racial patrimony with care. Their "Do Not Trespass" signs not only kept out local undesirables but kept the "good stock" in, kept their human fauna as undefiled as the club streams that were scrupulously stocked with noble "brookies." Indeed, the one thing, and maybe the only thing, these clubs had in common was their insistence on social exclusivity. A white upper-class elite bound by education, business and family ties, club connections, and city residences, a tribe that in the immigrant metropolis felt itself besieged, was, in the great park, confident and strong.[70]

In 1893, one-fourth of the new Adirondack Park, a total of 940,000 acres, was leased or owned by fifty private sportsmen's clubs. Within thirty years these exclusionary strongholds were joined by other kinds of enclaves that further buffed the park's high patrician tone: Great Camps, grand preserves, children's summer camps, lakeside multifamily compounds, country clubs, and residential colonies like the Lake Placid Club, founded in 1895 and eventually the biggest four-season recreational community in the nation. But while most of these have broken up and few function as they did, the reputation of the region as no place for Black people abides. In 2016, the Adirondack environmentalist Aaron Mair, then head of the Sierra Club, visited the Schroon River, and white rafters, drifting past, greeted him with a fusillade of racist slurs. In 2020, Nicky Hylton-Patterson, the Black director of the Adirondack Diversity Initiative, took a morning jog in Saranac Lake and on the railroad trestle above her trail was a newly sprayed comet of graffiti—"Go Back to Africa," and worse.[71]

It's not frequent. It's not even typical. It's that it doesn't go away.

Challenging the Narrative

There is no fast fix here, not for any piece of this. The wrongs that moved Gerrit Smith to do what he did in 1846 are all still with us: voter suppression tactics that block Black access to the ballot; a wealth gap that cleaves and destabilizes the world; systemic obstacles that stall the way to economic advancement and political empowerment. These were Gerrit Smith's concerns in 1846; and ours, too, every one. Gains are made, but never so securely that we dare to look away. The beam of justice is not steady. It shines, falters; it needs minding all the time. The opportunity to track the progress of that beam as it breaks ground on the floor of daily life, lighting up this victory, that loss, might be the Black Woods' best gift. History on a grand scale—an epic wartime presidency, a mass contagion, an economic crash—craves action, resolution, summary. But local history is different. Its capacity for paradox is huge. It makes room for the human factor, the slow mess that reminds us how easily derailed is the work of change.

In places with strong racial or ethnic populations (the Deep South, big cities, Indian reservations, intractably white suburbs, members-only residential communities), we grasp the work of racializing at a glance. But in places that have "lost" Black neighborhoods to arson, urban renewal, out-migration, redlining, or the insults of Jim Crow, a glance is not enough to call a missing narrative to mind. A more conscious kind of scrutiny is needed. And it's happening. In the Adirondacks, Vermont, Oregon, Wisconsin, Maine, and Iowa, lay and local historians recover evidence of long-gone neighborhoods and enclaves. Will their findings dislodge deep-sunk, hard-defended narratives, or just splash them with fresh paint? That is, will they contend with whiteness and how it built and reinforced the presumption of Black incapacity, or stop with rote assertions of diversity?[72]

It's not enough to call out and celebrate the missing. Why they went missing, how they were disappeared, is the much tougher question. And in the Black Woods, the grantees and their descendants did much more than diversify. They challenged the white wilderness, and they changed it. Their coming roused anxiety, uneasiness, and loyalty, and subverted a default racism in a hundred small, startling ways. White

Adirondackers soaked up race jokes in the *Malone Palladium* but scared off bounty hunters who came after a once-enslaved Black neighbor. Franklin farmers dubbed a river N—— Brook, yet when the time came to serve the Union, they took the Black Marylander James Brady into their company because—the law be hanged—they knew Brady and needed heads. When the penniless Lyme Epps had a stroke, Lake Placid villagers got up funds to help him, and when his impaired brother, Albert, died in the downstate institution where he'd lived most of his life, and no family was left to bring him home, Lake Placid saw to his return. He was an Eppes, after all. The town cemetery was where he had to be.

This dissonance clanged the other way as well. Recall the zeal of George S. Hale, who, with Francis Lee, chiseled John Brown's name so deep into the great rock Brown adored that "neither morbid relic-seeking tourists nor the storms of centuries can blot it out," yet, as a member of the Immigration Restriction League, labored to keep lesser races out. Or the volte-faces of the clubman Harry Wade Hicks, who championed John Brown and the Black pilgrims, rounded up pallbearers for Lyman Epps's funeral, got speakers for John Brown Day, and produced an elegant brochure for the Black-organized memorial at Brown's farm, yet kept lifelong faith with Melvil Dewey's high church of white supremacism. Or, for that matter, the vexed legacy of Lake Placid itself, which basked in its business dealings with the most restrictive club around yet cultivated an alliance with Black pilgrims devoted to a vigilante who made war on his own government.[73]

In John Brown country, the Adirondack surveyor Wait Lewis told a reporter he would like to see Gerrit Smith elected president—that's how white-hot was his progressivism—but on the job, in the field, Black settlers smelled a fake. Here, Clarence Darrow, Oswald Garrison Villard, and William Shirer spoke rousingly of equal rights for Black Americans, then repaired to the Lake Placid Club for solace of class and kind. We dream of reconciliation, some way to square the circle, give us reason to declare that because Harry Wade Hicks was a bigot, his regard for Brown and his affection for Lyme Epps were untrue. Or, conversely, that because he did so much for the JBMA, he could not *really* hold with Dewey's notions about racial purity. His colors showed at John Brown's grave in May. But he was both, and there is nothing reconcilable about it.

The Black Woods was both too: a beacon for a better idea, and a tangle of false, forgotten, or misremembered narratives. Repeatedly, historiography othered the Black experience to accommodate a racialized agenda. Instead of honoring the Black Woods' promise as a font of hope, a dream of something better, something transformational, writers and historians turned the story into a cautionary parable of Black incapacity. *Not here*, it said. *Not yours. Not for you*. And none of this was lost on John Thomas. "*I begin* to be regarded as an 'American citizen,'" he told Gerrit Smith in 1872 (italics mine). Thirty-two years after he fled enslavement, twenty-five years after the giveaway, ten years after legal emancipation, and he was just beginning to see justice, to be counted by his neighbors as a stakeholder in the republic.

But better, always better, than if he had stayed south. Relative to *that* road not taken, John Thomas had gained ground. No matter if Gerrit Smith gave up on the giveaway before Thomas harvested his first load of hay. He still stewarded his gratitude "for the interest you have always taken in the welfare of my people"—*always* because Thomas knew that Smith's giveaway was one effort in a long career of antislavery endeavors. And in declaring that he spoke "on behalf of my colored brothers generally," Thomas made the same point for himself. He, too, had a long career "breasting prejudice and opposition." *You and I*, he reminded his old benefactor, *are in it for the long haul—combatants fighting hard with the resources at hand. You, with money, politics, and power. I, with the work of my own life*. Bolstering his pride in his achievement was his memory of the hell he had left behind, a memory that few white Americans could grasp. To have been another's property, disposable as livestock—*I, too, have a trajectory*, the ex-slave reminded Smith. *My Adirondack chapter—it's one of many in my book, which, like your book, sir, is hard packed*. On one end, three decades of enslavement in Maryland. On the other, far from realized, the pursuit of full equality in the United States. The ascent from slave to fugitive to settler-farmer to citizen was more than the context for John Thomas's appreciation for Smith's gift. It was the continuum that helped him deal with Northern racism. Not to ignore it or excuse it, but to recall that things could be, had been, worse, and therefore could be, might get, better.

For whatever happened in the Black Woods was better than the day Mr. Merrick sold his wife, the reenslavement of Robert and Jacob McCray, or the age of neoslavery that dropped like a hood over the shards of Reconstruction. Adirondack bigotry could not be likened to a terrorist regime of systemic white supremacism. Black Adirondackers kept sight of the distinction.

They didn't glory in it, though. Not like their white neighbors. From Civil War days to the civil rights era, Adirondack newspapers thrilled to

Southern dispatches that confirmed the North's monopoly on justice and racial tolerance. Horrific stories documenting racialized atrocities in the South worked Northerners into a pious lather while diverting them from undone work at home. For how much easier it was for white Adirondackers to salute their own progressivism than to imagine the prospects of the Black grantee-settlers and their descendants if they had gotten, and early on, the backup, loans, credit, and good faith to go for more: to head a jury, raise a regiment or organize a company in the Civil War, serve as county supervisor, join the school board, run a sawmill, run a factory, feed a savings account, and other rote entitlements and perquisites of those who "did not see race." Some will offer that what might have been is none of history's concern. But the breach between what happened in the Black Woods and what could not have happened (because it was blocked, outlawed, jailed, dismissed, never offered, never had a chance) may be the greatest unresolvable contradiction of them all. And there is nothing to be done about this, no way to rectify that gap.[74]

But a gap is bridgeable. It may be spanned. To see it in the first place, walk its length, concede its depth—here, surely, is the start.

Epilogue

"How did I not know this existed?"

—Tiffany Rea-Fisher, executive director,
Adirondack Diversity Initiative and director of the
dance company, EMERGE125, on learning about
Timbuctoo

In mid-August 2018, the Adirondack Experience (ADKX), the renowned history museum in the heart of the Adirondack Park, brought a new artifact into its core exhibition hall. The boxy little structure came from a Schroon Lake music camp in eastern Essex County. The head of the Seagle Music Colony had it built on-site in 1957 for an aspiring voice student from Clinton, North Carolina. Fulton Fryar, newly graduated from his all-Black high school, had been invited to join Seagle to study voice and opera, and his hopes for this demanding and esteemed summer program were high. There would be top-flight instruction and a chance to sing in big productions. He'd make friends too, guys like him who loved putting voice to song.

Most expectations were well satisfied. At Seagle, Fryar studied hard, sang in operas, got good parts, and helped build sets. But there would be no downtime hanging with new buddies in the bunkhouse. When he got to the colony, bone tired from the bus ride, Fryar was directed up a brushy slope to a shedlike structure near the laundry. Finished just that day: his own bespoke back of the bus, a one-man shoebox with a window, bunk bed, and shelving. Fryar, the first and only Black student at the Seagle Music Colony, was astonished. This was the *North*. In the *North* this was not supposed to happen. Fryar found some paint and a brush. On the door in a bright, flowing hand, he wrote, "Always Welcome to

'The Closet,' the home of Fulton Fryar." For the two summers he spent at Seagle, this was where he slept.[1]

After Fryar left, "Fulton's Closet" was a storage unit and a utility shed. Then in 2018, when the Closet was slated for demolition, a visitor to Seagle read Fulton's welcome on the door and inquired about the backstory. It struck him strongly that there was something here worth keeping. Preservationists were contacted, and curators pricked up their ears. The ADKX moved this relic of Adirondack-style Jim Crow to its campus, and ever since, it has been stopping people in their tracks. Amid the wicker pack baskets, stuffed bear cubs, and bent-twig headboards from the Great Camps of tycoons, it's not what visitors expect. But it's where the Closet belongs, making its bleak point. This happened here, and more than here. It happened in the sportsmen's club, the jury box, the cure cottage, and the county board of supervisors. All were spaces, inside or out, where Black people in the Adirondacks were not, and where their absence spoke of white privilege and power.

There is a poem by Mark Strand called "Keeping Things Whole" I sometimes thought of while I was working on this book. The speaker describes himself in terms of where he isn't. Where there's a void, he fills the void, and his movement keeps things whole, plugs the gap that other people make and leave. This is what he does and all he does, and it often struck me that Blackness—for early Adirondackers in this story— seemed to register in just these terms—the absence of field, the negative space, the thing that gave what's visible its contour and distinction. But here's the difference. The speaker in Strand's poem enjoys the privilege of agency. *He* names his job; his movement is his choice. What went on in Adirondack country—the othering of Blackness that helped keep things whole, so to speak—was not Black chosen. It was white made and white enforced.[2]

And the aspiring opera singer Fulton Fryar never asked to be sequestered in a shed. It was his choice, however, to speak about the Closet at the ADKX in August 2018 to an auditorium packed to capacity, and to find, after sixty years, his experience firmly acknowledged as a part of Adirondack history. His story was now everybody's story, and the insult dealt out daily for two summers was no longer his to bear alone.

The inclusion of the Closet in the region's leading museum rides a surging trend. Since the beginning of this century, Adirondack activists and institutions have been laboring to build awareness of the Black

Adirondack experience, contend with legacies of racism, and ensure Black engagement in the process.

The ADKX has led the charge with programs that engage with social justice and inclusivity, and it looks like an exhibit on the Black Adirondack experience will find a home there too. Still going strong are several other projects that I mentioned in the preface. In 2016, Parks made John Brown Lives! its "Friends Group" for the John Brown Historic Site, which means more say in programming, site interpretation, and community outreach. The JBL! exhibit, *Dreaming of Timbuctoo*, continues to enlighten visitors with a story of nineteenth-century suffrage justice and the Black farming initiative that inspired Brown to move his family to his last and favorite home. The SUNY Potsdam archaeologist Hadley Kruczek-Aaron has expanded the reach of her Timbuctoo dig, which calls the Eppes family's world to life through the revelations of material culture. In 2022, her students tackled a shady midden behind the clapboard home of Anna Newman, the Philadelphia rusticator who fell hard for the Adirondacks, stayed for keeps, and hired Lyme Epps Jr. to tend her livestock. In 2023, Hadley's diggers will take their whisks and trowels to the presumed site of the Eppeses' second home.

In 2016, composer Glenn McClure followed his 2013 *Timbuctoo: An Abolition Oratorio*, with *Promised Land: An Adirondack Folk Opera*, once

Promised Land: An Adirondack Folk Opera. Photographer, Mark Kurtz. Northern Lights Choir, Saranac Lake, November 16, 2016. Composer, Glenn McClure. Artistic director, Helen Demong. Soloists, top left to right: George Cordes ("Paul Smith"), Kimberly Weems ("Martha Brown"), and Jorell Williams ("Lyman Epps").

again collaborating with musical director Helen Demong of the Northern Lights Choir in Saranac Lake. In the works, I'm told, is a full-bore opera honoring the Eppeses' frontier lives and friendship with John Brown.

Recent responses to the story include the elegiac 2021 documentary *Searching for Timbuctoo*, from the Albany filmmaker Paul Miller, who gives his narrative a rich, panoramic frame and deepens the history with interviews with historians academic and independent. Martha Swan of John Brown Lives!, and educators from the state archives and the Adirondack region, are cooking up lesson plans and field trips for grade schoolers that can steep them in a corner of New York history through a saga of Black pioneers and voting rights on the antebellum Adirondack frontier. Historic signs have been erected that mark the vanished neighborhoods of Timbuctoo and Blacksville. On maps and local signage, John Thomas Brook will replace the name of the stream that bore a racist name for 150 years.[3]

People want to make something of this story. They want the hope that fired it, and the faith that fanned it even after its originator left it for dead. After a visit to the exhibition, the New York City jazz pianist Eli Yamin wrote and recorded the lushly rolling "Timbuctoo Blues" with his band. Two installations from the artist-activist Ren Davidson

Memorial Field for Black Lives. Installation at John Brown Farm. Ren Davidson Seward, artist. Saranac Lake, 2021–. Photographer, Nancie Battaglia, Lake Placid.

Seward of Saranac Lake occupy the grassy traffic circle at the entrance
to the John Brown Farm. Under Pollia's bronze hero and his Black
friend, Davidson's Memorial Field for Black Lives documents the tie
that binds the antislavery struggle to antiracism work today. Her subject, Black Americans who were killed without cause by law enforcement
officers or vigilante mobs, makes its hard point in seventy knee-high
posterboards that rise in rows around the statue, each bearing a death
notice as parsed and taut as a haiku. And winding behind the first, a
second installation offers a chronology of Black voting rights granted
or denied.

On John Brown Day in 2022, the Memorial Field was the site of
an open-air dance performance from the Harlem-based dance company EMERGE125 (formerly Elisa Monte Dance of Manhattan). The
company has a long-standing summer residency in Lake Placid, but it
was sixteen years before the director-choreographer Tiffany Rea-Fisher
learned about Timbuctoo and its roots in a suffrage justice initiative.
In summer residencies since, she has choreographed a range of pieces
reflecting aspects of this story. On May 8, 2022, her company honored
John Brown's birthday. At dusk, in the long shadows of the memorial statue, and to an ethereal and haunting version of "John Brown's
Body," dancers swooped from lamentation to resolution, all soaring
leaps and light.[4]

Adirondack independent scholars and history buffs find fresh por-
tals in and out of this rich story, some of them astonishing. The research of the Plattsburgh reporter Robin Caudell inspired a monologue
about the suffrage activist Helen Appo Cook, a daughter of the Black
settler William Appo. In New Russia, Margaret Bartley's interest in the
Smith grantee Lafayette Mason has her scheming with a town historian
in South Dakota to get a proper veteran's headstone in the graveyard
where she believes he rests. Greg Furness, before retirement a historian
with NYS Parks, has, in addition to his deep-spaded genealogical work
on Adirondack abolitionists and grantees, quietly replaced or fixed broken, missing, or illegible headstones of Black Adirondackers who served
in the Civil War (and recently furnished William Appo Jr.'s stone with
a Civil War veteran's GAR marker). And bringing his forensic skills to
bear on the map of the Black Woods, the Adirondack paleoecologist
and science teacher Curt Stager has identified what might be cellar
holes for the Morehouse homestead on Loon Lake, and the location of
Hazzard family farmsteads. His digitization of Smith's gift lands will
point the way to an interactive map that we hope will let people see at

a keystroke just where the land lots were for grantees such as Frederick Douglass, Solomon Northup, and Willis Hodges. Another intriguing prospect: a self-guided hiking map that will get this story off the page and give it boots and blisters. Brother Yusuf Burgess, who introduced city kids from Albany and Troy to Adirondack camping and a dose of abolition history (see the preface), would be all in.[5]

Engaging with this story, too, are conservationists and stewards of Adirondack culture. In 2022, the nonprofit Adirondack Land Trust has pledged to bring more "cultural due diligence" to its research on land awaiting conservation action. So, more human history (like evidence of squatters, Native Americans, or here-and-gone Smith grantees) may figure in title searches of properties on what used to be Smith's gift land. Another august not-for-profit, Adirondack Architectural Heritage (AARCH), known mainly for its preservation advocacy and fine-grained tours of Adirondack landmarks (Great Camps, hunters' clubs, rustic boathouses, historic barns, etc.), now lists a driving tour of Timbuctoo in its long inventory, no small effort given the dearth of cabin sites and other proofs of occupancy.[6]

In 2022, two venerable environmental organizations, the Adirondack Council and Protect the Adirondacks! (PROTECT), hosted presentations on the story of Smith's giveaway—a tacit recognition of all that twenty-first-century environmental activists have in common with New York's Black agrarians before the Civil War. In addition to their mutual respect for the salving, transformational power of the wilderness, both activist generations share a recognition of the forest as a potential commons, and of wild nature as the image of democracy in action, blind to skin color, unimpressed with caste. True, the Black pioneer stalked his soul-forging regenerative moment with a rifle and an axe, and the twenty-first-century hiker-tourist with a day pass and a laminated map, but the expectation in each case of better health and spiritual refreshment in these still, fragrant woods is still very much the same.[7]

The early framing of the Adirondacks as a fount of Black replenishment and self-belief also inflects new projects and initiatives that aim to get Black New Yorkers to the Adirondack Park. Since 1991, Benita Law-Diao from the South Bronx and Albany, an organizer with the national organization Outdoor Afro, has been taking Black New Yorkers—teenagers, families, naturalists, women—into the Adirondacks for canoe trips and hikes. This is work she does for free and with a missionary fervor. "I want people to know what's here!" she says. "Oh my God, to see what it *does* for people. The *joy*." One vanload at a time, Law-Diao is making converts, among them, Governor Kathy Hochul, who in 2022 appointed Law-Diao to the Adirondack Park Agency. She is the first Black board member in its fifty-one years.[8]

The twelve-year-old Adirondack Diversity Initiative (ADI) is another group that has aimed to introduce Black urbanites to the Adirondack region. It can be a tough sell. BIPOC students from New York City at SUNY Potsdam, for instance, may be only fifteen miles from the Blue Line, but to many, the nearby wilderness can seem as distant as Duluth. One shrewd program offers not only outdoor expeditions but affordable provisions that can make the difference between a great first experience and a bust (think tents, sleeping bags, a good raincoat, and Smartwool socks). The ADI has also partnered with Black excursion outfits from Rochester, Albany, and the Bronx to facilitate day hikes, river trips, and tours of the Wild Center and the John Brown Farm.

Particularly hopeful is the Timbuctoo Climate and Careers Summer Institute from the SUNY College of Environmental Science and Forestry (ESF) in Syracuse. Paul Hai, director of the ESF's Adirondack Interpretive Center and an advocate for diversifying the Adirondack workforce, has long argued the benefits of giving Black city students access to a summer stint of experiential learning in the woods. Forest ranger, camp director, mycologist—these prospects need a spark. At Adirondack environmentalist Aaron Mair's suggestion, the "Timbuctoo Pipeline" will partner with Brooklyn's Medger Evers College, a CUNY Brooklyn school with a largely Black enrollment, to set up young Black scholars with boots-on-the-ground summer study at ESF and other upstate campuses. And if this downstate/Adirondack alliance invokes another visionary city-to-wilderness program that helped city Black New Yorkers find the woods in 1846, it should. Both Mair and Hai celebrate this legacy (Mair has introduced members of the Black, Puerto Rican, Hispanic, and Asian state legislative caucus to the Timbuctoo exhibit at the John Brown farm). In 2022, at the urging of the caucus, the state legislature awarded the "Timbuctoo Pipeline" $2.1 million, and gave the same amount again in 2023.[9]

All of these present-day initiatives (I've named only a few) can leave no doubt that the early promise of the Black Woods as a landscape of transformation retains its power to inspire. Not so enduringly charismatic has been the appeal of Black Adirondack farming. No "pipelines" are being organized to revive this part of Smith's old scheme,

Members (with family members) of the New York State Black, Puerto Rican, Hispanic, and Asian Legislative Caucus at the *Dreaming of Timbuctoo* exhibition, 2021. Photographer, Nancie Battaglia, Lake Placid.

and no field trips to Black-owned farms either. Of the eighty-five Black-managed farms in New York State on a recent map from Black Farmers United NYS, not one is in the six-million-acre Adirondack region. In the Finger Lakes, Hudson River valley, and Long Island are clusters of Black farmers. Inside the Blue Line there are none. Racial diversity does not distinguish this region's sixty farmers' markets, or the scores of locally supported small farms that constellate Essex County's eastern half. The nearest Black-owned farm I know of near the Adirondack Park is sixteen miles south of it. In Canajoharie's long-shuttered Beech-Nut baby food plant, E29 Labs will provide five hundred union jobs and a "cultivation facility" for "adult use" cannabis.[10]

We are a long way from Timbuctoo.

We are also a long way from exhausting the uses of this story for scholars. Much remains to be explored. Early in this book, for instance, I identified several Black settlement plans in New York that were inspired by Smith's announcement of 1846. But the reach of Smith's idea extended well beyond the border of his state. After the war, speculators and justice activists hoped to set up freedpeople on farm colonies in the South, and their bids to win Smith's backing ranged from the crudely opportunistic to the fervently altruistic, the grandiose to the shyly hopeful, and the one-page summary to the pamphlet-long petition. Smith heard from bankrupt enslavers wanting him to compensate them for their efforts to change up the plantation (*See how far we've come! No slaves! No overseers! All that bad business done with!*), even while their schemes subverted any prospect of Black-owned farms or homes, mobility, self-employment, or freedom from debt. Northern speculators in the South waxed eloquent about maximizing profits by systematizing labor, but this hardly benefited freedpeople or helped Black laborers gain holdings of their own.[11]

But some appeals were more generous and earnestly progressive, and a few were from abolitionists as long in the racial justice trenches as Gerrit Smith. The Yankee activist Charles Stearns purchased a 1,500-acre farm near Augusta, Georgia, and broke it into plots for Black ex-slaves and white Northerners alike (and Stearns dreamed big, aiming to plant "in every Southern County a New England colony" whose "influence [would] entirely renovate the South"). The devout abolitionist John Gregg Fee organized a Black residential community in Camp Nelson, Kentucky, selling modest house lots at one-fifth the market price to freedmen who were veterans of the US Colored Troops. And Smith said no to all of them, the speculators and idealists and his old Radical Republican allies in Congress who hoped for his support for government land confiscation. No project that might stiffen the animosity the vanquished white South bore toward the North would win his backing. He did not want to see this war revived.[12]

Can we discern the influence of Timbuctoo today? In the South in 2023, young radical agrarians preach the gospel of Black husbandry with the fervor of Charles Ray and Willis Hodges. And no less than the Black agents, they celebrate the links between Black farming, self-sufficiency, civic empowerment, and spiritual health.[13]

Smith's plan also speaks to—and might even be a forerunner—of affirmative action. This justice-driven strategy we call affirmative action wouldn't get its name until 1961, when President Kennedy introduced it in an executive order aiming to fight job discrimination against minorities (later this order would take on discrimination against women). The injustice Gerrit Smith targeted was Black enfranchisement, but his plan, too, strove to equalize a badly uneven playing field. Another commonality these two plans share: the criticism they invited, and do still, for seeming to reward the undeserving and for failing to provide sufficient capitalization, structure, and administrative support. Nor would either scheme be credited for everything it got (or is getting) right. An effort to contextualize Smith's project would both contemporize it and historicize affirmative action as a trend much older than we think.[14]

I glancingly observed the creep of Adirondack gentrification and its impact on the Black grantees, their children, and their communities, but after reading the Adirondack sociologist Eliza Darling's seven-part online essay on the attenuated history of Adirondack displacement and gentrification, I'm sorry I didn't push my inquiry harder. Darling's research has me wondering, for instance, whether, after the Civil War, Black and white families in the Black Woods were dropping from the census in equal measure. What about the comparative rates of bankruptcy and eviction? Would a close review of court responses to debt or petty crime reveal patterns of divergence? What uncomfortable and useful information might a more data-driven inquiry reveal?[15]

Another topic that begs for a deep dive: Smith's land philanthropy in the context of Native American land loss. We speak generally about settler colonialism on wild land from coast to coast, but Adirondack scholars have given this "exempted" region too quick a pass. In *Peter Smith of Peterboro: Furs, Land and Anguish*, Gerrit Smith's hometown biographer, Norman Dann, traces the early nineteenth-century upstate fur trader and land baron Peter Smith's massive land purchases and clears the way for further interrogation. Anecdotal yarns about his unforgiving landlordism are an old story; not so the pattern of opportunism and duplicity Dann notes in Smith Sr.'s long dealings with indigenous people. Put plainly, this speculator's land wealth was gained at the expense of the Haudenosaunee Confederacy, and the inherited wealth that enabled Gerrit Smith's ability to give away his land had roots in toxic soil. How we understand Gerrit Smith's land gifts to impoverished Black New Yorkers will gain from a consciousness of its indebtedness to other people's losses and displacement.[16]

The irony is that several of the leading settler colonizers who benefited from the land fortunes of the Smiths were themselves of indigenous descent. According to the town historian, Lyman E. Eppes's father was a "full blooded Indian." To Amherst census takers in 1900 and 1910, the Hasbrook family aligned itself with the Montauk branch of the Narragansetts (as would, in 1910, the family patriarch, Josiah Hasbrook Sr., from his last home in Sag Harbor). In Saranac Lake in 1910, Morehouses and Gordineers (also spelled Gardineer) claimed

Montauk ancestry (and, rather weirdly, a link to the "Arikara," a tribe in South Dakota). The affiliation is not repeated, but even if it showed up only in a few censuses, we might ponder what this meant to Adirondack families long identified as Black, and wonder, too, whether an allegiance to a native heritage informed their forebears' move to this frontier.[17]

In recent years, some scholars have discerned in the Black Woods a kind of lost utopia. Certainly Gerrit Smith's own Bible-fired perfectionism argues for this view. His first notion of the colony reflected the radical theology that joined his idea of what could be, and what ought to be, to a practical solution; it partook of the ideal from the first. His Black land agents also reveled in the millenarianism of Bible politics and sketched the prospective colony in utopian terms. But since the hopeful rhetoric never translated into a working model, or a plan for one, or the *hope* of one once settlers actually settled, the utopian reading is not mine.[18]

But exceptionalist readings of Adirondack history are a regional tradition, and they are going strong. An ADKX-sponsored webinar on Timbuctoo in 2022, for instance, counted fully *twelve* "Black Suffrage Communities" that Gerrit Smith "set up." And maybe there's no help for this. Maybe the happy habit of exceptionalism is baked into the region's DNA, and if I can learn to love the regional tradition, embrace hyperbole as heritage, I won't feel so confused. A town supervisor assures her audience on Franklin Pioneer Day, "We did not see race." *Really*? But she was speaking for her memory, a proud one, and good for her.[19]

She did not speak, however, for the Black chauffeurs in Saranac Lake's segregated boardinghouses, or the white proprietors of Adirondack cottage colonies, motor courts, and inns whose lodgings went unlisted in the *Negro Motorist Green Book* from 1936 to 1964. They saw race, I'm pretty sure. And the Boy Scouts, school principals, and firemen who blacked up for hometown minstrel fundraisers in every corner of the park did too. The Adirondack editor who wrote the headline, "Colored Man in E-Town Jail for Auto Theft" in 1926 when Marshall Morehouse's cousin stole a car saw race—skin pigment being, in this report, the first proof of criminality. And I'm guessing two Black schoolchildren, Oscar and Ann Morehouse, saw race when a white classmate was cast as a "Nigger Doll" in the Petrova Elementary School Christmas pageant in 1948—and this announced in the same issue of the *Adirondack Daily Enterprise* that reported with grave concern a Georgia governor's new "'white supremacy' program designed to keep 80 per cent of Georgia's negroes from the ballot."[20]

My question is, why idealize? Why gild the lily? It doesn't need the paint. What makes the integrated neighborhoods and hamlets of the Black Woods exemplary is that they *weren't* exceptional. Race was seen, felt, and noted. Why shun the history that was? The Black-founded settlements we know were on the ground were miracle enough without tripling their numbers. Even in the glory days of a rough parity on the frontier, Black and white frontiersmen commingled not from a heedful dream of racial justice but because cooperating made life easier and beat the inefficient alternative. James Brady was admitted to an all-white army company because he was pale enough to pass, and beefing up the company spared his town the burden of a draft. The innkeeper Iddo Osgood urged two Black men to move to North Elba because it didn't have a minister or doctor, and they could meet the need. When a tax collector needed proof that John Thomas owned and worked his property, Thomas's white neighbors gave it. Standing for the Thomases meant the Thomases would stand for them.

Charles B. Ray, who more than any agent trusted the genius of expediency, had it right all along. It would be the face-to-face encounter that sparked the intermittent bonfires of an equalitarian frontier. That's where I find the best of the Black Woods: in all the messy, needful dealings that make room for the human factor—dealings that often leave me a little hungry, because the closer-in the zoom, the more I want to know. *Too bad!* says history with a shrug. *I'm done here. You're on your own.* Simeon Hasbrook climbed Whiteface. This much we can be sure of. There's a letter that reports it. *But did he slow for blueberries? Could he see Vermont?* The Hampton Singers stayed with the Eppeses when they visited Lake Placid. *Were there fireflies that evening? Did they walk to John Brown's grave?* And the Alabama sharecropper Robert McCray who got $300 for his late father's Adirondack gift lot . . . *what did his wife say? What happened next?* John Brown wrote Willis Hodges thirty-five letters, almost all of these destroyed when Brown was put under arrest. *What was in them? Names of fugitives? Details of routes?* I want answers! Maybe, you as well. And the history won't get us there, won't say what wasn't saved.

But it gets us this far. It gets us to the point of asking—to wondering, and then imagining. Can there be a better view?

ACKNOWLEDGMENTS

If it weren't for Betsy Folwell, my longtime, now retired editor at *Adirondack Life* magazine, I would not have gotten started and then stuck on writing articles about Adirondack ethnic, social, and migratory history. And if I hadn't written what I did, Martha Swan, director of the social action group John Brown Lives!, wouldn't have urged me to curate the exhibit *Dreaming of Timbuctoo*, which gave rise to this book.

So thanks, first thing, to these two friends for their long faith.

As for other long companions: these books are in my bibliography, but even so, I name them here to salute their uncommon usefulness to me in this endeavor. *The Plains of Abraham*, by the late Lake Placid town historian, Mary MacKenzie, was never far from my desk. Notwithstanding our sometimes vastly different interpretations of the Black experience in the region, her long chapter on North Elba's Black community was the first to recognize the Smith grantees as Adirondackers and stakeholders in her town's story, and my debt to this pioneering dive is great. Philip Terrie's *Contested Terrain* and *Forever Wild*, touchstones of Adirondack cultural history, stretched my understanding of what the Black pioneers experienced, and the social historian Sally Svenson's wide-ranging *Blacks in the Adirondacks* offered a panoramic overview of regional Black history that helped me keep the Black Woods of Gerrit Smith in perspective.

On the great age of antislavery reform and resistance, I never stopped referencing Benjamin Quarles's many books, or the authoritative *Black Abolitionist Papers*, or checking in with John Stauffer's *The Black Hearts of Men*, for his inquiry into an interracial friendship among prominent radical reformers bound by their interest in Gerrit Smith's idea. No biography of John Brown was more helpful to me than David Reynolds's authoritative effort, or more respectful of the Black community in North Elba. And a few books that had nothing whatsoever to do with Adirondack history, like Patricia Limerick's *The Legacy of Conquest* and Jonathan Spiro's *Defending the Master Race*, gave me sturdy guideposts too.

That 2001 exhibition, *Dreaming of Timbuctoo*, the inspiration for this book project, was much enhanced by archival research from several volunteers, and many of their bold findings are represented here. So to Cliff Oliver, Charles Touhey, Jeff Jones, Suzy Doolittle, Claudia Blackler, Bill Herbert, Shirley Morgan, Mary Hotaling, Cherrie Burgess and her late husband, the beloved Brother Yusuf Burgess, and, always and again, Martha Swan of John Brown Lives!—my stubborn gratitude at the thought of how much we got done.

Assistance and encouragement met one request of mine after another in libraries and archives at the Adirondack Experience (formerly the Adirondack Museum); the Adirondack History Museum; New-York Historical Society; Morgan Library; New York State Archives and State Library; Hart-Cluett Museum, Research Room, in Troy; Special Collections Research Center, Bird Library, Syracuse University; Special Collections, Feinberg Library, SUNY Plattsburgh; the National Archives and Records Administration in Washington, DC; Saratoga Springs Public Library; Saranac Lake Free Library, Adirondack Room; Lake Placid Public Library; and of course, the county archives of Essex, Franklin, Herkimer, and Hamilton. The Essex County Archives in the courthouse is one especially sweet place to work.

All of the content-rich websites that now make primary material so accessible have been a blessing beyond measure. I leaned particularly hard on Ancestry.com, Accessible Archives, NYS Historic Newspapers, Fulton County History, the West Virginia Memory Project, and Newspapers.com—sleep-thieving, eye-blearing rabbit holes every one.

Shrewd leads came my way from John Brown biographer and scholar Lou DeCaro, Donna Burdick, town historian of Smithfield, NY, Cynthia Halberson of the Jones Library, Amherst, MA, and Patty Wiley of the Middlesex Historical Society in Vermont. Brendan Mills, supervisor of the John Brown State Historic Site, Debra Kimok of SUNY Plattsburgh's Special Collections, Margaret Gibbs, Jenifer Kuba, Lindsay Pontius, all of the Adirondack History Museum, and Jerry Pepper of the Adirondack Experience directed me to sources unexpected. To the long line of researchers and scholars who have benefited from the expertise of James Folts of the New York State Archives, I add my name and awe. The independent scholars Margaret Bartley, Karl Beckwith Smith, Tom Calarco, Norm Dann, David Fiske, Morris Glenn, Mary Hotaling, Carol Kammen, Hadley Kruczek-Aaron, Lee Manchester, Don Papson, Ken Perry, Curt Stager, Paul and Mary Liz Stewart, and John Warren all gifted me with great ideas and suggestions, and Greg Furness, especially, never met a query he couldn't run to ground.

Greg and Gladys Furness, Jane Haugh, Chris Jerome, John Stauffer, Phil Terrie, and Chase Twitchell read versions of this book. Each brought to it a discrete perspective and special expertise and alerted me to key points, thematic possibilities, and blunders I had missed. And for the last section on memory and memorials, I could have had no better reader than the late Michael Kammen.

I think it's fair to say the academy isn't famous for its warm regard for independent scholars, and of course, our own sullen expectation of indifference doesn't help. But I got very lucky with the anonymous readers who vetted this manuscript for Cornell University Press. They all know this territory well, and reviewed it with care and gratifying interest. They held it to a high standard, and gifted me with tough advice, most of which I took.

A Hackman Fellowship from the New York State Archives plunged me into the substantial bounty of the Essex County tax redemption records. Two grants from the Furthermore Foundation, an initiative of the J. M. Kaplan Fund, let me extend my research and grace the book with maps and artwork too. Two residencies at the Blue Mountain Center in Blue Mountain Lake were much valued. And thanks are owed to the editors Annie Stoltie, Lisa Bramen, and Niki Kourofsky, of *Adirondack Life*. Whether they gave me room to write articles that informed this book (on poorhouses, impoverished contract farmers, squatters, peddlers, blackface minstrel shows, conservation and eugenics, or the Klan) or the chance to rework research for this book into articles (on Black Civil War veterans, Smith's land agents, or the scuttling of a state plan for an interpretative center at John Brown's home), I have been one lucky freelancer, and am very much obliged.

My agent Malaga Baldi of Baldi Books has been all in from the day she finished reading the manuscript, and how this project might have fared without her good faith and straight talk is hard to imagine. Michael McGandy, my acquisitions editor at Cornell University Press, was for this book before it *was* a book, and for that confidence alone I am in his debt. Both book and writer were strengthened by his unsentimental rigor, his regard for organization, and his wide-angle perspective on this history. Associate editor Clare Jones, tasked with shepherding this slow learner through my management of image logs, permissions, TIFFs, and JPGs, had a thankless job she dispatched with steely calm.

Marketing is new to me but the mavens at CUP were not discouraged, and made this new world legible and fun. The book itself was much improved by the sharp eye of its copyeditor, Eric Levy. And I got really very lucky with my production editor Karen Laun, who fielded a blizzard of eleventh-hour tweaks and edits. Thanks also to my proofreader, Alan Berolzheimer, and to the challenge-loving reference librarians in my hometown public library, and most of all, to my friend and neighbor Mitch Cohen, who saw me through the long home stretch of readying this book for production with patience and unfailing cheer. May every digitally clueless author be so blessed.

Writers who work slowly ask a lot of people close to us. After a while, our friends get bored, and maybe frustrated or uneasy. *She's never going to finish, so don't ask.* It's from kindness, so no blame! But for my friends who did keep asking—Martha Swan, Dennis Johnson, Valerie Merians, Chris Shaw, Steve Stern, Debra Spark, Karen Brooks, Jane Haugh, Marc Woodworth, Susan Bokan, Bruce Kennett, Sylvia Davatz, Sally Brady, and Louise, Sara, and Carol (sister, sister-in-law, and cousin)—God bless. I did it. I hit send.

I could also thank my husband Jack Nicholson, and our son Jesse who grew up with this project, but it would be like thanking my own breath. That's how livening has been their interest and support.

NOTES

Preface

1. David Gibson, "A Living, Growing Memorial to Brother Yusuf," *Adirondack Almanack*, 9/12/2019; Lauren Stanforth, "Youth Leader, Brother Yusuf, 64," *Times Union* (Albany), 12/10/2014; Frederick Rasmussen, "Students Learn the Importance of a Bond with Nature," *Baltimore Sun*, 1/15/2011; Mark Frankel, "Xbox Detox," *Sierra*, 7/1/2010; Brother Yusuf Burgess, "Keynote Address," 2nd Annual Michigan No Child Left Behind Coalition Summit 2020, University of Michigan–Dearborn, 6/23/2010; Yusuf Burgess, conversations with the author, 1999–2012.

2. Morrison, *Playing in the Dark*, 39.

3. Worth recalling here is the historian George Frederickson's observation about German antisemitism—the linchpin of Nazi ideology at a time when the German Jewish population was less than 1 percent. Frederickson, *Racism*, 126–27. In the colonial era, whiteness underscored the white male's assertion of civic standing and entitlement. It did this for an ascendant master class of planters in Virginia (Morgan, *American Slavery, American Freedom*, 386), for white working men in the north (Roediger, *Wages of Whiteness*, 20), and for Irish immigrants striving for recognition as vote-worthy whites (Ignatiev, *How the Irish Became White*). Blackness, the go-to point of contrast for all things *un*-free and despised, underscored the value of white freedom, and Emancipation would not easily dissolve the conflation of Black skin with freedom's opposite; the idea of Blackness as freedom's counterpoint was too useful and entrenched. According to a search of NYS Historic Newspapers (https://nyshistoricnewspapers.org/), from 1840 to 1960, the word "nigger" appeared in Essex, Franklin, Warren, and Clinton County newspapers over two thousand times, and "Rastus," a stock character in minstrelsy and typically the butt of jokes he never gets, crops up a slew of times in Essex County newspapers between 1849 and 1960. Svenson, *Blacks in the Adirondacks*, 99–102, 151–52.

4. On the convergence of the eugenics movement with the Adirondack conservation discourse, see Godine, "Conservation's Dark Side."

5. Watson, *Military and Civil History*, 220; Sylvester, *Historical Sketches*, 139; Smith, *History of Essex County*, 664. David Reynolds (*John Brown, Abolitionist*, 164–65) observes that John Brown embraced the Puritan connection, and that his contemporaries reveled in it. Samuel Ridley Howe proudly pictured Brown as a representative "of the Puritan militant order." Howe's wife, Julia, dubbed Brown "a Puritan of the Puritans" (Reynolds, *John Brown, Abolitionist*, 292). Historian F. E. Chadwick (who declared North Elba as "wholly unfitted by climate

and production to the negro race," heralded Brown's "Puritan stock" in *Causes of the Civil War, 1859–1861*, v. 19 (Harpers, 1906, 69). Brown, mused the cultural critic and author Charles Eliot Norton in 1913, was "a man born out of time. . . . He belonged to the Covenanters, with the Puritans." Peterson, *John Brown*, 81, 179n1; Blight, *Race and Reunion*.

6. Jones, "They Called It Timbucto." Russell Banks's novel *Cloudsplitter* (HarperCollins, 1998) roused a surge of interest in Timbuctoo, most of it enthusiastic. But the North Elba historian Mary MacKenzie was no fan. Banks brought fugitives into his story. He killed off one character whose life, in actuality, was long. "Already [Banks's novel] has done irreparable damage to local history," MacKenzie wrote, "and caused me no end of trouble. . . . For 36 years I have labored very hard to eliminate the kind of nonsense that Banks spouts . . . and then [he] comes along and overnight destroys my efforts." (Mary MacKenzie, letter to the editor, *Orion*, 11/20/1997, LPPL archives; and MacKenzie, "Regarding Russell Banks's Novel, 'Cloudsplitter,'" in *More from the Plains*, 97–101.) But the outrage of a town historian who saw no value in "a fictitious biography of a famous man" was no match for public opinion. Banks's readers were looking for the gong of truth, not the rat-a-tat of fact, and did not miss what they weren't after. Banks's "nonsense" limned a world beyond the reach of historical method. If the novelist went where historians feared to tread, this was, after all, his job.

7. Caleb McDaniel (Rice), Hadley Kruczek-Aaron (SUNY Potsdam), Daegan Miller (Cornell), and Lynne M. Feeley (Harvard) have all plumbed the meanings of Timbuctoo and its representations. Kruczek-Aaron, an anthropologist, has for several years conducted field digs on the gift lot of the grantee Lyman Eppes, at John Brown's North Elba home, and on other nearby land with ties to Timbuctoo. In May 2014, the Northern Lights Community Choir performed the composer Glenn McClure's *Timbuctoo: An Abolition Oratorio* in the Adirondack hamlet of Saranac Lake. McClure's later composition, *Promised Land: An Adirondack Folk Opera*, also was inspired by stories of Timbuctoo. See Peter Crowley, "Hymns of a Promised Land," *ADE*, 5/18/2016. The North Country Underground Railroad Museum (https://www.northcountryunderground railroad.com/museum.php) opened in Ausable Chasm in May 2011. While its emphasis is on the stories of fugitives moving through the Champlain Valley toward Canada, it has also explored the stories of undocumented immigration in the region, and human trafficking today.

Introduction

1. Donaldson, *History of the Adirondacks*, 2:6.
2. GS to TW, CBR, and JMS, Peterboro, NY, 8/1/1846, GSP. Unless otherwise indicated, Smith's letters, speeches, discourses, and circulars referenced in this book are housed in the Gerrit Smith Papers at Syracuse University. Pamphlets, broadsides, speeches, and news articles are identified as such. The names of sender and recipient indicate a posted letter. When Lyman Epps Jr. mentioned Smith's land gifts, he did not invoke an equal voting rights campaign for Black New Yorkers. "'John Brown' by Gerrit Smith," broadleaf, 8/15/1867, JB/BBS Coll./WVMP, and Frothingham, *Gerrit Smith*, 253–59.

3. Gellman and Quigley, *Jim Crow New York*, 73–78, and Ned Benton, "Dating the Start and End of Slavery in New York," 2017, https://nyslavery.com mons.gc.cuny.edu/dating-the-start-and-end-of-slavery-in-new-york/#:~:text.

4. On Smith's life and career, see Frothingham, *Gerrit Smith*; Harlow, *Gerrit Smith*; Dann, *Practical Dreamer*; Stauffer, *Black Hearts of Men*, 1–7.

5. GS, "Gerrit Smith's Reply," *Peoples' Rights*, 7/8/1844.

6. Field, *Politics of Race*, app. B, 236–37. In 1846 Franklin County voters went 58.8 percent for suffrage, Essex County 70.6 percent, and Clinton 72.8 percent, the highest equal rights vote in New York. In 1860, New York voters, once again, shot down equal suffrage, and in these three Adirondack counties, support for Black voting rights was also in decline.

7. Editorial, *New York Herald*, 12/29/1874; editorial, *New York Daily Tribune*, 12/28/1874; "Obituary," "The Late Gerrit Smith," "The Era of Moral Politics," "Local Miscellany: The Late Gerrit Smith," *NYT*, 12/29–31/1874; "Gerrit Smith," *Christian Recorder*, 1/7/1875.

8. "Late Gerrit Smith"; Henry Highland Garnet, "Obituary," *New York Herald*, 1/1/1875.

9. "An Old Abolitionist Dead," *NYT*, 7/26/1884. Likely the two daughters who came to view Smith's body were Florence and Henrietta Cordelia. At this time, Ray's daughter Charlotte was in Washington, DC, practicing law.

10. Chaplain E. O. Glavis to GS, Newark, 7/15/1865; George W. Jennings to GS, NYC, 9/26/1873; Rhys Jones to GS, Utica, 8/2/1870; Godine, "Abolitionist and the Land Reformer."

11. See Cox, *Bone and Sinew*, on nineteenth-century Black settlements in the Old Northwest Territory; Vincent, *Southern Seed, Northern Soil*, on Black and mixed-race communities in Indiana; and "Malaga Island," Maine: An Encyclopedia, accessed 1/17/2023, https://maineanencyclopedia.com/malaga-island.

12. On historians and writers who claimed that Smith's 1846–47 land distribution plan was meant for Southern fugitives, see chap. 5, note 30.

13. Thomas Wentworth Higginson, "A Visit to John Brown's Household in 1859," in *Contemporaries*, 219–43.

14. Frothingham, *Gerrit Smith*, 112–13; Tanner, "Gerrit Smith," 32.

15. Du Bois, *John Brown*, 111; Dyson, "Gerrit Smith's Effort," 358. In 1923, this rote narrative was reinforced when the Black historian Carter Woodson ascribed the failure of Smith's giveaway to "the infelicity of the soil and the lack of initiative on the part of the Negroes" (*Chicago Defender*, 4/28/1923). On the routing of the New York State Historic Site's plans for an interpretive center at the John Brown farm in the late 1970s, see chap. 17, and Godine, "Ambushed."

16. Alice Paden's afterword to Svenson, *Blacks in the Adirondacks*, 247–74; and Alice Paden, interviews by the author, 1/31/2011, 12/9/2010.

1. He Feeds the Sparrow

1. Chapter 4, "Humanity," in Frothingham's *Gerrit Smith*, abounds with details of Smith's work routines and largesse.

2. John Thomas to GS, Bloomingdale, Essex County, 8/26/1872; L. D. Tanner to GS, NY, 7/21/1872; GS to President Andrew White, Cornell University, 5/8/1872.

3. In early 1846, Smith published a booklet advertising his sale land, much of it in northern New York. Smith, *Gerrit Smith's Land Auction*; *ECR*, 3/14/1846, 4/18/1846, and 4/25/1846; Gellman and Quigley, *Jim Crow New York*, 73–78; GS to TW, CBR, and JMS, 8/1/1846. The "mean and wicked" voter suppression ruling for Black New Yorkers would continue to keep them disenfranchised until the federal ratification of the Fifteenth Amendment in 1870, when New York's property requirement was nullified and equal voting rights for all New Yorkers was assured.

4. Gellman and Quigley, *Jim Crow New York*, 249–59; "About the Colored Conventions," https://coloredconventions.org/about-conventions/; GS to TW, CBR, and JMS, Peterboro, 11/14/1846.

5. GS to TW, CBR, and JMS, 8/1/1846.

6. "Gerrit Smith's Tour through Saratoga, Warren, Essex and Clinton," *AP*, 6/25/1845.

7. "The Suffrage Question—Who Are the Best Friends to the Negroes," *ECR*, 4/18/1846.

8. "Gerrit Smith's Response to the Colored Citizens of Albany," *AP*, 3/13/1846; GS to E. S. Bailey of Brookfield, A. Raymond of Eaton, and F. Rice of Cazenovia, 4/10/1846; Volpe, "Liberty Party"; and Kraut and Field, "Politics versus Principles," 102–3. On June 10, 1846, the *Albany Evening Journal* opined, "The admission of Texas, and the question of Free Suffrage, were in the hands of Abolitionists. The Liberty Party in this State could have given the country an Anti-Texas President in 1844; and in 1846 they could have obtained the Right of Suffrage for the colored man. But Mr. Smith and his 'editors and orators' strangely refused to act with the opponents of Texas and the friends of Free Suffrage. . . . As the fifteen thousand abolitionists amongst us gave the state to Polk—Polk to the People—Texas to the nation, and slavery to Texas, so they may now give a majority of the members of Congress to the loco focos, and *California to Slavery!*"

9. Hyde, *Gift*, 56.

10. Douglas Strong's *Perfectionist Politics* offers an elegant history of "Bible politics" in the Burned-Over District and its call for antislavery political engagement in daily life. Also see Gerrit Smith's "Discourse on Creeds, and Ecclesiastical Machinery," Peterboro, 2/21/1858, on the value of a place-based spiritual community unburdened by "creeds and churches and a clerical order of men."

11. Stauffer, *Black Hearts of Men*, 103–5.

12. See Frothingham, *Gerrit Smith*, 44–93, on Smith's conversion to "Bible politics" and the founding of the Church of Peterboro; GS, *Be Natural! A Discourse*, a twenty-four-page treatise, 11/20/1864.

13. Friedman, "Gerrit Circle," 23. Friedman notes that Smith and his upstate allies were cut from the same homespun: small-town men of middle age, descended mostly from New Englanders, educated, pious, friends of temperance, and compelled by the potential of local political action.

14. GS to Elder Kingsley, 9/1/1845; Sernett, *North Star Country*, 294n68; George Thomas, Esq., "Personal Recollections of Gerrit Smith," 1/5/1875, Onondaga County Public Library, NY; GS to "Mr. [Ba---son]," Peterboro,

3/16/1845; W. J. Wilbur to GS, Peterboro, 7/3/1871; GS to James Barnett, Peterboro, 4/14/1862; GS to Laura Bosworth, Peterboro, 2/27/1847.

15. JMS to GS, NYC, 2/6/1850.

16. JB to Owen Brown (his father), Springfield, MA, 1/14/1849, in Ruchames, *A John Brown Reader*, 67.

17. John Thomas to GS, Bloomingdale, 8/26/1872. John Thomas's thirty-three-line obituary in the *Malone Palladium* in 1895 identified Ezekiel Merrick of Queen Anne County as his enslaver. Thomas names Merrick as his enslaver.

18. Fields, *Slavery and Freedom*, 18, 174; *Minutes of the National Convention*, 39.

19. *The Emancipator*, 3/14/1842; Pasternak, *Rise Now*, 38; Calarco, *Underground Railroad*, 90, 196–97; Grover, *Make a Way Somehow*, 80.

20. *GSLB*, 88; Seaver, *Historical Sketches*, 173. Thomas's gift lot was at the northern border of Franklin Township on the town of Bellmont line. So plodding was the pace of settlement in Bellmont that in 1822 the state assembly offered land to anyone who cleared fifteen acres and built a house in Bellmont in five years' time. No other town in Franklin County made such an offer, perhaps because no other was so innocent of charm. Smith, *Map of Franklin County*.

21. John Thomas to GS, Bloomingdale, 8/26/1872.

22. Kezier King to GS, McGrawville, NY, 8/16/1861; Harriet Sykes to GS, Hannibal, NY, 10/26/1858; Mary Pryne to GS, Warners, Onondaga County, NY, 7/11/1870; John Lagrow to GS, New York Central College, McGrawville, NY, 8/12/1852; J. B. F. Walker to GS, Lincoln, VT, 4/4/1860; Robert Spring to GS, Philadelphia, 10/23/1871.

23. GS to Gov. Washington Hunt, 3/5/1852; Stauffer, *Black Hearts of Men*, 105–9. Though Smith broke with the Millerites after the "Great Disappointment," Stauffer discerns a lasting influence on Smith's thinking. His immersion in Millerite apocalyptic theology "contributed to Smith's acceptance of violence," thus easing Smith's eventual allegiance to John Brown.

24. On Smith's Congressional career, see chap 10; Douglass, *NS*, 5/18/1849.

25. "Proceedings of the New York Anti-slavery Convention, held at Utica, October 21, and New York Anti-slavery State Society, held at Peterboro, October 22, 1835," GSP. For a summary of this transformative moment in upstate abolition history, see Sernett, *North Star Country*, 49–53; Frothingham, *Gerrit Smith*, 164–68.

26. Burdick and Dann, *Heaven and Peterboro*; Frothingham, *Gerrit Smith*, 98.

27. Harrold, *Rise of Aggressive Abolitionism*, 123–39. Smith told convention-goers that the letter he read aloud was penned by a fugitive, knowing this would especially outrage and alarm proslavery Southerners. "The 'Black' Convention," *NASS*, 9/26/1850. See Humphreys, *"Agitate! Agitate! Agitate!"*; "Sinbadism Outdone," *Poughkeepsie Journal*, 8/24/1850. Among Southern newspapers that denounced Smith's convention were the *Clarksville (TN) Jeffersonian*, the *Tarboro (NC) Press*, the *Mississippi Free Trader* (Natchez), and the *Baltimore Sun* (Maryland).

28. "The 'Black' Convention," *Gallatin Tenth Legion*, Gallatin, TN, republished in the *National Anti-Slavery Standard*, 9/26/1850.

29. Sernett, *North Star Country*, 136–45; GS, *Address Reported by Gerrit Smith to the Jerry Rescue Convention: Held in Syracuse, October 1, 1857.*

30. GS, "Address of the Liberty Party"; GS, "Anti-Fugitive Slave Law Meeting" (printed document), Syracuse, NY, written 1/9/1851, Gilder Lehrman Collection, https://www.gilderlehrman.org/collection/glc0471716. Also see GS to CBR, 11/16/1848, and GS circular, 12/29/1848, GSP.

31. [GS], "Autobiographical Sketch of the Life of Gerrit Smith," n.d., 1856. For an inquiring reading of the essay-length autobiography Smith penned in middle age, see McKivigan and McKivigan, "'He Stands Like Jupiter'"; Editorial, *New-York Tribune*, 8/3/1857; "Letter from Gerrit Smith," 8/10/1857; GS to L. P. Brockett, Esq., 10/9/1861.

32. Salmon Brown to F. B. Sanborn, 8/8/1901, Portland, OR, JB/BBS Coll./ WVMP. Early biographies of Brown tear through his Adirondack chapter the sooner to plunge into his dramatic, insurrectionary career. Twenty-first-century biographies have accorded Brown's North Elba stay more respect. See Reynolds, *John Brown, Abolitionist*; Stauffer, *Black Hearts of Men*; Sernett, *North Star Country*; DeCaro, *"Fire from the Midst of You"*; and Laughlin-Schultz, *Tie that Bound Us*, on the Browns' years of homesteading and intermittent community building in North Elba.

33. "Gerrit Smith, on Kansas," speech, 8/8/1856; "Kansas," *New York Daily Times*, 7/11/1856. Smith addressed a Kansas convention at Kremlin Hall, Buffalo, NY, on July 10, 1856.

34. See Renehan, *Secret Six*, 122–23, 141–44, 153, 162–63, on Smith's contributions to this group and to Brown. Lead funders of Brown's militant agenda are described as well in Oates, *To Purge This Land*, 226–31; Reynolds, *John Brown, Abolitionist*, 248, 254–55, 258–59, 266, 283, 290; Stauffer, *Black Hearts of Men*, 198–200; and Sernett, *North Star Country*, 208–13.

35. Brown's warriors wounded nine men and killed four. His party lost ten men in the raid, including Brown's sons Oliver and Watson. Two more raiders were hanged with Brown: John Anthony Copeland Jr. and Shields Green. The historian Merrill D. Peterson notes four reasons why Brown's trial struck many as both spurious and rushed: Brown, badly injured, was not offered his own choice of lawyer. Nor was he in shape to mount his own defense. The State of Virginia was charging him with treason, but treason was a crime against a nation. And he could never hope for an impartial jury in Charles Town, only seven miles from Harpers Ferry. Peterson, *John Brown*, 12–13.

36. McKivigan and Leveille, "'Black Dream.'"

37. GS to Charles Sumner, 6/7/1860; McKivigan and Leveille, "'Black Dream.'" Smith's case manager during his stay at the Utica Psychiatric Asylum was John Perdue Gray, MD, a radical innovator in biological psychiatric theory and the esteemed director of the asylum from 1854 to 1886.

38. GS, speech in Albany, 2/27/1863, in GS, *Speeches and Letters*, 1:1864; "Letter to Mrs. Stanton on the Presidential Question," 6/6/1864, in ibid., 2:14–18; "Speech at Young Men's Mass Convention," Syracuse, 9/3/1863, in ibid., 1:45–51; A. L. Scott to GS, Oswego, 11/28/1863; Donna Burdick, "The Village Green," *Snippets: From the Hills of Smithfield*, Smithfield Community Association., 1995, vol. 2; "To-Day's Report," *Janesville (WI) Daily Gazette*, 3/20/1863.

39. GS to President Andrew Johnson, 4/24/1865; GS to Charles Sumner, 2/5/1866; "Speech of Gerrit Smith (to His Neighbors)," Peterboro, 6/22/1872.

40. "Gerrit Smith on the Duty of the North to the South," *Richmond Whig*, 7/19/1867; GS, "On the Fort Pillow and Plymouth Massacres, April 26, 1864," in GS, *Speeches and Letters*, 2:7–13.

41. Blight, *Race and Reunion*, 57–63.

42. Blight, *Race and Reunion*, 57–63.

43. "Southern Sentiment," *St. Lawrence Plaindealer*, 11/3/1874; GS to George T. Downing, "Equal Rights for Blacks and Whites," 3/6/1874. Smith published this letter to his friend as a one-page flyer for widespread circulation. See Syracuse University Libraries, Digital Collections, https://digitalcollections.syr.edu/Documents/Detail/gerrit-smith-to-george-t.-downing-on-equal-rights-for-blacks-and-whites/2513.

44. "'John Brown' by Gerrit Smith," broadleaf, 8/15/1867, JB/BBS Coll./WVMP. Smith's secretary, Caleb Calkins, visited the Browns' home; Smith apparently did not. Alexis Hinckley to GS, 7/24/1864, and "The Truth about John Brown's Farm," *ECR*, 2/29/1896; Charles M. Sherman to GS, Chenango County, NY, 6/15/1873; Frank M. Terry to GS, Liverpool, NY, 12/9/1873; William J. Fowler to GS, Rochester, NY, 12/12/1873; Victor Kingsley to GS, Onondaga County, NY, 8/14/1866; Robert Spring to GS, Philadelphia, 10/23/1871.

45. "Tale of Gerrit Smith behind Adirondack Suit," *NYT*, 11/19/1904.

2. Gerrit Smith Country

1. Sumner Stebbins to GS, Unionville, PA, 5/14/68; Frothingham, *Gerrit Smith*, 33.

2. GS to W. L. Chaplin, Saratoga Springs, NY, 5/26/1845, published as "Gerrit Smith's Tour through Saratoga, Warren, Essex and Clinton," *AP*, 6/25/1845; Frothingham, *Gerrit Smith*, 29–34; Stauffer, *Black Hearts of Men*, 102–3, 315; GS, "Gerrit Smith's Tour." Several of the land agents Smith visited on this tour were pioneers who had bought acreage from him years before. From Duxbury, Vermont, Thomas Nash took his family to the Plains of Abraham in 1839. Smith sold him land, and by 1857, Nash was urging Smith to float North Elba a loan for a road extension that might "open up a large tract of feasible land for farming purposes which will enable the [emigrant] to push back into the woods without *all* the disadvantages of a pioneer life," and would "not only help to make sales [of Smith's unsold land] but will greatly enhance the value." T. S. Nash to GS, *NE*, 7/20/1857.

3. Smith, *History of Essex County*, 660; GS, "Gerrit Smith's Tour."

4. GS, "Gerrit Smith's Tour"; Sterngass, "African American Workers"; Smith, *History of Essex County*, 663; Donaldson, *History of the Adirondacks*, 1:347; White, *Adirondack Country*, 195–96.

5. Brown, *Reverend Abel Brown*; Calarco, *Underground Railroad*, 84, 89–90. So impressed was Smith with the antislavery scene in Clinton County that he declared it would be "the first [county] in our State to throw off its political shackles and stand forth for the slave." GS, "Gerrit Smith's Tour."

6. John L. O'Sullivan on "manifest destiny," in *New York Morning News*, 12/27/1845, quoted in Meinig, *Shaping of America*, 2:211; William H. Prescott to Charles Sumner, 5/15/1846, in Wolcott, *Correspondence*, 596, 597; Meinig, *Shaping of America*, 2:222; Wilentz, *Rise of American Democracy*, 585.

7. Wilentz, *Rise of American Democracy*, 585-86, 594-601.

8. Wilentz, *Rise of American Democracy*, 598; Meinig, *Shaping of America*, 2: 299-301; Horton and Horton, *In Hope of Liberty*, 102-3; Hon. James Harlan, New York, speech, US Senate, 1/4/1860; Meinig, *Shaping of America*, 2:300-302; Wilentz, *Rise of American Democracy*, 594-601, 605-10, and DeVoto, *Year of Decision*, 297-99; Wilentz, *Rise of American Democracy*, 597; Foner, *Free Soil*, 266-67.

9. Frothingham, *Gerrit Smith*, 99-101; DeVoto, *Year of Decision*, 214.

10. DeVoto, *Year of Decision*, chap. 1, 4-48.

11. GS to TW, CBR, JMS, CBR, Peterboro, 8/1/1846; GS, *Address to the Three Thousand Colored Citizens*; William Tyson, Ulysses Vidal, Patrick Reason, Newport Henry, James McCune Smith, Theodore S. Wright, Charles B. Ray, and John Zuille to Wesley Bailey, "A Central Committee of Colored Citizens Organized for the Extension of the Right of Suffrage," *Utica Liberty Press*, 2/5/1846. Later in 1846, each of these signatories received a gift deed from Gerrit Smith.

12. GS to TW, CBR, and JMS, 8/1/1846; Lewis Tappan to GS, NY, 7/27/1846. James McCune Smith's many elegant and soulful letters to Gerrit Smith are collected in Stauffer, *Works*. Also see Stauffer, *Black Hearts of Men*, 68-69, 125-27, 144-55, 198-99, 275-77.

13. GS to TW, CBR, and JMS, 8/1/1846, 9/9/1846.

14. GS to TW, CBR, and JMS, 8/1/1846.

15. GS to TW, CBR, and JMS, 8/1/1846.

3. Three Agents and Their Reasons

1. Harris, *Shadow of Slavery*, 76. On disease and morbidity among Black city families at midcentury, see Freeman, *Free Negro*, 170-71; Hodges, *Root and Branch*, 194-96, 230-31; Litwack, *North of Slavery*, 169; and Harris, *Shadow of Slavery*, 265-66.

2. On McCune Smith and his work, see Stauffer, *Black Hearts of Men*, 65-69, 123-27; Stauffer, *Works*, xix-xlii; Peterson, *Black Gotham*, 130-32, 156-58, 168-70, 219-22; Blight, "In Search of Learning"; Charles Bennett Ray, "Black Churches in New York City, 1840," *CA*, published in *African American Religious History: A Documentary Witness*, ed. Milton C. Sernett (Duke, 1999), 220; Davis, *Problem of Slavery*, 216-25; JMS to GS, 12/17-18/1846, 12/28-31/1846.

3. Morgan, "Education and Medical Practice"; Litwack, *North of Slavery*, 154-55, 180. Litwack shares a story from Henry B. Fearon's 1818 *Sketches of America*: "After witnessing the ouster of a prospective Negro customer from a New York barber shop, an astonished English visitor requested an explanation from the Negro barber. 'Aye, I guess you were not raised here,' the barber replied. 'Now I reckon you do not know my boss [also a Negro] would not have a single gentleman come to his store . . . if he cut colored men.'"

4. AICP, *First Report*, 8. Also see Coleman, *Going to America*, 163; Freeman, *Free Negro*, 166; Green, *Glance at New York*, 175, quoted in Anbinder, *Five Points*,

82; *New York Tribune*, 7/1/1847, in Coleman, *Going to America*, 119; Clay Mc-Shane and Joel Tarr, "The Centrality of the Horse to the Nineteenth Century American City," in Mohl, *Making of Urban America*, 105–30.

5. Granick, *Underneath New York*, 16, 33, 40–41; Burrows and Wallace, *Gotham*, 787; Joseph Patrick Byrne, *Encyclopedia of Pestilence, Pandemics, and Plagues* (Greenwood, 2008), 101.

6. Stauffer, *Black Hearts of Men*, 66, 69; "Report on the Social Condition of the People of Color around New York City," *NS*, 4/10/1851; "Flight from the City," *NYT*, 6/3/1852; Burrows and Wallace, *Gotham*, 774.

7. CBR, "Prejudice," *CA*, 9/26/1840; Work, "Life of Charles B. Ray," 365–66; Freeman, *Free Negro*, 298–303; Burrows and Wallace, *Gotham*, 556–60, 596–98; CBR, *Eighth Annual Report of the City Missionary to the Destitute Colored Population* (1852), 2. Biographical information about Charles Ray is substantially drawn from a short memoir by his daughters Henrietta Cordelia Ray and Florence Ray (*Sketch of the Life of Rev. Charles B. Ray*) and the scholarly essay "The Life of Charles B. Ray," by M. N. Work.

8. Thomas Dresser, *African-Americans on Martha's Vineyard: From Enslavement to Presidential Visit* (Arcadia, 2010), 29, 43–44; Harris, *Shadow of Slavery*, 275; Ripley, et al., *Black Abolitionist Papers*, 3:470, 484n, 2n; Swift, *Black Prophets*, 19–46; *Rights of All*, 5/29/1829 and 6/12/1829; "Agricultural Pursuits," *CA*, 11/4/1837.

9. Harris, *Shadow of Slavery*, 275; Ripley et al., *Black Abolitionist Papers*, 3:95n6, 277n2; Swift, *Black Prophets of Justice*, 19–46; *Rights of All*, 5/29/1829 and 6/12/1829; "Agricultural Pursuits," *CA*, 11/4/1837. From 1837 to 1841, the *Colored American* published over fifty articles promoting farming, gardening, and country living. (See index in Jacobs, *Antebellum Black Newspapers*.) Many pieces were by the Quaker abolitionists Augustus and John Owen Wattles. Augustus Wattles was the chief purchaser and land agent for a thirty-thousand-acre colonization effort in Ohio, and a close friend of John Brown.

10. *New Yorker*, 6/3/1837; Meinig, *Shaping of America*, 2:222–36.

11. "Important Letter from Augustus Wattles," *CA*, 10/28/1837; "Ohio Memorial Extract No. 2," *CA*, 3/22/1838; ibid.; "Can't Take Care of Themselves," *CA*, 3/15/1838.

12. CBR, "Emigration of Colored People to Canada," *CA*, 11/18/1837.

13. CBR and Willis Hodges, "Report on Agriculture," Troy Colored Convention, Liberty Street Church, 10/6–9/1847; "Resolutions," *Model Worker*, 5/18/1848. Also see "Agricultural Pursuits," *CA*, 11/4/1837; "Domestic Habits," *CA*, 4/19/1838.

14. Paris Young, Caroline Draper, and Amanda Tuttle-Smith, "Freedom Seekers: Henry Highland Garnet," Slavery and Freedom at Washington College, accessed 2/9/2023, https://slaveryandfreedomatwashingtoncollege.org/freedom-seekers-3/; and "Henry Highland Garnet," Historical Society of Kent County, accessed 2/9/2023, https://kentcountyhistory.org/Henry-Highland-Garnet.pdf.

15. Among biographers who have tracked Henry Highland Garnet's epic odyssey from Maryland enslavement to leading advocate for Black militant abolitionism and Black rights are Joel Schor (*Henry Highland Garnet*) and Earl

Ofari (*"Let Your Motto Be Resistance": The Life and Thought of Henry Highland Garnet*). Also see chapter 6 ("Henry Highland Garnet, Charles Ray, and Black Action Programs in New York State in the 1840s") in David E. Swift's *Black Prophets of Justice,* and Garnet-focused chapters in Sterling Stuckey's *Slave Culture.*

16. TW to New York State Anti-slavery Society, *CA,* 7/8/1837; Scott Cady and Christopher L. Webber, *A Year with American Saints* (Church Pub., 2006), 108. On Garnet at the Noyes Academy, see Swift, *Black Prophets of Justice,* 117–18; and Stuckey, *Slave Culture,* 145–47, 161.

17. On Black students' experiences at the Oneida Institute, see Milton C. Sernett, "Common Cause: The Antislavery Alliance of Gerrit Smith and Beriah Green," *The Courier* 21, no. 2 (Fall 1986): 68.

18. "Religious Societies," Hart Cluett Museum, 2/3/2021, https://www. hartcluett.org/rensselaer-county-blog/religioussocieties?rq=%22Religious%20 Societies; HHG, speech, published in *National Negro Convention, Buffalo, 1843* (J. H. Tobitt, 1848). Garnet's influential speech may be read in full at the Colored Conventions Project, https://coloredconventions.org/garnet-address-1843; Ofari, "Roots of Black Radicalism."

19. Frothingham, *Gerrit Smith,* 57–63.

20. "Report, on the Best Means for the Promotion of the Enfranchisement of Our People," *Minutes of the Fifth Annual Convention of the Colored Citizens of the State of New York, Held in the City of Schenectady, on the 18th, 19th, and 20th of September, 1844,* published in the introduction to Garnet's *Memorial Discourse,* 37. In Troy, on August 1, 1846, Garnet again urged a Black retreat from urban life. *AP,* 9/1/1846.

21. "Extract from a Sermon, Preached at Troy, N.Y., to a Company of Mr. Gerrit Smith's Grantees, on the Eve of Their Departure to Their Lands, by Henry Highland Garnet, Pastor of the Liberty Street Church," *NS,* 5/12/1848.

22. JMS, introduction to *Memorial Discourse.*

23. GS to John Thomson Mason, 10/19/1846 and 11/6/1846; GS to George Thompson, 11/6/1846; GS to W. E. Whitney, Esq., 11/6/1846; GS to Mason, 10/19/1846.

24. GS to TW, CBR, and JMS, Peterboro, 9/10/1846; *New York Journal & Advertiser* (Auburn), 9/23/1846. The column would be referenced in the *Oswego Advertiser* and the *Rochester Advertiser.* The *Cortland County Whig,* 10/22/1846, reprinted derogatory reports from the Oswego and Rochester *Advertiser*s. *ECR,* 10/10/1846.

25. *GSLB,* 119–22. In these last pages of his *Land Book,* Smith registered the final tweaks and additions—some as late as 1853—that brought his count to the requisite three thousand. GS, *Address to the Three Thousand Colored Citizens.*

26. TW, CBR, and JMS to Smith grantees, *AP,* 10/28/1846.

27. Marx, *Machine in the Garden,* 23, 104–5, 113–15, 121–30; ibid., 127: "All of this makes more sense once we recognize the noble husbandman's true identity: he is the good shepherd of the old pastoral dressed in American homespun."

28. TW, CBR, and JMS to Smith grantees, *AP,* 10/28/1846.

29. TW, CBR, and JMS to Smith grantees, *AP,* 10/28/1846.

30. GS to TW, CBR, and JMS, Peterboro, 11/14/1846. In *Gerrit Smith: Philanthropist and Reformer* (246), Ralph Harlow suggests that Smith's land gifts were devised to "bring new strength—numerically at least—to his Liberty Party. Not only the grantees but their friends, relatives, and dependents would be under the strongest obligation to follow the political leadership of Gerrit Smith. Land grants in other words might be considered a substitute for the patronage as an element of party strength and solidarity." But Smith never imposed an obligation, and neither did his agents (though Garnet dropped hints). Harlow's assumption of Black indebtedness to Smith underestimates the independence of the Black electorate and distorts the *publicly* disinterested nature of Smith's benevolence. Hoping for Liberty votes (and Smith hoped hard) was not the same as openly demanding them.

31. See "Husbandry," *CA*, 3/22/1838. *Colored American* editor Samuel Cornish urged Black pioneers to respect "the privileged order of the land, and be careful that there are but two or three families of our people in any one place." In this same issue, the Geneva barber J. W. Duffin (later a Smith agent) implored Black homesteaders to "scatter ourselves over the country with our white brethren." Smith's giveaway of 1846, which gifted Black grantees with lots near white-owned farms, implied this same commitment to a thoroughgoing rural integration, a goal that likely took a cue from Black agrarians like Ray, Garnet, Cornish, and Duffin, and challenged the segregationist land policies of many white radical reformers.

32. Stauffer, *Black Hearts of Men*, 136–38.

33. Stauffer, *Black Hearts of Men*, 136–38. For years, the radical reformer Thomas Ainge Devyr clung to the hope that Gerrit Smith would bankroll the land reform movement of radical agrarians. Other white land reformers dreaded Smith's interest in their cause, predicting that it would estrange their backers in the South. Godine, "Abolitionist and the Land Reformer."

34. Godine, "Abolitionist and the Land Reformer."

4. Theories into Practice

1. Duffin to GS, Geneva, 9/7/1846; Jacob Benjamin to GS, Albany, 2/1848; Shotwell to GS, NYC, 9/21/1846; Mary E. Mills to GS, 9/18/1846; Amos Beman to HHG, from a letter HHG wrote Samuel Ringgold Ward, 3/2/1849.

2. GS to Cornish, 10/1/1846; Van Rensselaer to GS, 12/7/1846.

3. Samuel G. May to GS, 9/24/1846 and 10/12/1846; GS to Samuel Porter, 12/2/1846; Abel Seaton to GS, 12/10/1850; Jonathan Walker to GS, Ferrisburg, VT, 7/26/1852. John Greenleaf Whittier's poem "The Man with the Branded Hand" tells Walker's story.

4. GS to Samuel Cornish, 10/1/1846; GS to Porter, 12/2/1846. Among the women to whom Gerrit Smith gave grants in his giveaway of 1846 were Mary Kantine of New York City, Rebecca Hornbeck of Onondaga, Harriet [illeg.] of Williamsburg, Flora Fry of Gouverneur, and Elizabeth J. Mann of Suffolk County (*GSLB*, 86, 121, 82, 96, 100). Publicly identified fugitives who received gift lots were Frederick Douglass, still a Massachusetts resident when he got his deed from Smith (*GSLB*, 72), the antislavery lecturer Henry Bibb of Boston

(37), Utica's antislavery preacher James Fountain (71), the fugitive Richard J. Eusti[ss], Little Falls (29), Lewis Haydn, a "fugitive from Kentucky" (37), and the antislavery sibling lecturers and fugitives from Kentucky, Lewis, Milton, and Cyrus Clark, who were not living in New York when they got their deeds. Morgan, "Education and Medical Practice," 609–10. In 1846, Maryland's John Thomson Mason "let" Smith emancipate his property for $3,000, and then only if the judge could keep the freedmen on as his indentured servants for two years. It is unlikely that they were given gift lots in 1848. Stauffer, *Works*, 303, 323–24n12.

5. Amos Beman and Charles Beman of New Haven, CT, got deeds from Smith; CBR to GS, [3]/31/1848; CBR and JMS to GS, 7/1/1847; Jermain Wesley Loguen to GS, 7/2/1847; CBR and JMS to GS, 12/2/1847; Wesley Bailey to GS, 5/22/1847; CBR to GS, [3]/31/1848; CBR and JMS to GS, NYC, 7/27/1847; GS to TW, CBR, and JMS, 10/3/1846.

6. Dann, *Practical Dreamer*, 127–33.

7. Cooper, "Elevating the Race," 619. Cooper notes that Benjamin Quarles's pioneering history, *Black Abolitionists*, was "for the most part the record of the activities of a couple of dozen men." On the midcentury insularity of New York's Black reform elite, see Hutton, *Early Black Press*, 103–28; Anbinder, *Five Points*, 91–93; Peterson, *John Brown*, 181–82, 127–29; CBR, *Receipt Book* ("Receipt Book of land grants from Gerrit Smith to 'colored and poor white slaves from the South,' 1846," A1352), NYSA.

8. J. W. Duffin to GS, Geneva, 9/7/1846.

9. At their yearly meeting, New York's Black stewards and marine cooks toasted the temperance advocates William Lloyd Garrison and Arthur and Lewis Tappan with wine. *CA*, 5/2/1840, quoted in Harris, *Shadow of Slavery*, 203; FD, "Temperance and Anti-slavery," *Renfrewshire (Scotland) Advertiser*, 4/11/1846.

10. Anbinder, *Five Points*, 198–99.

11. Dann, *Practical Dreamer*, 102; Koeppel, *Water for Gotham*, 287.

12. The male tavern culture at midcentury held particular appeal for Black laborers in an era when so many more Black women were finding jobs as domestics than Black men were finding work. Harris, *Shadow of Slavery*, 99; Charles Loring Brace, *The Dangerous Classes of New York and Twenty Years Work among Them* (1872), 64–65, quoted in Anbinder, *Five Points*, 194.

13. JMS to GS, 12/17/1846.

14. GS, *Address to the Three Thousand Colored Citizens*, 7; *GSLB*, 119, 4/18/1851/119. "My Committee in the City of New York [JMS and CBR], informed me that they cannot find in [each] County as many suitable persons for temperance as I have called for. Hence, I permitted them to go into other Counties to supply the lack."

Most of the slots that had been held for takers in Putnam, Suffolk, Queens, and Richmond Counties went to Albanians, and residents of New York County and Brooklyn picked up gift deeds that were redirected from Westchester, Ulster, and Dutchess Counties. (Among the beneficiaries of the expanded search was "Lewis Pierce of North Elba," who got his second Adirondack deed in this exchange). From 1839 into the early 1840s, Henry Highland Garnet wrote and published the *Clarion*, an antislavery newspaper in Troy. Wesley Bailey, son and father of newsmen, merged the highly regarded *Friend of Man* with the smaller *Madison and Onondaga Abolitionist* to create the *Liberty Press* in 1842. William Chaplin of Massachusetts took over the *Albany Patriot* in 1846 when its editor, Charles Torrey, went to jail for helping fugitives. Charles Bennett Ray, a cofounder of New York City's *Colored American* in 1836, took it over in 1839 and remained its editor in chief until it folded on Christmas Day 1841. Samuel Ringgold Ward produced two radical abolition newspapers, the *True American and Religious Examiner*, from Cortlandville in central New York, ca. 1845–48, and the *Impartial Citizen*, from Syracuse and Boston, ca. 1849–51.

15. WPP to GS, 10/2/1847, 3/28/1848, 4/28/1848.

16. "Acknowledgment to Gerrit Smith," *NE*, 4/15/1847, and GS to Samuel Porter, 12/2/1846; E. M. Griffing to GS, Little Falls, 5/12/1848; Street Dutton to GS, Meredith, NY, 5/20/1850; Hiram Corliss to GS, Union Village, 10/28/1850 (so outraged was the radical abolitionist Corliss by John Brown's capture at Harpers Ferry that he urged Smith to fund a raid to spring Brown from the Charles Town jail); May, *Our Anti-slavery Conflict*, 325; William T. Torrey to GS, Holley, NY, 12/15/1846; Jabez Hammond to GS, Cherry Valley, NY, 10/30/1846, 4/6/1847; Timothy Jenkins to GS, Oneida Castle, 11/22/1849; William Slade to GS, Middlebury, VT, 7/31/1847; "Forty Families of Colored People," *Brooklyn Eagle*, 3/30/1848.

17. "The Chaplin Meeting," *Liberator*, 1/24/1851, and Sernett, *North Star Country*, 130. The 1840 Liberty Party slate included the senatorial candidate Nathaniel Safford, Hunt for state assembly, and the gubernatorial aspirant Gerrit Smith. *CA*, 10/10/1840. Two years later, Hunt ran for lieutenant governor on the abolition ticket; he got one vote. *Oneida Whig*, 11/22/1842. The erudite Lawson attended radical abolition conventions in Syracuse and organized the Free Democracy (Free Soil) Party in Oneida County. *Syracuse League*, 1851, n.d., and *FDP*, 9/10/1852; John Howard Brown, ed., *Lamb's Biographical Dictionary of the United States* (Boston, 1900), 162. The antislavery educator Beriah Green's response to Smith's giveaway was typical of many reactions from Smith's white admirers. A few lines of solemn praise ("I rejoice to hear of your . . . designs towards our Colored fellow-citizens. God bless you. . . . May their acres be well-cultivated under the guidance & with the blessing of Him who 'hath given the Earth to the children of men'!") briskly segued to the main concern: abolition politics, abolition above all. Beriah Green to GS, Whitesboro, NY, 8/28/1846; William Chaplin to GS, Albany, 11/26/1846.

18. "Grand Convention of Smith's Grantees," *AP*, 12/9/1846; JMS to GS, 12/17/1846; "Gerrit Smith, Esq. GREAT MEETING OF THE COLORED PEOPLE OF TROY," *American Freeman*, 11/17/1846. Also see Bell, *Negro Convention Movement*, 91–94.

19. "On Meeting of the Colored People of Troy," *AP*, 10/28/1846.

20. "Acknowledgment to Gerrit Smith," *NE*, 4/15/1847; "these presents": JMS and CBR to GS, 3/27/1848; CBR to GS, 5/24/1847.

21. CBR to GS, 5/24/1847; MacKenzie. *Plains of Abraham*, 17–19, chap. 15, 76–79.

22. JMS and CBR to GS, 7/27/1847.

23. Friedman, *Gregarious Saints*, 118–21.

24. "Gerrit Smith," *Model Worker*, 12/29/1848. The four resolutions praising Smith's land gifts were passed at the 1847 Colored Men's Convention, held in Troy from October 6 through 9. In late May 1847, Charles B. Ray shared these with Smith. Smith wrote his screed on November 16, 1847, and the *Model Worker*, a short-lived abolition paper in Utica, ran the convention resolutions and Smith's grim response the next month.

25. Lewis Tappan to GS, NYC, 4/15/1848.

26. Lewis Tappan to GS, NYC, 4/15/1848.

5. On Fat Lands under Genial Suns

1. Frothingham, *Gerrit Smith*, 29, and Tanner, "'Foe to Sad Oppression's Rod,'" 106, 11; Durant, *History of Oneida County*, 447; Osborn, "Tug Hill."

2. Jones, *Annals of Oneida County*, 149–50; ibid., 147; Wager, *Our Country*, 434; Riley, *Florence in History*; Jones, *Annals of Oneida County*, 149, 154.

3. FD, *NS*, 2/18/1848.

4. Ripley et al., *Black Abolitionist Papers*, 3:178–79n3; Quarles, *Black Abolitionists*, 172–73, 219–20; Paul Stewart, "Myers, Stephen (1800–1870), and Myers, Harriet (1807–1865)," in Hinks and McKivigan, *Encyclopedia of Antislavery*, 486–87; Stewart, "Underground Railroad"; "Runaway Slaves," *Charleston Mercury*, 2/12/1858.

5. GS to HHG, 6/10/1843. In 1843, Gerrit Smith regarded the influence of Myers's Albany Whig-supported broadsheet as so pernicious that he set up Reverend Garnet in Troy with a newspaper that would challenge it. (Myers's paper was the *Northern Star and Freeman's Advocate*; Garnet's was the *Clarion*.) Other papers Myers edited and copublished were the *Elevator*, the *Northern Star and Colored Farmer*, the *Pioneer*, the *American Reporter*, the *Impartial Citizen*, the *Telegraph and Temperance Journal*, and the *Voice of the People*. "To Gerrit Smith, Esq., and Other Leaders of the Liberty Party," *Northern Star and Freemen's Advocate*, 2/27/1846.

6. *GSLB*, 10. Among Albany activists who received Florence gift lots near Stephen Myers' lot were the tailors Thomas Vogelsang and William Topp and the newspaper publisher Charles Morton, *GSLB*, 10; "The Colored Settlement at Florence," from the *New York Evening Post*, 12/22/1848, was picked up by the *Baltimore Sun*, 12/27/1848; the *Farmer's Cabinet* (Amherst, NH) and *Times-Picayune* (LA), 1/1/1849; the *Lancaster (PA) Examiner*, 1/3/1849; the *Indiana State Sentinel*, the *Pennsylvania Freeman* and *National Era*, 1/4/1849; the *American Courier* (Washington, DC), 1/6/1849; the *Daily Constitutionalist and Republican* (GA) ("This settlement is doubtless intended as a sort of asylum for runaway negroes from the slave states"); the *Prairie du Chien (WI) Patriot*, 1/24/1848; and the *Tarboro (NC) Press*, 2/3/1849.

7. DD to GS, Florence, 2/21/1848; *IC*, 5/23/1849 (Myers's meeting with Black Uticans occurred on 12/26/1848); *NS*, 2/16/1849 and 2/23/1849.

8. Myers's endorsement of Smith's plan for the Black Woods in the *Northern Star and Colored Farmer* was approvingly republished in the *North Star* (1/4/1849) and the *Ram's Horn* (2/25/1848 and 3/10/1848). DD to GS, Florence, 2/21/1848; *IC*, 5/23/1849; *NS*, 2/16/1849; *NS*, 2/23/1849.

9. *NS*, 2/23/1849; *IC*, 5/23/1849, covering Myers's speech in New Bedford on 12/26/1848; *NE*, 1/4/1849; *NS*, 2/16/1849; DD to GS, 3/21/1849.

10. Lewis Tappan to GS, 4/15/1848; "Florence Convention," *NSCF*, n.d., cited in *NS*, 1/26/1849. Gerrit Smith's Black land agents Ray, McCune Smith, Loguen, Ward, and Topp each agreed to promote or seek donations for Myers's Florence settlement (and Douglass, early on, endorsed it too). Smith had given several of his agents gift lots in both the Adirondacks and Florence (*GSLB*, 56), and they may have felt their Florence acreage would gain the greater value if Myers's project caught fire. When the Albany agent William Topp was offered gift land in either Florence or the Adirondacks, he chose Florence. *GSLB*, 74; "The Florence Telegraph," *NYDT*, 1/30/1850.

11. Wm. H. Topp to FD, 1/10/1849, *NS*, 1/19/1849; *Journal of the Assembly*, 81, 117–18; *NSCF*, n.d., quoted in *NS*, 2/16/1849.

12. *NS*, 2/16/1849; *IC*, 3/4/1849; *NS*, 3/2/1849. Even before Bibb shared his concerns, Douglass had misgivings about Florence and its promoter. He had agreed to serve on a finance committee, but Myers had given him no details of the work. "We ought to know our duties if we are expected to act," Douglass grumbled to his readers. *NS*, 1/26/1849.

13. GS to FD, 2/24/1849, in *NS*, 3/2/1849.

14. "The Florence Settlement," *NS*, 3/30/1849; FD to Stephen Myers, *NS*, 3/16/1849; *IC*, 3/28/1849. Samuel Ringgold Ward, editor of the *Impartial Citizen*, softened his own retreat from Myers's settlement scheme with a potshot at the *Ram's Horn*, which, like the *North Star*, backed away from Myers' plan: "The Ram's Horn is edited by Thomas Van Rensselaer, and that is enough to indicate the importance of the denunciation."

15. Levin Tilmon to FD, *NS*, 3/30/1849.

16. Stephen Myers to FD, *NS*, 3/30/1849.

17. *Albany Argus*, 5/29/1849; "The Settlers on Smith's Lands in Oneida County," *NS*, 11/2/1849; "Sheriff's Sale," *Oneida Morning Herald*, 8/18/1851, 10/8/1851.

18. DD to GS, 2/16/1849 and 3/21/1849.

19. "Florence Settlement," *NS*, 2/23/1849; JMS to GS, 9/11/1850.

20. DD to GS, 2/16/1849. I am indebted to the independent scholar and history teacher Jessica Harney of Rome, New York, for sharing much of what she and her students have learned about the Florence colony after Stephen Myers left the scene and it fell from public view. Jessica Harney, "Index of Florence, NY Tax Assessor Records, 1853–1857" and "Black Residents of the Town of Florence, 1860 US Census" (unpublished); and Wellman, "We Took Ourselves to Liberty," 151–52, 171.

21. May, *Some Recollections*, 323; GS to W. L. Chaplin, Saratoga Springs, NY, 5/26/1845, published in the *Albany Patriot* as "Gerrit Smith's Tour through Saratoga, Warren, Essex and Clinton," *AP*, 6/25/1845; McKivigan and McKivigan, "'He Stands Like Jupiter,'" 193.

22. GS to L. A. Hine, 9/21/1852; *FDP*, 10/8/1852; GS to J. K. Ingalls, *The Landmark*, 8/15/1848; GS, letter and circular to John Cochrane, William L. Kenney, Isaac T. Hopper, George H. Evans, and Daniel C. Eaton, of NYC, 5/1/1849, published in *NYT* and *NE*, 5/17/1849.

23. Hyde, *Gift*, 21.

24. JMS to GS, NYC, 3/27/1848.

25. C. J. Morton, Benjamin Latimore, Peter Crummell, J. P. Anthony, Richard Thompson to GS, 11/4/1846.

26. On Wilson, see Ripley et al., *Black Abolitionist Papers*, 4:14n9; GS to Thomas Van Rensselaer, 2/11/1847; Van Rensselaer to GS, 5/26/1847.

27. James Blair Webb, George T. Downing, Samuel Cornish to GS, 6/1/1847. On the Black businessman and reformer George T. Downing, see Ripley et al., *Black Abolitionist Papers*, 4:312–14, 317–18n16; Quarles, *Black Abolitionists*, 219–20; Peterson, *Black Gotham*, 277–80; Logan and Winston, *American Negro Biography*, 187–88. On Webb and Caldwell's modest forays into justice activism, see the *Proceedings of the National Convention*, 3, 10, 12, and "Important News from Trinidad," *CA*, 4/18/1840; on Caldwell's wealth, see "The New York Expedition for Liberia," *FDP*, 11/25/1853. On Samuel Cornish's agrarianism and his dealings with Smith, see Cornish to GS, NYC, 3/24/1834 and 12/18/1834; GS to Cornish, 10/1/1846; Other stockholders in Webb and Caldwell's group were John A. Williams, a Wesleyan Methodist minister in Newark, New Jersey, who sometimes worked on suffrage issues with Troy's Garnet (*CA*, 6/27/1840, 11/20/1841), and the New Haven minister Samuel T. Gray (Ripley et al., *Black Abolitionist Papers*, 4:313, 321n24). The three female investors were Lydia Bosly, Sarah Augustus, and Lucy Harris. CBR and JMS to GS, 5/22/1847; CBR and JMS to GS, 5/20/1847; CBR and JMS to GS, 5/25/1847.

28. James Blair Webb, George T. Downing, and Samuel Cornish to GS, NYC, 6/1/1847.

29. Harris, *Shadow of Slavery*, 274–75; Calarco, *Underground Railroad*, 230; Strong, *Perfectionist Politics*, 178–79.

30. Among the Adirondack historians and memoirists who assumed that Timbuctoo was a hideout for fugitives were Sylvester (*Historical Sketches*, 137, 140; Bowditch ("Trips to the Adirondacks—Visit to John Brown's Grave," 1879, in *Bowditch, Life and Correspondence*, 2:79–80); Donaldson (*History of the Adirondacks*, 2:6); Brewster ("John Brown of North Elba," *New York History*, 10/1952); White (*Adirondack Country*, 195–96); Boyer (*Legend of John Brown*, 391); Bernstein (*Sticks*, 63); and Villard (*John Brown*, 73). James Blair Webb and Abraham Caldwell's land company initiated purchases of Adirondack land for George Wilson, Dennis Washington, William Smith, and Enos Cuthbert. George Wilson to GS, 12/6/1847; Wilson and Webb to GS, 3/10/1848). Also see "Gerrit Smith's Grants," *NS*, 6/23/1848, and Harris, *Shadow of Slavery*, 277. On the never-built Rush Academy, see D. D. Moore, *John Jamison, History of the A.M.E. Church in America* (Teachers' Journal Office, 1884), 308–14. See https://docsouth.unc.edu/church/moorej/moore.html; *78th Annual Report of the Regents of the University of the State of New York, made to Legislature, 2/16/1865* (G. Wendell Pub., 1865), 11.

31. "Brethren . . . ," *New York Tribune*, 12/1/1852. On Gerrit Smith's conception of Timbuctoo as an American alternative to African colonization, see Stauffer, *Black Hearts of Men*, 141.

32. "Convention of Colored Citizens," *NS*, 4/10/1851 (in this article, Caldwell was misidentified as Abraham Colville, an error he likely did not race to correct); *FDP*, 6/17/1853.

33. "Convention of Colored Citizens," *NS*, 4/10/1851. On the colonization-ist Abraham Caldwell in Africa, see Daniel H. Peterson, *The Looking Glass: Being a True Report and Narrative of The Life, Travels, and Labors of the Rev. Daniel H. Peterson, a Colored Clergyman; Embracing a Period of Time from the Year 1812 to 1854, and Including His Visit to Western Africa,* 1851; Moses, *Liberian Dreams,* 39–54, 74–75; "Missionary Intelligence from Africa," *Jersey City Sentinel and Advertiser,* 3/11/1854; William Nesbit, "Four Months in Liberia: or African Colonization Exposed," 1855, in Moses, *Liberian Dreams,* 91.

34. In 1849, press releases titled or concerning "Gerrit Smith's Colored Set-tlement" ran in papers from Albany to Alabama, and in many of them, Florence was said to enjoy the support of the prominent Whig politicos "Messrs. Fill-more, Fish, Morgan, Spencer, etc." Though Millard Fillmore, Hamilton Fish, Edwin Morgan, and John Spencer were none of them proslavery, neither were they ardent abolitionists or champions of the rights of free Black men. The radical abolitionist Gerrit Smith would have bridled at the suggestion of an alliance; GS to TW, CBR, and JMS, 11/14/1846.

35. On the shaping role of Romantic literature on the vision of the Black Woods, see Stauffer, *Black Hearts of Men,* 149–52, 182–86. Sturges, "Con-sumption in the Adirondacks," documents the geographic exceptionalism that shaped the Adirondack wilderness narrative from the early 1800s to the twenty-first century; William C. Nell, "Convention of Colored People," *NS,* 10/20/1848. The convention was in Cleveland, Ohio, 9/6–8/1848. It is hard to know whether the source of this quote was Nell (named as the article's author), Gerrit Smith (one of his subjects), or the editor George Bradburn (his paper, the *Lynn Pioneer,* was the source of the *North Star*'s clip).

36. *NS,* 2/18/1848; *RH,* 2/25/1848; *Northern Star and Freemen's Advocate,* quoted in *NS,* 4/1/1848.

37. Thompson, *Geography of New York State,* 374.

38. Cole, "Essay on American Scenery," 5.

39. Terrie, *Forever Wild,* 26; Stilgoe, *Common Landscape in America,* 206–7; Rev. Horace Bushnell, "The Age of Homespun," *Scribner's,* 1851, quoted in Bidwell, *Rural Economy,* 371.

40. *New York Forestry Commission Report, 1885,* quoted in Terrie, *Forever Wild,* 25–26; *New York Tribune,* 4/8/1857; Billington, *America's Frontier Heritage,* 33.

41. Crèvecoeur, "What Is an American?" (letter 3), in *Letters from an Ameri-can Farmer,* 91–105; Slotkin, *Fatal Environment,* 72.

42. JMS to GS, 12/28/1846; FD, *NS,* 1/5/1849; Albers, *Hands on the Land,* 107.

43. On Gerrit Smith's dealings with his Adirondack contract farmers, see Go-dine, "Occupied Territory"; "From the *Model Worker,*" *NS,* 1/12/1849. Douglass reprinted two letters in this column. The first was Charles Ray's letter to Gerrit Smith of 5/18/1848, thanking him for his land gifts on behalf of the 1847 Troy Colored Men's Convention, and listing the delegates' four resolutions that hon-ored him as well. The second letter was Smith's belated and unhappy answer of 11/16/1848.

44. Cole, "Essay on American Scenery," 3.

6. Something besides "Speechifying"

1. Hodges, *Free Man of Color*, xxii–xxv, 9–14, xxvi–xxvii. Hodges shared his memoir with his family. He did not publish it himself. In 1896, his son Augustus Hodges serialized it in the *Indianapolis Freeman*. In 1982, the University of Tennessee Press produced the authoritative edition with an introduction by Willard Gatewood.

2. Hodges, *Free Man of Color*, 16, xxviii, 38.

3. Hodges, *Free Man of Color*, 38–39; Douglass, *My Bondage and Freedom*, 335–41.

4. Hodges, *Free Man of Color*, 40–49.

5. "Troy Colored Men's Convention," *CA*, 9/11/1841; "Proceedings of the National Convention of Colored People and Their Friends," 10/6–9/1847, in Bell, *Minutes of the Proceedings*, 1–17; Hodges, *Free Man of Color*, 46.

6. Hodges, *Free Man of Color*, 78, xli–xlii, Villard, *John Brown*, 659–61, and Ruchames, *John Brown*, 69–72; Reynolds, *John Brown, Abolitionist*, 56–57; Hodges, *Free Man of Color*, 50–53.

7. Hodges, *Free Man of Color*, 53–55, xxix, 60–64, 58, 64–69, 58.

8. Hodges, *Free Man of Color*, 74, xliv, 50; *RH*, 2/25/1848; Hodges, *Free Man of Color*, xliv, 80.

9. *USFC 1850*, NE, Essex County; "J. H. Henderson Boot and Shoe Manufactory," *CA*, 3/30–5/11/1839; *CA*, 7/18/1840; *CA*, 10/17/1840; Freeman, *Free Negro*, 296; "Virginia or Vermont?," *USFC 1850*, NE, Essex County. Circumstantial evidence suggests that Henderson's mother was born in Virginia, but the census taker's spellings of "Vt." and "Va." are very much alike; On the same page of the *Colored American* that ran the ad for Henderson's "Manufactury" were many more ads from Black tradesmen, artisans, and reformers who all eventually got deeds from Gerrit Smith. Below Henderson's plug is a line about Dr. James McCune Smith's office hours. At the column's top is an alert for the Brooklyn rooming house of William J. Hodges, Willis Hodges's brother, who would get a gift lot too. In another column is a notice from Elizabeth Appo, a dressmaker and milliner whose husband, William Appo, a Philadelphia musician, bought land from Gerrit Smith in 1848. Near it is a notice from one of Smith's future land agents, J. W. Duffin. The co-owners of the paper, Samuel Cornish and Philip Bell, were Smith grantees, and Charles Bennett Ray, the paper's agent and frequent contributor, was a grantee and an agent. On Henderson's church work and his teaching in the city, see Freeman, *Free Negro*, 296; and *CA*, 7/18/1840 and 10/17/1840.

10. *CA*, 8/28/1841; Spann, *New Metropolis*, 123; "W. P. Johnson to the Editor," *CA*, 7/17/1841.

11. Schor, *Henry Highland Garnet*, 34–72; Henry Highland Garnet, "Call to Rebellion," National Negro Convention, Buffalo, NY, 8/1843.

12. Records, Liberty Street Presbyterian Church, Troy, NY. Minutes and membership lists for Troy's Liberty Street Church are accessible at the Presbyterian Historical Society, Philadelphia, https://www.history.pcusa.org. "Mrs. Henderson" was admitted on 5/25/1844, and her husband on 3/11/1847. "Rensselaer County Convention," *CA*, 11/20/1841; "Colored Citizens of

Troy," *Christian Freeman*, 5/5/1843; *NASS*, 1/26/1846; "To Gerrit Smith, Esq., and Other Leaders of the Liberty Party," *NASS*, 3/14/1846; HHG to GS, Troy, 9/20/1848, 9/16/1848; HHG to FD, 2/5/1849, and in *NS*, 2/16/1849; *GSLB*, 88–89. Deedholders with ties to Troy who settled in the Adirondacks were William Carasaw, Lyman Eppes, Thomas Jefferson, Samuel Jefferson, John Thomas, Wesley Murray, James H. Henderson, George Hamilton, and Stephen Warren Morehouse. Settler John Vinson held no deed, but was Troy-based. Stephen Warren Morehouse was a Saratoga County deedholder who in the early 1830s had made his home in Troy.

13. "On Meeting of the Colored People of Troy," *AP*, 10/28/1846 (also published in *American Freeman*, 11/17/1846). For all their early zeal, the grantees who made this exploratory trip never did settle on their land. "Address to Grantees by TW, CBR and JMS," *AP*, 10/28/1846; *NS*, 2/18/1848.

14. Ray and Hodges, "Report of the Committee on Agriculture," 1847, 29. Charles Ray's background may have informed his expectation that the farmer's life could "cauterize" racial divides, but Willis Hodges's Maryland experience suggested otherwise. In 1829, a reign of terror besieged his world when white farmers mobbed and vandalized the farms and homes of the Hodgeses and their Black neighbors. *GSLB*, 88–89.

15. "Extract from a Sermon, Preached at Troy, N.Y., to a Company of Mr. Gerrit Smith's Grantees, on the Eve of Their Departure to Their Lands, by Henry Highland Garnet, Pastor of the Liberty Street Church," *NS*, 5/12/1848; Grover, *Make a Way Somehow*, 80; Swift, *Black Prophets of Justice*, 169.

16. Diantha Gunn to fiancé, 7/29/1856, in Calarco, *Underground Railroad*, 123; Perry, *History and Genealogy*, 72–81.

17. Calarco, *Underground Railroad*, 117; Perry, *People of Lowly Life*, 219; *Court Docket Book*, 1848, Washington County Archives, Fort Edward, NY, 275; Tefft, *Story of Union Village*, 70.

18. Lemuel Knapp to GS, St. Armand, 4/10/1848; William Lathrop to GS, 11/22/1847; E. D. Culver to GS, Greenwich, 11/30/1849. On Culver's steadfast antislavery career, see "Erastus D. Culver," Wikipedia, last edited December 27, 2022, https://en.wikipedia.org/wiki/Erastus_D._Culver. Former congressman Culver's letter was endorsed by William H. Mowry, a leading founder of Union Village's integrated, antislavery Free Congregational Church, and a vice president of the Eastern New York Anti-slavery Society.

19. *General Index*, 426, 537, 586; Hurd, *Clinton and Franklin Counties*, 505; William Cowper, "The Task," in *Poems of William Cowper, Esq.: With a New Memoir* (1869), 62; *GSLB*, Washington County, 106.

20. "Family Name," Hasbrouck Family Association, accessed 10/17/2022, https://www.hasbrouckfamily.org/family-name/; John W. Barry, "Slavery's Hidden History in the Mid-Hudson Valley Coming to Light," *Poughkeepsie Journal*, 4/25/2018; Eric Roth, "Relations between the Huguenots of New Paltz, N. Y. and the Esopus Indians," Huguenot Historical Society, 3/15/1999.

21. "Historic House Tour along 'The First Highway' in New Paltz," Hudson Valley One, June 1, 2017, https://hudsonvalleyone.com/2017/06/01/historic-house-tour-along-the-first-highway-in-new-paltz/.

22. From Adirondack independent historians John Sasso and Mark Friden I learned that South Mountain was an early, now-forgotten name for the small mountain that today honors an Adirondack pioneer and trail builder, Henry Van Hoevenberg. Josiah Hasbrook, *GSLB*, Newburgh, Orange County, 78; *USFC 1840, Fishkill, Dutchess County; 1850; NYSC 1855*, NE. The Black laborer Charles Hasbrook, his wife, and his young son, Charles Jr., lived in Newburgh in 1840. Ten years later, Charles Jr. was living with Leonard Worts, a Smith grantee, and his wife, Diana Worts, in the Adirondack town of Keene. To the census taker Leonard Worts named Virginia as his birth state, but an 1885 death notice reported that he was born enslaved in New York ("Obituary," *VWSJ*, 8/26/1885). Hasbrook family genealogist, Donna Hasbrouck, has identified kinship ties between the slaveholding white Worts (or Wurtz) and Hasbrook families in and around Newburgh.

23. *GSLB*, 78; "The Founding of New Paltz," Hasbrook Family Foundation, 1999–2017; "Dutchess County," in Eisenstadt, *Encyclopedia of New York State*, 480; Washington, *Sojourner Truth's America*, 9–47. Washington's vivid portrait of daily life for enslaved African Americans in New York's Dutch-controlled Hudson River Valley makes plain why a fresh start on the Adirondack frontier held an allure for some grantees. Groth, *Slavery and Freedom*, 147–48. In the 1840s, the construction of the Hudson River Railroad attracted hundreds of Irish immigrants to Dutchess County. Relations between the newcomers and Black families in this neighborhood were strained and fractious. This, too, suggests a reason why the Adirondacks seemed to hold more promise.

24. To a census taker in 1855, the North Elba pioneer Lewis Pierce said that Virginia was his birth state. Long after his death, his daughter Lucy Pierce Miles disputed this. Her father, she told census takers, was from Louisiana. See Lucy Miles [LPM], *USFC 1880, 1900, 1910*, Middlesex, Washington County, VT; "The Philadelphia Slave Case," *NYHT*, 10/25/1848; *NE*, 11/2/1848; and *NS*, 11/3/1848.

25. See LPM, *USFC 1880, 1900, 1910*, Middlesex, Washington County, VT; "Thomas Earle," in *The National Cyclopaedia of American Biography . . .* , ed. James Terry White (J. T. White, 1901), 11:145–46, and GS to "My Dear Brother [unnamed]," 10/9/1840 (the Philadelphia abolitionist to whom Smith wrote did not like Thomas Earle, but Smith defended him, calling Earle "a gentleman of great moral character and a decided enemy of slavery"); "Philadelphia Slave Case."

26. *New York Tribune*, 10/20/1848, and "The Philadelphia Slave Case," *NYHT*, 10/25/1848; *GSLB*, 101, 105, and 119; *NYSC 1855*, NE. Pierce is listed as a Suffolk County grantee for both gift lots, but his place of origin is given as North Elba. Maybe, even after his self-emancipation was confirmed, Pierce felt at risk and sought to keep his Louisiana backstory out of sight. In Smith's *Land Book*, he is listed as a Suffolk County grantee, in one case living in North Elba, and elsewhere in Manhattan. (Smith gave Pierce two lots.)

27. CBR to GS, 5/18/1848, 6/5/1848; Joseph Romeo, "A Genealogical and Biographical Record of the Appo Family," n.d., unpublished, 12–26, and Southern, *Music of Black Americans*, 109–10, 112, 114; Payne, *Recollections of*

Seventy Years, 236; Southern, *Music of Black Americans*, 109, and *Morning Post*, 12/13/1837; Delany, *Condition, Elevation and Destiny*, chap. 14.

28. "Appeal of the Philadelphia Association," *NS*, 7/13/1849; "Day of Thanksgiving," *Pennsylvania Freeman*, 4/29/1847; "Great District Meeting," *CA*, 10/2/1841; *CA*, 3/28/1840; *Troy City Directory* (Tuttle), vol. 14 (William and Elizabeth Appo lived at 282 River Street, near the home of James Henderson, their future neighbor in North Elba); "Colored Citizens of Troy," *CF*, 5/5/1843; *NASS*, 1/26/1846, 1/29/1846; "Notice-Public Exhibition," *CA*, 9/14/1839.

29. *RH*, 2/25/1848 and 3/10/1848. The eight men (many of them with families) who moved to Blacksville were Willis Hodges, George W. B. Wilson, Samuel Drummond, W. B. Smith, E. H. Smith, G. W. Lott, Charles C. W. Brown, and Perry Williams (possibly Perry Weeks). The first four of these had deeds.

30. Villard, *John Brown*, 222; JB to GS, 4/8/1848.

7. Trailblazers

1. "Gerrit Smith's Land," Jermain Loguen to JMS, *NS*, 3/24/1848. In this letter, Loguen indicates that he left Syracuse for the gift lands in August 1847 and returned to Syracuse in September after seven weeks away. For the first leg of this he was a circuit rider, stopping here and there to preach to Methodist congregations in the Mohawk River valley before the great swing north. He came home, he wrote McCune Smith, to find his family "in deep affliction." A young daughter had died in his absence, and this loss "took entire possession" of his thoughts. This was why McCune Smith did not get a report from Loguen until mid-March 1848.

2. "Gerrit Smith's Land."

3. Loguen's white Adirondack helpers were, in Essex County, Alfred Spooner and Jesse Gay, Esq. (Elizabethtown), Uriah H. Mihill (Keene), Jesse Tobey Jr. (Jay), Wendell Lansing (Wilmington), and William Flack (Ausable Forks), and, in Franklin County, the Merrill family (Merrillsville), and Rensselaer Bigelow (Malone).

4. Hodges, *Free Man of Color*, 8.

5. "Mad Dogs—Hydrophobia," *New York Daily Herald*, 7/1/1848; "City Items—Hypothermia," *NYDT*, 7/1/1848; *NYDT*, 7/4/1848; "Incidents Connected with the Great Dog War of 1848," *New York Daily Herald*, 7/29/1848; JMS to GS, 7/7/1848.

6. JMS to GS, 7/7/1848.

7. *CA*, 1/20/1838. Provost's "fair living" would not ensure his family's security. Notwithstanding his prominent role in the city's "uplift" cohort (see "Philanthropic Order of Sons of Temperance," *NASS*, 7/16/1846; "Evening School," *CA*, 9/14/1839; "Right of Suffrage," *CA*, 12/30/1837), the Provost family moved at least five times during the 1830s and early 1840s. In 1846, the year he received his gift deed, Provost was living near the notorious Five Points. In Charles Ray's receipt book, Provost's address was in the Eighth Ward, a neighborhood favored by city cartmen. Hodges, *New York City Cartmen*, 160. Hodges's monograph explores the daily lives of cartmen, white and Black, with scrupulous and steady care.

8. On Anthony Provost's legal travails, see *CA*, 9/16/1837 and 5/9/1840, and *New York Globe*, 4/15/1846. Provost's experience is described as well in Hodges, *Root and Branch*, 233, and Harris, *Shadow of Slavery*, 217–19. On the city world of cart men in the first half of the nineteenth century, see Isaac S. Lyon, *The Recollections of an Old Cartman* (Newark, NJ, 1848), in Hodges, *New York City Cartmen*, 157–59.

9. Coleman, *Going to America*, 168, 274n.

10. "Excerpts from the Debate on Suffrage . . . , 1846," in Gellman and Quigley, eds., *Jim Crow New York*, 252–59. Quoted here are the city paint dealer, John A. Kennedy, 255: John Hunt, a city printer, 256–57; and the attorney Bishop Perkins from New York City, 258.

11. Swift, *Black Prophets of Justice*, 139–42; Field, *Politics of Race*, 61, 62, 236–37; Dodson, Moore, and Yancey, *Black New Yorkers*, 72.

12. Harris, *Shadow of Slavery*, 217–18; *Doggett's New York City Directory* (New York) lists Anthony Provost, "col'd," as a porter in 1846/47, a "laborer" in 1848/49, and again as a "porter" in 1853/54; "Stealing a Horse," *New York Tribune*, 7/12/1850. The reported theft of Provost's horse and wagon in 1850 by Lewis B. Brown (who was convicted) reveals that Provost did, at times, cart for a living, notwithstanding the city's attempt to stop him. Gellman and Quigley, *Jim Crow New York*, 257.

13. "Arrest for Receiving Abolition Papers," *Albany Evening Journal*, 1/9/1847. The arrest of John C. Pulley for picking up a New York abolition paper at his post office in Baltimore was reported in newspapers both pro- and antislavery. Penn, *Afro-American Press*, 62–65.

14. JMS to GS, 7/7/1848; "Gerrit Smith's Grants," *NS*, 6/23/1848.

15. Communipaw [James McCune Smith], "Moving in May in the City," *FDP*, 4/29/1859, cited in Stauffer, *Works of James McCune Smith*, 176.

16. JHH to GS, North Elba, 10/15/1850, 8/13/1851.

17. JB to Willis A. Hodges, *RH*, 3/10/1848; JB to Owen Brown, 1/10/1849.

18. JB to WH, 2/28/1848, reprinted in *New York Evening Post*, 12/20/1859; JB to WH, 1/22/1849, 12/20/1859. The *Post* published six letters that John Brown sent to Hodges while he was ensconced in Blacksville. The other letters Hodges got from Brown were reportedly destroyed when Brown was seized at Harpers Ferry.

19. Adams, "Black Flies," 7; Harold Weston, *Freedom in the Wilds: An Artist in the Adirondacks* (Syracuse, 1971), 3–5.

20. "Troy Grantees Meeting," *NS*, 11/10/1848; "Religious Societies," Hart Cluett Museum, 2/3/2021, https://www.hartcluett.org/rensselaer-county-blog/religioussocieties.

21. JMS to GS, 5/12/1848.

22. Hodges, *Free Man of Color*, xliv, 80. Three times cited in the Hebrew scriptures, most famously in the Book of Micah ("Everyone will sit under their own vine and under their own fig tree, and no one will make them afraid, for the LORD Almighty has spoken"), this phrase captivated abolitionists and land reformers alike. Jamie Bronstein, *Land Reform and Working-Class Experience in Britain and the United States, 1800–1862* (Stanford, 1999), 64–65; Hodges, *Free Man of Color*, xlvii, 80, and Augustus M. Hodges in the *Indianapolis Freeman*, 10/24/1896.

23. Hodges, *Free Man of Color*, 82.

24. Baumann, "Goldsmith."

25. "Gerrit Smith's Land," *NS*, 12/8/1848; "Meeting of the Rochester Grantees," *NS*, 12/15/1848.

26. FD, *NS*, 1/10/1849.

27. FD, *NS*, 1/5/1849.

28. "From the *Northern Star and Colored Farmer*, Essex County, Town of Keane [*sic*]," *NS*, 2/2/1849.

29. JHH to HHG, 1/29/1849, and "Mr. Waite [*sic*] J. Lewis and the Smith Lands," *NS*, 2/16/1849, with introductory letter by HHG to FD, 2/5/1849. Garnet's remarks implicitly reproached Douglass for not publishing Henderson's first letter. The jab was one more parry in a long-standing quarrel between these strongheaded power brokers, who for years took pains to challenge and discredit each other. Schor, *Henry Highland Garnet*, 105; Blight, *Frederick Douglass*, 222-23.

30. JHH to HHG, 1/29/1849, and "Mr. Waite J. Lewis."

31. Ruth Brown Thompson, "Pioneer Life in the Adirondacs," in Sanborn, *Life and Letters*, 101.

32. Higginson, "Visit to John Brown's Household." Higginson suggested that by this surveyor's "villainy the colony was almost ruined in advance, nor did it ever recover itself"; Smith, *History of Warren County*, 221-22. Keene school minutes and local newspapers document Wait Lewis's public service (*ECR*, 2/6/1847, 12/25/1847), and notwithstanding the grantees' concerns about his skill, his survey of a gift lot for the city grantee William Thomas was no different from another, older survey of the same lot by the respected Adirondack surveyor Stephen Thorn. See Adirondack Surveys Collection, LPPL; Norman Van Valkenburgh, interview by the author, 4/29/2005. Head of New York's Division of Lands and Forests from 1978 to 1986, Van Valkenburgh authored *The Forest Preserve of New York State in the Adirondack and Catskill Mountains* and several "Land Surveyor" mysteries set in northern New York.

33. HHG to FD, *NS*, 2/16/1849.

8. The Second Wave

1. Ripley et al., *Black Abolitionist Papers*, 3:302-3n; Philip Foner, "William P. Powell: Militant Champion of Black Seamen," in *Essays in Afro-American History*, 88-111, and Peterson, *Black Gotham*, 180-81, 195-96, 204-5, 237-39; JMS to GS, 2/6/1850, and Ripley et al., *Black Abolitionist Papers*, 4:42-47.

2. JMS to GS, 2/6/1850.

3. JMS to GS, 2/6/1850.

4. Ruth Brown Thompson, "Pioneer Life in the Adirondacs," in Sanborn, *Life and Letters*, 99-101.

5. Dana, "How We Met John Brown."

6. JMS to GS, 2/6/1850.

7. JMS to GS, 2/6/1850.

8. Thumbnail descriptions of these pioneering households in North Elba are corroborated or suggested in state and federal censuses, legal documents, local maps, and Gerrit Smith's *Land Book*.

9. MacKenzie, *Plains of Abraham*, 139–40.

10. *NYSC 1855*, NE; JB to Ruth and Henry Thompson, 10/6/1851, in Sanborn, *Life and Letters*, 108.

11. *USFC 1850*, Franklin, Franklin County. The Maryland origins of the Moore, Weeks, Morehouse, and Murray families are noted in this census; Stephen Morehouse lived in Troy, New York, in the early 1830s (*Troy City Directory*, 1832, 1834, and 1835), and got his gift deed from Gerrit Smith in 1847 while working as a boatman in Waterford, Saratoga County (*GSLB*, 92–93). Twelve men from Waterford received land from Gerrit Smith. Only the Morehouses moved north. On Stephen Morehouse's wife's names, see 398n3. On the grantee Daniel Thompson, see chapter 11.

12. *USFC 1850*, Duane, Franklin County, *Atlas of Franklin County*, 41.

13. McCune Smith's allusion to his daughter's death in his letter to Gerrit Smith echoed the bad news in Jermain Loguen's letter after his trip to the Black Woods the previous year. Like the city doctor, the Syracuse minister was late with his report because of a personal catastrophe; a child of his had died while he was away from home.

14. *NYSC 1855* reveals Black children attending school in Essex County's North Elba and in Franklin County's towns of Franklin and Bellmont; JMS to GS, 12/17/1846.

15. CBR to GS, 12/2/1847; Meinig, *Shaping of America*, 328, 332, 346, 307.

16. *USFC 1850*, Raisin Township, Lenawee County, MI; R. I. Bonner and William A. Whitney, *History and Biographical Record of Lenawee County, Michigan* (W. Stearns, 1879), chap. 15; Bonner, *Memoirs of Lenawee County*, 279–95, and Fuller, "Settlement of Michigan Territory"; Lindquist, *Antislavery-Underground Railroad Movement*; *USFC 1850*, Raisin Township, Lenawee County, MI; Lindquist, *Antislavery-Underground Railroad Movement*, 74; *USFC 1860*, Albion, Calhoun County, MI; Rev. John. W. Robinson, "Jonathan Mingo," *Albion Recorder*, 6/4/1869. The shape-shifting Mingos changed more than their address when they left New York. In Albion, Michigan, the slave-born Mingo identified his ancestry as Native American; his Black ancestors were not acknowledged. (Leslie Dick of the Local History Room, Albion Public Library, MI, provided me with details of Mingo Street and Mingo's Albion reputation.) At his funeral, Mingo was described as the "uneducated, barefoot Indian boy" who made good. Federal censuses in Michigan in the late 1800s represent the Mingo family as "Narraganset Indians." Mingo's sons served in white regiments in the Civil War. Nothing in this family's file in the Albion historian's office recognizes the Gerrit Smith grantee who attended Black uplift meetings, read the *Colored American*, and dreamed of farming in the Black Woods.

17. GS to Samuel Cornish, 10/1/1846, and GS to CBR, JMS, and TW, 10/3/1846; *Freedom's Journal*, 3/23/1827, 5/4/1827, 6/22/1827, 8/31/1827, 11/9/1827; *Rights of All*, 5/29/1829 and 6/12/1829; *CA*, 4/12/1838, 4/19/1838, and 6/22/1839; Samuel E. Cornish, *GSLB*, 56; Lapp, *Gold Rush California*, 69; Swift, *Black Prophets of Justice*, 31 and 31n. Within a year Cornish was back in New York City. While he did not farm his gift lot, he put it to use, speculating in the Smith Lands like many of his friends. Reuben Ruby, *GSLB*, 44; *New York Tribune*, 8/17/1849, cited in Lapp, *Gold Rush California*, 14; "Colored Association in

California," Samuel I. Davis to William Lloyd Garrison, *Liberator*, 2/15/1850; P. Brown to Alley Brown, 12/1851, from the California-Oregon Collection, Missouri Historical Society, cited in Lapp, *Gold Rush California*, 23; "Items—for the Gold Fields," *Essex County Reporter*, 2/8/1849, *New York Tribune*, 11/21/1849, Lapp, *Gold Rush California*, 13, 39, 276n.

18. JMS to GS, 2/6/1850.

19. Wardner, "Footprints on Adirondack Trails," chap. 8, "First Winter in the Adirondacks." Years before he moved to the Adirondacks, Wardner wrote, "I studied every farm I saw, the house, the barns, the arrangement of fences and all such details. In my mind I had a clear picture of my intended future home, even to the row of apple trees near the house with a dozen white bee hives on the ground near the apple trees. Also I had pictured a spring up in the woods, with a steady flow of water through pump logs down to the kitchen." Ibid.

20. E. M. Griffing to GS, 5/12/1848; CBR to GS, 5/12/1847.

21. "From the New York Tribune. A Christian Philanthropist," *NE*, 5/17/1849; circular, GS to John Cochrane, William L. Kemeys, Isaac T. Hopper, George H. Evans, and Daniel C. Eaton, Peterboro, 5/1/1849.

22. FD, *NS*, 1/5/1849; JMS to GS, 12/17/1847.

23. Work, "Life of Charles B. Ray"; Morgan, "Education and Medical Practice"; JMS to GS, 12/17–18/1846: "It is very sickly here. In addition to my ordinary practice, I have 17 children ill with measles." McCune Smith's note let Gerrit Smith know why he would not, *could* not, move to the Black Woods. Every day, his good work made the difference between life and death. JMS to GS, 4/9/1858; Peterson, *Black Gotham*, 156–58; Harris, *Shadow of Slavery*, 157; Ripley et al., *Black Abolitionist Papers*, 3:350–51; "Forgotten Books," 293; JMS, "A Dissertation on Influence of Climate on Longevity," *Office of Merchants' Magazine*, 1846, and "Physician's Report to the Managers of the Colored Orphan Asylum," 11/23/1851, Colored Orphan Asylum Records, NYHS.

24. James McCune Smith, "Convention of Colored Citizens," report, *NS*, 4/10/1851.

9. A Wider Cartography

1. Jacoby, *Crimes against Nature*, 33. There were, of course, exceptions. In the 1820s, the New York speculator Peter Smith bought North Elba acreage at auction and told the longtime squatters he would not sell them the land they had worked so hard to tame. Suddenly reduced to tenants, many moved away. That land baron was Gerrit Smith's father, whose hard-dealing legacy Gerrit labored to reverse. See Smith, *History of Essex County*, 663; MacKenzie, *Plains of Abraham*, 20–22.

2. Frederick Brown to "Brother Watkin" Brown, Osawatomie, KS, 11/10/1855, JBjrKS.

3. A comparison of gift lots in Gerrit Smith's *Land Book* with home locations noted in the state and federal censuses from 1840 to 1865 is one way to document the grantees' preference for land more to their liking than what they'd legally received. Mary MacKenzie tracks these moves in *The Plains of Abraham* (129–40), and in *Blacks in the Adirondacks*, Sally Svenson expands the reach

of this inquiry to Franklin; Baumann, "Goldsmith." The first Hunter's Home near Loon Lake was a farmhouse that the innkeeper Paul Smith rented in 1848. Four years later, he bought two hundred acres and built the better-known hotel of the same name. Tyler, *Story of Paul Smith*, 13–17; F. L. Turner, "Early Days in the Town of Franklin," *AR-EP*, 2/1930; Census takers knew Stephen Warren Morehouse's wife by many names, including Mary, Laura, Lara, Laney, and Lura. In the 1870s, she moved in with her daughter Jane Morehouse Jones in Malone, and lived with her for years. *NYSC 1875*, Malone, NY.

4. A speculative map of Timbuctoo is at the John Brown farm. The cartographer (maybe long-time site manager Ed Cotter) used J. H. French's 1858 town map as a base on which to flag the deeded land of eleven Black North Elba pioneers. Parks historian Maurice O'Brien included this map in his paper, "'Timbuctoo': An Attempt at Negro Settlement in the Adirondacks." 0/1/1977, PIA.

5. When Susan left her family, it wasn't from their first isolated cabin at South Mountain. In 1855, their home was a log cabin nearer to the frame home of Henry and Ruth Brown Thompson and handy to the home of Lyman Eppes as well. See Josiah Hasbrook, *NYSC 1855*, NE. Leonard Worts and Lewis Pierce's hunting excursions are documented in Worts's Vermont obituary, along with Worts's claim that he and Pierce got lost, then "found and rescued by John Brown." *VWSJ*, 8/26/1885.

6. *Records of the Association for the Benefit of Colored Orphans, Series III, Admission Records*, vol. 23, 174–76, vol. 24, #484, #485, #348, NYHS; LPM, widow's pension appeal, NARA. Lucy Miles (née Pierce) was born on 8/3/1859 in New York City.

7. LPM widow's pension; Susan Hasbrouck, *USFC, 1860*, Manhattan.

8. LPM widow's pension.

9. Jane Thompson to Belle Brown, 11/14/1865. Cited in Mackenzie, *Plains of Abraham*, 151.

10. MacKenzie, *Plains of Abraham*, 150–51; *USFC 1870*, NE; LPM widow's pension; JM military pension, deposition, 8/9/1898.

11. "Elizabethtown, the Oldest Adirondack Summer Resort, Still Stands at the Head," *EP*, 5/18/1899. Several Black North Elbans moved to Westport for short spells between 1850 and 1874. Among them were Josiah and Jane Ann Hasbrook, Samuel and Jane Jefferson, William and Jane Carasaw, Silas and Jane Frazier, Susan Hasbrook Pierce and her daughter Lucy, Jeremiah Miles, and Leonard and Deanna Worts. *USFC 1850, 1860, 1870*; *NYSC 1855, 1865, 1875*; and LPM widow's pension. On the migration of the Weeks family to Westport and points north, see Jones, "They Called It Timbucto."

12. Joseph James, *USFC 1850, 1860, 1870*, Westport, and *GSLB*, 33 and 104; "Mrs. Adeline E. James," *EP*, 1/7/1915. Westport history buffs Morris Glenn and Bill Johnston also generously shared with me their research on this family in 2001.

13. George W. Bell, *GSLB*, 79. Already an Essex County resident when he received his lot, George Bell crops up in Willsboro census reports from 1845 to 1875. On January 22, 1879, the seventy-five-year-old farmer left his log house for the county poorhouse, a not-unusual removal for poor, aging Adirondackers

in winter. Bell's place of birth, variously identified as Delaware, Washington, DC, and Maryland, hints at an early life in slavery.

14. Alexander Hasbrook is identified as a guide for the innkeeper Paul Smith in a photograph, "Guides at Paul Smith's Boathouse," SLFL. Josiah Hasbrook's neighbors note his several jobs besides farming in their affidavits for his military pension. On Carasaw, see MacKenzie, *Plains of Abraham*, 159; Edward Cotter to BBS, NE, 2/7/1966, JB/BBS Coll./WVMP; Merle D. Melvin to Norman Dann, 3/4/2005 (courtesy of Norman Dann, Peterboro); Egel, Kirshenbaum, and Malo, *Santanoni*, 37; Josiah Hasbrook, *NYSC, 1865*, Sag Harbor, NY.

15. *USFC 1870*, Franklin, Franklin County; Wardner, "Footprints on Adirondack Trails," 116–17; "Shooting in the Adirondacks" (1860, 1899); Tyler, *Story of Paul Smith*, 41–42. Local historian Helen Escha Tyler reports that the teenaged Warren Morehouse cooked for hunting parties led by the great guide Paul Smith in the early days of Smith's first inn, Hunter's Home. Morehouse also cooked at the nearby Rainbow Inn (Wardner, "Footprints on Adirondack Trails," 117–18), and, with his mother, helped out at Paul Smith's second inn before he went to Massachusetts to join his regiment (*USFC 1860*, Franklin). Back in Franklin after the war, Morehouse was a "waiting man" for the Franklin innkeeper Sarah Hill (*NYSC 1865*, Franklin). I am grateful to the independent scholar Don Papson for details of Morehouse's employment.

16. "Shooting in the Adirondacks."

17. Hardy, "Iron Age Community," 37; HHG, "Preached at Troy, N.Y., to a Company of Mr. Gerrit Smith's Grantees," *NS*, 5/12/1848.

18. *TS*, 8/16/1894; *ECR*, 3/1/1888; *NYSC 1855*, NE; *USFC 1860*, NE. Mary MacKenzie was the first historian to identify and honor Eppes's achievements beyond his friendship with John Brown. See MacKenzie, *Plains of Abraham*, 131–36; *GSLB*, 89. Eppes, like James Henderson, received his deed in Smith's distribution in 1847; *EP*, 3/29/1894.

19. David Rhinelander, "From Past to Present," *Hartford Courant*, 4/23/1999; Barbara W. Brown, "School for African American Children, Colchester," 2008, New London County Archives Society; Douglass Harper, "Slavery in Connecticut," Slavery in the North, 2003, http://slavenorth.com/connecticut.htm; Peter P. Hinks, "Gradual Emancipation Reflected the Struggle of Some to Envision Black Freedom," Connecticut History, 1/2/2020, https://connecticuthistory.org/gradual-emancipation-reflected-the-struggle-of-some-to-envision-black-freedom/; LEE to John Brown Jr. and Owen Brown, NE, 11/10/1885, JBjrOH, Frohman Coll., Rutherford P. Hayes Presidential Library, OH; NE school reports, 1857, ECCO. In 1857, five Eppes children attended school. A Worts and a Carasaw were the other Black youths in this class.

20. Brumley, *Guides of the Adirondacks*, 118, and Street, *Indian Pass*, 14; LEE to FD, NE, 7/12/1854, in *FDP*, 7/21/1854; BBS to George Marshall, 4/19/1962 ("power of Attorney executed by Silas Harris, NYC, to Lyman Eppes Sr. granting authority to control and supervise landed property in Franklin County, NY," 7/19/1888), JB/BBS Coll./WVMP; JB to Ruth and Henry Thompson, 12/29/1852, JB/BBS Coll./WVMP; "Excavation Reveals Clues about Timbuctoo," *LPN*, 7/31/2009.

21. *EP*, 7/21/1916; Ben F. Lewis, Plattsburgh, NY, to Marjorie Lansing Porter, 3/26/1955; MacKenzie, *Plains of Abraham*, 134: Ruth Brown Thompson to Wealthy Brown, 3/10/1850, NE, JBJr.

22. Porter, *Lem Merrill*, 15, reports that some neighbors of the Black grantees used this racial slur. Circumstantial evidence (headstone epitaph, age and census records, state of origin) intimates that Alexander Hazzard's wife was the same teenaged Mary Elizabeth Bailey who came north to Franklin with James, Louisa, and Samuel Brady in the 1850s.

23. MacKenzie, *Plains of Abraham*, 133. Federal and state censuses from 1850 to 1880 suggest the slave-state origins of Virginia-born Sally Henderson, and in Franklin to the north, the southern roots of James and Louisa Brady, Mary Elizabeth Bailey, and the grantee Wesley Murray. "She Was Once a Slave; Interesting History of a Colored Woman—Her Piety and Charity," *Troy (NY) Northern Budget*, 5/27/1888; SH military pension, affidavit, Josiah Hasbrook Jr.; "Bloomingdale," *Malone (NY) Palladium*, 3/8/1894; see chapters 1 and 8; Sanborn, *Life and Letters*, 100, 131–32. Brendan Mills, JBF site manager, estimates that the young fugitive Cyrus Thomas lived with the Browns for about eighteen months. Mills, interview by the author, 11/9/2018. On Adirondack writers who embraced the image of the Black Woods as a destination for fugitives, see ch. 5, note 30.

24. The letters of Jermain Loguen, James H. Henderson, John Brown, and Brown's daughter Ruth Brown Thompson all document bigotry on the frontier. It should be noted, however, that in the thirteen years between the passage of the Fugitive Slave Act and the start of the Civil War, no Black Adirondacker was seized by bounty hunters. No evidence suggests that Southern-born grantee-settlers were directly threatened by their neighbors. The charcoal wagons that reportedly trundled fugitives through the Adirondacks to Canada were not attacked. No Essex County deputy marched to North Elba to claim the fugitive Cyrus Thomas in the several seasons he was with the Browns. Bounty hunters who pursued the grantee-fugitive John Thomas to Franklin were deterred by his white neighbors, who warned them that if they tried to take this farmer, he would fight, and they would help. See chap. 11 in this book; Seaver, *Historical Sketches*, 6; and Papson, "The John Thomas Story."

25. "Honor to Gerrit Smith!," *Signal of Liberty*, 10/3/1846, and "Gerrit Smith's Donation," *Signal of Liberty*, 12/5/1846. This paper also promoted Black husbandry in Michigan, but the Washingtons needed more than Michigan's rich soil; they wanted a community representing principles of racial justice. The Black Woods fit that bill. D. Washington, "For the Voice of the Fugitive," Ann Arbor, 1/13/1852, in *The Voice of the Fugitive*, 1/29/1852. By March 1857, Dennis Washington had lost confidence in the leadership of the Refugees Home colony, his home in Chatham, Canada West. See the following in *PF*: "Refugees in Canada," 2/21/1857; "Letter No. 1," "Letter No. 2," 3/14/1857; "A Communication from Dennis Washington," 3/7/1857; "Correspondence," 4/18/1857; and "For the Provincial Freeman," 4/25/1857. Also see James Blair Webb to GS, 3/1848. The land broker Webb sent Smith forty dollars from Ann Arbor's Dennis Washington for "a deed for 40 acres in Township 11"; Dennis Washington to Henry Bibb, *Voice of the Fugitive*, 1/29/1852.

26. Bibb, *Life and Adventures*. On this charismatic reformer-activist, see Cooper, "Fluid Frontier"; and Bordewich, *Bound for Canaan*, 380–88; *GSLB*, 37. Bibb's forty-acre gift lot (near the lots of Douglass and the Boston activist William Wells Brown) was in Township 12, Old Military Tract, Lot 24, in Essex County; Henry Bibb to GS, 12/30/1848; Henry Bibb, "Florence," *NS*, 3/23/1849; "Correspondence," *PF*, 3/2/1857, 3/4/1857, 4/18/1857, and 4/25/1857. Winks, *Blacks in Canada*, 204–8, describes the work of Bibb's Refugee Home Society. For a wide-ranging cultural context for these settlements, see introduction, Ripley et al., *Black Abolitionist Papers*, 2:3–46; Out of slavery for nine years when the Fugitive Slave Act was enacted, Walter Hawkins recollected that he might have stayed to "fight it out" were it not for the risk to his family. But, "What if he was killed in battle? What would become of his wife and children?" If he were slain or seized, "there was a chance of them being taken south and sold on the auction block." Better to "enjoy his own liberty [and] secure the same for his wife and children than to live in fear." Edwards, S. J. Celestine, with Walter Hawkins, *From Slavery to a Bishopric, or, The Life of Bishop Walter Hawkins of the British Methodist Episcopal Church, Canada* (John Kensit, 1891), 112–22.

27. "On Meeting of the Colored People of Troy," *AP*, 10/28/1846.

28. See Bordewich, *Bound for Canaan*, chap. 15; ibid., 168–70; R. J. M. Blackett, "Freemen to the Rescue! Resistance to the Fugitive Slave Law of 1850," in Blight, *Passages to Freedom*, 133–47; Christianson, *Freeing Charles*, 69–70, 88–103; Campbell, *Slave Catchers*, 110–47, 199–207; Quarles, *Black Abolitionists*, 200; Lois Horton, "Kidnapping and Resistance: Antislavery Direct Action in the 1850s," in Blight, *Passages to Freedom*, 161; Quarles, *Black Abolitionists*, 200.

29. *The Fugitive Slave Law and Its Victims*, American Anti-slavery Society, NY, 1856; Douglass H. Shephard, "The 1851 Recapture and Trial of Harrison: A Compilation of Accounts between 1851 and 1944," 2014, https://chqgov.com/county-historian/underground-railroad; John P. Downs and Fenwick Y. Hedley, *History of Chautauqua County, New York and Its People* (American Historical Society, 1921).

30. "Moses Viney, Negro Bodyguard of Dr. Nott for Many Years, Continues Active and Reminiscent," *DG*, 1904; "Aged Moses Viney Claimed by Death," *DG*, 1/11/1909; Yetwin, " Odyssey of Moses Viney"; *GSLB*, 92; Genovese, *Roll, Jordan, Roll*, 143–44, 361–65. While Viney was in Canada, Eliphalet Nott covered the fugitive's taxes on his gift lot (*County Treasurers Sales in 1852 for Outstanding Taxes from 1849*, 1609, NYSA). After Nott purchased Viney's freedom for $250, Viney returned to Union College and resumed his work as Nott's teamster and valet. On Van Pelt, see Durkee, *Reminiscences of Saratoga*, 11; Samuel G. Boyd, *In the Days of Old Glens Falls—as I Remember It* (Zonta Club of Glens Falls, 1927); and "Another Fugitive Slave Case," *Glens Falls Free Press*, 9/17/1851.

31. Hunter, 331–35; Ripley et al, *BAP*, v. 4, 144n10, 402n8; On strategies and instances of kidnapping, see Siebert, *Underground Railroad*, 240, 295–96, 318; Bordewich, *Bound for Canaan*, 135–43, 172–78; and Foner, *Gateway to Freedom*, 60–70, 108–9; Curry, *Free Black*, 229–31.

32. Carl Beckwith Smith, conversation with the author, Loon Lake, NY, 5/13/2005; *ECR*, 10/25/1907; MacKenzie, *Plains of Abraham*, 151, 139; "Essex County, Town of Keane," *NS*, 2/2/1849; "A Talk by C. Walter Goff Given to

the Lake Placid–North Elba Historical Society—circa 1965," typescript, Special Collections, LPPL.

33. Charles H. Peck, *Plants of North Elba*, Bulletin of the New York State Museum, vol. 6, no. 28 (6/1899): 69, 81; H. Possons, "Mountains and Lakes," *Troy Daily Times*, 4/26/1890; Hayes, *Lake Placid*, 15; "A Talk by C. Walter Goff . . . ," LPPL. Franklin, too, held the trace memory of the Black Woods in the spoken map. A hundred years after Lt. Alfred Skiff brought the once-enslaved Walter Scott to Franklin, and long after the Scotts had moved away, neighbors called their farmstead the Scott place. See Tyler, ". . . In Them Thar Hills," 63.

34. MacKenzie, *Plains of Abraham*, 14; "The Old Slavery Days," *PR*, 3/28/1903, and "Reference to Gerrit Smith," *EPG*, 4/2/1903.

35. Andrew Williams, *Map to Accompany a Description and Historical Guide to the Valley of Lake Champlain and the Adirondacks, Tourists' Edition* (R. S. Styles, 1871), Special Collections, University of Vermont; Wardner, "Footprints," chap. 10, "Early Days at Rainbow," 6; Ahaz Hayes, *NYSC 1855*, St. Armand, Essex County.

36. "Spike" [Spike Schmeele], "Highlights of the Game," *LPN*, 3/31/1944. The derogatory local nickname for this cemetery, reportedly near Bear Cub Road in Averyville, south of North Elba, was confirmed by the Adirondackers Nathan Farb and Greg Furness, who heard it from older Placidians. The site of the cemetery is unknown today, and likely will remain so. No law requires the upkeep or protection of unmarked burial sites in New York. In an email (11/28/2000), retired historical interpreter Furness told me he "repeatedly" heard the "John Brown Farm referred to as 'The N— Site' or 'The N— Farm.'"

37. Letter. Mary MacKenzie to Mary Hotaling, 4/28/1994, Mary MacKenzie Collection, LPPL. J. F. French, "North Elba, 1858," from *The Map of Essex County, New York* (E. A. Balch, 1858).

38. JB to WH, Springfield, MA, 5/22/1848, 10/28/1848, and 1/22/1849, published in the *New York Evening Post*, 12/21/1859; JHH to HHG, Timbucto, West Keene, 1/29/1849, in *NS*, 2/16/1849; and John Brown Jr. to his mother, Mary Ann, Springfield, MA, 10/15/1849 ("We reached Keene a week ago. . . . [We] visited most of the important places. Such as Timbuctoo &c."), JBJr.

39. John Brown may not have known the more familiar spelling of "Timbuctoo." Spelling was not his strength. (Among words misspelled in letters to his wife are "verry," "hapiness," "immagination," "boddy," "equl," "kneed," and "midling.") On the mystery of Timbuctoo's first naming, see Caleb McDaniel's online essays "In Search of John Brown's Timbucto, Part I," 8/11/2010, https://www.owlnet.rice.edu/~wcm1/john-brown-timbuctoo-part1.html, and "In Search of John Brown's Timbucto, Part II," 9/3/2010, https://www.owlnet.rice.edu/~wcm1/john-brown-timbuctoo-part2.html.

Among the surnames these new marriages introduced to the Black Woods were Langley, Scott, Prince, Gardineer, Johnson, Smith, Anthony, and Miles (mostly Southerners and Vermonters). And some Black names belonged to hired hands and servants who lived in the homes of white people—interracial households that were compelled by frontier necessity. But the inclusivity of Black families represented something more. Invoking Herbert Gutman's research, George Frederickson notes that the "consciousness of being part of an extended family—including spouses, siblings, grandparents, aunts, uncles, and cousins—provided Afro-Americans with the foundations for a sense of community that could extend over time and across space. When in the nineteenth century original families were broken up and individual members carried [away], the effect was of course traumatic; yet the kinship ideal was not lost. When blood relationships were lacking . . . fictive kinship arrangements tended to take their place until a new pattern of consanguinity had time to develop." Frederickson, *Arrogance of Race*, 120.

In the Black Woods in 1855, Louisa and James Brady of Franklin made room for young Mary Bailey (very possibly a relative), and young Charles Hasbrook was the "adopted son" of Leonard and Deanna Worts. Five years later, the elderly Wortses took in the youthful Harriette Hasbrook and her older brother Josiah, whose parents had split up and moved away. After the Civil War, Private Josiah Hasbrook housed his half-sister Lucy Pierce (who for a while took his surname for her own). When he remarried, Charles Henry Hazzard made a home in St. Armand for his new stepdaughters. Genevia and Clara Smith (Southern-born and, like their mother, likely once enslaved). After Genevia's death and her husband's removal to Manhattan, Charles Hazzard and his wife took in their teenage grandchildren (and their descendants may live in Saranac Lake even now).

40. Donaldson, *History of the Adirondacks*, 2:6; MacKenzie, *Plains of Abraham*, 167–68. "They called it Timbuctoo?" was MacKenzie's stern response to both Donaldson and the Boston writer Katherine Butler Jones's essay on Timbuctoo in *Orion*, Winter 1998; Monmonier, *Squaw Tit to Whorehouse Meadow*, xi, 37, 69; JHH to HHG, Timbucto, West Keene, 1/29/1849, published in *NS*, 2/16/1849. In this letter Henderson reported, "I have been here for eight months," or since June or July 1848. Another letter dates his residency on Lot 93 in Township 12 to mid-May 1848. JHH to GS, 10/15/1850.

41. "Timbucktoo," *Hartford Courant*, 11/5/1879. Of the four newspapers indexed in Donald Jacobs's inventory *Antebellum Black Newspapers*, *Freedom's Journal* took the strongest interest in sub-Saharan Africa, covering European exploration, African culture, the slave economy, tribal life, and tribal governance. The Timbuctoo explorers Hugh Clapperton, Alexander Laing, and René Caillié invited multiple mentions, and more than a dozen columns were devoted to the Timbuctoo-born lecturer and Africanophile Prince Abdullah Rahaman. For articles regarding European exploration (and Timbuctoo), see *Freedom's Journal*, 3/16/1827, 4/6/1827, 12/26/1828, 10/10/1829, 2/26/1829, and 2/28/1828; for news of Africa's geography and tribal culture, 3/28/1829 and 4/6/1829; and for Rahahman's report on Timbuctoo, 10/24/1828. Appiah and Gates, *Dictionary of Global Culture*, 644–45; Lila Azam Zanganeh, "When Timbuktu Was the Paris of Islamic Intellectuals in Africa," *NYT*, 4/24/2004; de Gramont, *Strong Brown God*, 33.

42. McDaniel, "John Brown's Timbucto, Part I," offers a discerning summary of the imagery of Timbuctoo in early nineteenth-century poems, explorers' letters, colonization appeals, and articles in the Black press.

43. Kryza, *Race for Timbuktu*, 229–36; Howe, *Afrocentrism*, 151. In the nineteenth century, one to two thousand slaves were transported annually every

year from Timbuctoo across the Sahara. Homer, *The Iliad*, I-429; HHG, *Past and Present Condition*, 8; Moses, *Afrotopia*, 47–48.

44. Jacobs, *Antebellum Black Newspapers*, 542, 50n; Cooley, *Negroland of the Arabs*; Armistead, *Tribute for the Negro*; HHG, *Past and Present Condition*.

45. McDaniel, "John Brown's Timbucto, Part I."

46. Randall Rohe, "The Geography and Material Culture of the Western Mining Town," *Material Culture* 16, no. 3 (Fall 1984): 114–15; "Timbuctoo, Yuba County," *San Francisco Daily Evening Bulletin*, 11/28/1857; "Mining about Timbuctoo, Yuba County," *San Francisco Daily Evening Bulletin*, 1/14/1859; Lyght, *Path of Freedom*, 38–40, 68, 79. At "Global Timbuktu: Meanings and Narratives of Resistance in Africa and the Americas," a conference at Rutgers University, 3/24/2017, Guy-Oreido Weston, a genealogist and historian from Mount Holly, New Jersey, and the great-great-grandson of a founder of the New Jersey Timbuctoo, shared his research on this colony, represented, in a deed of 1829, as Tombuctoo, before this name was changed. Wood and Hageman, *Burlington and Mercer Counties*, 500–506.

10. We Who Are Here Can See and Know

1. John Warren, "A Short History of Adirondack Beaver," New York Almanack, 8/24/2021, https://www.newyorkalmanack.com/2021/08/a-short-history-of-adirondack-beaver/; Terrie, *Wildlife and Wilderness*, 59–60; Hurd, *Franklin and Clinton Counties*, 209. In *The Adirondack; or, Life in the Woods* (Baker, 1849), Joel T. Headley confidently asserted that "game of all kinds swarm the forest: bears, wolves, panthers, deer, and moose." Quoted in Terrie, *Wildlife and Wilderness*, 59; Brumley, *Guides of the Adirondacks*, 118.

2. *NYSC 1855*, NE, and MacKenzie, *Plains of Abraham*, 132–33; "The Late Elijah Simonds . . . ," *EP*, 7/21/1916; "Old-Time Adirondack Christmas Recalled," *Elizabethtown (NY) Times*, 12/26/1940; untitled news clipping, n.d., Adirondack newspaper, 7/1940, George Marshall Papers, SLFL.

3. Ruth Brown to Mary Ann Brown, West Keene, 10/31/1849; *ECR*, 1/7/52; *ECR*, 2/3/1850; Keller, *Adirondack Wilderness*, 91; "Laws Reached by the Board of Supervisors in Their Annual Meeting of 1849," *ECR*, 2/23/1850, and "Proceedings of the Board of Supervisors," *ECR*, 1/21/1854. The Saranac River was declared a public highway in 1846, the upper waters of the Hudson in 1849, and the Ausable River in 1853.

4. Reynolds, *John Brown, Abolitionist*, 89–91.

5. Carvalho, "John Brown's Transformation"; "The John Brown House," Summit County Historical Society of Akron, Ohio, 2020, https://www.summithistory.org/john-brown-house; JB to Mary Brown, Akron, 12/27/1852. Brown/Gee Collection, Hudson Library and Historical Society, Hudson, OH.

6. "Dear Editor," John G. Fay to *LPN*, 12/11/1942. In this same letter, Fay noted that his father, Gilman Taylor Fay, taught Black and white farm children in his North Elba schoolhouse.

7. Late in life, Josiah Hasbrook Jr. recalled his father's rescue, after "three days in the deep gorges and snowdrifts," by a party organized by John Brown (*Springfield Daily Republican*, 7/28/1915). But it is unclear whether this

happened before or after Henderson's own death. In her recollection of her father's near-fatal brush with hypothermia, Ruth Brown Thompson dated it to the winter of 1850 (Villard, *John Brown*, 73–74). Whether Henderson in his last distracted hour actually called to mind Brown's providential arrival at Robert Scott's cabin is, of course, unknowable. But he very likely heard about it, and perhaps it gave him hope.

8. "Dear Editor," *LPN*, 12/11/1942; JB to Ruth Brown Thompson, in Sanborn, *Life and Letters*, 104; "Colored Citizens of Troy," *Christian Freeman*, 5/5/1843, "Appeal for Rights," *NASS*, 1/29/1846; JHH to HHG, *NS*, 2/16/1849; "Evening School," *CA*, 10/17/1840; Mackenzie, *Plains of Abraham*, 144; JHH to GS, *NE*, 10/15/1850.

9. JHH to GS, *NE*, 10/15/1850; JB to GS, 11/8/1849. On one side of the 11/8/1849 letter from Brown to Smith is the agreement between Pliny Nash and Smith for the ten-installment payment plan for this land, and a note describing Samuel Jefferson's assumption of this payment plan from 8/29/1851 to 12/23/1853. JHH to GS, *NE*, 10/14/1848. The history of Lot 93 is tangled and somewhat troubling. James and Susan Henderson built their home on land that their white neighbor, Pliny Nash, owned and let them use while Nash was buying it on time from Gerrit Smith. The obliging Nash would have sold it to them, too, but a year before James Henderson died, John Brown devised a plan to buy the contract to all of Lot 93 from Smith directly, and to split it up between himself, his son Jason, the Hendersons, and the Jeffersons, with separate deeds for all. That was a good plan, but for some reason never stated, John Brown changed his mind and opted for another lot, transferring the purchase plan of 93 to the Jeffersons. This left Henderson in the lurch. John Brown had assured him that Gerrit Smith would sell him his piece in installments, and on the strength of this suggestion Henderson had built his farm. But white locals with long dealings with Peterboro told Henderson the rich man would never break up a forty-acre lot (Smith dealt in five-thousand-acre parcels, not five-acre shards), and Smith's secretary, Caleb Calkins, confirmed this.

10. *Report of Select Committee*, 44–45; Godine, "Poor View."

11. Colored Orphan Asylum Records, Association for the Benefit of Colored Orphans Records, series 3, vol. 23, 349–52, NYHS, https://digitalcollections.nyhistory.org/islandora/search/Colored%20Orphan%20Asylum%20Records?type=edismax&cp=islandora%3A130602; Harris, *Shadow of Slavery*, 136.

12. Harris, *Shadow of Slavery*, 160, 278; Henderson intake report, Colored Orphan Asylum Records, vol. 23, 349; Harris, *Shadow of Slavery*, 136, 158–59; Colored Orphan Asylum Records, 230, 58, 62–65; Anna Shotwell to GS, NYC, 9/21/1846, and Harris, *Shadow of Slavery*, 277; Colored Orphans Asylum Records, vol. 3. Susan Henderson's six children were admitted to the orphanage on 11/26/1852 and immediately determined to be "enjoying good health." Tellingly, while all six were admitted to the asylum on the same terms and day, the death of two of them within weeks of each other caused the record keeper to disavow the younger, Susan Henderson, an infant, as a legitimate inmate of the institution, "she being irregularly received . . . not recorded—[and] sick upon entering." The orphanage did not want the death of this infant on its books. On infant mortality in the orphanage, see Harris, *Shadow of Slavery*, 162–65.

13. Harris, *Shadow of Slavery*, 162; JMS to GS, NYC, 2/6/1850; "DIED," *CA*, 8/28/1841; Harris, *Shadow of Slavery*, 278, 336n. Benjamin Henderson died on 11/12/1852, less than two weeks after his infant sister, Susan A. Henderson. And after three years in the asylum, thirteen-year-old James G. Henderson was only ten days out of it when, on 4/29/1855, he "gave up the Ghost." Colored Orphans Asylum Records, vol. 23, 329. In light of the orphanage's response to his baby sister's death in 1852 (see note 12), one wonders if the orphanage wanted him out before he died.

14. "Charles E. Hodges (1819–after April 15, 1910)," Encyclopedia Virginia, 12/22/2021, https://encyclopediavirginia.org/entries/hodges-charles-e-1819-after-april-15-1910/. Charles Hodges, executor of his late father's family farm of 143 acres, owed taxes on the property and was urged by his attorney to get out of Virginia before creditors filed suit. Hodges, his mother, and some siblings moved to William Hodges's home in Brooklyn in 1851.

15. LEE to "Mr. Editor," *FDP*, 7/21/1854.

16. LEE to "Mr. Editor," *FDP*, 7/21/1854.

17. LEE to "Mr. Editor," *FDP*, 7/21/1854; FD, *NS*, 2/18/1848; JHH to HHG, "West Keene, Timbucto, Essex County," 1/29/1849, in *NS*, 2/16/1849. On slavery's effect on nineteenth-century Black America's relationship to land and farming, see Smith, *African American Environmental Thought*, 7, 8, 14, 66–67.

18. Fox, "Lumber Industry," 17; Meinig, *Shaping of America*, 246; "Northern Guide," *ECR*, 7/1/1852.

19. CBR and JMS, "To Gerrit Smith Grantees."

20. FD to Harriet Beecher Stowe, Rochester, 3/8/1853; "From the Minutes of the Colored National Convention," *FDP*, 12/2/1853.

21. FD to Stowe, 3/8/1853; "Hills, Lakes and Country Streams, or A Tramp in the Chateaugay Woods," excerpted in *FDP*, 6/9/1854.

22. "Help for the People of Color," *FDP*, 10/9/1851, from the *New York Independent*; Joseph C. Holly, *GSLB*, 32.

23. "News," *BDE*, 4/2/1853. In this issue, the *Eagle*'s readers would learn that "hundreds if not thousands of the parcels of land given away by Hon. Gerrit Smith to poor & worthy white & colored people in this State were advertised to be sold for taxes"; FD to Stowe, 3/8/1853; "From the Minutes of the Colored National Convention," *FDP*, 12/2/1853.

24. "Plan of the American Industrial School," *FDP*, 4/15/1854, 3/16/1855.

25. "The American Industrial School," *New-York Tribune*, n.d., in *FDP*, 5/26/1854; *Oberlin Times*, n.d., quoted in *FDP*, 4/15/1853; "The U.S. National Council," *Provincial Freeman* (Toronto), 8/5/1854; "Selections, from *New York Tribune*, National Council of the Colored People," *FDP*, 5/18/1855; "Scioto" to FD, Columbus, OH, 4/24/1854, published in *FDP*, 5/26/1854; "The Industrial School," *FDP*, 6/1/1855.

26. Peter Humphries Clark, *Herald of Freedom*, n.d., 1855, quoted by "Communipaw" [JMS] in *FDP*, 8/10/1855 and 9/21/1855. Clark's opposition to Douglass's proposed industrial college pained McCune Smith deeply. A barber's son in Cincinnati, the activist and writer Peter Clark once supported Liberian colonization but later embraced an ardent antiemigrationism. As the principal of a Black high school in the 1850s, Clark opposed desegregation (integrated

schools, he felt, would be taken over by whites). "No man was truer to his op-pressed people than Peter H. Clark," wrote the reformer William Wells Brown in 1882. Brown, *Rising Son*, 524. See Philip Foner on Clark's political career in Foner, *Essays in Afro-American History*, 155–77; and David A. Gerber's essay "The Dialogue of Hope and Despair," in Litwack and Meier, *Black Leaders*, 173–90.

27. Ripley et al., *Black Abolitionist Papers*, 3:345–51, 350n. In the 1850s, James McCune Smith used the pseudonym "Communipaw" (from Communipaw Flats, in New York City) in columns for *FDP* and *NASS*.

28. JMS to GS, NYC, 12/17/1846; JMS to GS, NYC, 2/6/1850; JMS to FD, "Our Leaders," *FDP*, 9/21/1855.

29. LEE to "Mr. Editor," *FDP*, 7/21/1854.

30. McGowen to GS, Albany, 10/1/1859; "Gerrit Smith," *New-York Tribune*, in *FDP*, 11/12/1852; John Brown to his children, 11/5/1852; BBS to Mary E. Cunningham, 6/5/1948; "Election of Gerrit Smith," *Liberator*, quoted in *FDP*, 11/19/1852; FD to GS, 11/10/1852; "Gerrit Smith," from *NYT*, in *FDP*, 11/12/1852; "Congressional Speeches," *NE*, 6/15/1854; "Speech of Gerrit Smith," *Daily Morning Advocate*, in *FDP*, 6/9/1854.

31. "Speed of Speech," *Semi-weekly Eagle* (Brattleboro, VT), 7/17/1848 ("Some of the reporters state that Daniel Webster speaks at the rate of eighty to one hundred and ten words per minute; Gerrit Smith from seventy to ninety...; Mr. Clay one hundred and thirty to one hundred and sixty; . . . Mr. Calhoun from one hundred and sixty to two hundred"). Other details of Smith's congressional career are drawn from Frothingham, *Gerrit Smith*, 212–26, and Harlow, *Gerrit Smith*, 312–25. In *The Field of Blood*, Joanne Freeman describes a culture of physical violence and intimidation in the antebellum halls of Congress as far from Gerrit Smith's calm domestic work culture as a battlefield.

32. "Letter from Gerrit Smith to Wm. Goodell," Peterboro, *FDP*, 11/1/1854; "The Appeal of the Independent Democrats in Congress, signed by Senators Salmon P. Chase and Charles Sumner, and U.S. Representatives Gerrit Smith, Joshua Giddings," *NE*, 1/14/1854. Other signatories included Edward Wade and Alexander De Witt. "The Appeal" was also published in the *Cincinnati Gazette* and the *New-York Tribune*. See https://web.archive.org/web/20070926214925/http://teachingamericanhistory.org/library/index.asp?document=945. Holt, *American Whig Party*, 815–16.

33. GS to Wm. Goodell, *FDP*, 11/10/1854. Smith had cause to worry. In his aggrieved letter to Goodell, he quoted a resolution from a National Colored People's Convention in Cleveland, Ohio, earlier in August 1854. "[We] hope, on due reflection," the delegates wrote, that Gerrit Smith "may yet consent to lose a meal of victuals, or an hour's sleep, for the cause of down-trodden and suffering humanity." "Letter from Hon. Gerrit Smith," *FDP*, 9/1/1854.

34. Harlow, *Gerrit Smith*, 334; "Letter from Gerrit Smith to Wm. Goodell," Peterboro, *FDP*, 11/1/1854; "Letter from Hon. Gerrit Smith," *FDP*, 9/1/1854. Clues to Smith's later sanction of antislavery militancy and violence animated the reformer's aggrieved defense of his congressional career in "Gerrit Smith to His Constituents," *FDP*, 8/18/1854: "Let it be remembered, that it is only while and where I am inside of the Government, that I acknowledge myself bound to bow to the will of the majority. I bow to it in the legislative hall and in the

court-room; and every where and always do I bow to it; until the purposed *execution* of the decree that is intolerable. Then I rebel." Out of Congress, and facing a repugnant law "which wrongs me greatly," he claimed every right "to decide whether to rebel against the Government, and to resist the enforcement."

35. In New York, most legal documents concerning nineteenth-century land tax sales by the state comptroller or the county treasurers, including notices of tax sales and redemptions, lists of tax-delinquent deedholders, appeals to redeem land from tax sales, applications to cancel tax sales, register of bids and sales, etc., are housed in the state archives in Albany. In 1999, the NYS Comptrollers Office transferred much of this documentary material to the state archives. For a summary of these holdings, see Jim Folts, "Land Title Records in the New York State Archives," draft 11, 17–19, at https://docslib. org/doc/1178699/land-title-records-in-the-new-york-state-archives-new-york-state-archives-information-leaflet-11-draft. Among the files I reviewed at the archives in Albany were A1352, "Receipt book of land grants from Gerrit Smith to 'colored and poor white slaves from the South,' " 1846, carbon copy of transcription of original records; BO846, Published Notices of Land Sold for Unpaid Taxes and Unredeemed, 1826–1905; BO847-85, Applications to redeem property from tax sales [Hamilton, Essex, Franklin Counties], 1846–1860; BO918, Certificates of land for sale for unpaid taxes, 1815–1928; B0934, "Lists of non-residents lands with unpaid taxes ca 1810–1850; BO940, County Treasurers' Statements of Non-Resident Lands Sold for Unpaid Taxes, 1849–1854; BO941-85, County Treasurers' Sales Tax Returns; A1411-77, "Applications for Cancellation of Tax Sales, 1841–1925," Comptroller's Office Land Tax Bureau; B1605-99, folder, "1852 Sale on 1849 Taxes, Vol. 1"; B1617 and B1619, Redemption Diaries, Comptrollers Office, NYSA, Albany, NY.

36. Nineteenth-century comptroller's records, now in the New York State Archives, document numerous Smith grantees and agents making up back taxes on gift lots not their own. B1605-99, "Registers of Non-Resident Lands Sold in Tax Sales by County Treasurers, 1852–1896, Vol. 1" and folder, "County Treasurer's Sale of 1853 Outstanding Taxes, Vol. 4"; B1609-99, "Daybook of Taxes and Redemption Payments to County Treasurer, 1850–1855" and folder, "County Treasurer's Sale of 1854 [for] Outstanding Taxes 1851, Vol. 1," NYSA.

37. Meinig, *Shaping of America*, 244. Eric Foner suggests that Charles Ray's zeal for speculation inflamed a rift between Ray and Lewis Tappan, one of Ray's codirectors on the New York State Vigilance Committee. Tappan suspected that committee head Ray used funds intended for a family of fugitives for a personal real estate investment of his own. Ray disputed these charges. Foner, *Gateway to Freedom*, 170–71; Stauffer, *Black Hearts of Men*, 146–48.

38. "Convention of Colored Citizens," *NS*, 4/10/1851.

39. "Tale of Gerrit Smith behind Adirondack Suit: Downing Heirs' Story Runs Back to Eccentric Philanthropist." *NYT*, 11/19/1904. Charismatic rumors about Underground Railroad activity on Gerrit Smith's land beguiled Adirondack Park historian Harold Hochschild (see Hochschild, *Township 34*, 61–62), and they continue to inspire research. In 2022, Pete Nelson, a lay historian and Adirondack activist, dove deep into Gerrit Smith's correspondence in hope of documenting an Underground Railroad water route that might have floated

fugitives to Canada by way of Eagle, Blue Mountain, and Utowana Lakes. Hard proof proved elusive, but Nelson's spirited talk on his quest, "Diversity in the Adirondacks: The Underground Railroad in Blue Mountain Lake," held an audience in thrall at the Blue Mountain Lake Art Center (8/24/2022).

40. "Tale of Gerrit Smith behind Adirondack Suit: Downing Heirs' Story Runs Back to Eccentric Philanthropist." *NYT*, 11/19/1904.

41. J. Clay Smith Jr., *Emancipation: The Making of the Black Lawyer, 1844–1944* (University of Pennsylvania, 1999), 38, 440.

42. "Tale of Gerrit Smith." See, among others, "The Adirondacks," *Boston Herald*, 11/17/1904; "Negroes Claim Big Estates," *St. Louis Post-Dispatch*, 11/18/1904; "Negroes Claim Adirondacks," *Fall River (MA) Evening Herald*, 11/18/1904; "Deeds in Hand," *NYDN*, 11/19/1904; and "Afro-American," *Seattle Republican*, 12/9/1904.

43. "Alleged Brooklyn Heirs to Adirondack Tracts," *Times Union* (Brooklyn), 11/16/1904. This piece ran in the *Commercial Advertiser* (Canton, NY), 11/29/1904, and the *Malone (NY) Farmer*, 11/23/1904. By the 1930s, new roads and state-built campgrounds in the Adirondack Park, along with rental cabins and other affordable tourist amenities, were democratizing the wilderness vacation and softening resentment of the region's old exclusionary social culture. Further, many of those old exclusive clubs and camps had fallen on hard times and closed.

44. These weekly legal notices appeared in the *Malone Farmer* and the *Elizabethtown Post and Gazette*. To the Lake Placid Kiwanis Club thirty years later, local attorney Robert F. Isham noted the "considerable trouble" that Gerrit Smith's "generosity" was still making for landowners seeking "clear title" to their lots. See "Clear Title of Land Goes Back to Slave Days," *LPN*, 4/11/42.

45. Communipaw [JMS] to FD, "Heads of Colored People," *FDP*, 4/15/1852; J. N. Still to "Mr. Editor," *FDP*, 4/22/1852.

46. Jason Brown, quoting JB to John Brown Jr., 2/15/1853, JBJr.

47. "Extract from a Sermon, Preached at Troy, N.Y., to a Company of Mr. Gerrit Smith's Grantees, on the Eve of Their Departure to Their Lands, by Henry Highland Garnet, Pastor of the Liberty Street Church," *NS*, 5/12/1848; Salmon Brown to F. B. Sanborn, Portland, OR, 8/8/1909, JB/BBS Coll./WVMP.

48. Sylvester, *Historical Sketches*, 1877.

11. I Begin to Be Regarded as an "American Citizen"

Epigraph: Excerpt from "Paul Robeson" by Gwendolyn Brooks reprinted by consent of Brooks Permissions.

1. Helen Tyler, "This 'n That," *ADE*, 8/10/1972: Galen Crane, "Our Towns: Vermontville," *AL*, February 1997.

2. Details of Isaac Lyon's Adirondack life are culled from mid-nineteenth-century US federal and New York censuses (1850-70); Helen Escha Tyler's history column, "This 'n That," in *ADE*, 4/7/1956, 4/29/1961, 5/24/1961, 8/10/1972; *FP*, 12/25/1851; and *MP*, 12/11/1862.

3. Tyler, "Early Days in Franklin," 22.

4. *USFC 1850*, Franklin, Franklin County.

5. Baumann, "Goldsmith," 110–12, and Teresa R. Eshelman, "Goldsmith's Continued," in *They Told Me So . . .* , vol. 2, August 1987; "Redemption Sale of 1859," Franklin County, Township 9, Old Military Tract, Lots 36 & 37; Township 10, Lots 99 & 100; and affidavits of Thomas Goldsmith and Simon Stickney, 6/30/1864, box 12, paper 41, CTSR (BO847).

6. James Folts, "Records Relating to Comptroller's Sales of Non-Resident Lands for Unpaid Taxes, 1786–1955," appraisal, n.d., NYSA.

7. Affidavit, Isaac Lyon Jr., CTSR (BO847).

8. "Redemptions—Sale of 1850," affidavits regarding Lot 282, Township 10, Old Military Tract, Franklin, Franklin County, CTSR (BO847).

9. "Redemptions—Sale of 1859" and "Redemptions—Comptroller's & Co. Treasurers Sales of 1853," CTSR (BO847); affidavits, J. J. Alexander and B. F. Lamson, 9/4/1863, defending John Thomas's right to his land on the east half of Lot 284, Township 10, Old Military Tract, Franklin, Franklin County. In the late fall of 1873, affidavits from nine white residents of Franklin, including Isaac, Freeman, and Richard Lyon, again confirmed Thomas's longtime occupancy of his farm. *USFC 1850, 1860, 1870*, Franklin, Franklin County; affidavit, John and Mary Ann Thomas, 1/29/1874, defending Isaac Lyon Jr.'s occupancy of his land on Lot 282, SE, CTSR (BO847). Lyon Jr. also had a village home in Vermontville. His contested farm was a few miles away.

10. "In matter of Lot 87, To. 11, O. M. Tract, Affts for Cancellation of Tax Sales of 1853–," Essex County, 6/5/1877, CTSR (BO847). In this year, affiants Judson C. Ware, a North Elba veteran of the Ninety-Sixth New York Infantry, Company K, and Joseph A. Titus, St. Armand town clerk and supervisor, confirmed the long-standing residency of grantee Avery Hazzard.

11. Town of Franklin Records, Adirondack Collection, SLFL. Local historian Shirley Morgan of Saranac Lake unearthed these important poll lists, and was good enough to share them with me. I am in her debt; *NYSC, 1855*, NE, Essex County. The citizenship category in this census confirmed a voter's eligibility. In St. Armand, in 1855, the *NYSC* identifies Avery Hazzard as a voter. That same year, in the Washington County village he left behind, only three Black residents out of sixteen were permitted to vote. None of the five Black male residents of Westport or the seven Black men in Elizabethtown are described in this 1855 census as voters, though a Black Westporter owned property in excess of $250. In Ward 3 of Troy, home to two dozen African Americans, three exercised the franchise in 1855.

The Black Woods stood out. Perhaps the antislavery culture of its poll keepers had something to do with this. The three white North Elbans who served as poll keepers in North Elba in 1849 were Iddo Osgood, the abolitionist who invited two Black land agents to move to his young hamlet, the farmer Timothy Nash whose extended family did business with James Henderson, and Robert Scott, who was putting up a Black grantee in his home. See "Laws Reached by the Board of Supervisors at Their Annual Meeting of 1849," *ECR*, 2/23/1850. By 1855, Iddo Osgood's son, Dillon, had taken over as North Elba's census enumerator and election manager.

12. Sylvester, *Historical Sketches*, 139–40; Bernstein, *Sticks*, 65.

13. Calarco, *Underground Railroad*, 41, 42; *ECR*, 11/14/1846. On responses to the North Elba election after Brown's hanging and burial, see *Daily Citizen and News* (Lowell, MA), 11/20/1860; *Providence Evening Press*, 4/5/1860; *Alexandria (VA) Gazette*, 3/26/1860; and *New Albany (IN) Daily Ledger*, 3/24/1860. If Democrats rejoiced, Republicans were outraged. John Thompson (of the abolitionist North Elba clan that sent two sons to Harpers Ferry) blamed the election of the Democrat Milote Baker, lumberman, on "intoxicating drinks, bullyism, and border-ruffianism," and claimed that "outsiders from lumber jobs turned the scale against us, being armed with slugshots, which were exhibited and flourished with threatening aspect." "Town Elections," *NS*, 3/15/1860, and *EP*, 3/24/1860.

14. "Shooting in the Adirondacks," 585.

15. See chap. 9 on Charles Dickens's unnamed stringer and Warren Morehouse.

16. *USFC 1850, 1860*, Franklin, Franklin County.

17. Hardy, "Iron Age Community," 51–52. Map, "Settlements Founded And/ Or Largely Nurtured by the Iron Industry, 1846–1850." Source: John Moravek, "Iron Industry," fig. 15. 91–90; Seaver, *Historical Sketches*, 361; Tyler, "Early Days in Franklin."

18. John Thomas to GS, Bloomingdale, Essex County, 8/26/1872, Cotter Collection, Special Collections, Feinberg Library, SUNY Plattsburgh. See chaps. 1 and 17 for more about this story. Family history records, Notre Dame Church, Malone, NY.

19. Seaver, *Historical Sketches*, 644–45.

20. Calarco, *Underground Railroad*, 158. Calarco notes that the turnout in Malone for abolition speakers in 1856 was sparse, and that town churches declined to host them, *PR*, 11/14/1846. In 1846, Franklin County gave a 225-vote majority to the Democratic gubernatorial candidate, Silas Wright. The Republican, John Young, won Essex County with a 650-vote majority. L. King to GS, 11/1/1850.

21. "Bloomingdale," *ECR*, 10/15/1871; Jacoby, *Crimes against Nature*, chap. 3; "Our Mines and Our Forests," *EP*, 3/14/1854; Hardy, "Iron Age Community," 89–91.

22. Town records, NE, 1851, and MacKenzie, *Plains of Abraham*, 144.

23. *USFC 1850*, Essex County. When he left North Elba, Josiah Hasbrook Sr. moved to New York City, Connecticut, and the village of Sag Harbor on Long Island. Susan Hasbrook joined another Smith grantee, the Louisianian Lewis Pierce, and they, too, lived briefly in Manhattan. (See chapters 6 and 9). Simeon, Josiah Jr., and Harriette Hasbrook lingered in North Elba when their parents moved away, and lived with neighbors, white and Black. On Silas Hicks, see JMS to GS, 3/37/1848; *GSLB*, 59; *USFC 1850, 1860, 1870*, Elizabethtown, Essex County, NY; and *NYSC 1855, 1865*; *GSLB*, 26; *USFC 1850, 1860, 1870*; and *NYSC 1855*, Elizabethtown, Essex County. On Harriet Hicks, see "Misc. Papers," ECCO.

24. JB to Ruth Brown Thompson, Akron, OH, 8/10/1852. Sanborn, *Life and Letters*, 152; *NYSC 1855, 1865*; *USFC 1860*, NE, Essex County. In 1850, forty-four-year-old Charles Willard lived with Charlotte Willard, twenty-six. Charlotte died a few years later. In 1855, Willard joined the abolitionist household

of Henry and Ruth Brown Thompson. By 1860, he was living in the home of a grantee's widow, Jane Craig. The substance of this interracial relationship is unclear. Willard was head of household in the census, but the cabin was Craig's. Sometime after 1865, Craig migrated to her sister's farm near Saratoga, and the aging Englishman went to Put-in-Bay, Ohio, perhaps at the urging of his former employers, Henry and Ruth Thompson, who had settled there and were cultivating grapes.

25. Jay's antislavery zealot, Jesse Tobey, was on Reverend Loguen's list of white Adirondack abolitionists whom Loguen judged trustworthy. Ruth Thompson recalls Cyrus Thomas in North Elba in Sanborn, *Life and Letters*, 100, 132; Lafayette Mason, *NYSC 185*, Elizabethtown, NY; George W. Bell, *GSLB*, 79, and *NYSC 1855*, Willsboro, NY.

26. For details of the Merrills' inn and Jerry Merrill's skills and reputation, see Porter, *Lem Merrill*, 10–11.

27. "Franklin County Land," *IC*, 7/25/1849. The preface to Merrill's letter was written by *Impartial Citizen* editor Samuel Ringgold Ward, Liberty Party zealot and one of Smith's agents. Another agent, Jermain Loguen, had appealed to Merrill for this report on March 20, 1849, and Merrill got the letter ten days later. On April 2 he answered Loguen, but not until July 25 would the *Citizen* publish Merrill's note. This was almost half a year after it was solicited—well past the spring moving season. Delays like this beleaguered the progress of the giveaway from its inception.

28. Teresa R. Eshelman, "Beginnings of Merrillsville," in *They Told Me So . . .*, vol. 2, 1987.

29. John Brigham to GS, Keeseville, 4/10/1856.

30. "Died," *MP*, 5/10/1895.

31. "Jacob Lane and Wife Caroline of Troy New York, Plaintiff First Part to Loring Ellis and John Brigham of Clintonville, NY, Plaintiff Second Part, for $660 . . . ," Book 00, p. 539, ECCO.

32. John Brigham to GS, 4/10/1856.

33. In 1859, Brigham and Caleb Calkins paid fifty dollars to the Poughkeepsie grantee William Vanderbilt and his wife for fifty acres of gift land, and twenty dollars for the lot of the Fishkill grantee Robert Williams. *Index of Deeds*, Franklin County, Book 30, FCA.

34. After 1846, a new voting bloc of naturalized immigrants in Essex, Franklin, and Clinton Counties drove "the sharpest proslavery declines in the state." Field, *Politics of Race*, 134.

35. Marjorie Lansing Porter reported the use of a racial epithet to describe the Smith grantees. Porter, *Lem Merrill*, 15.

36. Smith grantees are buried in many Adirondack cemeteries. Eppes and Appo family members are in the North Elba Cemetery in Lake Placid. In the Union Cemetery in Vermontville are Morehouses, Thomases, and Murrays. The Hazzard clan favored the Brookside Cemetery in Bloomingdale (see Svenson, "Brookside"). The Wortses and Fraziers rest in the Hillside Cemetery in Westport. Joseph and Adeline James are buried in the Riverside Cemetery in Wadhams, and in the county poorhouse cemetery in Whallonsburg are Harriet Hicks and a Willsboro grantee, George W. Bell. In none of these burial grounds

is racial identity suggested, except regarding military service. The headstones of Stephen Warren Morehouse (Union Cemetery) and Charles Henry Hazzard (Brookside) honor their service in the US Colored Troops in the Civil War.

12. If You Only Knew How Poor I Am

Chapter epigraph from the Gerrit Smith Papers.

1. *NYT*, 8/29/1856 and 9/7/1856, quoted in Reynolds, *John Brown, Abolitionist*, 195.

2. *ECR*, 9/8/1854; *USFC, 1850*, St. Armand, Essex County; "Movements in Favor of Freedom," *FG*, 6/10/1854.

3. Michael Fellman, *Inside War: The Guerrilla Conflict in Missouri during the American Civil War* (Oxford University Press, 1989), 15–19. For a proslavery perspective on the Emigrant Aid Company, see Johnson, "Emigrant Aid Company."

4. W. O. Lynch, "Population Movements in Relation to the Struggle for Kansas," *Studies in American History* (1926): 381–404, cited in Harlow, "Kansas Aid Movement," 25, 25n.

5. Chestina Bowker Allen, "Journey from Massachusetts to Kansas," unpublished manuscript, 1854–58, Kansas Historical Society, https://www.kshs.org/archives/6839; George O. Willard to (*Boston*) *Journal*, 1/7/1855, quoted in *Kansas Territorial Clippings*, 1:53–55, cited in Barry, "Emigrant Aid Parties."

6. Kansas Land Trust Company, advertisement, n.d., Kansas Memory (Kansas Historical Society), accessed 2/15/2023, https://www.kansasmemory.org/item/90770/page/1; Lemuel Knapp, "Testimony of Lemuel Knapp," recorded by National Kansas Committee, 1/5/1857, Kansas Memory, https://www.kansasmemory.org/item/90631; Lemuel Knapp, "Experiences of Lemuel Knapp," 1/5/1857, in Adams, Martin, and Connelley, *Transactions*, six pages. Thaddeus Hyatt Collection, Kansas Historical Society.

7. "Testimony of Lemuel Knapp."

8. "Experiences of Lemuel Knapp"; *USFC 1870*, Grant, Riley County, KS.

9. *ECR*, 9/8/1854.

10. *USFC 1850*, St. Armand, Essex County; "Board of Supervisors Report, St. Armand," *ECR*, 12/16/1848; Lemuel Knapp to GS, St. Armand, 4/2/1860; LK to GS, 2/26/1850; "Peterboro," *EP*, 2/18/1892; LK to GS, 4/10/1848.

11. LK to Caleb Calkins, 2/26/1850.

12. "Gerrit Smith," *ECR*, 10/10/1846, and "Land for the Landless," *ECR*, 5/28/1849; GS, "To the Persons Who Derive Title from Myself or My Late Father to Land in Charlotte River and Byrne's Tracts, in the Counties of Delaware, Otsego, and Schoharie," circular, 5/24/1844; Godine, "Abolitionist and the Land Reformer."

13. Stauffer, *Black Hearts of Men*, 102–4; Harlow, *Gerrit Smith*, 31–33.

14. Harlow, *Gerrit Smith*, 242; Stauffer, *Black Hearts of Men*, 138.

15. McKivigan and McKivigan, "'He Stands Like Jupiter.'" Smith's unpublished fourteen-page manuscript was not dated, but internal references suggest he wrote it in 1856 in Saratoga Springs, NY.

16. Chester Converse to GS, Schroon, 4/8/1847; William Griffing to GS, 3/15/1847. The spelling and punctuation in these appeals have been corrected.

17. Andrew Micklejean to GS, Fulton, 1/26/1846; Patrick Rine to GS, Rome, 12/22/1845; Merrit Fowler to GS, Butler, 5/1/1847.

18. Alden Speer to GS, Moriah, 4/22/1850.

19. Mason Whiting, Esq., to GS, Binghamton, 8/26/1845; GS to Whiting, Peterboro, 8/30/1845.

20. S. Huntington to GS, Franklin, n.d.; Sherburn brothers to GS, Keene, 3/9/1850; W. S. Sherwood to GS, Glens Falls, 6/14/1848; Joseph [illeg.] and Josephus Marshall to GS, Pottersville, 12/23/1847; W. F. Whipple to GS and Caleb Calkins, Johnsburg, 2/8/1848; Phineas Norton to Calkins, Keene, 4/23/1850; John Brown (not the abolitionist) to GS, Johnsburg, 2/14/1846; J. H. Van [illeg.] to GS, Pottersville, 2/15/1847; S. Huntington to GS, Franklin, 3/19/1847.

21. GS, "To the Persons Who Derive Title"; GS to TW, CBR, and JMS, 10/1/1846.

22. GS, circular, Peterboro, 5/1/1849; Daniel Cady to GS, 6/13/1849, quoted in Harlow, *Gerrit Smith*, 250. The pragmatic Cady bluntly doubted "whether a favor can be done to a poor man, black or white, by tempting him to emigrate to settle upon your northern lands. A poor man who has energy and enterprise enough to settle upon those lands and clear up a farm had better go west—a poor man without energy had better keep out of the northern lands . . . [and] the expense of removing from a southern county to a northern part of the state will equal the value of 50 acres of land."

23. Jabez Parkhurst, Henry B. Smith, and Sidney Lawrence, all Smith-appointed Franklin County appraisers of worthy white recipients for Smith's land in 1849, lived at an arduous remove from the "South Towns" (Franklin, Brighton, Harrietstown, Duane), and their choices reflected their preference for giftees who were easier for them to reach. In all of Franklin County, no white person from the southern townships got free land, LK to GS, St. Armand, 4/2/1850. St. Armand's Lemuel Knapp had much in common with his Kansas-bound neighbor, John Brown. Both men were Yankee homesteaders, friends of Gerrit Smith, small-time speculators who lost more money than they could spare, members of the New England Emigrant Aid Company, and helpers to the Black grantees. But what divided them bears noting too. When Brown left the Adirondacks in 1854, his monied friends made sure his Adirondack home stayed his. Knapp had no rich backers, and when he left, he left for good. "Gerrit Smith," *SL*, 9/11/1847; Harlow, *Gerrit Smith*, 239.

24. *GSLB*, 26. Born in 1822 to William Mason and Diana Robinson Mason in the Clinton County mining hamlet of Ellenburgh, Lafayette Mason was a collier before he took up farming. Contract, 1/23/1860, Box R-9, "Misc. Papers," ECCO. The price of this lot, No. 24 in Roaring Brook Tract, was $702. *New York Town Clerk's Register*, NYSA.

25. From Civil War Draft Registration Records and Civil War Muster Roll Abstracts, NYSA: Lafayette Mason enlisted on 12/21/1863, in Elizabethtown, NY, for Company G, 118th Infantry. In a hospital in Albany, he was transferred to the Ninety-Sixth Regiment in 1865, and honorably discharged because of disabilities. His son Lewis enlisted in Brooklyn on 12/10/1863 with

the Twentieth US Colored Infantry for three years. See also LM military pension; CM widow's pension; and MCM widow's pension.

26. "Notice of Motion and of Judgment/Foreclosure," 7/27/1869, Banker Box Q-37, ECCO.

27. "Notice of Motion and of Judgment/Foreclosure"; *USFC 1870*, Vernon Springs, IA; MCM widow's pension; Iowa affidavits, George W. Combs, 12/22/1892, and Job W. Hood, 12/27/1892, and "Homestead Proof," Bureau of Land Management, Federal Land Office Records, US Department of the Interior, NARA; LM military pension; CM widow's pension; MCM widow's pension; affidavit, M[. . .] Brown, Michigan, 7/31/1888.

28. "Board of Supervisors—2nd Session," *ECR*, 12/15/1849.

29. Jermain Wesley Loguen to JMS, *NS*, 3/24/1848; Watson, *General View*, 78, and Watson, *Military and Civil History*, 217–18. Don James McLaughlin explores the cultural history of the term "Negrophobia" in "The Anti-slavery Roots of Today's '-Phobia' Obsession," *New Republic*, 1/29/2016; "North Country," in Eisenstadt, *Encyclopedia of New York State*, 1119; Terrie, *Contested Terrain*, 16.

30. North Country," *Encyclopedia of New York State*, 1119; Terrie, *Contested Terrain*, Ch. 1, "A Broken, Impracticable Tract"; Hardy, "The Iron Age Community of the J.&J. Rogers Company," 99.

31. "Summons & Warrants," Business and Land Files, GSP. Smith sued Wait Lewis on 1/25/1853, Monroe Hall on 3/11/1852, and Samuel Warner on 3/27/1850. In the Warner (Cram) Cemetery near Crown Point, Warner's tombstone reads, "A Revolutionary Soldier and a Friend of the Slave." *AP*, 10/29/1845; *FDP*, 10/23/1851 and 8/12/1853; "Henry Clay and Slavery," Samuel Warren [*sic*] to FD, *FDP*, 5/6/1852.

32. GS, journal entry, 11/30/1843, *Gerrit Smith Letter Book L, 1848–1871*, GSP; SW to GS, Crown Point, 4/20/1850. Smith characterized land monopoly as slavery in speeches at Syracuse, 1/20/1848, Troy, 4/14/1851, Buffalo, 9/17/1851, and Washington, DC, 2/21/1854.

33. GS to SW, Peterboro, 4/24/1850; "Moses Clough," in Nathaniel B. Sylvester, *History of Rensselaer Co., New York* (Everts & Peck, 1880), 132.

34. "Gerrit Smith's Tour," *AP*, 6/25/1845, and JMS to GS, 2/6/1850; Marjorie Lansing Porter, "Earlier Day Essex and Clinton County Newspapers," *ECR*, 7/6/1951; "The Late Wendell Lansing," *PS*, 5/27/1887; "Wendell Lansing," in Hurd, *Clinton and Franklin Counties*, 130–33; *ECR*, 3/21/1924.

35. *ECR*, 10/16/1844; "The Offices," *ECR*, 7/26/1846; *ECR*, 4/11/1846, from the *Troy Whig*; Mr. Editor—:," *Essex County Times*, 10/31/1844; Marjorie Lansing Porter, "Earlier Day Essex and Clinton County Newspapers," *ECR*, 5/25/1951, 6/8/1951, 6/15/1951, and 7/6/1951; "The Late Wendell Lansing" and "Wendell Lansing," in Hurd, *Clinton and Franklin Counties*; "A Distinction to Be Remembered," *ECR*, 9/2/1854. Abolitionists would be blamed by Whigs like Tarbell not only for Polk's victory, but for the war with Mexico, the Texas land grab, and the ascension of Southern racists to federal positions. In the Civil War, Tarbell had a raucous career as a brevet brigadier general (only President Lincoln's intervention reversed his court martial for judging another officer "a Damned fool and Illiterate Whelp"). During Reconstruction, Tarbell took charge of a plantation in Mississippi and served locally as town marshal

and circuit judge—and here his white rage flared. He opined on Black "depravity . . . universal thieving and lying," declared "Negro suffrage . . . a measure of the most stupendous wildness and humbug of this or any other age," and dismissed Black soldiery as "a poor burlesque." Perhaps signaling his old contempt for Smith and his initiative, he offered, "Give the blacks the best State in the Union, with teams, seed, grain, farming tools, a year's supply of all things, and five hundred dollars in money each, and they would starve to death the second year, and relapse into barbarism in half a century." Thomas P. Lowry, *Curmudgeons, Drunkards, and Outright Fools, Court Martial of Civil War Union Colonels* (Lincoln, 1997), 213–18; "Northern Views of the Qualification of Negroes to Vote," *Fayetteville Observer*, 11/29/1866; *ECR*, 9/26/1872, 10/2/1872, and 10/24/1872.

36. While not dominant, the names of French Canadians and Irish are conspicuous in the "Summonses and Warrants" that Gerrit Smith dispatched to his Adirondack contract farmers at midcentury. (See reels 24 and 74, GSP.)

13. Nothing Would Be More Encouraging to Me

1. "Receipts," *FDP*, 11/2/1853; *ECR*, 8/13/1853. In a review of Northup's book, the *Essex County Republican* stressed the valor of Northup's white rescuer, Henry Northrop. In contrast, *Frederick Douglass' Paper* emphasized the kidnapped Northup's twelve-year ordeal and the brutality of slavery itself. *ECR*, 11/26/1853.

2. Quarles, *Black Abolitionists*, 187–90; Ripley et al., *Black Abolitionist Papers*, 4:153, 6n; William J. Watkins to FD, "Are We Ready for the Conflict?," *FDP*, 2/9/1855.

3. Watkins to FD, "Are We Ready?"

4. Watkins to FD, "Are We Ready?"; William Watkins to GS, 9/27/1858. "Like the great majority of Americans, white or Black, Douglass wanted his vote to count for something more than the affirmation of an abstract principle, however noble," observes Quarles in *Black Abolitionists*, 188.

5. "1856 presidential election: Revision History," Wikipedia, last edited 2/3/2023. Ripley et al., *Black Abolitionist Papers*, 4:401n. Perkal, "American Abolition Society," provides a sharp analysis of Gerrit Smith's failed bid for the governorship in 1858.

6. Perkal, "American Abolition Society," 63. Smith's campaign newssheets in 1858 were *The Hour and the Man* (Albany), the *State Leaguer* (Syracuse), and the *Gerrit Smith Banner* (New York City). Perkal, "American Abolition Society," 64. In 1858, the Republican incumbent and victor was Edwin D. Morgan. Amasa J. Parker stood for the Democrats.

7. Resolution No. 7, from the "Suffrage Convention of the Colored Citizens of New York, Troy, Sept. 14, 1858," *Liberator*, 10/1/1858, Colored Conventions Project Digital Records, accessed 1/4/2023, https://omeka.colored-conventions.org/items/show/239; Bell, "Some Reform Interests"; Quarles, *Black Abolitionists*, 187–88; "Supporting the New Republican Party, 1858," in Aptheker, *Documentary History*, 410–11.

8. An issue of *Voice of the People* (no. 5, 1858) is in the library of the New-York Historical Society, NYC.

9. "Wm. J. Watkins," *Troy Daily Times*, 10/12/1858 (and in *Voice of the People*, no. 5, 1858); HHG and James Duffin to GS, 9/16/1858; Ripley et al., *Black Abolitionist Papers*, 4:398–99 ("Watkins, poor Watkins, went over to the enemy, and is employed as their agent to stump the State for the Republicans"); *Troy Daily Times*, 10/12/1858.

10. William J. Watkins to GS, 9/27/1858; Ripley et al., *Black Abolitionist Papers*, 4:399–400.

11. Harlow, *Gerrit Smith*, 380.

12. Wm J. Hodge [*sic*] to Stephen Myers, *Voice of the People*, no. 5, 1858. Hodges's letter is dated 10/25/1858. The Democratic *Brooklyn Eagle* doted on Hodges's speeches with a gleeful condescension apparently due a Black minister who delivered sermons "in the classics, then in the French, and so on to the Timbuctoo dialect and the 'unknown tongue.'" See *BDE*, 11/26/1853, 12/16/1854, 12/28/1854, 6/8/1855, 9/24/1856, 8/2/1858, 9/29/1858, 12/27/1859, 1/5/1860, 6/6/1860, 8/2/1860, 8/3/1860, and 8/23/1860.

13. S. R. Scottron Jr. to Myers, *Voice of the People*, no. 5, 1858; Myers, "One Word More," *Voice of the People*, no. 5, 1858. The date of Scottron's letter, 10/25/1858, suggests that Myers cranked out the final issue of his campaign sheet just before the November 2 election. Scottron's manifold accomplishments as an activist, inventor, churchman, and Civil War soldier are noted in Willard Gatewood, *Aristocrats of Color: The Black Elite, 1880–1920* (Indiana University, 1990), 224–25, 305; and Taylor, *Black Churches of Brooklyn*, 18.

14. Smith's disdain for Myers was evident in a letter to Henry Garnet in June 1843. About Myers's Whig-favored Albany paper, the *Northern Star and Colored Farmer*, Smith griped, "Were this paper true to the holy cause of liberty its proslavery patrons would shrink from it, as from a snake." GS to HHG, Peterboro, 6/10/1843; Samuel Scottron, *GSLB*, 61. At a meeting of Black voters in Williamsburgh in late September 1858, "speeches were delivered by Wm. H. Hodges and Willis A. Hodges, both of whom denounced Gerrit Smith and the abolitionists generally, and advised colored voters to support the Republican ticket." "The Colored Voters," *BDE*, 9/29/1858.

15. Editorial, *New-York Tribune*, 8/3/1857.

16. "Letter from Gerrit Smith," 8/10/1857. In the weeks after Smith's disavowal of his land distribution scheme in the *Tribune*, papers picked it up in Wisconsin, Ohio, Illinois, Massachusetts, western New York, and Canada.

17. "Gerrit Smith and His Colored Friends," *NYT*, 10/7/1858.

18. "1858 New York State Election," Wikipedia, last edited 4/30/2022, https://en.wikipedia.org/wiki/1858_New_York_state_election.

19. Reynolds, *John Brown, Abolitionist*, 104, 111; JB to James Redpath, quoted in Redpath, *Public Life*, 206; Villard, *John Brown*, 55; JB to "Wife & Children every one," St. Catherine, Canada West, 4/6/1858, JB/BBS Coll./WVMP.

20. JB to "Wife & Children every one," 4/6/1858, JB/BBS Coll./WVMP; JB to "Wife & children every one," 5/1/1858. Beinecke Library Collection, Yale University, New Haven, CT.

21. "How John Brown Came—Reasons Which Brought Him to This State," *PS*, 10/31/1902; *Potsdam Commercial Advertiser*, 11/5/02; and other papers. In Thomas Higginson's essay about Brown, "His Family at North Elba" (Webb, *Life and Letters*, 224), the same point is made; Charles Dudley Warner, *Hartford Press*, 11/24/1866.

22. Reynolds, *John Brown, Abolitionist*, 193–96; "Pottawatomie Creek, Jan. 17th," *EP*, 3/27/1857.

23. Untitled typescript about Lyman Eppes by the Adirondack historian and folklorist Marjorie Lansing Porter, Special Collections, Feinberg Library, SUNY Plattsburgh. Porter interviewed Epps Jr. in 1939, a few years before he died. In her column, "Neighbors across the Lake" (*Burlington Free Press*, 7/28/1939), she wrote, "When visiting his North Elba home for the last time, he [John Brown] urged Lyman Epps Sr. to go with him on his departure. Mrs. Epps objected, but added that if $200 could be raised so that she could take the entire family back to New York, her former home, she might change her mind." Sanborn, *Life and Letters*, 497–98; JB to John Brown Jr., West Newton, MA, 4/15/1857, JB/BBS Coll./WVMP; JB to F. B. Sanborn, 5/15/1857, Peterboro, JB/BBS Coll./WVMP.

24. "Races at Lake Placid," *ECR*, 1/23/1896. Lyman Epps (son of the grantee) had poor luck that day. His horse, Prince E., which ran against three others in four races, placed fourth in every one.

25. Wells, "Lake Placid Childhood"; MacKenzie, *Plains of Abraham*, 133–34; and typescript on Lyman Eppes by Marjorie Lansing Porter. "Music was [the] most important thing in their lives. They formed a family singing group: Lyman Sr., tenor, Mrs. Eppes and Amelia, soprano; Albert and Lyman, Bass, and Evaline, also. They sang at weddings, funerals, kitchen parties, church affairs, and Sunday school." MacKenzie, *Plains of Abraham*, 134–35; Godine, "Noteworthy Mr. Appo."

26. JB to John Brown Jr., Akron, OH, 8/21/1854, quoted in Ruchames, *John Brown Reader*, 86; Villard, *John Brown*, 73; JB to GS, 6/20/1849, JB/BBS Coll./WVMP; "Want Memorial to John Brown," *Watertown Daily Times*, 8/30/1915; Sanborn, *Life and Letters*, 101; Dana, "How We Met John Brown"; Ruth Thompson to Franklin B. Sanborn, in Sanborn, *Life and Letters*, 99–101; JB to John, Jason, Frederick, and Daughters, Springfield, MA, 12/4/1850, quoted in Ruchames, *John Brown*, 81; Ruth Thompson to Wealthy Brown, NE, 4/16/1850, JBjrKS; Ruth Thompson to John Brown Jr., NE, 8/13/1851, JBjrKS; JB to WH, Springfield, MA, 1/22/1849, quoted in Villard, *John Brown*, 72–73; Ruth Brown to Mary Brown, 9/7/1849, JBjrKS; JB to Ruth Thompson, 8/10/1852, quoted in Sanborn, *Life and Letters*, 152; Ruth Thompson to John Brown Jr., NE, 8/13/1851, JBjrKS; Villard, *John Brown*, 72; Ruth Brown to Wealthy Brown, NE, 3/10/1850, JBjrKS.

27. Brendan Mills, site manager of the John Brown Farm, bases this estimate on his review of the Brown family's correspondence. Conversations with the author, 2015. Thomas Wentworth Higginson, quoted in Redpath, *Public Life*, 68.

28. JB to Ruth Brown Thompson, Akron, 8/10/1852, quoted in Sanborn, *Life and Letters*, 152; Ruth Thompson to Sanborn, quoted in Sanborn, *Life*

and Letters, 104; JB to Mary Brown, Springfield, MA, 11/28/1850, quoted in Ruchames, *John Brown*, 79–80; JB to Ellen Brown, Boston, 5/13/1859, in Ruchames, *John Brown*, 123.

29. Ruth Thompson to John Brown Jr., 5/30/1854, JBJr.; Henry and Ruth Thompson to Wealthy Brown and John Brown Jr., 5/7/1854, JBJr.; Henry Thompson to John Brown Jr., 8/15/1852, JBJr.

30. Abraham Lincoln, "Lincoln's Second Inaugural Address," 3/4/1865, Lincoln Memorial website, https://www.nps.gov/linc/learn/historyculture/lincoln-second-inaugural.htm.

31. Oates, *To Purge This Land*, 75–77.

32. JB to Brown family, 9/30/1854, Akron, OH, quoted in Ruchames, *John Brown*, 94–95.

33. Villard, *John Brown*, 714; Ruchames, *John Brown Reader*, 87; Boyer, *Legend of John Brown*, 527.

34. JB to Brown family, 9/30/1854, quoted in Ruchames, *John Brown*, 94; Reynolds, *John Brown, Abolitionist*, 121–28.

35. JB to Mary Ann Brown, Springfield, MA, 1/17/1851, quoted in Ruchames, *John Brown*, 83; John Brown, "Words of Advice," resolution presented to the League of Gileadites, Springfield, MA, 1/15/1851, quoted in Ruchames, *John Brown*, 85; HHG, "An Address to the Slaves of the United States," speech, National Convention of Colored Citizens, Buffalo, NY, 8/16/1843, Blackpast, 1/24/2007, https://www.blackpast.org/african-american-history/1843-henry-highland-garnet-address-slaves-united-states. Also see Henry Highland Garnet, *Walker's Appeal, with a Brief Sketch of His Life: And Also Garnet's Address to the Slaves of the United States of America* (J. H. Tobitt, 1848), 89–96. John Brown helped underwrite the cost of this publication.

36. Bondi, August, from "With John Brown in Kansas." Quoted in Reynolds, *John Brown, Abolitionist*, 189; JB to Mary Ann Brown, Springfield, MA, 1/17/1851, quoted in Ruchames, *John Brown*, 83; Reynolds, *John Brown, Abolitionist*, 270–71.

37. "Sambo's Mistakes," *RH*, 1847 or 1848, and published in Villard, *John Brown*, 659–61. No issue of the *Ram's Horn* that ran this essay survives. The Maryland Historical Society in Baltimore has Brown's handwritten copy; JB to George L. Stearns, 1/29/1859, Ruchames, *John Brown: The Making of a Revolutionary*, 163.

38. Katherine Mayo, "Brown in Hiding and in Jail," *New York Evening Post*, 10/23/1909; Ruchames, *John Brown*, 248.

39. Boyer, *Legend of John Brown*, 459; *NYSC 1855*, NE, Essex County. The 1855 New York census reported two Black settlers (Isaac Craig and Thomas Brown) in their fifties, one twenty-year-old (John Vinson), four men in their thirties (Thomas Jefferson, William Carasaw, Josiah Hasbrook, Silas Frazier), five in their forties (Leonard Worts, Lewis Pierce, Lyman Eppes, Henry Dixon [Dickson], and Samuel Jefferson), and three sixteen-year-old boys (Simeon Hasbrook, Charles Worts, and William Jefferson). The Hazzards of St. Armand (by 1855 well ensconced), had three young men at home ages twenty to twenty-seven: Leonard, George, and Charles Henry. Alex, not on hand for this census, was of age to fight as well. And that year in Franklin, five Black males between seventeen and forty-seven were in the census, too.

40. Higginson, "His Family at North Elba."

41. Reynolds, *John Brown, Abolitionist*, 66.

42. Obituary, Adaline Boynton, *MF*, n.d., 1902; "From Article in the Spring-field Union," n.d., in "John Brown's Body," typescript, Vergennes Town Historian's Office, Vergennes, VT; Oates, *To Purge This Land*, 241; Brewster, "John Brown of North Elba," *New York History*, 10/1952; Villard, *John Brown*, 413.

43. Gordon Sherman to Kristin Gibbins, 8/2/1984, New York State Parks, Recreation, and Historic Preservation; "Thomas H. Peacock Expires; Recalled John Brown Vividly," *AR-EP*, 6/13/1942; MacKenzie, *Plains of Abraham*, 113-17.

44. Wardner, "Footprints on Adirondack Trails," chap. 13, p. 2; ibid., chap. 10, p. 5.

45. Wardner, "Footprints on Adirondack Trails," chap. 13, p. 2.

46. Laughlin-Schultz, *Tie That Bound Us*, 52-53; Reynolds, *John Brown, Abolitionist*, 180-81, 293-95.

47. William Phillips, "Special Correspondent of the New York Tribune," in *Conquest of Kansas*, 332-42; Peterson, *John Brown*, 6-9.

48. Reynolds, *John Brown, Abolitionist*, 277, 279. On the Pottawatomie massacre, see Oates, *To Purge This Land*, 133-37; and Reynolds, *John Brown, Abolitionist*, 170-74. On the response to the massacre in the press, see ibid., 174-78. For all of Eppes's and other Black men's disinclination to join Brown in the field, I know of nothing that indicates any lessening of their respect or affection for John Brown or his family. See Hasbrook's obituary in the *Springfield Daily Republican*, 7/28/1915 ("Death of Aged Negro—Was Friend of John Brown"); MacKenzie, *Plains of Abraham*, 134.

49. Reynolds, *John Brown, Abolitionist*, 114.

50. JMS to FD, 5/4/1854, published in Ripley et al., *Black Abolitionist Papers*, 4:220.

51. "Lyman E. Epps, Sr.," from "Essex County, N.Y. Newspaper, March, 1897," in W. E. Connelley, *John Brown Scrapbook*, JB/BBS Coll./WVMP; "The Late Elijah Simonds," *EP*, 7/21/1916; *LPN*, 6/14/1940; P. F. Schofield to H. S. Harper, 11/29/1918, SLFL; Brumley, *Guides of the Adirondacks*, 118; "Lyman E. Epps, Sr."; "Negro with a History Dead, Lyman Epps Was Taken to Elba, N.Y. by John Brown," *NYT*, 3/27/1897.

14. To Arms! The Black Woods at War

1. "Death of an Aged Negro," *Springfield Daily Republican*, 7/28/1915; Ed Cotter to BBS, 5/23/1953, Edwin Cotter Collection, SUNY Plattsburgh.

2. Quarles, *Negro in the Civil War*, 26-29.

3. For details of Levi Hazzard's military service, see Revolutionary War Pension Applications, Washington County Archives, Fort Edward, NY.

4. Quarles, *Negro in the Civil War*, 30, and McPherson, *Negro's Civil War*, 163-66; campaign badge, 1868, Schomburg Center for Research in Black Culture, Photographs and Prints Division, NYPL, https://digitalcollections.nypl.org/items/62a9d0e6-4fc9-dbce-e040-e00a18064a66.

5. On Willis Hodges in the war, see Richard Lowe, "Willis Augustus Hodges," in Charles W. Calhoun, ed., *The Human Tradition in America from the*

Colonial Era through Reconstruction (SR Books, 2002), 302; On the war service of the sons of the grantees Thomas and Samuel Jefferson, see "Jefferson, Garrett," New York, Civil War Muster Roll Abstracts, http://www.archives.nysed.gov/ research/res_tips_004_civilwarabstracts.shtml; "Political Paragraphs," *Troy Daily Times*, 8/24/1880, 11/10/1888, 8/30/1892, and 7/22/1901; and William H. Chenery, *The Fourteenth Regiment Rhode Island Heavy Artillery Colored, 1861–1865* (Providence, 1898), 61, 216. When the war broke out years after their return to Troy, Thomas Jefferson's son Garrett enlisted with the Thirty-First New York Colored Volunteers and was made sergeant. Injured at Petersburg, Virginia, he lost his arm, but on his return to Troy he worked for decades as a teamster, campaigned for the Republicans, and promoted his city's chapter of the Grand Army of the Republic, a fraternal organization of Union veterans. His brother Samuel, much less fortunate, served with the Fourteenth Regiment, Rhode Island, Colored, Heavy Artillery. In Plaquemine, Louisiana, he and his two comrades were ambushed by Texas Rangers and stripped, shot, and left unburied where they fell.

6. William Appo, NE, Essex County, *New York, U.S., Registers of Officers and Enlisted Men Mustered into Federal Service, 1861–1865*, 6 vols. (NY Bureau of Military Statistics, 1865), NYSA, https://digitalcollections.archives.nysed.gov/ index.php/Detail/collections/36, https://ancestry.com.

7. "30th Infantry Regiment," in Phisterer, *New York*, New York State Military Museum and Veterans Research Center, Saratoga Springs, NY, 2078–87, https:// archive.org/details/phisterernewyork03fredrich/page/2078/mode/2up; Sam Smith, "Moments in Time: The Battle of Second Manassas—a Battle in Five Parts," American Battlefield Trust, accessed 10/20/2022, https://www.battlefields. org/learn/articles/moments-time-battle-second-manassas-battle-five-parts.

8. Mary MacKenzie, town and village historian, Lake Placid and North Elba, to Victor Roy, commander, American Legion, Lake Placid, 5/22/2001, and to Charles Thomas, Lake Placid, 5/31/2001, Mary MacKenzie Collection, LPPL.

9. Greg Furness, email to the author, 11/11/2022.

10. Seraile, *New York's Black Regiments*, 18–25; Gero, *Black Soldiers*, 23–24, 29–40.

11. *USFC* 1850, Franklin, Franklin County; Warren Morehouse, USCT Military Service Records, "Declaration of Recruit," NARA; Matthews, *Freedom Knows No Color*, 56; William Sidney Mount, *The Power of Music*, 1846, oil on canvas, Cleveland Museum of Art, https://www.clevelandart.org/ art/1991.110.

12. "Black Soldiers in the U.S. Military during the Civil War," NARA, last reviewed 9/1/2017, https://www.archives.gov/education/lessons/blacks-civil-war#:~:text=By%20the%20, educator resource; Seraile, *New York's Black Regiments*, 59–64; *Rosters of the New York Infantry Regiments during the Civil War*, New York State Military Museum and Veterans Research Center, https://museum.dmna.ny.gov/unit-history/conflict/us-civil-war-1861-1865/ rosters-new-york-volunteers-during-civil-war/rosters-new-york-infantry-regiments-during-civil-war.

13. J. Marsh to GS, NYC, 7/21/1863; Pasternak, *Rise Now and Fly*, 81; Bob Davern, "Surgeon and Abolitionist James McCune Smith: An African American Pioneer," *Readex Blog*, 4/17/2012, https://www.readex.com/blog/

surgeon-and-abolitionist-james-mccune-smith-african-american-pioneer;
McGruder, "'Fair and Open Field'"; Hodges, *Root and Branch*, 26.

14. "Lewis Henry Douglass," Wikipedia, last edited 5/15/2022, https://en.wikipedia.org/wiki/Lewis_Henry_Douglass; Lears, *Rebirth of a Nation*, 14; FD, "Should the Negro Enlist in the Union Army?," speech, *DM*, 7/6/1863.

15. "Robert Gould Shaw," National Park Service, accessed 10/20/2022, https://www.nps.gov/people/robert-g-shaw.htm. Several of Private Morehouse's Adirondack neighbors—Louisa Brady, John Thomas, Lewis Pierce, and Josiah and Susan Hasbrook—were once enslaved (and Morehouse would encounter more ex-slaves on his return to the Black Woods after the war). Bowditch, *Life and Correspondence*, 43–47.

16. Emilio, *Brave Black Regiment*, 255.

17. On Gerrit Smith's stumping for the Union during the war, see chapter 1, note 37. Emilio, *Brave Black Regiment*, 166, 301; Egerton, *Thunder at the Gates*, 284; Mass. Fifty-Fourth Regimental Records, NARA; "In Memoriam, Asa P. Isham, MD," *Lancet-Clinic* 107 (March 1912): 334; August V. Kautz, *Customs of Service for Non-Commissioned Officers and Soldiers* (Lippincott, 1864).

18. CHH military pension; *U.S. Civil War Draft Registrations Records, 1863–1865*, NY, Ancestry.com, accessed 1/7/2023, https://www.ancestry.com/search/collections/1666/; Alexander Hazzard of St. Armand registered for army service on 7/1/1863.

19. EC widow's pension; JH military pension; *U.S. Civil War Draft Registrations Records, 1863–1865*, NY; SH military pension; Whaling Crew List Database, New Bedford Whaling Museum, accessed 1/15/2023, https://www.whalingmuseum.org/online_exhibits/crewlist/search.php?term=simeon+hasbrook&by_name=on&by_vessel=on. Sanford Hasbrook, Josiah and Simeon's younger brother, also joined the navy (Navy pension, 310710). Sanford was ship's cook on the revenue cutter *Cuyahoga*. Like his brother Simeon, he stayed a seaman for years after the war. *USFC 1870*, Glastonbury, CT.

20. Private William Carasaw, NYCT, Carte-de-Visite, Cady Photo Gallery, Canal Street, NY, n.d., New York State Military Museum, Saratoga Springs; Seraile, *New York's Black Regiments*, 24–27; JMS, introduction to *Memorial Discourse by Henry Highland Garnet* (Washington, DC, 2/12/1865), 57–58; Hunter, *To Set the Captives Free*, 204. McCune Smith survived the war, but congestive heart disease diminished his activity in these years, and he died in 1865. Stauffer, *Works*, xxviii.

21. Dyer, *Compendium*, 1727–28; EC widow's pension. Carasaw's military physician used the catch-all term "Southern fever" for a range of illnesses. What saddled Carasaw with lasting asthma and a weak heart may have been the long-term effects of malaria, yellow fever, typhoid fever, or influenza. CHH military pension; JH military pension.

22. JSH widow's pension; ibid., and JSH, deposition for JH military pension; JH military pension; William Carasaw, affidavit for JH military pension; JH, CHH, and Eugene D. Chilson, affidavits for EC widow's pension.

23. Egerton, *Wars of Reconstruction*, 98–101; contract between Jeremiah Miles and Rienzi Bennett, Beaufort, 4/23/1866, in JM military pension; Rose, *Rehearsal for Reconstruction*, 223–28; Foner, *Reconstruction*, 51–54; Rose, *Rehearsal*

for Reconstruction 68; Egerton, *Wars of Reconstruction*, 116; White, *Republic*, 42–55; Egerton, *Wars of Reconstruction*, 117–18, 107–8, 112–13, 102–12, 126–27; Williamson, *After Slavery*, 80–81.

24. "A South Carolina Senator Murdered," *NYT*, 10/19/1868; Archie Vernon Huff, "Political Assassination in South Carolina," keynote address, 70th Annual Meeting of the South Caroliniana Society, Columbia, SC, 4/29/2006; and Foner, *Reconstruction*, 351, 548.

25. *USFC 1850*, Newburgh; *NYSC 1855*, NE, and MacKenzie, *Plains of Abraham*, 157–58; *USFC 1860*, Non-population Schedule, NE, Essex County; JF widow's pension; MacKenzie, *Plains of Abraham*, 151.

26. JF widow's pension; *Civil War Pension Index: General Index to Pension Files, 1861–1934*, NARA. In April 1874, the Bureau of Pensions granted Jane Frazier a widow's pension of eight dollars a month. Her pension notes reveal that her late husband was a "Cabin Cook" on the gunboat and cargo ship *Augusta Dinsmore* from 1864 to 1865.

27. The circumstantial evidence that suggests this party's roots in slavery was this: Louisa, James, and Samuel Brady, and Louisa's father, Josiah Bunion, all were Marylanders (Bailey came from Delaware) and all born decades before Emancipation. Louisa's 1894 obituary described her as a former slave, and anecdotal sources said her father had been enslaved as well. Her second husband, James Brady, could not name his parents when a Franklin town clerk interviewed him for the army (a response explainable by a childhood ruptured by enslavement). Further, New Jersey's Salem County, where the Brady clan resided when they left Maryland, was a hub of Underground Railroad activity, bustling with Quaker abolitionists and laced with routes for fugitives heading north. See LB dependent mother's pension; *1860 USFC*, Franklin, Franklin County; *USFC 1850*, Mannington, Salem County, NJ; *New York Town Clerk Registers of Men Who Served in the Civil War*, Franklin, Franklin County; "Bloomingdale," *MP*, 3/8/1894; Seaver, *Historical Sketches*, 644–45; Kelly Roncace, "Three Major Underground Railroad Routes Were in South Jersey," *South Jersey Times*, 2/6/2011.

28. *USFC 1850* and *1860* and *NYSC 1855*, Franklin, Franklin County. State and federal census records and tax records from midcentury and after reveal the residencies of the Thomases, Murrays, Morehouses, and Bradys, and the Bunion/Holland cabin. George Holland was a grantee from Westchester's White Plains, whose gift land (never used) was in Township 3, Totten & Crossfield Patent, Hamilton County (*GSLB*, 109.) In Franklin County, Holland squatted.

29. JBr military pension, and "U.S., Civil War Soldier Records and Profiles, 1861–1865," Ancestry.com, https://www.ancestry.com/search/collections/1555/; LB dependent mother's pension; Landon, *History of the North Country*, 1:441–42; *USFC 1860*, Franklin, Franklin County.

30. LB dependent mother's pension; Lewis Paye, affidavit, LB pension, 4/29/1891; Samuel Brady to LB, LB pension file, n.d; *New York State Town Clerks' Registers*, NYSA.

31. Matthews, *Freedom Knows No Color*, 55; Seraile, *New York's Black Regiments*, 59–60, 34; James McCune Smith, "Sketch of the Life and Labors of Rev. Henry Highland Garnet," introduction to Garnet, *Memorial Discourse*, 17–68.

32. Seraile, *New York's Black Regiments*, 35–42, 50–53; "The Twentieth U.S. Colored Regiment," *Harper's Weekly*, 3/19/1864; "The Fete to the 20th U.S. Colored Infantry," *Frank Leslie's Illustrated Newspaper*, 3/26/1864; "Grand Ovation to a Black Regiment in New York," *NYT*, 3/12/1864; *Atlantic Monthly*, 3/19/1864.

33. Seraile, *New York's Black Regiments*, 82–83, 60–63, app. 10, 144; Chaplain George Washington LeVere, "From the Twentieth Regiment U.S. Colored Troops," *AA*, 7/30/1864; "General Order No. 44," 9/2/1864, in *AA*, 10/22/1864; Terry L. Jones, "Brother against Microbe," *NYT*, 10/26/2012.

34. Samuel H. Brady military pension, USCT muster roll, NARA; and LB dependent mother's pension. Brady's headstone in the Chalmette National Cemetery is number 10716.

35. LB dependent mother's pension; Sara A. Muzzie to Private James Brady, 2/28/1865, courtesy of Susann Hoskins, Brady family genealogist, Binghamton, NY.

36. See *USFC 1870, 1880, 1890, 1900*, and *NYSC 1875, 1885*, and *1890 Veterans Schedules*, Malone, NY; *New York State Town Clerks' Registers*, NYSA. In this document, James Brady is described as "Mulatto," with a white parent and a Black one. And while this enlistee told the registrar he and Louisa were Samuel's parents, he gave her last name not as Brady but as Bunyan, her maiden name. Susann Hoskins, email to the author, 2/12/2006.

37. Hoskins, email, 2/12/2006.

38. From Willsboro on Lake Champlain, Long Island–born Horace Mingo enlisted with the Second New York Cavalry in 1864 (military pension, 109.846, 70391). The Adirondack-born grantee Lafayette Mason of New Russia enlisted with the 118th NY Volunteers in 1863. (MCM widow's pension.) The year before, the grantee Joseph James's son, Adolphus, also from Willsboro, joined Company F of the 118th. His brother, Harvey James, of the First Vermont Cavalry, died in an army hospital in Virginia in 1864.

Some upstate Black New Yorkers who weren't Adirondackers and served in white regiments were Ira Brum of Ithaca, an 1864 enlistee with the 185th NY Volunteers. Brum was "the only colored man in his company," his obituary reports. "[He] possessed the confidence and good will of his officers and comrades" *U.S., Union Soldiers Compiled Service Records, 1861–1865*, NARA, at ancestry.com, and Carol Kammen, "African American Men in White NY Civil War Units," *New York History*, 1/4/2012, https://www.newyorkhistoryblog.com/2012/01/african-american-men-in-white-ny-civil.html. From Delhi, William S. Law and Reuben Dyer joined the 89th NY Volunteers (Matthews, *Freedom Knows No Color*, 140–41), and Virgil Jackson of the Hudson River hamlet Fort Ann served with his neighbors in Company F, NY 169th, Troy Regiment. Perry, *People of Lowly Life*, 122.

The historian Carla Peterson observed the sometime humanizing influence of neighborly propinquity in a *NYT* online contribution, "Black Elites and the Draft Riots," 7/13/2013. https://archive.nytimes.com/opinionator.blogs.nytimes.com/2013/07/13/black-elites-and-the-draft-riots/. The many documented accounts of "unnamed neighbors who decided to help, to protect, to rescue" Black Manhattanites during the rioting "proved," Peterson suggests, "that if being a neighbor could unleash hatred and violence, it could also elicit acts of pure kindness. In fact, it seems that being an integral part of a neighborhood community was the one thing that could trump race."

39. MacKenzie, *Plains of Abraham*, 115. Among Adirondack officers with strong abolitionist convictions were Colonel George Hindes of the NY 96th, son of James Hindes, a Liberty Party candidate for Ausable supervisor in 1845 (*ECR*, 2/19/1845); and Colonel Oliver Keese Jr. of the 118th "Adirondack Regiment," part of a Quaker-descended Adirondack clan that helped numberless fugitives to Canada. The historian Tom Calarco suggests that as many as twenty-seven Clinton County abolitionists were Keeses by birth or marriage, and almost all belonged to antislavery societies (Calarco, *Underground Railroad*, 143). Elizabethtown's Captain Robert Livingston of the 118th shared a legal practice with the Liberty Party zealot Jesse Gay (Smith, *History of Essex County*, 483). The son of a farmer and a schoolteacher in Ausable Forks, both ardent abolitionists, Sergeant Myron A. Arnold of the 118th was poised to take command of a Black company when he was killed in 1864 at Drewry's Bluff (author's correspondence with Arnold family genealogist Barbara B. Lewis, Simi Valley, CA, 11/2000). Captain Rowland Kellogg, also of the 118th, was the son of Orlando Kellogg, one of the four Adirondackers who stood vigil over John Brown's coffin when it rested overnight in the Essex County Courthouse.

40. Seaver, *Historical Sketches*, 125; Phisterer, *New York*, 6:3095–97. Perhaps reflecting the reconciliationist convictions of his era, the late nineteenth-century historian H. Perry Smith deemed Wardner's abolitionism divisive. While acknowledging that Wardner was "a very zealous worker for the colored man," his antislavery church took "members from both of the other churches which left all three societies weak." (Smith, *History of Essex County*, 719). Untitled news clipping, n.d., 96th Regiment New York File, NYS Military Museum and Veterans Research Library.

41. *1860 USFC*, Westport, Essex County; MacKenzie, *Plains of Abraham*, 158; *USFC 1850*, Philadelphia; *NYSC 1855*, Essex County; Civil War Muster Roll Abstracts, NYSA; and Civil War Draft Records, NARA; LM military pension. An affidavit that Lewis Mason submitted to the pension office when he was sixty-three suggests he was fourteen when he enlisted.

42. *CA*, 4/1/1837, 8/4/1841, 8/21/1841, 9/4/1841, and 11/20/1841; *USFC 1860*, Albion, MI; Mingo obituary, *Albion Recorder*, 6/4/1869. The light-skinned descendants of James McCune Smith disavowed their Black ancestry. See Stauffer, *Works*, xvi–xix. Stauffer's preface includes an essay by McCune Smith's descendant Greta Blau, titled "How James McCune Smith Became White."

43. "John Brown's Birthday," *Burlington Free Press*, 5/22/1885; *USFC 1920*, Fresno, CA; BBS to Marjorie L. Porter, 9/9/1955, and BBS to E. N. Cotter, 8/27/1965, JB/BBS Coll./WVMP; Albertine Enid LaFollette, death certificate, City and County of San Francisco, and Joseph A. Romeo to Mary MacKenzie, 9/10/1992, Mary MacKenzie Papers, Lyman E. Eppes Collection, LPPL.

44. BBS to Marjorie Porter, 8/9/1955, BBS to George Marshall, 4/29/1962, BBS to E. F. Cotter, Lake Placid, 8/27/1963, Edwin N. Cotter Jr. Collection, Special Collections, SUNY Plattsburgh; Cotter to BBS, 6/13/1967 and BBS to Cotter, 7/5/1967, JB/BBS Coll./WVMP.

15. An Empowering Diaspora

1. MacKenzie, *Plains of Abraham*, 150. Private Hazzard returned to St. Armand with Julia Smith Hazzard and Julia's daughters, Clara and Genevia. Svenson, *Blacks in the Adirondacks*, 28–29; JSH widow's pension and JM military pension.

2. Tyler, ". . . *In Them Thar Hills*," 63; *NYSC 1875,* Franklin, Franklin County; Howard Riley, "The Town of Franklin's Black History," *ADE*, 6/6/2020. The movement of Black veterans and refugees into the Adirondack region is noted in town histories of Westport, Warrensburgh, Mayfield, Port Henry, Indian Lake, Wilmington, and Whitehall. Also see Svenson, *Blacks in the Adirondacks*, 46–52, and Perry, *People of Lowly Life*, 121, 133, 146–47, 169–70.

3. TE/TT military pension; *USFC 1870*, NE, Essex County; Mary MacKenzie, "The North Elba Men and Their Fates," *LPN*, 11/28/1997; JH military pension, affidavit, Benjamin Demmon, 7/28/1881. The farmer's son Ben Demmon reports that he and his young neighbor, Josiah Hasbrook Jr., worked together at Intervales, the Demmon farm, before the war and after; North Elba school records, ECCO; William W. Patton, "John Brown," marching song. In *John Brown, Abolitionist*, David Reynolds documents the surge of violence after Harpers Ferry that was directed at Southerners who supported Brown.

4. *USFC 1870*, NE, Essex County; TE/TT military pension, affidavits.

5. Shaffer, *After the Glory*, 104. Shaffer writes, "To be a real man was to be a legally married man, asserting the most basic of manhood rights—the authority of a household head—as a first step to asserting other manhood rights." Marriages among Black veterans in Essex and Franklin Counties are documented in military pensions for Civil War soldiers, their widows, and their dependents. Seven women in the Black Woods who got married after the war were Jane Ann Hazzard, Adaline Hazzard, Rachel Caroline Thomas, her sister Charlotte Ann, Mary Elizabeth Bailey, Harriette Hasbrook, and her sister-in-law, Lucy Pierce Hasbrook. On James Brady's marriages, see chapter 14. On William Appo's late-life marriage, see Godine, "Noteworthy Mr. Appo"; Howard Riley, "The Town of Franklin's Black History," *ADE*, 6/6/2023; LPM widow's pension; JH military pension. NARA military pension files note the marriages of the grantee Avery Hazzard's children.

6. On William Carasaw, see *USFC 1880*, Vergennes, VT; EC widow's pension, statements, Lewis Mott, 9/11/1888, and Eugene D. Chilson, 9/12/1888; and "Vergennes," *Middlebury Register*, 7/16/1880, 9/24/1886.

7. The Vermont Historical Society librarian, Paul Carnahan, and the Middlesex town historian, Patricia Wiley, confirmed Josiah Hasbrook's role as commander of GAR Hall Post 39 in 1893 in Worcester, Vermont; *Malone Palladium*, 5/29/1902, *Malone Farmer*, 1/18/1905, 11/14/1906; Carnahan and Wiley, emails to the author, 5/12/2015; CM widow's pension.

8. On Jane Craig, see *USFC 1860* and *NYSC 1865*, NE, Essex County; on Jane Frazier, see *NYSC 1865*, Westport, Essex County, and JF widow's pension; on Louisa Brady, see LB dependent mother's pension; on Julia Hazzard, see CHH military pension and JSH widow's pension.

9. Pension appeals for the Black Adirondack veterans Miles, Hasbrook, Hazzard, Morehouse, Carasaw, and Lafayette and Lewis Mason attest to

war-induced rheumatism. JM military pension, affidavits, C. H. Hazzard and Josiah Hasbrook. Private Hasbrook took lasting pride in how he nursed and revived his army friend Jerry Miles with poultices of "mayweed" (chamomile), a healing herb in lotions, salves, and teas. JH military pension; CHH military pension, affidavit, William Martin; Godine, "Battle after the War." Thanks to my editor, Annie Stoltie, from *Adirondack Life*, for permission to excerpt language from this article in this book.

10. Shaffer, *After the Glory*, 123–24, 127–31.

11. Shaffer, *After the Glory*, 123–24, 127–31, 132, 137; Pencak, *Encyclopedia of the Veteran*, 1:7–10, 95–96; SH military pension, statement, JH, 10/12/1904; JH military pension; CM widow's pension, claimant's affidavit; Pencak, *Encyclopedia of the Veteran*, 1:10, 95; JH, military pension, depositions, C. F. Branch, MD, Amherst, MA, 11/15/1902, and Capt. Carlos P. Lyman, Esq., Amherst, MA, to Pension Bureau, 12/3/1903 and 2/17/1905; recommendation, Sam Houston, Medical Referee, to Pension Bureau, 9/8/1904.

12. Shaffer, *After the Glory*, 55–56; Pencak, *Encyclopedia of the Veteran*, 1:10, 95–96.

13. CHH military pension, affidavits, Special Examiner Clement Sullivane to Commissioner of Pensions, Plattsburgh, 3/15/1889, and James E. Pipes, 3/11/1889.

14. JH military pension, affidavits, Samuel Dickinson, 7/26/1881; Betsy C. Torrance, 7/28/1881; Linton Deming, 7/27/1881; Dennis Dewey, 1/28/1891.

15. CAM widow's pension, affidavits from Joseph C. Merrill and Alburn Hathaway, 1/17/1891; Jane Bombard and Eunice Swinyer, 1/20/1892. Although pediatric hydrocephalus was not named as Henry Morehouse's affliction, his enlarged head, paralysis, and history of seizures point to this diagnosis.

16. If white Adirondack veterans suffered more than Black veterans, it was because they could; they had the opportunity to fight. Even after Black men were allowed to bear arms for their country, they saw much less combat than white soldiers. "Indeed," notes Donald Shaffer, "some Union authorities felt that African-American troops were suitable only for fatigue duty." Shaffer, *After the Glory*, 15. "Manly" warfare was deemed a privilege for white men alone.

17. CHH military pension, affidavit, Sylvester Reid, 3/5/1891; CAM widow's pension, affidavit, Eunice Swinyer, 1/20/1892.

18. The idea of an innate capacity that made Black people unfit for Adirondack pioneering pervades the Adirondack canon. See (among many others) Watson, *General View*, 78; Richards, *Romance of American Landscape*, 235–36; Sylvester, *Historical Sketches*, 140; Stoddard, *Adirondacks*, 68–69; Smith, *History of Essex County*, 188–89; and, most influentially, Donaldson, *History*, 2:3, 6.

19. *NYSC 1855*, Brooklyn, NY; "Willis A. Hodges (1815–1890)," *Encyclopedia Virginia*, 1/12/2022, https://encyclopediavirginia.org/entries/hodges-willis-a-1815-1890/. Hodges returned to New York City no later than 1853, the year he married Sarah Ann Corprew Gray.

20. Josiah Hasbrook to Pension Bureau, 12/6/1888, in JH military pension. Not the census but Josiah Hasbrook's Civil War pension file is my source of information about his family's many moves. In a letter detailing his need

for medical attention, Hasbrook named his doctors and addresses. Censuses, loose-woven sieves at best, did not pick up his years in Westport or Wadhams.

21. "The Homestead Act, May 20, 1862," National Archives, last reviewed 7/22/2019, https://www.archives.gov/legislative/features/homestead-act; "African-American Homesteaders in the Great Plains," National Park Service, accessed 10/21/2022, https://www.nps.gov/articles/african-american-home-steaders-in-the-great-plains.htm; Daniel P. Barr, "Westward Migration," Dictionary of American History, accessed 10/21/2022, https://www.ency clopedia.com/history/dictionaries-thesauruses-pictures-and-press-releases/ westward-migration.

22. Josiah Hasbrook Jr.'s stint in Glastonbury with his father revealed no migration. Only a few weeks after the census found him in Connecticut, another census taker recorded him at home with his family on his North Elba farm. Josiah Hasbrook Jr., *USFC 1870*, Glastonbury, CT, and NE; JF widow's pension; *USFC 1870*, Westport; Jane Craig, *USFC 1870–1910*, Saratoga; George Holland, *USFC 1870–1900*, Canandaigua, Ontario County.

23. In his town history, *Mostly Spruce and Hemlock*, the Tupper Lake historian Louis J. Simmons mentions the early residency of Black pioneer and Smith grantee Enos Brewer. By 1875, Brewer was living in northern Franklin County, where he farmed and hired out. Enos Brewer, *NYSC Census*, Dickinson, Franklin County; James Brady, *USFC 1870, 1880*, Malone, and *Malone Farmer*, 11/14/1906; Alexander Gordon, *USFC 1880*, Monmouth County, NJ; Wesley and Phebe Murray, residential poll tax records, Town of Franklin Archives, Franklin County. (Wesley Murray died in 1867. His Franklin poll taxes were paid in 1863, 1864, and 1867.) Avery Hazzard's children who took up full- or part-time farming were Charles Henry, Alexander, Lovinia, Jane Ann, and Adaline. Josiah Hasbrook's half sister Lucy Pierce married Private Jeremiah Miles; they farmed in Middlesex, Vermont. Private Alexander Butler, husband of Josiah's sister Harriette, was a sometime farmer in Connecticut. And Harriette's daughter Hester married a farmer, Private Henry Prince of the Massachusetts Fifty-Fourth Volunteer Infantry. Before he took up cooking in earnest, and ten years after he left his own farm in North Elba, Josiah Sr. picked up farm work in Connecticut. *USFC 1870*, Glastonbury, CT; and *NYSC 1865*, Sag Harbor, Easthampton, NY.

24. "Black Abolitionists and the Republican Party," in Ripley et al., *Black Abolitionist Papers*, 4:402n8.

25. Sojourns in Wadhams and Vergennes after the Civil War are documented in Josiah and Jane Ann Hasbrook's applications for pension relief. The Hasbrooks' first home in Middlesex may have been a farmhouse rented from their neighbor, Charles Pierce. "The Late Middlesex Shooting Affray," *VWSJ*, 9/1/1875.

26. In *Discovering Black Vermont*, Elise Guyette argues that Vermont's well-burnished antislavery reputation is exaggerated. While Vermont outlawed slavery early on, the state constitution sanctioned the gradual emancipation of children, which stretched out Vermont's enslavement long after slavery was presumably abolished. Guyette, *Discovering Black Vermont*, 6–7, 120–21; Tom Calarco, "The Fresh Air of Freedom: The Underground Railroad

in Vermont," accessed 10/21/2022, https://www.academia.edu/42782201/The_Fresh_Air_of_Freedom_The_Underground_Railroad_in_Vermont.

27. GAR membership book, Hall Post 39, Worcester, VT (X369.151 H14), Vermont Historical Society, Montpelier. Hasbrook was commander of this post in 1893. "Was Friend of John Brown—Death of Josiah Hasbrook, Once of Bear Swamp Section of Middlesex," *Montpelier Evening Argus*, 7/29/1915.

28. "Was Friend of John Brown"; EC widow's pension, statement and affidavit from JH, 1888, 1889; *VWSJ*, 11/7/1883.

29. "A Silver Celebration," *VWSJ*, 11/15/1893; Ray and Hodges, "Report of the Committee," and "Resolutions," *Model Worker*, 5/18/1848.

30. See note 43, below; *USFC 1930*, Amherst, MA; "Frank L. Miles Dies," *Burlington Free Press*, 11/8/1934; *VWSJ*, 12/12/1894.

31. *A&P*, 10/14/1896; JH military pension.

32. Gallagher, *Breeding Better Vermonters*, 45–46; Walter M. Rogers, "Vermont's Deserted Farms," *Stray Leaves from a Larker's Log*, 1897, quoted in "Vermont Eugenics: A Documentary History," https://www.uvm.edu/~eugenics/roots.html (Nancy Gallagher also explores this in her online essay "Vermont Eugenics," ibid.); *A&P*, 10/14/1896.

33. "Shady Rill," *Vermont News*, 11/9/1897.

34. "Notice of Foreclosure," *VWSJ*, 1/26/1898.

35. *Amherst (MA) Directory*, 1905; *Massachusetts, U.S. Death Notices, Amherst, 1901*, https://www.ancestry.com/search/collections/3659/; JH military pension. A picture of Josiah Hasbrook Jr., cropped from a group photograph of Civil War veterans at a GAR parade (photographer unknown), hangs in the Jones Library in Amherst.

36. *A&P*, 4/6/1887; *VWSJ*, 7/27/1887, 11/15/1893; *Springfield Daily Republican*, 7/29/1915.

37. MacKenzie, *Plains of Abraham*, 163–64.

38. *USFC 1870*, NE, Essex County. Elliott, age twenty-four in 1870, was twenty when he mustered out, and sixteen when he escaped enslavement and joined the army in Virginia; Hardy, "Iron Age Community"; Moravek, "Iron Industry," fig. 15, "Settlements Founded and/or Largely Nurtured by the Iron Industry, 1846–1860," 91–90; Seaver, *Historical Sketches*, 361; Tyler, "Early Days in Franklin"; Smith, *History of Essex County*, 721; Deed Book 84, 3/15/1882, 252, ECCO.

39. Hardy, "Iron Age Community," 138–234; *NYSC 1875*, North Hudson and New Russia, Essex County. On different days in 1875, census takers found Elliott living in these towns. *USFC 1880*, Elizabethtown, Essex County.

40. TE/TT military pension. Thomas Thompson was not the only Black person who left the Adirondack region to find a Black spouse. Lyman and Annie Eppes's daughter Kate met her spouse in New York City. Lyman Epps Jr. told a reporter that he might have married if he had met a Black woman in North Elba who was available, but since he didn't wish to move, marriage was not an option. He recognized bachelorhood as the price of living in a community where interracial marriage was apparently unthinkable. Margaret Bartley, "Researching Adirondack Diversity," lecture, Adirondack History Museum, 10/12/2018. Bartley's census work on Black households in Essex

County from 1840 to 1930 reveals that while interracial marriages were not frequent in Essex County's eastern half, neither were they unheard of. "Fred. Douglass Married," *EPG*, 1/31/1884. Many newspapers made Douglass's wedding an occasion to stoke white fear of race mixing. Blight, *Frederick Douglass*, 650–51.

41. TE/TT military pension, including affidavits. The US Bureau of Pensions assessed the legitimacy of claims from Union veterans who used aliases, including fugitives-turned-soldiers who hoped a name change would make it hard to track their old enslavement, veterans who dropped old slave names during or after the war for new identities as free men, and repeat "bounty jumpers" who enlisted, claimed their pay, deserted, and reenlisted under false names (in this fashion, one enterprising huckster collected thirty-two bounties; see Murdock, "New Civil War Bounty Brokers," 266).

42. TE/TT military pension, including affidavits; Martha [Riddick] Thompson, widow's pension; MacKenzie, *Plains of Abraham*, 212–15. Three antislavery families owned this property: John Brown's good friends the abolitionist Thompsons, who bought their land from Gerrit Smith; Palmer Havens, a radical reformer and speculator; and the Demmons, Elliott's employers. The Brewster clan, who bought it next, sold the whole place to the Lake Placid Club in 1905. Weigand, *Irrepressible Reformer*, 324, 352. The Lake Placid Club Stores, Inc., was buying up former properties of Black grantees and their children as late as 1950. Legal notices soliciting descendants of Maud Eppes Appo with regard to a parcel in Lake Placid ran in the *Lake Placid News* in April and May of 1950.

43. MacKenzie, *Plains of Abraham*, 163–65.

44. Vaughan, *Abandoned Farm Areas*, 8–12, and Stradling, *Nature of New York*, 63–65; Hedrick, *History of Agriculture*, 438; Beatty, *Age of Betrayal*, 105, 108; Guyette, *Discovering Black Vermont*, 120–21.

45. Military pensions show that for long spells, the veterans Miles, Hazzard, Hasbrook, and Frazier were confined to bed by war-caused illness. In these hard seasons and beyond, their wives and mothers and older children ran their households and took jobs.

46. Laughlin-Schultz, *Tie That Bound Us*, 80–90, and Special Collections, Concord Free Public Library, Concord, MA. According to Laughlin-Schultz, offers of help for Annie and Sarah's schooling came from Rebecca Spring, Parker Pillsbury, Theodore Weld, and Franklin Sanborn. In the end, it was Sanborn, Gerrit Smith, and Wendell Phillips who paid for the Brown girls' tuition at Sanborn's Concord School. On Lucy Pierce's youthful marriage to Jerry Miles in Wadhams, see LPM widow's pension, affidavit, 7/20/1913.

47. *Rural Vermonter*, 6/18/1886; *VWSJ*, 5/9/1894; *Montpelier (VT) Morning Journal*, 3/13/1906; *Montpelier (VT) Evening Argus*, 4/21/1913; *Montpelier Morning Journal*, 4/21/13; Patricia Wiley, "Middlesex Residents' Memories and Stories about the Hasbrook and Miles Families," 8/2021, courtesy of Middlesex (VT) town historian.

48. Federal and state censuses from 1880 into the Depression identify these jobs with John Thomas's descendants. See Svenson, *Blacks in the Adirondacks*, chap. 5; Vincent, *Southern Seed, Northern Soil*, xiii–xv; David A. Gerber, "Local

and Community History: Some Cautionary Remarks on an Idea Whose Time Has Returned," in Kammen, *Pursuit of Local History*, 217–18.

49. Menand, *Metaphysical Club*, 49–69, 97–148. Scientific racialism is not the focus of Menand's intellectual history, but his pages on American scientists who embraced theories of racial hierarchy expand the context for considering the racialized social culture of the postbellum Adirondacks. "Professor Agassiz on the Negro," *EP*, 6/27/1867. Whether about mummies, coral reefs, or "negro body types," the Harvard scientist Louis Agassiz's opinions were well represented in Adirondack newspapers until his death in 1873.

50. Rosa Scott, *USFC 1900*, Franklin, NY, and *USFC 1920*, Englewood, NJ; Richard Scott, *USFC 1910*, Franklin, *USFC 1920*, Tupper Lake, and World War II draft registration card, 1942, Hightstown, NJ, https://www.ancestry.com/discoveryui-content/view/7413359:1002; John Carasaw, *USFC 1880*, Vergennes, and *USFC 1900*, Burlington; James Carasaw, *USFC 1880*, Vergennes, *Troy City Directory*, 1901, 1907, 1911, and *USFC 1930*, NYC; Frederick Carasaw, *USFC 1800*, Vergennes, and *USFC 1910*, Worcester; CM widow's pension; Dabel, *Respectable Woman*, 66–74, and Jenny Carson, "Laundry," in Eric Arnesen, ed., *Encyclopedia of U.S. Labor and Working-Class History* (Taylor & Francis, 2007), 777–83. US and state census records link the following descendants of grantees to laundry work and housecleaning in the first third of the twentieth century: Rosa Scott, Mary Hazzard, Elizabeth Hazzard, Mary Morehouse, Kathleen Morehouse Prince, and Libby Morehouse Hazzard. Laundry work paid badly in the first place, and no laundresses were paid as poorly as Black women, who were typically restricted to flatwork ironing and pressing. Carson, "Laundry," 781; "Marshall Morehouse," *ADE*, 3/4/1964; my own phone conversations with Robert Lagroome, 2010–20, Baltimore; "George Hazzard Dies; Native of Saint Armand," *ADE*, 9/29/1948.

51. James Morehouse, World War II draft registration card, 1942, https://www.ancestry.com/discoveryui-content/view/411183:1002; *USFC 1930*, Corona, Queens.

52. CM widow's pension; *MP*, 5/10/1894; *Adirondack Chronology*, https://digitalworks.union.edu/cgi/viewcontent.cgi?article=1000&context=arlpublications.

53. JMS to GS, 7/27/1847. Susan Clark and Woden Teachout explore the role of mutual need and collaboration in small communities in *Slow Democracy*. Invoking the small-town culture of citizen participation that distinguished an earlier United States, they make a spirited defense of place-based local activism as an agent of effective change.

54. "Johnson vs. Hazzard," ECCO, and Record of Commitments, Essex County Jail, Archives, Adirondack History Museum, Elizabethtown. Charles Henry Hazzard, farmer, age sixty, went to jail on March 17, 1886, for "debt," and was released on May 14 of that year.

55. Record of Commitments.

56. Svenson, "Integrated Cemetery"; *EP*, 12/14/1893; "James H. Pierce," Historic Saranac Lake LocalWiki, accessed 1/9/2023, https://localwiki.org/hsl/James_H._Pierce; "Captain Pierce," *ADE*, 3/16/1964; "Judson C. Ware," obituary, *EP*, 10/29/1908; Annie Brown to John Brown Jr., 7/18/1857, JBjrKS.

57. "Affidavits for Cancellation of Tax Sale of 1853 . . . In Matter of Lot 87, To. 11., O.M. Tract," Redemptions, Tax Sales, Box 11, #36, NYSA; Byron Pond to GS, 1/12/1854. Pond litigated a complicated sale of family property belonging to the extended Hazzard clan in 1861. "Charles H. Hazzard and Juliana Hazzard agnst. Margaret Ann Hazzard, Alexander Hazzard [etc.]," Supreme Court, 9/4/1861, ECCO; *NYHT*, 3/12/1896; "Ex-Assemblyman Alembert Pond," *NYT*, 3/12/1896; *EP*, 3/2/1899, 2/6/1903; *AR-EP*, 4/22/1926.

58. Byron Pond to Franklin Rowe, n.d., ECCO.

59. Clark and Teachout, *Slow Democracy*, 27–30.

60. Jacoby, *Crimes against Nature*, 39; William F. Porter, Jon D. Erickson, and Ross S. Whaley, eds., *The Great Experiment in Conservation: Voices from the Adirondack Park* (Syracuse University, 2009), 51. In this compendious 2009 anthology of environmental essays on the Adirondack Park, contributors do not consider the relevance of small-scale agriculture to the park's conservation mission. A long-standing bias against farming in this region is ripe for interrogation, especially in light of the contributions of community-supported family farms to the Adirondack economy.

61. Fifteen-year-old Richard N. Thomas died on June 24, 1860, and was buried in the Union Cemetery, Vermontville, Franklin County. Smith, *History of Essex County*, 667; "Indenture," John Thomas to Orin Otis, 1/7/1889, Deed Records, FCA; *USFC 1900*, Franklin, Franklin County; MacKenzie, *Plains of Abraham*, 133.

62. Thompson, *Body, Boots and Britches*, 304; Marjorie Lansing Porter, "Neighbors across the Lake," *Burlington Free Press*, 7/28/1939; *TS*, 1/30/1908; Ben Lewis to Marjorie Lansing Porter, 3/26/1956, Feinberg Library, Special Collections, SUNY Plattsburgh; "John Brown's Old Home to Be Made Memorial," *AR-EP*, 8/5/1921, and "Sang at Brown's Funeral, and Again Yesterday," *LPN*, 5/10/1938.

63. "Editorial Notes," *PR*, 9/2/1899; Katherine McClellan, "John Brown, His Raiders and Their Resting Place," *EP*, 8/31/1899; "43rd Anniversary of Battle of Osawatomie" and "John Brown's Men Reburied," *NYT*, 8/31/1899.

64. Thomas Featherstonhaugh, "The Final Journey of the Followers of John Brown," *New England Magazine*, 4/1901, JB/BBS Coll./WVMP; McClellan, "John Brown"; Pamela Merritt, "John Brown's Other Bodies," Saranac Lake, 10/27/2015, https://www.saranaclake.com/story/2015/10/john-browns-other-bodies.

65. As many as seven clubs and fraternal organizations in New York called the gregarious Potter a member. George Hodges, *Henry Codman Potter, Seventh Bishop of New York* (New York, 1915). No advocate for racial justice, this John Brown Day speaker enraged Black activists with his advocacy of African colonization and his refusal to condemn lynch law in the South. Michael Bourgeois, *All Things Human: Henry Codman Potter and the Social Gospel in the Episcopal Church* (University of Illinois, 2010), 78–82; "Summer Retreats When Old Money Was New," *NYT*, 8/12/2010.

66. "Blow Ye the Trumpets Blow," *PS*, 9/1/1899; Oates, *To Purge This Land*, 164–65.

67. McClellan, *A Hero's Grave in the Adirondacks*.

68. "Saranac Lake, Spring Resorts," *BDE*, 5/4/1902; "Hazzard agst. Hazzard," Supreme Court, Franklin County, NY, 7/22/1904, Franklin County Records; William A. Langley, *NYSC 1905, USFC 1910*, St. Armand; *EP*, 11/2/1911, 11/19/1911, 11/23/1911, and 11/30/1911; *A Tuberculosis Directory* (National Association for the Study and Prevention of Tuberculosis, 1916), 86.

69. McClellan, *A Hero's Grave in the Adirondacks*.

70. Charles W. Linnell, Albany, to Commissioner of Pensions, Washington, DC, 3/6/1899, in CHH military pension file; JM military pension; LPM widow's pension. Seeking to validate the claim of Lucy Miles, Linnell interviewed Lucy's Adirondack neighbors, including Lyman E. Eppes. Linnell would conclude that Hazzard "has the best of reputations. He owned two farms earned by his labor, and is respected by the white people of his neighborhood." On 9/27/1899, three weeks after the ceremony at John Brown's farm, Charles Henry Hazzard died. *TS*, 12/14/1877, 2/17/1898.

71. Martin Luther King Jr. used this phrase in his "I Have a Dream" speech on 8/28/1963, and again at Riverside Church in New York City on 4/4/1967, in his sermon "Beyond Vietnam: A Time to Break Silence."

16. White Memory, Black Memory

1. Stoddard, *The Adirondacks Illustrated* [1874 edition]. This travel memoir not only inclined lawmakers to approve the Adirondack Park, noted Banks, but "made the region in the public imagination a permanent part of the state." "New York State Writers Institute Announces First Ten Selections of Its '25 Uniquely New York Books' List," press release, SUNY Albany 11/16/2009.

2. Stoddard, *Adirondacks*, 68–69.

3. MacKenzie, *Plains of Abraham*, 11.

4. Stoddard, *Adirondacks*, 70, 66; LEE to "Mr. Editor," *FDP*, 7/21/1854; "Sang at Brown's Funeral and Again Yesterday," *LPN*, 5/10/1935.

5. Watson, *General View*, 725; "John Brown as Farmer," *Syracuse Daily Courier*, 11/10/1859. This editorial, which deemed Smith's effort "an utter failure" and observed the "sorrow and suffering" it inflicted on the grantees, shows the reach of Watson's harsh assessment of 1853. While more gentle, Katherine McClellan's *A Hero's Grave in the Adirondacks* (1896) also invoked "inherent causes" for the giveaway's demise ("As these negros . . . had been taught only indoor pursuits, they could not cope with nature in this rugged clime, and gradually they fell sick, became discouraged, died, or returned to their former homes, with one notable exception [Lyman Eppes]."); "Gerrit Smith's Insanity," *Baltimore Sun*, 11/14/1859, quoted in the *Troy Budget*, n.d.; "The Insanity of Gerrit Smith," *Baltimore Sun*, 11/17/1859, quoted in the *Albany Journal*, n.d.

6. "Historians and Other Writers," in "John Brown (Abolitionist)," Wikipedia, last edited 2/14/2023, https://en.wikipedia.org/wiki/John_Brown_(abolitionist)#Viewpoints; GS, *Manifesto*, Peterboro, 8/15/1867, GSP, and in Frothingham, *Gerrit Smith*, 258.

7. Charles and William Mali to GS, NY, 8/28/1867; Charles Calverley to GS, NYC, 4/9/1873; George L. Brackett to GS, Albany, 5/26/1862; Louis Ransom to GS, Utica, 9/15/1860; James Edgerly to GS, Great Falls, NH, 9/21/1874;

Dr. C. D. Griswold to GS, Columbus, OH, 9/25/1862 (before he moved to Ohio, Griswold published the *Sunbeam*, a Spiritualist newspaper in Buffalo, NY); George W. Gandry to GS, Vergennes, VT, 8/28/1863. In 1798, John Brown, a Quaker shipping magnate from Rhode Island, paid $33,000 for 210,000 acres in the southwestern Adirondacks. On many New York maps, this swath of land was named "John Brown's Tract." Though well south of the land that Gerrit Smith gave his grantees, it was frequently mistaken for Smith's gift land, and Smith's land agents lamented the confusion. Z. Eastman to GS, Elgin, IL, 2/3/1874. Franklin William Scott reports that Eastman edited several anti-slavery newspapers in Illinois before the Civil War, among them the *Genius of Liberty* (1840–42), the *Western Citizen* (1845), and the *Daily Times* (1852). Scott, *Newspapers and Periodicals*.

8. "Rally Round the Flag! The People's National Convention!," *PS*, 6/14/1872.

9. Frothingham, *Gerrit Smith*, 258; Quarles, *Allies for Freedom*, 4.

10. Reynolds, *John Brown*, 188, 472.

11. Isaac A. Gates to GS, Cresco, IA, 1867.

12. "'John Brown' by Gerrit Smith," broadleaf, 8/15/1867, JB/BBS Coll./WVMP, and in Frothingham, *Gerrit Smith*, 253–59; Alexis Hinckley to GS, 7/24/1868 ("I am about to offer the John Brown Farm for sale & I should prefer to sell it to some of the friends of John Brown, or friends of the antislavery course. Would it not be the best way to [have/handle] the place owned by the Society or friends of the Society. Please do consider this & talk with some of your friends. Mrs. Brown would greatly prefer to have the place sold in that way. Respectfully, Alexis Hinckley, NE"); *ECR*, 3/5/1896.

13. Whiting, *Kate Field*, 224.

14. Kate Field to William Claflin, Newport, RI, 9/7/1869, in *Kate Field: Selected Letters*, ed. Carolyn J. Moss (Southern Illinois University, 1996), 50; R. W. Emerson to Field, in Whiting, *Kate Field*, 243.

15. Field's bold bid to save Brown's North Elba home is closely tracked in Scharnhorst, *Kate Field*, 68–75; Schecter, *Devil's Own Work*, 326–28, 337–38. After the withdrawal of federal protection, atrocities against Black civilians in the South stepped up markedly. Between 1877 and 1950, over four thousand Black Southerners were lynched. Laura Bliss, "A Comprehensive Map of American Lynchings," Bloomberg CityLab, 1/17/2017, https://www.bloomberg.com/news/articles/2017-01-17/this-map-of-u-s-lynchings-spans-1835-to-1964.

16. "Drives among the Mountains and Lakes," *PS*, 6/30/1879, and "John Brown's Adirondack Farm," *BDE*, 8/2/1896, both laud the bloodless triumph of historic preservation.

17. Gobrecht, *National Historic Site*.

18. Travelers' impressions of the caretakers at the John Brown Farm ranged from rattled to disgusted. A visitor in 1875 shrank from the resident farm family's "mercenary" entreaties and the "entrancing inscription" of their entrance sign ("John brown Farm, chicken or trowt 50 cents and loging [*sic*]"). *Express and Standard* (Newport, VT), 6/22/1875. In "Camp Lou" (*Harper's Magazine*, 5/1881), Marc Cook derided locals who knew less about their hometown hero than did visitors from afar. Margaret Sidney (*Adirondack Cabin*, 248–51) was

more impatient still. The caretaker's wife, wrote Sidney, pressured pilgrims to buy pictures and candy, regaled them with misinformation about Brown's life, then worried they might vandalize the site. The state built a site manager's cottage in 1926. Chamberlin, *John Brown*, 34; John O. Collins, *Four-Track News*, 5/1903; "In the North Woods," *New-York Daily Tribune*, 6/3/1903; Henry W. Shoemaker, "John Brown the Lumberman: An Address Delivered by Henry W. Shoemaker to the Freshman Class at the State Forest School, Mont Alto (Funkstown) Pennsylvania, March 1, 1929," *Times Tribune Press* (Altoona, PA), 1931, 22 pp.; Shaw, "John Brown."

19. "The Virginia Rebellion," John Brown to "A Quaker Lady," *NYT*, 11/7/1859. This spare headstone from Connecticut honored five of the Browns: John Brown's grandfather, who shared his name; Brown himself; his son Frederick, who was killed and buried in Kansas in 1856; and Oliver and Watson, who died at Harpers Ferry. In "Manufacturing Martyrdom: The Antislavery Response to John Brown's Raid," the historian Paul Finkelman documents the unavailing efforts of abolitionists to "canonize Brown as a crucified martyr for the cause of the slave" and get Brown buried at the storied Cambridge cemetery where, as Henry C. Wright wrote, "an *appropriate* monument might be erected to him." Wright to the *Liberator*, 8/31/1860, and "Arrival of JB's Remains at Troy," *NYT*, 12/6/1859. See Finkelman, *His Soul Goes Marching On*, 41–66.

20. Nineteenth-century travelers' accounts that give stress to the difficulty of simply getting to the farm include "Among the Adirondacks," *NYT*, 8/5/1867; Mayo, "Adirondacks in August"; Dana, "How We Met John Brown"; Gould, "John Brown at North Elba" (on Adirondack pilgrimage patterns from the antebellum era to our time, see Sturges, "Consumption in the Adirondacks," which considers how the pilgrimage as a literary trope shaped an image of the region and eased its transformation into the excursionist's parkland and preserve); "Letter from Henry C. Wright," *Liberator*, 8/1860 ("No monument . . . could so fitly . . . perpetuate the memory of such a man as the bold, stern, defiant mountains"); "Celebration at North Elba," *DM*, 9/1860; Charles Dudley Warner, "Adirondack Notes," *The Press* (Hartford, CT), 11/24/1866 ("The whole region seems somehow consecrated with his spirit"); Street, *Indian Pass* ("Old Whiteface, and . . . the great Tahawus [were] truly two grand grave-stones . . . between which John Brown sleeps, reared in everlasting rock by the great God himself"); "Celebration," *DM*, 9/1860. In his 1963 "I Have a Dream" speech at the Lincoln Memorial, Martin Luther King Jr. declared, "Let Freedom ring from the mighty mountains of New York." The environmental activist Peter Bauer suggests that King wrote this with Brown's Adirondack resting place in mind. Peter Bauer, "From the Mighty Mountains of New York," *Lake George Mirror*, 1/2009.

21. "Letter from Henry C. Wright."

22. George S. Hale, "Ode to John Brown," *ECR*, 3/19/1896, from an article by Francis W. Lee, "Why Is a State Monument Necessary?," Boston, 3/12/1896.

23. "Celebration at North Elba," *DM*, 9/1860; "Funeral Oration of Wendell Phillips," *New York Tribune*, 12/12/1859; "Celebration at North Elba"; "Distribution of the John Brown Fund," *DM*, 10/1860; "All Compromises Useless," *Liberator*, 12/28/1860.

24. "Proceedings of the Board of Supervisors," *EP*, 12/11/1858; "Annual Fair of the Essex County Agricultural Society," *ECR*, 8/5/1854. On John Brown's wide-ranging Adirondack network: marriage ties hitched his family to the Thompsons, Brewsters, and Hinckleys, all longer-rooted in North Elba than Brown's clan. Warner, "Adirondack Notes"; Stoddard, *Adirondacks*, 79; Street, *Woods and Waters*, 325; Hoffman, "Pilgrimage." In 1898, New York assemblyman Martin Ives made a grand tour of the Adirondacks. In his chapter about John Brown's home, not a sentence notes the Black pioneers Brown came to help or any part of Brown's antislavery career outside his "foolhardy," "hopeless and rash" plans for Harpers Ferry. Ives, *Adirondacks in Eighteen Days*, 41–47.

25. For apolitical celebrations at Brown's home and grave, see "A Tramp and Tarry among the Adirondacks and Lakes," *NYT*, 7/24/1866; "His Soul Is Marching On," *NYT*, 9/29/1890; Nichols, "Adirondack Pilgrimage."

26. Warner, "Adirondack Notes"; GS, "Among the Adirondacks," *NYT*, 8/5/1867.

27. Smith, "William Cooper Nell"; Nell to GS, Boston, 6/7/1860; Nell to GS, Rochester, NY, 12/28/1847.

28. Susann Owens to GS, New Haven, 8/6/1861; T. D. Trumbull to GS, Ausable Forks, 1874 nd; John J. Jenkins to GS on behalf of Rachel Webb, NYC, 8/12/1869. James Blair Webb was the city speculator who, in 1849, partnered with Abraham Caldwell to buy wilderness land from Smith and resell lots to Black New Yorkers (see chap. 5). One Adirondack lot was sold to Dennis Washington, an escaped slave in Michigan. When Washington never claimed his land, the property reverted to Webb, and on Webb's death his widow, unable to find the title, asked Smith to replace it. William Wells Brown to Wendell Phillips, London, 9/29/1849, 9/1/1852, Houghton Library, Harvard University.

29. "Willis A. Hodges (1815–1890)," Encyclopedia Virginia, accessed 2/18/2023, https://encyclopediavirginia.org/entries/hodges-willis-a-1815-1890.

30. "Affidavit" for "literal transcription of the Nelson-Hodges lineage and records . . . as researched and compiled by Alexander Augustus Moore, 5/21/1876–9/18/1959, a descendant." Notarized in Kings County, NY, 7/6/1973, Edwin Cotter Collection, Special Collections, Feinberg Library, SUNY Plattsburgh. Also see Karl Beckwith Smith III, "Loon Lake, Franklin County, New York, An Introduction," 2001, http://loonlakehoa.org/llhisto ryks.pdf.

31. Algernon F. Jones to GS, East Brooklyn, 4/23/1855; John J. Johnson to GS, NYC, 4/28/1874; Nathan Johnson to GS, New Bedford, 2/18/1873.

32. A white surveyor-speculator, Lem Merrill, bought this lot (it was his grandfather, the surveyor "Jerry" Merrill, who described a "Smith Lot" for the *Impartial Citizen* in 1849. See chap. 11). Deeds (power of attorney assigned by Silas Harris, NYC, to Lyman Eppes, NE, witness James Pierce, 7/19/1888), FCA and JB/BBS Coll./WVMP.

33. *GSLB*, 105; CBR, "Receipt Book of Land Grants from Gerrit Smith to Colored and Poor White Slaves from the South," A1352–77, vol. 1, Comptroller's Office, NYSA.

34. GS, "To the Slaves of America," address to the Anti-slavery Convention of New-York, Peterboro, 1/19/1842.

35. Blackett, *Beating against the Barriers,* 1–87; Swift, *Black Prophets of Justice,* 204–43; Phipps, *Mark Twain's Religion,* 172; Blight, *Frederick Douglass,* 84–85; *GSLB,* 63; Pennington, *Fugitive Blacksmith,* xv.

36. CBR, *Receipt Book,* NYSA. The 1850 *USFC* names no Stephen Pembroke, white or "col'd," living in Ulster County; Smith gave James Pennington the north two-thirds of the west half of Lot 157, Township 11, Old Military Tract, in Essex County. These forty acres were within a few lots of his brother Stephen's bigger lot.

37. Foner, *Gateway to Freedom,* 22–23.

38. Novalis (Georg Philipp Friedrich Freiherr von Hardenberg), from *Fragmente und Studien: Die Christenheit oder Europa* (1922); Roth, *Why Write? Collected Nonfiction, 1960–2014* (Library of America, 2017).

39. Webber, *American to the Backbone,* 244–49. Webber's pages offer a lively, deft account of the Pembrokes' escape and capture.

40. Webber, *American to the Backbone,* 244–49.

41. Webber, *American to the Backbone,* 244–49.

42. "Story of Stephen Pembroke," *PF,* 8/5/1854; *FDP,* 6/2/1854, 6/9/1854, 6/16/1854, 6/23/1854, 3/16/1855, and 5/11/1855; "Slave Catching Revived," *FDP,* 6/2/1854; Stephen Pembroke to James Pennington, Sharpsburg, MD, 5/30/1854, in *FDP,* 6/16/1854; Herrin, "From Slave to Abolitionist"; "Letter from J. W. C. Pennington," *FDP,* 5/11/1855; Thomas H. S. Pennington to William Still, Philadelphia, "Capture, Trial, and Return of the Fugitives Stephen Pembroke and His Two Sons to Slavery, Brother and Nephew of the Rev. James W. C. Pennington, D.D.," Lancaster County (PA) Historical Society, 1893; May, *Fugitive Slave Law,* 37–38. Pennington's attorney was the antislavery Whig Erastus D. Culver, formerly of upstate Washington County (and an advocate for the grantee Avery Hazzard). In his New York City practice, Culver defended several fugitives. After the horrific outcome of the Pembrokes' case, his antislavery militancy hardened. "The Late Fugitive Slave Case," *NYT,* 5/29/1854.

43. "A Slave Made Free," *Salem (MA) Register,* 7/3/1854, "Stephen Pembroke, the Returned Fugitive," *New Orleans Times-Picayune,* 7/7/1854; *U.S. City Directory, Brooklyn,* 1868; *NYDT,* 7/1/1854 and 7/29/1854; on taxes paid on Pembroke's lot, see note 52 below; *NYSC 1865,* Brooklyn; "Personal," *BDE,* 5/22/1869. The McCray brothers, who never saw their father after they were reenslaved, told Mary Abel's agent that Pembroke died in 1859 ("Abel v. Brewster," *New York Supplement,* vol. 12, *Containing the Decisions of the Intermediate and Lower Courts of Record of New York State,* 1891, 332). William Still, who tracked the movements of fugitives after they were freed, put Pembroke in Florida as late as 1870 ("Transcription of Capture, Trial and Return of the Fugitives, Stephen Pembroke and His Two Sons, to Slavery," Lancaster County Historical Society, n.d.). The Abels suspected that Pembroke died in New York City in the 1880s, but their inquiries in the *Christian Recorder* brought no replies ("Information Wanted of Stephen Pembroke," *Christian Recorder,* 2/14/1889 and 2/21/1889).

44. *GSLB,* 105. As a witness for the plaintiff (Mary Abel), Oliver Abel Jr. recalled camping on Lot 177. "Supreme Court . . . , Mary E. Abel v. Benjamin Brewster, Case on Appeal," 12/9/1889, ECCO. Further details of this fight for

prime Adirondack land may be found in "Abel v. Brewster, Misc. Records, T-20," 5/17/1887, ECCO; and "Abel v. Brewster," *New York Supplement*, 333. On Oliver Abel's family history of Adirondack innkeeping, and his and Mary's forays into backcountry hospitality, see *EP*, 6/4/1914; and *ECR*, 10/26/1923, 1/29/1939.

45. CHH, military pension file, St. Armand.

46. *New York Tribune*, 10/24/1885; Foner, *Gateway to Freedom*, 227.

47. William E. W. Yerby, *History of Greensboro, Ala., from its Earliest Settlement* (Paragon, 1908), 127–28.

48. In the 1870, 1880, and 1900 federal censuses, Robert and Jacob McCray of Greensboro, AL, were farm laborers. When Greensboro attorneys deposed Robert McCray in the late 1880s, he shared details of his livelihood, his arrival in Alabama, and his parents' stories. (Jacob was not part of these proceedings.) See "Abel v. Brewster, Misc. Records," 1887, 1889, ECCO; CBR to James E. Webb, 1/25/1883; "Abel v. Brewster," ibid. In his letter to Webb, Ray clarified his "anxious" expectation that the McCrays would be served "with promptness and [illeg.] with no expense."

49. Eric Taunton, "Over 800,000 Alabamians Live below Poverty Line; Sixth Poorest State in the Nation," *Birmingham Times*, 6/14/2018 (in 2022, this ranking had not changed); Donna J. Siebenthaler, "Hale County," last updated 7/20/2022, *Encyclopedia of Alabama* http://www.encyclopediaofalabama.org/article/h-1330; James Agee and Walker Evans, *Let Us Now Praise Famous Men* (Houghton Mifflin, 1941); and "Of Poor Farmers and 'Famous Men,'" *NYT*, 11/26/2011. The website for the Safe House Black History Museum (https://safehousemuseum.org) describes the modest home in Greensboro where King took refuge with his movement allies.

50. Blackmon, *Slavery by Another Name*; "The Rich Blacks of New York," *New-York World*, reprinted in *Buffalo Morning Express*, 12/11/1876. The withdrawal of federal oversight of Klan activity was catastrophic. In 1882 alone, forty-nine Black Southerners were lynched, five of them in Alabama. See "Lynching in Alabama," Alabama Memory, accessed 1/10/2023, https://alabamamemory. as.ua.edu/source/lynching-in-alabama/.

51. "Supreme Court . . . , Mary E. Abel v. Benjamin Brewster, Case on Appeal." See Mackenzie, *Plains of Abraham*, 215–23, on Brewster's career as an innkeeper in Lake Placid (the Manhattan children's rights reformer Charles Loring Brace was one of Brewster's faithful guests). The Brewsters and the Abels had more in common than their zest for hospitality. Like the Thompsons, Hinckleys, and Nashes, these families took lasting pride in a connection to John Brown. Mary Abel's father, Elisha Adams, was the county sheriff who hosted Wendell Phillips and Mary Brown at his inn when they escorted Brown's coffin to North Elba in 1859. John Brown's son Oliver, who fell at Harpers Ferry, was married to a Brewster. But between John Brown's coming to North Elba and *Abel v. Brewster* yawned three tumultuous decades, and in the 1880s, bragging rights about a local tie to John Brown signified no zeal for racial justice (if indeed they ever had).

52. North Elba tax assessment rolls in the Essex County Archives (ECCO) show Brewster making five tax payments on Lot 277 from 1863 to 1893, Stephen Pembroke paying taxes on it in 1855, and an unidentified "non-resident,"

who may have been James Pennington or Charles Ray, stepping up from 1850 to 1858. *PS*, 12/20/1889.

53. Ray and Ray, *Sketch of the Life*, 20–22; "Supreme Court . . . , Mary E. Abel v. Benjamin Brewster, Case on Appeal," and CBR to GS, 5/24/1847. The school-teacher Florence Ray was living with her parents in Manhattan when her father helped the Abels and McCrays (Florence Ray, *USFC 1880*, NYC).

54. "Biographical History," in Gerrit Smith Miller Papers, Special Collections, Syracuse University, revised 9/29/2015, https://library.syracuse.edu/digital/guides/m/miller_gs.htm.

55. *ECR*, 12/13/1883. The case was also noted in the *Whitehall Chronicle* and the *Plattsburgh Sentinel*, 12/20/1889; W. Freeman Galpin, "Gerrit Smith Miller, a Pioneer in the Dairy and Cattle Industry," *Agricultural History*, 1 (1931).

56. Renee Lettow Lerner, "The Rise of Directed Verdict: Jury Power in Civil Cases before the Federal Rules of 1939," *George Washington Law Review* 81, no. 2 (February 2013): 448–525; "Abel v. Brewster," *New York Supplement*; "Circuit Court," *ECR*, 12/19/1889; "North Elba," *ECR*, 9/28/1871. Brewster was much favored in local coverage of this case. On June 2, 1892, the *Essex County Republican* greeted Judge Russell's ruling for the defendant with relief, noting that this case "of unusual interest . . . involved the question of title to land from colored persons formerly in slavery, . . . the plaintiff claiming title through them." Brewster's attorney, George W. Smith of Upper Jay, won praise for his "ceaseless efforts in behalf of the defendant."

57. "Abel v. Brewster," *New York Supplement*, 333.

58. "William L. Learned," in D. A. Harsha, *Noted Living Albanians and State Officials: A Series of Biographical Sketches* (Weed, Parsons, 1891), 217–25; "Abel v. Brewster," *New York Supplement*, 133.

59. Blight, *Race and Reunion*, 217; In 1891, Oliver Abel went to Sharpsburg, Maryland, to interview Stephen Pembroke's neighbors about his marriage to Surena Pembroke, the mother of their sons. More depositions would follow. Most witnesses described Stephen and Surena Pembroke as a married couple. ("They were considered man and wife in the community of Sharpsburg. . . . [T]hey were looked upon as married; this repute continued as long as she lived with him which was up to the time of her death," offered the Sharpsburg druggist Grafton Smith.) See "Abel v. Brewster, Misc. Records."

60. Webber, *American to the Backbone*, 248; THSP, Hospital Steward, military pension file. Pennington's service saddled him with dysentery, malaria, and heart disease. Frustrated when he could not get his pension upgraded despite ample evidence of need, Pennington wrote President William McKinley, charging the government and the Pension Bureau with "a different standard of disability for the members of the Afro-American regiments." THSP to William McKinley, 2/24/1899, THSP military pension. Pennington wrote two essays and a letter about his uncle's ordeal and his father's providential role in Pembroke's emancipation. See Pennington, *Capture, Trial, and Return*, and THSP to Marianna Gibbons, 1897, Archives, Lancaster (PA) Historical Society.

61. *USFC 1880*, Sharpsburg, MD.

62. "Justice Russell Dead," *NYT*, 2/4/1903, and "Memorial of Leslie W. Russell," *Association of the Bar of the City of New York, Annual Report* (1905), 148–50.

63. Penningroth, *Claims of Kinfolk*, 158. I am indebted to the legal historian Paul Finkelman for his helpful response to my inquiry about this prolonged case (Finkelman, email to the author, 1/6/2014). Groth, *Slavery and Freedom*, 71; MacKenzie, *Plains of Abraham*, 217; "Ben Brewster Poses for Moving Picture," *LPN*, 7/13/1914.

64. Robert McCray in "Voter Registration, 1867, Hale County, Alabama," 281. In March 1867, Congress passed the Reconstruction Act. Officers in Alabama's military districts had six months to register males twenty-one and older for the vote (after each made a loyalty oath to the government). That year, at the direction of the Alabama House of Representatives, the publisher J. K. Green printed a book-length list of Alabama voters. From 1867 to 1874, Black Alabamians enjoyed equal suffrage. When Grant's administration withdrew federal troops from the South and Democrats regained control of Alabama's government, de facto disenfranchisement took hold hard. See Michael W. Fitzgerald, "Congressional Reconstruction in Alabama," *Encyclopedia of Alabama*, last updated 10/24/2017, http://www.encyclopediaofalabama.org/article/h-1632; C. G. Gomillion, "The Negro Voter in Alabama," *Journal of Negro Education* 26, no. 3 (Summer 1957): 281–86.

65. *Reconstruction in America*; "Abel v. Brewster, Misc. Records," deposition of Robert McCray, 5/10/1887, Greensboro, Hale County, AL. I know of one twentieth-century Adirondack history that invokes this court case. In 1946, Arthur W. Hayes's *Lake Placid: Its Early History and Developments* dismissed the deed the McCrays secured from the Abels as "a forgery." Hayes, "Citizen, Guide, and Building Contractor," also suggested that the Black Woods was meant to give a "home for the Slaves where they could live as free people," but they left it for "a warmer climate"—those few, that is, "who got out before they froze to death." Hayes, *Lake Placid*, 6, 5.

17. Pilgrims

1. John R. Spears, "An Adirondack May," *NYT*, 6/1/1902.

2. JMB, "A Pilgrimage to John Brown's Farm," *TC*, 8/1922.

3. "North Elba," *ECR*, 5/11/1873. "John Brown," author of the ECR's "North Elba" column, was Reuben Conger, an Essex County farmer. "Monument to John Brown," *NYT*, 7/22/1896; "The G.A.R. Reunion," *ECR*, 2/6/1903; "Brown Day Deferred," *LPN*, 8/20/1915; *LPN*, 9/17/1915, "John Brown Memorial," *LPN*, 7/21/1916; *LPN*, 8/20/1915; and Byron R. Brewster to Mrs. J. B. Remington, JB/BBS Coll./WVMP, 1/31/1916.

4. "John Brown Day a Matter of History," *LPN*, 8/25/1916. Inspired by the massive turnout for Theodore Roosevelt at the dedication of John Brown Memorial Park in Osawatomie, Kansas, in 1910, Byron Brewster hoped to book Roosevelt for his headliner. At this he failed, but the lineup he pulled together was impressive. Brown's biographer Franklin H. Sanborn had been one of Brown's quiet supporters. From Manhattan but an Adirondacker by birth, John Milholland founded the antiracist Constitutional League and, with his friend W. E. B. Du Bois, organized the NAACP when race riots racked Springfield, Massachusetts, in 1908. Morton Sosna, "The South in the

Saddle: Racial Politics during the Wilson Years," *Wisconsin Magazine of History* (Autumn 1970): 37 (of Wilson's era, Sosna wrote, "Not since the days of the Fugitive Slave Act and the Dred Scott decision had the federal government so thoroughly humiliated Black men"); *LPN*, 8/25/1916. The Reform rabbi Stephen Wise, a founding member of the NAACP, summered in Lake Placid. On Waco's lynching incident, see Patricia Bernstein, *The First Waco Horror: The Lynching of Jesse Washington and the Rise of the NAACP* (Texas A&M Press, 2006), 87–137, 157–72.

5. "A Dirge Written to Other Music," *LPN*, 9/1/1916.

6. See NYS Historic Newspapers (http://nyshistoricnewspapers.org) for mentions of lynchings in Adirondack papers between 1916 and 1922; Brophy, *Reconstructing the Dreamland*, 23–62; *Survey Journal* (NYC), 1/15/1916. Notwithstanding public outrage about the lynching epidemic, the Southern-dominated Senate rejected legislation that would make lynch mobs liable for murder, require federal court trails for lynching cases, and offer federal protection for Black prisoners at risk of being mobbed, seized, and murdered. "Pilgrimage of J. Brown Assn.," *LPN*, 5/16/1924; David Fiske, "Pilgrimages Part of John Brown's Farm History," New York Almanack, 5/23/2019, https://www.newyorkalmanack.com/2019/05/pilgrimages-part-of-john-browns-farm-history/. The NAACP would organize a separate one-time John Brown pilgrimage to Harpers Ferry in 1932.

7. *LPN*, 5/13/1927; "J. Max Barber Writes on Prejudice and Depression," *PC*, 10/3/1931; "Lay Plan for Co-operative Purchasing System in Philly," *PC*, 11/7/1931; JMB to HWH, 5/14/1924, 4/12/1925, 4/17/1925, and HWH to JMB, n.d., 1925, HWHC; JMB to HWH, 3/26/1927, and HWH to JMB, 3/28/1927, HWHC; Quarles, *Allies for Freedom*, 185–92; JBMA file in HWHC; JBMA Archives, Special Collections, LPL; "Colored People Honor Memory of John Brown," *LPN*, 5/1/1925, "Third Annual Pilgrimage to John Brown's Grave," "Nation's Editor [Oswald Garrison Villard] Hits President in Fiery Speech," *LPN*, 5/15/1925; Darrow could afford to taunt. His complexion gave him license for the sly, breezy banter. When Max Barber matched Darrow's challenge with his own—"John Brown's mantle has fallen on your shoulders. . . . [Are] you giving the full measure of devotion to the cause of justice and right?"—he did not goad his audience into examining its conscience. He flattered it. Darrow could locate North Elba in Calvin Coolidge's racist America, but if Barber wanted his pilgrimage to succeed, he would keep John Brown country idealized, a gilded land apart. "Outdraws Jazz" and "Darrow Makes Stirring Plea for the Negro and Memory of John Brown in Powerful Address," *LPN*, 5/13/1927. Darrow spoke about Brown so often he prompted the archivist Boyd B. Stutler to observe to another Brown scholar, "Clarence had but one story—he strung it out over a period of seventeen years." BBS to Louis Ruchames, 8/30/1957, JB/BBS Coll./WVMP; BBS to William Lloyd Imes, 11/11/1957, JB/BBS Coll./WVMP. Besides Darrow, Villard, and Randolph, other name speakers in the first decade of the pilgrimage were William Pickens, a renowned orator and the field branch director of the NAACP; the Tennessee-born Rev. William Lloyd Imes, civil rights activist and speaker; Stutler of West Virginia, a John Brown lay historian who aided generations of scholars and biographers; Charles

V. Roman, MD, historian and founder-advocate of the Black national physicians group, the National Medical Association; and Leonard Ehrlich, author of *God's Angry Man*, an acclaimed novel about John Brown.

8. JBMA brochure, 1927, HWHC; "John Brown's Birthday to Be Celebrated May 9th," *PC*, 4/21/1928; Du Bois, *Darkwater*, 228–30, and Hale, *Making Whiteness*, 125–38. (In a letter to Douglass, Gerrit Smith lamented the precarity of Black travel in 1874: "Alas, how many a colored brother and colored sister have felt their hearts die within them, whilst traveling, or attempting to travel, through this still caste-cursed and still satan-swayed land!" GS to FD, 6/27/1874.) "The 'Jim Crow' Issue," *NYT*, 4/10/1908. In this article, the young Max Barber told a Black political convention in Chicago, "We want to smash the 'Jim Crow' car, and if we cannot smash them, we will undertake to smash the party which, being in power, tolerates them." Cohen, *At Freedom's Edge*, 248–73.

9. JBMA brochure, 1928, HWHC; JMB, "Plans for Pilgrimage to Honor John Brown at Resort, Set Again," *PC*, 5/7/1932. Barber wrote a weekly column for the *Pittsburgh Courier* from 1930 to 1933. Founded in 1907, this paper once boasted the widest circulation of any Black paper in the nation.

10. Sorin, *Driving While Black*, 36–42; Kahrl, "Political Work of Leisure," 62–63.

11. *LPN*, 5/16/1924.

12. Johnson, "Freedom and Slavery," 37–46; Bobby J. Donaldson, "'More Than a Mere Magazine': J. Max Barber, Booker T. Washington, and *The Voice of the Negro*," paper presented at the annual meeting of the Organization of American Historians, San Jose, CA, 3/2005; Harlan, "Booker T. Washington," and Driskell, *Schooling Jim Crow*, 64–66, 93–99, 257–58n; Lewis, *W.E.B. Du Bois*, 319, 329; Norrell, *Up from History*, 389.

13. Lewis, *W.E.B. Du Bois*, 319; "Will Honor John Brown," *Washington Post*, 8/13/1906; speech, Ransom C. Reverdy, "The Spirit of John Brown," in Quarles, *Blacks on John Brown*, 79–84.

14. Dray, *Hands of Persons Unknown*, 162–67; Johnson, "Freedom and Slavery," 42–43; Johnson and Johnson, "Away from Accommodation," 329–32; Driskell, *Schooling Jim Crow*, 64–66, 94–99, 101–5; "Barber Took to His Heels—Posing as a Martyr," *New York Age*, 10/25/1906; Harlan, "Booker T. Washington," 56–62, and Norrell, *Up from History*, 321, 318, 386–93.

15. Du Bois, *Souls of Black Folk*, 44.

16. JMB, "A Pilgrimage," *TC*, 8/1922, 167–69. The exaggerated report of the pilgrims' unexpected reception was a cherished feature of the JBMA's origin story.

17. JMB, "John Brown, the Forerunner and Prophet of Emancipation," unpublished manuscript, 1922, NAACP archives; *LPN*, 5/12/1922.

18. Norrell, *Up from History*, 52, 70–71, 98–99, 200–202, 365–67; "Rough Sketches," *Voice of the Negro*, 11/1905, described in Johnson and Johnson, *Propaganda and Aesthetics*, 23 (the author of this story was John Henry Adams); "The Negro Farmer," *TC*, 5/1922.

19. "An Interview in the St. Paul Dispatch," 1/14/1896, in Harlan, Kaufman, Kraft, and Smock, *Booker T. Washington Papers*, 102.

20. See note 22, below; JMB, "John Brown," from "John Brown in Bronze, 1800–1859, Containing Program and Addresses of the Dedicatory Ceremony and Unveiling of the Monument of John Brown," Lake Placid, 5/9/1935, in Quarles, *Blacks on John Brown*, 110. Among Barber's misconceptions: Black farmers bought their land from Gerrit Smith; John Brown was Smith's land broker; Brown's League of Gileadites originated in North Elba (it was Springfield); Smith was a governor of New York; on constraints on early abolition scholarship, see Fladeland, "Revisionists vs. Abolitionists," 1–3, and Goggin, "Countering White Racist Scholarship," 355–59; Frothingham, *Gerrit Smith*, 112. The Black scholar Zita Dyson reiterated this verdict in her 1918 essay on Smith's land grants, "Gerrit Smith's Effort"; Du Bois, *John Brown*, 110–12, 119, 127; Villard, *John Brown*, 73. The scrubbing of the history of Black Adirondack farmers has still to be examined in the context of a long-established, wider pattern of effacement of farm history from the Adirondack narrative. See Harris, "Hidden History of Agriculture," 165–71.

21. Every twentieth-century newspaper account of Lyman Epps Jr. exalts his tie to John Brown. Mostly that connection was framed as a childhood acquaintance, but sometimes it bubbled into something more, and Epps, a young teen when Brown left Essex County, would signify Brown's "protégé," "good friend," and "confidante." In 1936, Albert W. Santway dedicated his *Brief Sketch of the Life of John Brown, the Martyr-Emancipator* to Epps because he was "the only man living who knew this great man who sacrificed his life to destroy human bondage." Clarence Gee to Charles B. Briggs, 8/22/1958, JB/BSS Coll./WVMP; "Sung by Lyman Epps of Lake Placid," Marjorie Lansing Porter Collection, Feinberg Library, SUNY Plattsburgh; JMB, "Pilgrimage to John Brown's Farm." Epps never tired of living in Brown's reflected glory. His memory of Brown taking him on his knee before he went away invites comparison with Thomas Hovendon's famous painting of Brown stooping to kiss a Black baby on his way to the gallows. Both scenes were fiercely cherished, and neither ever happened. *LPN*, 11/8/1940; Thompson, *Body, Boots and Britches*, 304; "John Brown's Body," *Commercial Advertiser* (Canton, NY), 5/13/1941; "John Brown's Neighbor Now 101," *NYT*, 6/20/1941.

22. See chap. 12; *EP*, 3/29/1894, *Mountain Mirror*, 3/24/1894; Brumley, *Guides of the Adirondacks*, 118; MacKenzie, *Plains of Abraham*, 134; LEE to Owen Brown and John Brown Jr., 11/10/1885, JBJrOH; "Receipts," *FDP*, 12/2/1853; Silas Harris to LEE, power of attorney, 7/19/1888, "Deeds," Franklin County Clerk's Office, Malone; John Brown to "Wife & Children every one," 4/6/1858 and 5/1/1858, St. Catherine's, Canada West, JB/BBS Coll./WVMP; Mackenzie, *Plains of Abraham*, 132; Marjorie Lansing Porter, "Our Folks," *ECR*, 1/31/1969; *EP*, 5/26/1887, 3/29/1894, 7/18/1901; *TS*, 8/19/1894; MacKenzie, *Plains of Abraham*, 128.

23. Before Lyman Jr.'s ill health forced his removal to the county home, he boarded with a widow's family in North Elba. *USFC 1920*, NE, Essex County; Ben Lewis to Marjorie Lansing Porter, Plattsburgh, 3/26/1955, Marjorie Lansing Porter Collection, SUNY Plattsburgh; "John Brown's Home to Be Made Memorial," *AR-EP*, 8/5/1921; *EPG*, 12/7/1905, 12/10/1908, *TS*, 1/30/1908; *AR-EP*, 8/5/1921.

24. John Brown Memorial Association, *John Brown in Bronze,* pamphlet, 1935, 18; *LPN,* 6/14/1940, 9/13/1940, 11/8/1940, and 6/27/1941; "Negroes Pay Tribute at Grave of John Brown," *Oswego Palladium-Times,* 5/9/1942, 11/21/1942; LEE to Ruth and Henry Thompson, 8/29/1895, Lake Placid, JB-jrOH; *LPN,* 11/5/1937. On burial plans for Albert Eppes, see letters between HWH and Dr. John Ross, Max Barber, and Eva Franklin, HWHC. When Harry Wade Hicks of the Lake Placid Club learned of Albert Eppes's death at the Harlem Valley State Institution at Wingdale, and that Lyman Epps Jr.'s poverty was so great he could not pay $150 to bring his brother home, he urged Wingdale's Dr. John R. Ross and Max Barber of the JBMA to assume the cost. Both Ross and Barber felt this was Lake Placid's responsibility. In the end, the Lake Placid chapter of the JBMA and the Town of North Elba (Lake Placid) paid for Eppes's burial in the family plot. Eva Franklin to HWH, Brooklyn, 11/8/1937, HWHC.

25. "John Brown's Tenor Dies at the Age of 102," *Utica Daily Press,* 11/21/1942; "Man Who Knew John Brown Dies at the Age of 102," *New York Age,* 11/28/1942; "Up-state Negro Sang at the Funeral of John Brown," *NYT,* 11/28/1942; "Hymn Singer for John Brown Succumbs," *Fresno Bee,* 11/28/1942; *LPN,* 6/11/1943; "Dedicate Epps Marker," *AR-EP,* 9/16/1943; *LPN,* 6/11/1943; Anne A. Heald, "The Shadow of John Brown," *Negro Digest,* 7/1962, and Matthew B. Clark to George Marshall, 3/26/1962, SLFL.

26. "Pilgrimage to Grave of John Brown Given Up," *Tupper Lake Herald,* 5/24/1934; HWH to Willis Wells, 3/--/1927 and HWH to Roger C. Holden, 3/24/1927, HWHC; *LPN,* 5/8/1925, and HWH to JMB, 4/13/1926 (telegram) and 4/17/1926, HWHC. See Svenson, *Blacks in the Adirondacks,* 134–38, and 170–74, on Black-owned boarding houses and health-seeking households in Saranac Lake in the first half of the twentieth century. JMB to HWH, 4/10/1931, 4/22/1933, HWHC. In 1931, Barber wrote Hicks from Philadelphia, "Since December we have had thirty bank failures here. . . . On one of the banks I had my little all and in another we had our local funds for the John Brown monument." All Black urban populations were devastated. The Black unemployment rate in Harlem was as high as 50 percent, and in Barber's Philadelphia, it peaked at 56 percent. In 1933, Barber told Hicks starkly, "No place was hit harder by the depression . . . and no group hit harder than ours." Langston Hughes, "The South," in Hughes, *Selected Poems,* 173; JMB to Mary Ovington, 5/11/1922, *Papers of the NAACP,* Du Bois Papers; JBMA membership drive letter, Philadelphia, n.d., 1924, Du Bois Papers.

27. See Svenson, *Blacks in the Adirondacks,* 122–33. Klan sightings or enlistment efforts in Essex, Franklin, and other Adirondack counties were noted in "Order against Klan Now in Effect," *ECR,* 8/24/1923; "The Fiery Cross in the Mountains," *TS,* 9/23/1923; "KKK Activity Reported in Area in 1924," *Gloversville Leader-Herald,* 9/23/1924; "Ku Klux Klan Meeting at 'Ti' a Farce," *AR-EP,* 11/6/1924; "Ku Klux Klan Startles Eagle Bay," *LPN,* 8/24/1924; "Find Dynamite Near Fiery Cross," *LPN,* 11/14/1924. In 1924 alone, twelve Klan-related dispatches ran in the *Glens Falls Post-Star.* Also see "Ku Kluxers Invade Westport," *TS,* 2/19/1925; "State Officials Investigate Klan," *AR-EP,* 3/5/1925; "Moriah," *ECR,* 9/2/1927; "Newspaper versus the Ku Klux Klan," *TS,* 2/27/1927; "Kondemned by the Konklave" and other editorials, *ADE,* 1/8/1927, 1/11/1927,

1/14/1927; "Mass Out of Doors," *LPN*, 6/5/1942; and "New School Hopes to Exorcize Old Ghosts," *LPN*, 8/30/1996 (the Wilmington Klan clubhouse was also a town office building and, briefly, a Waldorf school). A vivid account of an Adirondack Klan meeting in the late 1920s appeared in Gordon and Gordon, *On Wandering Wheels*, 56–71.

28. Godine, "Punishment and Crimes"; "Merry Minstrels Repeat Success," *LPN*, 5/7/1915; Amy Godine, "The History of Blackface in the Adirondacks" (lecture), Adirondack Experience, 8/20/2019, https://www.theadkx. org, 8/20/2019; "John Brown's Letters" and the advertisement "Minstrelsy and Vaudeville Happy Hour" ran in adjacent columns in the *Lake Placid News*, 4/9/1915. "K. of C. Minstrel Echoes," *AR-EP*, 11/10/1927; "Huge Crowds Greet Elaborate Pageants Here," *LPN*, 8/14/1936. From 1916 into the twenties, D. W. Griffith's *The Birth of a Nation* played in movie houses in Saranac Lake, Malone, Lake Placid, Ticonderoga, and Plattsburgh.

29. Barber, "Forerunner and Prophet"; *LPN*, 5/12/1922.

30. For a probing history of the Lake Placid Club and its controversial founder, see Wiegand, *Irrepressible Reformer*, 251–63, 315–78. Other resources are Campbell, *Inside the Club*; and Ackerman, *Lake Placid Club*.

31. Wiegand, *Irrepressible Reformer*, 318, 323, 315, 251, 323–24.

32. Wiegand, *Irrepressible Reformer*, 56–57, 56n, 251–53, 315, 324; Campbell, *Inside the Club*, 71–77, 163–64; Wiegand, *Irrepressible Reformer*, 255, 324, 334, 352, 260, 264, 271; Spiro, *Defending the Master Race*, 182. In 1912, the Cornell economist Jeremiah Jenks and his protégé W. Jett Lauck published *The Immigration Problem* (Funk & Wagnalls). Jenks served on the Immigration Restriction League and the US. Immigration Commission, which paved the way for the draconian anti-immigration laws of 1924. Leonard, *Illiberal Reformers*, 149–50; Spiro, *Defending the Master Race*, 199, 208; Leonard, *Illiberal Reformers*, 112, 117, 148; Spiro, *Defending the Master Race*, 183, 190, 339. Pastor of the Plymouth Church of the Pilgrims in Brooklyn and summer chaplain at the Lake Placid Club, Newell Dwight Hillis lectured widely on race betterment. "Dr. Hillis on Eugenics," *NYT*, 11/24/1913; and *LPN*, 8/19/1927.

33. In his 1998 *Lake Placid Club*, David Ackerman's reading of Melvil Dewey's racism is a cursory dismissal: "Whether someone, or some particular incident in his earlier days triggered Dewey's stand regarding the private Lake Placid Club's selectivity, an explanation is lacking other than it may have 'reflected the times.'" The historian Barbara McMartin invokes this same rationale in *The Privately Owned Adirondacks*, while conceding that Dewey may have "carried it to an extreme." Burton Bernstein's Essex County profile, *The Sticks*, also uses the fig leaf of convention to "contextualize" Dewey's bigotry, and in *The Plains of Abraham*, the town historian Mary MacKenzie skirts the subject altogether. Wiegand, *Irrepressible Reformer*, 114, 252, 315, 324, 334, 352, 358–59, 287.

34. On Harry Hicks's dealings with the JBMA and Jesse Max Barber, see the Harry Wade Hicks Collection (HWHC) at the JBFSHS, and the JBMA collection at LPPL. Information about Hicks's environmental legacy and his advocacy of winter sports and the 1932 World Winter Olympics is archived at the Adirondack Experience and the Adirondack Research Library at the Kelly Adirondack Center in Schenectady, NY. Little is revealed of Hicks's interest in

the JBMA in the Lake Placid Club Collection, LPPL. The annual Black pilgrimage was not featured in the club's program notes, newsletters, and internal
memos. Did the club not recognize Hicks's work on behalf of the pilgrimages?
Or was it Hicks who chose to keep this interest separate from his club work?
The Black pilgrims never saw them separately. In their view, Hicks and his
great club were one.

35. Wiegand, *Irrepressible Reformer*, 350, 254, 374; Ackerman, *Lake Placid
Club*, 130–31. See Hicks's correspondence with Boyd Stutler, JB/BBS Coll./
WVMP; *LPN*, 11/4/1921; "John Brown and Abraham Lincoln: Response to the
John Brown Memorial Association in Its Presentation of a Picture to the Lake
Placid Club, Delivered by Rev. William E. Barton, D.D., at the Club, on May 9,
1928," *LPN*, 5/18/1928. One wintry Sunday in 1921, sixty-two club guests visited the farm. *LPN*, 2/25/1921. Over the years, Harry Hicks continued to welcome Black pilgrims to the club for limited tours, visits to the club library,
organ recitals, and the like. He introduced John Brown Day speakers, and made
speeches too. HWH to BBS, 5/21/1953.

36. As a public servant (New York's state librarian from 1888 to 1905),
Dewey came under heavy scrutiny for his unconcealed antisemitism and track
record of sexual harassment; the threat of legal action always loomed. See Wiegand, *Irrepressible Reformer*, 264–311.

37. JMB to Melvil Dewey, Philadelphia, 5/14/1925; HWH to JMB,
6/10/1925; JMB to HWH, 4/12/1925; HWH to JMB, 4/15/1925; JMB to HWH,
4/13/1926; HWH to JMB, 4/13/1926, 4/17/1926, and 4/26/1926; JMB to HWH,
2/10/1927; HWH to JMB, 2/12/1927, HWHC; Godfrey Dewey, "Sixty Years of
the Lake Placid Club," *Lake Placid Club Notes*, 8/4/1955; 1927 JBMA appeal,
JBMA circular, n.d., HWHC; Thomas A. Teal, Chairman of Pilgrim Committee,
to "Friend," 1927, HWHC; JMB to HWH, 3/9/1927, HWHC.

38. F. B. Kirkbride to HWH, 6/25/1934, HWHC. Among Kirkbride's pub-
lications was "The Right to Be Well-Born," an argument for segregating "cre-
tins," "imbeciles," and other "degenerates," "during the entire reproductive
period" to spare "well-born" humanity from ruination. American Philosophi-
cal Society, 3/2/1912, http://www.eugenicsarchive.org/eugenics/view_image.
pl?id=350.

39. On Pollia, see Regina Soria, *American Artists of Italian Heritage, 1776–
1945: A Biographical Dictionary* (Fairleigh Dickinson, 1993), 178. In the early
1930s, JBMA benefits for the John Brown Memorial were held in many cities
and publicized in Black newspapers. In "John Brown Memorial Statue" (*New
York History*, 7/1935, 329), New York State Historian Alexander C. Flick observed that donations for the statue mostly came from poor Black city people with little cash to spare. "Show Model of Memorial to John Brown," *LPN*,
8/31/1934, and "John Brown Memorial for Lake Placid," *AR-EP*, 9/6/1934.
Barber's plan was also flagged in the *Massena Observer*, 9/27/1934. In the era
of Black Lives Matter, what Barber understood as an unambiguous expression of Black America's lasting gratefulness to the white freedom fighter scans
less clearly. Barber's hoped-for message of Black gratitude gets muddied when
the figuration of the statue suggests Black dependency—and a Black America
not quite caught up, but *eager! educable! evolving!* The paternalism in Pollia's

narrative, unobjectionable to a Black civil rights group in 1935, seems somewhat out of step today. See Bay, *White*, 193–94.

40. William G. Howard to HWH, Albany, 3/27/1935, HWHC; JMB to HWH, 4/4/1935, HWHC.

41. The Northern New York Tombstone Transcription Project (https://www.nnytombstoneproject.net/) identifies all people buried, or simply honored, in John Brown's quarter-acre "shrine." Gobrecht, *National Historic Site*.

42. HWH to JMB, 3/25/1935 and 4/4/1935, HWHC.

43. JMB to HWH, 4/4/35; HWH to William G. Howard, Conservation Department, NY, 4/10/1935; HWH to Mayor George Owens, Lake Placid, 4/10/1935; HWH to JMB, 5/7/1935; HWH to Mrs. William H. Taylor, 4/11/1935; HWH to A. B. See and Mr. King (potential underwriters), 4/18/1935; and HWH to JMB, 5/7/1935, HWHC. Hicks pressed Lithgow Osborne to make sure the traffic circle got some landscaping, an improvement he was confident would "in a measure atone for the disappointment Dr. Barber may feel because of the now approved site." HWH to Osborne, 4/8/1935, HWHC.

44. Dr. Alexander Flick, "John Brown—Nonconformist," from John Brown Memorial Association, *John Brown in Bronze*, pamphlet, 1935, 33. Also see Flick, "John Brown Memorial Statue." In his speech, "Brown, the Man Manifest" (*John Brown in Bronze*, 36), Judge Brewster offered, "I think most are agreed that had natural economic causes been allowed to work out the problem, slavery would have disappeared in the South long since." Karen L. Cox, "Lost Cause Ideology," Encyclopedia of Alabama, last updated April 25, 2022, http://encyclopediaofalabama.org/article/h-1643; and Fladeland, "Revisionists vs. Abolitionists," 1–13.

45. "His Soul Is Marching On," *NYT*, 9/29/1890.

46. JMB, "John Brown," from "John Brown in Bronze," in Quarles, *Blacks on John Brown*, 109–15.

47. "The Ku Klux Klan Parade," *Greensboro Watchman*, 4/30/25; Barber's columns for the *Courier* were as brashly spiky as his public speeches at North Elba were restrained. In "The Negro Horoscope" (9/19/1931), he wrote, "If Christianity means brotherhood, charity, equality, there is no Christianity among white people"; In February 1865, the radical abolitionist Thaddeus Stevens "venture[d] to predict" that John Brown's name would grow so bright that "the State of Virginia . . . by its own freedmen and its own freedom, will . . . raise a monument to [Brown's] memory upon the very place where his gallows stood." *Vermont Phoenix* (Brattleboro), 2/10/1865. This hasn't happened, and it seems unlikely that it might.

48. "To Erect Bronze Plaque at Grave of John Brown," *LPN*, 7/19/1946. On the nonappearance of Du Bois: when the pilgrimage was launched, Barber urged his mentor to attend. He never would, which was a pity. John Brown Day could have used the blessing and celebrity of Black America's leading intellectual, a John Brown biographer, and the editor of *The Crisis*. (Du Bois, who held the cult of Nordicism in fierce contempt and counted several Jewish activists among his friends, may have shrunk from Barber's alliance with the white supremacist Lake Placid Club.) Barber would also be dismayed to learn that after the first year, he could not count on the NAACP to share the work of raising

funds for a Black-subsidized monument (even while Du Bois and the NAACP lobbied for a John Brown statue in Harpers Ferry, which would not be built).

See Du Bois to Horizon Board of Control, 3/18/1909, Du Bois Papers; JMB to Du Bois, Philadelphia, 2/25/1918, ibid.; JMB to Wm. Pickens, 6/18/1930, ibid., cited in Lewis, *Du Bois: The Fight for Equality*, 230; *PC*, 5/28/1932. Over the decades, some keynote speeches by John Brown Day speakers did catch fire. A few months before Dr. Martin Luther King Jr.'s speech at the March on Washington in 1963, Alexander Allen of the Urban League gave a talk in North Elba on the value of Brown's principles for civil rights activists in Allen's time that spoke for all of Max Barber's first high hopes. Alexander J. Allen, "Action from Principle," typescript, 5/26/1963, West Virginia Department of Arts, Culture and History, https://archive.wvculture.org/history/wvmemory/images/jb/RP09-0084G.jpg.

49. "Plan to Stress Significance of Brown's Grave," *TS*, 8/28/1947.

50. *ECR*, 6/28/1946; *Ogdensburg Journal*, 3/27/1948; *North Countryman*, 4/1/1948.

51. Kim Smith Dedam, "Generations of Freedom: Legacy of John Thomas Lives On through Family," *PPR*, 2/18/2007; Robin Caudell, "Two Sisters Born in Saranac Lake Return to Unknown Maryland Roots," *PPR*, 2/18/2007; Howard Riley, "Celebration in Vermontville," *ADE*, 7/14/2007; Don Papson, "Descendants of Black Adirondackers Reunited after Nearly 50 Years," *North Country Lantern*, Summer–Fall 2007.

52. "John Morehouse, 82, Dies in Saranac Lake," *ADE*, 11/28/1959, and federal and state census reports on Franklin and Saranac Lake Village in Franklin and Essex Counties from 1880 to 1940; "Empire State Notes: News of Northern New York," *ECR*, 11/5/1920; "Saranac Youths Sentenced," *TS*, 3/17/1927; "Indictments Returned by Grand Jury," *Adirondack News*, 3/19/1927.

53. Details of late twentieth-century Morehouse family history are drawn from the author's conversations with the Morehouse descendant Robert Lagroome of Baltimore from 2015 to 2018; Robin Caudell, "After Nearly 50 Years Apart, Family Reunites," *P-R*, 8/12/2007; "Saranac Lake Resident Dies of Cancer," *ADE*, 2/3/1956.

54. "Scout Charter Is Presented Lions; Investiture Held," *ADE*, 4/9/1948; "Petrova's Pre-Xmas Festivities," *ADE*, 12/18/1948; Bob McKillip, interview by the author, Saranac Lake, NY, 2009; Conversations, Amy Godine and Robert Lagroome, 2015–2018.

55. "Saranac Lake Resident Dies."

56. "Saranac Lake Resident Dies"; Caudell, "Family Reunites"; Don Papson, remarks, Vermontville Pioneer Day, Franklin, Franklin County, NY, 7/21/2007.

57. 1910 Indian Population Schedule, Harrietstown, Franklin, *USFC 1910*. Harrietstown, the largest town by area in Franklin County, overlaps with Saranac Lake village. Papson, remarks.

58. Mary Ellen Keith, Town of Franklin Supervisor, remarks, Vermontville Pioneer Day, 7/21/2007.

59. Spiro, *Defending the Master Race*, 356–57, 362–65; Stevenson, *Just Mercy*, 14–18.

60. "What's Wrong with the South," *AR-EP*, 6/1/1961.

61. Godine, "Ambushed." The author thanks the editors of *Adirondack Life* for permission to use language from this article.

62. Kristine Gibbins, Program Analyst, Historic Preservation, to Ed Cotter, Superintendent, JBF, 11/2/1977, PIA.

63. Mary MacKenzie, "Against Proposal to Make John Brown's Farm Site into a Visitors Interpretive Center," in MacKenzie, *More from the Plains*, 102-9; "Comments by Edwin N. Cotter, Jr.: 'Response to Maurice O'Brien's "Timbuctoo": An Attempt at Negro Settlement in the Adirondacks.'" PIA.

64. "State Planning to 'Resurrect' Brown Farm," *P-R*, 6/6/1978; "Chapman Says He Is Opposed to State Planned Uplift at John Brown Farm," *LPN*, 4/27/1978; "Farm Petitions," *LPN*, 5/25/1978; Harold Faber, "Plans to Alter John Brown Memorial Arouse Protest Upstate," *NYT*, 7/10/1978. Quoted in the article on the "desecration" of this site was Daisy Stringer, head of the JBMA chapter in Lake Placid. Editorial, "Let's Leave John Brown's Body Alone," *NYT*, 7/13/1978; "Brown Farm Project," *LPN*, 7/13/1978; "Albany Putting Aside a Program to Improve John Brown Site," *NYT*, 7/21/1978; "John Brown's Farm Won't Be Commercialized," *P-R*, 7/22/1978; "To the Editor," *LPN*, 7/27, 1978; "A Dissenting View on the State's John Brown Farm Modernization," *LPN*, 8/24/1978. One memory that drove local suspicion about the proposed interpretive center was the building of two ski jumps in 1977. Although these towering concrete and steel extrusions off Route 73 were for the coming Olympic Games, and Lake Placid could not host the games without them, the brute pragmatism of their design and their domination of the landscape underscored the dependency of Adirondackers on outside interests and outside plans. And this far from Albany, state agencies had a way of looking all the same. To her garden club, MacKenzie intimated that what might come to the John Brown Farm could be as bad as or worse than the ski jumps: "We were promised the towers would be pleasing in appearance, would shade into the environment, and would not detract from the beauty of the landscape. Now look what we're stuck with." (MacKenzie, "Against Proposal," *More from the Plains*, 13). It was Parks' misfortune that its designs on the historic site followed so closely on this other out-of-Albany initiative.

65. On 8/9/2008, in Saratoga Springs, I interviewed Mark Lawton, a retired administrator from New York's Department of Historic Preservation, about the scuttled plan to build a historical interpretive center at the John Brown Farm. Lawton's memories were sharp. "Any time you went anywhere doing a simple improvement at the John Brown Farm, hackles were raised. The site was in stasis. We'd had no success for years. The state ignored it," Lawton told me. "The Bicentennial was the first time we could get funds for the Trust site system. And the tourist potential of the Olympics was the ticket to getting people into the farm. But there was a curious thing about the local folks. They didn't want to hear about it. People had an idea about what a site meant, and if it didn't comport with reality, you had a big job on your hands. . . . We got clobbered. Blindsided like you wouldn't believe."

66. "Convention of Colored People," *NS*, 10/20/1848. The column by William C. Nell that includes this trenchant remark does not clarify who said it;

Simpson, "Wilderness in American Capitalism," 560; Brown, *Pleasant Valley*, 63; Donaldson, *History of the Adirondacks*, 2:6.

67. Watson, *General View*, 714.

68. Found in Charles B. Davenport and Albert G. Love, *Drafted Men: Statistical Information Compiled for the Draft Record* (Washington, DC, 1920), 250; editorial, *NYT*, 8/9/1864; Marcus, "Dangers of the Geographical Imagination," 36–56, *Geographical Review*; Grant, *Passing of the Great Race*, 150.

69. Proceedings of the Second National Conservation Congress at Saint Paul, 9/5–8/1910, cited in Mitman, "In Search of Health," 201, 209n.

70. The Adirondack historian Barbara McMartin (*Privately Owned Adirondacks*, 28–34) has observed how American clubs, estates, and game preserves appropriated the social culture of their much older English counterparts. And in *An Entirely Synthetic Fish* (chap. 6), the journalist Anders Halverson notes how the reverencing of hierarchy by an Anglocentric elite extended even to fish. Sluggish, mud-loving bottom feeders (catfish, crappies, bullheads) were presumed to be a natural fit for "lesser races" (poor Southern whites and ex-slaves), while gentlemen and sportsmen laid claim to the hard-fighting athletic natives (silvery "brookies" and rainbow trout).

71. McMartin, *Privately Owned Adirondacks*, 134; W. J. Andrus, Forest, Fish and Game Commissioner, NY, *Forest and Stream*, ca. 1892, quoted in McMartin, *Privately Owned Adirondacks*, 69; some Great Camps that have repurposed themselves as nonprofits with a strongly public-spirited agenda are Eagle's Nest in Blue Mountain Lake, Great Camp Sagamore near Inlet, and Camp Santanoni on Newcomb Lake; on racist incidents inside the Blue Line, see Brian Mann, "Are Black Visitors Really Welcome in the Adirondack Park?," North Country Public Radio, 8/26/2016; James M. Odato, "Aaron Mair," *AL*, 12/2016; Gwendolyn Craig, "Diversity Official Said She Will Stay in Post despite Racist Graffiti Incident," *Adirondack Explorer*, 7/9/2020; Michael Hill, "In White Adirondacks, Racism May Be Toughest Hill to Climb," Associated Press, 9/14/2020.

72. Editor Richard H. Schein's introduction to *Landscape and Race in the United States* offers a geographer's perspective on the subtle and pervasive influence of racialization on built environments and landscapes. Schein, *Landscape and Race*, 1–21.

73. Footnote to letter, Henry I. Bowditch to "Mrs. H—," Saranac Lake, 7/27/1865, quoted in Von Holst, *John Brown*, 203; Ward, "Immigration Restriction League," 639. John Higham's *Strangers in the Land* (102–10, 152) profiles Boston's nationally influential Immigration Restriction League. See also Colm Lavery, "Situating Eugenics."

74. Among the many Adirondack dispatches that painted derogatory portraits of the postbellum South were "'The Great Law of Ham'" and "Carl Schurz's Report," *MP*, 1/25/1866; "Slavery Continues in Kentucky," *MP*, 1/2/1868; "Smoking Out the Ku Klux Klan," *ECR*, 10/26/1871; "Life in Mississippi," *ECR*, 10/24/1872; "Politics in the South," *MP*, 9/11/1884; "The Clay Eaters," *Hamilton County Press*, 12/15/1888; "No 'Jim Crow' Cars," *Plattsburgh Daily Press*, 8/6/1909; and "Guardsmen Save Negro from Mob," *Plattsburgh Daily Press*, 8/16/1933.

Epilogue

Epigraph: From "Telling the Story of Timbuctoo through Dance" by Naj Wikoff, in the *Lake Placid News*, 8/27/2020. Rea-Fisher became the director of the Adirondack Diversity Initiative in 2023.

1. The author thanks the editors of *Adirondack Life* for permission to paraphrase and use language from my article, "The Closet."

2. Strand, "Keeping Things Whole," in *Collected Poems*, 78.

3. Riddle, "Finding Timbuctoo"; Andy Flynn, "The Dig," *LPN*, 8/4/2022.

4. Naj Wikoff, "Telling the Story of Timbuctoo through Dance," *LPN*, 8/27/2020.

5. Robin Caudell, Maggie Bartley, Greg Furness, and Curt Stager each described their independent projects to me in phone calls and emails in 2022.

6. Mary Thill, Adirondack Land Trust, email correspondence with the author, 8/22–23/2022; "Looking for Timbuctoo," Adirondack Architectural Heritage, accessed 1/12/2022, https://aarch.org/tours/looking-for-timbuctoo/. Elizabethtown history buff Maggie Bartley and I developed this daylong driving tour in 2019.

7. On 10/29/2022, the Adirondack Council sponsored Hadley Kruczek-Aaron's presentation after a screening of *Searching for Timbuctoo* at Paul Smith's College. On 7/16/2022, I spoke about the Black Woods at the annual meeting of Protect the Adirondacks! at the John Brown Farm.

8. Benita Law-Diao, conversations with the author, 8/7/2022, 8/13/2022; Kim Dedam, "Benita Law-Diao Confirmed as APA Commissioner," *Community Sun-News*, 6/15/22.

9. Susan Arbetter, "Lawmakers Looking to Create a Student Pipeline to the Adirondacks to Confront Racism and Climate Change," State of Politics, 3/7/2022, https://nystateofpolitics.com/state-of-politics/new-york/politics/2022/03/07/lawmakers-look-to-create-a-student-pipeline-to-the-adirondacks-to-confront-racism-and-climate-change-; Paul Hai, conversations with the author, 8/14/2022.

10. For an online map of Black-managed farms in New York State, see Black Farmers United NYS (https://www.blackfarmersunited.org); Adam Dewbury, local food system director, Adirondack North County Association (ANCA), interview by the author, 10/27/2022; Joshua Thomas, "Cannabis Business Interested in Canajoharie Site," *Daily Gazette* (Schenectady, NY), 4/20/2021.

11. To cite a few instances of "begging letters" from Smith's white Southern petitioners after the war (all from GSP): Union army veteran C. T. Torrey from Smith's own Madison County discerned a "golden opportunity" in the conversion of a run-down plantation outside Natchez into a cattle ranch, if only Smith could see his way to lending him $5,000; John Taylor, a "repentant rebel" from Chatterton, Virginia, needed $500 "to put me on my feet again" so he could hire his ex-slaves to build him a new steamship landing—for surely it was the job of "the philanthropists of the North" to "[take] care of this unfortunate people" and save them from starvation. T. D. Tredway of Prince Edward County, Virginia, waist deep in debt, drastically shorthanded, and unable to offload his land, wanted Smith to buy half his estate directly, then convey half

of *that* half to a dozen families in fee simple, at which point Tredway would provide them with food for a year, as well as a schoolhouse and a church. But this plan would not make his ex-slaves self-providing farmers. Smith declined them all.

12. On Laura Stebbins, see the Emily Howland Papers, Manuscripts and Archives, Cornell University; the Pratt Family Papers, Clements Library, University of Michigan; the Laura W. Stebbins Papers, Special Collections, Duke University; and Laura Stebbins to GS, 8/3/1869. A range of small presses have kept Charles Stearns's 580-page polemic, *The Black Man of the South, and the Rebels; or the Characteristics of the Former, and the Recent Outrages of the Latter*, in print. More biographical information may be found in McPherson, *Struggle for Equality*, 414–16; and McPherson, *Battle Cry of Freedom*, 203–4. On John Gregg Fee, see Howard, *Evangelical War*; and Sears, *Utopian Experiment*.

13. On the revival of Black agrarianism in the South, see Marcus Washington, "Black Agrarianism in America," Rhodes Farms (blog), 3/2/2021, https://rhodesfarms.org/blog/the-decline-and-resurgence-of-black-agrarianism; King et al., "Black Agrarianism"; and Williams and Gimenez, *Land Justice*.

14. See *Encyclopaedia Britannica Online*, s.v. "affirmative action," last updated 10/26/2022, https://www.britannica.com/topic/affirmative-action; and Jackie Mansky, "The Origins of the Term 'Affirmative Action,'" *Smithsonian Magazine*, last updated 11/1/2022, https://www.smithsonianmag.com/history/learn-origins-term-affirmative-action-180959531/.

15. Eliza Jane Darling, "Adirondack Gentrification," parts 1–7, New York Almanack, 8/1–6/2021, https://www.newyorkalmanack.com/tags/Adirondack-Gentrification; and "The Rest of the Story," parts 1–2, *Adirondack Daily Enterprise*, 4/24/2021 and 5/1/2021.

16. Dann, *Peter Smith of Peterboro*, 15–28, 43–66.

17. MacKenzie, *Plains of Abraham*; Josiah Hasbrook, *USFC 1900* and *USFC 1910*, Amherst, MA.

18. On Timbuctoo as a utopia, see Reynolds, *John Brown, Abolitionist*, 83, 131; Stauffer and Trodd, *Tribunal*, xxvi; Miller, *This Radical Land*, 70. The historian and biographer David Reynolds discerns the utopian heart of Smith's giveaway in Brown's interest in socialist cooperation, suggested, he believes, by Brown's asking his Black neighbors how they felt about him leaving North Elba for another field of action. (My reading of this episode argues for another interpretation.) Stauffer and Trodd point to John Brown's radical egalitarianism in North Elba, but the racially progressive family culture of one household does not a wider utopia make. The environmental historian Daegan Miller perceives the utopian soul of the Black Woods in the radical agrarianism of Smith's agents and in Smith's interest in agrarian reform, and, indeed, the allure of utopian ideology for Black leaders who supported Smith's initiative ran deep. How or whether that ideology suggested a selling point for the grantees before and especially after they moved to the frontier, however, is unclear. Paper hype was one thing; the pioneers' expectations and their experience in the woods were something else.

19. Mary Ellen Keith, town supervisor, remarks, Vermontville Pioneer Day, 7/21/2007. In an ADKX-sponsored webinar, "Nineteenth-Century Black

Settlements & Environmental Justice in the North Country," on 5/14/2022, Aaron Mair named twelve "free Black hamlets or Black Suffrage Communities" that Gerrit Smith "set up" in the Adirondacks. Included in this dozen were four Adirondack townships, and the hamlets of St. Armand, Vermontville, and Bloomingdale. But the townships show up on Adirondack maps when Gerrit Smith was four (and in any case, townships did not designate communities or towns). St. Armand, Vermontville, and Bloomingdale were settled by Canadians and New Englanders. St. Armand's first and only Black family for several years was the Hazzards, who touched down in 1851. Further, the four Black-originated communities we can name in the Black Woods (Timbuctoo, Freeman's Home, Blacksville, and Negro Brook) were settled by grantees with no help or direction from Smith or his agents. Smith never named them in a letter (and neither did his agents) and took no interest in their welfare. Mair additionally offers that this was the first effort to link Black suffrage rights with land purchases. It may have been the first such effort in New York. As early as the 1830s, however, suffrage rights activists were establishing Black settlements in the Northwest Territories with an eye to eventually securing Black voting rights ("Ohio Memorial Extract No. 2," *CA*, 3/22/1838; "Can't Take Care of Themselves," *CA*, 3/15/1838; and Cox, *Bone and Sinew*, 86–90). As it stands, this latest Adirondack utopia is less a provable thesis than another instance of Adirondack exceptionalism and aspirational speculation.

20. "Colored Man in E-Town Jail for Auto Theft," *AR-EP*, 7/29/1926; "Petrova Elementaries Give Gay Christmas Program" and "Georgia Moves to Bar 80 per cent of Negro Ballots," *ADE*, 12/18/1948.

BIBLIOGRAPHY

Archives

Adirondack Collection, Adirondack Research Room, Saranac Lake Free Library, NY

American periodicals, 1741–1900, Schomburg Center for Research in Black Culture, NYC

Archives and Library, Adirondack Experience, Blue Mountain Lake, NY

Beinecke Library Collection, Yale University, New Haven, CT

Edwin N. Cotter Jr. Collection on John Brown, Feinberg Library, Special Collections, SUNY Plattsburgh

Essex County Clerk's Office (archives, land and court records), Essex County Courthouse, Elizabethtown, NY

Franklin County Archives, Franklin County Courthouse, Malone, NY

Gerrit Smith Papers, Special Collections Research Center, Syracuse University Libraries, Syracuse, NY

Gilder Lehrman Collection, John Pierpont Morgan Library, New York City

Hamilton County Archives, Hamilton County Courthouse, Lake Pleasant, NY

John Brown Memorial Association/Harry Wade Hicks papers, at John Brown Farm State Historic Site Archives, North Elba, NY

John Brown Farm Archives, New York State Department of Parks, Recreation, and Historic Preservation, Division of Historic Sites, Peebles Island, NY

John Brown Jr. Papers, 1826–1948, Kansas Historical Society, Topeka

John Brown Jr. Papers, Ohio Historical Society, Columbus, OH

John Brown Jr. Papers, Frohman Collections, Rutherford B. Hayes Presidential Library, Fremont, OH

Lake Placid Public Library Special Collections. Includes Adirondack Surveys collection; John Brown Memorial Association Collection; Lake Placid Club Archives; Lyman E. Eppes collection; and Mary MacKenzie Archives

Liberty Street Presbyterian Church (Troy, NY) records, Presbyterian Historical Society, PA

Marjorie Lansing Porter Collection of Ballads and Lore, Feinberg Library, Special Collections, SUNY Plattsburgh

National Archives and Records Administration, Washington, DC

New-York Historical Society library, newspapers collection, and *Records for the Benefit of Colored Citizens, Series III, Admissions Records*, New York Colored Orphan Asylum, NYC

New York State Archives, Albany

456 **BIBLIOGRAPHY**

US Civil War Pension files, National Archives and Records Administration, Washington, DC

W. E. B. Du Bois Papers, Special Collections and University Archives, University of Massachusetts, Amherst

Books

Ackerman, David H. *Lake Placid Club: An Illustrated History*. Lake Placid Education Foundation, 1998.

Adams, Franklin George, George Washington Martin, and William Elsey Connelley. *Transactions of the Kansas State Historical Society*. Kansas State Historical Society, 1900.

Albers, Jan. *Hands on the Land: A History of the Vermont Landscape*. MIT, 2000.

Anbinder, Tyler. *Five Points: The 19th-Century New York City Neighborhood That Invented Tap Dance, Stole Elections, and Became the World's Most Notorious Slum*. Simon & Schuster, 2002.

Appiah, Kwame Anthony, and Henry Louis Gates Jr., eds. *A Dictionary of Global Culture*. Knopf, 1997.

Armistead, Wilson. *Tribute for the Negro*. William Irwin and Charles Gilpin, 1848.

Bay, Mia. *The White Image in the Black Mind: African-American Ideas about White People, 1830–1925*. Oxford, 2000.

Beatty, Jack. *Age of Betrayal: The Triumph of Money in America, 1865–1900*. Knopf, 2008.

Bell, Howard Holman. *A Survey of the Negro Convention Movement, 1830–1861*. Northwestern University, 1953.

Berlin, Ira, Joseph Patrick Reidy, and Leslie S. Rowland, eds. *Freedom's Soldiers: The Black Military Experience in the Civil War*. Cambridge University, 1998.

Bernstein, Burton. *The Sticks: A Profile of Essex County, New York*. Dodd, Mead, 1972.

Bibb, Henry. *Narrative of the Life and Adventures of Henry Bibb, An American Slave, Written by Himself*. Self-published, 1849, University of North Carolina, 2018.

Bidwell, Percy Wells. *Rural Economy in New England at the Beginning of the 19th Century*. The Academy, 1916.

Billington, Ray Allen. *America's Frontier Heritage*. Holt, Rinehart & Winston, 1966; University of New Mexico, 1974.

Blackett, R. J. M. *Beating against the Barriers: The Lives of Six Nineteenth-Century Afro-Americans*. Cornell University, 1989.

Blackmon, Douglas A. *Slavery by Another Name, The Re-enslavement of Black Americans from the Civil War to World War II*. Doubleday, 2008.

Blight, David W. *Frederick Douglass: Prophet of Freedom*. Simon & Schuster, 2018.

———. *Frederick Douglass' Civil War*. Louisiana State University, 1991.

———. ed. *Passages to Freedom: The Underground Railroad in History and Memory*. Smithsonian, 2004.

———. *Race and Reunion: The Civil War in American Memory*. Belknap of Harvard, 2001.

Bonner, Richard Illendon. *Memoirs of Lenawee County, Michigan.* Western Historical Association, 1909.

Bordewich, Fergus. *Bound for Canaan.* HarperCollins, 2005.

Bowditch, Vincent Yardley. *Life and Correspondence of Henry Ingersoll Bowditch.* 2 vols. Houghton, Mifflin, 1902.

Boyer, Richard O. *The Legend of John Brown: A Biography and a History.* Knopf, 1972.

Brophy, Alfred L. *Reconstructing the Dreamland: The Tulsa Riot of 1921.* Oxford, 2002.

Brown, C. S., ed. *Memoir of Reverend Abel Brown.* Self-published by C. S. Brown, Worcester, MA, 1849.

Brown, George Levi. *Pleasant Valley: A History of Elizabethtown, Essex County, New York.* Post and Gazette, 1905.

Brown, William Wells. *The Rising Son; or, The Antecedents and Advancement of the Colored Race.* A. G. Brown, 1873–1874.

Brumley, Charles. *Guides of the Adirondacks: A History.* North Country Books, 1994.

Burrows, Edward G., and Mike Wallace. *Gotham: A History of New York City to 1898.* Oxford, 1998.

Calarco, Tom. *The Underground Railroad in the Adirondack Region.* McFarland, 2004.

Campbell, Barbara A. *Inside the Club: Stories of the Employees of the Former Lake Placid Club.* Troy Book Makers, 2008.

Campbell, Stanley W. *The Slave Catchers: Enforcement of the Fugitive Slave Law, 1850–1860.* University of North Carolina, 1970.

Carrier, Peter. *Holocaust Memorials and National Memory Cultures in France and Germany since 1989.* Berghahn Books, 2005.

Carton, Evan. *Patriotic Treason: John Brown and the Soul of America.* Free Press, 2006.

Chamberlin, Joseph Edgar. *John Brown.* Small, Maynard, 1899.

Christianson, Scott. *Freeing Charles: The Struggle to Free a Slave on the Eve of the Civil War.* University of Illinois, 2010.

Clark, Susan, and Woden Teachout. *Slow Democracy: Rediscovering Community, Bringing Decision-Making Back Home.* Chelsea Green, 2012.

Cohen, William. *At Freedom's Edge: Black Mobility and the Southern White Quest for Racial Control, 1861–1915.* Louisiana State University, 1991.

Coleman, Terry. *Going to America.* Pantheon, 1972.

Cooley, William Desborough. *The Negroland of the Arabs Examined and Explained; Or, An Inquiry into the Early History and Geography of Central Africa.* J. Arrowsmith, 1841.

Cox, Anna-Lisa. *The Bone and Sinew of the Land: America's Forgotten Black Pioneers and the Struggle for Equality.* PublicAffairs, 2018.

Crèvecoeur, Hector St. John de. *Letters from an American Farmer; and, Sketches of Eighteenth-Century America.* Davies & Davis, 1782.

Curry, Leonard P. *The Free Black in Urban America, 1800–1850.* University of Chicago, 1981.

Dabel, Jane E. *A Respectable Woman: The Public Roles of African American Women in 19th-Century New York*. NYU, 2008.

Dann, Norman K. *Peter Smith of Peterboro: Furs, Land and Anguish*. Log Cabin Books, 2018.

———. *Practical Dreamer: Gerrit Smith and the Crusade for Social Reform*. Log Cabin Books, 2009.

———. *When We Get to Heaven: Runaway Slaves on the Road to Peterboro*. Log Cabin Books, 2008.

Davis, David Brion. *The Problem of Slavery in the Age of Emancipation*. Knopf, 2014.

de Gramont, Sanche. *The Strong Brown God: The Story of the Niger River*. Houghton Mifflin, 1976.

DeCaro, Louis A., Jr. *"Fire from the Midst of You": A Religious Life of John Brown*. New York University, 2002.

———. *John Brown: The Cost of Freedom*. International Publishers, 2007.

———. *John Brown: The Man Who Lived; Essays in Honor of the Harper's Ferry Raid Sesquicentennial, 1859–2009*. LuLu, 2009.

Delany, Martin R. *The Condition, Elevation, Emigration, and Destiny of the Colored People*. Self-published, 1852.

DeVoto, Bernard. *The Year of Decision: 1846*. Little, Brown, 1943.

Dodson, Howard, Christopher Moore, and Roberta Yancey, eds. *The Black New Yorkers: The Schomburg Illustrated Chronology*. Wiley, 2000.

Donaldson, Alfred L. *A History of the Adirondacks*. 2 vols. Century, 1921.

Douglass, Frederick. *Life and Times of Frederick Douglass: Written by Himself*. De Wolfe & Fiske, 1892.

———. *My Bondage and My Freedom*. Miller, Orton & Mulligan, 1855.

———. *Selected Speeches and Writings*. Edited by Philip S. Foner, and Yuval Taylor. University of Chicago, 2000.

Dray, Philip. *At the Hands of Persons Unknown: The Lynching of Black America*. Random House, 2002.

Driskell, Jay Winston, Jr. *Schooling Jim Crow: The Fight for Atlanta's Booker T. Washington High School and the Roots of Black Protest Politics*. University of Virginia, 2014.

Du Bois, W. E. B. *Darkwater: Voices from Within the Veil*. Harcourt Brace and Howe, 1920.

———. *John Brown*. George W. Jacobs, 1909.

———. *Souls of Black Folk*. A. C. McClurg, 1903.

Duberman, Martin, ed. *The Antislavery Vanguard: New Essays on the Abolitionists*. Princeton, 1965.

Durant, Samuel W. *History of Oneida County, New York*. Everts & Fariss, 1878.

Durkee, Cornelius E. *Reminiscences of Saratoga*. Reprinted by *The Saratogian*. Higginson Book Co., 1928.

Dyer, Frederick H. *A Compendium of the War of the Rebellion*. Dyer, 1908.

Egerton, Douglas R. *Thunder at the Gates: The Black Civil War Regiments That Redeemed America*. Basic Books, 2016.

———. *The Wars of Reconstruction*. Bloomsbury, 2014.

Eisenstadt, Peter, Laura-Eve Moss, and Carole F. Huxley, eds. *Encyclopedia of New York State*. Syracuse University, 2005.

Ellis, Arthur Blake. *George S. Hale, A.M.: A, Prepared for the Proceedings of the Massachusetts Historical Society*. J. Wilson & Son, 1899.

Emilio, Luis F. *A Brave Black Regiment: History of the Fifty-Fourth Regiment of Massachusetts Volunteer Infantry*. Boston Book Co., 1894.

Engel, Robert, Howard Kirshenbaum, and Paul Malo, eds. *Santanoni: From Japanese Temple to Life at an Adirondack Great Camp*. Adirondack Architectural Heritage, 2000.

Eshelman, Teresa R., ed. *They Told Me So . . .* Vols. 1-9. Town of Franklin Journal, Vermontville, NY, 1986-1999. https://www.townoffranklin.com/journals.html.

Field, Phyllis F. *The Politics of Race in New York: The Struggle for Black Suffrage in the Civil War Era*. Cornell, 1982.

Fields, Barbara Jeanne. *Slavery and Freedom on the Middle Ground*. Yale, 1985.

Fields, Karen E., and Barbara J. Fields. *Racecraft: The Soul of Inequality in American Life*. Verso, 2012.

Finkelman, Paul, ed. *His Soul Goes Marching On: Responses to John Brown and the Harpers Ferry Raid*. University of Virginia, 1995.

Foner, Eric. *Free Soil, Free Labor, Free Men: The Ideology of the Republican Party before the Civil War*. Oxford, 1970.

———. *Gateway to Freedom: The Hidden History of the Underground Railroad*. W. W. Norton, 2015.

———. *Reconstruction: America's Unfinished Revolution*. Harper & Row, 1988.

———. *The Story of American Freedom*. Norton, 1998.

Foner, Philip S. *Essays in Afro-American History*. Temple, 1978.

Fox, William F. *History of the Lumber Industry in the State of New York* (first published in the *Sixth Annual Report of the New York Forest, Fish, and Game Commission*, 1901). Harbor Hill Books, 1976.

Frederickson, George M. *The Arrogance of Race: Historical Perspectives on Slavery, Racism and Social Inequality*. Wesleyan, 1988.

———. *Racism: A Short History*. Princeton, 2002.

Freeman, Joanne. *The Field of Blood: Violence in Congress and the Road to Civil War*. Farrar, Straus & Giroux, 2018.

Freeman, Rhoda Golden. *The Free Negro in New York City in the Era before the Civil War*. Garland, 1994.

Friedman, Lawrence J. *Gregarious Saints: Self and Community in American Abolitionism, 1830–1870*. Cambridge University, 1982.

Frothingham, Octavius Brooks. *Gerrit Smith: A Biography*. G. P. Putnam's Sons, 1878; repr. Negro Universities Press, 1969.

Fuller, James. *Men of Color, To Arms!: Vermont African-Americans in the Civil War*. iUniverse, 2001.

Gallagher, Nancy. *Breeding Better Vermonters: The Eugenics Project in the Green Mountain State*. University Press of New England, 1999.

Garnet, Henry Highland. *A Memorial Discourse by Rev. Henry Highland Garnet Delivered in the Hall of Representatives, Washington City, D.C., on Sabbath Feb. 12, 1865*. Introduction by James McCune Smith. J. M. Wilson, 1865.

———. *The Past and Present Condition, and the Destiny of the Colored Race: A Discourse Delivered at the Fifteenth Anniversary of the Female Benevolent Society of*

Troy, N.Y., Feb. 14, 1848. J. C. Kneeland, 1848. https://archive.org/details/pastpresentcondi00garn/page/n43/mode/2up.

———. *Walker's Appeal, with a Brief Sketch of His Life. And Also Garnet's Address to the Slaves of the United States of America.* J. H. Tobitt, 1848.

Gellman, David N., and David Quigley, eds. *Jim Crow New York: A Documentary History of Race and Citizenship, 1777–1877.* NYU, 2003.

Genovese, Eugene. *Roll, Jordan, Roll: The World the Slaves Made.* Pantheon/Random House, 1974.

Gero, Anthony F. *Black Soldiers of New York State: A Proud Legacy.* SUNY, 2009.

Glenn, Morris F. *The Story of Three Towns: Westport, Essex, and Willsboro.* Printed by the author, Alexandria, VA, 1977.

Gordon, Jan, and Cora Gordon. *On Wandering Wheels: Through Roadside Camps from Maine to Georgia in an Old Sedan Car.* Dodd, Mead, 1928.

Granick, Harry. *Underneath New York.* Rinehart, 1947.

Grant, Madison. *The Passing of the Great Race, or The Racial Basis of European History.* Scribner's, 1916.

Green, Asa. *A Glance at New York: Embracing the City Government, Theatres, Hotels, Churches, Mobs, Monopolies, Learned Professions, Newspapers, Rogues, Dandies, Fires and Firemen, Water and Other Liquids, &C., &C. . . .* Published by the author, 1837.

Groth, Michael E. *Slavery and Freedom in the Mid-Hudson Valley.* SUNY, 2017.

Grover, Kathryn. *Make a Way Somehow: African-American Life in a Northern Community, 1790–1965.* Syracuse University, 1994.

Guyette, Elise A. *Discovering Black Vermont: African American Farmers in Hinesburgh, 1790–1890.* University of Vermont, 2010.

Hale, Grace Elizabeth. *Making Whiteness: The Culture of Segregation in the South, 1890–1940.* Vintage/Random House, 1998.

Halverson, Anders. *An Entirely Synthetic Fish: How Rainbow Trout Beguiled America and Overran the World.* Yale, 2011.

Harlan, Louis R., Stuart Kaufman, Barbara Kraft, and Raymond Smock, eds. *The Booker T. Washington Papers.* Vol. 4, *1895–1898.* University of Illinois, 1975.

Harlow, Ralph Volney. *Gerrit Smith: Philanthropist and Reformer.* Henry Holt, 1939.

Harris, Leslie M. *In the Shadow of Slavery: African Americans in New York City, 1626–1863.* University of Chicago, 2003.

Harrold, Stanley. *The Abolitionists & the South, 1831–1861.* University of Kentucky, 1995.

———. *The Rise of Aggressive Abolitionism: Addresses to the Slaves.* University of Kentucky, 2004.

Hayes, Alfred W. *Lake Placid: Its Early History and Developments.* Adirondack Resorts, 1946.

Hedrick, Ulysses. *A History of Agriculture in the State of New York.* J. B. Lyon, 1933.

Higginson, Thomas Wentworth. *Contemporaries.* Houghton Mifflin, 1899.

Higham, John. *Strangers in the Land: Patterns of American Nativism, 1860–1925.* Rev. ed. Rutgers, 1992.

Hinks, Peter P., John R. McKivigan, and R. Owen Williams, eds. *Encyclopedia of Antislavery and Abolition*, 2 vols. Greenwood, 2007.

Hochschild, Harold K. *Township 34*. Adirondack Museum, 1976.

Hodges, Graham Russell. *New York City Cartmen, 1667–1850*. New York University, 2012.

——. *Root and Branch: African Americans in New York & East Jersey, 1613–1863*. University of North Carolina, 1999.

Hodges, Willis Augustus. *Free Man of Color: The Autobiography of Willis Augustus Hodges*. Edited and with an introduction by Willard B. Gatewood Jr. University of Tennessee, 1982.

Hoffman, Charles Fenno. *Wild Scenes in the Forest and Prairie*. William H. Colyer, 1843.

Holt, Michael F. *The Rise and Fall of the American Whig Party*. Oxford, 1999.

Hornaday, William Temple. *Our Vanishing Wildlife: Its Extermination and Preservation*. Scribner's, 1913.

Horton, James Oliver, and Lois E. Horton. *In Hope of Liberty: Culture, Community and Protest among Northern Free Blacks, 1700–1860*. Oxford, 1997.

Howe, Stephen. *Afrocentrism: Mythical Pasts and Imagined Homes*. Verso, 1998.

Hughes, Langston. *Selected Poems*. Knopf, 1971.

Hunter, Carol. *To Set the Captives Free: Reverend Jermain Wesley Loguen and the Struggle for Freedom in Central New York, 1835–1872*. Garland, 1993.

Hurd, Duane Hamilton. *History of Clinton and Franklin Counties, New York*. J. W. Lewis, 1880.

Hutton, Frankie. *The Early Black Press in America, 1827 to 1860*. Greenwood, 1993.

Hyde, Lewis. *The Gift: Imagination and the Erotic Life of Property*. Vintage, 1999.

Ignatiev, Noel. *How the Irish Became White*. Routledge, 1995.

Isenberg, Nancy. *White Trash: The 400-Year Untold History of Class in America*. Viking, 2016.

Ives, Martin B. *Through the Adirondacks in Eighteen Days*. Wynkoop Hallenbeck Crawford, 1899.

Jacobs, Donald M., ed. *Antebellum Black Newspapers*. Greenwood, 1976.

Jacoby, Karl. *Crimes against Nature: Squatters, Poachers, Thieves, and the Hidden History of American Conservation*. University of California, 2001.

Johnson, Abby Arthur, and Ronald Maberry Johnson. *Propaganda and Aesthetics: The Literary Politics of African-American Magazines in the Twentieth Century*. University of Massachusetts, 1979.

Jones, Pomroy. *Annals and Recollections of Oneida County*. Printed by the author, 1851.

Kammen, Carol, ed. *The Pursuit of Local History: Readings on Theory and Practice*. AltaMira, 1996.

Keller, Jane Eblen. *Adirondack Wilderness: A Story of Man and Nature*. Syracuse University, 1980.

Koeppel, Gerard T. *Water for Gotham: A History*. Princeton, 2000.

Kryza, Franz. *The Race for Timbuktu: In Search of Africa's City of Gold*. HarperCollins, 2006.

Landon, Harry F. *History of the North Country.* 3 vols. Historical Publishing Co., 1932.

Lapp, Rudolph M. *Blacks in Gold Rush California.* Yale, 1977.

Laughlin-Schultz, Bonnie. *The Tie That Bound Us: The Women of John Brown's Family and the Legacy of Radical Abolitionism.* Cornell, 2013.

Lause, Mark A. *Young America: Land, Labor, and the Republican Community.* University of Illinois, 2005.

Lears, Jackson. *Rebirth of a Nation: The Making of Modern America.* HarperCollins, 2009.

Leonard, Thomas C. *Illiberal Reformers: Race, Eugenics, and American Economics.* Princeton, 2016.

Lewis, David Levering. *W. E. B. Du Bois: Biography of a Race, 1868–1919.* Henry Holt, 1993.

———. *W.E.B. Du Bois: The Fight for Equality and the American Century, 1919–1963.* Henry Holt, 2000.

Limerick, Patricia Nelson. *The Legacy of Conquest: The Unbroken Past of the American West.* W. W. Norton, 1987.

Lindquist, Charles N. *The Antislavery-Underground Railroad Movement in Lenawee County, Michigan, 1830–1860.* Lenawee County Historical Society, 1999.

Litwack, Leon. *North of Slavery.* University of Chicago, 1961.

Litwack, Leon, and August Meier, eds. *Black Leaders of the Nineteenth Century.* University of Illinois, 1988.

Logan, Rayford W., and Michael R. Winston, eds. *Dictionary of American Negro Biography.* W. W. Norton, 1982.

Lyght, Ernest. *Path of Freedom: The Black Presence in New Jersey's Burlington County, 1659–1900.* E. & E. Pub. 1978.

MacKenzie, Mary. *More from the Plains of Abraham.* Edited by Lee Manchester. Lake Placid Public Library, 2011. Ebook/PDF. http://www.slideshare.net/LeeManchester/more-from-the-plains-of-abraham.

———. *The Plains of Abraham: A History of North Elba and Lake Placid.* Edited by Lee Manchester. Nicholas K. Burns, 2007.

Marx, Leo. *The Machine in the Garden.* Oxford, 1964.

Matthews, Harry Bradshaw. *Freedom Knows No Color: African American Freedom Journey in New York and Related Sites, 1823–1870.* Africana Homestead Legacy, 2008.

May, Samuel Joseph. *Some Recollections of Our Anti-slavery Conflict.* Fields, Osgood, 1869.

McManus, Edgar J. *A History of Negro Slavery in New York.* Syracuse University, 1966.

McMartin, Barbara. *The Great Forest of the Adirondacks.* North Country Books, 1994.

———. *The Privately Owned Adirondacks.* Lake View Press, 2004.

McPherson, James M. *Battle Cry of Freedom: The Civil War Era.* Oxford, 1988.

———. *The Negro's Civil War: How American Blacks Felt and Acted during the War for the Union.* Random House, 1991.

———. *The Struggle for Equality.* Princeton, 1964.

Meinig, D. W. *The Shaping of America*. Vol. 2, *Continental America, 1800–1867*. Yale, 1993.

Menand, Louis. *The Metaphysical Club*. Farrar, Straus & Giroux, 2001.

Miller, Daegan. *This Radical Land: A Natural History of American Dissent*. University of Chicago, 2018.

Mohl, Raymond, ed. *The Making of Urban America*. Rev. ed. Scholarly Resources, 1997.

Monmonier, Mark. *From Squaw Tit to Whorehouse Meadow: How Maps Name, Claim, and Inflame*. University of Chicago, 2006.

Morgan, Edmund S. *American Slavery, American Freedom*. W. W. Norton, 2003.

Morrison, Toni. *Playing in the Dark: Whiteness and the Literary Imagination*. Vintage/ Random House, 1992.

Moses, Wilson Jeremiah. *Afrotopia: The Roots of African American Popular History*. Cambridge University, 1998.

——, ed. *Liberian Dreams: Back-to-Africa Narratives from the 1850s*. Penn State, 1998.

Murray, William H. *Adventures in the Wilderness; or, Camp-Life in the Adirondacks*. Fields, Osgood, 1869.

National Cyclopedia of American Biography. Vol. 11. James T. White & Co., 1901.

Norrell, Robert. *Up from History: The Life of Booker T. Washington*. Belknap of Harvard, 2009.

Northup, Solomon. *Twelve Years a Slave: Narrative of Solomon Northup, a Citizen of New York, Kidnapped in Washington City in 1841, and Rescued in 1853*. Auburn, Derby & Miller, 1853; repr., edited by Henry Louis Gates Jr. and Kevin M. Burke, W. W. Norton, 2016.

Oates, Stephen. *To Purge This Land with Blood: A Biography of John Brown*. University of Massachusetts, 1984.

Ofari, Earl. *"Let Your Motto Be Resistance": The Life and Thought of Henry Highland Garnet*. Beacon, 1972.

Otis, Melissa. *Rural Indigenousness: A History of Iroquoian and Algonquian Peoples of the Adirondacks*. Syracuse University, 2018.

Painter, Nell. *The History of White People*. W. W. Norton, 2010.

Pasternak, Martin B. *Rise Now and Fly to Arms: The Life of Henry Highland Garnet*. Garland, 1995.

Payne, Daniel. *Recollections of Seventy Years*. A. M. E. Sunday School Union, 1888.

Pencak, William A. *Encyclopedia of the Veteran in America*. 2 vols. ABC-CLIO, 2009.

Penn, I. Garland. *The Afro-American Press and Its Editors*. Wiley, 1891.

Penningroth, Dylan C. *The Claims of Kinfolk: African American Property and Community in the Nineteenth-Century South*. University of North Carolina, 2003.

Pennington, James W. C. *The Fugitive Blacksmith; or, Events in the History of James W. C. Pennington, Pastor of a Presbyterian Church, New York, Formerly a Slave in the State of Maryland, United States*. Charles Gilpin, 1849.

Perry, Kenneth. *People of Lowly Life: Early Persons of African American Heritage in Washington County, N.Y.* Troy Book Makers, 2019.

Peterson, Carla L. *Black Gotham: A Family History of African Americans in Nineteenth-Century New York City*. Yale, 2011.

Peterson, Merrill D. *John Brown: The Legend Revisited*. University of Virginia, 2002.

Phillips, William A. *The Conquest of Kansas by Missouri and Her Allies*. Phillips, Sampson, 1856.

Phipps, William E. *Mark Twain's Religion*. Mercer University, 2003.

Phisterer, Frederick. *New York in the War of the Rebellion, 1861–1865*. 6 vols. 3rd ed. J. B. Lyon, 1912.

Porter, Marjorie Lansing. *Lem Merrill: Surveyor-Conservationist*. Privately published, 1944.

Prescott, William H. *The Correspondence of William Hickling Prescott, 1832–1857*. Edited by Roger Wolcott. Houghton Mifflin, 1925.

Quarles, Benjamin. *Allies for Freedom: Blacks and John Brown*. Oxford, 1974.

——. *Black Abolitionists*. Oxford, 1969.

——, ed. *Blacks on John Brown*. University of Illinois, 1972.

——. *The Negro in the Civil War*. Russell & Russell, 1968.

Rael, Patrick, ed. *African-American Activism before the Civil War: The Freedom Struggle in the Antebellum North*. Routledge, 2008.

Ray, Henrietta C. [Cordelia], and Florence T. Ray. *Sketch of the Life of Rev. Charles B. Ray*. J. J. Little, 1887.

Redpath, James. *The Public Life of John Brown, with an Auto-biography of His Childhood and Youth*. Thayer & Eldridge, 1860.

Renehan, Edward, Jr. *The Secret Six: The True Tale of the Men Who Conspired with John Brown*. University of South Carolina, 1997.

Reynolds, David S. *John Brown, Abolitionist: The Man Who Killed Slavery, Sparked the Civil War, and Seeded Civil Rights*. Knopf, 2005.

Richards, T. Addison, *The Romance of American Landscape*, Leavitt and Allen, 1855.

Riley, Thomas Michael. *Florence in History to 1953*. Pub. by author, 1953, and Town of Florence Historical Society, 1985.

Ripley, C. Peter, Roy E. Finkenbine, Michael E. Hembree, Donald Yacovone, eds. *The Black Abolitionist Papers*. Vols. 3 (1830–46), 4 (1847–58), and 5 (1859–65). University of North Carolina, 1991. https://www.uncpress.org/book/9781469624389/the-black-abolitionist-papers/. This definitive five-volume documentary collection also includes seventeen microfilm reels, a 571-page guide at http://www.worldcat.org/title/black-abolitionist-papers-1830-1865/oclc/39092386, and an online database at http://bap.chadwyck.com/marketing/.

Roediger, David R. *The Wages of Whiteness: Race and the Making of the American Working Class*. Rev. ed. Verso, 1999.

Rose, Willie Lee. *Rehearsal for Reconstruction: The Port Royal Experiment*. Oxford, 1976.

Ruchames, Louis. *John Brown: The Making of a Revolutionary*. Grosset & Dunlap, 1969.

——, ed. *A John Brown Reader*. Abelard-Schuman, 1959.

Sanborn, F. B., ed. *Life and Letters of John Brown, Liberator of Kansas, and Martyr of Virginia*. S. Low, Marston, Searle & Rivington, 1885.

Scharnhorst, Gary. *Kate Field: The Many Lives of a Nineteenth-Century American Journalist*. Syracuse University, 2008.

Schecter, Barnet. *The Devil's Own Work: The Civil War Draft Riots and the Fight to Reconstruct America*. Walker, 2005.

Schein, Richard H., ed. *Landscape and Race in the United States*. Routledge, 2006.

Schor, Joel. *Henry Highland Garnet: A Voice of Black Radicalism in the Nineteenth Century*. Greenwood, 1977.

Sears, Richard. *A Utopian Experiment in Kentucky: Integration and Social Equality at Berea, 1866–1904*. Greenwood, 1996.

Seaver, Frederick J. *Historical Sketches of Franklin County and Its Several Towns*. J. B. Lyon, 1918.

Seraile, William. *New York's Black Regiments during the Civil War*. Routledge, 2001.

Sernett, Milton C. *North Star Country: Upstate New York and the Crusade for African American Freedom*. Syracuse University, 2002.

Sewell, Richard H. *Ballots for Freedom: Antislavery Politics in the United States, 1837–1860*. Oxford, 1976.

Shaffer, Donald R. *After the Glory: The Struggles of Black Civil War Veterans*. University of Kansas, 2004.

Sidney, Margaret. *An Adirondack Cabin: A Family Storytelling of Journeyings by Lake and Mountains, and Idyllic Days in the Heart of the Wilderness*. D. Lothrop, 1890.

Siebert, Wilbur H. *The Underground Railroad from Slavery to Freedom: A Comprehensive History*. Macmillan, 1898.

Simmons, Louis J., *Mostly Spruce and Hemlock*, Vail-Ballou Press, 1976.

Slotkin, Richard. *The Fatal Environment: The Myth of the Frontier in the Age of Industrialization, 1800–1890*. Atheneum, 1985.

Smith, Gerrit. *Speeches and Letters of Gerrit Smith on the Rebellion*, vol. 1, John A. Gray, 1864; vol. 2, American News Co., 1865.

Smith, H. P. *History of Essex County: With Illustrations and Biographical Sketches of Some of Its Prominent Men and Pioneers*. D. Mason, 1885.

——. *History of Warren County, New York*. D. Mason, 1885.

Smith, Kimberly K. *African American Environmental Thought*. University of Kansas, 2007.

Sorin, Gretchen. *Driving While Black: African American Travel and the Road to Civil Rights*. Liveright/W. W. Norton, 2020.

Southern, Eileen. *The Music of Black Americans: A History*. W. W. Norton, 1971.

Spann, Edward K. *The New Metropolis: New York City, 1840–1857*. Columbia, 1981.

Spiro, Jonathan Peter. *Defending the Master Race: Conservation, Eugenics, and the Legacy of Madison Grant*. University of Vermont, 2009.

Stauffer, John. *The Black Hearts of Men: Radical Abolitionists and the Transformation of Race*. Harvard, 2002.

——, ed. *The Works of James McCune Smith: Black Intellectual and Abolitionist*. Oxford, 2006.

Stauffer, John, and Zoe Trodd, eds. *The Tribunal: Responses to John Brown and the Harpers Ferry Raid*. Belknap of Harvard, 2012.

Stevenson, Bryan. *Just Mercy: A Story of Justice and Redemption.* Spiegel & Grau, 2014.

Stewart, James Brewer. *Holy Warriors: The Abolitionists and American Slavery.* Rev. ed., Hill & Wang, 1996.

Stilgoe, John R. *Common Landscape in America, 1580 to 1845.* Yale, 1982.

Stoddard, Seneca Ray. *The Adirondacks: Illustrated.* 1st ed., Weed, Parsons, 1874, and Applewood, 2008.

Stradling, David. *The Nature of New York: An Environmental History of the Empire State.* Cornell, 2010.

Strand, Mark. *Selected Poems.* Knopf, 1980.

Street, Alfred Billings. *The Indian Pass.* Hurd & Houghton, 1869.

——. *Woods and Waters, Or, The Saranacs and Racket.* M. Doolady, 1860.

Strong, Douglas M. *Perfectionist Politics: Abolitionism and the Religious Tensions of American Democracy.* Syracuse University, 1999.

Stuckey, Sterling. *Slave Culture: Nationalist Theory and the Foundations of Black America.* Oxford, 1987.

Svenson, Sally E. *Blacks in the Adirondacks: A History.* Syracuse University, 2017.

Swift, David E. *Black Prophets of Justice.* Louisiana State University, 1989.

Sylvester, Nathaniel Bartlett. *Historical Sketches of Northern New York and the Adirondack Wilderness.* W. H. Young, 1877.

Taylor, Clarence. *The Black Churches of Brooklyn.* Columbia University, 1994.

Tefft, Grant J. *The Story of Union Village.* Vol. 1. Greenwich Journal, 1942.

Terrie, Philip G. *Contested Terrain: A New History of Nature and People in the Adirondacks.* Syracuse University, 1997.

——. *Forever Wild: A Cultural History of Wilderness in the Adirondacks.* Syracuse University, 1994.

——. *Wildlife and Wilderness: A History of Adirondack Mammals.* Purple Mountain, 1993.

Thompson, Harold W. *Body, Boots and Britches.* Lippincott, 1940.

Thompson, John H., ed. *Geography of New York State.* Syracuse University, 1977.

Tyler, Helen Escha. "... *In Them Thar Hills*": *Folk Tales of the Adirondacks.* Currier, 1968.

——. *The Story of Paul Smith: Born Smart.* North Country Books, 1988.

Villard, Oswald Garrison. *John Brown, 1800–1859: A Biography Fifty Years Later.* Houghton Mifflin, 1911.

Vincent, Stephen. *Southern Seed, Northern Soil: African-American Farm Communities in the Midwest, 1765–1900.* Indiana University, 1999.

Von Holst, Hermann. *John Brown.* Cupples and Hurd, 1889.

Wager, Daniel. *Our Country and Its People: A Descriptive Work on Oneida County, New York.* Boston History Co., 1896.

Washington, Margaret. *Sojourner Truth's America.* University of Illinois, 2009.

Watson, Winslow C. *A General View and Agricultural Survey of the County of Essex: Taken under the Appointment of the New-York State Agricultural Society.* Albany, 1852.

——. *The Military and Civil History of the County of Essex, New York.* Munsell, 1869.

Webb, Richard D., ed. *The Life and Letters of Captain John Brown.* Smith, Elder, 1861.

Webber, Christopher. *American to the Backbone: The Life of James W. C. Pennington, the Fugitive Slave Who Became One of the First Black Abolitionists.* Pegasus Books, 2011.

Wellman, Judith, with Jan DeAmicis, Mary Hayes Gordon, Jessica Harney, Deirdre Sinnott, and Milton Sernett. *"We Took to Ourselves Liberty": Historic Sites Relating to the Underground Railroad, Abolitionism, and African American Life in Oneida County and Beyond; A Historic Resource Study.* National Park Service, 2022.

White, Richard. *The Republic for Which It Stands: The United States during Reconstruction and the Gilded Age, 1865–1896.* Oxford History of the United States. Oxford, 2017.

White, William Chapman. *Adirondack Country.* Knopf, 1967.

Whiting, Lilian. *Kate Field: A Record.* Little, Brown, 1899.

Wiegand, Wayne A. *Irrepressible Reformer: A Biography of Melvil Dewey.* American Library Association, 1996.

Wilentz, Sean. *Chants Democratic: New York City & the Rise of the American Working Class, 1788–1850.* Oxford, 1984.

———. *The Rise of American Democracy.* W. W. Norton, 2005.

Williams, Justine M., and Eric Holt-Giménez eds. *Land Justice: Re-imagining Land, Food, and the Commons in the United States.* Food First Books, 2017.

Williamson, Joel. *After Slavery: The Negro in South Carolina during Reconstruction, 1861–1877.* University of North Carolina, 1965.

Winks, Robin W. *The Blacks in Canada: A History.* Yale, 1971.

Woodward, E. M., and J. F. Hageman. *History of Burlington and Mercer Counties, New Jersey: With Biographical Sketches of Many of Their Pioneers and Prominent Men.* Everts & Peck, 1883.

Articles, Papers, Unpublished Manuscripts, Dissertations, Speeches, Convention Proceedings, Pamphlets, Government Publications, Archival Collections, and Maps

AICP (New York Association for Improving the Condition of the Poor). *First Report of a Committee on the Sanitary Condition of the Laboring Classes in the City of New York with Remedial Suggestions.* John F. Trow, 1853.

Allen, Garland E. "'Culling the Herd': Eugenics and the Conservation Movement in the United States, 1900–1940." *Journal of the History of Biology* 46, no. 1 (Spring 2013): 31–72.

Annual Report of the New York Forest Commission. 2 vols. New York Forest Commission, J. B. Lyon, 1894.

Aptheker, Herbert. *Documentary History of the Negro People of the United States.* Citadel, 1951.

Atkinson, Eleanor. "The Soul of John Brown: Recollections of the Great Abolitionist by His Son." *American Magazine* 68 (October 1909): 633–43.

Atlas of Franklin County, New York. D. G. Beers, 1876.

Barry, Louise. "The Emigrant Aid Parties of 1854." *Kansas Historical Quarterly* 12, no. 2 (May 1943): 115–55.

Baumann, Amelia S. "Goldsmith, Mill Town of Long Ago." *Franklin Historical Review Collection 2*, vol. 7 (1970): 110–12.

Bell, Howard Holman, ed. *Minutes of the Proceedings of the National Negro Conventions, 1830–1864*. Arno, 1969.

———. "Some Reform Interests of the Negro during the 1850s as Reflected in State Conventions." *Phylon* 21, no. 2 (1960): 173–81.

———. *Survey of the Negro Convention Movement, 1830–1861*. Northwestern University, 1989.

Blight, David W. "In Search of Learning, Liberty, and Self-Definition: James McCune Smith and the Ordeal of the Antebellum Black Intellectual." *Afro-Americans in New York Life and History* 9, no. 2 (July 1985): 7–26.

Brechin, Gray. "Conserving the Race: Natural Aristocracies, Eugenics, and the U.S. Conservation Movement." *Antipode* 28, no. 3 (July 1996): 229–45.

Burdick, Donna Dorrance, and Norman K. Dann. *Heaven and Peterboro: The Current Relevance of 19th Century Peterboro to Human Rights Today*. Gerrit Smith Estate National Historic Landmark, Peterboro, NY. Pamphlet. Privately published, 2003.

Bushnell, Rev. Horace. "The Age of Homespun." Sermon, Litchfield, CT, August 1, 1851. published in *Work and Play*, A. Strahan, 1864.

Carvalho, Joseph, III. "John Brown's Transformation: The Springfield Years, 1846–1849." *Historical Journal of Massachusetts*, Winter 2020, 46–95.

Civil War Muster Roll Abstracts, 1861–1900. NYSA.

Coates, Peter. "Eastenders Go West: English Sparrows, Immigrants, and the Nature of Fear." *Journal of American Studies* 39, no. 3 (December 2005): 431–62.

Cole, Thomas. "Essay on American Scenery." *American Monthly Magazine*, no. 1 (January 1836): 1–12.

Cooper, Afua. "The Fluid Frontier: Blacks and the Detroit River Region—a Focus on Henry Bibb." *Canadian Review of American Studies* 30, no. 2 (2000): 127–48.

Cooper, Frederick. "Elevating the Race: The Social Thought of Black Leaders, 1827–1850." *American Quarterly* 24, no. 5 (December 1972): 604–25.

Dana, Richard Henry, Jr. "How We Met John Brown." *Atlantic Monthly*, July 1871.

Deluca, Kevin, and Anne Demo. "Imagining Nature and Erasing Class and Race: Carleton Watkins, John Muir, and the Construction of Wilderness." *Environmental History* 6, no. 4 (October 2001): 541–60.

Dyson, Zita. "Gerrit Smith's Effort in Behalf of the Negroes in New York." *Journal of Negro History* 3, no. 4 (1918): 354–59.

Fladeland, Betty. "Revisionists vs. Abolitionists: The Historiographical Cold War of the 1930s and 1940s." *Journal of the Early Republic* 6, no. 1 (Spring 1986): 1–21.

Flick, Alexander C. "John Brown Memorial Statue." *New York History* 16, no. 3 (July 1935): 329–32.

Folts, James. *Appraisal Job 87-01: Records Relating to Comptroller's Sales of Non-resident Lands for Unpaid Taxes, 1786–1955*, p. 3, n.d. NYSA.

Friedman, Lawrence J. "The Gerrit Smith Circle: Abolitionism in the Burned-Over District." *Civil War History* 26, no. 1 (March 1980): 18–38.

Fuller, George N. "Settlement of Michigan Territory." *Mississippi Valley Historical Review* 2, no. 1 (June 1915): 25–55.

General Index to the Laws of the State of New York 1777–1901. J. B. Lyon, 1902.

Gobrecht, Lawrence E. "National Historic Landmark Nomination: John Brown Farm and Gravesite." National Historic Landmarks Survey, National Park Service. November 21, 1997. PDF.

Godine, Amy. "The Abolitionist and the Land Reformer: Gerrit Smith and Tom Devyr." *Hudson River Valley Review*, Spring 2014.

———. "Adirondack Blackface." *Adirondack Life*, January/February 2021.

———. "Ambushed." *Adirondack Life*, November/December 2009.

———. "The Battle after the War." *Adirondack Life*, November/December 2015.

———. "Conservation's Dark Side." *Adirondack Life*, January/February 2015.

———. "Legacies of Slavery." *Adirondack Life*, January/February 2022.

———. "The Noteworthy Mr. Appo." *Adirondack Life*, November/December 2003.

———. "Occupied Territory." *Adirondack Life*, Collector's Issue, 2007.

———. "A Poor View." *Adirondack Life*, July/August 2019.

———. "Punishment and Crimes." *Adirondack Life*, July/August 2004.

Goggin, Jacqueline. "Countering White Racist Scholarship: Carter G. Woodson and *The Journal of Negro History*." *Journal of Negro History* 68, no. 4 (Autumn 1983): 355–75.

Gould, Elizabeth P. "John Brown at North Elba." *The Outlook*, November 21, 1896, 909–10.

Hardy, Philip J. "The Iron Age Community of the J.&J. Rogers Company, Au Sable Valley, New York, 1825–1900." PhD diss., Bowling Green State University, 1985.

Harlan, Louis R. "Booker T. Washington and *The Voice of the Negro*, 1904–1907." *Journal of Southern History* 45, no. 1 (February 1979): 45–62.

Harlow, Ralph V. "The Rise and Fall of the Kansas Aid Movement." *American Historical Review* 41, no. 1 (October 1935): 399–412.

Harris, Glenn. "The Hidden History of Agriculture in the Adirondack Park, 1825–1875." *New York History* 83, no. 2 (Spring 2002): 165–202.

Herrin, Dean, "From Slave to Abolitionist: James W. C. Pennington of Washington County, Maryland." Paper presented at the Millennium Crossroads Conference, Frederick Community College, Frederick, MD, 9/30/2001.

Hoffman, Charles Fenno. "A Pilgrimage to John Brown's Mountain." *The Knickerbocker, or New York Monthly Magazine*, March 1862, 232–37.

Humphreys, Hugh C. "'*Agitate! Agitate! Agitate!*' The Great Fugitive Slave Law Convention and Its Rare Daguerreotype." *Madison County Heritage*, no. 19 (1994): 3–64.

John Brown Memorial Association. *John Brown in Bronze, 1935.* Commemorative brochure, Lake Placid. JBMA/Harry Wade Hicks Collection, John Brown Farm State Historic Site Archives, North Elba, NY.

Johnson, Abby Arthur, and Ronald M. Johnson. "Away from Accommodation: Radical Editors and Protest Journalism, 1900–1910." *Journal of Negro History* 62, no. 4 (October 1977): 325–38.

Johnson, Bethany. "Freedom and Slavery in the Voice of the Negro: Historical Memory and African-American Identity, 1904–1907." *Georgia Historical Quarterly* 84, no. 1 (Spring 2000): 29–71.

Johnson, Samuel A. "The Emigrant Aid Company in the Kansas Conflict." *Kansas Historical Quarterly* 6, no. 1 (February 1937): 21–33.

Jones, Katherine Butler. "They Called It Timbucto." *Orion*, Winter 1998: 27–33.

Journal of the Assembly of the State of New York. Vol. 1, 72nd Session. Weed & Parsons, 1849.

Kahrl, Andrew W. "The Political Work of Leisure: Class, Recreation, and African American Commemoration at Harpers Ferry, West Virginia, 1881–1931." *Journal of Social History* 42, no. 1 (Fall 2008): 57–77.

King, Katrina Quisumbing, Spencer D. Wood, Jess Gilbern, and Marilyn Sinkewicz. "Black Agrarianism: The Significance of African American Landownership in the Rural South." *Rural Sociology* 83, no. 3 (September 2018): 677–99.

King, Miriam, and Steven Ruggles. "American Immigration, Fertility, and Race Suicide at the Turn of the Century." *Journal of Interdisciplinary History* 20, no. 3 (Winter 1990): 347–69.

Kraut, Alan M., and Phyllis F. Field. "Politics versus Principles: The Partisan Response to 'Bible Politics' in New York State." *Civil War History* 25, no. 2 (June 1979): 101–18.

Kruczek-Aaron, Hadley, "Race and Remembering in the Adirondacks: Accounting for Timbucto in the Past and the Present," *The Archaeology of Race in the Northeast* (April 2015): 134–149.

Landon, Fred. "Henry Bibb, a Colonizer." *Journal of Negro History* 5 (1920): 437–47.

Lavery, Colm. "Situating Eugenics: Robert DeCourcy Ward and the Immigration Restriction League of Boston." *Journal of Historical Geography* 53 (July 2016): 54–62.

Lee, Mary. "John Brown Rests amid the Mountains." *New York Times Magazine*, October 20, 1929.

Lehman, Orin. "To Make History Live Again at John Brown's Farm." Letter. *NYT*, July 25, 1978.

Longstreth, T. Morris. *Lake Placid and an Experiment in Intelligence.* Pamphlet, 1918, with introduction by Melvil Dewey of the Lake Placid Club. Likely published by the club, this pamphlet reprints chap. 10 from Longstreth's book, *The Adirondacks* (Century Club, 1917), 231–57.

Marcus, Alan P. "The Dangers of the Geographical Imagination in the U.S. Eugenics Movement." *Geographical Review* 111, no. 1 (2021): 36–56.

Mayo, A. D. "Adirondacks in August." *Old and New* 2 (September 1870): 342–52.

McGruder, Kevin. "'A Fair and Open Field': The Responses of Black New Yorkers to the New York City Draft Riots." *Afro-Americans in New York Life and History* 37, no. 2 (July 2013): 7–40.

McKivigan, John R., and Madeleine Leveille. "'The Black Dream' of Gerrit Smith, New York Abolitionist." Syracuse University, *Library Associates Courier* 20, no. 2 (Fall 1985): 51–76.

McKivigan, John R., and Madeleine McKivigan, "'He Stands Like Jupiter': The Autobiography of Gerrit Smith." *New York History* (April 1984): 188–200.

McLaughlin, Don James. "The Anti-Slavery Roots of Today's '-Phobia' Obsession." *New Republic*, 1/29/2016.

Metcalf, C. L. "Black Flies and Other Biting Flies of the Adirondacks." *New York State Museum Bulletin*, 289 (January 1932): 6–58.

Miller, Daegan. "At Home in the Great Northern Wilderness: African Americans and Freedom's Ecology in the Adirondacks, 1846–1859." *Environmental Humanities* 2 (May 2013): 117–46.

Minutes of the National Convention of Colored Citizens, Held at Buffalo, NY, 1843. Piercy & Reed, 1843.

Mitman, Gregg. "In Search of Health: Landscape and Disease in American Environmental History." *Environmental History* 10, no. 2 (April 2005): 184–210.

Moravek, John. "The Iron Industry as a Geographic Force in the Adirondack-Champlain Region of New York State, 1800–1971." PhD diss., University of Tennessee, 1976.

Morgan, Thomas M. "The Education and Medical Practice of Dr. James McCune Smith (1813–1865), First Black American to Hold a Medical Degree." *Journal of the National Medical Association* 95, no. 7 (July 2003): 603–14.

Murdock, Eugene C. "New York's Civil War Bounty Brokers." *Journal of American History* 53, no. 2 (September 1966): 259–78.

Nichols, May Ellis. "An Adirondack Pilgrimage." *National Magazine* 18, no. 4 (July 1903): 476–79.

O'Brien, Maurice. "'Timbuctoo': An Attempt at Negro Settlement in the Adirondacks." Unpublished manuscript, 1977. JBF files at Parks, Recreation, and Historic Preservation, Division of Historic Sites, PIA.

Ofari, Earl. "The Roots of Black Radicalism." *Black World/Negro Digest* 18, no. 10 (August 1969): 18–22.

Osborn, Elinor. "Tug Hill, Land of Water." *Northern Woodlands* (Winter 2004): 44–50.

Papson, Don. "The John Thomas Story: From Slavery in Maryland to American Citizenship in the Adirondacks." Six-part series. *Lake Champlain Weekly*, October 18, October 25, November 1, November 8, November 29, 2006.

Pennington, Thomas H. S. *Capture, Trial, and Return of the Fugitives Stephen Pembroke and His Two Sons to Slavery, Brother and Nephew of the Rev. James W. C. Pennington D. D.* n.d. This six-page report was sent with a letter dated August 1, 1897, to Marianna Gibbons of Bird-in-Hand, PA. Document Collection Archives, Lancaster County Historical Society.

———. *Prominent Events in Life of Rev. J. W. Pennington, D. D. by His Adopted Son, Thomas H. Sands Pennington of Saratoga Springs, N.Y.* n.d. Document Collection Archives, Lancaster County Historical Society.

Perkal, M. Leon. "American Abolition Society: A Viable Alternative to the Republican Party?" *Journal of Negro History* 65, no. 1 (Winter 1980): 57–71.

Perlman, Daniel. "Organizations of the Free Negro in New York City, 1800–1860." *Journal of Negro History* 56, no. 3 (July 1971): 181–97.

Perry, Kenneth A. *Some Notes towards a History and Genealogy of the African-American Population of Washington County, New York.* Privately published, 2005. Washington County Historian's Office, Fort Edward, NY.

Proceedings of the National Convention of Colored People and Their Friends, Held in Troy, N.Y., on the 6th, 7th, 8th and 9th October, 1847. J. C. Kneeland, 1847.

Proceedings of the National Liberty Convention, Held at Buffalo, N.Y., June 14th &
15th, 1848. Public domain, via Wikimedia Commons.

Ray, Charles Bennett. "Receipt Book of Land Grants from Gerrit Smith to
Colored and Poor White Slaves from the South, 1846." Copy of typed
transcription of the original record. New York State Comptroller's
Office, Land Tax Bureau, certified and dated, Mary F. Parillo, 1936. NYSA.

Ray, Charles B., and Willis Hodges. "Report of the Committee on Agriculture."
In *Proceedings of the National Convention of Colored People*, Troy, NY, 25–30.

Ray, Charles B., and James McCune Smith. "To Gerrit Smith Grantees. : Redeem Your Lands!!" Broadside, October 4, 1854. Gerrit Smith Collection, Special Collections, Wichita State University, KS.

Reconstruction in America: Racial Violence after the Civil War. Research report.
Equal Justice Institute, 2020.

Report of Select Committee Appointed to Visit Charitable Institutions Supported by the
State and all City and County Poor and Work Houses and Jails of the State of New
York. C. Van Benthuysen, 1857.

Riddle, Holly. "Finding Timbuctoo." *Adirondack Explorer*, December 18, 2021.
https://www.adirondackexplorer.org/stories/finding-timbuctoo.

Rome, Adam. "Nature Wars, Culture Wars: Immigration and Environmental Reform in the Progressive Era." *Environmental History* 13, no. 3
(July 2008): 432–53.

78th Annual Report of the Board of the Regents of the University of the State of New
York, Made to the Legislature, Feb. 16, 1865. G. Wendell, 1865.

Shaw, Albert. "John Brown in the Adirondacks." *Review of Reviews* 14, no. 3 (July–
December 1896): 311–17.

"Shooting in the Adirondacks." *All the Year Round* 1 (September 1860): 585–88.

Simpson, Charles R. "The Wilderness in American Capitalism: The Sacraliza-
tion of Nature." *International Journal of Politics, Culture, and Society* 5, no. 4
(Summer 1992): 555–76.

Smith, Gerrit. "Address of the Liberty Party to the Colored People of the United
States." In *Proceedings of the National Liberty Convention, Held at Buffalo,*
N.Y., June 14th and 15th, 1848, 10–13.

———. *An Address to the Three Thousand Colored Citizens of New York Who Are the*
Owners of One Hundred and Twenty Thousand Acres of Land in the State of
New York, Given to Them by Gerrit Smith of Peterboro, September 1, 1846.
Pamphlet. New York (n.p.), 1846. See Lehigh University, https://digi-
talcollections.lib.lehigh.edu/islandora/object/digitalcollections:rare-
book_1049#page/2/mode/1up. Includes Smith's August 1 and Sep-
tember 9 letters to Rev. Theodore H. Wright, Rev. Charles B. Ray, and
Dr. J. McCune Smith, their response to his proposal, and their advice to
the grantees. The contents of this pamphlet were also published in the
Albany Patriot, 10/28/1846, and the *Liberty Press* in Utica, 11/18/1846.

———. *Gerrit Smith's Land Auction: For Sale, and the Far Greater Share at Public Auction,*
about Three Quarters of a Million Acres of Land, Lying in the State of New York,
1846. Pamphlet, 54 pages. GSP, Special Collections, Syracuse University.

———. *Land Book (J), 1844–1877, v. 88, or Account of My Distribution of Land among*
Colored Men, ca. 1846–53. GSP, Special Collections, Syracuse University.

Smith, Robert P. "William Cooper Nell: Crusading Black Abolitionist." *Journal of Negro History* 55, no. 3 (July 1970): 182–99.

Smith, Robert Pearsall. *Map of Franklin County, New York, from Actual Surveys.* Taintor, Dawson, 1858.

Sterngass, Jon. "African American Workers and Southern Visitors at Antebellum Saratoga Springs." *American Nineteenth Century History* 2, no. 2 (June 2001): 35–59.

Stewart, Paul. "The Underground Railroad According to Stephen Myers." *Freedom Seeker* (Summer 2013): 1–3.

Sturges, Mark. "Consumption in the Adirondacks: Print Culture and the Curative Climate." *New York History* 100, no. 1 (Summer 2019): 109–35.

Svenson, Sally E. "Brookside: An Integrated Adirondack Cemetery." *New York Archives* 21, no. 4 (Winter 2018): 31–36.

Tanner, E. P. "Gerrit Smith: An Interpretation." *Quarterly Journal of the New York State Historical Association* 5, no. 1 (January 1924): 21–39.

Tanner, Kevin P. S. "'A Foe to Sad Oppression's Rod': The Story of Gerrit Smith." PhD diss., SUNY Binghamton, 2008.

"To Gerrit Smith, Esq., and Other Leaders of the Liberty Party." *Northern Star and Freeman's Advocate*, 2/27/1846. NYSL.

Tyler, Helen Escha. "Early Days in Franklin." *Franklin Historical Review* 6, no. 1 (1969): 19–25.

Vaughan, Lawrence M. *Abandoned Farm Areas in New York.* Bulletin 490, Cornell Agricultural Experiment Station, 1929.

Volpe, Vernon L. "The Liberty Party and Polk's Election." *The Historian* 54, no. 4 (June 1991): 691–710.

Ward, Robert De Courcy. "Open Letters: An Immigration Restriction League." *The Century* 49 (February 1895): 639–40.

Wardner, James M. "Footprints on Adirondack Trails." With Charles A. Wardner. Unpublished typescript, Adirondack Experience Library, Blue Mountain Lake, NY.

Wells, Leila M. "A Lake Placid Childhood." *York State Tradition*, Spring 1972.

Wohlworth, Charles. "Conservation and Eugenics: The Environmental Movement's Dirty Secret." *Orion*, July/August 2010.

Work, M. N. "The Life of Charles B. Ray." *Journal of Negro History* 4 (October 1919): 361–71.

Yetwin, Neil. "The Odyssey of Moses Viney." *Schenectady County Historical Society Newsletter.* 37–39, no. 1–10, Six-part series, 2001, 2002.

Websites

Accessible Archives databases (https://www.accessible-archives.com)

The Adirondack Chronology. Adirondack Research Library, Union College. Last revised 12/26/2021. Richard E. Tucker, senior editor (https://digitalworks.union.edu/cgi/viewcontent.cgi?article=1000&context=arlpublications)

Adirondack Experience (https://www.adkx.org)

Adirondack Experience Collections database (https://adirondack.pastperfectonline.com/archive)

Ancestry (https://www.ancestry.com)

Chronicling America: Historic American Newspapers (https://chronicling america.loc.gov/)

Civil War muster roll abstracts of New York State Volunteers, United States Sharpshooters, and United States Colored Troops (https://digitalcollec tions.archives.nysed.gov/index.php/Detail/collections/4138)

Colored Conventions Project (https://coloredconventions.org/)

The Crisis Collection (https://archive.org/details/pub_crisis?tab=collection)

Digital records of the Colored Conventions Project (https://omeka.colored conventions.org/)

Encyclopedia Virginia (https://encyclopediavirginia.org/)

Fold3 (https://www.fold3.com/)

Gerrit Smith Papers: Inventory (https://library.syr.edu/digital/guides/s/smith_ g.htm)

John Brown/Boyd B. Stutler Collection, West Virginia Memory Project Data-base (https://archive.wvculture.org/history/wvmemory/imlsintro.html)

New York State Archives, Land Records (http://www.archives.nysed.gov/ research/land-records-guide)

New York State Heritage Digital Collections (https://nyheritage.org/)

New York State Newspaper Project (https://www.nysl.nysed.gov/nysnp/)

New York Times, 1851–2015, with index, 1851–1993 (https://www.proquest.com/ scholarly-journals/proquest-historical-newspapers-new-york-times/ docview/217892515/se-2)

Newspapers.com (https://www.newspapers.com)

Old Fulton New York Postcards (https://fultonhistory.com)

INDEX

Page numbers in *italics* indicate figures

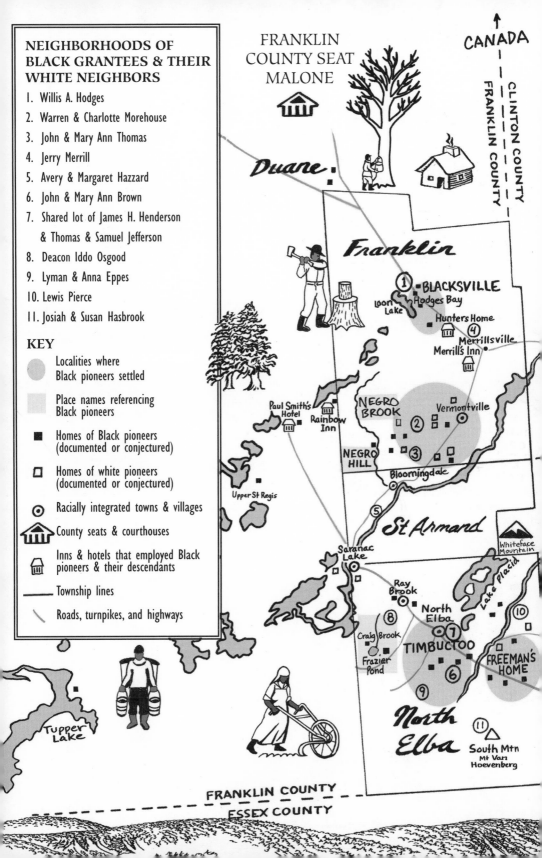

NEIGHBORHOODS OF BLACK GRANTEES & THEIR WHITE NEIGHBORS

1. Willis A. Hodges
2. Warren & Charlotte Morehouse
3. John & Mary Ann Thomas
4. Jerry Merrill
5. Avery & Margaret Hazzard
6. John & Mary Ann Brown
7. Shared lot of James H. Henderson
   & Thomas & Samuel Jefferson
8. Deacon Iddo Osgood
9. Lyman & Anna Eppes
10. Lewis Pierce
11. Josiah & Susan Hasbrook

KEY

Localities where Black pioneers settled

Place names referencing Black pioneers

■ Homes of Black pioneers (documented or conjectured)

□ Homes of white pioneers (documented or conjectured)

⊙ Racially integrated towns & villages

County seats & courthouses

Inns & hotels that employed Black pioneers & their descendants

— Township lines

╲ Roads, turnpikes, and highways

CANADA

FRANKLIN COUNTY SEAT MALONE

CLINTON COUNTY
FRANKLIN COUNTY

Duane

Franklin

① ■ BLACKSVILLE
Loon Lake
Hodges Bay
Hunters Home
④
Merrillsville
Merrill's Inn

Paul Smith's Hotel
Rainbow Inn

NEGRO BROOK
②
Vermontville

NEGRO HILL
③

Bloomingdale

Upper St Regis

⑤
St Armand

Whiteface Mountain

Saranac Lake

Ray Brook

North Elba
⑦

⑧
Craig Brook
Frazier Pond
TIMBUCTOO
⑥

⑨

FREEMAN'S HOME
⑩

North Elba

Tupper Lake

⑪
South Mtn
Mt Van Hoevenberg

Lake Placid

FRANKLIN COUNTY
ESSEX COUNTY